ABSTRACTS
OF
THE WILLS OF EDGECOMBE COUNTY
NORTH CAROLINA
1733-1856

By
Ruth Smith Williams
and
Margarette Glenn Griffin

Southern Historical Press, Inc.
Greenville, South Carolina

This volume was reproduced from
an 1956 edition located in the
Publisher's private library
Greenville, South Carolina

This direct ALL correspondence and book oreders to:
Southern Historical Press, Inc.
PO Box 1267
375 West Broad Street
Greenville, S.C. 29602-1267

Originally printed & ©: Rocky Mount, N.C. 1956
Reprinted by: Southern Historical Press, Inc.
          Greenville, S.C.
ISBN #0-89308-830-7
Printed in the United States of America

D E D I C A T I O N

We dedicate this book with af-
fection to our respective families,
who have been so patient and understanding during these many months
spent on the intensive and pains-
taking effort in its preparation.

A U T H O R S '   P R E F A C E

So many have asked, "Why are you abstracting the wills of Edgecombe County?" that we feel an explanation is due.

In doing genealogical research, it is absolutely necessary to have correct family data. Only from wills, deeds, census, marriage, tombstone and Bible records can this be had. When there is doubt in kinship, frequently the problem is solved by referring to old wills, in which a man or woman bequeaths property to "my son", "my grandson", "my great nephew", etc. No one can question that statement of record through the years.

Frequent trips to the Archives in Raleigh, or to Court Houses in Edgecombe and other counties, have convinced us that abstracts of wills, placed in libraries and available at all times, would be invaluable to researchers.

Many, whose ancestors had their roots deep in old Edgecombe, have scattered throughout the nation, and since World Wars I and II there has been a noticeable increase in family research from distant areas. These abstracts will be most helpful to their widely dispersed descendants.

The bequests of horse, bridle and saddle to almost every member of a family recalls the mode of travel commonly used in days when roads were hardly more than paths, and horseback was the most convenient.

Almost without exception every will contained bequests of one to half a dozen featherbeds and furniture to heirs. In order to conserve space we have omitted the featherbeds and furniture, but feel we should explain the meaning of "furniture" in this connection. In early times, beds in most instances were of the tester type, the furniture included featherbed, bolster, pillows, homewoven sheets, blankets and coverlets and

handmade quilts, and curtains for the top and under-
neath the bed.

It was customary to bequeath one's clothes, and
this can be understood when one realizes that cotton
and wool were home-grown products, and much labor went
into the spinning and weaving, to say nothing of the
handstitching necessary for making it into garments.
Clothing was appreciated and treasured, and not quickly
cast off.

So many customs have passed away that, for the sake
of preserving bits of homely information, we have included the enumeration of such articles as cotton cards,
woolen and flax wheels, box-irons (hand irons with an
arrangement for opening the iron and putting live coals
inside for heating, which was ultra modern a century
or more ago,) and piggins, (small wooden vessels of
many uses, one of which was washing the hands). Pewter
dishes were treasured for their wearing qualities;
looking glasses were not easily obtained. Trunks were
valued for their storage and the safety of family keep-
sakes. A still and worm were part of every plantation's
equipment for the manufacture of whisky or brandy. Iron
pots, spiders, and skillets were standard cooking utensils and important kitchen equipment. Riding chairs
were luxuries, and cart wheels were necessities, as
were hunting, regular and side saddles, flax and cotton
seed, and bee hives and bees.

Misspelling of names and articles have been re-
tained in many instances because of their quaintness.
When a name appeared in a will incomplete, or was illegible, and was found to be correct and complete in
the probate notes by the Clerk of Court, the Clerk's
interpretation has been used in our abstracts.

To conserve space, the names of the slaves have
been omitted, the names, in most instances being
Biblical or for historical persons, such as Solomon
or Caesar, reflecting consideration and thought. We
were impressed with the many kind references to beloved and faithful servants, not as slaves, but as

"My negro man Timothy" or "my negro woman Sarah". In
many instances they were given their freedom and provided with a house and parcel of land, and instructions
given that they not be required to work; that care be
given, and that they not be allowed to lack for clothing or food, nor be molested.

Most wills, it appears, were made a short time before death, or when the testator was old and infirm
and unable to sign, except by touching the pen or by
making a cross. We are convinced that the majority
were not illiterate, and, not wishing to stigmatize,
we have omitted his or her "x" mark. We have also left
off the seal following a testator's name, as it was
nothing more than legal form, few actually possessing
family seals for such formalities.

It has been our aim and desire to preserve any
historical or genealogical fact or statement in these
wills for the help it may be to researchers.

Ruth Smith Williams
Margarette Glenn Griffin

July 1, 1956
Rocky Mount, North Carolina

A C K N O W L E D G E M E N T S

We acknowledge with deep appreciation the interest
and courtesy shown us by Dr. C. C. Crittenden and his
staff while we were abstracting the original wills in
the State Archives. We wish, especially to thank Mrs.
Mary Rogers, of the Search Room, who was unfailingly
helpful, patient and ready to decipher any difficult
date or name.

We also appreciate the cordial assistance received
in the Court House of Edgecombe County from Mr. Don
Gilliam, Jr., Clerk of the Superior Court, and from
Mrs. Ruth Mason and other members of his staff.

We are indebted to Mrs. Ruth Jeffreys of the Braswell Memorial Library, Rocky Mount, who gave us steady
encouragement by reminding us of the importance of this
historical contribution to posterity, and especially
to Mr. Hugh B. Johnston, Jr., Historian for Wilson
County, who suggested the book, served as our advisor
throughout the undertaking, and prepared the map of the
principal changes in the boundaries of Edgecombe County.

We are deeply grateful to Dr. Albert D. Bell,
minister, historian and author, whose experience was
graciously shared with us.

We appreciate the interest and patience of Mr.
and Mrs. L. D. Thomas, publishers, who have striven
with us to make this book as nearly perfect as possible.

We are grateful to The News & Observer, The Evening
Telegram and other newspapers that have given us pub-
licity and praise.

Ruth Smith Williams
Margarette Glenn Griffin

CLERKS OF THE SUPERIOR COURT

OF

EDGECOMBE COUNTY, NORTH CAROLINA

1760 - 1956

James Hall	1760 - 1772
Edward Hall	1772 - 1819
Michael Hearn	1820 - 1837
Joseph Bell	1837 - 1849
John Norfleet	1849 - 1855
M. A. Jones	1856 - 1864
Irvin Thigpen	1864 - 1868
John Norfleet	1868 - 1874
H. L. Staton, Jr.	1874 - 1878
W. A. Duggin	1878 - 1882
J. J. Atkinson	1882 - 1882
H. L. Staton	1883 - 1886
B. J. Keech	1886 - 1890
Ed Pennington	1890 - 1906
A. T. Walston	1906 - 1945
W. S. Babcock	1946 - 1955
Don Gilliam, Jr.	1955 - 19_

ABBREVIATIONS

A	acres
Adm.	administrator
Bro.	brother
Chil.	child/children
C. C.	Clerk of Court
Ct.	court
Dau.	daughter
Dec'd.	deceased
Exr.	executor
Extx.	executrix
Gr. dau.	granddaughter
Gr. neph.	grandnephew
Gr. niece	grandniece
Gr. son	grandson
Gdn.	guardian
Neph.	nephew
₤	pounds
Prob.	probate
Ref.	reference
S.	shillings
Sgd.	signed
Wit:	witnesses

Nunc. placed after dates of wills indicates that the will is nuncupative.

I N T R O D U C T I O N

It might be a matter of considerable interest to
discuss the general background of old Edgecombe County
in the period covered by these abstracts of its early
wills, but anything of real value would be sufficiently
long to divert the attention of the reader from the
principal work, while encroaching upon the materials
of any future historian who might wish to prepare a
corrected and enlarged version of the "History of
Edgecombe County" published thirty-six years ago by
J. Kelly Turner and John L. Bridgers, Jr. Since a map
has been included to show the geographical boundaries
possessed by Edgecombe County at various times during
the period of the present volume, some additional de-
tails of these territorial changes will undoubtedly
make the best possible Introduction.

Although Edgecombe County did not enjoy a truly
independent organization until Northampton County was
severed from Bertie County in 1741, it had been estab-
lished as an effective Precinct, to all practical pur-
poses, on May 16, 1732, and had been named for Sir
Richard Edgecombe, later Baron Edgecombe, who was Lord
of the British Treasury at that time. The Edgecombe
County wills actually began with one in the year 1733
and were probated by the Clerk of the Bertie County
Court prior to 1741, but after that date Edgecombe
County had its own Clerk and Court.

The colonists who petitioned the Governor and
Council for this new Precinct resided on Fishing Creek
and adjacent areas south of Morotock (or Roanoke)
River as far as the mouth of Conoconaro Creek. Governor
George Burrington and His Majesty's Council readily
approved (to the expressed annoyance of the General
Assembly of North Carolina) their request, with Roanoke
River as the northern boundary with Bertie County, a
straight line from Conoconaro Creek through Blount's
Old Town on Tar River to Neuse River as the eastern
boundary with Beaufort (later Pitt) County, and a rather
nebulous line northwesterly past the North East Branch
of Cape Fear River as the southern boundary with

Craven County (later Johnston and Wayne Counties).

As the result of a new petition on October 31, 1732, the Governor and Council pivoted the beginning of the middle line eastward to the Rainbow Banks (near the present Hamilton) on Roanoke River. On November 11, 1734, a Bill to establish Edgecombe Precinct was finally introduced into the General Assembly; it appears never to have been enacted into a Law, and yet Edgecombe was and continued to be a functioning Precinct (and later, County) in the records of all parties concerned. There was no question about its northern boundary, but its eastern and southern boundaries had never been formally surveyed. On February 22, 1739/40, ineffectual Bills were introduced for establishing Edgecombe as a County and for ascertaining the true course of the line shared with Beaufort County.

Edgecombe finally achieved the full status of a County of the Colony of North Carolina on April 4, 1741, and all of it was included in Edgecombe Parish. In the official Act, the Roanoke River continued as the northern boundary, from which a line beginning at Jenkin Henry's upper corner went straight past the mouth of Cheek's Mill Creek on Tar River to "the middle grounds" between Tar River and Neuse River, and then northwesterly between them "as nigh as may be". The Beaufort County line was fairly well known, and Commissioners were supposed to determine more precisely the division with Craven County, but for some reason the latter boundary remained uncertain and troublesome even after "Granville's Line" was surveyed between the holdings of King George II and the Earl of Granville in the year 1743.

On April 6, 1748, therefore, the General Assembly was forced to appoint Mr. Joseph Howell and Mr. Joseph Lane as new commissioners to finish running the line from the mouth of Cheek's Mill Creek on Tar River, straight to the mouth of Tosneot Swamp on Contentnea Creek, and then up Contentnea Creek as far as a point opposite the mouth of Cypress Creek on Tar River. This point was the one from which a straight line had been drawn by Commissioners William Eaton, William Person, James Macklewean, and Francis Stringer through the mouth of Cypress Creek N. N. E. to the

mouth of Stonehouse Creek on Roanoke River, as had
been authorized on June 28, 1746, by the Act to set
apart all the western area of Edgecombe County as a
new Parish named St. John and County named Granville.
This represented the first of the four major divisions
of Edgecombe County.

By an Act dated October 13, 1756, Edgecombe Parish
was divided and the lower part became St. Mary's Parish.
The line of division began where the old Parish Line
crossed Conetoe Creek, followed the Creek to its head,
took a straight course to Fishing Creek at the Michael
Dorman place, and then proceeded up Fishing Creek to
the line that separated Edgecombe Parish from St. John's
Parish in Granville County. On December 8, 1758, this
same line served to divide the newly created Halifax
County and Edgecombe Parish on the north from Edgecombe County and St. Mary's Parish on the south. All
the Edgecombe County records prior to January 1, 1759,
remained in the old Court House at Halifax, and those
beginning at a later date soon settled down at Tarboro
(with the exception of those that have been deposited
lately in the North Carolina State Archives at Raleigh).

St. Mary's Parish was divided on March 2, 1774,
by running a straight line from James Cane's plantation on Fishing Creek to Redmond Bunn's place on Tar
River and thence to Christian Rowe's Ferry on Contentnea Creek. The area lying west of this line would
henceforth be known as St. Elizabeth's Parish. The
third division of Edgecombe County was effected by an
Act dated April 8, 1777, which appointed Commissioners
Joseph Clinch, Arthur Arrington, Henry Horn, Jr.,
Daniel Ross, and Isaac Horn to run a line from the
Cool Springs at John Powell's plantation on Fishing
Creek to the Falls of Tar River and thence to the
Widow Rowe's Ferry on Contentnea Creek. The new County
named Nash lay on the west side of this line and embodied St. Elizabeth's Parish approximately, although
the Episcopal Parish system expired with many other
British Colonial regulations at the beginning of the
Revolutionary War.

On January 29, 1779, there was annexed to Edgecombe County a small piece of Halifax County lying
below a line run from the Wall–Crocker corner on

Fishing Creek to John Wall's back corner, directly to
the fork of Marsh Swamp near Matthew Parker's place,
down the Swamp to Deep Creek, across the mouth of
Indian Branch, and along this Branch to the Martin
County line. On May 29, 1784, Commissioners were appointed to "extend" the line from the old Edgecombe-
Halifax line at the Benjamin Cotton place directly to
the Martin-Pitt line at the Charles Council place.

In 1793 Edgecombe County was again increased
slightly by the part of Martin County southwest of a
line running from the Edgecombe-Halifax-Martin junc-
tion to the Wolf Pond near Indian Branch, thence to
the Great Cypress Pond in Williams's wilderness,
directly to Thomas Taylor's place, and then due south
to the Pitt County line. In 1801 Pitt County surren-
dered to Edgecombe County the acreage removed by running a line from the point at which the old Edgecombe
County line crossed Conetoe Creek near Samuel Crisp's
home, down the Creek to the Christopher Harrell plantation, and then nearly west to the said Edgecombe
County line.

The fourth and last major division of Edgecombe
County occurred on February 13, 1855, when the area
north of Contentnea Creek and between the counties
of Nash and Pitt was included in the formation of
Wilson County. Beginning in the Pitt County line about
a half-mile southwest of the head of Lang's Mill Run,
a straight line was run by Surveyor Redden S. Petway
northwest five miles to Pender's Hill, thence N. N. W.
to Town Creek at the mouth of Colonel David Williams's
Mill Branch, up the Branch to the Mill, and northwest
past the home of William Adams, Sr., to the Nash
County line near Sharpsburg.

In 1871 that strip of Edgecombe County west of the
Wilmington & Weldon Railroad and between the Halifax
and Wilson County lines was annexed to Nash County.
On March 12, 1883, a new line was authorized to be
run north from the Rake Straw Place to the bridge on
Williams's Branch on the road leading from Upper Town
Creek Church to Temperance Hall Church, up the Branch
to its head, northwesterly to the Sharpsburg Road near
the house of E. G. Hales, down this road to the Wilmington & Weldon Railroad, and then south along the

Railroad to the original Wilson County line. This survey added only a small amount of territory to the northeastern part of Wilson County, and represented the last appreciable alteration to the boundaries of modern Edgecombe County.

In conclusion, I wish to express my personal pride and pleasure in having been of some small assistance to my friends, Mrs. Ruth Smith Williams and Mrs. Margarette Glenn Griffin, in the planning and preparation of this book. Both ladies are exceptionally capable and intelligent, as will be evidenced abundantly by the accuracy and uniformly high quality of their work. They have performed an invaluable service for posterity in making available to every genealogist and historian the large, varied, and valuable mass of information buried in the wills of old Edgecombe County between 1733 and 1856. I venture the opinion that theirs will prove the most important single volume of will abstracts published in the South down to the present date.

Hugh B. Johnston, Jr.

Wilson, North Carolina
July 1, 1956

ABSTRACTS
OF
THE WILLS OF EDGECOMBE COUNTY
NORTH CAROLINA

ABINGTON, PENELOPE

Sept. 9, 1846. Nov. Ct., 1855. Bk. G, p 144. JOHN S. DANCY, $200, bed, bedstead and curtains and my sunflower bed quilt. Friends: HELEN RAGSDALE, $100; MARY WILSON, $30 and my star and garter bedquilt; MRS. SARAH FOXHALL, broadcloth cloak; MARGARET LEWIS, merino scarf; SUSAN SMITH, French blanket shawl; NANCY DANCY, wife of WILLIAM F. DANCY, all land and other property to be sold, proceeds together with notes, money, bonds, etc. held in trust by Adm., interest paid annually to NANCY DANCY, reversion to her 4 daus. Wit: JOHN H. MATHEWSON, N. MATHEWSON. Codicil: Sept. 28, 1846. Bequeath to WILLIAM F. DANCY, buggy and harness, value $150. Wit: JOHN H. MATHEWSON, N. MATHEWSON. No Exr. JOHN S. DANCY, Adm. Bond $8000. WM. NORFLEET & N. MATHEWSON, Securities.

ADAMS, HOPEWELL

Oct. 18, 1794. May Ct., 1799. Sons: JAMES, all the lands of which he is now possessed and my still; HOPEWELL, two negroes. Son & Exr: WILLIAM, plantation whereon I live. Daus: SARAH, one mare colt; JANE TENNISON, wife of ABRAHAM TENNISON, 5 S and this to be their full share of my living. Wit: JOHN LITTLE, JOHN HINES.

ADAMS, JAMES

Feb. 4, 1818. Feb. Ct., 1820. Bk. E, p 233. Son: JAMES, 1 negro, remaining slaves to be divided between 3 sons; Son & Exr: HENRY; Son: HOPEWELL. Daus: PEGGY BELL, SALLY KNIGHT, MERIA (MARIA) PRICE, $10 each. Wit: THOMAS EDMONDSON, SR., G. FOOTE. Will Caveated by ALLEVANY, EMELINA, BETHANY, ELINZA, JULIA & HUGH HUDSON BELL, by JOSHUA BELL, their next friend; CHARLES KNIGHT, in right of his wife, SALLY; JOHN PRICE, in right of his wife MARIA and BRITTAIN SAVIDGE.

1

ADAMS, READING
Aug. 10, 1808. Aug. Ct., 1808. Bk. D, p 326. Wife:
SINEY, mare, her bridle and saddle, and three wheels.
Lend 1 negro and all remaining estate until eldest
child attains maturity, unless my wife should sooner
marry; in either case, I request that my land be equally divided between my sons, CULLEN & WILLIAM, at the
same time the balance of my property shall be equally
divided among all my children (unnamed). Exr:
CHRISTOPHER HARRELL. Wit: HENRY P. TOOLE, JAMES ADAMS.

ADDAMS, WILLIAM
June 7, 1824. May Ct., 1829. Wife: ELIZABETH, all
property both reyal (real) personal and perishable.
After her death all property shall be divided between
ALLEN JONES, ASA JONES, FREDERICK JONES & ELIZABETH
BELL, these being my wife's children. Exr: ALLEN JONES,
ASA JONES, FREDERICK JONES. Wit: M. W. MAYO, WILLIAM
GRIMES.

ALLEN, JAMES
Dec. 4, 1733. Feb. Ct., 1733. Legatee: JAMES KELLEY.
Exr: JOHN NAIRNE. Wit: WILLIAM BELL, ANNE STONE, JOHN
STONE. Impression of head on seal. (Grimes's Wills).

ALLEN, JOHN
Oct. 20, 1763. Oct. Ct., 1763. Wife & Extx: ALICE,
estate to be sold and after debts are paid, bequeath
to wife, all the remainder to raise her children upon
(unnamed). Wit: ELISHA BATTLE, RACHEL COLEMAN and
SARAH COLEMAN.

ALLEN, ROGER
June 5, 1762. June Ct., 1762. Wife & Extx:
ELIZABETH, plantation and all land; also, remainder of
estate provided she maintains my daughter MARY during
her life with sufficient meat, close and lodging. Daus:
ELIZABETH GANDY, 10 ᏞProclamation money and cow and
calf; MARY. Wit: DUNCAN LAMON, JOHN DORMAN, EDWARD
GANDY.

ALLIN, SAMUEL
Jan. 13, 1763. Jan. Ct., 1763. Nunc. Will. SAMUEL

ALLIN before his discease made a statement that he
wished to appoint one CALEB HOLLIS of Pitt County, to
be manager of his estate, take his books and accounts
and get in all his debts and likewise pay all the debts
that he, SAMUEL ALLIN, owes. Furthermore ALLIN says
there is a new camblet coat and briches of mine that
it is my desire that ye aforesaid CALOB HOLLIS should
take them and dispose of them for the use of his children, and as for the rest of my close, I give them to
my son; and as for my bed and furniture, I reserve the
use of them to my wife; and as for the other part of
my estate after my debts is paid, it is my will and
desire that it shall be equally divided between my son
DEMCY ALLIN and the aforesaid CALOB HOLLIS. Certified
by CAPT. JOSEPH HOWELL, Esq. Sworn to before WM. HAYWOOD.

ALSOBROOK, PARTHINIA
    May 26, 1808. Aug. Ct., 1812. Bk. E, p 40. Dau &
Extx: MILLEY ALSOBROOK, my side saddle, chest, trunk;
remainder household goods and two cows to be sold, proceeds to MILLEY. Daus: PRISSY HUDNALL & RHODAY WEEKS,
5 S each. Wit: JOHN GATER, SAMUAL GATER, GRACE GATER.

AMASON, DELANA
    Sept. 4, 1841. Nov. Ct., 1841. Bk. F, p 262. Wife:
JEMIMA AMASON, Lend land whereon I live, purchased of
THEOPHILUS GAY and wife. Dau: JEMIMAH AMASON, 1 horse,
1 negro, 2 cows and calves, 2 sows and pigs, 6 sheep.
working tools, plow, gear, cart, furniture, ½ doz.
mulberry chairs, ½ doz. chairs purchased of HENRY
WOODARD, 1800 wt. pork, 75 bbls. corn, 7 stacks fodder.
Daus: ELIZABETH AMASON, $20; ALSA JOHNSON, 6 plates,
2 bowls; DELANA AMASON, geese, woolen wheel, linen
wheel, loom, which I purchased of SALLY DICKENSON. Son
& Exr: ISAAC URIAH AMASON, balance of land purchased
of HENRY WOODARD, sheep and oxen. Sons: JOHN AMASON,
$1; DAVID WILLIAMS AMASON, all my land except that
lent to wife, JEMIMA; 2 year old colt, blue chest,
notes now on hand. Gr. dau: PENNINA JANE ROGERS, my
riding saddle; MARTHA ANN DELANA ROGERS, blue chest
purchased of SALLIE DICKINSON. Gr. chil: WILLIAM W.;
THOMAS J. & ELISHA AMASON, each $1; MARY ANN, HARRIETT
& MARIAH GAY, each $1. Wit: LEWIS ELLIS, JESSE
APPLEWHITE.

3

AMASON, ELLENDOR
Aug. 18, 1829. Feb. Ct., 1832. Bk. F, p 131. Dau:
SALLY WARD, $10; Gr. dau: ELEANOR WARD, $50. Son: WM.
AMASON, $10. Gr. dau: ELIZA M. AMASON, $50. Sons:
NATHAN AMASON, $50; ELBERT AMASON, 1 negro, blacksmith
tools, ½ brandy made this year and Colt, my sorrel mare
is in foal with; ASA AMASON, 2 negroes and barrel of
brandy. Daus: NANCY AMASON, negro boy; POLLY & ELIZABETH,
lend 2 negroes. Wit: JAMES BARNES, COFIELD ELLIS.

AMASON, THOMAS
Sept. 25, 1792. Nov. Ct., 1792. Daus: PRISCILLA
WHITLEY, stone pitcher and sundial; MARY AMASON, ANN
SINGLETON, SARAH HALL, 5 S each; MILLACENT WHITLEY,
dish, bason, plate and all my sheep; CHRISTIAN JOHNSON,
remainder of estate. Son & Exr: WILLIAM, my manner
(manor) plantation and all land belonging to it. Exr:
ELI AMASON. Wit: EDWARD MAYO, LUKE BOLTON, JEMIMA
BOLTON.

AMASON, WILLIAM
Apr. 11, 1793. No probate date. Wife: SARAH AMASON,
lend plantation on which I live; also residue, Sons:
JAMES AMASON, JESSE AMASON, 1 ewe and 70 A of land,
which he hath already had by deed of gift; Son & Exr:
JOHN AMASON, my plantation, after his mother's death.
Daus: PATIENCE BARNES (BONNER?), 5 S beside what she
hath already had; OBEDIENCE BAGGET; ELIZABETH BRANTLEY;
MARTHA BAGGET, 2 ewes which she hath allredy in her
persesion. Exr: ELI AMASON. Wit: _____THOMAS, NATHAN
BARNES, ETHELDRED AMASON.

AMASON, WILLIAM
Mar. 10, 1811. Aug. Ct, 1811. Son & Exr: ELI, plantation whereon I live; Son: MINOAH AMASON, land lying
on Long Branch, brandy still and grindstone. Chil of
MINOAH AMASON, all property of mine now in persession
of MINOAH AMASON. Daus: ALICE BENTLEY, 1 negro; ADAY
DAVIS, 2 ₺ current money. Residue to be divided thus:
1/5 to ELI AMASON, 1/5 to children of JEMMIMAY BOLTEN,
1/5 to children of MINOAH AMASON, 1/5 to ALICE BENTLEY,
and 1/5 to children of ADAY DAVIS. Exr: GARRET KNIGHT.
Wit: JONATHAN ELLIS, ASHLEY TURNELL, WILLIAM JOHNSTON,

ANDERSON, HENRY
Nov. 24, 1801. Feb. Ct., 1802. Wife: CHARITY, lend
½ of land and ½ personal property with reversion to 5
sons: Sons: WILLIAM, ALLEN, JOHN, HENRY (Exr),
FREDERICK. Daus: VINEY, POLLY, $30 each. Exr: DRURY
MAY. Wit: P. PUGG (PEGG?), JOHN LITTLE.

ANDERSON, WILLIAM
Nov. 29, 1789. May Ct., 1790. Bk. 3, p 145. Wife:
MOURNING, lend all land on S side Tarr River, N side
Iyancokey Swamp and on Faulk's Branch together with
residue of estate, except 28 A lying N of Tarr River.
Daus: ABASALA VAUGHN, MARTHA STALLINGS, wife of JOHN
STALLINGS. Sons: GEORGE, JAMES, WILLIAM, (son of my
former wife, MARTHA), WILLIAM (son of my present wife,
MOURNING), CHARLES, HENRY, reversion of all land. Daus:
RACHEL, MOURNING, PENELOPE, MARY, bequeath to each
child except HENRY, 5 S. Exr: JESSE DELOATCH, JOHN
SHERROD, ELIJAH PRICE. Wit: L. RUFFIN, ELIJAH HORN,
JOSEPH PITMAN.

ANDREWS, ELIZABETH
Apr. 4, 1767. Jan. Ct., 1768. Daus: ELIZABETH,
MARY & SARAH, all wearing clothes to be equally divi-
ded between 3 daus., except one blue and white striped
cotton gownd and one white cotton pettycoat bordered
with calico which I give Gr. dau: SARAH NICHOLSON. Son
& Exr: BENJAMIN NICHOLSON, remainder of my estate. Wit:
SAM'L TANNER, PAMELA NICHOLSON, JAMES (?) GRAY.

ANDREWS, ELIZABETH MAUN
Oct. 21, 1820. Nov. Ct., 1820. Sons: JONAS
JOHNSTON BELL $25; RICHARD BELL $25 each; WILLIAM
JOHNSTON ANDREWS, negro boy and $300; ABNER, negro
boy and $300. Daus: MARTHA MAUN ANDREWS, 2 negro girls
and $300; MARGARET MAUN ANDREWS, 2 negro girls and
$300. I will that my land and plantation be sold to-
gether with negro girl Bedett and her child. The Marsey
(marshy) Branch field whereon my mother's dower ex-
tends should be sold separately, and it is my wish
that COL. PETER HINES purchase it for particular con-

siderations from me to him. It is my wish that all my
negroes not herein named should be divided, and my 2
sons, WILLIAM J. ANDREWS & ABNER ANDREWS share 1/3
divided, between them, and my 2 daughters MARTHA &
MARGARETT should have the other 2/3 equally divided
between them.

When my youngest dau. MARGARETT shall arrive at
the age of 18 yrs. or marry, there should be a general
division and not before. I will that my Exrs. should
retain in their hands the sum of $600 for the main-
tainance of my 2 old negroes Sam and his wife Nannar
so long as they live, and that they be permitted to
have a house and garden plot. The $300 left each
ANDREWS child was according to contract with THOMAS
NORFLET. Exrs: JOHN SCARBOROUGH, ELIAS CARR. Wit:
RAWLEY REASONS, WILLIE EDWARDS.

ANDREWS, JESSE
    Nov. 15, 1771. Aug. Ct., 1772. Bk. Q, p 198. Wife
& Extx: MELIA, lend whole estate. Sons: ALLEN, CULLEN.
Daus: ELIZABETH, JEAN. Reversion of lands purchased of
SAMUEL WILLIAMS, joining lands of JEREMIAH HILLIARD &
WILLIAM HORN to 2 sons. Exr: ELISHA BATTLE, Esq. Wit:
LYDIA WHITE, SARAH LANCASTER, WM. WILLIAMS.

ANDREWS, JOHN
    July 2, 1809. Nov. Ct., 1809. Bk. D, p 352. Wife
& Extx: ELIZABETH MAUND ANDREWS. Exr: PETER EVANS,
HENRY J. TOOLE. Wit: H. HAYWOOD, JAMES HOWARD.

ANDREWS, WHILDON
    Jan. 20, 1823. May Ct., 1823. Bk. E, p 327. Wife:
Unnamed. Sons & Exr: WALLACE, land; HENRY, land, still,
colt and $100; Son: GRAY, land. Dau: PATSY, cow and
calf and chest. Lands lying along Best's line, Sugg's
Branch, Pool's line, Pitt County line and Piney Island.
Wit: WILLIAM W. ANDREWS, HENRY MATTHEWS.

ANSLEY, JOSEPH
    Mar. 23, 1826. May Ct., 1826. Bk. F, p 57. Sis:
SOPHIA BELL, $150. Niece: JOANN AMBROSE, 1st dau of
my bro ZACARIAH AMBROSE, $150; Bros: DAWSON, JORDAN,
JOHN, PETER & ABROSE, $450 each. Exr: REDDIN SUGG; Wit:

DAVID DANCY, BENJAMIN BOYKIN.

ARCHER, ZACHARIAH
   Dec. 14, 1813. Feb. Ct., 1818. Bk. E, p 179. Wife
& Extx: JOANNA, 1/3 entire estate. Bros: JEREMIAH,
JOHN, 5 S each. Friend and Exr: ZACHARIAH DEW, remain-
der of estate. Wit: STARLING WALLER, WARREN WALLER.

ARMSTRONG, ROBERT
   Sept. 3, 1798. Nov. Ct., 1798. Wife: MARY, lend
plantation. Sons: GRAY, plantation at mother's death;
MATTHEW, land bought of JACOB BATTLE. Legatees: JOHN
LONG, JOSEPH ARMSTRONG, ELIZABETH LAND, MARY LONG,
SARAH BRAKE. Extrs: JACOB BATTLE, JOSEPH ARMSTRONG;
Wit: ANDERSON STURDIVANT, WM. FAULK.

ASKEW, JOSIAH
   Oct. 10, 1818. Nov. Ct., 1818. Wife: Unnamed. PEGGA
BARRON. Sons: ELIE, ENOS, horse; WILLIAM, $300; JOSIAH,
$50; DAVID 10 S. Exr: None named. Wit: EGBERT H.
WILLIAMS, EDWIN GARDNER. Adms. apptd: JOHN WILKINSON,
AARON ATKINSON. Bond securities: JESSE C. KNIGHT,
LAMON DUNN.

ATKINSON, AARON
   Jan. 1, 1842. May Ct., 1848. Bk. F, p 392. Wife:
SALLY, lend land whereon I dwell, also 2 negroes. Re-
version to heirs excepting NANCY WALSTON. Dau: NANCY
WALSTON, land whereon she and her husband dwell, pur-
chased of AMOS WALSTON, adjoining JOHN P. PITT: 9 ne-
groes to be sold, monies equally divided among unnamed
heirs excepting wife and NANCY WALSTON. Exr: WILLIE
ATKINSON, THEOPHILUS ATKINSON. Wit: B. G. H. WEAVER,
JOAB P. PITT.

AUSTIN, HENRY
   July 10, 1843. Feb. Ct., 1845. Wife: LYDIA, 4 negroes, $4000, lend Town Lot No. 17 where we now reside,
lot 12, all furniture, carts, wagon, horse, mule, acr-
riage, harness, also pinney woods land near town. Reversion to youngest dau: MARY JANE AUSTIN. Son & Exr:
ROBERT H., $5000, negro woman, 6 negroes, also Lots 48,
73, 74 and 63 in Tarboro. Daus: MARTHA ANN DOWD $2000,

6 negroes, land purchased of HENRY TAYLOR and $2000 to
be held in trust for her benefit and kept free of control of husband by Exr. Reversion to her children.
CATHERINE ELIZABETH CRENSHAW, $2000, 5 negroes and lots
2 and 23 in Tarboro and $2000 held in trust by Exr. and
free from control of husband. Reversion to her children;
MARY JANE AUSTIN, $2000, 4 negroes, town lots No. 12
and 17 whereon I live and $2000. Reversion to her heirs.
No witnesses. Proven in Ct. by oaths of HENRY T. CLARK,
JAMES WEDDELL, JAMES M. REDMOND.

AUSTIN, LYDIA
    Sept. 29, 1852. Feb. Ct., 1853. Son & Exr: ROBERT
H. AUSTIN, $400. Daus: MARTHA ANN DOWD (?), 2 negroes;
CATHERINE E. CRENSHAW, MARY I. MATHEWSON, residue di-
vided equally.

AVERITT, JAMES (Sr.)
    Nov. 15, 1822. Nov. Ct., 1823. Bk. F, p 4. Wife:
EDAH. Son & Exr: EDWIN, land after death of Mother.
Sons: THOMAS & KINTCHEN, $10 each; JAMES, land after
death of Mother. Daus: ELSEY BUNTYN, $5. Chil of ELSEY
BUNTYN: BENJ., EVERITT, JAMES, AMY & SALLY, 1/7 of es-
tate. LEVINIA SMITH. Chil of LAVINA SMITH, 1/7 of es-
tate. CLARACY MANNING, Chil of CLARACY MANNING:
HARRIETT, MARINA, LAVINA, 1/7 of estate; LUVYCE SMITH,
1/7 of estate; ELENER MATTHEWS, 1/7 of estate; SALLY
GODARD, 1/7 of estate; EDAH BATON, 1/7 of estate. Wit:
JOHN BEST, SALLY BEST, WILLIAM BEST.

BAILEY, JOHNATHAN
    No date. Feb. Ct., 1852. Bk. F, p 470. Daus: LUCY
BRAZWELL, 1 negro; POLLY TAYLOR, her heir, 1 negro;
SALLY JORDAN, lend land whereon she lives, and 1 negro,
reversion to her children; NANCY RUFFIN, lend land
whereon she lives and also 1 negro. Reversion to her
children; REBECCA MAY, lend negro girl, reversion to
her children; MARTHA AMASON, 5 negroes; DILLY, (dec'd?)
her children; DAVID LAWRENCE WILLIAMS (Gr. son);
ELIZABETH WILLIAMS (Gr. dau), 1 negro and $120 to be
divided between them. Sons: BENJAMIN, his heirs to
have land on N side road and adjoining MATTHEW
WHITEHEAD, JEREMIAH BATTS; also 1 negro. Exr: THOMAS

AMASON, JEREMIAH BATTS. Wit: D. WILLIAMS & THOMAS FLY.

BAKER, DAVID G.
    Sept. 12, 1844. Nov. Ct., 1844. Bk. F, p 313. Wife
unnamed. Residue for support of wife and infant children. Exr: & Gdn of Chil: MOSES BAKER. Wit: D. WILLIAMS,
WM. S. BAKER. Codicil, Sept. 22, 1844. Exr: to buy beloved wife a trusty negro fellow, skilled in management
of farm and repairing emplements. Wit: WM. S. BAKER,
JOHN PITT.

BAKER, ELIZABETH
    Aug. 29, 1831. Nov. Ct., 1831. Bk. F, p 130. Son:
BENJAMIN P. PORTER, 2 negroes and a mare, Daus: ANN T.
PORTER, it is my will and desire that my family remain
and live together and that my son BENJAMIN try to raise
the young negroes, and stock and cattle be kept for
use of family. Exr: FIGURES PHILIPS. Wit: RICHARD
BAXTER, EDWD. POWER.

BAKER, JESSE
    Sept. 1787. Jan. Ct., 1788. Bk. B, p 65. Wife:
MARTHA. Sons: JONATHAN, MOSES, AARON & DAVID. Exr:
THOMAS MERCER, RICHARD STROTHER. Wit: S. RUFFIN,
JOSEPH PITTMAN, ETHELRED RUFFIN.

BAKER, JULIA
    May 18, 1790. Nov. Ct., 1790. Bk. 3, p 148. Nunc.
Will. Bros: BENJ. BLAKE BAKER, 1 negro; WILLIAM, 1
negro. Nephs: BENJ. BEVERLY BAKER (son of RICHARD, 1
negro; RICHARD HENRY BAKER, 1 negro. Niece: MARY BAKER
(dau of RICHARD), 4 negroes; Friends: SARAH BENTON, 1
negro girl, also bureau and worked toilet cloths. Sis:
EMILY BAKER, MARTHA LOUISA BAKER, wearing apparel.
Bro-in-law: DR. JOHN LEIGH, watch. Division to be
made by MRS. ELIZABETH BAKER, MRS. JUDITH BAKER, MRS.
CATHERINE BAKER. Written by THOMAS BLOUNT and proved
in court by oath of ĄANN HARVEY'.

BAKER, MOSES
    Dec. 1, 1781. Nov. Ct., 1786. Bk. C, p 28. My 7
eldest children having already had their full portion
of my estate, I leave 5 S to each of the following:

Gr. son: MOSES, eldest son of my eldest son, MICHAEL;
Son: MOSES; Gr. dau: ELIZABETH, dau of my son, AARON;
THOMAS, JOSHUA. Daus: ANN, wife of RALPH VICKERS &
MARY, widow of MICAJAH STINSON. Son & Exr: JESSE BAKER,
all land and remainder of estate. Wit: WILLIAM BRAND,
CHRISTIAN BRAND, BENJ. BRAND.

BALDIN, (BOLDEN?), JONATHAN
    Jan. 18, 1781. May Ct., 1781. Wife & Extx: SARAH.
Exr: ANDREW IRWIN. Wit: PECK (?) PROCTOR, SMITH BRYON,
SARAH LOW.

BANDY, JAMES
    Sept. 26, 1807. Nov. Ct., 1812. Bk. E, p 50. Wife
& Extx: SUSANNAH. Exr: ETHELRED EXUM. Wit: FREDERICK,
PHILIPS.

BANDY, SUSAN
    Jan. 8, 1840. Nov. Ct., 1842. Bk. F, p 270.
Friends: HENRY HYMAN, 10 slaves "In consideration of
the high regard and esteem I have for him, and from
the full confidence that he will treat well and take
good care of all my slaves, I wish that he should have
them." SARAH KNIGHT, wife of JAMES C. KNIGHT, 1 negro
woman, Tempe, wife of his man Arnold. Neph: MATTHEW
EXUM, son of JOHN EXUM, 1 negro. MARTHA ANN FORT, infant dau of JOHN FORT, $50. LAURA BAKER, dau of WM.
S. BAKER, property which descended to me from my sister
MARY DURLEY (?). Exr: HENRY HYMAN. Wit: EPHRAIM DICKEN,
JAMES M. REDMOND.

BANKS, THOMAS
    June 15, 1829. Nov. Ct., 1829. Bk. E, p 108. Wife:
PATSY, entire estate, lands from Wyatt's bridge to
Mount Prospect, adjoining lands of HENRY BRYAN, pur-
chased of AARON JOHNSTON. Exr: HENRY AUSTIN, Esq. Exr.
refused to serve. Wit: LOUIS D. WILSON, EZEKIEL STATON;
Adm. granted LUNSFORD R. CHERRY. Securities: JOHN P.
MANNING, WILLIE BRADLEY.

BAREFOOT, JEPTHAH
    May 13, 1799. Feb. Ct., 1800. Wife: MARGARET, plan-
tation, furniture & stock. Son: MAT(?), plantation

whereon he lives; Gr. sons: SENETH, JEPTHAH, MAT, JOHN,
orphans of dec'd son NOAH, 150 A; JOHN 150 A; WILLIAM,
Gr. son, JONATHAN, son of WILLIAM, 25 A; STEPHEN, Gr.
son, DILLIN, son of STEPHEN, 150 A. Exr: JEPTHAH
BAREFOOT, JOHN BAREFOOT. Wit: CHAS. COLEMAN, WILLIAM
BOND WHITEHEAD.

BAREFOOT, JEPTHAH
     Feb. 7, 1805. Feb. Ct., 1805. Bk. D, p 221. Sons:
THOMAS, NOAH, all lands and plantations equally di-
vided. Daus: MARGARETT, SARAH, remainder of property.
Exr: CHAS. COLEMAN. Wit: STEPHEN BAREFOOT, JOHN
BAREFOOT, DEMSEY JORDAN.

BARFIELD, CHARLES
     June 9, 1809. Aug. Ct., 1809. Bk. D, p 349. Wife:
ELIZABETH, $50. Sons: FEDRICK, horse, bridle and saddle
which equals $100; HOPKIN (?), horse which equals $80.
Dau: VINAH ANDRY. JOHN ANDRY, son of dau VINAH ANDRY,
$50 which is daughter's part. Residue to be divided
between wife and dau. Exr: WILLIE STANTON. Wit:
BENJAMIN AMASON, WILLIAM ELLIS.

BARFIELD, DICEY
     July 19, 1851. Feb. Ct., 1852. My natural son:
HENRY BARFIELD, all of my estate. Exr: ROBT. H. AUSTIN,
Esq. Wit: T. L. LAWRENCE, JOHN L. KNIGHT.

BARFIELD, EPHRAIM
     Mar. 10, 1848. Feb. Ct., 1853. Bk. F, p 496. Son:
BYNUM BARFIELD, $5 - has had an equal part; Son & Exr:
HORACE ELY BARFIELD, all my land and 9 negroes, stock,
cattle, household and kitchen furniture, utensils, corn,
fodder, cotton, peas and wheat and all money due me.
Gr. dau: TABITHA ANN BARFIELD, dau of BYNUM BARFIELD, 1
negro. Exr: HARMON WARD. Wit: WILSON HOWARD, ARTHUR B.
HYMAN.

BARFIELD, JAMES
     Dec. 9, 1770. Probated, 1770. Wife: ANN, lend use
of plantation, whereon I live and 3 negroes. Sons:
DANIEL, plantation whereon he lives, also reversion in
1 negro; MILES, reversion in 2 negroes; SAMUEL, re-

version in young horse; JAMES, reversion in plantation
whereon I live. Daus: ELIZABETH BOON, 3 ₺ money;
CATHERINE BARTLEY, 2 cows & calves; CRESSEY BARFIELD,
cow and calf. Exr: BENJAMIN AMASON. Wit: WILLIAM
DANIEL, EPHRAIM BARNES, JOHN THOMAS, SR.

BARFIELD, JOHN SR.
July 29, 1845. Nov. Ct., 1846. Bk. F, p 349. DICY
BARFIELD, mare, cow & calf, 8 shoats, 1 ewe & lamb,
beehive and corn.. Lend my house field, wheete patch
field for her life. Residue sold and divided among
lawful heirs. Exr: GERALDUS GARRETT, HORACE ELI
BARFIELD. Wit: ALFRED EDMONDSON, HARMON WARD.

BARFIELD, LYDIA
Oct. 17, 1828. Nov. Ct., 1828. Bk. F, p 95. Dau
& Extx: DICY BARFIELD, 1½ dozen plates, bowstrate and
pitcher, wooling and flax wheals, 2 dishes, 1 bason,
4 setting chears, pot, loom, 2 pare harnesses, 3
earthen bowls, 1 set tea cups and sawsers. Wit: THOS.
EDMONDSON, ASA EDMONDSON.

BARKSDALE, DANIEL
No date. Nov. Ct., 1835. Bk. F, p 179. ASA WILSON,
for his friendship and services, tract on N side of
White Oak Swamp on lines of FIGURES PHILIPS, WILLIAM
E. BELLAMY, CALEB ETHERIDGE. Also 5 negroes. Residue
sold and divided in 3 parts, 1/3 to chil of sis
ELIZABETH BRADFORD, wife of JOHN BRADFORD; 1/3 to be
divided between HENRY EELBECK, and JOHN BRADFORD'S
chil by his wife, POLLY, formerly POLLY EELBECK, and
THOMAS BRADFORD'S chil by his wife ELIZABETH, formerly
ELIZABETH EELBECK; the other 1/3 between BENJAMIN F.
HALLSEY'S chil by his wife CLEOPATRA, formerly
CLEOPATRA BARKSDALE. Exr: BENJAMIN F. HALLSEY. Wit:
WILLIAM F. BELLAMY, WILLIAM L. HUNT.

BARLOW, DAVID
Nov. 29, 1789. Feb. Ct., 1790. Bk. 3, p 130. Sons:
LUIS, all lands divided equally between 3 sons;
DAVID, still, negro; BENJAMIN. Dau & Extx: SARAH, 1
negro Jim, and gray mare; BECCA, 1 negro and 18 pounds
specia. Exr: SMITH BRYANT. Wit: JOHN BATTS, HARDY

BRYAN, WILKERSON MABREY.

BARLOW, LEWIS
    Feb. 7, 1831. Aug. Ct., 1831. Bk. F, p 127. Son:
BILLY BLUNT BARLOW, lend 3 negroes.. if no heirs, then
to my dau, LOUISA KNIGHT, or heirs. PETER E. KNIGHT be
Gdn. to my son BILLY BLUNT KNIGHT: In case of his
death, BENJAMIN BATTS. JOSEPH KNIGHT is to act as my
Special Agent in the State of Kentucky, with power to
sell a tract of land in the County of Livingston, and
collect debts. In case of his death, then PETER E.
KNIGHT is appointed. Money collected to be put on interest for my dau LOUISA KNIGHT. Wit: JAMES BIGGS,
(Second Wit, Illegible).

BARNES, ABSALOM
    Feb. 29, 1792. May Ct., 1792. Wife: MARTHA, Residue.
Sons: NOAH, land east and south of Great Branch; JACOB,
remainder of land. Exr: EPHRAIM BARNES, MARTHA BARNES.
Wit: JOHN AMASON, ETHELRED AMASON.

BARNES, ARCHILOUS
    Feb. 4, 1807. Feb. Ct., 1807. Bk. D, p 264. Wife:
PEGGY, land adjoining ELISHA WOODARD, LEMUEL DANIELS
& JOHN BARNES on Contentnea Creek. Dau: SUCKEY THOMAS,
1 negro, 1 horse, bridle and saddle, 2 cows and calves.
Son & Exr: EDWIN, land whereon he lives, formerly oc-
cupied by JONATHAN ROBERTSON, 1 negro, 1 horse, bridle
and saddle, 2 cows and calves, and 2 sows and pigs;
ARCHILOUS, reversion in land left his Mother, 1 negro,
1 horse, bridle and saddle, 2 cows and calves, 2 sows
and pigs, also brandy still provided his brother,
EDWIN, shall always have use of still without toll.
Dau: SALLY, 1 negro, 1 mare, bridle, saddle, also 2
cows and calves. Exr: ICHABOD THOMAS, son-in-law. Wit:
BENJAMIN AMASON, JAMES BARNES, JESSE FARMER.

BARNES, AZIEL
    July 29, 1804. May Ct., 1805. Bk. D, p 230. All
land divided between Sons and Exrs: SOLOMAN, JOSIAH;
Daus: ELIZABETH BARNES, mare; SARY SPAIGHT, colt; Gr.
dau: PLEASANT BARNES, cow and calf. Wit: JESSE FARMER,
GARRIET KNIGHT, JACOB BARNES.

BARNES, BRITON

Feb. 14, 1818 (?) May Ct., 1818. Bk. E, p 191. Son:
BENJAMIN, loom and guir, pine chest, looking glass,
flax wheel, 4 puter basons, 2 dishes, 7 plates, 2 doz.
puter spoons, canister, stone butter pot, 2 bottles, 2
small trunks, chirm, water pail and piggin, 3 pots,
Dutch oven, riler, bowl, earthen butter pot, 2 milk
cups, 6 cattle, 1 half-pint tankard, 2 weeding hoes,
2 axes, handsaw, drawing knife, augur, 3 chizels, $20
that is due me from JOHN W. BARNES, frying pan, skillet
and large trunk; Dau: ELIZABETH PITMAN, wife of EDWARD
PITMAN, a feather bed; Son: MILZA, walnut table, puter
dish and $20 due me from JOHN W. BARNES; Dau: LUCY
PITMAN, wife of JESSE PITMAN, a feather bed; all lands
to be divided between sons: MILZA, BURWELL, JOHN AND
BRITTAIN. Division to be made by JACOB HORN and JOHN
HORN. Exr: Sons, BURWELL BARNES, JOHN BARNES. Wit:
EGBERT H. WILLIAMS, MARTIN PITMAN.

BARNES, BRYAN

July 20, 1839. No probate date. Bro & Exr: WILLIAM
BARNES, 1 negro. Niece: MARY COBB, wife of EDWARD COBB,
1 negro. Friend: EDWIN BARNES, 1 negro. My lands in
Nash Co., house, stock, crop, etc. be sold. Residue
divided among heirs. Wit: (illegible), WILLIAM KNIGHT.

BARNES, CHARLIE

Oct. 22, 1840. Feb. Ct., 1841. Bk. F, p 252. Wife:
Lend for life, or widowhood, 1 negro, horse (choice),
2 cows and calves, sow and 8 pigs, 8 year-old hogs,
4 ewes, clock, chest (choice), 30 bbls. corn, 10 bu.
wheat, 1200 lbs. pork or bacon, 30 lbs. sugar, 10 lbs.
coffee, 8 gal. molasses, -- year's provisions and
Brandy still. Sons: JOHN D. BARNES and the child my
wife is now pregnant with --; ROBERT BARNES, son & Exr.
Gr. chil: $100 each: MARY E. ALFORD, NATHAN, CHARLES
C., BENNETT, MARTHA BARNES, REBECCA BARNES & SARAH
BARNES. Residue divided between chil: ROBERT, JOHN and
unborn child. Wit: ORREN D. CALHOUN, ANDREW (?) A.
CALHOUN, RICHARD GAY.

BARNES, DEMPSEY

Mar. 25, 1807. Aug. Ct., 1807. Wife: SARAH, land,

14

½ brandy still, ½ cydercasks, ½ orchards, furniture,
flax wheel, hackel, cow and calf, horse, bridle and
saddle, and residue of estate; Son & Exr: JOSEPH, land;
Son & Exr: JESSE, land; Son: THOMAS, land; Son: JAMES,
land on Toisnot Swamp adjoining Robert Coleman; Son;
JOHN, land, other half still, casks, etc; Dau:
SUSANNAH DANIEL, $40, also property already received;
Dau: POLLY BARNES, $300, 2 cows and calves, 1 colt and
saddle; Dau: ELIZABETH APPLEWHITE, $75 silver and all
property already received; Dau: SARAH BLACKBURN. Gr.
son: NATHAN BLACKBURN, son of SARAH, horse, saddle, 2
cows and calves and $300. Wit: Z. W. BAKER, WILLIAM
WHITE.

BARNES, EDITH
    Sept. 26, 1848. Sept. - Aug. Ct., 1849. Bk. F,
pp 433-7. Gr. Chil: EDITH DEW, WRIGHT BARNES, WELTHY
BARNES, JESSE BULLUCK, REBECCA BARNES, $200 each;
JESSE BARNES, son of DEMPSEY D. BARNES, 1 negro boy;
$400 cash and furniture. My old negro, Isaac, has priv-
ilege of choosing his master, either of my three sons:
ELIAS, WILLIAM OR JOSHUA, his wife VILET, to go with
him and sufficient sum of money to support them their
lifetime. If they cannot agree on amount to support
them, I wish my friends, JAMES D. BARNES, LARRY D.
FARMER & JACOB TAYLOR shall say what would be suffi-
cient. Son: JOSHUA, 2 negroes valued at $600. Residue
to be divided between my three sons and exrs, ELIAS,
JOSHUA and WILLIAM. JESSE BULLUCK caveated. Jury Em-
pannelled: DAVID HOWELL, SR., DAVID HOWELL, JR., WELLS
DRAUGHAN, WILLIAM HARRELL, JESSE CRISP, JOHN HARRELL,
JOHN A. VINES, JAMES REDDICK, LITTLEBERRY BRADLEY,
JOHN KNIGHT, SR., WILLIAM ADAMS, REDDING LEWIS.

BARNES, EDWARD
    Dec. 15, 1760. Mar. Ct., 1762. Wife & Extx: SARAH,
all residue of estate, both real and personal, during
her widowhood. Sons: NATHAN, WILLIAM, JACOB and
ABRAHAM; Dau: MOURNING,FIVEASH, CHARITY SIMS, MARY
SIMS, ELIZABETH LEIGH, SARAH AMASON, 1 S each; Dau:
PATIENCE BARNES, reversion in plantation whereon I
live. Dau: ELIZABETH BARNES, 1000 A plantation on
Chowan River whereon she now lives, reversion to my

Gr. son: JACOB BARNES. Son: JACOB. Gr. daus: BARBERY
WIGGINS and FERREBY WIGGINS, 2 cows each; Gr. son:
MICHAEL BARNES, tract land lying on Chowan River, join-
ing plantation his mother lives on called Myery Mash.
Wit: JAMES BARFIELD, ELIZA BARFIELD, THOS. EDMUNDSON.

BARNES, EDWIN
    Aug. 21, 1807. Nov. Ct., 1807. Bk. D, p 298. Wife:
SALLEY, ½ land including home, in case of any children
the other ½ to go to them. Otherwise entire estate to
my wife. Exr: ICHABOD THOMAS, WILLIE STANTON. Wit:
ARCHELAUS BARNES, MARTHA SIMS.

BARNES, EDWIN
    Oct. 4, 1843. Nov. Ct., 1843. Nunc. Will. Not
proved. Land I purchased at Tarborough of the Estate
of JAMES J. BARNES, dec'd, be sold. Residue given children of my sister SALLY BARNES. Note: MRS. TREASY
BARNES, wife of EDWIN BARNES, notified she might offer
objection in Nov. Term of Court, 1843. Wit: JOSHUA
BARNES, JULIAN JORDAN, MOSES FARMER.

BARNES, ELIZABETH
    June 6, 1789. May Ct., 1794. Neph: THEOPHILUS, son
of my Bro: SAMUEL SKINNER. Gr. dau: ANN WATKINS, dau
of JOHN RICKS, my side saddle & bridle. The two Gr.
daus to inherit all remaining estate. Gr. dau: MARY
HORN, wife of ABISHAI HORN. Exr: ABISHAI HORN, JOSEPH
SUMNER. Wit: MARTHA SUMNER, HANNAH PITMAN.

BARNES, JACOB
    Jan. 16, 1764. Jan. Ct., 1764. Wife: JULAND, lend
use of plantation whereon I live. All residue of estate to wife, it to be divided between youngest chil:
PATTY and ABRAHAM. Son & Exr: JESSE, plantation whereon he lives with all cattle, hogs, maers, and household stufe and 1 negro. Son & Exr: JAMES, plantation
I had of JOHN WIGGINS with all cattle, hogs and horses,
our household stufe and land belonging thereto; 1 negro
boy, My stell cap and worm, only his mother to have
use of said stell during her lifetime to stell her one
licker. Daus: BRISSULLA WILLIAMS, 2 negroes, mare and
colt; Dau: JERUSHA BARNES, 1 negro, young mare and new

sidesaddle and fore cows and calves. Son: JOSEPH, all
land bought of JACOB DUNN, all cattle, hogs, mars,
household stufe belonging thereto; also negro. Son:
JACOB, ½ land lying on N side Contentnea Creek, being
the upper part and ½ hogs, cattle, one horse and 1 negro; ARCHELAUS, ½ land lying N of Contentnea Creek, being lower part, ½ cattle, hogs, 1 maire, and 1 negro.
Dau: PATTY, 1 negro; Son: ABRAHAM, 1 negro. Exr: JOHN
THOMAS. Wit: NATHAN BARNES, JAMES ROGERS, ELIZABETH
LEE.

BARNES, JAMES
     Mar. 12, 1805. May Ct., 1805. Bk. D, p 223. Wife:
JULAN. Son & Exr: WILLIE (WILEY) and son: WILLIAM to
have plantation whereon 1 live also 640 A on White Oak
Swamp, adjoining BENJ. JOHNSTON and ABNER EASON. Son &
Exr: REDDICK, 470 A on Poplar Branch on JEMIMA MEADE'S
line, 320 A adjoining STEPHEN BARNES and D. ELLIS. Son:
BRYAN, 350 A land S side of Toisnot Swamp, adjoining
lines of GEORGE BLACKWELL, JESSE PITMAN, MARY COREY,
JOHN MORRIS; 550 A on Little Swamp adjoining lines of
HENRY VIVERETTE & WM. WHITEHEAD; 40 A west of Toisnot
Swamp, 300 A in Nash Co., adjoining GEO. BLACKWELL,
DEMSEY BARNES, JOHN MORRIS, PHILIPS & HENRY FLOWERS.
Also Mills on Harmony Swamp and 6 A land adjoining them.
Son & Exr: JOHN; Son & Exr: JAMES, $2000 cash, bay colt.
Remainder of estate divided between four daus and wife:
MARY BRIDGERS, SARHA (SARAH) BARNES, ELIZABETH BARNES,
AND SUSANNA BARNES. Wit: GARREOT KNIGHT, WILLIAM
BRIDGERS.

BARNES, JAMES A.
     Oct. 14, 1848. Feb. Ct., 1849. Bk. F, pp 425-28.
Wife: SARAH BARNES, lend land on Big Contentnea Creek
adj. JOHN BARNES, 100 A land... on Gum Swamp... whereon ELIZA BASS lives, the THEOPHILUS BASS Place, household furniture, ½ brandy still and barrels, 10 negroes,
1 chest, mare, and colt, mule, 2 calves (choice) heifers,
etc. Neph: THEOPHILUS BASS, privilege of using ½ A of
land whereon he lives, also whole of the 150 A JACOB
BARNES tract, reserving part of this land to my wife
during her lifetime. Also give unto THEOPHILUS BASS
forever certain lot of land I drew in settlement of

17

estate of JOHN BARNES, adjoining WILLIE SIMS near Gum
Pond, a Swamp, JACOB S. BARNES to cover all the land
near Broken Leg for the purpose of straightening out
his line-- to SARAH BARNES line. Also negroes loaned
my wife, etc. My wife and THEOPHILUS BASS to receive
money coming in from the hire of negro fellow Charles.
MARTHA TOMLINSON, wife of DANIEL TOMLINSON, TREASY
DARDEN, dau of McKINLEY (?) DARDEN, 1 negro. My negro
man Tom may choose his master. Sis: BEEDY (BESSIE)
WOODARD of the State of Georgia, 1 negro now in her
possession. THEOPHILUS BASS (dec'd), three children:
GEORGE WASHINGTON BASS, THOMAS WARREN BASS & JESSE
JACKSON BASS, 8 negroes to be bound to pay notes for
fifty or sixty dollars I gave to JACOB S. BARNES, Adm.
of JAMES BASS, ELIZA BASS, widow of JAMES BASS to have
use of and occupy all lands I own on E side of Big Contentnea Creek; etc; bequeath 1 negro. Niece: MARGARET
EVANS of Georgia, $300.50. Friend: WYATT MOYE. Wit:
WOODARD COOK, EDWIN BARNES.

BARNES, JAMES W.
Aug. 23, 1844. Nov. Ct., 1845. Bk. F, p 324. Sons:
JAMES, land on Toisnot; STEPHEN, land on Harmony Swamp;
DEMPSEY and wife TERESA. Daus: SALLY DANIEL, POLLY
JORDAN, ZILPHA BAREFOOT. Remaining property to be di-
vided equally between my Daughters and children of son
DEMPSEY BARNES. Property to be valued by friends:
JAMES D. BARNES, WILLIE ROUNTREE, SIMON ROBBINS . Exr:
Neph: JOSHUA BARNES. Wit: SIMON ROBBINS, JAMES FARMER,
PENNY FARMER.

BARNES, JESSE
June 30, 1841. Nov. Ct., 1843. Bk. F, p 296. Wife:
EDITH, 6 negroes, furniture, horse, saddle and bridle,
3 cows and calves, 3 sows and pigs, 4 ewes and lambs--
lend land on which I live & $500. Gr. son: WRIGHT BARNES,
lend land lying on S side Toisnot Swamp on line of
heirs of DEMPSEY BARNES-- also lend 1 negro, and $400.
JESSE BULLUCK, lend 1 negro - $500, Horse, bridle and
saddle. To each Gr. dau I lend 1 negro and $400:
EDITH BARNES, WELTHY BARNES, DELPHA BARNES, SALLY
BARNES, REBECCA BARNES. Gr. son: JESSE BARNES, son of
DEMPSEY D. BARNES, $ 300. Sons & Exr: ELIAS, WILLIAM,

JOSHUA and son THOMAS. Dau: NANCY FARMER. Wit: JAMES
D. BARNES, JOHN COLEMAN, WILLIAM BARNES.

BARNES, JOHN
    Apr. 9, 1823. No probate date. Bk. E, p 342. Land
and plantation to be sold and money divided between 6
older children (unnamed). Exr: Bros: JOSEPH BARNES
and JESSE BARNES. Wit: W. BARNES, HENRY HORN.

BARNES, JORDAN
    Sept. 19, 1822. Nov. Ct., 1822. Bk. E, p 309. Wife:
SARAH, 1/3 income from land on Drake Creek, Sumner Co.,
Tennessee, either rent or from sale, which I have empowered my brother NATHAN BARNES to sell. If sold she
to have $150. Also large iron pot, small ditto, iron
potrack and chest; Be it known that JOHN ANDERSON
BARNES and ELIZABETH ANDERSON BARNES are children of
my wife, SARAH BARNES, before wedlock--but I have
good reason to believe they are my children also. It
is my wish that above children should share equally
in my estate with their mother. She to have $150 cash
if land is sold and balance divided between children.
Son: JOHN ANDERSON BARNES, all working tools. Dau:
ELIZABETH ANDERSON BARNES, cloth loom. Exr: Friends,
MOSES PRICE, ELIJAH HORN. Wit: JOEL BATTLE, ABSALOM
HORN.

BARNES, JULAN
    Oct. 23, 1823. May Ct., 1824. Bk. F, p 20. Son &
Exr: BRYAN, cow and calf; son: WILLIAM, 1 negro boy;
dau: SALLY, 1 negro, 1 pine chest; Children of dec'd
son: JOHN, 50 cents cash; children of Dec'd son:
WILLIE, 50 cents cash; Dau: MARY BRIDGERS, 50 cents
cash; Son: JAMES and son: REDDICK, 50 cents cash. Dau:
ELIZABETH BELCHER $300. The remainder to be equally
divided between four youngest children: BRYAN, WILLIAM,
SALLY BARNES and ELIZABETH BELCHER. Wit: W. THOMAS
AMASON, REDDICK BARNES.

BARNES, JOSEPH
    May 11, 1824. Aug. Ct., 1824. Wife: SARAH, 3 ne-
groes, mare, riding chair, $300 cash and 300 A plan-
tation whereon I live. Daus: ELIZABETH DEW, all pro-

perty she hath already received; POLLY ROBBINS, all
property she hath already received; SALLY HORN, all
property she hath already received; NANCY, 2 negroes
and $75 cash; PENNY, 2 negroes and $75 cash; CELIA,
2 negroes and $75 cash; TREECY, 2 negroes, enough cash
to get her a saddle and bridle worth $16 and $75 cash;
TEMPERANCE, 2 negroes, cash to get her saddle and bridle
worth $16 and $75 cash; MARTHA, 2 negroes, cash to get
her saddle worth $16 and $75 cash. Sons: JAMES, all
lands, except 300 A whereon I now live, which goes to
my wife SARAH, to be divided between two sons, JAMES
& DEMPSEY, when youngest reaches 21 yrs... each son to
have: $75 cash, 2 cows and calves, 2 sows and pigs,
saddle and bridle, 1 horse, enough money to give him
six months schooling and 1 soot of clothes. DEMPSEY..
to also have brandy still after his mother's death.
Any money arising from sale of property at wife's
death, to be equally divided between all children except sons, JAMES and DEMPSEY. Exr: Son-in-law:
FREDERICK ROBBINS; Bros: JESSE BARNES, JAMES BARNES.
Wit: ARTHUR ROBBINS, SIMON ROBBINS.

BARNES, NANCY
     May 23, 1835. Aug. Ct., 1835. Bk. F, p 178. Bro-
in-law: FREDERICK F. ROBBINS, 1 negro. Heirs of Bro-
in-law: THOMAS HORN (THORN), 1 negro. Bro-in-law:
JAMES DEANS, 2 young negroes. MARTHA BARNES, dau of my
bro: DEMPSEY BARNES, $100. NANCY ROBBINS, dau of
FREDERICK F. ROBBINS; Bro: JAMES BARNES & Bro-in-law:
JOHN DEW Residue of estate. Sis: POLLY ROBBINS & PENNY
DEANS. Exr: DEMPSEY D. BARNES. Wit: JOSHUA BARNES,
HENRY HORN (THORN?)

BARNES, NATHAN
     Apr. 1777 probated. Wife and Extx: (unnamed). Res-
idue. Daus: SARAH DANIEL, NANNIE BRUCE (?), SELAH
BARNES, 1 cow, 1 yearling, 4 sheep. Sons & Exr: EPHRAIM
BARNES, 10 S each; son: LEMON BARNES, 1 cow and calf,
1 ewe and lamb; Sons: ABASALOM AND AZIEL, 10 S each.
Gr. sons: LEMUAL BARNES and ELIAS DANIELL, 10 S and a
parcil of hogs each. Wit: EPHRAIM BARNES, ABASALOM
BARNES, AZIEL BARNES.

BARNES, PATIENCE

July 5, 1818. Aug. Ct., 1818. Bk. E, p 202. Gr. son: DUKE W. HORN, chest painted red. Gr. dau: HARRIET HORN, chest painted green and all my wearing apparel. WHITMEL HORN, all residue of estate to be his for the purpose of raising and educating him. In case of his death before maturity to revert to his sister, HARRIET. Exr: JOEL BATTLE. Wit: JONATHAN THOMAS, JOAB HIATT.

BARNES, PEGGY

Mar. 2, 1816. Aug. Ct., 1816. Bk. E, p 143. Daus: SUSANNA THOMAS, SALLY TARTT. Son & Exr: ARCHELAUS BARNES, all residue of property sold and equally divided between son and 2 daughters. Gr. chil: TEMPA THOMAS, PEGGY THOMAS, POLLEY R. THOMAS, 10 Ŀ each. Exr: ICHABOD THOMAS. Wit: JAMES BARNES, JOHN BRANTLEY.

BARNES, POLLY

Oct. 18, 1845. Nov. Ct., 1845. Land shared equally as long as children are amind to live together. When son GEORGE W. becomes of age, if all are willing, it may be sold and money equally divided. Exr: BURWELL BARNES, son. Wit: ORREN D. CALHOUN, J. W. CALHOUN.

BARNES, POLLY

Jan. 31, 1845. May Ct., 1848. Bk. F, pp 397-8. Dau: POLLY HARPER, $450 to be left in the hands of my son, JAMES D. to loan out, interest to be paid POLLY HARPER, and her alone, annually, as long as she lives. Reversion to her children. Residue to be divided between my heirs: EDWIN BARNES' children, one share: ARTHUR D. BARNES, SALLY BARNES, JAMES D. BARNES, ELIZABETH FARMER. Exr & Son: JOHN D. BARNES. Wit: E. H. WOODARD, L. D. FARMER.

BARNES, REDDICK

Oct. 26, 1835. Nov. Ct., 1835. Bk. F, p 181. Wife: MARTHA, 2 negroes, 2 cows, table, 3 sows and pigs. Lend ½ of my old plantation, mare & saddle. Son & Exr: JAMES, plantation whereon I live, purchased of JOHN R. BARNES, also tract adjoining my old plantation, purchased of DEHORITY ELLIS; also 1 negro, horse, walnut table, clock, ¼ of all turpentine taken this year, 2 cows and yearlings and all hogs called his. Dau: POLLY, plan-

tation whereon I formerly lived, ½ at my death, the
other half at her mother's death - 2 negroes, 2 cows
and yearlings, horse and gig, walnut table, chest and
half my sitting chairs. Gr. dau: MARTHA BARNES, 1 negro. Chil. of my son, WILLIE: MARTHA, PENNINAH,
ELIZABETH and POLLEY, plantation whereon said WILLIE
BARNES lives, also 1 negro. Wit: BRYAN BARNES,
BENJAMIN BYNUM, WILLIAM BARNES.

BARNES, SARAH
    Dec. 23, 1833. Aug. Ct., 1834. Dau: TRESEE FARMER,
2 negroes and dining chairs; MARTHA BULLUCK, 2 negroes,
my "burow, also my hors." Gr. son: JOSEPH SHEARWOOD,
mare; Gr. dau: SALLEY SHEARWOOD, bed and furniture;
Gr. son: DEMPSEY SHEARWOOD, colt. Exr: Sons-in-law,
ISAAC FARMER, BENNET BULLUCK. Wit: DEMPSEY D. BARNES,
ARTHUR ROBBINS.

BARNES, SARAH
    Apr. 5, 1849. May Ct., 1854. Bk. G, p 57. Neph:
LEVY HOWELL, 1 negro. Sis: TEMPA JORDAN, wife of
JAMES JORDAN, 2 negroes; ELIZA BASS, 1 negro and ½
brandy still; JUDEA COOK, wife of WOODARD COOK, 1 ne-
gro; reversion to nephews: BUNNION BASS and WILLIAM
BASS. Residue to sisters. Exr: WILLIAM BARNES, bro of
ELIAS BARNES. Wit: WILLIE SIMS, EDWIN BARNES.

BARNES, STEPHEN
    Mar. 26, 1823. Aug. Ct., 1823. Bk. E, p 340. Wife:
ELIZABETH, plantation and all residue of estate. Son:
WILLIAM, land south of Whiteoak Swamp, it being land
purchased from JETHRO BARNES, JR. Dau: NANCY, $90,
cow and calf and 2 ewes and lambs. Son & Exr: JAMES,
reversion of land between Whiteoak Swamp and Bear
Branch, it being a piece given to me by HENRY GAY,
and by him purchased of JACOB BARNES. Dau: ELIZABETH,
$10, cow and calf and 2 ewes and lambs. Son: REDDICK,
reversion in lands lying on north of Bear Branch of
Whiteoak Swamp, horse, cow & calf, 2 ewes and lambs.
also another $50. Dau: TABITHA, $10. Wit: JAMES BARNES,
WILLIAM BARNES.

BARNES, THOMAS

Feb. 13, 1761. June Ct., 1761. Wife: ANN residue
of estate during her lifetime. If daughter JULIAN is
living at mother's death it shall revert to daughter
ANN, provided she take care of her sister JULIAN. If
JULIAN should die before her mother, then mother's
part shall pass to sons WILLIAM and BRITTAIN, and dau
ANN BARNES. Son: WILLIAM, plantation whereon I live
with appurtenances belonging thereto, 2 cows and calves,
2 sows and pigs, 2 pewter basons, pewter dish and ½ doz
pewter plates. Son: BRITTAIN, 4 cows and calves, 4 sows
and pigs, 2 pewter basons, pewter dish, ½ doz plates,
and 5 Ꮭ cash money. Dau: MARY TUCKER, cow and calf;
Gr. dau: AMERICA BARNES, 1 cow and calf and 1 sow and
pig. Exr: THOMAS BARNES, JOHN BARNES. Wit: DUNCAN LAMON,
JACOB FLOWERS, SR., PHILIP THOMAS.

BARNES, WILLIAMSON
    May 19, 1814. Aug. Ct., 1814. Bk. E, p 66. Wife:
PATIENCE, lend all land on S side of Tar river with
reversion to Gr. son: DUKE WM. HORN; 2 negroes with
reversion to dau: TABITHA, 1 young mare, 2 walnut
tables, chaney press, green chest, safe, ½ doz sitting
chairs, 1 cart and pr wheels, 2 cows and calves, 6
sheep, 10 hogs, sow and pigs, 40 barrels corn. All this
for her lifetime. Dau: TABITHA HORN, all land on N side
of Tar river and still on said land, with reversion to
my Gr. son: DUKE WM. HORN. The land I own in state of
Georgia should be sold and proceeds equally divided
between wife and daughter. Exr: MALACHI BARNES, BYTHAL
HORN. Wit: JORDAN BARNES, JOSHIAH HORN.

BARRON, THOMAS
    July 23, 1776. July Ct., 1777. Wife & Extx:
MOURNING, lend measured plantation whereon I live, bequeath to her 2 negro wenches.. the first child that
shall be born of either to belong to son WILLIAM. remainder of their increase to be divided equally between
my oldest 4 children: JAMES, THOMAS, BARNABY & MARY.
Son & Exr: JAMES, negro and tract of land whereon I
live, beginning at Cabbun Branch, it being the upper
end of my said land. Son: THOMAS, 1 negro; my right of
labor that I have done on the land lying between MARTIN
HORN and THOMAS FARMER; 2 two year old heifers and 1

horse. Son: BARNABY, reversion in land whereon I live,
also he shall have all the improved land in his possession when he reaches 21 years; 1 negro, my still, except that I reserve the use thereof to the stilling of
what liquor is made on the plantation. Dau: MARY, 1
negro, 2 cows and calves, 2 two-year old heifers. Dau:
MARTHA, 1 "molatta" boy. Wit: BENJAMIN BRAND, JACOB
PAGE, BARNABY BARRON.

BARROW, (BARRON?), WILLIAM
    Oct. 20, 1758. Dec. Ct., 1758. Wife: PRISCILLA.
Son & Exr: WILLIAM, plantation on Kehuky Swamp. Dau:
ANNA FORT. Gr. dau: ELIZABETH FORT. Wit: JAMES BARNES,
DREW SMITH, WILLIAM BARNES.

BASSFORD, ALEXANDER
    Oct. 20, 1789. Feb. Ct., 1791. Bk. 3, p 161. Wife:
ANN, plantation whereon I live for her lifetime, at her
death to be equally divided between MARY, ALEXANDER,
JAMES AND GEORGE. Also all residue of estate not already
given. Daus: MARY, PEGGY, 1 S each current money. Sons:
JAMES and GEO. to have plantation on this side of swamp.
Son & Exr: ALEXANDER, tract of land on N side Moore's
Swamp, part of a tract entered by JOSHUA SEBRELL and
indentured to me. Wit: ARRON COLEMAN, ISHAM O'NEAL.

BAT(E)MAN, JOHN BATMAN
    Aug. 11, 1803. Nov. Ct., 1803. Wife: KEZIA, lend
her land and plantation whereon I live during her life
or widowhood. Son: ASHAL, land after his mother's death.
Dau: POLEY, cow and calf. Sell mare and upper part of
tract of land to pay debts. Leave all the rest of estate to be equally divided between my wife, and two
children. Exrs: ISAAC FARMER, JESSE FARMER. Wit:
MICAJAH PETTAWAY, WILLOBY ETHERDGE, JEREMIAH ETHERDGE.

BATTLE, DEMSEY
    Mar. 9, 1815. May Ct., 1815. Bk. E, p 91. Son &
Exr: CULLEN, land lying on S side of Fishing Creek, in
Nash Co., which I bought of HARDY CAIN and land bought
of JAMES CAIN, 15 negroes, also stock and other property
in his possession. Dau: AMELIA, ½ of my land in state
of Georgia, bought of SILAS MERCER, 17 negroes, mare,

her colt, bay philly, buroe, 1 dieping (Dining?) table,
6 mulberry chairs, $950 and 1 horse worth $35. Son &
Exr: ANDREWS, ½ of my land in State of Georgia bought
of SILAS MERCER, 15 negroes - 4 horses, other things
I have given into his possession. 15 cattle, 6 sheep,
6 chairs and $500. Son: JOHN, land whereon I live,
which my father gave me by deed of trust, 10 negroes
when he shall arrive at the age of 21 yrs, 1 Philly,
which he claims for his, and $600. Wit: JACOB BATTLE,
JER. (EMIAH) BATTLE, JOSEPH S. BATTLE.

BATTLE, ELISHA
Feb. 6, 1799. May Ct., 1799. Dau: ELIZABETH CRUDUP,
2 negroes and their increase and $225. Gr. dau: CLOE
LEE, 2 negroes. Sons & Exrs: ELISHA, all negroes and
their increase and other things which I have given
into his possession; JACOB, all negroes and their increase and other things which I have given into his
possession; Son & Exr: JETHRO, all negroes and their
increase, and other things which I have given into his
possession. Son & Exr: DEMSEY, all the negroes and
their increase and other things I have given him in
his possession, also my part of the plantation which
I and my sons JACOB and JETHRO BATTLE leased of ELIAS
FORT during the term of the lease. Gr. sons: ISAAC
BATTLE, 1 negro and $60 silver; JOEL BATTLE, 1 negro
and $50 silver; Gr. dau: ANN ROSS, 1 negro and $65;
Gr. dau: MARY ANDREWS, her three children: JESSE
ANDREWS, JOHN ANDREWS and ELIZABETH ANDREWS, $100
silver each. All remaining part of estate to be
equally divided amongst my 5 children: ELIZABETH
CRUDUP, ELISHA BATTLE, JACOB BATTLE, JETHRO BATTLE
and DEMSEY BATTLE, provided that my daughter, SARAH
HORN'S 6 children (to wit) JEREMIAH HILLIARD,
ELIZABETH FORT, PURITY FORT, CHARITY BUNN, SEELY SUGG,
and HENRY HORN come in for 1 equal share with my 5
children to be equally divided among them, and also
provided that my son JOHN BATTLE'S children (to wit)
JOSIAH BATTLE, DAVIS BATTLE and ELISHA BATTLE come in
for one equal share with my 4 sons and 1 daughter.
It is not intended that the debts which any of my
children and grandchildren may be owing me at the time
of my death shall be included in their legacies. Wit:

NATHAN GILBERT, JOSEPH SUMNER, DUKE WM. SUMNER.

BATTLE, FRANCES
     Apr. 23, 1806. Aug. Ct., 1806. Bk. D, p 253. Son
& Exr: JOSHIAH BATTLE; son DAVIS BATTLE, ELISHA BATTLE,
son & exr: All my negroes to be equally divided between
my three sons. Gr. dau: ELIZABETH ANDREWS, all my wearing apparel, including, Buckles, Buttons, Rings, Natts
(?) and the like, 3 trunks, a piece of muslin which is
in the house, what striped and checked cloth there is
in the house, a piece of cloth wove N 13 & O's, also
a new bed and bedstead cord and Wikor Matt, which stands
in the shed; 2 good coverlets, 3 good blankets, 3 sheets,
and a bolster and 2 pillows, a small walnut table, my
new looking glass, my riding saddle, and bridle, and
a new bed quilt which is sewed together in order to
quilt, made of new stuff; a case of small knives and
forks, which have flowered handles and the forks, three
prongs, also ½ of my earthen or glassware which is
commonly kept in the upper part of the Boefat; a dozen
new pewter spoons, my newest lining wheel. In case
ELIZABETH ANDREWS should die before maturity, all my
wearing apparel be equally divided between my daus-in-
law, JANE BATTLE and MARGARET BATTLE. NATHAN GILBERT:
$10. Remainder of estate to 3 sons, JOSIAH, DAVIS AND
ELISHA, each to have a ¼ part and my 3 Gr. chil: JESSE
ANDREWS, JOHN ANDREWS and ELIZABETH ANDREWS - they to
share equally in the other ¼ part. Exr: ELISHA BATTLE,
SR., JACOB BATTLE. Wit: JACOB BATTLE, BURREL BATTLE,
MICHAEL THOMAS.

BATTLE, JACOB
     Mar. 17, 1815. May Ct., 1815. Bk. E, p 96. Son
& Ext: JAMES S. BATTLE, 300 A lying on Beach-Run Swamp
and Huckley Marsh, another tract east of Beach-Run
lying mostly in the fork of Beach and Falling Run
Swamps, purchased of EXUM S. SUMNER. Also all my wearing apparel and my watch. Dau: BETSEY, remaining part
of land in Edgecombe Co. including all which was given
me by my father, except about 50 A which I have given
JAMES S. BATTLE and CULLEEN BATTLE deeds for and all
purchased of WM. DANCEY and WM. HORN; other lands purchased of EXUM S. SUMNER, DANIEL SUMNER, JETHRO BATTLE

and DUKE W. SUMNER which lieth in the bent of Tar River.
Also 2 work horses, 4 colts, 80 cattle, 30 sheep, 80
hogs and provisions for herself and family for yr. also
her stock for 1 yr. One walnut Boefat, and furniture
including all my glass and chiney, earthen ware, 3
walnut tables, 1 buroe, 2 pine chests, one cherry chest,
2 trunks, 1 saddle and bridle, 1 doz silver table spoons,
1 doz tea spoons, 4 pare fire Doggs, 1 doz Siting chares.
     All remaining estate, real and personal I give to
son JAMES and daughter BETSEY provided they shall pay
$400 annually for support and maintenance of my son
MARMADUKE BATTLE. Exr: Neph, CULLEN BATTLE. There being
no witnesses, this will was admitted to probate and
proven by oaths of JEREMIAH BATTLE, JOSEPH BATTLE,
JESSE BATTLE. Codicil or deed of gift from JACOB BATTLE
to daughter BETSEY gives her twenty-two negroes. Mar.
17, 1815.

BATTLE, JAMES S.
     Dec. 8, 1847. Aug. Ct., 1854. Bk. G, p 71. "I give
and devise to the deacons and their successors in office
of the predestinarian baptist church at the Falls of
Tar River, Nash Co. NC (in trust), so long as the doc-
trine and principles now held and advocated in sd church
and no longer (if ever such principles should be aban-
doned), $1250, to be loaned out with good security,
interest annually arising therefor to be given to the
pastor of sd church, the principal to remain as perpet-
ual monument of the donor, a poor dependent sinner, if
saved at all, entirely and solely by Grace. Sons & Exrs:
JAMES M., WILLIAM S. and TURNER W. BATTLE; Daus: MARY
E, PENELOPE B., MARTHA A. BATTLE. Gr. son: JOHN PAUL
JONES BATTLE. Exr: TURNER P. WESTRAY. No Wit: Proven by
oaths of JOHN S. DANCY, REDDING S. PETWAY, DEMPSEY
TREVATHAN & THOMAS L. MAINER. The long and interesting
will of a very wealthy man.

BATTLE, JOHN
     Jan. 22, 1774. Apr. Ct., 1774. Bk. (?), p 211. Son
& Exr: WILLIAM, 140 A plantation on N of Swift Creek,
land bought of THOMAS FLOYD; 12 negroes provided he
maintain my sister ELIZABETH BATTLE, horse, bridle and
saddle, all hogs, all this provided he allows my

daughter SARAH BATTLE sufficient maintenance for life.
Son & Exr: JOHN, 5 negroes; son, JAMES, 5 negroes; dau:
AMY BELL, 100 L proclamation money; dau: SARAH, bed. Gr.
son: JOHN BATTLE (son of my son JOHN), 145 A plantation
lying on S side of Poplar Swamp in Sussex Co., Va., and
1 negro. Gr. son: THOMAS BATTLE, 1 negro; Gr. son:
EPHRAIM BATTLE, 30 L proclamation money. Exr: WILLIAM
HILL. Wit: W. T. MEARNS, JAMES BATTLE, F. (?) THOMPSON.

BATTLE, JOHN
    Jan. 28, 1796. Feb. Ct., 1796. Wife: FRANCES lend
part of tract of land whereon I live, being 75 A along
with another tract adjoining CULLEN ANDREWS, also another I bought of STEPHEN WATKINS, all this, for her
lifetime. Son & Exr: JOSIAH, all my land bought of
JEREMIAH HILLIARD, lying in Nash and Edgecombe counties, between Swift Creek and Beach Run. Son: DAVIS,
all my land north of Tar River and Piney land in Nash
Co. bought of JOEL PITMAN and THOMAS WILLIAMS' Heirs-
piney land west of HORN'S Creek and a mare. Son: ELISHA,
remainder land in tract lent wife., all my piney land
not aforementioned; ½ my still. To DAVIS and ELISHA my
part of saw mill at Falls of Tar River. Son: JOHN, all
land lent wife and ½ still. Daus chil: JESSE ANDREWS,
JOHN ANDREWS, ELIZABETH ANDREWS, $100 each. EMANUEL
SKINNER and NATHAN GILBERT $25 each. Exr: DEMSEY BATTLE
(bro). Wit: CULLEN ANDREWS, ELISHA BATTLE, JR., JESSE
FORT.

BATTLE, JOSEPH S.
    Dec. 5, 1844. Aug. Ct., 1847. Bk. F, p 366. Wife
(unnamed), 8 negroes, all furniture, ½ livestock in
N. C., $200, berouk and gear. Lend land on E side lane
including house, lands south of road; land west of
lane, not including Taylor, Mason and Harrison land,
also 2 negroes. Remaining property including that in
Miss. to children. Codicil Dec. 7, 1844. Ordering com-
pletion of new house to be paid for out of estate.
Manager for NC property JAMES J. PHILIPS. Manager for
Miss. property JAMES M. BATTLE. Widow, MARY ANN BATTLE
relinquished right to administer, requesting Court to
appoint JAMES J. PHILIPS, Adm. Bond $50,000. JAMES S.
BATTLE & JESSE H. POWELL, Securities.

BATTS, BENJAMIN
    Mar. 18, 1806. Nov. Ct., 1807. Bk. D, p 290. Son
& Exr: ISAAC, land bought of THOMAS WELLS, that bought
at JOHN BATTS' sale with ½ place known as Crockers Hole,
4 negroes and $200 cash. Lend use of Sein place belong-
ing to plantation whereon I live. Dau: POLLY, land and
plantation whereon I live, including all my land in
bend of Tar River, all stock, household & kitchen furniture, all produce belonging to said plantation, 4 negroes and $200 cash. Wit: JAMES SOUTHERLAND, D.RANDOLPH.

BATTS, ELIZABETH
    July 31, 1845. Feb. Ct., 1849. Bk. F, p 411. Niece:
LUCINDA SUGG, 3 negroes along with other estate. Exr:
PHESINGTON SUGG. Wit: JARRETT HOPKINS, TAYLOR MEEKS.

BATTS, JOSEPH
    Jan. 9, 1807. Nov. Ct., 1807. Bk. D, p 292.
ELIZABETH JOYNER, lend land and plantation whereon I
live, 2 negroes, 2 horses, 4 cows and calves, 4 sows
and pigs, all furniture, pewter, pots, frying pans,
plows, plowhoes, 2 axes, and still, all her natural
life. It is my will that she shall not sell, rent or
dispose of any of above property. At her death my estate shall be divided as follows: Daus: MARTHA HARRIS,
ELIZABETH BATTS, SARAH BATTS, MARY BATTS, 350 A of
land and plantation lying in Springs Percosen to be
sold, and money divided between 4 daus. Sons: JOSEPH,
GERALDOUS, plantation where I live, left to ELIZABETH
JOYNER, also 200 A plantation in pineywoods, purchased
of JOHN LAWRENCE; fishing place known as Crockers Hole,
also tract bought of DAVID LAWRENCE and still, all to
be equally divided between sons JOSEPH and GERALDOUS,
at her death. Son: WILLIAM, 25 S. Exr: ISAAC BATTS,
JOSHUA LAWRENCE. Wit: ISAAC BATTS, LUCY BATTS, NATHAN
MATHEWSON, (another illegible).

BATTS, LUCY
    Mar. 15, 1847. Probated 1847. Son & Exr: BENJAMIN
BATTS, 6 negroes, walnut table, buffet, Brandy still,
cidar mill, casks; right, title and interest in his
crop, stock, and provisions, farming utensils, etc. Gr.
son: ISAAC BATTS, sideboard; Dau: MILDRED (?) LAWRENCE,
wife of JOHN LAWRENCE. 4 negroes, walnut table, chest,

etc. Wit: PETER E. KNIGHT, BENJAMIN W. KNIGHT.

BATTS, WILLIAM
    1806. Nov. 27, 1806. Bk. D, p 225. Wife, CHEASEA,
lend plantation with reversion to 5 youngest sons,
cattle, hogs, household and kitchen furniture and 1
horse; Sons: JOHN, (1 or 2 youngest sons), 1 mare;
BENJAMIN, (1 of youngest sons), 1 colt. Wit: JOHN
BARNES, BRITON BARNES. (Son: WILLIAM proven by deed).

BELCHER, BEVERLEY
    Feb. 24, 1820. Nov. Ct., 1821. Bk. E, p 283. Gr.
son: ROBERT BELCHER, 110 A including house wherein I
live on Long Branch, Cool Spring Branch on THOMAS
DUPREE'S line; Gr. son: LEWIS BELCHER, residue of land
containing 100 A. Their father, JOHN BELCHER, take care
of and have use of plantations, rent free, until they
come of age. Dau: MARTHA PARROT, wife of JOSEPH PARROT,
4 negroes. Gr. daus: MARY, ELIZABETH and SARAH BELCHER,
daus of JOHN BELCHER and wife ELIZABETH, cow and calf
each, when marry or come of age. Gr. sons: ROBERT,
WILEY and LEWIS BELCHER, 1 negro each. Son: JOHN, 4
negroes. All other negroes to be divided between gr.
sons, except 3 divided between gr. daus. All my household and kitchen furniture to be divided between gr.
daus. at death of their father and mother. Exr: THOMAS
DUPREE, GEORGE A. SUGG. Wit: SAM RUFFIN, WM. RUFFIN.

BELL, BATHANA
    Oct. 17, 1844. Nov. Ct., 1845. MARGARET ROUNTREE,
1 slave. Should she die without issue, to my sister
EMELIZA ROUNTREE, residue of my estate. Sister: EMELIZA
ROUNTREE, $10. Wit: JO. LAWRENCE. Will presented 4th
July 1843, before one witness; Court refused to admit
said will to probate.

BELL, BYTHAL
    Sept. 30, 1793. Nov. Ct., 1803. Wife: MARY, lend
plantation whereon I live, 5 negroes, horse, bridle &
saddle, 2 sows and pigs, 10 sheep, 2 cows and calves,
10 chairs, walnut table, walnut desk, all earthenware
belonging to my Bow Fatt, and 50 barrels corn during
her lifetime. All other lands to be equally divided

between 4 sons: MARMADUKE, NORFLEET, HENRY CLINCH &
WILLIAM WESLEY BELL. All negroes and perishable estate
to be divided between 6 children. Whole estate remain
in possession of mother, each child to receive his
share as he comes of age or marries. If any abuse takes
place to any child or his estate, executors have power
to act as will be to greatest advantage to children.
Daus: ELIZABETH and MARGARET. Exr: WILLIAM BELLAMY,
WHITMILL BELL. Since will had no witnesses, was proved
by oaths of EDWARD HALL, THOMAS GUION and BLAKE BAKER.

BELL, ELENZY
    Sept. 27, 1850. Feb. Ct., 1851. (ELENZY BELL was of
Halifax Co., N. C.) Sister: ILEY DREW, lend 3 slaves,
with reversion to her heirs; if none, to heirs of my
bro: RICHARD BELL. Sis: MARGARET DREW. Bro: RICHARD
BELL'S lawful heirs, one negro. Exr: Friend, WILLIAM
R. CHERRY. Wit: JOHN B. BELL, LEMUEL S. SAVAGE.

BELL, FREDERICK
    Feb. Ct., 1803. Wife & Extx: SALLY GOLDSMITH BELL,
3 negroes, walnut table and her riding saddle. Sons:
REDDICK and FREDERICK, 40 shillings each; son: JOSHUA,
4 negroes and their increase, and negro Peter, should
he redeem him; son: NOAH, 2 negroes and bay colt, 1 yr
old; son: PARSONS, 2 negroes, and filly 2 yrs old; son:
HUTSON, 3 negroes; son: MARMADUKE NORFLET BELL, 1 negro and 1 square table; son: WILLIAM, 3 negroes and
their increase. Exr: THOMAS BELL. Wit: WRIGHT BELL,
JAMES JOHNSON.

BELL, FREDERICK
    Jan. 28, 1844. Probated, 1846. Bk. F, p 337. Dau:
LUCY BULLUCK, wife of WHITMEL K. BULLUCK, slaves and
other property already in her possession. Gr. dau:
ELIZABETH DANDRIDGE, dau of said WHITMEL and LUCY,
slaves. Son: BENNETT H. BELL, property now in his
possession. Gr. son: MacGILVERY BELL, slave. Dau:
POLLY BULLUCK, wife of WILLIAM G. BULLUCK, property,
during her life, and slave, reversion to their son,
WILLIAM BULLUCK. Dau: PHEREBY KNIGHT, wife of PETER
KNIGHT, property and slaves during her life, reversion
to their dau ELIZABETH KNIGHT. Dau: ELIZABETH, widow

31

of WILLIAM BELL, property in her possession and slaves;
Dau: EMILY CHERRY, wife of THOMAS B. CHERRY, life est.,
property already possessed, and slaves. Son: LORENZO D.
BELL, property placed in his possession, all debts due
me, and slaves. Dau: EUGENIA McGEE, wife of WILLIAM
McGEE, slaves and property, life estate, reversion to
their dau, LAURA McGEE; dau: LAVINIA M. BELL, life
estate, property and slaves. Son-in-law: WILLIAM McGEE,
all debts he is due me cancelled. Exr: R. CHAPMAN. Wit:
PETER KNIGHT, BRITAIN HOWELL.

BELL, GEORGE
     Dec. 21, 1751. Feb. Ct., 1752. Sons: ARTHUR, GEORGE,
WILLIAM. Dau: ELIZABETH FLOYD. Gr. dau: MARTHA BELL,
dau of JOHN BELL. Exr: FRANCIS FLOYD, ARTHUR BELL. Wit:
WILLIAM PORTIS, THOMAS BELL, THOMAS FLOYD.

BELL, GEORGE
     Feb. 18, 1755. May Ct., 1755. Wife & Extx: SARAH
Son & Exr: JOHN, 160 A plantation whereon I live. Sons:
DAVID, 150 A land; GEORGE, 150 A on Deep Creek. Wit:
ARTHUR BELL, GEORGE BELL, RAFE CHANNEL.

BELL, JOHN
     Dec. 20, 1793. Feb. Ct., 1794. Wife: ELIZABETH,
lend her her choice of all my plantations, 2 negroes
during her widowhood, mare, 1 bridle and saddle, 2
cows and calves, 2 sows and pigs, all kitchen and
household furniture. Sons: JONAS JOHNSTON BELL, all
lands S side of Tar river, 2 negroes and their increase;
RICHARD, 2 negroes and their increase and all my lands
lying N side of Tar river, negro woman Dinah and her
child Sue to be equally divided between JONAS and
RICHARD when RICHARD shall arrive at lawful age. Residue to be divided between sons. Exr: PETER HINES, AMOS
JOHNSTON, JOHN ELLIS. Wit: HENRY HINES, JOSIAH BULLUKE
(BULLUCK), SELAH HINES.

BELL, JOSHUA
     July 4, 1793. Nov. Ct., 1793. Wife & Extx: PHERIBY,
lend her during her widowhood, 3 negroes; give her
5 L money. Sons: FREDRICK, lend 300 A "purchase pattern"
land bought of JAMES ATKIRSON, also 130 A bought of

32

JOSEPH MOORE, and 10 S, reversion to his son: FREDERICK;
WILLIAM, negro man now in his possession; BYTHAL, negro
man now in his possession; REASON WRIGHT BELL, 200 A
land during natural life, 1 negro now in his possession;
should he die without issue, land to return to son
BENJAMIN; JOSHUA, land which he now lives on, also land
which I bought of THOMAS WATSON and 1 negro; THOMAS lend
plantation he lives on during natural life, and 1 negro
now in his possession; ARTHUR, 2 negroes now in his possession; WHITMIL, land and plantation bought of ARTHUR
MOORE. Dau: PHEREBY DREW, wife of JOHN DREW, 1 negro
woman, now in her possession; Gr. dau: ABSILLA BRYANT;
Gr. son: WILLIAM BRYANT, 1 negro now in father's possession. Dau: ABSILLA LAWRENCE, 1 negro and 5 ᗷ money.
Son & Exr: BENJAMIN, all land and plantation NATHAN
BRIDGER lives on, 4 negroes, horse, desk, trunk and
gun I had of Tool. If BENJ. should die without lawful
heirs, all I gave him should return to my son, JOSEPH.
Son & Exr: JOSEPH, plantation I live on, the land and
plantation I lent my son THOMAS BELL, I give to son
JOSEPH and his heirs, also 32 A bought of ELIZAH
HOBGOOD, my mill and 7 negroes. In case my son JOSEPH
should die without lawful heirs, what I gave him should
return to my son BENJ.; all cattle bought of JAMES(?)
sider still and worm, black stock gun, round barrel
gun, grinding stone, handmill, desk, black walnut table
and chist, mare and colt that I had for PETER KNIGHT,
mare and colt I had for ROBERT SAVAGE, horse, all plowhoes and weeding hoes and axes, all sider, hogheads,
and corn that is in the barne, all growing in fields,
also wheat and all pewter and pots. All cattle and
hogs not given, and rest of estate divided between
BENJAMIN & JOSEPH. Gr. son: WHITMIL (?), 1 negro. Exr:
WM. HAYNES. Wit: WM. HAYNES, JOHN HUDNALL, WILLIE
HUDNALL and HENRY ALSBROOK.

BELL, MARMADUKE
    Jan. 24, 1830. Feb. Ct., 1830. Bk. F, p 111. I
leave my friends: J. S. BATTLE and BAT MOORE and my
father-in-law: GEORGE BODDIE to settle my business and
to sell any or all property, land or negroes as they
may think best. I wish the present crop to be made before any sale. MARMADUKE BELL.

The above offered for probate by JAMES S. BATTLE
& BARTHOLOMEW F. MOORE, GEORGE BODDIE having relin-
quished his right as Exr. and proved by oaths of
JOSEPH S. BATTLE, HENRY BRYAN and WILLIAM C. BELLAMY.

BELL, NANCY
    Feb. 6, 1822. Feb. Ct., 1822. Bk. E, p 293. Mother-
NANCY BELL - all estate for her lifetime. At her death,
estate goes to my infant dau SALLY ANN. If she should
die before maturity, estate to be equally divided between my sisters: CATHERINE BELL and SALLY DANCY and
my nephew FRANCIS HENRY KNIGHT and my 2 nieces
ELIZABETH STOKES KNIGHT and WILLIAM ANN KNIGHT. It is
my will that my friend CHARLES KNIGHT take guardian-
ship of said infant dau SALLY ANN. Exr: CHARLES KNIGHT.
Wit: BENJ. B. HUNTER, HONOR BRADLEY.

BELL, RICHARD
    Sept. 26, 1783. May·Ct., 1790. Bk. 3, p 140. Wife
& Extx: MILDRED, plantation whereon I live, all negroes stock, and furniture for life, reversion to sons.
Son & Exr: BENJAMIN, 1 negro, reversion in 2 negroes
and all that part of my estate he has in his possession.
Son & Exr: JOHN, reversion in all land, 3 negroes, 1
doz pewter plates, 1 horse, bridle and saddle, 2 cows
and calves, 2 sows and pigs .and 1 dish. Wit: PETER
HINES, JR., WILLIAM QUIN, JOSIAH WILLS.

BELL, SALLY G.
    Feb. 8, 1825. Nov. Ct., 1825. Bk. F, p 47. Son &
Exr: MARMADUKE N. BELL, 3 negroes, 1 tea kettle and 1
saw. If he should die without lawful heirs, property
shall return to children of my sons FREDERICK, HUDSON,
and WILLIAM BELL. Son & Exr: FREDERICK, 10 S; Sons:
HUDSON and JOSHUA, 10 S each; Gr. sons: LORENZO BELL
and FREDERICK JOSEPH BELL, 1 negro each. Son: NOAH,
1 negro; Gr. dau: ELIZABETH G. BELL, 1 negro; Son:
WILLIAM, 1 sow & pigs; Gr. dau: BETSY BELL, all wearing apparel to her and her mother. Bed clothes to
FREDERICK, HUDSON and MARMADUKE. If after remainder of
property is sold and debts paid there is any balance,
I wish it to be given to WILLIAM LANDIN, son of
MARMADUKE N. BELL and POLLY LANDIN. I wish $50 to be

raised from my estate for the benefit of PARSON BELL
for 1 yr only. Wit: BENJ. B. HUNTER, DAVID BARNES.

BELL, THOMAS
    Jan. 8, 1761. July Ct., 1763. Wife & Extx: MARTHA,
use of plantation, also residue of estate during life
or widowhood. In case she should marry I give her an
equal share with my children: CAROLINE, PRISCILLA and
BRITTAIN. Gr. Son: JACOB SAUL BELL, 5 S current money
(son of KATHERINE BELL in Va.); Son: BRITTAIN BELL,
reversion in 221 A plantation whereon I live. Wit:
JOHN GRIFFIN, CATHERINE CARVER.

BELL, WHITMILL
    Mar. 24, 1824. Nov. Ct., 1824. Bk. F, p 26. Wife:
BETSY, all property in wife's hands during her life,
after death to be equally divided among 6 youngest
children. Dau: WINNY HARREL, 4 negroes and their increase and $20; Son: JARROT, $50; Son: WHITMILL, horse,
bridle and saddle and $125. Sons: JOSEPH, BENNETT,
WILLIAM, DAVID, JAMES, NEWSOM. Dancy land to be sold
to pay debts and balance to be used for schooling and
supporting 6 youngest children. Exr: Bro, JOSEPH BELL,
DAVID BARNES. Wit: PATRICK MCDOWELL, WILLIAM SAVAGE.

BELL, WILLIAM
    Dec. 1, 1752. May Ct., Aug. Cts, 1754. Son & Exr:
ARTHUR, 190 A plantation whereon he dwells, also 390
A in River Islands and adjoining MARMADUKE NORFLEET
and JOHN DREW. Son & Exr: JOSHUA, plantation where he
dwells; Dau: MARY PYRENT and ANNE BELL. Gr. dau: SARAH
PYRENT. Wit: JAMES ATKINSON, WILLIAM CAIN, REBECAH
CAIN.

BELL, WINNIFRED
    Sept. 18, 1837. Probated 1837. Son: BYTHAL R. BELL,
1 negro. Son: MARMADUKE H. BELL, 1 negro and her increase. Dau: MARGARET ANN HEARN. Residue divided between sons. Witness: W. D. STATON.

BELLAMY, JOHN
    May 3, 1796. Aug. Ct., 1797. Wife & Extx: SALLY,
lend 10 negroes, plantation whereon I live, 1/3 all

stock, cattle, horses, hogs, sheep utensils, and furniture during her life. Reversion to my children. Son: WILLIAM, reversion in plantation whereon I live; Son: JOHN, my land and plantation on Swift Creek which I bought of MATTHEW KINCHEN, also land on Tar River. Exr: Bros: WILLIAM BELLAMY, ALEXANDER BELLAMY. There being no witnesses, will was proven in court by oaths of JOHN HUDSON, JOHN WILLIAMS, EXUM LEWIS.

BELLAMY, WILLIAM
   June 27, 1779. Nov. Ct., 1780. Wife & Extx: lend 2 negroes, 10 cattle, 20 hogs, 1 horse, saddle and bridle, all furniture and utensils and plantation for life; Dau: ELIZABETH KINCHEN, 3 negroes; the lands on Tar River purchased of WILLIAM HOLT to sons, JOHN and WILLIAM, JOHN to have his choice; remainder of estate to be divided between children: MARY, LUCA, JOHN, WILLIAM, ALEXANDER and MARGET. Exr: JOSEPH J. CLINCH, MATTHEW KINCHEN, ETHELRED PHILIPS. Wit: SER'D (SHERWOOD) HAYWOOD, STEPHEN COLEMAN, ROBERT CARLILE.

BENTLEY, JOSHUA
   July 16, 1799. Aug. Ct., 1799. Wife: MARTHA BENTLEY, 5 negroes, Brandy still, cap and worm, stock, plantation, other lands and articles inside and out. MARTHA PURNAL, plantation bought of WILLIAM DANIEL, til her son JOSHUA PURNAL comes of age; ELIZABETH PURNAL, bed & furniture; CLAREY ANDREWS, 1 negro; CULLEN ANDREWS, horse, bridle and saddle; ASHLEY PURNAL, 10 Ł current money. Exr: THEOPHILUS THOMAS, ICHABOD THOMAS. Wit: JESSE FARMER, JAMES T. ENNIS, WILLIAM ROBERTSON.

BENTLEY, MARTHA
   Dec. 18, 1804. Nov. Ct., 1808. ASHLEY, son of JOHN and MARTHA PURNAL ŦURNŁLŤ, plantation where I live, 50 A of my new survey lying over the branch, green beaufat, house desk, red chest and ½ brandy still; JOHN ROBERTSON, son of HENRY ROBERTSON and wife CLARY, all land above Deep Branch between HENRY ROBERTSON and THOMAS SPARKMAN; JAMES F. ENNIS and wife CLARY, lifetime use of land in my new survey, reversion to their son JESSE T. ENNIS; Bro: JOHN JARREL,

1 negro, reversion to his son THOMAS JARREL; BETSEY
PURNAL, 1 negro, 1 horse and riding chair; JOSHUA
PURNAL, ½ brandy still, ELIJAH DANIEL and HENRY
ROBERTSON to have lifetime use of it to still their
own liquor; JEREMIAH BENTLEY, 1 negro; POLLY ROBERTSON
and MILICENT ROBERTSON, 1 cow and calf each. Residue
divided between BETSY ,**PURNAL** and my brother JOHN
JARRELL'S sons: ISAAC, THOMAS and JOHN JARRELL. Exr:
Trusty friends: JOSEPH FARMER and AVERITT PEARCE. Wit:
JESSE FARMER, AVERITT FARMER, WILLIAM POLLACK.

BENTON, ABSALOM
    Mar. 13, 1795. Feb. Ct., 1806. Bk. B, p 241. Wife:
CHARITY, choice of horse, bridle, saddle; lend 1 negro,
stock, cattle at plantation of MOSES KNIGHT and linen
wheel; dau: CHRISTIAN WHITAKER, 3 negroes with their
increase; son: JAMES BENTON, 100 A land purchased of
JOHN BRANCH, Esq., 5 negroes, 1 horse, bridle, saddle;
6 cattle, musket and little gun; desk; 3½ ft table;
case and bottles. Dau: ELIZABETH BENTON, 509 A land,
purchased from JOHN BRANCH, Esq., 6 negroes, horse,
bridle, saddle, 6 cattle, walnut table, 3½ ft chest
of drawers, china cups & saucers; 6 silver tea spoons,
walnut chest and 1 linen wheel made by JOHN YOUNG. Gr.
son & Exr: ELI BENTON WHITAKER, 6 negroes and increase;
beaufatt; large walnut table, blue chest; my long gun.
Use of syder still to son, JAMES BENTON, Gr. son:
JAMES WHITAKER; negro man to gr. son. Exr have management & Education of my two children JAMES BENTON and
ELIZABETH BENTON until of age. Exr: JOHN WHITAKER,
(son-in-law); CARY WHITAKER, friend. Wit: K. KNIGHT,
JAMES KNIGHT, ISAAC FORMAN.

BENTON, CHARITY
    Apr. 5, 1818. Aug. Ct., 1818. Bk. E, p 22. Son
& Exr: JAMES BENTON, 1/3 of whole estate – reason:
Attended to me and my business. Dau: PHERABA, 20 S,
already provided for. Gr. daus: SALLEY NICHOLSON and
EVELINA B. BENTON, 1 dress each. Son: ALLEN KNIGHT;
Daus: ELIZABETH C. BENTON and POLLY CORBIN; dec'd
dau: SALLY; dec'd sons: KINDRED KNIGHT, JOHN C. KNIGHT;
dec'd dau: ELIZABETH NICHOLSON. Wit: JOHN JENKINS,
WILLIAM HOWERTON.

BENTON, JAMES
Feb. 6, 1821. Feb. Ct., 1821. Bk. E, p 263. Property for support of my family (unnamed), 4 negroes to be sold. Exr: GRISHAM C. PITTMAN, SPIER C. COFFIELD, SPIER WHITAKER. Wit: REDDIN LINCH, EZEKIEL HOWERTON.

BENTON, JETHRO
June 21, 1774. Jan. Ct., 1775. Bk. B, p 229. Nunc. Will. 20th day of this inst. SAM'L SANDS made oath before me that on the 3rd day of this inst. he heard the above JETHRO BENTON give his estate as follows: Sis: CHRISTIAN SPIER, 1 negro woman; Bro: ABSALOM BENTON, 1 negro girl; Sis: JERUSHA PARKER, 1 negro boy. Balance of estate be sold and debts paid. Remainder divided between bro and sisters. Sworn before me ELISHA BATTLE.

BIGGS, JOHN
Aug. 12, 1789. Nov. Ct., 1789. Wife: BETHIA and children, negroes. Balance to be divided equally. Son: JAMES, land (200 A) FRANCIS HAYNES lives on; son: WILLIAM, land where I live; Daus: SARAH, NANCY & LOVIE, 1 negro each. Dau: ELIZABETH, 1 negro and 50 ℔ money. Son: TULLY, three notes against WILLIAM SIMONDS, one against JAMES SIMONDS; one against JOHN SIMONDS, 1 horse, 1 maire, 1 ewe, 1 lamb. Also 1 horse to be sold. Exr: FRANCIS LAWRENCE HAYNES, JONTHIA SPINKS.

BIGNALL, ELIZABETH
Dec. 27, 1794. My Ct., 1795. Son: ROBT. EDWARD BIGNALL, all my estate. If dies without heirs, to my cousin ZADOCK BAKER, also my riding horse if I die possessed of one. In case of his decease, I give all to cousin HENRY BAKER. Cousin: SALLIE BAKER, wearing apparel. Exr: Bro: JOB BIGNALL. Wit: W. CLEMENT, SALLY BAKER.

BIGNALL, ROBERT
June 5, 1786. Oct. Ct., 1787. Dau: ANN SPEED, 2 negroes and their increase and 150 ℔ in hard money. Dau & Extx: SARAH, 7 negroes; 6 large silver table spoons; one half my silver tea spoons; one Tea Board; One largest China bowl; one Dressing Glass, that commonly stands in my Bedroom; other Looking Glass commonly

kept in the Little Room; ½ of all chairs, tables, Trunks,
etc. and 300 pounds specie. Dau: PEGGY, 6 negroes and
their increase, 6 silver Table Spoons; half my Silver
tea spoons; Large China Bowl; one salad bowl, large
look'g glass and one dressing glass -- one half my chairs
and Tables, trunks, etc. 300 Ŀ in hard money; sons:
ROBERT and EDWARD, in equal shares, 10 negroes with increase, when son ROBERT comes of age. Request Carsel
and her children to be in one group; also to share the
land I purchased from Rev. Mr. HENRY MOIR. Desire sons
kept in school and no expense be spared for good education. Gr. son: JOSEPH SPEED, 1 negro girl 10 or 12
years old. Exr: son: ROBERT BIGNALL. Son-in-law, JOSEPH
SPEED, to be Exr and Gdn to my 2 sons. Wit: SAM BROWN,
JR., HENRY IRWIN, JOHN SPEED.

BIGNALL, ROBERT,
Jan. 27, 1793. May Ct., 1793. All real estate to be
sold and land purchased in healthier climate for home
for wife and son. Property hers til son comes to lawful
age; he to be educated ; Payments of debts urged. Exrs:
Wife: ELIZABETH BIGNALL; Friend, JOHN HUDSON, BLAKE
BAKER, Wit: JOHN JOHNSTON, ZADOCK BAKER.

BILBERY, DUEL
May Ct., 1837. Bk. F, p 200. Wife & Extx: NANCY
shall possess my property of every description - to
her I give it to be at her disposal forever. Wit: LEVI
WILKINSON, B. WILKINSON.

BILBERRY, NATHANIEL
Aug. 21, 1830. May Ct., 1836. Bk. F, p 191. Wife:
MARY, 2 horses, riding chair and harness, side saddle,
1500 lbs pork, 30 bbls corn, 30 lbs sugar, 15 lbs coffee, 5 bu salt, 30 lb fodder shucks, 10 gal molasses,
12 bu wheat. Also lend her 3 negroes, ½ all stock, ½
household furniture, goods and tools. Also lend land,
including mill. Reversion to son-in-law REDING BONNER.
Lend another 80 A tract bought of JOSHUA SASNETT adjoining lands of COL. HENRY RUFFIN and ZACKERIAH
GRIFFIN -- Reversion to Bro: DUEL BILBERRY. Dau:
FRANCES KILLEBREW (wife of GEORGE KILLEBREW), land S
side of road to Tarborough adjoining COL. HENRY

RUFFIN and JOHN GRIFFIN, it being the land bought of
MARMADUKE BELL and whereon I live. Dau: MARY (wife of
REDING BONNER of Warren Co. Tenn.) Bro: DUEL BILBERRY.
Exr: BENJAMIN WILKINSON, GEORGE KILLEBREW. Wit: S. L.
HART, JOSIAH SPIER.

BILBRE, MARGET
    Apr. 1, 1785. Apr. Ct., 1787. Son: ELEXANDER
(ALEXANDER) BILBRE, 160 A plantation. 80 A bordering
old patent to HUDNALL CORNER and 1 horse; Dau: SARAH
BILBRE, 1 horse. Balance property equally divided. Exr:
JOHN BATTS. Wit: ROBERT HUDNALL, JOSEPH HARRIS, JAMES
HARRIS.

BILBY, NANCY
    May 9, 1839. May Ct., 1843. Sis: POLLY MOORE and
POLLY PITT, (wife of ARCHIBALD PITT) to have residue
of my property. Reversion to THOMAS C. PITT, son of
POLLY PITT, and NANCY PITT, dau of POLLY PITT. Exr:
JESSE C. KNIGHT, MOSES BAKER. Wit: THOMAS GRIFFIN,
BENNET BRADLEY.

BILLEPS, ISOBEL
    Dec. 31, 1847. Feb. Ct., 1850. Bk. F, p 437. Dau:
PENNY, bed and furniture; Dau: EMILY DEAL, Remainder
estate; Gr. son: GRAY PHILIPS, 1 horse. Exr: Son-in-
law, JAMES DEAL. Wit: JOSEPH COBB, EDMUND ALFORD.

BLACKBURN, WILLIAM
    Mar. 5, 1803. Feb. Ct., 1804. Gr. son: WILLIAM,
son of GEORGE BLACKBURN, ½ of all money due me for
notes, and money from sale of mare, cattle or stock.
Gr. son: BURREL, son of GEORGE BLACKBURN, 3 books:
"Burket on the New Testament", "Humphrey on the Bible"
in 2 vol., writing desk I keep my papers in. MARY
BLANFORD, no part of personal property to be sold as
long as she chooses to, live on it, all increase in
stock if she raise any, all corn and meat to support
herself and dau CHERRY and negro woman Jenny. CHERRY
BLANDFORD, she and her mother, MARY BLANDFORD, the
interest on $300 yearly, until CHERRY, born 15th of
June, 1801 comes to age of 15. Interest on $200 to
CHERRY until she is 21, and if she behaves herself
well and marries careful and sober man, I then give

her the principal, during life -- reversion to Gr.
sons: WILLIAM BLACKBURN and BURREL BLACKBURN.
    I desire my negro woman Jenny be set free, and if
she cannot support herself, she shall be supported out
of my estate. Cloth to be given her for clothes. Barrels and iron tools to remain on plantation. Exr: ISAAC
FARMER, JESSE FARMER. Wit: ROLON ROBBINS, WILLIAM
ROBBINS, FREDERICK ROBBINS. (Interesting will).

BLACKLIDGE, LOUISA
    Nov. 3, 1786. Oct. Ct., 1789. Neph: BLOUNT BLOUNT,
(son of WILLIAM BLOUNT), two lots of ground in Town of
Tarborough No. 104 & No. 105. Niece: MARY LOUISA BLOUNT,
9 negroes. Bro: READING BLOUNT, 16 negroes. Hus: RICHARD
BLACKLIDGE, Gold sleeve buttons, wedding ring. Use of
lots No. 104-105 in Town of Tarborough, 26 negroes his
lifetime. Niece: SARAH BRANTON, negro girl, Patience,
after time has expired she has to live with MRS. CONNER
of Craven Co. at age of 12 years. Sis: ANN HARVEY, all
my clothes. Exr: JOHN SITGRAVES, Esq. Wit: J. LEIGH,
CHARLES EVERARDE, G. L. SCHENCK.

BLACKWELL, GEORGE
    Mar. 30, 1763. No probate date. Wife & Extx: ANN,
lend manner (manor) plantation with reversion to sons,
EDMOND (EDWARD?), WILLIAM and GEORGE, JR. and no more
of estate; Children: MARY, FANNE, JESSE, SELAH and
GEORGE, 1 S each. Son: HARDEA, plantation on Bell
Branch, S side maccason, 20 lbs. feathers and the crea-
tures already given him with my mark, 3 dishes, 2
basons, 3 plates, 1 horse branded with a cross, and
bridle and saddle; remainder estate to children:
ABRAHM, PATIENCE, FARABEA, JAMES, AMEA, DORCAS, EDMOND
(EDWARD?) and WILLIAM. Exr: Son: GEORGE BLACKWELL. Wit:
THOMAS HORN, SR., DANIEL JOHNSON, CORNELIUS JORDAN.

BLAKE, NANCY
    June 20, 1825. Nov. Ct., 1825. Bk. F. Friend:
JOSHUA LAWRENCE, $50; Friend & Extx: MRS. ELIZABETH
HUNTER; CHARLES GERARD HUNTER, son of MRS. ELIZABETH
HUNTER. Wit: BEN M. JACKSON.

BLOODWORTH, WILLIAM

Dated 1793. Feb. Ct., 1795. Wife: (unnamed), plan-
tation, horse, bridle and saddle etc. Daus: BETSY
HORNE, MARY BLOODWORTH and SELAH BLOODWORTH, 1 negro
each. Son: WILLIAM, land S side of Mill Branch. Sons:
HARDY, JESSE & TIMOTHY, land to each. Daus: AMEY &
PURETY. Wit: WILLIAM THOS., JAMES THOMAS, MARY THOMAS.

BLOUNT, JOHN G.
    Sept. 3, 1828. Nov. Ct., 1828 & Feb. Ct., 1829. Bk.
F, p 95. Wife: SALLEY, lands and houses; Bro: THOS. H.
BLOUNT, negroes; Exr: SHERWOOD HAYWOOD. Wit: R. P.
HAYWOOD, DELIA HAYWOOD.

BLOUNT, MARY S.
    Apr. 22, 1822. Feb. Ct., 1823. Bk. B, p 319. Leg-
atees: COL. HUTCHINS G. BURTON, of Halifax and lady
MRS. SALLY BURTON, all my negroes; object of this be-
quest is none shall be sold, and to render the subjects
as happy as is compatible with the state of slavery.
DUNCAN CAMERON, Esq., of Orange Co. Rev. WILLIAM HOOPER,
Fayetteville, money for Protestant Episcopal Church in
Raleigh; JOHN W. EPPES, Esq. Buckingham Co., Va. and
MRS. MARTHA B. EPPES, lands in Tenn. SPENCER D. COTTON,
Esq. and wife MARGARET of Tarboro, lands in Ohio and
City of Raleigh. MOSES MORDICIA, land in Wake Co. N. C.
and Tennessee. MRS. JULIA R. SNEED, wife of JUNIUS
SNEED, Esq. of Rowan Co., stock in Bank of New Bern;
COL. DUNCAN L. CLINCH, stock in Bank of N. C.; ROBERT
STUART, formerly of Tarboro, now N. Y. and wife MARY,
money; BENJAMIN M. JACKSON, Tarborough, money; MRS.
SARAH TOOLE (formerly MRS. GILMOUR), money; MARY S.
CLARK, dau of JAMES W. CLARK, plate and money; MRS.
MARY VAN NESS, friend, of Wash. D. C. $1000; MRS.
BARROW, wife of BENNET BARROW, formerly of Tarboro,
$500; MARTHA BARROW, dau of BENNETT BARROW, Esq., $400;
MRS. HUNTER, wife of HENRY HUNTER of Edgecombe Co.;
CATHERINE DARBY: NANCY BLAKE: MARY, dau of THOS. TAYLOR,
Richmond, Va.; ELIZABETH, wife of JOHN LITTLEJOHN, Esq.
of Edenton, N. C.; ANN BLOUNT, of Edenton; MARY ELIZA
TOOLE and METHUSELAH TOOLE, children of late HENRY
TOOLE, money; Elder MR. CHEVROLLIE, of Richmond, Va
and his lady; MARY LITTLEJOHN, dau of JOSEPH LITTLEJOHN,
Esq., of Granville; MARY POLK, wife of WILLIAM POLK of

Mecklenburg; MRS. L. B. PROSSER, of Miss.; JACOB HUNTER,
of Warren; MRS. ANN FALCONER, of Raleigh; ELIZABETH
HUNTER; JOSEPH R. LLOYD; GEO. W. MORDICIA; ELLEN, dau
of MOSES MORDICIA, JULIA JANE SNEED, dau of JUNIUS
SNEED; JOHN S. RUSHWORM (?); MRS. ANN B. HARDY, OLIVIA
L. BLOUNT and PATSY B. BLOUNT, daus of JOHN G. BLOUNT,
Miniature, ring, breast pin; MRS. MARTHA B. EPPES, of
Buckingham, my carriage; MRS. ANN E. MIDDLETON, of S. C.,
India Shawl, rings, point lace; ELLEN MORDICIA, neck-
lace, breast pin, head pin and bracelets; MARY S. CLARK,
jewelry; MARY, ELISA, and CAROLINE, daus of JOHN W.
EPPES, Esq.; HANNAH PITMAN, of Edgecombe; THOMAS H.
BLOUNT, portrait and legacy; MRS. SALLY BURTAIN, MRS.
JULIA R. SNEED, MARGARET G. COTTON, all bed and table
linen; HARRIET JOINER; ANN W. LANE, mahogany dressing
case; MRS. ELIZABETH LOWE, watch; MRS. M. G. COTTON,
Book; MOSES MORDICIA, my interest in estate of my bro:
THOMAS E. SUMNER, also my portrait; land in Warren Co.
sold to pay bequests. Slaves to be liberated; Rochester,
who served Master well, $300; Monument to be erected
to father, GENERAL JETHRO SUMNER, "hero of 1776"; Fund
for the poor in Edgecombe Co.; Relief of widows and
orphans. Exr: MOSES MORDICIA, of Wake Co; COL. HUTCHINS
G. BURTON, of Halifax; SPENCER D. COTTON; BENJAMIN
M. JACKSON, Tarbourough. Wit: LOUIS D. WILSON, DAVID
BARNES.

BLOUNT, THOMAS
    Aug. 2, 1808. May Ct., 1812. JACKEY S. BLOUNT,
land in Halifax, negroes. (Her dec'd brother, McKINNIE
H. SUMNER) Children of my Bro: JOHN G. BLOUNT; Neph:
JOHN GRAY BLOUNT (son of JOHN GRAY BLOUNT), land at
Tarborough and in Tennessee, on Duck River, near the
mouth thereof, from my bro: WILLIAM BLOUNT. Neph: THOS
HARVEY BLOUNT, land in Pitt Co. Nieces: ANN BLOUNT
TOOLE and MARY BLOUNT MILLER, land in Tennessee. Bro:
WILLIAM BLOUNT, land in Tennessee. Exr: JOHN GRAY
BLOUNT, WILLIE BLOUNT, THOMAS H. BLOUNT, WILLIAM J.
BLOUNT.

BLOXSOM, RICHARD
    Feb. 26, 1828. Nov. Ct., 1828. Bk. F, p 94.
TIMOTHY FERRELL, have settlement of my estate. Exr:

TIMOTHY FERRELL. Proved by oaths of MOODY WILLIFORD, BENNET BUNN.

BOLTON, RICHARD
 Apr. 27, 1787. Feb. Ct., 1789. Wife: FERIBY (with small children); Son: RICHARD, land bought of WILLIAM DANIEL; Son: JOHN, land and plantation bought of ABSALOM CASSWAY; Dau: MARY, land bought of AMERSON, money; son: ISAAC, land received of LEONARD LANSTON, in fork of Panter Branch; Son: LUKE, land N. W. Side Main Road leads from Contentony to Tarboroy Town; Dau: ELIZABETH WARD, money, also cattle at JAMES BARROW'S. Exr: JAMES BARROW, MARMADUKE BRANTLEY. Wit: JOHN SINGLETON, JR., ELIZABETH BRANTLEY.

BOLTON, RICHARD
 Apr. 27, 1818. Aug. Ct., 1820. Bk., E, p 241. Wife: & Extx: TATHA, plantation, horses, stock, cattle, ne- groes. Chil: JOEL, ELIZABETH WOOTEN, TABITHA WOOTEN, ELSEY COBB, FANNY WOOTEN, already provided for: Dau: SARAH BOLTON, land and 1 negro; Dau: ZILPHIA BOLTON, land, furniture and money; Son: SETH, land N side Burton's Branch, east end of it; Son: GERALDUS, land S Side Burtons Branch; Son & Exr: ASA, land and negroes. Wit: JOHN MILBURN, HARMON EDWARDS.

BOND, HENRY
 Jan. 26, 1761. Mar. Ct., 1761. Wife & Extx: ROSNAR, plantation, negroes, money and stock. Legatees: eldest sons of my 3 bros: LEWIS BOND, HANCE BOND (dead), WILLIAM BOND, Exr: WILLIAM HAYWOOD. Wit: JOSEPH WOMBLE, JR., FRANCIS ELLINOR, GREGORY STALLIANS.

BONNER, LUTEN
 Dec. 26, 1815. May Ct., 1819. Bk. E, p 213. Wife & Extx: CLARY, "all mi estate". Wit: E. CROMWELL, JOSIAH COBB.

BOOTH, JAMES
 Aug. 9, 1806. Feb. Ct., 1808. Bk. D, p 303. Wife & Extx: ELIZABETH, plantation N side Indian Creek; Son: JAMES, land S side Indian Creek; Son: LAMON, land N side Indian Creek; Dau: ELIZABETH. Son & Exr: JOHN.

Chil: SARAH BATTS, NANCY PATON & ELIZA BOOTH. Wit:
STARLING WALLER, WILLIAM CLARK.

BOOTH, THOMAS (SR)
    May 19, 1777. Nov. Ct., 1786. Son: JOHN, Curent
money of Va.; Son & Exr: JAMES, money; land; 1 negro
girl. Son & Exr: BENJAMIN, land on S side of Tar River,
1 negro man. Son: ROBERT, plantation. Daus: DORCUS &
HANNAH. Wit: BEVERLY BELCHER, JAMES BOOTH, BENJAMIN
BOOTH.

BOOZMAN, JAMES
    Sept.13, 1784. Probated, 1784. Wife & Extx: MARTHA,
Estate; Chil: JAMES, SAMUEL, MEEDA, BRITON, JESSE,
ETHELDRED. Dau: PATTY, cow and calf, 4 sheep, chest and
1 horse; Son & Exr: JOSIA. Wit: JOHN COLWELL, SAMUEL
TEASTER (?).

BOWEN, ARTHUR
    Mar. 1, 1763. Apr. Ct., 1763. Legatee: Cousin ARTER
(ARTHUR) BOING, land, tenements, negroes (illegible)
lying in Northampton Co. Exr: JOILE (JOEL?) BOING. Wit:
WILLIAM LASITER, THOMAS HARDEMAN, WM. HARRIS.

BRADDY, JOSEPH
    Oct. 17, 1802. Nov. Ct., 1804. MARY ALSOBROOK, plan-
tation bought of JESSE WALL and 1 negro; FRANK ALSOBROOK,
son of MARY, land bought of ROBERT HODGE; Dau: SUKEY
KNIGHT, 2 plantations bought of THOMAS KEA and DAVID
PENDER; Dau: HEPSEBAH MABRY, land S side Gum Swamp and
2 negroes; Gr. chil: JOSEPH POPE, 535 A plantation and
negroes; ANNA KNIGHT; REBECCA MABRY; CHARITY ALSOBROOK;
REBECCA ALSOBROOK; MARY KNIGHT, 2 plantations S side
Swamp; PHILIP POPE. Exr: NONE, JOSEPH POPE, MARY
ALSOBROOK, SUKEY KNIGHT Adm. Wit: JOB BRADDY, MARY
BRADDY.

BRADDY, PATRICK
    June 20, 1781. Feb. Ct., 1782. Son: JOB, plantation.
Daus: ANNIE TEEL BRADDY, OLIVE BRADDY, MARGARET BRADDY
& MARY BRADDY. Exr: WILLIAM HACKNEY. Wit: JOSEPH BRADDY,
MOSES HARGROVE.

BRADFORD, NATHANIEL

Oct. 2, 1756. Feb. Ct., 1757. Wife: SARAH. Son &
Exr: JOHN, plantation whereon I live, also 50 A marsh
land; Son: NATHANIEL, remainder my lands; Dau: MARY &
PATIENCE. Exr: JOSEPH LANE. Wit: SAMUEL HARVEY, JEMIMA
SIMMONS.

BRADLEY, AGY

Nov. 14, 1820. Nov. Ct., 1820. Bk. E, p 248. Wife:
HONOUR. Son: ALEXANDER, lands from his gr. father,
JAMES DILLIARD; Dau: CATHERINE, land purchased of JAMES
DANCY, joining RICHARD HARRISON, WM. KEA and JOSEPH
BELL. Exr: ELIJAH HORN, REUBEN BRADLEY. Wit: JARROTT
BELL, SOLOMON BRASWELL.

BRADLEY, BENJAMIN P.

June 25, 1854. Aug. Ct., 1854. Bk. G, p 76. Wife:
(unnamed); Son: ROBERT JOHN; other children (unnamed);
Exr: JOSEPH CUTCHINS, JESSE H. POWELL. Wit: J. J.
JOHNSON, HENRY NEWSOME. Note: - Complicated, detailed,
legal angles.

BRADLEY, BURWELL

July 17, 1837. Aug. Ct., 1838. Gr. son: RUBIN
WATSON, household and kitchen furniture; stock of all
kinds, tools, utensils, shot gun, crop. RIDY MARSHENGALE,
one blue chest. Wit: PATRICK McDOWELL, D. BRYAN.

BRADLEY, DAVID

Jan. 27, 1850. May Ct., 1852. Bk. F, pp 477-78.
Son: ROBERT WILLIAM BRADLEY, of Tennessee, $300 in
addition to what I have given him; Son: BENJAMIN P.
BRADLEY, 200 A land, for which I have given him a
deed of gift. I desire he pay to my estate principal
of note I hold against him -- but not the interest;
Son: JONATHAN BRADLEY, 200 A of land, for which I gave
him deed of gift; Son: HARDY BRADLEY, land on which I
live, and by this gift consider him made equal in land
to sons: BENJAMIN P. and JONATHAN BRADLEY. Also, in
consequence of his afflictions, $200. Dau: MARGARET
ANN BRADLEY, $200. Residue divided, my daus: CHARLOTTE
WHITE, MARGARET ANN BRADLEY and my gr. dau: MARTHA
ELIZABETH LEGGITT, receive amounts equal in value to

the legacies made my two sons: BENJAMIN and JONATHAN
BRADLEY. No Exr named. REDDIN PITTMAN apptd Adm. Wit:
JOSEPH HIGGS, WILLIAM ADKINS.

BRADLEY, JONATHAN
    May 4, 1817. Nov. Ct., 1844. Bk. F, p 312. Father
& Exr: RICHARD BRADLEY, lend all land purchased of
DAVID COFFIELD - known as Harper tract - All property
and negroes to be sold and all divided between bros &
sis: DAVID, ELIZABETH, PRISCILLA, NONNA, ROSY, ABSILLA,
SARAH, RICHARD. Give to sis: POLLY and her dau: ZYLPHA
one equal share. Sis: SUKEY'S share to go to her children. Exr: Bros: DAVID BRADLEY, RICHARD BRADLEY. Wit:
RICHARD HARRISON, STEPHEN BRADLEY.

BRADLEY, JOHN
    Feb. 17, 1772. May Ct., 1772. Dau: SARAH PARIT,
cow and calf; Son: RICHARD, cow and calf; Son: STEPHEN,
mare, sow and pigs; Son: BURRELL, cow and calf, horse
and colt; Wife & Extx: ELIZABETH, all lands and estate
not already given away, reversion to my children, hereafter named: LUCY, AVAIR, JOHN, JOSEPH, ELIZABETH. Wit:
HENRY JOHNSON, ELIZABETH ALLEN JOHNSON, LUCY BELL.

BRADLEY, NANCY
    Mar. 27, 1851. Nov. Ct., 1854. Property to be sold.
ELIZABETH DENTON, wife of CONNEL DENTON, to be paid by
my Executor, $205.30. Nieces: SALLY JOHNSON and
ELIZABETH DENTON, receive interest on proceeds. Exr:
JOHN F. SPEIGHT. Wit: JOSHUA LYON, BENNET T. LYON.

BRADLEY, PENELOPE
    Mar. 26, 1846. Probated, 1847. Bk. F, p 372. Niece
& Extx: ELIZABETH DENTON, property of every description
which I have acquired since the death of my husband.
Wit: LUNSFORD R. CHERRY, CAMPBELL DENTON.

BRADLEY, PRISCILLA
    Aug. 5, 1839. May Ct., 1842. Bk. F, p 267. Sisters:
NANCY BRADLEY, SARAH BRADLEY. Sisters to have whole
estate, reversion to: SARAH JOHNSON and ELIZABETH
DENTON. No Exr. Wit: JAMES SAVAGE, PATRICK McDOWELL.

47

BRADLEY, RICHARD

Mar. 21, 1826. Nov. Ct., 1827. Son: JONATHAN, cow
and calf; Sons & Exr: DAVID and RICHARD, all my lands,
equally divided. Daus: PRISCILLA, NANCY and SARAH, each
dau to have cow and calf and the three of them to have
riding chair, harness, brood mare; choice of my stock;
also lend them while single one negro boy Anthony lands
from Jones line to Moore Swamp - 100 A. Dau: ROSEY
(RONEY?), $20. Balance to be sold and divided between
my chil: ELIZABETH, MARY ABSALA, DAVID, PRISCILLA,
NANCY, SARAH and RICHARD, reserving one Eleventh -- I
intended to give my dau SUKEY -- but for reason best
known to myself --leave this to discretion of my executors for use in her support — should her present
husband die, she shall receive it, etc. Exr: JOHN
MANNING, Wit: WILLIE BRADLEY, FIGURES PHILIPS.

BRADLEY, SALLY

June 18, 1845. Feb. Ct., 1847. Sis: NANCY BRADLEY,
life estate in all my property - tract adjoining land
of DAVID BRADLEY & SILAS WEEKS; 4 negroes Tom, Lorenzo,
Dicey and Hogar -- After her decease, property sold
and money divided between my neices SALLY JOHNSON and
ELIZABETH DENTON. My negro Tom to be permitted to se-
lect the person he wishes to buy him. Exr: PATRICK
McDOWELL, JOHN F. SPEIGHT. Wit: JOSHUA L. LYON, BENNET
T. LYON.

BRADLEY, STEPHEN

July 22, 1829. Feb. Ct., 1830. Bk. F, p 112. Wife:
PENELOPE, household and kitchen furniture, 3 cows and
calves, choice of ten hogs, choice of mare and colt.
Son & Exr: WILLIS, 1 mare. Gr. son: JOHN H. BRADLEY,
$10. Gr. dau: PENELOPY HOWINGTON, $10. Gr. dau: AGNES
FLETCHER, $10. Balance not before given divided between
my living sons. Wit: D(EMPSEY) BRYAN.

BRAKE, JACOB, SR.

Jan. 26, 1827. Aug. Ct., 1830. Bk. F, p 118. Wife:
MORNING, cloth loom and wollen wheel, iron pot, iron
oven and lid, 2 pare pot hooks, one iron pot rack, pare
fire tongs, one shovle, iron griddle, large pewter
bason, bread tray, pewter dish, two meal stands, small

piggin, case of bottles, 3 setting chairs, one spice
menter (?), one cow - (first choice) Sow and pigs, 2
sheep, 2 pewter plates, and 2 flat irons. Chil: JESSE,
WINNIFRED JACKSON and JACOB, $2 each. ANDREW C. JACKSON,
son of ELISHA W. JACKSON, 2 sheep. Balance my estate
unto: BENJAMIN, SPENCER, JOSIAH, JAMES, AMOS and
APSALA BRAKE, chil of my son JACOB BRAKE, when they
come of age. Exr: MOSES PRICE, Wit: MOSES SPICER,
ARCHIBALD WHITFIELD.

BRAKE, PATIENCE
     Mar. 4, 1854. Nov. Ct., 1854. Bk. G, p 94. Daus:
PENNINA CLARK, quilt, one half my wearing apparel. Son
& Exr: WILLIAM BRAKE, residue of estate, including
stock, provisions, household and kitchen furniture,
also all monies. Wit: WILLIE RICKS, THEO. THOMAS.

BRACEWELL (BRASWELL), ABNER
     Apr. 9, 1807. May Ct., 1807. Bk. D, p 279. Wife:
NANCY, one half my Estate; Dau: ZILPHA, other half
when she comes of age. Exr: JAMES SOUTHERLAND,
SHADARACK COLLINS. Wit: LEWIS FORT, JOHN WILLIAMS.

BRASWELL, BENJAMIN
     Feb. 25, 1789. May Ct., 1792. Wife: MARY, lend
plantation, stock, reversion to JAMES and JOHN; negroes, reversion to chil. Son & Exr: JAMES, all that
land below Watery Branch, and on N side of Mill Branch.
Son: JOHN, 125 A land on Town Creek, joining THOS.
MERCER; Remainder of land on Watery Branch. Plantation
lent to their mother as near as can be divided equally
between my last mentioned sons. Son: SIMON, negro boy.
Gr. dau: POLLY RUFFIN, dau of MILLIE RUFFIN. Dau:
SELAH RUFFIN, wife of SAMUEL RUFFIN, 5 cattle and 5
sheep. Dau: WINNEY, 1 negro girl. Wit: THOS. MERCER,
THOMAS WILLIAMS. Also sons: Permenter, Sudon & Zadock

BRASWELL, BYTHAL
     Jan. 21, 1841. Feb. Ct., 1842. Bk. F, p 266. Wife:
LOUISA. Estate equally divided between all my children,
viz: JACKEY D. PEAL, WILLIE BRASWELL, CALVIN BRASWELL,
SERENY HU?NALL (HUDNALL), FRANCES BRASWELL, Exr: MOSES
PRICE, ROBERT BARNES. Wit: REDMON CURL, EASON WILLIAMS.

BRASWELL, CRISSEY

Sept. 8, 1848. Feb. Ct., 1853. Bk. F, p 498. Dau:
POLLY CALHOUN, $400, carriage and harness, 2 horses,
spinning wheel, bed and furniture left me by her
father, JAMES BRASWELL, - also 1/5 of my lands she and
Gr. daus to divide wearing apparel and bedclothes; Gr.
dau: MARY ELIZABETH ARMSTRONG, 1/5 my land, 2 negroes -
reversion to her children - also $150; Gr. son: JAMES
GRAY ARMSTRONG, 1/5 my land, 2 negroes and $50; Gr.
dau: CRISSY ARMSTRONG, 1/5 my land, 3 negroes - rever-
sion to her children and $50; Gr. son: GEORGE
WASHINGTON ARMSTRONG, 2 negroes and $50. Exr: WILLIAM
D. PETWAY, JAMES F. JENKINS. Wit: JESSE MERCER, DAVID
T. (?) MERCER. Codicil, May 13, 1852. Bequeath negro
to MARY ELIZABETH BARNES, if she leave no heir to
CRISSY ARMSTRONG and her heirs..Wit: JESSE MERCER,
GEORGE W. KILLEBREW.

BRASWELL, JAMES

Sept. 27, 1760. Jan. Ct., 1765. Wife: Unnamed.
Chil: JOSEPH, JAMES, BENJAMIN, SARAH CAIN AND OLIVE
STINSON. Son & Exr: SIMON, reversion in 400 A plan-
tation I live on, all stock, cattle, hogs, horses,
all household goods and furniture. Wit: SAMUEL RUFFIN,
JOHN DAVIS, NATHANIEL RUFFIN.

BRASWELL, JAMES

Oct. 2, 1783. Nov. Ct., 1783. Wife: UNITY, 15 S
specie; Son & Exr: NATHAN, 100 A tract purchased of
ISHAM HUMPHREY and negro boy; Son: JAMES, 100 A tract
lying between SOLOMON BRASWELL and JOSEPH FORT, also
late entry of 300 A adjoining JACOB FORT, WILLIAM SUGG
and ANTHONY BACON, 1 negro and horse; Son: ABNER, 132
A tract on Hendrix Creek and adjoining SOLOMON BRASWELL,
Cowlick Creek, GRICE'S line and JOHN SOUTHERLAND, also
60 A purchased of JOSEPH HOWELL adjoining JOHN
SOUTHERLAND, ROBERT BIGNALL and HENRY IRWIN, 1 negro
and horse; Son: BURRELL, plantation where I live and
tract purchased of THOMAS GRICE, land entry, between
P. GRICE'S line and ROBERT BIGNALL, 1 negro and horse.
Daus: FERIBY, CHARITY, RACHAEL, ELIZABETH and SARAH,
1 negro each. Exr: JOHN SHERROD, ROBERT DIGGS. Wit:
NOAH SUGG, JOHN SOUTHERLAND, JOSEPH BORDEN.

BRASWELL, JAMES
   Nov. 20, 1821. May Ct., 1824. Bk. F, p 18. Wife &
Extx: CRISSEY, all my lands and negroes of every Class.
All stock, together with plantation utensils etc. Son:
HENRY B. BRASWELL, 1 colt and reversion in land. Residue
not already given away be divided equally among my daus:
HARRIET, POLLY, BETSEY and CRISSEY BRASWELL. Exr: JOHN
MERCER. Wit: E(DWIN) BULLUCK, HENRY GRIFFIN.

BRASWELL, PERMENTER
   Oct. 23, 1827. Nov. Ct., 1830. Wife: MARGARET, lend
all land with reversion to chil ROBERT and ANN; all ne-
groes with reversion to chil. Son & Exr: BENJAMIN. Gr.
Chil: EGBERT WILLIAMS, MARTHA ANN WILLIAMS, and BLAKE
WILLIAMS, $30 each. Exr: ROBERT BARNES. Wit: LOVITT
KILLEBREW, SAMUEL MOORE.

BRASWELL, RICHARD
   Dec. 7, 1767. Jan. Ct., 1772. Bk. 4 p 193. Wife &
Extx: ELIZABETH, lend all remaining property, reversion
to children. Son: SAMPSON, land on Tar River and Nah-
unta Path; Son: SOLOMON, plantation; Son: RICAHRD;
Son & Exr: JAMES; Son: WILLIAM; Daus: SARAH, MARY and
ELIZABETH, 5 S proclamation money each. Wit: THOMAS
BRYANT, WILLIAM SHERROD, JOSEPH FORT, SAMSON DILLARD,
JAMES GRAY.

BRASWELL, RICHARD
   Aug. 27, 1804. Feb. Ct., 1807. Bk. D, p 267. Wife:
CHARLOTTA and children, Estate Exr: JOSEPH BELL, JAMES
SOUTHERLAND. Wit: MALACHI DENNY, DAVID RANDOLPH.

BRASWELL, ROBERT R.
   Dec. 11, 1845. Aug. Ct., 1848. Bk. F, pp, 402-04.
Wife: ANSEYLINA, household and kitchen furniture,
horse, mule, cart, gig, farming tools, all my land on
E side of my Canal; 3 negroes; yoke oxen; and support
for one year. Son & Exr: JOSEPH J. BRASWELL, 89 A
called the Moor land and $100 cash; Son & Exr: BENJ.
G. BRASWELL, my Lovit Long plantation; my storehouse

and contents, except notes and accounts; and blacksmith tools. Son: THOMAS P. BRASWELL, the plantation on which my mother now lives and Brady still; Son: ROBERT S. BRASWELL, two tracts I bought of JESSE C. KNIGHT and LAWRENCE MOORE. Youngest son: JOHN D. BRASWELL, my home plantation at decease or marriage of wife. Dau: MARGARET BRASWELL, 1 negro and $100; Dau: ELIZABETH, 1 negro; Dau: ARRIETTER BRASWELL, 1 negro; Dau: ANCELYLINA LANCY BRASWELL, 1 negro. After division of my mother's Estate and my part of WINNEY WILLIAMS estate takes place, both my shares of these estates to be sold and money divided among my living children and lawful heirs. Wit: WM. H. HINES, J. W. CALHOUN.

BRASWELL, ZADOC
    Mar. 13, 1851. May Ct., 1852. Bk. F, p 473. Wife: MARY, lend 1 negro, horse, 20 hogs, 2 cows and calves, 3 ewes and lambs, 1 dz sitting chairs, walnut table, walnut chist, kitchen furniture, loom, 2 pr cards, 2 spinning wheels, 2 carts and wheels, tools, etc. 100 A including houses etc., poultry, year's support, set knives and forks, doz plates. One negro to be sold to pay debts - reversion of land to all children: LUCINDA THORNTON, FRANCES WINNEFRED, ZADOC R. BAKER, SPENCER L. MARY P., SALLY, JULY, MARTHA. No Exr. Admin. granted to BAKER BRASWELL. Wit: DAVID WILLIAMS, BYTHAL G. BROWN.

BRIDGERS, BRITON
    Sept. 28, 1795. Nov. Ct., 1795. Wife: (unnamed), 4 negroes, 3 horses, half my hogs, sheep and geese, all land on N side Williams' Branch with reversion to son JOHN, all necessaries now provided for building and furnishing house - to complete; Son: WILLIAM, land N side Town Creek purchased of RALPH WEAKS and sheriff of sd County and tract purchased of JOHN MORRIS on N side Town Creek at mouth Mill Branch and 5 negroes, colt, philley, saddle and bridle, 6 cows and calves, 6 ewes and lambs, 7 sows and pigs, when he marries or reaches 21; Son: JOHN, 7 negroes and their increase. Exr: WILLIAM ROUTH, LEMMON RUFFIN, JAMES BARRON, WILLIAM BRIDGER, Wit: JOSEPH PENDER, THOMAS WILLS. WILLIAM GUARDNER.

BRIGGS, JOEL
    Nov. 27, 1780. Aug. Ct., 1783. Wife & Extx:
ELIZABETH, all my estate - Reversion to my 4 children
(unnamed). Exr: ETHELDRED GRAY, friend. Wit: AQUILLA
COHOON, JAMES GRAY.

BRINKLEY, ABRAHAM
    Oct. 4, 1835. Aug. Ct., 1838. Son: HENRY, all lands
in Edgecombe Co., 1 negro and the clock; Dau: BARSHEBA
DARNOLD, 1 negro with reversion to her chil: WILLIAM
and KINCHEN DARNOLD; Dau: SALLY LLOYD, 1 negro with re-
version to my daus: HULDAH, GILLEY and ELIZABETH
BRINKLEY; Remaining chil: GILLEY, ELIZABETH, NANCY,
HULDAH and HENRY, 1 negro each. Wit: JO P. PITT, WATSON
HARRELL.

BROADRIBB, THOMAS
    Mar. 15, 1794. May Ct., 1794. Son: MICHAEL BELL
BROADRIBB, all estate after payment of debts. Exr:
WILLIAM ROBT. GRAY. Wit: NOAH WOODARD, ELISHA VANN,
HARDA STALLINGS.

BROWN, JAMES
    May 7, 1795. May Ct., 1797. Wife: SELAH, plantation
where I now live; reversion to son JAMES; 4 cows and
calves, 4 ewelambs, 2 sows and piggs; 2 dishes and half
a dozen plates, half a dozen chears, 2 pots, a spider,
table, 2 chests, loom and gear, 2 water poles and one
washing tub; lend her 2 negroes her lifetime or widowhood. Son: JAMES, still; two other plantations; one
purchased of JAMES WATKINS, the other of ANTHONY MOORE.
Gr. son: JOHN RODNEY CASWELL, horse, bridle and saddle;
1 suit of clothes at the age of 21 years; residue of
my estate to be sold and money divided between SARY
CASWELL and SAMUEL BROWN and JAMES BROWN. Exr: AARON
COLEMAN, JOHN WILLIAMS. Wit:STEPHEN COLEMAN.

BROWN, JAMES
    Mar. 26, 1773. Mar. Ct., 1774. Son: JAMES, my plan-
tation; Daus: MOLLEY, SALLY, ANNY. Exr: BENJAMIN AMASON.
Wit: JAMES AMASON, JESSE AMASON, WILLIAM AMASON

BROWN, JOHN

Mar. 13, 1758. June Ct., 1759. Wife: PATIENCE. Son:
NATHAN, land, still and cider hogsheads; Son: HARDY;
Dau: PATIENCE POPE, ELIZABETH EDWARDS, PRISCILLA BROWN,
HENRIETTA BROWN, OLIVE BROWN. Gr. Son: BURAL SHELTON.
Exr: NATHAN BROWN, SAMUEL EDWARDS, LODAMON_____?
Wit: JOHN POPE, GEORGE CRUDUP, NICHOLAS DIXON. Proven
in Halifax Court.

BROWNRIGG, GEORGE
     July 30, 1782. Feb. Ct., 1784. Son & Exr: GEORGE
BROWNRIGG, JR., (a certain young man born of MARY
BYRAN), 200 A plantation where I dwell, bought of
NICHOLAS SESSIONS, 150 A plantation bot of JOHN SHELP,
on Tar River, 12 negroes, all cattle, hogs, etc. furniture -- all personal estate.
     In case GEORGE BROWNRIGG should be at sea, or a
great distance at time of my death, I will and desire,
authorize and impower PETER HYNES, JR. and HENRY HYNES
to take into their care my estate until such time as
GEORGE BROWNRIGG, JR. return home. Then deliver it to
him. Wit: RICHARD WILLIAMS, WILLIAM WILLIAMS, MICHAEL
GERMAIN, GEO. EVANS.

BROWNRIGG, OBEDIENCE
     Apr. 6, 1839. Probated 1840. Bk. F, p 242. Dau:
PENNINAH WATSON and MARY RUFFIN, the two best beds in
my house; Son: JAMES TART, two large looking glasses
and all my setting chairs; Son: THOMAS E. TART, 10 S;
Son: EDWIN BROWNRIGG, 10 S; Son: WILLIE BROWNRIGG, 10
S: Dau: MARIA BURDEN, 7 negroes her life time; Son:
ALFRED BROWNRIGG, 1 negro girl; Dau: OBEDIENCE WRIGHT,
8 negroes and all my table and teaspoons. Gr. dau:
MARTHA A. TART, all my china; Gr. dau: PENNINAH TART,
my dining table, dressing table, looking glass; it is
my desire that the labor of Joe shall support the old
woman Cloe her lifetime. Gr. dau: MARGARET TART, residue. Exr: JAMES B. WOODARD, WILLIAM WOODARD. Wit:
ELIZABETH WOODARD, JEREMIAH FARROW.

BRUCE, GEORGE
     Dec., 1806. May Ct., 1807. Bk. D, p 278. Chil:
ABSALOM, ELIZABETH JOHNSTON, JAMES, AZIEL and SARAH
LLEWALLING, 12 S each; SEALY and PATSY, 1 negro each

and rest of property divided between them; JORDAN, Exr:
PATSY BRUCE, JORDAN BRUCE. Wit: GARRIOT KNIGHT, NOAH
BARNES, KENNEDAY CONTECH.

BRYAN, DEMPSEY
	Feb. Ct., 1847. Bk. F, p 352. Wife: MARY, all lands,
17 negroes, 15 shares stock in Bank of Tarboro, Branch
of the Bank of the State of N. C., household furniture-
Barauch, harness, buggy, harness, 2 horses, 4 mules
(her choice) 60 head hogs, 6 head cattle, 20 head sheep,
2 wagons and harness, yoke stears and cart, log chains,
large iron kettle, plantation tools of every kind --
for life or widowhood. Reversion at her decease to my
son & Exr: HUGH BLAIR BRYAN; 175 bbls. corn, 30 stacks
fodder, 7000 lbs. pork, 20 bu. of salt; 300 lbs. sugar;
100 lbs. coffee; 5 bbls flour for her and family support.
Negroes. Dau: LUCY, wife of BENJAMIN BATTS, 12 negroes,
10 shares stock in Tarboro Bank, Branch of State of
N. C. Gr. son: WILLIAM HENRY KNIGHT, slaves in trust,
10 shares stock in Tarboro Branch of the Bank of State
of N. C., profits arising for benefit and support of
his mother -- profits arising yearly. Gr. son: WILLIAM
HENRY KNIGHT, slaves (7); two tracts of land bought of
RICHARD (of Florida), on S side of Fishing Creek,
Edgecombe Co., on both sides of Griffin's Swamp. Dau:
PENNINA BRYAN, 17 negroes, 10 shares in Tarboro Branch
State Bank of N. C.; $1000 cash; furniture. Dau; Mary,
wife of THOMAS MAYO, 12 negroes. Ten shares of stock
in the Tarboro Branch of the Bank of State of N. C.,
$500 cash. Dau: MARTHA, wife of REDDIN PITMAN, 14
negroes and $1000. Son & Exr: WILLIAM D. BRYAN, 16
negroes, 10 shares stock in the Tarboro Branch of
State Bank of N. C.; Dau: NANCY, 11 negroes; ten
shares of stock in the Wilmington and Raleigh Rail-
road Co.; 10 shares in the Tarboro Branch of State
Bank of N. C., $500 cash; furniture. Wit: JOHN F.
SPEIGHT, PATRICK McDOWELL, LUNSFORD R. CHERRY. Codicil:
May 5, 1845. Bank stock and negroes lent beloved wife
MARY, be sold and divided between LUCY BATTS, SARAH
KNIGHT, PENNY BRYAN, MARY MAYO, MARTHA PITMAN, WILLIAM
D. BRYAN, NANCY BRYAN and HUGH B. BRYAN.

BRYAN, DREWRY

Jan. 11, 1843. Feb. Ct., 1843. Bk. F, pp 277-8.
Wife: SUSAN BRYAN, lend 112 A land whereon I live; also
the Bradley Place on the W side of Fishing Creek 111 A,
all the Mill Field, on Fishing Creek, houses, etc.
household and kitchen furniture; 3 horses, mare, 2 cows,
calves, 6 head sheep, etc; my barouch, harness and 5
negroes; Son: WILLIAM BRYAN, $500; Son & Exr: JOSEPH
BRYAN, land in Halifax Co., 5 negroes and 3 horses;
Dau: PENELOPE MABRY, 5 negroes; my 4 sons: HENRY,
BLOUNT, GRAY and ETHELDRED BRYAN, all my land. Should
either die before reaching legal age or having heirs,
property reverts. Exr: CHARLES MAYBREY. Wit:
BENJAMIN BATTS, WILLIAM DICKENS.

BRYAN, ELIAS
July 25, 1821. Nov. Ct., 1821. Bk. E, p 276. Wife:
ROSA, 2 negroes reversion to son ELIAS should either
die or become afflicted another of same value -- so
they can support their mistress. Reversion to estate.
Choice of horses, land of her choosing for her support;
large iron kettle - then to son ELIAS. My faithful men
servants - Jim and Bill, remain until death of my wife-
benefit wife & two youngest children. They may then
choose which of my children they will belong to. My
faithful woman slave, Chaney, also be permitted to
chose, etc. Estate kept together for education of my
three youngest children, support their mother, and
family, until coming of age of ROBT. Son & Exr: HENRY
BRYAN, land I purchased of BENJAMIN PHILIPS, JOSEPH
HOUSE, ISAAC HOUSE, and ROBERT ROSE, SR., lying on the
S side of Swift Creek; cattle, sheep, half the hogs,
which shall be fattened -- and balance of crop-- one
mare, mule colt, bay colt horse, 9 negroes - 5 of them
to remain on my NORSWORTHY MIALS plantation until January, 1824, for the benefit of my estate. Dau:
ELIZABETH B. PITMAN, land on S side of Swift Creek
known by the name NORSWORTHY MIALS plantation - at
age 21 - also 2 cows and calves, 2 sows and piggs, 20
bbls of corn, 7 negroes. Son: ROBERT, land on N side
of White Oak Swamp known as Harris plantation -- on
ensuing January his coming of age. ELIAS, lands and
plantation whereon I live. Lands I purchased of
MATTHEW KINCHEN, JOHN WIGGINS and THOMAS WIGGINS, JUNR.

889 A & 100 A on S side of White Oak Swamp, by name of
JOHN MIALS place, which I purchased of JOHN EXUM, when
he comes of lawful age. Dau: MARY H. BRYAN, 7 negroes.
Exr: DEMPSEY BRYAN, worthy friend, HENRY BRYAN. Wit:
JOSEPH PHILIPS, THOS. WIGGINS. Caveated by ROBERT
McMULLEN as to whether it was last will. It was found
to be -- & probated. (A long and thoughtful, considerate
will.)

BRYAN, JOHN
    Dec. 3, 1801. May Ct., 1803. Son & Exr: HARDY, 50
A joining land of ROBERT McMULLEN and JONAS PARKER.
Son & Exr: WRIGHT, 50 A adjoining PHILIP POPE and JOB
BRADDY. Son & Exr: ROBERT, 50 A adjoining WRIGHT BRYAN
land and FREDERICK SAVAGE all rest of my estate. Son &
Exr: ISHAM, 50 A adjoining ROBERT BRYAN and WILKERSON
MABRY. Heirs of son: JESSE, 10 S. Dau: PHERIBY McMULLEN,
10 S. Wit: PERSON GLOVER, HARDY BRYAN, ELIZABETH HARKNEY.

BRYAN, ROSA H.
    Mar. 7, 1850. No probate date. Dau: MARY H. BUNN
and her chil: 1 doz chairs, walnut table, mohogany
table, 3 chests and their contents, 2 mules, 4 cows
and calves, 12 sheep, 12 geese, all curtains and 240 A
tract called the Exum land; Grt. Gr. dau: ROSA WILLIAM
FAIRCLOTH, 1 negro. Residue divided between lawful
heirs. Exr: BENJAMIN F. KNIGHT. Wit: J. E. LINDSEY,
B. F. KNIGHT. Not proved. Rejected by court. See minutes May term, 1850.

BRYAN, SMITH
    Sept. 18, 1809. May Ct., 1811. Bk. E, p 14. Wife:
MARTHA, land, S side Fishing Creek, Mouth of Purcosin
Branch, adjoining lands of SILAS BRYAN; 3 negroes. Re-
version to dau NANCY - negroes, riding chair, harness,
and money; Son: JAMES, land bought of TURNER BRYAN and
JOSHUA LAWRENCE, negroes, etc. Son & Exr: DEMSEY, ne-
groes and money; Dau: CATEY MURPHY, money; Son: SILAS,
land bought of JACOB PROCTOR, negroes, still, money;
Son: DRURY, land, cash, negro. Exr: JOSHUA LAWRENCE.
Wit: BRITAIN JONES, TURNER BRYANT.

BRYAN, THOMAS

Feb. 15, 1785. May Ct., 1785. Wife: FAITHFUL BRYAN, 18 head hoggs, 6 sheep, 3 cattle, all geese, Also lend dwelling house, outhouses; ½ part of 200 A land. She to have all land not given away her life time or widowhood. Son: JOHN, 100 A land, 1 negro; Son: WILLIAM, 100 A land and 3 negroes; Son: HUDSON, 200 A land, 2 negroes, 30 hoggs, and colt (sorrel) after decease of wife. Dau: ELIZABETH COFFIELD, 2 negroes; Dau: DELILAH BRYAN, 1 negro; Dau: ANN BRYAN, 1 negro. Wit: THOMAS FOXHALL, JOHN FOXHALL, JOHN OAKEY.

BRYANT, EVIN
Aug. 27, 1808. Nov. Ct., 1810. Bk. E, p 1. Evin BRYANT, WILLIAM BRYANT, MARY BRYANT and ELIZABETH BRYANT, sons and daughters of my brother JOHN BRYANT, dec'd, 5 S each; Sis: DELILAH WOODARD, wife of NOAH WOODARD, 5 S; Sis: NANCY JONES, wife of JESSE JONES, 5 S; lands, on N side of Tar River, negroes and personal property to be sold -- cash give to my brother WILLIAM BRYANT and my niece POLLY COFFIELD, dau of THOMAS CAFFIELD. Exr: WHITMEL BELL, LAWRENCE O'BRYAN. Wit: JAMES PEAL, WILLIS PEAL.

BRYANT, FAITHFUL
Oct. 12, 1803. May Ct., 1804. Bk. D, p 208. Dau: POLLY CLARK, a note against JESSE CLARK; Gr. dau: CHARLOTTE CLARK,_____, 1 heifer; Gr. dau: DELILAH JONES, bed; Dau: NANCY JONES, residue of my estate not already given away. Exr: JESSE JONES. Wit: EXUM LEWIS, HANNAH JONES.

BRYANT, GAYLE
Apr. 8, 1788. Nov. Ct., 1793. Wife & Extx: ELIZABETH, land, mare, bridle and saddle all my hogs and cattle - household goods, and clothes, until her decease or marriage. Reversion to my children. Dau: SARAH BRAND, lining wheel; Dau: EDAH JORDAN, all land and manner (manor) plantation; loom and weaving gear. Gr. son: NAZARETH ALLEN, small shot gun. Exr: JOSEPH JORDAN. Wit: JESSE PITMAN, MOURNING PITMAN, THOMAS EDWARDS.

BRYANT, JOHN

Sept. 14, 1734. May Ct., 1735. Lend wife ELIZABETH,
1 mullato wench, her own bed & furn - also another bed
& furn. which hath tick to it, black walnut safe and ½
doz turned frame Rush chairs, 1 trunk, large iron pot
with a still made upon it, 1 small iron pot, 1 brass
skillett, fire tongs & shovel, box iron, small "chaffing"
dish, 1 gelding, bridle & saddle mare & colt, 25 cattle,
4 sheep, 2 basons of "putre", 2 dishes, 4 plates, ½
doz spoons, 1 iron spit; Son & Exr: WILLIAM, land called
Ballards lying in Cypress Swamp, tract on Deep Creek
upon the Indian Path, tract on Beaver Dam Swamp and
Fishing Creek - 2 negroes, 1 large & 1 small iron pot,
black walnut round table, 4 "leathorn" chairs, 1 new
case of bottles, 2 pewter basons, 2 dishes (pewter),
4 plates, ½ doz spoons, 1 Bukaneer Gun - whatever
cattle, hogs, horses & mares that are called his, also
15 head of my own stock, also 4 stears at Canahoo; all
rest of my stock at Canahoo to be divided between him
& JOHN FORTE. Further bequeath him a bay mare, new
saddle & bridle, 4 horses, 4 sheep and 7 pounds current
money of Va. Son: ARTHUR, plantation whereon I live
adjoining that given WM., another plantation on Deep
Creek where RICAHRD CAMP now liveth, also 100 A in
Cohukee Swamp, 2 negroes, black walnut square table,
4 leathron chairs, 2 iron pots, 2 pewter basons, 2
dishes, 4 plates, iron spit, 6 horses, all cattle &
stock where RICHARD CAMP lives to be divided between
him & RICHARD CAMP, also 25 head of my home cattle,
4 sheep, 7 pounds Va. current money, 1 silver sack
cup, 1 small trunk and iron bound case of bottles.
Son & Exr: DAVID HOPPER, 160 A lying in fork of Beaver
Dam Swamp joining land given son WM., 20 pounds Va.
current money owed to me by JAMES BARNES by a note in
his own hand, to be paid at MR. THEOPHILUS PUGH'S.
also 2000 weight of pork. Friend JOHN FRYE, 100 A on
Cahukee Swamp where ROBT. WRIGHT liveth; Friend JAMES
TURNER, living in Va.; remainder of that tract left
to son DAVID HOPPER. Wit: ROB'T REDFORD, ARCHBALD
THOMPSON, ANN FRAZIER.

BRYANT, WILLIAM
    Sept. 21, 1748. Feb. Ct., 1749. Sons: JOSEPH and
WILLIAM, 1 negro each; Dau: PATIENCE, my house, land

and plantation, mill, 1 negro, new bedtick, green rug,
Dutch blanket, mare, 6 cows and calves; Dau (?): SARAH
MYHAND, 1 negro; Gr. son: JAMES McDANIEL, cattle, 1 ne-
gro; Friend: THOMAS HUYANDINE, my bareskin coat; Friend:
SARA?, horse and side saddle, "if she recovers of the
sixness she now lise under"; Residue to be divided be-
tween RATCHEL McDANIEL and my 4 children. Exr: ABRAHAM
DEW, EDWARD BROWN. Wit: THOMAS POPE, WILLIAM ANDREWS,
JAMES MYHAND.

BRYANT, WILLIAM
    May 15, 1761. Nov. Ct., 1761. Nunc. Will. THOMAS
FOXHALL, aged thirty seven years, first duly sworn
before BENJ. HART, said a few hours before the death
of WILLIAM BRYANT, he said that he gave to his son
SMITH BRYANT, land on Fishing Creek, below the Road
that crosses at his landing -- etc.
    That he gave to his son ARTHUR BRYANT, land be-
ginning at the yellow hill on the cove, and up the
cove to the mouth of the pine pocosin branch. That he
gave to his son WILLIAM BRYANT, the plantation whereon he then lived, at the mouth of Crooked Swamp, etc.
after death of his wife SARAH BRYANT. That he gave to
his son BRITTAIN BRYANT, land lying on the upper ridge
of the Crooked Swamp, beginning at the mouth of a branch
opposite the briary old field, etc. Also he gave all
his land that lies below the Crooked Swamp he had not
disposed of to his son JOHN BRYANT. All his land that
lieth above Crooked Swamp above the land that he gave
to his son BRITTAIN, he desired sold and rest of estate to his wife SARAH BRYANT for to raise his children -- and farther, saith not. Certified before me
this 5 day of May, 1761. Benj. Hart.

BRYANT, WILLIAM
    May, 1762. Jan. Ct., 1763. Mercht. Goods to be
valued and sold -- about 30 head of cattle, 5 head of
horses and mares. Wife have use of house and plantation, outhouses, gardens, horse, saddle, 1 negro,
12 cows and calves. Wife bring up my children. Son:
SAMUEL, Reversion in house and plantation. Son:
BENJAMIN, my plantation on Little River, stock and
cattle thereon; Son: WILLIAM, Plantation on Buffalo

Creek, Johnston Co., 5 cows and calves. Dau: PATTY, 1
negro woman, 4 dishes, 4 basins, 1 doz. plates, horse
& saddle; Dau: NANNIE, 1 negro boy, 4 basins, 1 doz
plates, horse & saddle. JOHN HILL, for faithful discharge of business, the sum of twenty pounds current
money. All my hogs, horses, cattle, sheep, geese to
be sold, money put to use of my children at the discretion of my loving wife and Executors. Exr: WM. LANE
(friend), ALEX BRODIE, NEWT LANE, EDWARD LANE.

BRYAN, WILLIAM
    Aug. 12, 1797. Aug. Ct., 1797. Wife & Extx:
LIZANAR, lend plantation whereon I live — to raise
children on, reversion to sons TURNER BRYAN and BAT
BRYAN. Perishables to be sold and divided among my
four daus: PATTY, POLLY, CANADAH and BARBARY BRYAN.
Wit: JOHN BATTS, WILKINSON MABREY, BENJAMIN HART.

BULLOCK, DAVID
    Sept. 15, 1774. Wife & Extx: (unnamed). Lend plan-
tation where I live now for her lifetime. Reversion
to son ROBERT. Lend unto wife all remaining part of
estate her lifetime. Then to be equally divided bet-
ween chil: Son: JOHN; Daus: MARY HAMBY, SARAH RUFFIN,
SUSANNAH; Son: NATHANIEL; Dau: PATTY; Son: ROBERT
HOOD BULLOCK; Daus: BETTY, AGNES. Sons: EDWARD &
DAVID BULLOCK and Dau: ELIZABETH JONES, 5 S each. Son:
ROBERT HOOD BULLOCK, plantation where I dwell. Exr &
Son: JOHN BULLOCK. Wit: NOAH SUGG, JAMES PERMENTER,
LEWIS DODGE.

BULLOCK, DAVID (JR.)
    Mar. 20, 1815. May Ct., 1815. Bk. E, p 100. Bro:
WHITMELE BULLOCK, I lend for two years my land and
plantation, stock, hogs, sheep; all crops left for
support of farm, also 1 negro. Bro & Exr: JONATHAN
BULLOCK, and plantation where I live. All else sold
and money divided among my brother and sister, GRAY
BULLOCK and ORRIN BULLOCK. Wit: DEMPSEY JENKINS,
RICHARD PEEL.

BUMPASS, JOHN
    Oct. 11, 1849. Nov. Ct., 1855, Bk. G, p 115. Wife:

MARTHA, whole estate; reversion to children. Daus: PHEREBY, MARY, MARTHA. Son & Exr: JOHN W. Wit: JACOB ING, WILLIAM B. HORNE.

BUNN, JOHN
    May, 17, 1760. June Ct., 1760. Son: DAVID, 200 A land and plantation where I live, with Mill, 2 cows and calves, large iron pot, 2 sows and pigs, large chest, "riffle" gun and 6 plates. Son: JOHN, 2 negroes, 2 cows and calves, smooth gun; small door pot, hand saw; augor and gauge, large chest, dishes, plates, 2 sows and pigs. ANN BUNN (?), remainder of my estate. Exrs (?) and Bros-in-law: JAMES RICK, JOHN RICKS. Wit: EDWARD MOORE, JOHN BARNES, WILLIAM JOHNSON.

BUNTIN (BUNTING), JOHN
    May 16, 1837. Nov. Ct., 1846. Bk. F, p 348. Wife: CREASY, lend 1/3 estate - reversion to MARY BUNTIN and WILLIAM BUNTIN. Dau: MARY BUNTIN, 1/3 estate. Gr. son: WILLIAM BUNTIN, son of RICHARD BUNTIN, 1/3 estate. Exr: DANIEL HOPKINS. Wit: ELISHA PORTER, JARRETT HOPKINS. Exr: Dec'd Adm. granted JESSE STANCIL, Esq. Bond $500. WILLIAM C. LEIGH and ELISHA PORTER, Securities.

BURN, MICHAEL
    Feb. 28, 1780. Feb. CT., 178? Wife & Extx: ANN, all estate, reversion to sons: AARON and MICHAEL, and FREDERICK SWINSON, son of my wife. Exr: ROBERT BIGNALL. Wit: R. BIGNALL, JAS. STOCKDALE, DENNIS STOCKDALE, ANNE RENN (?).

BYNUM, JOSEPH
    May 23, 1841. May Ct., 1841. Bk. F, pp 259-60. Wife: SALLY, lands purchased from LEMON WARD, 200 A tract I live on, tract of 130 A (boundaries deed show), 8 ne- groes; half my stock; cattle, hogs, sheep, all poultry, brandy still, cider casks, riding carriage, harness, 2 horses, farming utensils, yoke of oxen, household and kitchen furniture; all bacon, corn, fodder and peas, bees, notes and money. Dau: NANCY WILKINSON, $50, and what I have given her. Son & Exr: ALLEN BYNUM, $300 in addition to what I have given him. Son: REUBEN BYNUM, 1 negro in addition.. Dau: SALLY APPLEWHITE, 3 negroes,

1 mare, and $100 cash. Dau: JULIA BYNUM, 3 negroes,
$200 cash, and trunk. Dau: ELIZABETH VINES BYNUM, 4
negroes and $100 cash. Son: SAMUEL VINES BYNUM, 100 A
land I bought of NEEDHAM WARD, 50 A land bought of
JAMES B. WOODARD (boundries in deeds). My interest in
200 Aland I leased of ELBERT AMASON, Gdn. to hers of
JOHN R. THOMAS, deceased... lands loaned my beloved
wife, half my stock and cattle, sheep, all my horses,
etc., 2 negroes, $300 in cash, trunk, bridle, saddle
and sulky. Dau: ABSALA BYNUM, 3 negroes, trunk, riding
gig, harness and $200 cash. Wit: LEMUEL O'BERRY, JACOB
S. BARNES.

BYNUM, SAMUEL, V.
    Sept. 5, 1848. Nov. Ct., 1848. Bk. F, p 408. Sis:
ELIZABETH V. BYNUM, all my lands, including my piney
woods tract, 1 negro, farming utensils, buggy, harness,
household and kitchen furniture, cart and wheels, stock,
horses, cattle, hogs, sheep; all my crop. Bro: REUBEN
BYNUM, my sulky and harness. Sis: APSILA C. BYNUM, 1
negro. Fifty dollars out of my estate to wall in graveyard on this place. Residue divide between my sisters.
Exr: Bro-in-law, COUNCIL APPLEWHITE. Wit: W. THOMPSON,
NATHAN P. DANIEL.

BYRUM, THOMAS (SEN'R)
    May 8, 1837. Aug. Ct., 1837. Wife: WINNEFORD, plan-
tation, all lands, personal estate her widowhood, or
life, only Executors be vested with power to sell such
part as wife may choose, to pay debts. Son & Exr:
JACOB BYRUM; Sons: JOHN, THOMAS. MOSES BYRUM'S heirs,
$1.00.

CAIN, HARDY
    Dec. 21, 1754. May Ct., 1755. Wife & Extx: RACHEL,
for benefit of raising my children, I bequeath all
cattle, hogs and household goods. Dau: ISOBEL, 150 A
plantation whereon I live; Dau: PEURITY, entry of land
in Johnson Co.; Dau: SARAH, 1 negro. Exr: Bro: JAMES
CAIN. Wit: WALLIS JONES, JAMES CARRELL.

CAIN, JOHN
    Feb. 9, 1755. Feb. Ct., 1757. Son & Exr: JONATHAN,
plantation bought of CHARLES HORN, also all lands I

hold on Maple Swamp except small piece I promised to
let JOSEPH MOORE, SR. have, where THOMAS RANER now
lives; also 1 negro, all cattle I had of WILLIAM HILL
ANDREWS, horse, saddle, bridle, and gun. Son: ABIJAH,
home plantation, also plantation whereon JAMES DEHORTY
lives. Dau: ZIPPORAH, all cattle of mine which ANDREW
VANCE has, also breeding mare. Dau: JERUSHA, 5th colt
of ZIPPORAH'S mare. Wit: JAMES DEHORTY, JOHN TANNER,
REBEKAH DEHORTY.

CAINE, HARDY
    Apr. 12, 1774. July Ct., 1774. Bro & Exr: JAMES
CAINE, my land; 3 negroes, 3 horses, all cattle and
hogs. All money in hands of my Gdn, EDWARD MOORE. Wit:
ISAAC HICK, WILLIAM WALKER.

CAINE, JAMES
    Mar 3, 1761. June Inferior Ct., 1761. Dau: DELILAH,
3 negroes, 5 cows and calves, and mare, when at age of
18 years; Dau: PENELOPE, 3 negroes and linen wheel;
Dau: ELIZABETH, 2 negroes, and linen wheel at age of
18; Dau: MARY, 2 negroes, 4 cows and calves, and linen
wheel at age 18; Son: JAMES, 600 A plantation and land
where I live, and half the new Survey, 2 negroes, my
still, walnut table and great pot, great Bible, 10
cattle and mare; Dau: ANN, 2 negroes, 2 large pewter
dishes and 10 cattle to be possessed at age of 18;
Son: HARDY, mill and plantation 160 A land, and half
of my new entry; 10 cattle, iron pot, and a young mare;
Son: JACOB, 320 A plantation in Johnson Co., 2 negroes,
50 L current money, 6 L Virginia money to buy him some
cattle, and an iron pot, and riffle gun..(Balance too
indistinct to road} Sole Exr: _____? WALKER. Wit:
CHARLES DANIEL, ISHAM WEAVER, DAVID PHILIPS.

CALHOON, ANDREW A.
    June 28, 1847. May Ct., 1849. Bk. F, p 428. Wife:
NANCY, $15 to buy mourning dress; land whereon I live
for natural life or widowhood; bequeath 2 negroes, 2
horses, mules, wagon, pork, sheep, hogs, etc. sideboard,
clock, Bible and Song Book, 2 chairs, etc. Remainder
divided between children. Desire Gdn to give boys common education to transact common business, and to girls

education to read and write. Reversion to children.
Gdn: WILLIAM D. PETWAY. Exr: WILLIAM H. HINES, REDDING
G. PETWAY. Wit: N. J. PITTMAN, S. D. ARMSTRONG.

CALHOUN, PHERABE

Dec. 13, 1839. Nov. Ct., 1845. Bk. F, p 326. Son:
ANDER A. CALHOUN, 1 negro.. ANDER to pay HARDY G.
CALHOUN, $25. ORREN D. CALHOUN note I hold against him
for $58.83, if found in my possession. Son: JOHN W.
CALHOUN $75, horse, etc. Son: HARDY, mare, bridle and
saddle, Etc. DELILAH SPICER, ORREN D. CALHOUN, POLLY
WILLIFORD, PIETY JOINER, JOHN W. CALHOUN, HARDY G.
CALHOUN, Residue. Exr: ? Wit: ROBERT R. BRASWELL.
JESSE LANCASTER.

CANE, WILLIAM

Aug. 13, 1757. June Ct., 1761. Wife & Extx: SARA
JANE, lend plantation where I live and residue with
reversion to children. Son: ELISHA, all cattle, S side
of Neuse River. Son: ARCHEY, reversion in plantation
where I live and half the land belonging to the tract,
pot, and mare. Son: WILLIAM, other half of tract where
I live. Exr: EDWARD MOORE. Wit: WILLIAM RICKS, THOS,
WHITFIELD, SR., JACOB BARNES,

CARLILE, ROBERT

Sept. 26, 1786. Nov. Ct., 1786. Wife & Extx: SARAH,
use of plantation, where I live, all personal property
for herself and in raising my children. Daus: SUSANNA,
MARY ANN, SARAH and RHODA. Sons: SIMON and EDWARD
(EDWIN?), lands, houses, orchards. Son: COLEMAN, 56 A
tract of land whereon LEMON O'NEAL now lives, debt
due me from RICHARD STROTHER, and double Britch gun.
Exr: ROBERT DIGGES. Wit: ELIJAH STALLINGS, JOHN BELL.

CARLILE, ROBERT

Sept. 27, 1808. Feb. Court, 1815. Bk. E, p 81.
Wife & Extx: NANCY, lend plantation stock and house
during life or widowhood. Dau: REBECCA JACKSON, 5 S;
Dau: LIDDY CARLILE, 5 ₤ currency; Dau: NANCY RILEY;
Son: JOHN; Dau: POLLY BELLFLOWER; Dau: EDEA SEALF;
Son: CLARK; Son: ROBERT; 5 S each. Son: JOSEPH, rever-
sion in half of land. Son: CARY, reversion in remain-
der of land. Wife's Dau: feather bed and furniture.
Exr: JAMES SIMMONS. Wit: JAMES HOGAN, JAMES DOWNING.

CARLILE, SARAH

July 13, 1772. Jan. Ct., 1776. Dau: MILLIE; Dau: SARAH BALDWIN and Dau: ELIZABETH BRADLEY, my wearing apparel. Son: ROBERT, one cow he now has in his possession. Son: WILLIAM CARLILE, 20 S Virginia money. Son: WM. BELL; Son & Exr: RICHARD BELL and son JOSEPH BELL, all rest of my estate. Wit: JAS. HILL, WILLIAM MORING, HENRY KEA.

CARLILE, WILLIAM

Apr. 5, 1769. May Ct., 1769. Wife: SARAH, one half my personal estate. Estate to be finally divided between my 2 sons. No sale — settled among themselves. Son & Exr: ROBERT, plantation and land whereon he now liveth, my wife shall have life estate in same; Son: WILLIAM. Wit: WILLIAM BELAMY, HARTWELL PHILLIPS, BENJAMIN BELL.

CARLISLE, CARY

Aug. 22, 1831. No probate date. Bk. F, p 130. Mother: NANCY CARLISLE, all money and claims, lending her all my land for life, then to my sister: MARTHA CARLISLE. Exr: CHARLES MABRY. Wit: ALSTON SAVIDGE, JOHN MABRY.

CARR, CELIA

Feb. 21, 1839. Nov. Ct., 1840. Bk. F, p 246. Son & Exr: JONAS J. CARR, 4 negroes, family Bible; Son: RICHARD HINES, interest on note; Dau: ESTHER J. BLOUNT, remainder estate divided between ESTHER J. BLOUNT and living children of LUCILLIA PRINCE. Dau: LUCILLIA PRINCE, Books, wearing apparel, furniture and $1000 to ESTHER J. BLOUNT. Exr: Neph: WILLIAM J. ANDREWS. Wit: R. H. BLOUNT, JOHN W. FARMER.

CARR, ELIAS

Feb. 8, 1822. Feb. Ct., 1822. Bk. E, p 289. Wife: CELIA, 8 negroes, 1/5 of my corn, fodder, peas, bacon, and lard, 1/5 of my stock, farming utensils, 1/5 plantation whereon I live, dwelling, beginning at Tar River, whole of household and kitchen furniture, for life or widowhood, dividends on Eleven Shares of stock in State Bank of N. C. Son: JONAS J. CARR, plantation

and in State of Georgia, which I purchased of the
PAYNES and WILLIAM JIMMERSON, on which JOSHUA THIGPEN
now lives and 7 negroes on arrival at lawful age; Son:
WILLIAM, reversion in land and plantation where I live,
also to son: WILLIAM, property and stock devised to
his mother. To each of my children: Dau: ESTHER J.
BLOUNT, WINNEFRED W. CARR, LUCRETIA CARR, $2000. Bal-
ance of my negroes in Jones County, Georgia under care
of ERWIN HART to be sold. Codicil: JONAS J. CARR: Farm
utensils, horses, hogs, cattle at my Georgia plantation,
shot gun. WILLIAM CARR: Shot gun. Gr. son: ELIAS BLOUNT,
negro boy Demsey. Exr:?. Wit: ROBERT WILLIAMS, JAMES
NORVILLE.

CARR, JONAS J. (PLANTER)
     Mar. 27, 1843. May Ct., 1843. Bk. F, pp 289-292.
Dau: MARY B. CARR, the gold watch that belonged to her
mother; bureau with her mother's wearing apparel, negro girl, also my Pig Basket plantation in Nash Co.,
negroes, etc. In Case MARY dies without heirs,   reversion to my sons WILLIAM B. and ELIAS CARR, etc.   Sons:
WILLIAM B. and ELIAS, to receive property from Gdn. at
legal age, including negroes. ELIAS to have double
barrel gunn, sword that belonged to my Grandfather
COL. JONAS JOHNSTON, my family clock that belonged to
my father, etc. To each of my children bed, bedstead,
furniture, etc. Exrs to preserve certain possessions
until children are old enough to appreciate their
value. Library to be divided between them. Sufficient
of my negroes to be kept for the cultivation of farm
where I now reside .. Piney Woods portion to be rented
out.   Education and supervision of Dau: MARY left to
my friend MRS. M. K. WILLIAMS, of Warren Co. Suitable
iron railings to be placed around family graveyard
and tombstones over each grave as have none. Exr:
Friend, DR. ROBERT F. G. H. WILLIAMS of Pitt County.
Friend, RICHARD WILLIAMS, of Pitt Co., Test. Gdn. of
my three children: MARY B., WILLIAM B. and ELIAS CARR.
Wit: ELIAS F. BLOUNT, JESSE JONES. Codicil: In case
RICHARD WILLIAMS refuse to act as Gdn., I appoint
JOHN B. WILLIAMS, of Warren Co. If he refuses I appoint
my bro. RICHARD HINES, Apr. 3, 1840.

CARR, WILLIAM
    Sept. 1, 1827. Nov. Ct., 1827. Bk. F, p 77. Bro:
JONAS CARR and Sis: LUCRETIA CARR, the whole of my
estate, negroes and all property, including notes. Adm.
granted to JONAS J. CARR. Wit: JOHN F. HUGHES, BENJ.
R. HINES.

CARSON, SARAH
    Oct. 30, 1847. Feb. Ct., 1851. Gr, son & Exr:
AUGUSTINE I. M. WHITEHEAD, have all money 1 am entitled
to; 2 negroes, 2 large looking glasses, brass kettle,
household and kitchen furniture. Wit: MOSES BAKER, E. G.
ARMSTRONG.

CARTER, JESSE
    July 6, 1778. Feb. Ct., 1779. Mother: SARAH MORGAIN,
the plantation whereon I live, and land adjoining. All
rest of my estate real and personal. Exr: EXUM LEWIS,
JOHN WHITAKER. Wit: EXUM LEWIS, JOHN WHITEHEAD, SARAH
MORGAN (JUNR).

CARTER, JOHN J.
    Nov. 3, 1833. Feb. Ct., 1834. Bk. F, p 155. Neph:
JOHN J. CARTER GRISSOM, son of sister; whole estate
with exception of $50. WILLIAM A. SMITH, $50 for use
of Missionary Society of the Va. Conference of the
Methodist Episcopal Church. Exr: WILLIAM W. WILLIAMS,
Wit: MOLAN DAVIDSON.

CARTER, KINDRED
    May 14, 1777. Oct. Ct., 1777. Nov. Ct., 1810. Feb.
Ct., 1819. Wife: MARY, 6 negroes. Plantation where I
live, all land, stock, household furniture and remainder of my estate, except otherwise devised, reversion
to my Gr. son: MOSES CARTER KNIGHT. Dau: PRISCILLA
KNIGHT, 4 negroes; Dau: CHARITY KNIGHT, 5 negroes,
likewise negroes now in her possession during life of
herself and husband MOSES KNIGHT. Dau: WINNEFORD TAYLOR,
4 negroes; Dau: PENELOPE WHITAKER, 4 negroes. Exr:
JAMES KNIGHT, CAREY WHITAKER. Wit: EXUM LEWIS, COULAM
WINSTEAD, PETER TATUM.

CARTWRIGHT, JOHN
    Oct. 12, 1780. Nov. Ct., 1780 Wife: SARAH, lend

plantation, one horse or mare; 2 cows and calves, pot, 2 hogs. Use of my negro fellow Primus, reserving the use of 20 A adjoining orchard, with my daus: SUSANNAH and SARAH, one half to be cleared land. Son: PETER, 1 sow and piggs; Son: JOHN BAPTIST CARTWRIGHT; Son & Exr: MATTHEW, cow and calf; Dau: MARY CAULWELL, one heifer; Dau: SUSANNAH, cow and calf; Dau: SARAH, cow and calf; Son & Exr: THOMAS NOTLY CARTWRIGHT, land lying between lines of PETER HINES, SEN'R and PETER CARTWRIGHT, adjoining Town Creek; cow and calf. Son & Exr: HEZEKIAH, reversion in plantation whereon I live, tract of land bought of CHARLES EVANS, except land given my son: PETER, by Deed of Gift. Also give to my said son, 80 A of land bought of JACOB JOHNSON joining my plantation; 1 horse or mare, cow and calf. HEZEKIAH and THOMAS CARTWRIGHT (my sons), 220 A land between my plantation and JOHN'S BRANCH; my lands in Johnston Co. to be divided between surviving children. My whip saw and Cross Cut Saw, carpenter's tools to be kept by my four sons, PETER, MATTHEW, THOMAS and HEZEKIAH. Also grinding stone for use on plantation. Wit: PETER HINES, JR., HENRY HINES.

CAUSEY, LEAVIN
Nov. 10, 1793. Nov. Ct., 1793. Wife & Extx: NANCY, 2 negroes, sorrel horse, stock of cattle and hogs, household and kitchen furniture. Son: LEAMON; (No land mentioned). Exr: PHILIP CAUSEY, JUN'R. Wit: STARLING WALLER, JOHN MORGAIN.

CAUSEY, PHILIP
Nov. 29, 1824. No probate date. Bk. F, p 35. Wife: RACHEL, land, plantation, horse, 2 cows and calves, 3 sows and pigs, desk, walnut table, pine table, 2 chests, ½ doz Windsor chairs, all bottomed chairs; riding chair and gear, kitchen furniture, and one bofat and furniture; all fowls; pair fire dogs, loom, with all apparatus, 1000 lbs. pork, corn and fodder and potatoes sufficient; and 2 negroes. Son: CULLEN. Son: GREENBERRY. Exr: ISAAC NORFLEET. Wit: JOSEPH FREEMAN, NATHAN SESSOMS. Note: ISAAC NORFLEET refused; JOSIAH FREEMAN and MOSES BAKER qualified.

CAVENA, CHARLES

Apr. 8, 1756. Feb. Ct., 1757. Son: DAVID, 1 S;
Son: NEEDHAM, 50 A on Beech Run; Son: AQUILLA, 60 A
on W side of Beech Run; Son: NICHOLAS, 1 S; Son:
ARTHUR, 60 A joining to NEEDHAM land on the River; Son:
CHARLES, ½ remaining land; Son: HENRY, ½ remaining
land. Dau: MARY, 300 A on S side Northuntee (Nahunta)
Marsh; Dau: MEMORIAL. No Exr: Wit: JOHN FOUNTAIN, JOHN
MURPHREE, ABIGAIL PITTMAN.

CAVENAH, MARY

July 12, 1793. Feb. Ct., 1794. Bro: CHARLES, 50 A
land and plantation and 1 mare. MARY WOMWELL, wife of
BENJAMIN WOMWELL, 5 hogs and 5 cattle. PATIENCE TAYLER,
widow of WILLIAM TAYLER, 5 cattle and 6 hogs. Cousin:
SUSSANNAH POLLARD, 3 cattle and 4 hogs. Cousin: THOMAS
POLLARD, (son of THOMAS POLLARD, dec'd), 3 cattle and
6 hogs. Neph: WILLIAM CAVENAH, (son of my bro. HENRY
CAVENAH), money. Exr: JOHN DANCY. Wit: ABISHA HORN,
JAMES WILLIFORD, TEZIA MOORE.

CHERRY, AARON

Jan. 16, 1835. Nov. Ct., 1835. Bk. F, p 182. Wife:
ELIZABETH, lend land whereon I reside, all negroes,
stock and furniture. Son: LUNSFORD R. CHERRY, 1 negro;
Son: LEWIS K. CHERRY, reversion in land whereon I re-
side. 1 negro. Dau: SARAH R. JONES, 2 negroes. Exr:
CHARLES W. KNIGHT, JESSE C. KNIGHT. Wit: ASA EDMONDSON,
JAMES H. SAVAGE, EDWARD POWER.

CHERRY, DAVID

Jan. 29, 1833. May Ct., 1833. Bk. F, p 145 Wife:
SARY, whole estate. JAMES BARROW, son of JOHN BARROW,
$400. Exr: EGBERT H. WILLIAMS. Wit: DAVID WILLIAMS,
JOHN R. PITT. Exr. refused; Adm. granted DAVID WILLIAMS.
Bond $4000. Securities: STEPHEN TAYLOR and _____?
WILLIFORD.

CHERRY, ELIZABETH

Mar. 12, 1840. Feb. Ct., 1841. Bk. F, p 250. Dau:
SALLY D. JONES, all my property of every description..
good notes amounting to $1000 to heirs of LEWIS K.
CHERRY, deceased. Wit: HENRY AUSTIN.

CHERRY, ROBERT

Oct. 1, 1809. Nov. Ct., 1820. Bk. E, p 254. Wife: MARY, lands and negroes, household and kitchen furniture, all kinds grain, stock of every kind; Dau: PEGGY, 5 negroes; Son: JOHN, land I bought of WILLIAM CONIGA; 2 negroes and money. Sum of 200 ₺. Dau: MARY, 5 negroes Son: THEOPHILUS, land and plantation with tract I bought of JOSEPH PIPPEN, negroes. Exr: JOHN M. MAYO, JESSE KNIGHT. Wit: JESSE KNIGHT, ALLEN KNIGHT, JOHN CHERRY.

CHERRY, SAMUEL

Oct. 2, 1805. Feb. Ct., 1810 (?). Bk. E, p 126. Wife: CLARY (CLARA), plantation, household and kitchen furniture, all horses, corn, hogs, stock, cattle, sheep, beef, riding cheer (chair), harness, 2 negroes and Tools. Son: CHARLES, Maintenance out of estate; Son: THOMAS B. CHERRY, all my property at death of wife CLARY. Plantation where BENJAMIN POWELL now lives. Exr: RODERICK CHERRY, BENJAMIN WHITFIELD. Wit: JOHN MOORING, Jr., FREDERICK MAY. Adm. granted to CLARY CHERRY; Bond $3000. With DEMPSEY EURE, WILLIAM COUNCIL and BENJAMIN WHITFIELD, Securities.

CHERRY, SOLOMON

Oct. 29, 1808. No probate date. Bk. D, p 340. CLARY (CLARA), 240 A land, 3 negroes, 3 horses, stock of cattle, household and kitchen furniture, 1 shotgun, 2000 lbs pork unless she marry again. Younger children to be supported without charge; Dau: SARAH, 100 A land S side Town Creek, adjoining land whereon I live and JOHAM HALLOMON lives, being property purchased of BRIDGER PITT; negroes; Dau: TABITHA, 2 negroes; Son: SAMUEL, 242 A plantation whereon I live, negroes. The infant my wife carries to be named DAVID or CLARY, 3 negroes. JOHN and DAKESS (DORCAS) SMITH, remainder of estate and $75 cash, 4 cattle and negro. Son: WILLIAM; Dau: MARTHA ROSS; Dau: ELIZABETH MANNING; Dau: LIDDY STANCIL; Dau: SUSANNAH CHERRY, 10 shillings each. Exr: DAVID FORE, JAMES PITT. Wit: H. WALLER, JOHN WILKINSON, SAMUEL CHERRY.

CHURCHWELL, MARY (POLLY)

Nov. 6, 1845. Feb. Ct., 1846. To HENRY L. BATTLE, (son of JOSEPH S. BATTLE), my hair trunk and contents, except my notes and other papers. To MARY CUTCHINS, (dau of ELI CUTCHINS), my bed and furniture, chest and clothes except dresses given POLLY PRICE. To POLLY PRICE, widow, 2 of my best homespun dresses, To HENRY L. BATTLE, son of JOSEPH S. BATTLE, two thirds and to RICHARD H. BATTLE, one third of money that belongs to me. $426.95. Exr: RICHARD H. BATTLE. Wit: THOS. M. WILKINS, THOS. NEWBY.

CLARK, HENRY
Oct. 15, 1784. Feb. Ct., 1785. Wife: FRANCES, plantation, stock of all kind; household goods and furniture; Sons: CHARLES, HENRY, RICHARD, and daus: GRACE SCARBOROUGH, FRANCES PROCTOR, DILILAH (DELIA) NORSWORTHY, 5 S each. Son: NATHAN, plantation where I now live after death of Wife. Dau: SENEY, balance of estate to be divided between son NATHAN and dau SEALEY CLARK. Exr: WILLIAM BLOOD (?), JOHN STRINGER. Wit: JOHN PROCTOR, HENRY CLARK, JOHN STRINGER.

CLARK, HENRY
Aug. 15, 1787. Nov. Ct., 1788. Wife: PENNY, mare, my land til my sons come of age. All my estate not mentioned in my will, to her. Son: HENRY, long gun; Son & Exr: RICHARD, place called "Swimming hole neck"; My little gun, all my tools; Daus: CLARY and FRANKY. Exr: JOHN STRINGER. Wit: SAMUEL NORSWORTHY, RICHARD CLARK.

CLARK, JAMES W., TARBORO
Nov. 1, 1843. Feb. Ct., 1844. Bk. F, pp 302-3. Wife: ARABELLA E. CLARK, dwelling adjoining lot, furniture, carriage, horses, wagon, gear, 2 cows and calves, 12 months provisions, and 5 negroes; life estate; Son & Exr: HENRY T. CLARK, my books, papers, guns, rifle, walking sticks, watch that was my father's and negroes heretofore advanced him; Dau: MARIA T. CLARK, 2 negroes; Dau: MARY S. CLARK, 2 negroes and increase; Dau: LAURA P. COTTON, of Florida, negroes heretofore advanced her. Remainder of my negroes in North Carolina and Alabama, with balance of my real

estate not before named, to be equally divided be-
tween wife and 4 children. Land in Weakley County,
Tenn. to be sold to ALFRED GARDNER. Request burial in
Episcopal Churchyard, Tarboro, and neat monument with
simple inscription of birth and age placed over grave.
Wit: TH. PARKER, BEN M. JACKSON, JAS. BLOUNT CHESHIRE.

CLARK, ROBERT
Dec. 12, 1752. Aug. Ct., 1753. Wife: JEAN; Son:
WILLIAM, to share with son MOSES, 200 A of land, it
being my share, equal with LOTT ETHEREDGE; Son: AARON,
100 A of land; Son: ROBERT to share with son LEVI,
plantation whereon I live. Daus: ANN TATUM, JEAN
CLYBUN, MARY DOUGLIS, RACHEL ETHEREDGE, AGNES ETHEREDGE,
and HANNAH UNDERWOOD. Exr: THOMAS TATUM. Wit: WILLIAM
WIGGINS, MARY WIGGINS.

COBB, EDWARD
Nov. 28, 1812. Nov. Ct., 1817. Bk. E, p 167. Wife:
WINIFRED, All my property her lifetime. Son & Exr:
STEPHEN; Son: GRAY; Son & Exr: JOHN. Dau: SALLY THIGPEN,
Reversion in 5 cattle; Dau: FANNY MAYO, Reversion in
5 cattle. Son: JONAS, Reversion in ½ of plantation and
residue; Son: EDWARD, Reversion in ½ plantation and
residue. Wit: HARMON EDWARDS, BRYANT EDWARDS.

COBB, JOHN
May 18, 1837. May Ct., 1837. Bk. F, p 198. Wife:
WINEFRED, land whereon I now live, livestock, household
and kitchen furniture; 5 negroes, for life or widow-
hood. Sons & Exrs: AMOS W. COBB and STEPHEN COBB, the
skinner tract of land, equally divided. Dau: LOUISA
CRISP, 1 negro and other articles now in her posses-
sion; Dau: LYDIA LUELLA COBB, 1 negro; Dau: LUCINDA
COBB, 1 negro; Dau: FANNY ELIZA COBB, 1 negro. Sons:
EPHRAIM EDWARD COBB, DAVID MONROE COBB and JONAS GRAY
COBB, reversion in land whereon I live and all stock.
Wit: EATON COBB, LACY ALFRED.

COBB, THOMAS N.
June 2, 1825. May Ct., 1829. Bro & Exr: EDWIN
GARDNER, all my estate. Wit: JO. P. PITT, ELISHA
ELLIS.

COCKBURN, GEORGE
  Mar. 14, 1799. May Ct., 1799. Wife & Extx: FRANCES,
lend all estate. Dau: ELIZABETH, at her marriage, 1
negro girl, chest, hunting saddle, all the cattle that
is at this time called hers. Dau: MARY, 1 negro girl,
hunting saddle and chest. Son & Exr: GEORGE, I will my
executors to make a line through my lands beginning at
what is now called CHAS. OWEN'S corner thru to Indian
well, where Edgecombe, Martin and Halifax counties
join. I give George land on W of line, running thru
line of tract I bought of THOMAS WEATHERBY and other
tract bought of MICAJAH LITTLE called Blackwell land;
18 A bought of ROBT CARLILE, 60 A bought of ROBT
SAVIDGE, 25 A lying on Mill (or mile) Swamp adjoining
Mill (Mile) Dam - also 1 A bought of JOHN OWEN (?) -1
negro, set blacksmith's tools, also my part of the
mill. Son: THEOPHILUS, all rest of my lands except
home plantation and land adjoining same which I will
my beloved wife to have during her natural life... 1
negro, still, cap and worm. The land where his mother
lives, after her death, 4 slaves to continue with
wife until WINNIFRED reaches 18 years of age, then
they and all residue of estate to be divided between
wife and 3 daus: WINNIFRED, FRANCES and MARIE. Exr:
WILLIAM HYMAN, SR. Wit: ELI HOWELL, MARY BIRD.

COFFIELD, BENJAMIN
  Oct. 24, 1770. Nov. Ct., 1770. Wife: ROSEANNAH, I
lend 4 negroes and all rest of estate not before given.
Reversion to my 5 children. Son: GRESHAM, plantation
whereon he now lives with the lands lying over Creek
in Halifax County, 5 negroes. Dau: ANN JONES, 3 negroes; Gr. son: ALLEN JONES, negro boy; Dau: PENELOPE,
5 negroes, 6 pewter plates, 2 basons and 2 dishes;
Son: BENJAMIN, plantation and land whereon I live
with the great mill thereunto annexed, 5 negroes and
1 desk; Dau: MARY, 3 negroes, 6 pewter plates, 2
basons and 2 dishes. Exr: Bro, SPEIR COFFIELD; Wit:
ABSALOM BENTON,_____? WHITAKER, JETHRO BENTON.

COFFIELD, BENJAMIN
  July 18, 1837. Aug. Ct., 1838. Gr. son: DAVID C.
WARD, of the State of Tennessee, 8 negroes with in-

crease; Gr. dau: ELIZABETH P. PENDER, 15 negroes with
increase, the Piano-Forte, clock and Brandy still attached to tract of land devised to her; Gr. dau:
MARTHA C. FORT, 14 negroes with increase, Brandy still
attached to land devised to her. Should she die without heirs, estate to be divided between Gr. son:
DAVID C. WARD and Gr. dau: ELIZABETH P. PENDER. I also
bequeath to my Gr. dau: ELIZABETH P. PENDER, plantation
whereon I now reside, beginning at Fishing Creek, Speir's
Old Bridge.. below where bridge now stands - along road
leading from said Bridge to Bell's Bridge on Tar River.
805½ A (See Deed of Conveyance), Gr. dau: MARTHA C.
FORT, land on Fishing Creek below, on E side of Speir's
Old Bridge to Bell's Bridge on Tar River, 672½ A. It
is my will that my two old negro men, Jim and Charles,
remain on the Plantation as long as they live and be
supported out of my estate, etc. Exr: Friends: WILSON
C. WHITAKER, REDDIN PITTMAN. Wit: G. C. PITTMAN,
STEPHEN COKER.

COFFIELD, DAVID
    June 3, 1817. Feb. Ct., 1818. Bk. E, p 180. Wife:
ELIZABETH, 6 negroes, being all negroes I ever rec.
from her, horse, colt, sorrel, gigg horse, gigg, best
harnes, 5 cows and calves; also lend thru widowhood
8 negroes, land necessary for negroes to cultivate,
including houses, etc. where I now live. ROB'T PITMAN
have charge working negroes. (?) JULIA MCDANIEL, leave
in trust for her, 3 negroes, mare, saddle and bridle
provided she marries with consent of my Exrs: Sons:
SPIER WILLIAM and JOHN W., lands on Fishing Creek to
be divided; each to have a negro woman and children
of equal value. All property reverts to sons at end
of widowhood of wife. Exrs to be Gdns of chil. Exr:
ROBERT JOHN PITMAN, BENNETT BARROW, JAMES BENTON. Wit:
ALEXANDER COTTON, WILLIAM DANCY.

COFFIELD, ELIZABETH
    Apr. 21, 1835. May Ct., 1835. Bk. F, p 170. Dau-
in-law: SARAH COFFIELD, window curtains, table-cloths
and towels. Son (dec'd): SPIER W. COFFIELD. Gr. dau:
ELIZABETH W. COFFIELD, bureau, bed and bedstead in
my room, my black trunk, silver teaspoons marked E. C.,

1 dining table; Gr. dau: MARTHA C. COFFIELD, dining
table, mate to the one given Gr. dau: ELIZABETH; Gr.
dau: SARAH SPIER WILLIAM COFFIELD, dining table bought
of MILES NASH also all silverware except spoons marked
E. C.; Niece: SARAH WHITAKER, Exrs to furnish her $25
per year for clothing, until she arrives at the age of
21; Neph: WILLIAM B. WHITAKER, 1 horse and $100; Neph:
L. H. B. WHITAKER, colt, also to have privilege of
buying my carriage and harness; Neph: JAMES C. WHITAKER,
my "gigg" and harness. Residue to be divided between
my 3 Gr. daus: ELIZABETH W., MARTHA C. and SARAH S. W.
COFFIELD. In case of death of all three without issue,
residue to be divided between my bros and sisters. Bro:
ABSALOM B. WHITAKER, have care of 2 negro children until they reach 14 or 15 years age; Sis: MOURNING
ETHERIDGE, have care of 1 negro child until she reaches
12 yrs. Exr: Bros: CARY WHITAKER, ABSALOM B. WHITAKER,
WILSON C. WHITAKER. Wit: SPENCER D. COTTON, NOAH
THOMPSON,

COFFIELD, SPIER
    Jan. 22, 1770. May Ct., 1771. Wife & Extx: (unnamed),
lend 7 negroes. All other negroes remain with wife until children come of age, provided she gives them good
education and good maintenance. Residue estate during
widowhood, reversion to chil. Dau: PRISCILLA WEST
COFFIELD, 3 negroes; Son: DAVID, 3 negroes; Dau:
ELIZABETH ANN COFFIELD, 3 negroes. Exr: _____? HAYNES.
Wit: THOMAS HYATT, JA (JAMES?) SPIER, PRISCILLA DUKE
(DUCK?).

COFFIELD, SPIER W.
    Oct. 12, 1825. Nov. Ct., 1825. Bk. F, p 46. Wife:
SALLY, child's part of negroes including those which
her father gave her - property she received of her
father - her beauro, my gig and harness and her choice
after my mother takes hers. Lend land in Halifax Co.
Residue left for use of my mother, wife and chil. Exr:
H. B. WHITAKER. Proved by oaths of SPENCER D. COTTON,
ELI B. WHITAKER, WILSON WHITAKER.

COFFIELD, THOMAS
    Feb. 6, 1812. Nov. Ct., 1812. Bk. E, p 45. Wife:
NANCY, lend plantation adjoining WM. TELFAIR for life

or widowhood, 1 negro, reversion of negro to Dau:
POLLY PITT. Bequeath horse, choice of stock, side
saddle and bridle, 2 cows and calves, 2 sows and pigs,
iron pot, skillet, sufficient pewter to keep house with.
Dau: POLLY PITT, wife of ARCHIBALD PITT, 3 negroes,
all land not lent wife, adjoining lands of JACOB
BRASWELL and ENOCH RAINOR. Residue of stock, Residue
of all property. Gr. son: WILLIAM COFFIELD PITT, son
of ARCHIBALD PITT, 1 negro girl. Exr: ARCHIBALD PITT,
STARLING WALLER. Wit: JOHN SASNETT, JOSHUA SASNETT.

COFFIELD, WEST
    Sept. 10, 1778. No probate date. Son: DAVID, still,
casks, barrels, 1 mare, 2 filleys, bridle and saddle,
5 cows, 5 cattle, 1 hat, 2 stears, 1 gold ring, 1 pr
silver shoe buckles, 1 grindstone, 1 bead and furniture, chest and pair knee buckles; Dau: PRISCILLA
WEST WEST; 2 negroes, bofett, walnut table, bridle
and saddle, pine chest and trunk; Dau: ELIZABETH, 3
negroes, chest, table, desk, horse or mare, bridle,
saddle, and residue of estate divided between daus.
Exr: Son-in-law: ISRAEL WEST. Wit: LUCY HAYNES,
PRISCILLA WEST WEST, XPHER (CHRISTOPHER) HAYNES.

COHOON, JOHN
    No date. Feb. Ct., 1789. Bk. 3, p 82. Wife & Extx:
PRISCILLA, lend all residue, Reversion to children.
Son & Exr: JOEL, plantation whereon he lives (except
50 A) and 1 negro; Dau: MARY, 1 negro; Dau: CHARITY,
1 negro; Dau: AVY, 1 negro; Son: SIMON, plantation
whereon I live with the 50 A taken off tract given
JOEL — with all land belonging to plantation whereon I live, reserving it for my true and loving wife
her lifetime. At mothers death to have 2 negroes. Wit:
MARY MORRIS, MOLLEY PROCTOR.

COHOON (clerk has CALHOUN), JOHN W.
    Mar. 7, 1837. Aug. Ct., 1847. Bk. F, p 374. Bro:
HARDY COHOON, all land, 1 colt bought of BENJ.
WILKINSON'S sale. Mother: PHARABA COHOON. All residue.
Exr: ORREN D. COHOON, ANDER A. COHOON, HARDY G. COHOON.
May Court, 1847. When offered for probate DELILA SPICER
came into court & declared it not the last will and

testament of JOHN W. COHOON. At Aug. Court, 1847, jury
impanelled was: BAKER (?) STATON, RICHARD SESSUMS,
HENRY APPLEWHITE, JAMES FLEMMING, JOHN HEARN, JAMES G.
WILLIFORD, WILLIAM ADAMS, JONAS WALSTON, JOHN W. PURVIS,
NATHANIEL A ?, WILLIAM C. LEIGH, HENRY BRINKLEY.

COHOON, WILLIAM (SR.)
      Jan. 3, 1789. Feb. Ct., 1790. Bk. 3, p 121. Wife
& Extx: (unnamed), Plantation and all on it during
her life or widowhood - Reversion to youngest dau
TRASY (?); Son & Exr: WILLIAM, oldest living son, 5
S; Daus: MARY, CHARITY, SARAH, PRISCILLA, PENELOPY,
5 S each; JACOB JOYNER, 5 S; Dau: TRASY, Residue after
mother death, except mare and 8 A to son: SOLLOMAN.
Exr: WILLICE McDEAD. Wit: EDWARD YOUNG (?), JACOB
HOLLAND, AARON PROCKTOR.

COKER, CALEB
      June 11, 1748. Nov. Ct., 1748. Wife: MARY. Sons:
RICHARD, JAMES, THOMAS; Daus: MARY NARRON, ANN BRUN,
FRANCIS WALL, ELIZABETH SPIER, SARAH COKER and AGNES
COKER. Exr: JAMES SPIER. Wit: MARGARET COKER, JAMES
COKER.

COKER, CALEB
      Apr. 6, 1785. Aug. Ct., 1785. Wife & Extx:
ELIZABETH. Son: JACOB, plantation whereon I live, also
75 A on Whiteoak Swamp (obtained) from my father
JAMES COKER. Son: EZIEKIEL, 57 A on Whiteoak Swamp
purchased of DEMSEY SPEIR, also 125 A survey of own
entry, Oct. 28, 1782. Exr: BRUMBLEA COKER. Wit:
JAMES BOYKIN, NATHANIEL COKER.

COKER, JAMES (SR.).
      Sept. 2, 1796. Nov. Ct., 1796. Wife: MARY, Lend
land, plantation, remainder estate during life or
widowhood; Son: NATHANIELL, Reversion in 550 A plantation whereon I live, including 200 A part of tract
granted by Earl of Granville, Aug. 4, 1761; Son:
WILLIAM, Reversion in 2 negroes; Dau: ANN SMITH, Reversion 1 negro; Dau: SELAH PEARMAN, Reversion in 2
negroes; Dau: MOLLEY JACKSON, Reversion in 2 negroes;
Son: RICHARD, negro Bess, provided he pay 1/3 her val-

ue;   Son: CALEB, his heairs 10 S; Son: DAVID, 10 S;
Son & Exr: BRUMBLY, 10 S; Son & Exr: JAMES, 10 S;
Dau: (?) SARÁH NUNNERY, her 6 chil. Ł 40. Wit: JAMES
NELSON, JOHN HARE.

COKER, JAMES
     Feb. 16, 1830. May Ct., 1830. Bk. F, p 118. Dau:
ANNIS MARKS, all land, i. e., 440 A. Reversion to her
sons, JAMES C., JOSEPH and NAT. In case of the death
of all three without issue, reversion to my bro:
DAVID COKER. All residue estate. Exr: JOHN P. MANNING,
ELI B. WHITAKER. Wit: JOHN EXUM, JAMES T. WATKINS,
JAMES BOYKIN.

COKER, JAMES
     Aug. 28, 1846. Nov. Ct., 1848. Bk. F, p 409. (?)
OLIVE & MARTHA COKER, $1; Sons: JOHN, STEPHEN and
WILLIAM COKER, $1; Dau: REBECCA MOORE, $1. Chil of
WILLIAM COKER to have all land, viz: DENTON tract,
BENJAMIN PORTER tract and tract on the road whereon
SARAH BRITT lives (she to have a home as long as she
lives). Exr: REDDING PITTMAN. Wit: WESLEY MANNING,
JOHN MANNING. Exr. refused to serve. Adm. granted
JOHN COKER. Bond $1000. LUNSFORD R. CHERRY and HENRY
HYMAN, Securities.

COKER, OLIVE
     Nov. 7, 1854. May Ct., 1855. Bk. G, p 108. Chil:
JOHN, STEPHEN, WILLIAM and REBECCA MOORE, $1.00 each;
Gr. dau: SUSAN FLORIDA ANN MOORE, and Dau: PATSEY
COKER, Residue of my property. Wit: HENRY PITTMAN,
WILLIE PITTMAN.

COKER, RICHARD
     June 19, 1807. Feb. Ct., 1808. Bk. D, p 305. Son:
JAMES, All land, and brandy still; Dau: TIRZAH, 2 ne-
groes; Dau: ABI, 2 negroes; Gr. dau: SARAH McCOOM
POWER, 1 negro; Gr. dau: MARIA POWER, 1 negro. Exr:
BENJAMIN COFFIELD. Wit: G. C. PITTMAN, WILLIAM
MANNING, JOHN R. MANNING. Codicil, date 19 of June,
ordering that family live together on plantation un-
til estate settled, with sufficient supplies - any

profits from operation of plantation over and above expense of family to go to son: JAMES COKER. Wit: G. C. PITTMAN, JOHN R. MANNING, WILLIAM MANNING.

COKER, WILLIAM
    Oct. 10, 1797. Feb. Ct., 1798. Bro: RICHARD COKER, 2 negroes; Any residue after Exrs receive ⅄ 5 each. Exr: FREDERICK COTTEN, RANDOLPH COTTEN. Wit: I. (or J.) PAVATT, NATHAN HARRIS.

COLEMAN, AARON
    July 6, 1796. Feb. Ct., 1800. Wife & Extx: HARDE, land & plantation, 3 negroes, silver tankard, set large silver tablespoons, set silver teaspoons, all household and kitchen furniture - plantation utensils, all stock; Sell blacksmith tools and watch to pay debts. BARTHOLOMEW BROWN: Shop joiners and silver tools. Exr: FREDERICK PHILIPS. Wit: BROWN EDWARDS; WILLIAM BRYANT.

COLEMAN, CHARLES
    Apr. 2, 1761. June Ct., 1761. Son: AARON, rifle gun, Residue divided between son and daughter. Dau: ABAGAL, 200 A S side Beach Run; Bro: JONATHAN, all land on Beach Run between that given dau ABAGAL and ELISHA BATTLE. Father & Exr: CHARLES COLEMAN, SR., all land lying on N side of Beach Run. Wit: ELISHA BATTLE, JON MURPHREE, RACHAEL COLEMAN.

COLEMAN, CHARLES
    Apr. 12, 1761. June Ct., 1761. Wife & Extx: RACHEL, all personal estate. Son & Exr: JONATHAN, 160 A plantation whereon I live and land lying N of Beach Run between my line and JOHN STALLENS. Gr. son: AARON COLEMAN, 100 A plantation whereon his father lived. Dau: PATIENCE, 192 A plantation on Beach Run. Wit: JOSEPH SUMNER, ELISHA BATTLE, JOHN MURPHREE.

COLEMAN, HARDE
    Oct. 18, 1807. Nov. Ct., 1807. Bk. D, p 294. Relation: NANCY EDWARDS, 3 negroes, 6 tablespoons, 12 silver teaspoons, silver tankard, pine chest, black walnut chest, all wearing apparel, pr silver shoe

buckles, gold broach and 2 rugs; Kinsmen: BARTHOLOMEW
BROWNE, 1 pr gold sleeve buttons, desk, watch, table
and all usually kept therein. Residue to be divided
between kinsman BARTHOLOMEW BROWNE and NANCY EDWARDS.
My wish that they continue on plantation together as
long as they can agree. If relation NANCY EDWARDS die
without issue, her negroes to be sold, money divided
between PATIENCE WEST DIXON and BARTHOLOMEW BROWNE.
Exr: FREDERICK PHILIPS, DEMSEY BRYAN. Wit: RICHARD S.
HART, GREEN DIXON.

COLEMAN, MOSES
     Mar. 2, 1760. June Ct., 1760. Wife: MARY, Lend land
& plantation whereon I live, Reversion to son, AMOS.
Son & Exr: JOHN, land & plantation whereon he lives,
household goods & chattels in his possession; Son &
Exr: MOSES, land lying both sides HOMINY Swamp, bay
gelding hors and all catel and hogs now called his,
also 1 smooth gun (?). Dau: CHRISTIAN; Son: AMOS. Wit:
THOMAS ROBINS, JR., SAMUEL GODWIN, JR., JOHN GOBLE
(CABLE?).

COLEMAN, ROBERT
     Jan. 10, 1761. Mar. Ct., 1761. Wife & Extx: SUSANOR,
Lend use plantation whereon I live for her natural life;
Reversion to son ROBERT. Son & Exr: AARON, 30 L cash.
Son & Exr: CADAR, Remainder land on Swift Creek sur-
veyed by WILLIAM HAYWOOD; Son & Exr: STEPHEN; Dau:
SARAH; Son: ROBERT, Reversion in plantation whereon I
live, also 100 A surveyed by WILLIAM HAYWOOD and
"muscate gun I hunt with". Son: JOSIAH; Dau: SUSANOR;
Dau: JACONIAS; Dau: GRACE; Dau: SELY; Son: HARDY; Dau:
SILPHA. Residue divided equally between wife and 12
chil. Wit: WILLIAM HAYWOOD, JOSHUA WOMBWELL, JO (?)
WILLIAMS.

COLEMAN, ROBERT
     Oct. 5, 1790. Feb. Ct., 1795. Son: JOHN, all land,
382 A; all ready money, notes and entire estate. Sis
& Extx: GRACE COLEMAN, use of boufett during her life,
in case not agreeing with rest of family she may cause
a house to be built on the land where she chooses,
cost to be paid from estate. Exr: JACOB BATTLE, NOAH

81

WOODARD. Wit: AARON COLEMAN, SELA COLEMAN.

COLEMAN, ROBERT (SR.)
    Nov. 13, 1806. May Ct., 1807. Bk. D, p 276. Wife:
MARY, lend 2 negro girls and 20 A land including
houses; Son & Exr: CHARLES; Gr. sons: (sons of CHARLES),
WILLIE, reversion in 1 negro girl; ALLEN, reversion in
land and 1 negro girl; ROBERT, reversion in 1 negro.
Son & Exr: ROBERT. Gr. sons: (sons of ROBERT), CHARLES,
1 negro; JOHN, 1 negro. Wit: L. W. BAKER, WILLIAM WHITE,
MARSHALL WHITE.

COLEMAN, STEPHEN
    Mar. 29, 1803. Aug. Ct., 1803. Wife: ESTHER, all
estate, real and personal to wife during her life or
widowhood, provided she makes a support for family and
children and keeps them together. At her marriage or
death, estate to be equally divided between children
or their heirs. Exr: EXUM LEWIS. Wit: JAMES BANDY,
FREDERICK PHILIPS.

COLEMAN, WILLIAM
    Dec. 29, 1749. Feb. Ct., 1752. Wife & Extx: JANE;
Son: SAMUEL, plantation whereon I live with 100 A be-
longing to same. Son: SAMPSON, remainder of land; Daus:
SARAH and SUSANNAH. Exr: Bro: ROBERT COLEMAN. Wit:
MOSES COLEMAN, CORNELIUS JORDAN, ELIN JORDAN.

COLLINS, SHADRACH
    Jan. 8, 1807. Probated, 1817. Wife: ELIZABETH,
lend 198 A land whereon I live, adjoining WILLIAM
CORBETT, NICHOLAS CORBITT, SAMUEL HARRIS and JOHN
WEBB, SEN., for her widowhood, reversion to 2 sons:
JOHN and SHADRACH, also 3 horses, all cattle, hogs
and personal estate. Exr: JOHN OWENS. Wit: PENNY
HADDOCK, POLLY RETTOR (RITTER?).

COLLINS, SHADRACK
    Oct. 25, 1814. Nov. Ct., 1814. Wife: GRIZZY, lent
but not to have the privilege of moving out of the
county, 5 negroes; plantation whereon I live, 3 horses,
2 carts, 4 fluke hoes, 4 half shares, 4 weeding hoes,
2 yoke oxen, 2 oxchains, 2 milk cows and calves, 4

sows and pigs, 8 sheep, 2 dining tables, 1 breakfast
table, desk, ½ doz. chairs, ½ of kitchen furniture, ½
crockery and glass, 2 looking glasses, 1000 lbs. seed
cotton, all flax, 5 beehives, full sufficiency of pork,
corn, fodder and peas for 1 yr. Reversion of all personal property to children. Son: JOHN, 1 negro. All
land to be divided between sons: BLOUNT and JOSIAH;
dau: ALLEY, 2 negroes; dau: ELIZABETH, 2 negroes. When
son BLOUNT becomes of age 9 negroes to be divided between BLOUNT, JOSIAH, ALLEY and ELIZABETH, they to
also have residue of estate. Should all 4 die, property
to go to GUILFORD and SPENCER MURPHY. Exr: HENRY AUSTIN,
JOSEPH BELL. Wit: EDWARD HALL, JOEL BURGESS, SALLY
MALLARD and EDWIN DANCY. Codicil Nov. 9, 1814. Whereas youngest son: JOSIAH COLLINS is dec'd, I give all
land bequeathed to him to his surviving bro: BLOUNT
COLLINS. All personal property given JOSIAH to be divided between wife, ALLEY, BLOUNT, and ELIZABETH. I
lend to wife, GRIZZIE, all silver plate during her
natural life. Wit: EDWARD HALL, EDWIN DANCY and
WILLIAM S. MURPHY.

COLWELL, JOHN
     Feb. 4, 1762. June Ct., 1762. Wife & Extx: SARA,
lend land and plantation whereon I live, 2 negroes
and mare during her life; Son: WILLIAM, reversion in
½ land (150 A upper end) and 2 negroes; Son: JOHN, reversion in other 150 A of land and 2 negroes; dau:
MARY, 2 negroes; dau: SARAH WILKINSON COLWELL, 1 negro.
Exr: OWEN FRANKLIN, FRANCIS BARNES. Wit: JOSEPH HOWELL,
JR., and JOHN GIBSON.

CONNELL, THOMAS
     Dec. 21, 1769. No probate date. Wife & Extx:
CATHERINE, lend plantation and all movable estate
during her life, reversion of plantation to dau: JANE
BURROUS, movable estate to wife's disposing; eldest
son: WILLIAM, all "wearing cloaths"; son: SIMON and
Dau: JANE BURROUS, 5 S proclamation money each. Wit:
ARTHUR DAVIS, BENJAMIN DAVIS.

COOPER, BLOUNT
     Sept. 13, 1849. Feb. Ct., 1854. Bk. G, p 49. Wife:

SOPHIA, land whereon I live together with all other estate. Exr: CHARLES MABREY. Wit: TURNER BASS. Signature of TURNER BASS proven by oaths of JOHN H. DANIEL, L. B. CUSHING.

COPPEDGE, AUSGUSTIN
    Jan. 20, 1793. May Ct., 1793. Wife: WILLMUTH, lend all estate, real and personal, plantation, etc. for life. Reversion to my chil: CHARLOTTE, GRIFFIN, MARY and AUGUSTIN, and the one my loving wife is with at this time. Exr: JOHN WILLIAMS. Wit: JOHN WILLIFORD, JOHN BELL, MARY GILL.

CORBIT, JOHN.
    Jan. 2, 1807. Feb. Ct., 1807. Bk. D, p 270. Wife (unnamed); son: WILLIAM, 150 A where he now lives; son & Exr: NICOLAS, 150 A including manor plantation; son: JOHNSTON, horse, crosscut saw, set of coopers tools, ax, hoe, gun, grubbing hoe, and saw; Wife, remainder estate during widowhood, reversion to my 5 daus: ANN, SARAH, WINIFRED, MARY and TEMPY. Wit: ROBERT FELLOWS, RICHARD CORBIT.

COTTEN, ALEXANDER
    May 12, 1823. May Ct., 1826. Bk. F, p 56. Dau: MARY, all perishable estate I am entitled to by will of FREDRICK COTTEN, also 4 negroes; son: ARTHUR, 40 S residue divided between son and dau. Exr: RANDOLPH COTTEN, SPENCER COTTEN. Wit: SPIER COFFIELD, THOMAS LYON. SPIER COFFIELD being dead in May, 1826, his handwriting was proved by oath of GRISHAM P. PITMAN.

COTTEN, AMOS
    Aug. 1, 1781. Aug. Ct., 1781. Wife: ZILPAH, use of estate during her widowhood and bequeath 1 negro; son: GEORGE, plantation where DAVID FOUNTAIN lives to be equally divided between sons: GEORGE and WIMBERLY, 1 mare and 1 negro each; son: WIMBERLY, 1 negro, horse and smith's tools; son: JOSEPH, part of tract whereon I live touching Spring Branch, it being the dividing line to be made by GEORGE WIMBERLY and/or ELIAS FORT, 1 negro and a mare; son: JAMES, remainder of plantation whereon I live, 1 negro and my still and worm; dau:

SALLY, 1 negro; dau: PHERIBE, 2 negroes; dau: ELIZABETH,
1 negro. Exr: GEORGE WIMBERLY, ROBERT DIGGES, ELIAS FORT.
Wit: JOHN FOUNTAIN, SOLOMON FOUNTAIN, WILLIAM ELENOR.

COTTEN, BENJAMIN
    Aug. Ct., 1789. Bk. 3, p 105. Nunc. Will. Proved
by oaths of THOMAS GARRET, NATHAN BRIDGERS and AMY
STEWART within 24 hours of death of BENJAMIN COTTEN
and entered in writing June 28, 1789. Dau: SALLY STEWART,
his child by AMY STEWART, 1 cow and calf, colt, dish,
3 plates, bason, linnen wheel, looking glass, box iron
and heater, chest and "chares"; JOEL WATSON, 2 cows
and calves, 3 plates, dish, bason iron pot, 6 earthen
plates, chest, weeding hoe, grubbing hoe, pair still-
ards, shoemakers' tools and carpenters' tools; ARTHUR
COTTEN: Residue divided between his 2 sons. Sworn to
before JAMES B?

COTTEN, FANNY
    Dec. 30, 1817. No probate date. Bk. E, p 193.
Mother: ELIZABETH COTTEN, old negro woman Dorcas, also
1 other negro, reversion to sister MARY COTTEN. Exr:
Bro. SPENCER D, COTTEN. Wit: RANDOLPH COTTEN

COTTEN, FREDERICK
    Nov. 17, 1814. May Ct., 1815. Bk. E, p 102. Mother:
ELIZABETH, lend all my property, real and personal,
for her more easy support and use — to be conducted to
her through and under immediate care and consideration
and direction of my bro: SPENCER D. COTTEN. Reversion
thus: Neph: FREDERICK PITMAN, son of ROBERT J. PITMAN,
and ELIZABETH, his wife and my sis., $500; Bro & Exr:
SPENCER D. COTTEN, all landed property; Sis: MARY
COTTEN, 1 negro. Residue divided between SPENCER D.
COTTEN and MARY COTTEN. Wit: RICHARD HARRISON and
ALEXANDER COTTEN.

COTTEN, GODWIN
    Mar. 28, 1834. Feb. Ct., 1837. Bk. F, p 201.
JAMISON GODWIN COTTEN, son of ARTHUR C. COTTEN, $250;
EDWIN WHITEHEAD, son of JOSEPH WHITEHEAD, $250; MARY
GODWIN COTTEN, dau of JOSEPH WHITEHEAD, $250;
FREDERICK R. COTTEN, MARY COTTEN, WILLIAM H. WILLS,
and ELIZA PITTMAN, dau of ROBERT JOHN PITTMAN, my

85

house and lot in Tarborough to be sold and money divided; LAURA P. COTTEN, wife of JOHN W. COTTEN, ELIZA
THOMPSON. wife of NOAH THOMPSON, and EPHRAIM DICKENS,
of Tarborough, all my negroes, except one, to be equally divided; I bequeath unto my negro man, Eli, his
freedom and $300 left in hands of Exr. for his support
in case of accident or need; Bequeath to George and
Mary, (2 mulatto chil.) $400. It is my will that
EPHRAIM DICKENS, LAURA P. COTTEN and ELIZA THOMPSON
procure the freedom of George and Mary, (2 mulatto
chil), the property of SPENCER D. COTTEN and that they
are protected in case of need; residue equally divided
between HENRY IRWIN, THOMAS B. IRWIN and CHRISTOPHER
S. DICKENS. Exr: SPENCER D. COTTEN, WILLIAM H. WILLS,
EPHRAIM DICKENS. Wit: ISAAC B. BRADLEY, COFFIELD KING.
Caveated by JOSEPH B. WHITEHEAD, JOHN EXUM, CANADA
HOWELL, JOHN WHITEHEAD, CLINCH HOWELL.

COTTEN, RANDOLPH, Tarborough
     July 9, 1847. Aug. Ct., 1852. Bk. F, p 482.
ELIZABETH COX, lots 15 and part of 26, dwelling house,
furniture, dividens from stock in Bank of Cape Fear.
Neph: FREDERICK R. COTTEN of Fla., son of SPENCER D.
COTTEN, all my bank stock except the 9 shares in Bank
of Cape Fear mentioned above. JOHN W. COTTEN, infant
son of my neph. the late JOHN W. COTTEN, 520 A land
I purchased of MICHAEL HEARN called "Sutton Place" on
N side Tar River adjoining Dr. C. L. DICKEN, ALLEN
JONES and JOHN DANIEL excepting 1 A on which school
house stands, and 3 negroes. MARY DENNING, wife of
_____? DENNING of Washington Co. (Fromerly MARY
COTTEN, Dau of the late ALEXANDER COTTEN), all cloth-
ing and furniture also my walnut desk. Nics: ELIZABETH
POWELL, wife of JESSE POWELL, side board; sis:
ELIZABETH PITTMAN, $50; RANDOLPH PITTMAN, only child
of my neph. SPIER PITTMAN of Halifax, $150;
FREDERICK R. PITTMAN, son of my sis ELIZABETH, $250.
Residue divided between all chil of neph. JOHN N.
COTTEN: MARGARET ELIZA COTTEN, ARABELLA CLARK COTTEN,
FLORIDA COLL COTTEN, JOHN W. COTTEN. A comfortable
frame house with plank floor and brick chimney shall
be built for each of my aged slaves: King and Primus,
also to have enough cleared land to support them and

their wives. In case they are unable to support themselves, my Exrs shall see they are cared for. Exr:
JESSE POWELL, HENRY J. CLARK, WILLIAM NORFLEET. Wit:
HENRY HYMAN, S. E. MOORE. June 23, 1849. Codicil:
Exchanging Bank Stock. To JOHN W. COTTEN, infant son
of my neph, the late JOHN W. COTTEN, 160 A land purchased of HENRY T. CLARK. (Same Wit). June 26, 1851,
Codicil revoking $50 bequest to sis: ELIZABETH PITTMAN
and giving it to RANDOLPH C. PITTMAN, infant son of
SPIER PITTMAN in addition to that already given him in
will. (Same Wit). July 19, 1852, 3rd Codicil, Reversion
of land lent ELIZABETH SCOTT to JOHN W. COTTEN and
MARY DENNING. (Same Wit).

COTTEN, WILLIE
    Oct. 24, 1805. Aug. Ct., 1807. Bk. D, p 269. Aunt:
ELIZABETH COTTEN, $1000 paid thru daughters FANNY
COTTEN, BETSEY COTTEN and POLLY COTTEN. Bros and Exrs:
HARRY COTTEN TART and JOHN COTTEN, Equally share all
remaining property. Wit: R. COTTEN, WILLIAM H.
SHALLINGTON.

COUNCIL, CHARLES
    July 6, 1805. Nov. Ct., 1806. Bk. D, p 236. Wife:
DICE, lend 2 negroes, household furniture, 3 cows and
calves, 3 ewes and lambs, all hogs, during life or
widowhood; son: JOSHUA COUNCIL, his heirs, 5 S; Dec'd
son: WILLIE COUNCIL, heirs, 5 S; Dec'd dau: TEMPY, heirs
5S; dau: ELIZABETH BLOUNT (BUNTING?), heirs, 5 S; dau:
CLEARY CHERRY, 10 S also lend her 2 negroes, reversion
equally divided between JOHN SMITH and DORCAS SMITH.
Dau: CHARLOTTE CHERRY, 5 S, lend her 2 negroes, reversion to her children. Son & Exr: JOHN, ½ land whereon I live and 2 negroes; son: WILLIE, ½ land whereon
I live, 2 negroes; son: WILEY, 1 negro; son: REDDICK,
negro Ben; Gr. son: BENNET COUNCIL; sons: HARDY,
CHARLES, and dau: SILVIA $100 silver each. Residue to
CHARLES, SILVIA, HARDY, JOHN, REDDICK & WILLIE. Exr:
COL. NATHAN MAYO. Wit: WILLIAM HYMAN, JR., JOSEPH
TAYLOR, WILLIAM CHERRY, WILLIAM TAYLOR. (It is im-
possible to tell whether WILEY and WILLIE are the
same).

COUNCIL, JOSHUA
Sept. 5, 1772. Apr. Ct., 1774. Wife: CHRISTIAN, all estate, reserving that she raise, maintain and educate my 3 daus: CLAREY, TEMPERANCE and MARY. Exr: HENRY HORN. Wit: LEWIS HINES, JACOB HORN, JOSEPH SUMNER.

COWELL, BERNARD
July 24, 1825. Feb. Ct., 1829. Bk. F, p 96. Wife & Extx: DRUSILLA, lend all property real and personal, reversion to WILLIAM TANNER, Gr. son of wife DRUSILLA; Exr: RICHARD HARRISON. Wit: DAVID HOLLAND, JAMES PENDER.

COX, JOSEPH
Jan. 25, 1821. Feb. Ct., 1825. Wife: JEMIMA, all land whereon I live, all stock, reversion to 5 chil: ROB'T, SETHE, POLEY HOWELL, JEMIMA BASEL and NANCY BASEL. Son: JOHN, $1; Son: WILLIAM, $1; Gr. dau: PATSEY COX, cow and calf, ewe and lamb; Gr. son: NATHAN COX, $1; Dau: NANCY BASEL, mare; Son & Exr: ROBERT; Exr: JONATHAN BASEL (Son-in-law). Wit: DAVID F. JONES, JESSE JONES.

CRAVEY, JAMES, of Northampton County
Dec., 1758. Probated Dec., 1758 in Edgecombe Co. Bequeath to the Parson or Parsons of the Parish that is or shall come after to save the people, where the land is all my lands that was my father's in the bounds of the old Battran (Patent?) that was his for an easement to the people of the Parish, for a gleabe for their "minestrour" from generation to generation for ever - not that they should make sale of same. MARY BROWN, my soposed (supposed) dau, 310 A bought of DRURY STOKES, 20 cattell, 100 hogs, feather bed & furn. that is my "yousing bed whereon I ly, my mear, too iron pots, half my puter, case of knives & forks, ovell table, 6 chears, iron spit, peare of sad irons, to her and her heirs lawful begotten of her body." In case of death of MARY BROWN, her part of estate shall be equally divided between my sister's chil. JEAN ALLEN, Niss (niece), 100 A bought of COLLIN WILLIAM BAKER, 20 cattle, 100 hogs, fether bed and furniture which has lately had a new tick, meare and colt, two iron

pots, half my puter, case of knives and forks, 6
chears, chest that was my father's. In case of death
of JEAN ALLEN without issue her part estate shall be
equally divided between my sister's chil. OWEN BROWN,
my "sposed" halfe brother, all tame bees and hives,
gun, horse, all wearing close; HUGH CRAVEY, half Bro,
1 Riffell, 2 guns and all reddey money and horse.
SARAH CRAVEY JORDEN, that unhappy woman — the beds
she bought, 1 rugg, bed sheats, spinning wheal, linnen
wheel, 4 pare cards, puter dish, plate, 3 basons, box
iron and heaters, cloth loom, 3 shutters, pare working
bars and boxes, 3 stays and harness, pare sezors, working iron, rolling pin, chest, box trunk, too stays and
harness and as for chears and hogs she has destroyed,
and raised not aney, I give her 2 bedtrays, 1 squeare
table, a pasell of stools and if this do not content
her & she should sue for her 1/3, you may find recepts
of dets I have paid for my father, & you will find she
has no right at all, and I order that it shall be tried
by law. Exr: ROBERT WARREN, his son, KICHEN WARREN. No
Witnesses.

CRISP, JESSE (SR.)
    Dec. 30, 1829. Aug. Ct., 1831. Bk. F, p 129.
Having sometime ago given away all my property but a
remnant, to my chil., I now dispose of said remnant
as follows: Sons: Exr: SPIER, negro boy, SPIER to
keep my old Negro man, Bristow and maintain him as
long as he lives; dau: ELEANOR BENNET'S heirs, negro
girl; dau: NANCY BENNETT, of Tennessee Wit: JOHN
W. CRISP.

CRISP, JESSE
    Sept. 8, 1836. Feb. Ct., 1837. Wife: ELIZA, life
or widowhood, all my lands and plantations, 2 negroes
gray mare, 1 mule, 2 sows, cow and calf, household
and kitchen furniture. My chil: NANCY ANN, BENJAMIN
FRANKLIN and ELENDER CRISP, my negro woman TABITHA
Junior, and her two chil. Newbern and Wilson, and
property I have lent to my wife, at her decease; Exr:
Friends, BENJAMIN WHITFIELD, JOHN MOORING. Wit:
BENONI M. WILKINSON, THOMAS BEST.

CRISP, SAMUEL (SR.)
June 10, 1829. Nov. Ct., 1829. Wife. (unnamed), 2
negroes to wait on her, reversion to son JESSE provided he care for negroes and not sell to pay his indebt-
edness. JESSE & SAMUEL to take care of mother; all land
to be divided between JESSE & SAMUEL and they to have
apple mill and grist mill. The following children already given their part of estate by deeds of gift made
1822: WM., FRANCIS, THOMAS, WHITLEY, REDDEN, MARY ODOM
of Tennysee; SARAH WHITLEY, of Tenn.; ELIZABETH
WHITEHERST, FANNY NELSON, LYDA WEATHERBY, PATSY NELSON.
Exr: Sons-in-law: JONAS NELSON, KINCHEN NELSON. Wit:
SPIER CRISP, JOHN W. CRISP.

CRISP, THOMAS
July 12, 1825. Aug. Ct., 1825. Wife: REBECCAH, 4
negroes, lend house and plantation, stock, utensils
for widowhood or life, reversion to children: POLLY,
NANCY and JORG, SAMUEL, JESSE, LYDA, SINDA RILEY CRISP,
and child my wife may have within 9 mo of my death.
Exr: JONAS NELSON, FREDERICK MAYO. Wit: BENJAMIN
WHITFIELD, JESSE CRISP.

CRISP, WILLIAM
Aug. 25, 1819. Nov. Ct., 1819. Bk. E, p 230. Wife:
(unnamed), lend all estate during widowhood. If she
should marry I lend her part of land, 2 negro women
her natural life; reversion to children (unnamed).
Exr: RODERICK CHERRY, THOMAS CRISP. Wit: SPIER CRISP,
SAMUEL CRISP.

CROCKER, DREWRY (Of Halifax County)
Nov. 11, 1779. Nov. Ct., 1779. Sis & Extx: ANNE
CROCKER, plantation with all stock whereon I live; Sis:
SALLY CROCKER, plantation whereon my Mother lives.
Should she die without issue, reversion to sis: MARY
PENDER. Remainder estate equally divided between sis-
ters. Sis: MILLEY PERRY; Sis: MOLLEY PENDER. Exr:
DAVID PENDER, ISAAC SESSUM. Wit: AMOS TURNER, R.
COTTEN.

CROCKER, PETER

Oct. 24, 1752. Aug Ct., 1753. Wife & Extx: SARAH.
Children mentioned but not named. Exr: FRANCIS
WILLIAMSON. Wit: JAMES WILLIAMSON, THOMAS BARRON,
JOSEPH BRIDGERS.

CROCKET, WILLIAM
    Jan. 27, 1851. Probated, 1852. Bk. F, p 475. Sis-
ters: ELIZABETH CROCKET, 50 L semi-annually; should
my sister, JEAN, outlive sister, ELIZABETH 50 L sterling to be continued to her, also 1000 L sterling to
the Magistrate in Dumfries in trust for my sister
ELIZABETH CROCKET, 4000 L sterling, to be invested at
general rate, and interest paid sisters JEAN and
ELIZABETH, half-yearly during their lives; To the magistrate, for the benefit of the Dumfries and Galloway
Infirmery.. 3000 L, $100.00 to Vestry of Calvary Church,
Tarboro for a burial place. To good friend, JAMES
WEDDELL, the residue of my estate. Exr: JAMES WEDDELL.
Wit: MATTHEW WEDDELL, WM. L. HART.

CROMWELL, ALEXANDER
    Aug. 19, 1788. Jan. Ct., 1788-89. Bk. C, p 66.
Sons: ALEXANDER, and THOMAS, Joyner's and Carpenter's
tools divided between them, no more. Dau: COMFORT
LAWRENCE, feather bed & furn., no more; Gr. daus:
SARAH LAWRENCE, and MARY LAWRENCE, 30 L current money
each at marriage. Chil: MARY HODGES, SARAH BALLARD,
BOLLING and PROVIDENCE MARLOW, 5 S each; Dau & Extx:
VENETIA BOOTH, ½ pewter and pots. Son-in-law & Exr:
ROBERT BOOTH, he and wife VENETIA to have use of all
stock, cattle, horses, etc. until VINSON SMITH comes
of age. Gr. son: VINSON SMITH, dwelling plantation
whereon I live, ½ puter, all furniture, farm tools,
gun, bridle and saddle and 1 negro when he reaches
21 yrs. Wit: JOHN HINES, JAMES BOOTH, FANEY BONNER.

CROMWELL, ELIZABETH
    Nov. 2, 1838. Probated 1840. Dau: CINDERELLA
PETWAY, 120 A tract I purchased of my son NAPOLEON
CROMWELL; dau: MARY McDOWELL, $750. son: PATRICK
CROMWELL, $750; dau: LAVINIA THIGPEN, 1 negro, also
$350; son: NAPOLEON CROMWELL, my 3 negroes. Son & Exr:
EPENETUS CROMWELL, my 2 negroes, 114 A tract of land

purchased of JOHN RICE; dau: MARTHYAN KNIGHT, 2 negroes; son: ELISHA CROMWELL, 75 A tract of land purchased of my son THOMAS CROMWELL and 4 negroes. Property remaining sold. Exr: Son-in-law: WILLIAM D. PETWAY. Wit: BEN M. JACKSON, F. D. LITTLE.

CROMWELL, THOMAS
    Sept. 12, 1795. Nov. Ct., 1795. Wife & Extx: SELAH, lend land bought of JONATHAN THIGPEN until son ELISHA reaches 21 yrs; lend land bought of JOHN THIGPEN until son, OLIVER reaches 21 yrs; lend plantation whereon I live, 2 negroes, and still to raise children on, reversion to son CHARLES; lend all remaining property, reversion to 3 youngest children; son & Exr: ELISHA, land, 1 negro, cow and calf, sow and pigs, at 21 yrs; son: OLIVER, land, 1 negro, cow and calf and sow and pigs when he reaches 21; dau: PARTHENAY, 1 negro, cow and calf and sow and pigs; Son: & Exr: CHARLES, plantation; dau: REBEKAH, 1 negro; dau: TABITHA, 1 negro. Wit: SAMUEL WREN, THOMAS NEWSOM. Codicil: Bequeath VINCENT SMITH, horse and saddle and 10 pounds money. Wit: OBED CHERRY, NED KEIL.

CULPEPPER, BENJAMIN
    Apr. 15, 1767. Aug. Ct., 1772. Wife: ELIZABETH, lend during widowhood 2 negroes, 5 cows and calves and maer. Dau: RAHAB WHITEHEAD, 1 negro, and 312 A N side of Mockson Creek; dau: MARTHA MANNING, 1 negro and 200 A S side Peachtree Creek; dau: ELIZABETH, 1 negro and 200 A N side Peachtree Creek; Son & Exr: ARASMAS, 320 A S side Fishing Creek, 7 negroes after the Old woman's death or widowhood. Wit: THOMAS WHITEHEAD, NATHAN WHITEHEAD.

CURL, SARAH
    Jan. 1, 1820. Feb. Ct., 1820. Bk. E, p 231. Dau: SILETER, all corn, cotton, brandy, 2 ewes and lambs, 2 cows and calves, mare; all money owed me by SAMSON NEWSOME to be equally divided between my youngest daughters, SILETER and PATSY. Residue estate to be divided equally between all 5 children: SILETER, PATSY, REDMOND, CATY WILLIAMS, CHARRITY WILLIFORD. Exr: EATON GAY. Wit: KINCHEN GAY, DEMPSEY JENKINS.

CURL, THOMAS
Feb. 18, 1848. Aug. Ct., 1854. Bk. G, p 86. All
estate to 4 sisters: ELIZABETH CURL, NANCY CURL,
MARTHA H. CURL and MOURNING CURL; Mother, lend one ne-
gro, Diamond. Proven by oaths of ROBERT-LONG,
BENJAMIN H. BRASWELL, JESSE PRICE and BURREL W. BARNES.

CURL, WILLIS
Jan. 25, 1810. Feb. Ct., 1811. Bk. E, p 5. Wife:
SARAH, lend during widowhood 300 A plantation whereon I live, 2 negroes, mare, colt, 6 cattle, 20 hogs,
6 sheep, also ½ plantation tools, cart, wheels, plough
frames. Reversion to CHARITY, SELETER and PATSY - Residue divided between wife and children. Son: REDMOND,
300 A plantation bought of FULGUM WESTER, Daus: CATY,
CHARITY, SELETER, PATSY. Exr: WILLIE BUNN. Wit: REDMOND
BUNN, SALLY CURL, NANCY FORT.

CUTCHIN, HUMPHREY
Oct. 15, 1773. July Ct., 1774. Bk. D, p 225. Dau
& Extx: SARAH BRYANT, 2 negroes, lifetime, reversion
to Gr, sons: GEORGE BRYANT and WILLIAM BRYANT. Gr.
daus: ANN WELLS, FAITH WELLS, SARAH BRYANT, CATY
BRYANT, 1 negro each. Wit: ROBERT DIGGES, THOS. BRYANT,
JOHN BRYANT.

CUTCHIN, THOMAS
July 29, 1781. Nov. Ct., 1781. Wife: MARY, plantation for life, reversion to son THOMAS; residue
equally divided between children (unnamed). Son &
Exr: THOMAS. Wit: JNO (JOHN) HUDNALL, SARAH HAYNES.

CUTCHIN, THOMAS
Sept. 8, 1821. Feb. Ct., 1827. Bk. F, p 64. Wife:
PHEREBE, all estate for widowhood of life, reversion
to children (unnamed). Exr: ELI HOWELL, JOSIAH
CUTCHIN. No witnesses. Proven by oaths of JAMES
DOWNING, JAMES KNIGHT, SOLOMON T. BRADDY.

DANCY, ARCHIBALD
Sept. 24, 1798. Nov. Ct., 1800. Wife & Extx:
(Unnamed) lend all estate during widowhood or life.
Reversion to children. Daus: REBEKAH, NANCY, BETSEY

and SALLY. Son: SAMUEL. Wit: M. DANCY, STEPHEN COLEMAN, PATIENCE TAYLOR.

DANCY, FRANCIS L., Tarboro
Sept. 20, 1845. Aug. Ct., 1848. Bk. F, p 404. Wife: CHARLOTTE, 339 A tract, called Harris Place, S side Tar River adjoining DAVID BULLUCK, THEOPHILUS PARKER and MRS. MARY GREGORY, bought of THOMAS HARRIS, deed Nov. 15, 1817; 190 A tract called Parker Place E side of Hendricks Creek, adjoining LEWIS D. WILSON and THOMAS H. HALL, bought of JOHN PARKER, Aug. 1, 1828; in Tarboro-Lots 5,6,7,8. Reversion lots 5 & 6 to son JOHN. Son & Exr: WILLIAM F., 1041 A tract called Strabane on N side Fishing Creek adjoining CHARLES MABRY and heirs of DREW BRYAN - bought of the late EDMUND MACNAIR - deed Dec. 31, 1834; also lots 18 & 29 in Tarboro with understanding dau: ELIZABETH M. BATTLE, wife of WM. S. BATTLE shall have carriage house which stands on Lot 29 whenever she chooses to remove it; also all movables pertaining to ginhouse at Strabane and all books belonging to law library. Dau: DELHA M. FOREMAN, 503-3/4 A tract known as Batts place, N Side Tar River adjoining BEN J. BATTS. bought of JOSEPH BATTS, deed May 16, 1818; also 494 A tract bought of NORFLEET, Clerk of Ct., in making partition between COLLINS bros. and others, deed Mar. 22, 1841; also lot 83 in Tarboro adjoining GEO. HOWARD. Son & Exr: JOHN S., 584 A tract N side Tar River adjoining EPHRAIM DICKEN, SOLOMON PENDER & JOHN WILLIAMS bought of WM. H. HODGE, deed Jan. 2, 1833; 262 A tract bought of MICHAEL HEARN & wife MARTHA, deed Mar. 14, 1842; Lot 102 in Tarboro - also all movables appertaining to gin house on lot 102. 414 A Tract opposite Strabane to DELHA M., WILLIAM F., JOHN S. - formerly belonged to ALEXANDER SESSOMS; deed by Sheriff SPENCER L. HART to me. Oct. 14, 1820. Wit: HENRY T. CLARK, WM. NORFLEET, WM. GEO. THOMAS.

DANCY, LUCY
Oct. 1, 1820. Nov. Ct., 1820. Bk. E, p 249. Son: EDWIN, negro; 3 negroes to be equally divided between sons: EDWIN and FRANCIS; Dau: SARAH WILKINS, keep negro Harriet until she is 13 yrs., then deliver to EDWIN. Exr: ROBERT JOYNER. Wit: FRANCIS DANCY.

DANCY, WILLIAM

Mar. 1805. Nov. Ct., 1807. Bk. D, p 299. Son: EDWIN,
5 negroes; Son: WILLIAM, 5 negroes, also lands on Fishing Creek including the Ship Place, Peris Place containing 844 A, all stock in his possession. Son: FRANCIS,
697 A lands on Tyan Coky Swamp, also lands on Town Creek
leased of MRS. MILLY BLOODWORTH with appurtenances
thereupon; also 8 negroes, desk, walnut table, beufatt,
horse, filly, colt, mare, 20 prime cattle, and 13 sheep.
Gr. dau: NANCY JACKSON, dau of J. J. JACKSON and MARY
ANN JACKSON; Gr. dau: MARY HORN, dau of WILLIAM HORN
and ELIZABETH, his wife; 3 negroes; Gr. son: WHITMELL
HORN, son of WILLIAM HORN and ELIZABETH, his wife; 3
negroes. Gr. chil: (Chil of JOHN DANCY): WILLIAM DANCY,
AGNES DANCY, JOSEPH JOHN DANCY. Exr: FRANCIS DANCY.
Wit: DEMPSEY JENKINS, JOS(EPH) PITT, LAMON RUFFIN.

DANCY, WILLIAM

Nov. 2, 1838. Nov. Ct., 1840. Bk. F, p 247. I have
this day made deeds to JOHN ROBERT DANCY, son of
ELIZABETH PRICE, by me, and to JAMES ALEXANDER DANCY,
son of ELIZABETH PRICE by me, for lands known as Lot
1 and Lot 2 shown in survey made by EDWARD L. MOORE
on Spring Branch. Son: JOHN ROBERT DANCY, Lot 1 of
survey, also 2 negroes. Son: JAMES ALEXANDER,
Lot 2 of survey, also 2 negroes. Dau: ELIZABETH DANCY,
dau of ELIZABETH PRICE by me, 4 negroes. Dau: MARTHA
ANN DANCY, dau of ELIZABETH PRICE by me, 4 negroes.
ELIZABETH PRICE, dau of SAMUEL PRICE, during term of
10 yrs from date of my death, 4 negroes, furniture,
lend 2 beds, 2 horses, 10 sheep, 3 cows and calves,
3 sows and pigs, all poultry during that time. At the
end of 10 yrs, all property to children Exr: LAWRENCE
HENRY HEARN, JOSEPH J. W. POWELL, JOSEPH R. LLOYD.
Wit: RUSSEL CHAPMAN, HENRY HYMAN, THEO (?) HYMAN. Exr
refused to serve Adm. granted to HENRY HYMAN. Bond
$10,000, S. L. HEARN, ANDERSON COHOON & ORREN D.
COHOON, Securities.

DANIEL, AARON

Sept. 22, 1761. Sept. Ct., 1761. Verbal Will.
L 4 - 4 S to DAVID BRASSELL. All wearing close, tools,
and saddle bags divided between DAVID & SAMUEL BRASSELL.

95

Taken before me (signed) ELISHA BATTLE. Wit. and proved
DORCAS POWELL on oath of D. POWELL.

DANIEL, ASA
    Apr. 5, 1813. Aug. Ct., 1813. Bk. E, p 61. Wife:
JUDITH, lend all property for life or widowhood, excepting horse, bridle and saddle to LEVI. Son: LEVI,
reversion in ½ land, horse, saddle and bridle; Son:
ISAAC, reversion in ½ land. Residue to be divided equally between all children. Dau: MARTHA BARNES, upon
division of estate to pay out of her equal part, $30
to ELIZABETH. Exr: Bro: EPHRAIM DANIEL; Son-in-law,
JAMES BARNES. Wit: JOSEPH FARMER, L. ROGERS.

DANIEL, JOSEPH
    Apr. 4, 1800. Nov. Ct., 1800. Wife: SARAH, lend
2 negroes, household and kitchen furn. ½ of all land
including plantation and houses where I live, during
her life or widowhood. Son: NATHAN, 1 negro; 2 negroes
divided between sons JOSIAH and ASA. Son & Exr: ASA;
dau: ZILPAH DICKESSON, 1 negro; Son: STEPHEN, 1 negro;
son: LEVI, 1 negro; dau: DELANAH BARNES, 1 negro; dau:
MARTHA DAUDNA, 1 negro; dau: SALEY DANIEL, at mother's
marriage or death, negro and colt; Son & Exr: EPHRAIM,
reversion in all lands, plantation and 1 negro. Household furn. all stock, money, etc., equally divided between all children. Wit: JESSE FARMER, ARCHELAUS BARNES.

DANIEL, JUDIETH
    Aug. 24, 1837. Aug. Ct., 1837. Dau: JUDIETH BASS,
all my lands and mare. Dau: SARAH BARNES, 1 negro; dau:
TEMPERENCE JORDAN, 1 negro; dau: ELIZA BASS, 1 negro;
dau: DELANA BOSWELL, $300.00 and balance $300.00 to be
paid out of money raised from sale of property. Gr. son:
LINUS (LIAS?) HOWELL, maire, bridle and saddle. Exr:
Son-in-law: JAMES A. BARNES. Wit: WRIGHT EDMONDSON,
ABNER TISON (TYSON).

DANIEL, LEMUEL
    Sept. 20, 1821. Feb. Ct., 1822. Bk. E, p 286. Wife:
ANA (AVA?) lend land lying S side of Little Swamp and
W side of Toisnot Swamp, residue of stock and 6 negroes.
Son: JOSIAH, land adjoining LUCY DANIEL and ARCHELAUS

BARNES and after mother's marriage or death, to have
all land lent to her, horse, bridle, saddle, all farming tools to JOSIAH & JAMES. Son & Exr: JAMES, land W
side Toisnot Swamp and N side Little Swamp, horse,
bridle, saddle, and cow and calf. Dau: JULAN WOODARD,
mare, chest, cow and calf, yearling, 6 sheep and 1 negro; dau: MARY JORDAN, mare, cow and yearling, 6 sheep,
chest, bridle and saddle and 2 negroes at mother's
death; dau: NANCY DANIEL, horse, bridle, saddle, cow,
calf, 6 sheep, chest and 2 negroes at mother's death;
dau: TRESEY SIMMS, horse, bridle, saddle, cow and calf,
6 sheep, chest and 2 negroes at mother's death. Wit:
DEMPSEY DANIEL, STEPHEN BARNES.

DANIEL, SIMON
    May 26, 1768. July Ct., 1768. Wife & Extx:
ELIZABETH, Residue of estate, cattle, hogs, horses and
sheep, also household goods during widowhood, then to
be divided between children. Son & Exr: WILLIAM, cow
and calf; son: SIMON, 2 cows and calves; son: ELIJAH,
mare, cow and calf, rifel gun; daus: MARY and DARKIS,
cow and calf each. Wit: JOHN STANSELL, WILLIAM BENTLEY,
JOSHUA BENTLEY.

DANSBE, DANIEL
    Jan. 21, 1749, 1750. Aug. Ct., 1750. Wife & Extx:
ELIZABETH, 490 A plantation in North Hampton Co. to
be sold; son: ISOME, my plantation; daus: MARY,
ELIZABETH and CLEAREMON, residue; Exr: DAVID ROZIER.
Wit: ROBERT TAYLOR, DAVID COLLINS, REUBEN ROZIER.

DAUGHTERY, ELIZABETH
    Sept. 29, 1817. Nov. Ct., 1817. Bk. E, p 170. Gr.
son & Exr: GERRALGRUS (GERADLDUS) DAUGHTERY, 11 cattle,
all hoggs, 2 puter dishes, 6 puter plates and horse;
Gr. daus: ELIZABETH DAUGHTERY, dau of son JOSEPH, her
share of residue of estate sold & put at interest for
ELIZABETH. Daus: ELIZABETH SMILLY; MARY HOOD?; ADA
WARD, wife of ELIJAH WARD; SALLEY PRICE, 20 S each;
Heirs of son SAMUEL DAUGHTERY, 20 S. Exr: MOSES SPICER.
Wit: RICHARD BLOXSAM, JESSE BRAKE.

DAUGHTERY, SAMUEL (SR.)

Aug. 28, 1787. Oct. Ct., 1787. Wife & Extx:
ELIZABETH, lend plantation whereon I live during widow-
hood or life, reversion to JOSEPH, lend residue of es-
tate for widowhood or life, reversion to 2 eldest sons.
Son: JOSEPH, mare; Gr. son: KINTCHEN GAY; Dau: MARY
GAY, puter dish; Dau: OLIVE, 5 S; dau: SCAROUGH
(SCARBOROUGH), 5 S; dau: ELIZABETH, ewe and lamb; son:
SAMUEL, 20 S; son: WILLIAM, 20 S. Exr: SAMUEL SKINNER.
Wit: WILLIAM HEALY, JAMES SPICER.

DAUGHTERY, SAMUEL
Feb. 22, 1805. May Ct., 1805. Bk. D, p 222. Wife:
MARY, lend mare, bridle, saddle, household furniture,
cattle, hogs for 5 yrs—all land for widowhood or until children come of age. Son: JOEL, reversion in 163
A plantation whereon I live, mare, 2 stears and 1 cow;
son: JOSIAH, reversion in 200 A land where my mother
now lives and also cow and gun; daus: ELIZABETH and
NANCY, cow each. Remainder estate divided between 2
daus. Exr: CHARLES BARNES. Wit: NATHAN BRAKE, JESSE
BRAKE.

DAUGHTIS, DEMPSEY
Note: —DAUGHTY in Clerk's hand. _____12, 1761. May
Ct., 1778. Bk. 3, p 70. Bros and Sis: WILLIAM, FRANCIS,
JETHRO, ELIZABETH PENDER, SUSANAH ASHBURN, MARY RADOCK,
1 shilling each. Bro & Exr: DANIEL, all other estate.
Wit: ROBERT ROBISON, DEMPSEY SPIER, JOHN SPIER, JOHN
HARGRAVE.

DAVIS, EMORY
Oct. 1, 1795. No probate date. Wife: RACHEL, lend
1 negro, mare, 4 cattle during widowhood or natural
life, reversion to son DAVID. Daus: MARTHA ROLLINGS,
SARAH ELLENER, ELIZABETH DILLIARD; son: THOMAS; daus:
DELILIAH GRIFFIS (GRIFFIN), MILLEY RUFFIN, SELAH
STRINGER — 5 S each; son: RIGHTSON, to have 1st child
borne by negro woman Dorcas; dau: RACHEL CAUSWAY, 5 S;
son: WILLIAM, cow and calf, ewe and lamb, gun, grubbing
hoe, 1 jug; son: DAVID, land and manner plantation
whereon I live, 2 negroes, still, horse, colt, all stock
of every kind, all furniture, tools and utensils. Exr:
WILLIAM BELL, BYTHAL BELL. Wit: JOHN STRINGER, RICHARD

CLARK, RICHARD POWELL.

DAVIS, JOHN
   Aug. 14, 1794. Feb. Ct., 1799. Wife & Extx: ANN,
lend plantation whereon I live, all stock, etc, during
natural life. Daus: ANN WILLIAMS and LEVINY GATER, 10
S each; dau: DIANNER HOWARD, feather bed & furn. son:
JOHN 10 £; dau: LEUCRESY, 10 S; Gr. son: AARON HOWARD,
plantation where I live, at my wife's death and 2 sows
and pigs. Residue of estate divided equally between
daughters and grandson. Exr: AARON DAVIS, BOAZ KITCHING.
Wit: HARDY HOWARD, JOHN OWENS, BOAZ KITCHING.

DAVIS, JOHN
   Nov. 18, 1822. Feb. Ct., 1824. Bk. F p 15. Wife:
PHERABY, share all estate for her lifetime with daughters until they marry or die, land on N side of Contentnea Creek, reversion to son JONATHAN. Dau & Extx:
JUDEA (INDIA?); dau: EADITH, cow and calf, sow and pigs
to JUDEA and EADITH each; Son & Exr: JONATHAN, lend
land whereon he lives and reversion in land lent his
mother & sisters. Daus: MILBRY ODOM, NANCY SKETRE ?;
DICY BAGGETT. Wit: DAVID DANIEL, WILLIE ROGERS, H. J.
G. RUFFIN.

DAVIS, JOSEPH
   Feb. 8, 1799. Feb. Ct., 1799. Wife & Extx: KEZIAH,
2 slaves, horse and colt, cows and calf, sows and pigs,
lend her 1 slave, reversion to NOAH. Son: NOAH, plantation and 1 slave; Dau: ELIZABETH, 2 slaves. Exr:
GARRY FORT. Wit: RANDOLPH COTTEN, SAMUEL WREN.

DAVIS, RACHEL
   July 31, 1800. Nov. Ct., 1800. Son & Exr:
WRIGHTSON, crop; JOHN GRIFFIS (GRIFFIN), 2 bbl corn;
LOVEY LONG, $45 silver; Sons & Daus (unnamed). Exr:
PHILIP CAUSEY. Wit: DEMPSEY JENKINS, DAVID A. TELFAIR.

DAWSON, JOHN
   Nov. 22, 1748. May Ct., 1749. Wife & Extx: MARY.
Sons: DEMEY (DEMSPEY?), SOLOMON. Daus: MARTHA, PATIENCE.
Wit: BENJAMIN CHAMPION, FRANCIS BYTHAL HAYNES, THOMAS
DAVIS. Also son: John

DEAL, MARY
    Jan. 24, 1834. Feb. Ct., 1834. 23½ A land divided
between 3 sons. Son: JOBY, mare and 2 shoats; son:
JAMES, sow and 5 pigs, 1 shoat; son: BENNETT, 2 shoats;
daus: ELIZABETH, MARY and SARAH, 3 geese each. ELY?
Two other daughters unnamed. Exr: WM. THIGPEN. Wit:
HENRY KEAL, TABITHY KEAL.

DEAVER, THOMAS
    May 13, 1805. May Ct., 1805. Bk. D, p 227. Wife
& Extx: PENELOPE, during widowhood lend plantation
whereon I live, including 200 A woodland across the
rd., 4 slaves; give her 1 slave, riding chair & harness,
mare, horse, 30 hogs, 15 cattle, black walnut chest
and $200. I will that $700 be raised by Exr to complete
house started. If unborn child is boy to share equally
with brothers; if dau, to have $500. Dau: MARY ANN
McFIELD DEAVER, $500 silver. Sons: JOHN M. and JAMES
M. reversion in all land. Exr: JACOB BATTLE, JAMES
BARROT of North Hampton Co. Wit: SIMEON HORN, ELIJAH
HORN, SIMON WILLIFORD.

DELOACH, MARY
    Jan. 4, 1773. Apr. Ct., 1774. Son: WILLIAM, 5 S;
dau: AVERILLA RUFFIN, wife of RICHARD RUFFIN, 5 S;
son: JESSE all I've already given him and 5 S; Son &
Exr: SAMUEL, all I've already given him and cow and
calf; and 2 ewes and lambs; dau: SELAH BARNES, all I've
already given her and 5 S; Son & Exr: JOHN, 320 A land,
part of tract purchased of SOLOMON BOYKIN, also my
great desk, square walnut table, painted chest, largest
linen wheel, mare, horse, 20 lbs. feathers and 30 geese;
dau: MILLY BLOODWORTH, all I've already given her, also
my wearing close and saddle; son: SOLOMON, smallest
desk, pine table, case of bottles, 5 cattle, 5 "Bread-
ing" sows, 1 linen wheel, mare, colt, and L 5; Gr. son:
WILLIAM BRASWELL, 5 shillings. I will that WM.
BLOODWORTH and ELIJAH HORN and two others divide property between sons: JOHN and SOLOMON. Wit: JOHN FAULK,
HANAH FAULK, SARAH FAULK.

DELOACH, SAMUEL
    Jan. 30, 1764. Apr. Ct., 1764. Wife & Extx: MARY,

land left by my father-in-law FRANCIS BOYKIN of North
Hampton Co. mare, & side saddle; lend all plant'n
whereon I live, still, all slaves for the raising,
maintaining and schooling of my children, for her life
or widowhood, all chattles, and tenements until children come of age. Son & Exr: WILLIAM, all that part
of my estate he's already possessed of and 10 S; dau:
AVERILLA RUFFIN, all that part of my estate she's
already possessed of and 10 S; dau: MOLLEY BRASWELL,
all that part of my estate she's already possessed of
and 10 S; Son & Exr: JESSE, that land joining MOSES
HAIR; colt, cattle, sows and 1 slave; son & Exr:
SAMUEL, plant'n purchased of JOHN STINSON, mair, cattle
sows, and 1 slave; dau: SELAH, 5 cattle, etc.; son:
JOHN, land purchased of JOHN STRINGER, mair, colt,
cattle, sows and 1 slave; dau: MILLIE, 5 cattle, etc.;
son: SOLOMON, plant'n whereon I live, still, and 1
slave. All remaining slaves and increase at wife's
death to be divided between 4 daus. Wit: JOHN GASNEY,
THOMAS BRYANT, JOHN FAULK.

DEW, ARTHUR
    Sept. 13, 1816. Nov. Ct., 1816. Bk. E, p 149.
Sis: MARTHA SIMMS, $1000; sons & daus: of Bro: JOHN
DEW, $1000; ELIZABETH FARMER, $500; Relatives: JOHN
BARNES, THOMAS BARNES, and NANCY BARNES, $50 each;
Bro & Exr: WILLIAM DEW, residue of Estate. Exr:
WILLIE ROUNTREE. Wit: W(ILLIA)M SHALLINGTON, ENOS
TART, FREDERICK PHILIPS.

DEW, JOHN, of North Hampton Co.
    Sept. 2, 1749. Probated 1762. Son & Exr: ABRAHAM
(Incomplete); son: ARTHUR, 200 A between JACOB RICKS
& JOHN WORREL, also land without bounds of Reedey
Branch & Coopers Branch; dau: ELIZABETH, (torn), cow
and calf. Remainder divided between 6 chil: ABRAHAM,
ARTHUR, JOHN, SARAH, PRISCILLA, & MARY. Wit: (Torn)
BENJ. HILL (?). Proven by oath of JOHN WORREL, one of
the witnesses.

DEW, MARY
    Jan. 17, 1801. May Ct., 1801. Gr. chil: JOHN,

NANCY and THOMAS BARNES, 10 S each as they received
their portion of Gr. father's estate. Remainder of
estate to be divided between chil: JOHN, ARTHUR, WILLIAM,
ELIZABETH FARMER and MARTHA SIMMS. Exr: JOHN DEW (son);
JACOB HORN. Wit: JESSE FARMER (one those persons called
QUAKERS), ENOS FARMER, ZYLPAH FARMER.

DEW, MILICENT
     Apr. 24, 1786. May Ct., 1786. Dau: MARTHA DE
WALL, (DUVALL), estate which fell to me from my father
ABRAHAM DEW, dec'd of Nash Co. Also cow and calf and
remaining wearing apparel; bro: WILLIAM DEW, 1 striped
cotton gound; SALLEY RODGERS, 3 white linen caps, 2 pr.
wooling stockings, 1 pr. cotton stockings. Exr & Gdn
for dau MARTHA DEWALL, THOMAS VIVRETTE. Wit: JESSE
PITMAN, PETER VANLANDENHAM.

DEW, WILLIAM
     Sept. 8, 1802. Marked – not to be recorded yet –
1802. Wife: FANNY, lend tract lying on Town Creek &
called Pitman Place also tract lying in fork of Town
Creek adjoining WILLIAM DIXAN & JOSEPH WINSTEAD, 5
slaves, mare, horse, 2 cows and calves, 2 sows and pigs,
hogs, 1/2 household furniture for her lifetime, then to
be divided between my 2 daus. Dau: TEMPY, mill and
plant'n I live on at mother's death and 5 slaves; dau:
JACKEY, tract called "dark Pocosin" consisting of 640 A
by deed from BENNETT BARROW and 4 slaves. Bro: SANULET
(SAMULET ?) VIVRETT, Blue suit. Bro: JAMES VIVRETT,
all other wearing close; bro: MICAJAH VIVRETT, note
against him of about $30. No Witnesses. Exr: JOHN
ROBBINS, JACOB HORN, JESSE FARMER.

DICKEN, BENJAMIN
     May 16, 1794. May Ct., 1794. Wife: CATHERINE,
lend all estate, each dau. to have same as JEAN when
they come of age; dau: JEAN DICKEN, trunk and saddle;
daus: SALLEY, MARGARET, CHATHERINE & MARY DICKEN, ALL
personal & perishable estate at mother's death; son:
JAMES TURNER DICKEN, reversion in land also plant'n in
Georgia. Exr: LEWIS DICKEN, VINSON JOHNSTON. Wit:
EPHRAIM DICKEN, SAMUEL JOHNSON, MARY DICKEN.

DICKENS, BENJAMIN
     May 1, 1847. Nov. Ct., 1851. All my lands to be
offered to my friend, JOSEPH I. W. POWELL at $300.00.
If he refuses, lands to be sold, and proceeds used in
manner explained. It is my wish that my Executor carry,
or send, my negroes to some free State, or Saint Domingo,
or the British West Indies. I give $9000.00 out of my
Estate, together with $3000.00 from land, for trans-
porting my negroes in a comfortable manner, and settl-
ing them agreeably, with their full freedom, freely
and cheerfully given by me. Friend: JOSEPH I. W.
POWELL, $5000.00, also horses, hogs, corn, produce,
plantation utensils, household and kitchen furniture,
buggy, carts, etc. Exr: JOSEPH I. W. POWELL. Wit:
JOHN KEA, STEPHEN HARPER. Codicil, May 1, 1847. There
being doubt as to what construction might be put upon
contents of my will, etc. Niece: ELIZABETH A. HARRISON,
The note I hold against JOSHUA L. HORNE, for about
$1200.00. WM. R. SAVAGE, the note I now hold against
him for about $90.00. ELIZABETH JOYNER, the note I
hold against ROBERT JOYNER. Remainder of property to
Exr: JOSEPH I. W. POWELL in Special Trust and confidence to be used in freeing and removing my slaves to
some suitable place, dividing the balance amongst them,
and give him full powers to use same for the purpose
of emancipating said slaves. Wit: STEPHEN HARPER,
EDMOND D. L. FAULK.

DICKEN, CHRISTOPHER
     May 13, 1779. Nov. Ct., 1779. Dau: MARY KEY, 2
slaves and land; son: EDMUND DICKEN, ₤ 10 money, 2
shirts, 2 pr. trousers, 1 pr. breeches, shoes, stockings; gr.son: CHRISTOPHER HAINS; dau: ANN; 4 gr.chil
(not named). Exr: EPHRAIM DICKEN, ISAAC SESSUMS. Wit:
BEN DICKEN, ELIZABETH CALAND, JESSE WALL. (Very indistinct).

DICKEN, EPHRAIM
     Nov. 14, 1790. Feb. Ct., 1791. Bk. 3, p 159.
Father: All estate. Bros & Exrs: BENJ. DICKEN, LEWIS
DICKEN. Wit: EPHRAIM DICKEN, JOHN GOODMAN, WILLIAM
DICKEN.

DICKEN, EPHRAIM
     Nov. 15, 1845. Nov. Ct., 1845. Bk. F, p 323.
C. F. DICKEN, 1 1/2 lots in Tarboro on which I live,
all land purchased of MICHAEL HEARN and wife, tract
purchased of Dr. T. H. HALL (or HALE), another tract
purchased of MATHEW DICKEN, 66 negroes, all horses,
mules, cattle, sheep and whole estate. No Exr. Wit:
A. H. MACNAIR, ROBERT H. AUSTIN, THOMAS A. MACNAIR.

DICKENS, WILLIAM
     Jan. 26, 1852. Nov. Ct., 1852. Bk. F, pp 488-89.
It is my wish and desire there shall be no sale of my
property. Dau: SUSAN SAVAGE, 2 negroes; gr.dau: LUCY
BRYAN, negroes. Grt.gr.chil: Children (unnamed) of
J. J. SAVAGE, decs'd, $1500.00; gr.son: WM. R. SAVAGE,
1 negro, $500.00; gr.dau: ELIZABETH ANN HARRISON, 3 ne-
groes; grt.gr.chil: Children of ELIZABETH ANN HARRISON,
negroes, 6 slaves; gr.dau: ELIZABETH JOYNER, 2 negroes
and $2500.00; son: CHRISTOPHER L. DICKEN, all my lands
on both sides of the Creek, balance of negroes not disposed of, all stock and crop, household and kitchen
furniture. Exr: CHRISTOPHER L. DICKENS. Wit: ETHELDRED
M. BRYAN, JOSEPH KNIGHT. Codicil, July 24, 1852. Re-
voked legacy to gr.son WILLIAM R. SAVAGE. Bequest of
negro girl to gr.dau: ELIZABETH ANN HARRISON and $200.
Bequest to dau: SUSAN SAVAGE, $150.00; gr.dau: ELIZABETH
JOYNER, $150.00; Wit: LEWIS M. ALSBROOK, JOSEPH KNIGHT.

DICKINSON, AVA.
     Aug. 1, 1837. May Ct., 1838. Dau: MARY DILLIARD,
all my estate whatsoever. Exr: ROBERT BARNES. Wit:
DORIS BRAKE, JAMES G. BARNES.

DICKINSON, JOHN
     Aug. 4, 1779. Feb. Ct., 1980. Wife & Extx: JANE,
all estate during lifetime; son & exr: THOMAS, all land
& plant'n; son: WILLIAM; dau: SARAH; daus: MARY TYE (?),
FANNY DILLARD, ELIZABETH FORT, JANE FORT, MARTHA JENKINS,
already provided for. Wit: W. HAYWOOD, SHERWOOD HAYWOOD,
JR.

DICKSON, RETISON (?)
     June 22, 1778. Aug. Ct., 1779. Wife: MARTHA,

estate during life or widowhood, reversion to dau,
MARTHA; son: THOMAS, 5 S. Exr: ISAAC SESSUMS. Wit:
SAMUEL BRIDGERS, FRANCES PIKE (?), THOMAS HODGES.

DIGGES, ROBERT.
        Nov. 17, 1786 Nov. Ct., 1789. Wife & Extx:
ELIZABETH, use of all estate during her life or widowhood; dau: SARAH WIMBERLEY, slaves; son: STARLING, land
& plt'n whereon I live also 300 A in Edge. Co. on Town
Creek adjoining BENJ. LANCASTER'S line. Remainder to
be divided between 4 chil: FRANCES, ELIZABETH, STARLING
and CATY. Exr: JACOB DICKINSON, GEORGE WIMBERLEY. Wit:
ELIAS FORT, ROGER LANCASTER.

DICKINSON, TURNER
        Nov. 30, 1835. Feb. Ct., 1836. Bk. F, p 183.
Wife & Extx: SALLEY DICKINSON; my crop of corn and cotton, horse, mare, and her increase; cow and 2 calves,
all stock, hogs, pair of stillyards, set of Wooden
ware, Walnut table, 9 setting chairs, looking glass,
plates, side saddle, frying pan, Dutch oven, waffle
irons, griddle, earthen dish, 19 geese, cart and wheels,
furniture & farming utensils. After wife's decease to
dau: MAHALY DICKINSON, large book, "The Life of Christ".
Son-in-law: WILLIE SANDERS, colt, briddle and saddle,
and my razor. Exr: Friend, JAMES B. WOODARD. Wit:
JACOB BARNES, WILLIAM BARNES, JR., THEOPHILUS GAY.

DILLARD, ELIZABETH.
        Nov. 25, 1817. Nov. Ct., 1817. Bk. E, p 172.
Dau: DOLLY ALSOBROOK, crop, cart & wheels, flax wheel,
flax hackle, stays, side saddle, 2 hogs and 6 shoats;
gr.dau: ELIZABETH MOORE, 10 S; daus: CHARITY SASNETT,
NEWTON MOORE. Exr: DEMSPEY BRYAN. Wit: ADY BRADLEY,
AARON COLEMAN.

DILLARD, JAMES.
        Nov. 27, 1789. No Probate date. Dau: SARAH
DILLARD, chest, mother's wearing clothes, tea kettle,
pare flat irons; personal property and land sold after
2 yrs, money divided between son, JAMES and dau, SARAH.
Exr: JOHN BATTS. Wit: BARNABA DILLARD, POLLEY DILLARD,
MARY DILLARD.

DILLARD, JOHN
Mar. 16, 1779. Feb. Ct., 1780. Wife: Whole estate
for lifetime. Divided among chil (unnamed) at her
death. Exr: ROBT. DIGGES, JAMES DILLARD. Wit: BETTY
DIGGES, JOHN SIKES.

DIXON, COFFIELD
Oct. 29, 1833. Nov. Ct., 1838. Son: HENRY, 150 A
of land adjoining his land, known as the REDLEY DIXON
land, also 60 A adjoining ASAEL FARMER'S; 1 negro; son:
RANDOLPH, 350 A of land whereon I live after the death
of self and wife. It is my wish RANDOLPH remain where
he now lives, having privilege of clearing and having
what he can make on the N side of the Mill Swamp;
another tract known as the MOSLEY place; tract of 11 A
purchased of BENJAMIN CRUMPLER; tract of 107 A, etc.,
Brandy still; dau: KEZIAH DIXON, 1 negro; MERIT JOYNER
and his wife SARAH, negro boy, Ned; GUILFORD HORN and
his wife MARY, 1 negro; BURWELL MOORE and his wife
PENNY, negro girl; THOMAS WINSTEAD and wife ELIZABETH,
negro woman; GUILFORD JOYNER and wife NANCY, 2 negroes;
Wife: MARY, her choice of stock, household and kitchen
furniture. Exr: JOHN G. WILLIAMS, WRIGHT W. JOYNER.
Wit: WRIGHT W. JOYNER, E. H. WILLIAMS.

DIXON, GREEN
Jan. 20, 1809. Feb. Ct., 1809. Wife: ELIZABETH,
lend South part of land during her lifetime; give her
1 cow, calves, mare, bridle, saddle, furniture, sitting
chears, 1 lum (loom), & gear, stock, hogs, sheep, geese,
3 chests, small squirrel gun, wollem & flax wheels.
Father: WILLIAM DIXON, all land he left to me to be
divided. Mother: OLIVE DIXON, mother to live on N Division on Whiteoak Swamp; sis: PATIENCE WEST DIXON,
land, being part of North division of father's land;
dau: NANCY, South division, 1 slave. Residue applied
to education of NANCY. Exr: WILLIAM BELLAMY, DAVID
COFFIELD. Wit: MOSES SMITH, WILLIAM C. KING.

DIXON, THOMAS
Sept. 14, 1790. Nov. Ct., 1790. Son & Exr: THOMAS
JR., ₤ 40 hard money, also all cattle I have at his
house; gr.son: NICHOLAS DIXON, HICKMAN DIXON, THOMAS

DIXON, JR., all cattle at NICHOLAS DIXON'S; gr.son:
WILLIAM DIXON, son of WILLIAM DIXON, 2 slaves; son &
exr: WILLIAM, 800 A plantation whereon I live, all
cattle, which is at JOHN MORRIS', living on Alston's
Mill Branch; daus: ELIZABETH MOUNTGOMARY and JEMIMAH
COHOON (CAHOON ?), 5 S each; Wit: JESSE PITMAN, THOMAS
WELLS, SALLEY DIXON.

DIXON, WILLIAM
    July 4, 1800. Aug. Ct., 1800. Wife & Extx: OLIVE,
estate for life or widowhood, to be divided thus: Son:
JOHN, 20 S; each of his 3 children, 1 years schooling;
son & exr: GREEN, all land, horse, bridle, saddle, gun,
cow, yearling, heiffer, sows, pigs, table, safe, new
Bible, 6 chairs, large iron pot, 1/2 cold water still;
dau: PATIENCE WEST DIXON, mare, saddle, bridle, cow &
calf, chest, linnen wheel, wooling wheel, walnut table,
loom & geer, looking glass, iron pot, 1/2 cold water
still, L 120 in dollars at 6 S apiece; gr.dau: PENELOPE,
dau of J (?) DIXON, bed and furniture provided she live
with her grandmother OLIVE DIXON (my wife). Exr: NATHAN
HARRIS. Wit: ANN BRADLEY, MARY BUTLER, HOSEA DURLEY.

DONALDSON, ROBERT
    Apr. 13, 1803. Feb. Ct., 1804. Friend & Exr: J. G.
S. SCHENCK, $1000.00; friend & Exr: JOHN HUDSON, my
store and lot (both residents of Tarborough). Son:
ROBERT, late of Downpatrick in Ireland, residue of my
estate. In case of his demise, to 1st Cousin: WILLIAM
DONALDSON, late of Jamaica, address to the care of
Messrs. Hibbert & Taylor, and in case of his decease,
to his next of kin - formerly of the Town of Aberdeen
in Scotland. Testators: THOMAS BLOUNT, NATHAN MATHEWS,
BENJAMIN BRECKELL. Codicil: Dr. THOS. PILLSON, the
sum of 100 guineas for services to my son. Wit:
JEREMIAH BATTLE, H. HAYWOOD.

DONALDSON, WILLIAM, of Tarborough.
    Apr. 18, 1817. May Ct., 1819. Bk. E, p 214. dau:
SARAH ANN DONALDSON, all my personal property: Bank
Stock, of the State, New Bern, or Cape Fear Banks; negro slaves. To Executors: My lot of land in this town
known as Number 69 in trust to be sold for benefit of

my daughter SARAH ANN. Parcel of land on S side of
Swift Creek purchased from JOHN WARD in name of SARAH
DONALDSON, my late wife, proved in August Court, 1814,
registered in Book 15, p 93, in trust for my daughter
SARAH ANN. Should SARAH ANN die without heirs, then to
ANN PHILLIPS, one half of the negroes that came to me
by her sister, my late dec'd wife, in consideration of
her love and attachment to her. The remainder of said
negroes I wish divided in 3 parts, one of which I give
and bequeath to the heirs of EXUM PHILLIPS, the other
to the heirs of MOODIE PORTER, by his wife ELIZABETH,
and the other to the heirs of FIGURES PHILIPS. Exr:
EXUM PHILLIPS, of Nash Co., N. C., EXUM LEWIS, of
Edgecombe Co, N. C., ROBERT DONALDSON, of the City of
New York. Also I nominate and appoint Dr. JOHN F.
WARD, of this town in case he is married to MARY
PHILIPS, of Orange Co., as Guardian of my child SALLY
ANN DONALDSON. .If he is not married, JAMES MOORE,
of Halifax Co., in same capacity. Expense of main-
tenance provided for child. Wit: ALEXANDER JOHNSON,
ROBT. PERRY.

DOOLES, THOMAS
    Nov. 28, 1756. May Ct., 1757. Wife: PATIENCE.
Son & Exr: JOSEPH, 300 A plantation whereon I live;
son: JOHN, 200 A adjoining JOEL ADAMS, 240 A adjoining
son JOHN, Kehukee and where the PURYEARS live to be
divided between 3 daus: SARAH, CATTEREN and BITHA.
Devisee: ROBERT PURYEAR, 100 A adjoining ROBERT HILLIARD.
Exr: ROBERT PURYEAR. Wit: JAMES MYHAND, MOSES HORNE,
JOSEPH DOOLES.

DORMAN, MARY
    Feb. 20, 1796. May Ct., 1801. Sons: DAVID, ROBERT,
REUBEN and JAMES HARPER, to have 1 A land adjoining
his own; son: JAMES HARPER. BANNISTER HARPER. Remain-
der of land to be divided among 4 sons, cattle, stock,
household furniture, and $50.00 in cash. NANCY
BATCHELOR, MARY BATCHELOR, WRIGHT WILLIAM BATCHELOR,
LYDIA HOBDY and MARY ACREE, 5 S each. Exr: JOHN
BATTS, DAVID HARPER, ROBERT HARPER. Wit: ALEX SESSUMS,
R. H. SESSUMS, ELIZABETH SESSUMS.

DORTCH, LEWIS I., of Nash County, N. C.
Oct. 24, 1838. Probated, 1838. Neph: RICHARD
HILLIARD, all my personal Estate. Exr: Friend and
Bro: WILLIAM H. HILLIARD. Wit: JACOB ING.

DOWNING, JAMES, SR.
Mar. 17, 1808. Aug. Ct., 1808. Daus: CHRISCHANEY
LITTLE, LYDIA EDMONDSON and ELIZABETH JOHNSON, 5 S
each; dau: MARY DOWNING, mare, cow, sow and pigs, loom
and all pots, 1 pair cart wheels, all the rest of my
household furniture not disposed of, 2 weeding hoes,
1 grubbing hoe, all my corn, fodder, and sider casks.
Sons: JAMES, JOSEPH and GEORGE DOWNING, and dau:
COURTNEY COOK, 5 S each. Exr: FRANCIS PURRIE, JAMES
DOWNING. Wit: THOMAS EDMONDSON, WILLIS EDMONDSON,
DINAH VANCE.

DRAKE, JESSE.
Mar. 26, 1796. Aug. Ct., 1796. Wife & Extx:
MARGARET, use of my estate of whatever nature during
widowhood, to raise my children. JEMIMAH SCARBOROUGH,
5 S, already provided for. Sons to be bound to learn
good trade at 15 yrs. Exr: Bro, WILLIAM DRAKE. Wit:
AMOS JOHNSTON, DREWRY DRAKE.

DRAKE, LAZARUS
Nov. 4, 1774. Feb. Ct., 1785. Wife: SARAH DRAKE,
the bed she now lies on, use of the plantation I live
on; all my household furniture and stock of whatever
nature during her life or widowhood. Also use of my
negroes. Son: JESSE, £ 5 Proclamation money. ANN
wife of BENJAMIN MARLEY, 20 S; son: WILLIAM, my tools
belonging to my trade, sons DAVID and HINES to have
use of tools; son: DREWRY, reversion in plantation.
If no heirs, then to son HINES; if he dies without
issue, to DAVID; daus: ELIZABETH and SALLY. No Exr.
Wit: JOHN BULLOCK, ALLEN HINES, SOLOMON ANDREWS.

DRAKE, SARAH
Mar. 19, 1804. May Ct., 1804. Nunc. Will. MARY
RIGHLAND, of lawful age, appeared before me, AMOS
JOHNSTON, one of the Justices of said County and de-
posed, and sayeth: She was at the house of SARAH DRAKE,

dec'd a few days before she died, and in the presence
of DREWERY DRAKE and his son LAZARUS, heard SARAH DRAKE
say it was her will and desire her son DREWERY DRAKE
have use of her feather bed and all the furniture belonging to the bed until his son LAZARUS came of age.
Said the bed was her own. That DREWERY (his son) have a
as many of her clothes as he could wear, the rest to be
cut down for children of DREWERY DRAKE; and her 2 gold
rings were to go to BETSEY DRAKE and TEMPY DRAKE, daus
of DREWERY DRAKE.

DRAKE, WILLIAM
    Feb. 14, 1827. May Ct., 1827. Bk. F, pp 69-71.
Son & Exr: LEVI DRAKE, son of ELINOR EDWARDS, dec'd,
all my estate. Exr: PETER EVANS, JOHN GARRETT. Wit:
BENJAMIN WEAVER, JAMES BARRON.

DRAUGHAN, WILLIAM
    Feb. 5, 1835. Aug. Ct., 1835. Bk. F, p 170. Wife:
Lend all lands (200 A), furniture, stock and tools.
Reversion of land to ROBERT and MILES; dau: MARTHA
HAY, $10; dau: EDNY, 20 A land lying S side of Cross
Branch along lines of WILLIAMS and PETWAY, formerly
HARDY FLOWERS; son: WILLIAM, 80 A land E side WILLIAM-
SON'S Branch on lines of JAMES DRAUGHAN; son: JOHN &
wife, WINNIFRED, 25 A land S side of road leading from
WILLIAM MERCER'S to Union Meeting House on lines of
MILES DRAUGHAN and WM. PETWAY; son: ROBERT; son: MILES,
(illegible). Exr: MATTHEW WHITEHEAD, AUGUSTIN WHITE-
HEAD. Wit: MARK BENNETT, BENJAMIN WILLIAMS.

DRUMMOND, THOMAS SR., Gentleman
    Nov. 3, 1813. Feb. Ct., 1815. Bk. E, p 89. Wife:
ELIZABETH, have provision and equal share; son: THOMAS,
JR., note for $28.40. Children of THOMAS DRUMMOND, JR.
(unnamed). Exr: BENJAMIN COFFIELD, SENR., ORRANGE
LINCH. Wit: H. PERKINS, JOHN BATCHELOR.

DUNFORD, PHILIP
    Mar. 5, 1821. May Ct., 1829. Wife: ELIZABETH, all
my land and plantation, stock, household and kitchen
furniture, plantation utensils; son & exr: JAMES,
horse, bridle, saddle and 1/2 my tract land; son: JOHN,

1/2 my land, furniture at Mother's discretion and $50.
If no heirs, reversion to son JAMES; dau: MARY SUMRELL,
$2. Exr: JOHN R. SCARBOROUGH. Wit: SETH PARKER
KINCHEN CHERRY.

DUNFORD, THOMAS
Oct. 7, 1841. Feb. Ct., 1842. Bk. F, p 264. Wife
& Extx: SALLY, lend all land and negroes; dau: SUSANNAH
HARRELL, 1 negro; son: WILLIAM, reversion in land, 1
negro; dau: LUNDY, (or LUCINDY ?), 1 negro; dau:
TABITHA, 1 negro. Wit: AMOS WOOTEN, SR., R. T. EAGLES.
Extx. refused to qualify. R. T. EAGLES Adm. Bond
$10,000. Securities: JOHN HARRELL, JONATHAN T. EASON,
WILLIAM B. PHILIPS.

DUNFORD, WILLIAM
Apr. 7, 1807. Aug. Ct., 1807. Bk. D, p 288. Son:
WILLIAM, 5 S; son: PHILIP; dau: SUSANNAH, choice cow
and calf, choice of linen wheels and woolen wheels,
and a pair of cards; son: THOMAS, lands and plantation
where I now live, bounded by lines of SAMUEL RUFFIN,
KEATON EVERETT, PHILIP DUNFORD, and JAMES SCARBOROUGH;
also young mare. After payment of debts, money from
sale of remainder to my children: sons; JOHN, JESSE,
and DANIEL. Exr: SAMUEL RUFFIN. Wit: ALLEN NETTLE,
JOHN NETTLE.

DUNN, ANN
Aug. 24, 1809. Nov. Ct., 1809. Bk. D, p 351.
Gr.son: JOSHUA DUNN, son of LAMON DUNN, 1 feather bed
on which I lie; gr.son: ANSON DUNN, son of NICHOLAS
DUNN, 1 cow and yearling; dau: LURANEY DUNN, 1 small
iron pot; dau: SELAH DUNN, my hunting saddle. Exr:
LAMON DUNN. Wit: DEMPSEY JENKINS, JOHN WILKINSON.

DUNN, DILLY.
Apr. 17, 1853. Aug. Ct., 1853. Bk. F, p 508. I
lend unto my friend POLLY DUNN, wife of JAMES DUNN,
all my lands and tenements, household furniture and
all stock, her lifetime, independent of any and all
claims against her husband, JAMES DUNN. I give and
bequeath to ELIZABETH, dau of POLLY DUNN, all my land,
tenements and stock, etc. Exr: J. R. PITT. Wit: B. S.
TAYLOR.

DUNN, JOHN

Jan. 26, 1793. Aug. Ct., 1793. Wife & Extx: ANN,
plantation whereon I live during widowhood, all stock,
during years of raising and maintaining my children,
also negroes; dau: MILLY CARR, 5 S; dau: LURANEY DUNN,
1 heifer; dau: MARY STRICKLAND, 5 S; son: JACOB, 5 S;
son & exr: NICHOLAS, 1 cow and my cabinet of joyner's
Tools; son: STEPHEN, 110 A of land, with plantation
where he now lives, etc; gr.dau: NANCY DUNN, 1 cow;
son: PHILLIP, 1 cow and 1 filly; dau: SEALY DUNN,
heifer; son & exr: LAMON DUNN, 130 A on Great Branch,
joining the old line and STEPHEN'S lines, and 1/2 my
estate after my debts are paid and decease of my wife;
son: JONAS DUNN, 240 A plantation where I live, at 19
years of age and other 1/2 my estate I have not given
away, and negroes. Executors sell barrel apple brandy
and 3 barrels sider to pay lawful debts. Exr: WILLIAM
BLOODWORTH. Wit: HARDY SCARBOROUGH, RICHARD CLARK,
ABSOLOM GARDENER.

DUNN, PENNY

Feb. 21. 1844. Aug. Ct., 1847. Sister: DELLIA
DUNN, 40 A land, all notes in my possession at my de-
cease, and all rest of my property. Wit: L. S. DUNN,
B. S. TAYLOR.

DUPREE, WILLIS

Oct. 15, 1844. Feb. Ct., 1849. Bk. F, p 430. "It
is my will and desire and I hereby direct that my old
negro man, Tom shall be allowed to spend his time
wherever he may think proper and labour for no person
more than he think proper, and if he is at any time in
want of any of the neccessaries of life, that whatever
he may need shall be furnished him during his life by
my executors." ? REDMOND R. DUPREE and neph, JAMES
DUPREE, whole estate; Exr: REDMOND R. DUPREE, ROBERT
F. J. H. WILLIAMS. Wit: ROBERT F. J. H. WILLIAMS,
RICHARD WILLIAMS. Feb. Ct., 1849. Will caveated by
LEWIS B. DUPREE and LAFAYETTE DUPREE. May Ct., 1849,
Widow, ELIZABETH DUPREE dissented. Jury which ordered
will probated: MICAJAH BRADLEY, STEPHEN HARPER, EDWARD
L. COTTEN, WILLIAM F. MERCER, HANSEL WILLS, MAYO
WORSLEY, LITTLEBERRY BROWN, JOHN KEY, WILLIAM TAYLOR,

JAMES BARNES, WILLIAM POWELL.

DURLEY, MARY
Sept. 20, 1834. Feb. Ct., 1835. Nunc. Will. Sister: SUSAN BANDY, $25, also my bed, bedclothes and all
wearing apparel; residue for burial. Proven by oath of
PRISCILLA BROUN, Sept. 22, 1834. Wit: EDWIN L. MOORE.

EASON, ABNER
Mar. 8, 1819. Aug. Ct., 1819. Bk. E, p 223. Wife:
MARTHY, all lands on N side of Little Contentnea Creek,
E side of Baget's Branch, negroes; Brandy still, stock,
horses, hogs, sheep, household and kitchen furniture,
corn, fowls, utensils, etc. during widowhood; son:
ABNER, negroes, cows, hogs, horses, and land from the
mouth to the head of the Branch; son: JONATHAN, land,
negroes; dau: CATHERINE SPEIGHT, negroes; son: ELNATHAN
T. EASON, 1 horse, briddle, saddle, 2 cows and calves,
land, property now in his possession; dau: SALLY GARY
(GAY ?), briddle, saddle, furniture, 2 cows and calves
sheep, money now in her possession. Exr: GARRETT KNIGHT,
$5000 bond. Wit: A. P. THIGPEN, JOHN THIGPEN.

EASON, COBURN
Jan. 18, 1801. Nov. Ct., 1803. Wife: ELIZABETH,
all lands and Plantation, and profits for 10 years;
only 1/3 of the Brandy, negroes, Horse and 6 brandy
barrels to be sold & money used for wife & children:
JOSHUA, MARTHA, MARY, MILLICENT, ELIZABETH, BENNETT
and SELETY EASON. Son: BENNETT, plantation and lands
and 1/3 of Brandy. Exr: Father-in-law, JOSHUA BARNES;
Bro, JOHN EASON. Wit: JAMES SCARBOROUGH, RICHARD LYON.

EDMONDSON, ANN
Aug. 17, 1820. Nov. Ct., 1822. Bk. E, p 307. Son:
JAMES HODGES, $5.00; gr.dau: NANCY BEST, side saddle;
gr.chil: NANCY BEST, JULY BEST, LEWISINDA BEST, CALVIN
BEST, wearing apparel; son & exr: POLLARD EDMONDSON,
all my estate not willed away. Wit: WM. R. LONG,
FRANCIS HATTON.

EDMONDSON, WILLIAM
Mar. 14, 1804. May Ct., 1804. Bk. D, p 201. Wife:

ORPHA, land and plantation during her widowhood; land
on N side of road to be sold; mare and colt, cattle,
hogs, sheep, geese, household and kitchen furniture,
hives of bees and tools. Son: WILLIS, horse, colt;
sons: WILLIAM and ELIAS H., reversion in land and
plantation; daus: NANCY, CHLOE, ORPHA and EUNICE. Gun
and shot bag to be sold. After wife's death or marriage, estate to be sold and divided. Exrs and bros: JOHN
EDMONDSON, THOMAS EDMONDSON. Wit: SAMUEL GATER, PENNY
EDMONDSON, WILSON HOWARD.

EDMUNDS, ELLIS
_____1808. No Probate date. Nunc. Will. Bk. D,
p 320. JOSIAH LODGE and JESSE BOZEMAN, JR. on 2 May
1808 depose; Were called by ELLIS EDMUNDS, decs'd, and
heard him make gifts of his property. To BENJAMIN
HINES, a young mare; to WILLIAM HINES, old mare and
her colt; to ROBERT WILLIAMS, 1 negro; balance to be
divided between his sisters. Gave his largest gun to
GEORGE WASHINGTON WILLIAMS, son of ROBERT WILLIAMS, on
condition he (ELLIS EDMUNDS) did not recover from
present illness. ROBERT WILLIAMS and WILLIAM HINES
to settle his business. JOSIAH LODGE and JESSE BOZMAN
appeared before AMOS JOHNSTON one of the Justices, and
made oath, the 3rd of May 1808.

EDWARDS, BETSEY (SR.)
July 14, 1816. Feb. Ct., 1818. Bk. E, p 177.
Nieces: BETSEY EDWARDS and POLLY EDWARDS, "my two
affectionate nieces", my land and plantation and all
profits thereon; household and kitchen furniture,
waring apparel, stock of all kinds. LEVEY DRAKE, bed,
etc. Negroes to be sold and money from father's estate
divided among my bro, NATHAN EDWARDS' children. Exr:
WILLIAM DRAKE. Wit: WM. BALFOUR, ELISHA WIGGINS.

EDWARDS, BRITAIN
May 11, 1813. Nov. Ct., 1817. Bk. E, p.165. Dau:
BYTHA EAGLES, $138.00; son & exr: HARMON, all of my
land, messuages, crop, sider barrels, working tools,
negro, it being his brother, GRAY EDWARDS' part; cow
and calf; 2 ewes, 1 lamb instead of a suit of clothing;
dau-in-law: CIELY EDWARDS; dau: NANCY, 1 negro, cow

and calf, 2 ewes and lambs; son: SILLAS W. EDWARDS, 1
negro, furniture, cow and calf, and lambs; son: BRYANT;
dau: SALLEY W. DUNFORD; dau: LUCINDA NORVILL; son & exr:
SILEY; son-in-law: THOMAS DUNFORD, 1 negro, cow and
calf, 2 ewes and lambs; son-in-law: CHAPMAN NORVILL,
1 negro, 1 cow and calf, 2 ewes and lambs; $9 instead
of a clock. Wit: EDWARD COBB, JR., JONAS COBB.

EDWARDS, HENRY
     Jan. 14, 1758. June Ct., 1758. Sons: NATHAN,
BRITAIN, JESSE (my plantation); sons & exrs: SAMUEL &
HENRY. Wit: ARTHUR BOWIN, JOHN NORWOOD.

EDWARDS, KINCHEN
     Jan. 30, 1847. May Ct., 1851. Wife: RACHEL, I
lend during life the whole 382 A plantation on Town
Creek, known as CHARLES LAND'S tract, 6 negroes, household and kitchen furniture, 2 horses, 3 cows, calves,
3 ewes and lambs, her choice of all stock, Brandy still,
cidar and brandy casks, cart and wheels, riding gig and
harness and year's provision. Son: RANDOLPH, I lend
541 A on the N side of Tar River; reversion to chil;
son: (?) MOSES, I lend other half of tract of land on
N side of Tar River, half of which is lent to my son
RANDOLPH, and 3 negroes; 3 gr.sons: HILLIARD, REDDING
and SION A. DAWSON, sons of my dau, NELLY, to have
293 A tract known as the EDWIN MOORE land, adjoining
lands of JACOB ROBBINS and WILLIAM W. WEAVER; and to
each $50 after death of my wife; 2 gr. daus: MARGARET
and CATHERINE DAWSON, daus of my dau NELLY, 1 negro
and $50 each. My youngest son: KINCHEN, 254 A land
lying on the S side of Tar River known as the JETTY
HAMMOND, WILLIAM A. JOYNER and WILLIAM W. PRIDGEN land,
adjoining the lands of JONATHAN JOYNER & MOSES JOYNER,
also plantation whereon I live. Exr: Trusty friends,
MOSES JOYNER, JOHNATHAN JOYNER. Wit: W. I. ARMSTRONG,
JACOB D. ROBBINS.

EDWARDS, MICAJAH
     Dec. 11, 1795. Feb. Ct., 1796. Wife & Extx:
ELIZABETH, plantation where I live life estate; 1 negro for support and schooling of my children; horse;
cupboard and what is in it; 25 barrels corn; 1200 lbs

pork; iron pots, ploughhoes, ploughs, 2 sows, 15 shoats, 8 sheep; pewter, wheels and cards, and Bible; reversion to LITTLEBERRY; dau: ELIZABETH, 1 chest; dau: SUSANNA; dau: MARY, cow and calf; 6 chears. Exr: BENJAMIN BATTS, PERSON GLOVER. Wit: BOAZ KITCHING, JOB BRADDY, JONES PARKER.

EDWARDS, NANCY

Oct. 5, 1853. Feb. Ct., 1855. Bk. G, p 99. CELIA EDWARDS, wife of Bro, HARMON EDWARDS, $200; SINDARILA EDWARDS, $25; WM. FAIRCLOTH, in right of his wife, SUSAN; my niece, $5; BASSET SYKES, in right of his wife, MARY ANN, my niece, $5. Residue of estate divided equally among: bros: BRITON EDWARDS, BRIANT EDWARDS, sis: LUCINDA NORVILLE and chil of following bros and sisters: TABITHA EAGLES, SILAR WOOTEN, SALLY DUNFORD, HARMON EDWARDS and SILEY EDWARDS (except SUSAN and NANCY). Exr: R. T. EAGLES. Wit: JOAB P. PITT, JAMES NORVILLE.

EDWARDS, NATHAN

Dec. 20, 1812. Nov. Ct., 1814. Bk. E, p 75. Dau: BETSEY, negro girl, Leah and ₤ 100; dau: ELEANOR, furniture; gr. daus: BETSEY and POLLY EDWARDS, daus of ELEANOR EDWARDS, dec'd, ₤ 100 each and furniture; dau: DELIA SHERLEY, 1 negro; gr. dau: BETSEY EDWARDS, dau of JONES EDWARDS, dec'd, 5 S; son: NATHAN EDWARDS, 5 S; gr. son: LEVY DRAKE, ₤ 10; gr. dau: DELILA PEELE, ₤ 10. Residue divided between sons EDMOND and TYTUS. Exr: EDMOND EDWARDS, JAMES WALSTON. Wit: W. BALFOUR, JOHN LEE.

EDWARDS, SILEY

Apr. 2, 1841. May Ct., 1843. Bk. F, pp 298-300. Wife: NANNY, my stock, horses, mules, hogs, cattle, sheep to dispose of as she pleases; lend her land, poultry, geese, bees, money and notes kept on interest, negroes to use for support of family. Daus: JENNETTY, POLLY W., PERMELIA and ELIZA EDWARDS, each to receive 1 negro out of my estate; SUSAN FAIRCLOTH, ELIZABETH TEAL, MARYANN SIKES, 1 negro each; son: ELI W. EDWARDS, gray mare; son: LEVI W. EDWARDS, mare, feather bed & furniture; son: JOHN S. EDWARDS, 1 negro and furniture.

Sons: ELI and LEVI EDWARDS shall have my land. . . .take
care of mother. Exr: AMOS WOOTTEN, SR., ELI W. EDWARDS,
LEVI W. EDWARDS. Wit: JOEL EDWARDS, MANSEL WOOTTEN,
AMOS WOOTTEN, SR. Caveated at May Ct., 1843 by BASSETT
SIKES and WILLIAM FAIRCLOTH. Nov. Ct., 1843. Jury:
PETER E. KNIGHT, JOEL GARDNER, JOHN BARFIELD, STEPHEN
COKER, THOMAS GRIMES, SIMON JONES, WILLIAM PIPPIN,
JAMES HINTON, WILLIE BRASWELL, WILLIAM H. HINES, JAMES
PITT, and ELISHA LANDING found the Will of SILEY
EDWARDS signed by him and it was ordered recorded.

EDWARDS, STOURTON (STANTON ?)
Oct. 14, 1783. Feb. Ct., 1784. Wife & Extx: ANN,
life estate, she to barter and sell to benefit children
with advice of JOSEPH EDWARDS, son of JOSEPH. Daus:
SARAH, ELIZABETH, JEANE, ANN; son: KENLIN HARRISON
EDWARDS; dau: JEAN, negro boy. Wit: JOHN DELVIN, JOHN
GOODMAN.

ELLINER, FRANCIS
July 13, 1769. Aug. Ct., 1769. Wife: HONOUR, life
estate in property, not hindering my 2 sons selling land
in any other place. Sons: WILLIAM, 100 A plantation I
purchased from GEORGE WIMBERLEY N side of Tar River,
another tract containing 440 A known as Cold Springs,
on GEORGE WIMBERLEY'S line, corner of COLEMAN'S Pocosin,
to AMOS COTTON'S path, at the road, to a pond, to
SAVAGE'S line; THOMAS and FRANCIS, the remainder of
said 440 A Cold Springs land. Friend: SHERWOOD HAYWOOD,
all money, bills, notes, bonds, on book accts. until
sons are of age, or can lay out money in negroes. In
case HAYWOOD should be robbed, he not to make good to
Estate. Estate to be divided between wife and 3 sons.
Exr: SHERWOOD HAYWOOD. Wit: JACOB DICKINSON, GEORGE
WIMBERLY, DANIEL WOODARD.

ELLINER, JAMES
Jan. 19, 1845. Feb. Ct., 1845. Bk. F, pp 318-20.
I wish my Executor to pick and pack my cotton, dispose
of all perishable property that can be spared from
plantation, reserving sufficient provisions for benefit
of my hands for the year; all hands to remain present
year, to make crop and complete engagement entered into

with PATRICK McDOWELL. Executor to pass over to
COFFIELD KING my negro man Eli the first of January for
duration of Eli's life. Dau: of my dec'd wife:
MARGARET CROMWELL, 10 negroes obtained by my marriage
with my last wife, MARTHA CROMWELL. Residue to sons of
my friend, PATRICK McDOWELL, to wit: JOHN, WILLIAM and
ELISHA McDOWELL. Exr: PATRICK McDOWELL, PHEASANTER
SUGG. Wit: R. HARRISON, G. A. MEEKS (WEEKS ?).

ELLINOR, WILLIAM
    Mar. 16, 1798. May Ct., 1798. Wife & Extx: SARAH,
lend land and plantation whereon I formerly lived,
called "The Old Place"; also Tavern and land joining
thereto; 2 horses, utensils, furniture, cattle, hogs,
and 3 negroes. ELIZABETH GRIFFIS, ₤ 10 current
money. Son: JAMES, 100 A on Tar River, 10 ₤ currency.
Dau: CATEY, 3 cattle, 2 cows and 1 yearling; Linning
wheel, woman's saddle, 1 chest, and ₤ 10 currency.
Son: ETHELRED, land and plantation where I formerly
lived; negro girl; if he dies, reversion to son
BENJAMIN. After ETHELRED arrives at 21 yrs., a brandy
still; until that time I lend use of said still to my
son & exr: JAMES, and SARAH (my wife). "Still to be
in same place she now stands and applied towards sav-
ing their own liquor". Son: BENJAMIN, the Tavern
Place, 50 A; 1 horse, colt, negro girl. If BENJAMIN
die without heirs, Tavern land falls to son ETHELRED;
if both deceased, to son JAMES. Daus: SALLY, furniture,
saddle, lining wheel, and 10 ₤ currency; CHRISSY, walnut table; HONOUR, 1 seel skin trunk. Wit: JOHN
DILLARD, F. PHILIPS.

ELLIS, COFFIELD
    Jan. 28, 1854. Feb. Ct., 1854. Bk. G, p 51. Wife:
PENINAH, bequeath 24 slaves, reversion, 2 to WILLIAM.
Remainder to SALLY & LOUISA, tract land known as the
NANCY Tract division of ELI AMERSON'S (dec'd) land,
tract known as NATHAN low grounds, also tract on which
I live on S prong of Tasthen (?) Branch, piney tract
on White Oak Swamp, known as ROGERS Land. Reversion
to son WM. Son & Exr: WILLIAM, all remaining land including that on Bear Branch and Panther Branch, my son
to complete canal to Toisnot Swamp, also 2 slaves; dau:

SALLY, wife of WILLIAM BARNES, $1000; dau: LOUISA, wife
of JAMES BARNES, $1000; niece: UNITY ELLIS; JAMES M.
COBB, if he continue to live with my wife until he is
of age, he is to have horse, bridle and saddle. Wit:
MACON MOYE, REUBIN BYNUM.

ELLIS, ELISHA (SR.)
     Sept. 12, 1824. Nov. Ct., 1824. Bk. F, p 25.
Wife: CHARITY ELLIS, plantation, life estate, horse,
3 cows and calves. Reversion to all Chil: ELIZABETH
RITTER; DENNIS ELLIS; son & exr: JOHN ELLIS; POLLY
JENKINS; ELISHA ELLIS; son & exr: LEWIS ELLIS;
EMILLIA ELLIS; LITTLE NANCY STALLING; CHARLES ELLIS.
Wit: JO P. PITT, JOHN RITTER.

ELLIS, JEAN (JANE ?)
     Sept. 12, 1815. Probated Sept. 26. Recorded Nov.
4, 1815. Bk. E, p 118. Dau: MARY OWEN; gr. son (?):
ELIJAH OWEN, 7 head cattle with balance of worldly
estate. No Executor. No Witnesses.

ELLIS, JOSEPH
     Sept. 13, 1802. May Ct., 1803. Son & Exr: JOHN,
negro man; son: EDWIN, negro girl; son & exr: WILLIAM,
negro man, 2 cows; son: BENJAMIN, negro man. Residue
divided. Wit: AMOS JOHNSTON, PETER HINES.

ELLIS, UNITY
     Dec. 26, 1817. Feb. Ct., 1818. Bk. E, p 176.
Son: WILLEY, all my land; gr. dau: UNITY ELLIS, "All
money from SPICEY ELLIS' Eastait"; 1 feather bed and
furniture, and stid of ELIZABETH ELLIS'; PIETY BARNES,
my mare; son (?): COFEL ELLIS, 1 basin and 2 boles,
$30; SPICY ELLIS, 1 bason; and 1 bole; my close and my
dau SPICY ELLIS' close to be divided between fore gr.
daus: UNITY, ELIZABETH, SPICY and SALLY ELLIS. All the
rest of my estait to be divided amongst all my sons.
Exr: ELI AMASON. Wit: ELEANER AMASON, SALLY JONES,
PIETY BARNES.

ELLIS, WILLIAM (SR.)
     Dec. 24, 1812. Feb. Ct., 1813. Bk. E, p 51. Wife
& Extx: UNITY, use of plantation in fork of the Mill

on Panther's Branch, and Toisnot Swamp, and on N side
of Branch; reversion to son: WILLIE, also 3 negroes
and their increase, horse, briddle, saddle and brandy
still. Son: COFFIELD, land between Contentney and S
side Mill Branch adjoining lands belonging to WOODARD'S
Orphans, JOSEPH COKER and ELI AMASON; also mill on
Panther's Branch, horse bridle and saddle and blacksmith's tools. Son & Exr: DIXON, 1 negro, plantation
where I formerly lived, county of Edgecombe, on waters
of Whiteoak Swamp, also tract adjoining lands of JOHN
WEBB and JETHRO BARNES. Son: JOHN, plantation and land
on main road from Tarboro to Stanton's Bridge, land I
had of EDWARD MAYO; 100 A, called ROGERS' land, I had
of JESSE ROGERS, and RICHARD GAY, adjoining lands of
JOSHUA JOHNSTON; and 1 negro. Son: GRAY, 1 negro,
225 A land near Tarboro adjoining lands of HENRY HUNTER
and EDWIN DANCY provided he has heirs, otherwise, land
near Tarboro, I give and bequeath to my son JONATHAN.
Son & Exr: JONATHAN, 1 negro, plantation, called the
THOMPSON land on main road from Tarboro to Greenville,
I had of STERLING WALLER and $1000. 150 A; dau: SPICY,
100 A tract on Toisnot Swamp, on main road from Stanton's Bridge to Tarboro, 4 negroes, horse, bridle,
chest, and trunk. Wit: HENRY I. J. RUFFIN, JOSEPH COX.

ETHERIDGE, CADER (CATOR ?)
     Apr. 18, 1825. May Ct., 1825. Bk. F, p 37. Wife:
CEDDY, land lying on a large Branch on lines between
me and my brother FREDERICK ETHERIDGE and along line
to SIMON EDWARDS; cattle, sheep, cows, all live stock,
household, kitchen furn., etc. Exr: THOMAS THORN
(HORN ?). Wit: JOHN W. BARNES, GERALDRUS SHERROD.

ETHERIDGE, CALEB
     May 20, 1826. Nov. Ct., 1826. Bk. F, p 63. Wife:
MARY, negroes, horse, 2 cows and calves, sow and pigs,
desk and buffet, 1 chest, small trunk, table and 6
chairs, case knives and forks, 2 basins, 2 dishes,
skillet, griddle; 2 weeding hoes, grubbing hoe, side
saddle, riding chair and harness, new still, 5 cider
hogsheads, 5 cider barrels and 1 year's allowance of
provisions; land on S side of GRIFFIN'S Swamp, PACE
tract; part of NICHOLSON Tract to be sold and money

divided. BRADLEY MORRIS and POWELL tracts to be
rented. Dau: MARTHA BUMPASS, wife of JOHN BUMPASS,
her chil. Sons & Exrs: JESSE ETHERIDGE, JAMES
ETHERIDGE. Wit: WILLIAM BELLAMY, CORNELIUS FOREMAN.

EVANS, ABRAHAM
     May 14, 1762. June Ct., 1762. Bk. A, p 95. Wife
& Extx: ELIZABETH, remainder of estate to be divided
between wife and all my chil. Sons & Exrs: JOHN, 250 A
land on Sappony; ABRAHAM, 250 A plantation on Tare
River. Daus: SARAH, LEDY, AMMY and ELIZABETH. Wit:
MOSES ATKINSON, SR., LEDY EVANS, THOS. DIXON ?.

EVANS, CHARLES
     June 1, 1759. June Ct., 1759. Son: JACOB, parcel
of land in Beaufort Co. which JEFFERS (?) claims a
title to. Sons: BENJAMIN and CHARLES, land on Tar
River and Town Creek. Dau: MARY BETTIS. Gr. chil:
CHARLES EVANS, son of BENJAMIN; JOHN EVANS, son of
CHARLES and ELIZABETH; ANN EVANS, dau of CHARLES and
ELIZABETH. Wit: JOHN TISON, CHARLES EVANS, JR.

EVANS, SUSANNA
     Aug. 2, 1803. Nov. Ct., 1807. Bk. D, p 296.
Mother & Extx: ANN SPUIL (SPRUILL ?). Wit: PETER
HINES, PETER HINES, JR.

EVENS, ELIZABETH
     Feb. 28, 1766. Oct. Ct., 1766. Bk. A, p 155.
Estate to be equally divided between my 5 chil; sons
& exrs: JOHN and ABRAHAM; daus: SARAH EVENS, LEADY
BALLARD, ELIZABETH EVINS. Wit: RACHEL PRICE, TOBIAS
SEELEY, SHERWOOD HAYWOOD.

EVERITT, EADIETH
     Mar. 23, 1834. Feb. Ct., 1837. Friend: FREDERICK
DAVENPORT. Son: JAMES EVERITT, all my property of
every description after debts are paid. The balance
of my chil have received their shares. Exr: JOHN
MOORING. Wit: FREDERICK TAYLOR, WILLIAM L. MOORING.

EVERITT, KETON
     Jan. 8, 1823. May Ct., 1823. Bk. E, p 326. Daus:

SALLY FAIRCLOTH, ELIZABETH EVERITT, MARY DOWDEN
(DARDEN ?). NANCY SUMERELL; sons: JOHN, EADY, LEHUR (?),
JORDAN, KETON, JOSHUA (Exr). Divide equally. Exr:
son-in-law, NEWSO (?) (NEWSON) FAIRCLOTH. Wit: PHILIP
DUNFORD, THOMAS DUNFORD.

EVERITT, SILAS
    Nov. 21, 1835. No Probate date. Wife: REBECCA,
100 A bought of JAMES LEWIS; 205 A bought of JAMES
LEWIS and HOWELL LEWIS whereon I live; lend her 173 A
land left by my father, JERRYSIAH (JEREMIAH) EVERITT,
adjoining ALLEN WARREN and others. Bequeath 1/2 all
negroes except Ned, 1/2 all money, hogs and horses,
1/2 all remaining property with exception of land I
have not disposed of. (?) SUSANNAH M. W. P. BROWN, negro Ned and furniture. Neph: KENNETH EVERITT, 370 A
land adjoining ALLEN WARREN left me by my father at
death of my wife. Remaining property divided between
4 sisters: POLLY MASON, MILLY WATERS, DEBROUGH STUBBS,
PENELOPE BOWEN. Exr: WM. C. LEIGH. Wit: WILLIS KNIGHT,
ALLEN COBB.

EVINS, ELIZABETH (Wife of ABRAHAM EVANS ?)
    Feb. 28, 1766. No Probate date. Son-in-law: DAVID
PRIDGEN, "heffer"; son & exr: JOHN EVINS; son & exr:
ABRAHAM; daus: SARAH EVINS, LEADY (LEDY) BALLARD,
ELIZABETH EVINS. Remainder, divide equally. Wit:
RACHEL PRICE, TOBIAS SEALEY. Note: SEAL is interesting.

EWING, GUSTAVUS
    Nov. 11, 1777. Feb. Ct., 1778. Wife & Extx:
JUDITH, 1/3 estate; son: JOHN EWING; dau: ELIZABETH
EWING, living in Virginia, eastern shore. Remainder
divided equally between 2 chil. Exr: SIMON PARKER,
JAMES CAIN. Wit: JAMES KNIGHT, ARTHUR FOREMAN.

EXUM, BARNEBY
    Apr. 9, 1792. Nov. Ct., 1796. Eldest Son:
WILLIAMSON, all land provided he pay son WILLIAM 1/2
value of land; dau: SIMMA; remainder divided between
3 chil. Exr: NATHAN HARRISS. Wit: MATTHEW KINCHEN,
ELISABETH KINCHEN.

EXUM, ETHELRED.
    Undated. Probated, Aug. Ct., 1779. Wife: RACHEL,
mare, bridle & saddle; lend wife and chil (not named),
slave, horse, filly, mare, all stock of cattle, hogs
and sheep, all household & kitchen furniture, plantation tools - to be kept on plantation until son
ETHELRED becomes 20 yrs, 4 slaves to be hired out.
Land lying between Moore's Swamp & Maple Swamp to be
sold; also horse, mare and barrel of brandy to be sold.
Son: ETHELRED, plantation whereon I live and all adjoining land except I lend 100 A to my daus. so long as
they are unmarried; also to ETHELRED, mare, still, gun,
bridle & saddle. Exr: WILLIAM BELLAMY, JAMES WILLIAMS,
ETHELRED PHILIPS. Wit: ETHELRED PHILIPS, EXUM PHILIPS,
MATTHEW KINCHEN.

EXUM, JOHN
    Jan. 23, 1775. Apr. Ct., 1775. Son: BENJAMIN, 1/7
of slaves, plantation whereon I live, purchased of
THOMAS BROWN & JOHN BROWN on Swift Creek; gr. son:
BENJAMIN, plantation purchased from JAMES CARTER, lands
purchased from JAMES SPIER, and tract joining CHARLES
PORTER, WILLIAM GEORGE, on Hugh's Marsh, adjoining
JOHN MIALS and WILLIAM KINCHEN; son: BARNEBY, L 20 Va.
Currency; dau: SARAH MIALS, wife of THOMAS MIALS, 10 s;
son: (dec'd) THOMAS - MARY EXUM, widow of son THOMAS,
1/6 of remainder of estate to be divided between her
and her chil. Son & Exr: ETHELRED; remainder estate
divided between son ETHELRED, gr. son BENJAMIN and
daus: SARAH PHILIPS, MARTHA JOHNSON and ELIZABETH
WILLIAMS. Gr. son: BENJAMIN to pay to his sisters L 5
cash. . .TABITHA EXUM, MARTHA EXUM, L 5. Exr: son-in-
law, JAMES WILLIAMS. Wit: WILLIAM KINCHEN, ETHELRED
PHILIPS, SARAH KINCHEN, REBEKAH POPE.

EXUM, JOHN
    Oct. 29, 1805. Nov. Ct., 1806. Bk. D, p 339.
Wife: PRISCILLA, to have entire estate until GREEN
reaches 20 yrs. Sons: EDWIN and GREEN. Exr: GREEN
LEWIS, BARTHOLOMEW LEWIS. Wit: THOMAS BANKS, JAMES
PHILIPS, GREEN LYNCH.

EXUM, MICAJAH
Apr. 11, 1785. Aug. Ct., 1785. Son & Exr: JOHN; son: WILLIAM; dau: SUSANAH; sons: MICAJAH, THOMAS and BARNABY. Exr: FIGURES LEWIS, NATHAN HARRIS. Wit: EXUM LEWIS, CALEB COKER, WILLIAM EXUM.

EXUM, WILLIAM
Oct. 26, 1790. Feb. Ct., 1795. Wife & Extx: MARY, lend plantation whereon I live and 6 negroes; give 1/2 all debts or moneys owed me; lend 1/2 stock of all kinds, also household & kitchen furniture and plantation utensils. Dau: SARAH BELLAMY, 4 negroes, 1/2 stock to receive mother's part at her death; gr. son: WILLIAM BELLAMY, 4 negroes. Exr: son-in-law, JOHN BELLAMY. Wit: MATTHEW KINCHEN, WILLIAM ROLLINGS.

EXUM, WILLIAMSON
Dec. 13, 1802. Feb. Ct., 1803. Wife: SALLEY, whole estate for life. Reversion to 3 chil: POLLY, BRYAN and WILLIAM. Exr: WILLIE JONES. Wit: WYATT BALLARD, LEVI DENTON.

FAIRCLOTH, NEWSOM
July 3, 1830. Feb. Ct., 1831. Bk. F, p 123. My youngest sons: JOHN and NEWSOM FAIRCLOTH, all the lands I now possess; should either die without heirs his part shall go to my son BRIGHT FAIRCLOTH. Residue divided between my 10 daus: LUCY, SUSAN, FEREBE, JENNY, CHERRY, WINNEFRED, ANNY, METILDY, WRITTA (RITA), WRIDLEY (RIDLY). Exr: JOHN R. SCARBOROUGH. Wit: R. T. EAGLES. (illegible).

FARMER, BENJAMIN
Mar. 16, 1825. Feb. Ct., 1827. Bk. F, p 65. Wife: ELIZABETH, 6 negroes, household & kitchen furniture, farming utensils; 225 A including DELOACH tract, also all on N side Tarborough Rd., which belonged to NEWBERN Tract; reversion to WILLIAM, 2 horses, 4 cows and calves, 4 ewes. Son & Exr: WILLIAM D., land N side Harmony Swamp; son: BRASSWELL, 214 A N side Toisnot Swamp joining lands of MOSES FARMER and ARTHUR D. FARMER, being part of land drawn by my wife & me by death of WILLIAM DEW. Dau of BENJ. FARMER: SALLY

HOLLOWELL, 40 S. Heirs of JOHN BARNES: THOMAS, BETSY, SALLY, BUDY, DEMPSEY, NANCY, $24 to be divided equally between the 6 of them. Balance of negroes be divided between following Heirs: sons, ABSOLOM, DEW, BRASWELL, JACOB, ARTHUR D. and WILLIAM D. FARMER; daus: BEEDY, WHITE, NANCY DEW and ELIZABETH AMASON. Wit: ISAAC F. WOOD, HANSEL D. GRIFFITH.

FARMER, BRASWELL of Lawrence Co. Tenn.
May 29, 1827. Filed in Robertson Co., Tenn. Nov. Ct., 1827 and in Edgecombe Co., N. C., 1853. Wife: NANCY FARMER, all that belongs to me after WILLIAM WHITE, my bro-in-law, and DEW FARMER are paid for their trouble in handling my business, and $1 to all and every one of my bros. and sisters in the State of North Carolina. Exr: WILLIAM WHITE. Wit: JOHN D. FARMER, AXUM FARMER.

FARMER, ELIZABETH
Jan. 29, 1844. Nov. Ct., 1852. Bk. F, p 490. Dau: ELIZABETH, tract of land on N side Toisnot Swamp on lines of MOSES FARMER and ARTHUR D. FARMER, Dec'd, it being a part of land which fell to me by death of my bro, WM. DEW. Residue to lawful heirs. Exr: LARRY D. FARMER, friend. Wit: JAMES D. BARNES, LARRY DEW.

FARMER, ISAAC
Nov. 13, 1800. Feb. Ct., 1805. Bk. D., p 220. Wife: (not named), 1 slave, horse, feather bed & furniture; lend her 1 slave, reversion to child she is supposed to be pregnant with; 100 A where JOHN ROSS lives, to go to unborn child. Property my wife brought with her when we were married may be sold to pay her debts, remainder to be hers. Sons: JOHN, 400 A including plantation whereon I live, also 1 slave; JOSIAH, 400 A, 1 slave; dau: PATIENCE, 1 slave; son & exr: ASAEL, money due me from JAMES WILLIAMS. Exr: bro, BENJAMIN FARMER. Wit: WM. BLACKBURN, WILLIAM DEW, JEREMIAH BATEMAN.

FARMER, JESSE
July 9, 1808. Aug. Ct., 1812. Bk. E, p 38. Wife: (not named), lend 1/3 plantation, 4 slaves, all stock,

furniture, utensils; reversion to son and exr: JOSEPH,
also remainder estate. Exr: CHARLES COLEMAN. Wit:
none. Proven in Ct., by oaths of FREDERICK COTTEN,
SPENCER S. HART.

FARMER, MOSES
     No Date. Nov. Ct., 1844. Bk. F, p 317. Wife:
ELIZABETH. Sons: MOSES; SAMUEL B., land whereon he
lives to be sold and added to estate for $1250 if
possible. Exr. to complete contract made with JOHN
HARPER, relative to dressing mill stones and putting
in trunk and wheel in DEW'S Mill, also charge LARRY D.
FARMER and JONATHAN DEW to guard their proportionable
parts for same. Remaining estate divided between wife
and children except LARRY D., until they become equal
with that given son and exr: LARRY D. Dau: JERUSIA;
sons: JAMES, JOHN A. and WALTER. Bro: SAMUEL FARMER.
Wit: RICHARD SHORT, WILLIAM D. FARMER.

FARMER, SAMUEL
     Mar. 21, 1814. Apr. Ct., 1817. Bk. E, p 158.
Wife: JERUSHA, plantation whereon I live, remainder of
slaves. Son & Exr: SAMUEL, 1 slave, $100; dau: RHODA,
1 slave; son & exr: MOSES, 1 slave, land on Miry Swamp,
known as Parish Place; dau: ANN SHARP, 1 slave; son:
ISAAC, 1 slave, plantation whereon I live after his
mother's death. Wit: _____? FARMER, ISAAC FARMER.

FARMER, THOMAS
     Nov. 16, 1784. Probate Date, 1785. Sons: THOMAS,
128 A plantation whereon I live; JOSEPH, 250 A (This
being newly entered); sons & exrs: JESSE, 250 A (This
being newly entered), and JOSHUA. Wit: JOSHUA FARMER,
AZIEL BARNES, DANIEL HIGHSMITH.

FELTS, WILLIAM
     Sept. 9, 1853. Feb. Ct., 1854. Bk. G., p 92.
Eldest son: JAMES W., $5; sons: JOHN B., $200; GEORGE
G., $150; Eldest dau: ELIZABETH M. SMITH, wife of
SYPA (?) SMITH, $500; Youngest son: GARRY P., land
whereon I live provided 3 youngest daus. shall be allowed to live with him and be supported from products
of the lands until they marry. Daus: PENELOPE J.

FELTS, $400; SARAH (SARAH ?) N. FELTS, $300; LAURA F.
FELTS, youngest dau: $400. Residue divided between
son: WILLIAM W.; dau: MARY A. EDMONDSON, wife of
RICHARD EDMONDSON; NANCY M. BERGMAN, wife of JOHN
BERGMAN and 3 unmarried daus. and youngest son. Exr:
JOSHUA SPEIGHT. Wit: R. C. D. BEAMON, STEPHEN SPEIGHT.

FERGUSON, ISAAC
    Mar. 6, 1764. July Ct., 1764. Wife & Extx:
ELIZABETH, lend 1 slave, also lend remainder my estate
her natural life. Son: JOHN, ₺ 12 when he reaches 21
yrs. Wit: WILLIAM KERBY, DANNEL LESLEY.

FERGUSSON, JAMES
    Oct. 1, 1763 or 68. Feb. Ct., 1769. Wife & Extx:
MARGRIT, use of estate during widowhood. Sons: JAMES,
JOHN and dau: SUSANNA, 10 S sterling each; sons: JOSEPH,
plantation whereon I live; BENJAMIN, 1 slave; daus:
MARY, MARTHA, EADY, ELIZABETH, 1 S sterling each. Wit:
JOHN TANNER, JAMES (FURGUSON ?), EDWARD MOORE.

FLANAGIN, JOHN
    Jan. 3, 1793. Aug. Ct., 1793 Wife: MARGARET;
Chil. by CHARITY MITCHEL: CORNELIUS, MARGARET, EDWARD,
DAVID, JAMES, JOHN, MATTHEW and CHARITY MITCHEL. Lend
to wife MARGARET and CHARITY MITCHEL, all my estate,
provided they live "quiet and contented together." In
case they do not, they shall have their part separate
and distinct from each other. After their deaths plantation to be sold & proceeds divided equally among
chil. of CHARITY MITCHEL begotten of my body. Exr:
CORNELIUS MITCHEL, EDWARD MITCHEL. Wit: WILLIAM
COTTEN, H. HARRISON, FREDERICK COTTEN.

FLEMING, CHARLES
    Nov. 27, 1824. Mar. Ct., 1829. Bk. F, p 105.
Wife & Extx: ELIZABETH. Exr: WILLIAM DRAKE. Wit:
HENRY DRAKE, LEVI DRAKE.

FLEMING, FREDERICK
    Sept. 4, 1855. Nov. Ct., 1855. Bk. G, p 116.
Wife: MARY ANN, whole estate, reversion to chil:
BALZARAH, ABSALOM, LEONORA, ANN ARSENA, GEORGE ELLA

(dau ?), and if there be another within 10 mo. after my death. Adm: AMOS W. COBB. Wit: A. B. NOBLES, E. E. COBB. Note: filed as "F. D. L. FLEMING'S Will."

FLEMING, WILLIS
Apr. 9. 1850. Feb. Ct., 1855. Bk. G, p 96. Wife: SARAH, 1/3 of all lands, dwelling and out houses, 8 slaves during widowhood; dau: ARCENA L. SKINNER, wife of ANDREW, slaves and property revert to next of kin. Dau-in-law, NANCY ANN FLEMING, wife of my son JESSE L. FLEMING, in trust of JOHN NORFLEET, 220 A tract of land in Halifax County, and 1 negro; reversion to family. Dau: ZILLA ANN PEEL, wife of HENRY W. PEEL, property left in trust of JOHN NORFLEET, If no heirs, reversion to my legal heirs; sons: FREDERICK D. L. and NINNIAN B. FLEMING, young negro each, etc; dau: SALLY ANN F. FLEMING, negro girl, etc. Exr: FREDERICK D. LITTLE, WILLIAM THIGPEN. Wit: WM. H. HINES, JOHN R. HINES. Codicil, witnessed by J. D. ROUNTREE and GEO. HOWARD, JR. SARAH FLEMING qualified, entered $10,000 Security Bond with WILLIAM THIGPEN and BENNETT PITT. Note: A very long and complicated will, disposing of much property.

FLOWERS, EDWARD, of Elizabeth Parish.
June 19, 1775. May Ct., 1778. Sons & Exrs: HENRY and EDWARD, 10 S Proc. money each; dau: MARY TISDALL, walnut chest, bought of ROB'T SHEFFERT. Son & Exr: JOHN FLOWERS, remainder of estate. Wit: DUNCAN LAMON, ARCHIBALD LAMON, CHARLES WILLIAMS.

FLOWERS, JACOB
July 14, 1766. Oct. Ct., 1766. Wife: MARY, lend 4 slaves, mare, horse, 11 cows and calves, 17 hogs, also lend plantation whereon I live. Son & Exr: JACOB, 7 slaves, still & worm, residue of stock; daus: ELIZABETH CALHOON, 3 slaves, 4 cows and calves; PRISCILLA CALHOON, 3 slaves and a cow and calf; gr. son: HARDY FLOWERS, tract. on N side Tarr River•the Great Branch, Main Road that leads to Lamon's Ferry, 1 slave, 4 cows and calves, 4 sows and pigs, bed & furniture and 1 horse. Exr: son-in-law: JOHN CALHOON. Wit: EDWARD MOORE, SAMUEL WILLIAMS, JOHN TANNER.

FLOWRY, LAZARUS (FLOWERS?)
No date. May Ct., 1799. Wife: WINNEY, mare, 2
cows, 2 sows and pigs, "lining" wheel, "wolling"
wheel. Lend residue estate for widowhood or until
youngest comes of age 21 yrs. Then to be equally
divided between 7 chil. Sons: JESSE, all land in
state of Cumberland; WILLIAM, land on Cabbin (Cabin)
Branch, joining BENJ. THORNALL; RICHARD; EPHRAIM;
BENJAMIN; dau: MARY; son: ENOCH. Exr: WILLIAM ELLIS,
JACOB POWELL, JOHN WILLIFORD, JAMES BARNES. Wit:
JOHN WILLIAMS, THOMAS WILLIFORD.

FLOYD, FRANCIS
Dec. 30, 1760. Mar. Ct., 1761. Wife & Extx:
ELIZABETH, Use of plantation, land & mill during widowhood, bed and furniture. Son & Exr: PARRAMAN
(PARAMAN). Note: Old's Abstracts, PARHAM. Reversion in
plantation whereon I live with mill and 140 A on N
side, Swift Creek, and mare; chil: CYRUS, remainder of
land and mare; DELILAH; BENJ.; SADISHA; ELIZABETH. Wit:
SAMUEL HARRIS, MATTHEW LOWRY, JR., WILLIAM DRAKE.

FOORT, ELIZABETH (FORT)
June 4, 1814. Aug. Ct., 1817. Bk. E, p 155. Gr.
dau: NANCY FOORT, entire estate. Exr: JAMES GREY,
JEREMIAH BATTLE. Wit: HENRY COTTEN, JAMES GREY.

FOORT, GEORGE (FORT?)
July 1761. Dec. Ct., 1761. Wife & Extx: MARY, use
of plantation whereon I live, reversion to son JACOB,
use of 2 negroes, reversion to sons JOSEPH & JACOB,
give 1 slave. Son & Exr: ELIAS, cow and calf; Son:
JACOB, plantation whereon I live, still to be shared
with my son JOSEPH; Daus: MARY BUNN, ELIZABETH DAVIS,
MARTHA BARNES, cow and calf each; Dau: ORFEE BARNES,
cow and calf, also 150 A land lying in Dobbs & Johnston Co. Son: JOSEPH, tract land surveyed by JOSEPH
LANE, also 100 A I had of my brother, ELIAS FOORT;
Dau: PRISCILLA, land surveyed by CHAS. YOUNG lying in
Dobs & Johnston Co.; Gr. son: JACOB, son of JOHN
FOORT, dec'd, part of tract of land on Hacher's Swamp
taken up by BENJAMIN BUNN, also 3 cows and calves and
mare. Exr: BENJAMIN BUNN. Wit: WM. HAYWOOD, ELIAS

FOORT, GEORGE LINCH.

FOREHAND, SOLOMON
    Mar. 3, 1798. Aug. Ct., 1802. Son: AMOS; Son and
Exr: DREWRY, to both sons all land upon head of Ruty
(Rooty?) Branch it being plantation where I formerly
lived. Son: JORDAN, land that lies on road where
SHADRICH SCARBOROUGH lived, 1 slave, horse and colt;
?: CLOAH ANDREW, wife of JOSEPH ANDREW; Son: DAVID,
plantation whereon I live, or money to buy one, slave
and horse; Daus: SARAH FURNIVALL, 5 S; RACHEL, 5 S;
SEALY, 1 slave; LYDIA, 1 slave; SUSANNA, 20 S; Exr:
CHARLES DILDAY. Wit: REUBEN ELLIS, JORDAN FOREHAND.
One Exr refusing to qualify, Adm. as granted WM. DRAKE.

FOREMAN, GEORGE
    Dec. 29, 1802. Nov. Ct., 1803. Wife: CRISSE, lend
all land given to JAMES during her natural life, 1
slave, 2 mares, all perishable & personal estate. Sons:
JACOB, 500 A land lying on Whitaker Swamp bought of
ISAAC FOREMAN, also 1/3 low ground on Swift Creek,
horse, cow and calf and 1 slave; CORNELIUS, lower part
of land bought of JACOB KNIGHT on Reedy Branch between
JACOB KNIGHT and MOORE KNIGHT on Swift Creek and Whiteoak Swamp adjoining lands of EXUM LEWIS, also 2 slaves,
horse, cow and calf, pewter dish, 1 bason and 6 "plaits"
also ½ profit from young "orched" on JAMES FOREMAN'S
land, provided he takes care of orched & helps to save
fruit until JAMES comes of age. Son: JAMES, all remaining land, containing upper part plantation next to
TIMOTHY M. NICHOLSON'S land, also 1/3 low ground adjoining T. M. NICHOLSON, 1 slave, 1 pewter dish, bason,
6 plaits, cow and calf, bed and furn.; Daus: SALLY,
slave when she marries or comes of age, horse, colt,
cow and calf, pewter dish, bason, 6 plaits; ELIZABETH,
cow and calf, pewter dish, bason, 6 plaits, 10 £ Va.
money when she comes of age or marries, also a sorrel
filly. Exr: CALEB ETHERAGE. Wit: T. W. NICHOLSON,
ADLEY MORRIS, HILLERY MORRIS.

FORT, ELIAS
    Jan. 14, 1761. Mar. Ct., 1761. Wife: CATTRON
(According to OLDS Abstracts, CATHERINE), lend entire

estate during widowhood at end of which divide as
follows: Son: JOSEPH, 2 slaves; Son & Exr: WILLIAM,
100 A on Tar River beginning at Chappel Door, also
170 A on opposite side of river, 2 slaves; Son & Exr:
ELIAS, plantation on which I live, 3 slaves, cyder
still; dau: SARAH WIMBERLEY, 2 slaves; Gr. son: JACOB
DICKENSON, cow and calf. Residue divided between 3
sons, JOSEPH, WILLIAM, and ELIAS. Wit: BENJ. HART,
AMOS COTTEN, SARAH HUBBARD.

FORT, JANE
Mar. 23, 1818. Nov. Ct., 1822. Bk. E, p 314. Dau:
LUCY RUFFIN, $1, residue to be divided between sons
WM. & EDWIN; Daus: CRESSY BROWNE, 1 saddle, $1; JANE
ELLINOR, $1; Son: EDWIN FORT, horse, colt. Exr. Bro:
THOMAS DICKINSON. Wit: FREDERICK PHILIPS, HENRY BRYAN.

FORT, JOHN
Feb. 15, 1761. Mar. Ct., 1761. Son: JACOB, land on
Hatcher's Swamp, all money, 1 slave, furniture, all
horses, mares and cattle. In case he has no lawful
heirs, estate goes to brothers. Bros: JOSEPH FORT,
JACOB FORT. Exr: Father, GEORGE FORT and BENJ. BUNN.
Wit: WILLIAM JOHNSON, THOS (?) UNDERWOOD, SOLOMON
BRACEWELL.

FORT, JOHN
Apr. 22, 1776. May Ct., 1780. Wife & Extx: (not
named), all land and residue estate lent her during
her life. Reversion of land to sons. Dau: ELIZABETH,
slave, cow and calf, sow and pigs, yew and lam, black
warnut table, 2 dishes, 2 basons, 6 plates, all new;
2 iron pot, large pine chest, warnut wheal, horse and
sadale and 5 S; Son & Exr: WILLIAM, 5 S Proc. money;
Sons: JOHN, still (other two sons to have use as long
as they wish); FREDERICK, 40 L current Va. money. Wit:
XPHER (CHRISTOPHER) HAYNES, WM. NOBLEN, DAVID HOLLAND.

FORT, JOSEPH
July 9, 1790. Feb. Ct., 1791. Bk. 3, p 163. Wife:
ELIZABETH, use of plantation and all land during widowhood, reversion to son GEORGE, the plantation
whereon I live, it being on road from T____t's Bridge

131

to Tarborough adjoining JAMES BRASWELL, Herrick Creek,
Raccoon Branch, ISHAM HINES to ELIAS FORT'S line. Lend
wife use of all slaves, reversion to children. Sons:
GEORGE, plantation whereon I live; JOHN, other plantation and remainder of land. Each dau (not named)
when marry, 2 cows and calves, horse, value of 10 L,
1 saddle. Exr: JOHN BATTLE, WILLIAM ROBERT GRAY. Wit:
JAMES WILLIFORD, CHARLES GRAY,_____? MANN.

FORT, MARY
     June 3, 1782. Aug. Ct., 1782. Sons: GARRY, colt;
LEWIS, 5 slaves. If these 2 sons should die before
maturity theirs to be divided between brother LEWIS
BARNES and SARAH, the wife of ELIAS FORT. Gr. daus:
ESTHER and KATY FORT, daus of ELIAS and SARAH FORT;
saddle; my wearing apparel. Exr: GEORGE LINCH, ELIAS
FORT. Wit: WILLIAM FORT, NOAH SUGG, DANIEL COTTEN.

FORT, MICAJA
     Feb. 14, 1799. Feb. Ct., 1799. Wife: ANN, 3 slaves;
Son: JOSEPH JOHN, 2 slaves. Bros: DAVID FORT, ELIAS
FORT, SPEAR FORT. Exr: DAVID COFFIELD, BENJAMIN
COFFIELD. Wit: STEPHEN W. CARNEY, RICHARD (?) CARNEY.

FOUNTAIN, HENRY
     Jan. 28, 1797. Feb. Ct., 1797. Chil: SALLY WIATT,
ELIZABETH SPEAR; HENRY and THOMAS, 10 S each; Son:
WILLIAM, all remaining estate. Exr: Bros, JAMES
FOUNTAIN, STARLING DIGGES. Wit: JAMES BRYAN, STARLING
DIGGES.

FOUNTAIN, JAMES
     May 1, 1824. May Ct., 1824. Bk. F, p 19. Estate
left to children of HENRY ADAMS: JAMES, MARGARET,
ALEXANDER and MARTHA ANN ADAMS. Gdn. of Chil: RICHMOND
DOZIER. Exr: FIGURES PHILIPS. Wit: JOHN POPE, HENRY
ADAMS.

FOUNTAIN, LODERICK
     Feb. 24, 1849, May Ct., 1850. Wife & Extx: lend
all estate; reversion to children. Son: RICHARD; Dau:
EMMILA illegible; Son: LAWRENCE, illegible; Dau: MARY
ELIZABETH; Son: ALMOND. Wit: WILBUR BRADLEY. Not pro-

ven; rejected by court. See Minutes May Term, 1850.

FOXALL, JOHN
   Nov. 1, 1789. No probate date. Wife: NANCY, horse,
bridle, saddle, cow and calf, sow and pigs, ewe and
lambs, lend 1 slave; reversion to son ROBERT, 2 slaves,
and residue, reversion to ROBERT and SARAH. Exr:
THOMAS FOXALL, BRITAIN BRYANT. Wit: BYTHAL BELL,
ROBERT THORTON.

FOXHALL, THOMAS
   July 6, 1791. Aug. Ct., 1792. Wife: SARAH, give 1
slave, pine Chest, small trunk; woollen wheel, one
pair Cotton Cards, looking glass, teapot, punch bowl,
ewe and lamb, loom, stay and harness, 1 setting chair,
1 qt. bottle, 5 barrels good corn, 300 wt. of pork, 1
breeding sow, pewter porringer, 2 small pewter basons,
6 spoons, small iron pot and rack. I lend 1 slave, 1
pewter dish, 2 plates, 2 case knives, 2 forks, linnen
wheel, washing tub, milk pail, cow and calf; reversion
between JOHN, THOMAS and dau MARY THORNTON. Son & Exr:
JOHN, plantation whereon he lives, purchased of GEORGE
BRYANT, also land lying between JOHN BRYANT, EVIN
BRYANT, BYTHEL BELL, and the Owl Pond Branch, also
small still, worm, and tub, smith's tools, crosscut
saw and 1 slave; Son & Exr: THOMAS, remainder of land,
largest still, worm and tub, best whipsaw, large iron
bound chest, narrow ax, broad hoe, 2 slaves and small
gun; Dau: MARY THORNTON, 1 slave, trading gun and 50 L;
Gr. dau: ANN FOXHALL, 1 slave, 20 L; Gr. dau: SALLY
FOXHALL, 1 slave, 30 L; Gr. dau: POLLY PITT, 1 slave,
40 L; Dau: JOANA SURGERNOR, 1 slave, 50 L, reversion
to her children. Exr: BRITON BRYANT, WILLIAM BELL Wit:
WILLIAM R. GRAY, ELIZABETH FORT, WM. FORT, BYTHAL BELL,
WILLIAM BELL, WHITMILL BELL.

FOXHALL, THOMAS
   Sept. 28, 1793. Feb. Ct., 1798. Wife & Extx: LUCA
(LUCIA); according to Old's Abstracts, LUCY. Lend tract
of land my father bought of MR. LANE, 5 slaves, pott,
tea kettle, coffee pott, set cups and sassers, teapott,
6 silver spoons, 1 case of knifes & forks, 6 pewter
spoons, looking glass, horse, 5 cattle, 2 sows and

pigs, 10 shoats, 6 sheep, 6 chairs, walnut table, chest,
5 barrels corn for her life. If the child she is now
with is boy wish land divided between him and son
WILLIAM; if a girl, land all goes to son WILLIAM. Exr:
BYTHAL BELL, JOHN BELLAMY. Wit: ELIZABETH KINCHEN,
SARAH FOXHALL, SALLY SESSUMS, ANN FOXHALL.

FREEMAN, JOSIAH
     Dec. 28, 1838. Probated 1838. Wife & Extx: SARAH
FREEMAN, ½ home tract bought of JOSEPH DAVIS, PHILIP
CAUSWAY, STERLING WALLER, EDWARD WALLER, MARGARET
WALLER, JESSE PARKER and wife, 829 A; 9 negroes, gig,
harness, 2 mules (her choice), 2 cows, 2 calves, 4
ewes and lambs, 2 sows and pigs, brandy still, sideboard and furniture, 1 doz. Winzer (Windsor) chairs,
carpet, 1 pr. hand irons, her chairs, shovel and tongs,
1 pair cards, one loom, 2 walnut tables, kitchen furniture, $300 in money. Son-in-law: WILLIE SUMMERLIN
and ELIZABETH, his wife, negroes, but should ELIZABETH
die without heirs, said negroes shall be returned to
legal heirs; $2676.00 has been paid my son-in-law,
WILLIE SUMMERLIN, balance of $84 to be paid at my
death. Son-in-law: JAMES BRIDGES and my dau: MILLISON,
his wife, 7 negroes, and $842; Son-in-law: WILLIAM
KNIGHT and my dau: EMERLINA, his wife: 12 negroes; Son
& Exr: JOSEPH JOHN FREEMAN, 643 A tract of land lying
on Fishing Creek which I bought of STEPHEN D. COTTEN,
and 16 negroes, blacksmith tools, sulky and harness,
2 mules, 2 horses, 2 sows and pigs, ½ doz. setting
chairs, brandy still, at SARAH FREEMAN'S death; Gr.
son: AUGUSTUS WHITEHEAD, the remaining half of tract
of land at the death of my beloved wife, SARAH
FREEMAN, 7 negroes, $200 to be applied to his educa-
tion. Gr. chil: The RHODES tract of land bought of
PATEY FLEETWOOD be sold, proceeds divided between chil.
of ELIZABETH SUMMERLIN and MILLISON BRIDGES. Exr:
REDDING SUGG. Wit: JAMES BILBRY, SEN'R, JOSIAH
LAWRENCE.

GADDEY, THOMAS
     July 28, 1787. Nov. Ct., 1788. Bk. 3, p 73. Wife:
LUCIE, plantation and residue of estate for life; Son:
THOMAS, already given land, 5 S; Daus: ELIZABETH

JOLLEY, DRUSILAH COOPER, LUCIE BROWN, ALLEY WARD,
FRANCES GADDEY, JERIAH GADDEY, MERRIAM GADDEY, each
dau. left 5 S. Son & Exr: ITHAMAR, reversion in 164 A
plantation. Exr: Son-in-law, SOLOMON BROWN. Wit: JOHN
ROSS, SR., ELIZABETH ROSS, JOHN ROSS, JR.

GAINER, MARY
Oct. 1751. Nov. Ct., 1751. HESTER GAINER. Sisters:
MARTHA GAINER, LIDDY GAINER, ELIZABETH FORMAN; Bro &
Exr: WILLIAM GAINER. Wit: ARTHUR BELL, MARTHA GAINER,
ESTER BELL.

GAINER, WILLIAM
Mar. 11, 1746. Nov. Ct., 1750. Wife & Extx: HESTER.
Sons & Exrs: WILLIAM and JOSEPH. Daus: MARTHA, LYDDA,
ELIZA, ELIZABETH FOURMAN. Wit: JOHN COLLINS, WILLIAM
BELL, MATTHEW LOWRY.

GARDNER, MARGARET
Nov. 2, 1839. No probate date. Son & Exr: MARTIN,
1 filly; Dau: LIEUCIA (illegible), mare, "wearing re-
parrells", also spotted breeding sow and black milk
cow. Perishable estate to: Daus: PENNY and LYRAH, and
Son, SOLOMON. Wit: L. S. DUNN, ELIE GARDNER.

GARDNER, GEORGE
Dec. 30, 1786. May Ct., 1789. Bk. 3, p 97. Wife:
MARY, use of all land and personal property during
widowhood or life; Son: MARTIN; Daus: MARY SEEBERY,
ANN PITMAN, ZYLPHY WILLIFORD, PHEREBY PITMAN, PHEBE
PROCTOR, 5 S each;Sons: WILLIAM, reversion in plan-
tation whereon I live, also all land I own E side
Great Mill Branch; GEORGE, reversion in all land W
side Great Mill Branch and MARTIN GARDNER'S line;
JULIAN; Dau: LUCREESE, reversion in personal property
divided between 4 youngest chil: WILLIAM, GEORGE,
JULIAN and LUCREESE. Note: Olds Abstracts shows only
MARY, WM. & GEO. Exr: BRITON BRIDGER, THOMAS MERCER.
Wit: RICHARD STROTHER, MARTHA MERCER, JAMES DRAUHON.

GARNER, ABSOLOM
Apr. 17, 1798. Aug. Ct., 1798. Sons: JESSY, plantation called AMBER'S Place, 2 slaves and a cow; JOHN,

3 slaves and a cow; LASENS (LAZARAS), plantation
whereon I live, 2 slaves, 1 cow, 2 slaves, who are to
have 25 A and house where they live to maintain themselves, and are to have all their cattle, hogs, horses
and household prop. Exr: RICHARD CLARK, WILLIAM RUTH.
Wit: SAMUEL NORSWORTHY, JONATHAN GARDNER, DEMPSEY
SKINNER. Exrs refused to administer. WM. DRAKE granted
administration.

GARNER, JOHN
     Sept. 25, 1760. Dec. Ct., 1760. Wife & Extx: MATHA
all working hands & personal estate during widowhood;
Daus: SARAH WRIGHT, 1 slave; JAYN GARNER, 1 slave and
137 A "Manner" plant'n. Son & Exr: JOHN, 1 slave; Sons:
JONATHAN, 1 slave, 100 A where WM. WRIGHT lived. ABSALOM,
1 slave and 100 A lying between 2 bros. Daus: LEDDY, 1
slave; ONNER (HONOR), youngest dau., 1 slave; MATHEW,
5 S; Gr. son: WILLIAM FARCLOATH, 25 S. Wit: WILLIAM
WRIGHT, THOMAS CLARK, REID BOLTEN.

GARNER, SABRA
     July 23, 1800. May Ct., 1801. PEGGY MATHEWSON, 1
slave; ABBY PECK MATHEWSON, 1 slave; Bro. & Exr:
GERALDUS TOOLE, 5 slaves, household furniture and
residue; Sis: JEAN BODDIE, 50 L money, wearing apparel,
1 suit of curtains & Bed Quilts; SABRA HEARN, 50 L
money; Sis: ELIZABETH OBRYAN, 50 L money. Wit: N.
MATHEWSON (NATHAN), P. MATHEWSON.

GATER, SAMUEL (Sr.)
     Feb. 24, 1820. Aug. Ct., 1820. Bk. E, p 236. Wife:
CHLOE, ewes, lambs, 10 geese, cow and calf, pot and
hooks, spinning wheel, sows and pigs, shoats, 12 bbl
corn, skillet, loom & gear, bee hive, 3 powdering tubs,
meal gum (?), washing tub, tray, water pail, 2 chests,
4 rush bottom chairs, 4 boals, 6 plates, 2 dishes, 1
set tea cups & sausers, 2 mugs, pewter dish, 6 puter
spoons, table, stand, case knives and forks, 1 pr.
cotton cards, pr. wool cards, stone jug, 100 wt. cotton
seed, 900 lb. Bacon, weeding hoe, ax, pr. flat irons,
24 lbs. hog lard, 1 gal. bason, frying pan. Lend land
along road to my son JOHN'S fence, including house.
Son: JOHN, reversion in land whereon I live and jug;

Daus: GRACEY, chest, woolen & linen wheels; LEVINIA
D., chest, bason and jug; Son: JAMES, ewe lamb and
jug; Dau: SARAH, chest, puter dish and jug; Son & Exr:
SAMUEL, 3 shoats, sow and jug; Daus: PENELOPE, puter
dish and jug; NANCY ROADS, bason and chist. Exr: WM.
R. LONG. Wit: POLLARD EDMUNDSON, EPHRAIM BAIRFIELD.

GATOR, JOHN
    Mar. 28, 1849. Aug. Ct., 1851. Bk. F, pp 457-8.
Sister: GRACEY HOWARD, all my land, stock of all kinds,
household and kitchen furniture, farming utensils, bees
and other property. After death of my sister I give to
HORACE ELY BARFIELD 15-1/4 A which I had of JOHN HOWELL.
Wit: H. WARD, KENNETH GATOR.

GATLING, ANN
    Aug. 8, 1814. Aug. Ct., 1814. Bk. E, p 65. Gr. dau:
NANCY ANDERSON (illegitimate dau. of my son BENJAMIN).
Son: BENJAMIN: 2 sheets, 1 blanket, all wearing apparel
except 1 habit and 1 petticoat, and ½ residue; Friend:
LEVINIA ANDERSON, habit and petticoat; Gr. son: WILLIAM
GATLING, son of WM. GATLING, SR., 5 ₤ money; Gr. son:
EDWARD GATLING, son of BENJAMIN, ½ residue. Exr: ISAAC
NORFLEET. Wit: SALLY DUNN, (ALEXANDER) FRYER.

GAY, DEMPSEY
    Mar. 30, 1840. Feb. Ct., 1841. Bk. F, p 251. Dau:
NANCY ELLIS; Sons: LEVIN, HENRY, DEMPSEY, ISAM, $1
each. MARTHA ANN MILLICENT EDWARDS, dau. of POLLEY
EDWARDS, $100; Son: PERREY, land whereon I live. Exr:
JACOB MERCER, JR. Wit: JOHN D. MERCER, DENNIS MERCER.
Will caveated May Ct., 1840, by JOHN ELLIS (wife NANCY)
LEVIN GAY, HENRY GAY, DEMPSEY GAY and ISAM GAY. Aug.
Ct., 1840, JOHN ELLIS, Adm.; Bond $1000, Securities:
JOHN CARTER, JACOB MERCER.

GAY, JOHN
    Mar. 24, 1759. June Ct., 1761. Wife: SARY, use of
estate lifetime. THOMAS PITMAN, son of eldest sister.
Exr: JOSEPH PITMAN, JR. Wit: MOSES PITMAN, JOSEPH
PITMAN, DANIEL BASS, JESSE GREEN.

GAY, HENRY
    Feb. 24, 1788. Aug. Ct., 1792. Wife: ?. remainder;

STEPHEN BARNES, plantation, 4 cows and calves, tools,
12 new chars, chist and mair; PATTY BARNES, 2 cows
and calves, chist; WM. GAY, son of JOHN GAY, SR., 5
S. Exr: JAMES BARNES, JETHRO BARNES, STEPHEN BARNES.
Wit: ABSALOM BARNES, AZIEL BARNES, NATHAN BARNES.

GAY, JOHN
    Mar. 21, 1761. Probated 1761. Wife: MARTHA, re-
mainder estate; Son & Exr: WILLIAM, plant'n whereon
I live, still and worm, new chest, money seals, brass
cock (clock?), stone jug and 6 bottles; Son: JOHN,
pr. hand millstones, whipsaw, pr. iron wedges and hoe;
Dau: MARY, cow and calf. Wit: EDWARD MOORE, JONATHAN
COLEMAN, MICHAEL HORNE.

GAY, WILLIAM
    May 6, 1782. Feb. Ct., 1798. Wife & Extx: ANN,
whole estate. Wit: JOHN WILLIAMS, JOSEPH FARMER,
BENJAMIN WILLIAMS.

GEORGE, ELIAS
    Jan. 16, 1771. May Ct., 1771. Wife & Extx: MARTHA,
estate lifetime, reversion to WM. Sons: WILLIAM, 1
slave, 10 £ money; JESSE, 1 slave, if he returns; Son
& Exr: ELIAS, 1 slave; Daus: SARAH, REBECCY, ELIZABETH,
ANNY, 5 S. Wit: JOSEPH HART, JOHN BARBER.

GEORGE, ELIZABETH
    Nov. 11, 1833. Nov. Ct., 1833. Dec'd Husband;
MICHAEL BARNES. Son: ELIAS GEORGE, land lent me by
dec'd husband reverting to son ELIAS, was given to
me by son ELLIS, it being ½ plantation whereon I live.
Son: FREDERICK. Dau: MARY E. GEORGE, lend land given
me by son ELIAS, reversion to son FREDERICK and my
cousin JAMES H. SAVAGE, cows, etc. 1 beaufat, walnut
table, desk, 8 chairs, the large chest, all earthenware,
3 pewter dishes, 3 pewter basons, 6 pewter plates, 1
linen wheel, cotton wheel, 1 pr. cotton cards, middle
and small pots, small oven, 3 bbls. corn, wheat, pork,
etc. Gr. son: LEMUEL N. LANGDON. Cousin & Exr: JAMES
H. SAVAGE, lend furn., black lead colore chest and all
plantation utensils. ELIZABETH LANGDON, sow and pigs
for support of Gr. son, LEMUEL N. LANGDON. Exr: WILLIS

BRADLEY. Wit: EDWARD POWER, EPHRAIM DICKEN. Codicil,
Nov. 11, 1833. Annulled all bequests to cousin JAMES
H. SAVAGE and took him off as Exr. Bequested land intended for JAMES H. SAVAGE to son FREDERICK and personal property to dau MARY E. GEORGE. Bequeath $30
to Gr. son LEMUEL N. LANGDON for education. Wit:
EDWARD POWER, STEPHEN BRADLEY, SR.

GEORGE, JOHN
     May 12, 1816. May Ct., 1816. Bk. E, p 131. Wife:
Land; MATTHEW PHILIPS tract adjoining MIALS land, to
be sold for debts, all other lands for her (wife's)
life; reversion to 4 sons: JAMES, THOMAS, WILLIAM and
JOSEPH J. Dau: POLLY, 2 slaves. Exr: ELIAS BRYAN, Bro.
MICHAEL GAY. Wit:_____? JACOB ING.

GEORGE, MICHAEL
     Oct. 25, 1823. Nov. Ct., 1823. Bk. F, p 6. Wife:
ELIZABETH, lend remainder land, reversion to 2 youngest
chil. MARY and ELIAS, 2 slaves, stock, cattle, furn.,
tools, loom and gear, riding chair and harness, corn
and pork. Dau: MARY, land joining THOS. BANKS, ELIAS
BRYAN (dec'd), and HARRIS plantation, also 1 slave;
Son: ELIAS, land joining THOS. WIGGINS, OLIVE DIXON,
ELIAS BRYAN, JR., MIALS land and HENRY J. EXUM; filly,
saddle and bridle. Sons: WILLIAM and FREDERICK. Exr:
DAVID BRADDY, HENRY BRYAN. Wit: THOMAS WIGGINS, JR.,
THOMAS BENSON.

GEORGE, SELAH
     Written 1806. May Ct., 1808. Dau: REBEKER COKER,
wearing apparel, chest and 1 slave; Gr. chil: WILLIAM
COKER, 1 slave; NANCY COKER, 1 slave; GEORGE COKER,
horse; LOVEY COKER, f. bed and furn.; Son: THOMAS,
money from sale of slave; Gr. son, oldest son of THOMAS,
slave; Gr. son: 2nd son of THOMAS, horse. Son & Exr:
MIKIAH (MIKAH), 5 hogs. Gr. sons: WILLIAM GEORGE and
FREDERICK, cow and calf. Son & Exr: JOHN. Gr. son:
JAMES GEORGE, son of JOHN, $10. Wit: HARDY MANNEN
(MANNING), CHARLOTTE MANNEN (MANNING).

GERHARD, CHARLES
     Mar. 2, 1797. Aug. Ct., 1798. Wife: ELIZABETH,

land, colts and negroes received as her portion of her
father's estate; also 4 negroes; 300 A land whereon I
live, together with my half grist mill, all household
and kitchen furn., provisions, farming utensils, choice
of any two naggs, all stock of cattle, hoggs, sheep
which I own in this county. Mother: DINAH SIMON, all
stock of horses, cattle, hoggs, and sheep, furn., utensils and provisions which I own in Beaufort Co., Lend
her during her life 1 negro, 170 A land whereon she
lives, also 80 A tract which will more fully appear by
deed from SAM'L JASPER to FORBES GERRAD; also 100 A
tract adjoining above will more fully appear by a patent from State to FORBES GERRAD, also 108 A tract adjoining above, will more fully appear by deed from
MOSES MAULE to me. BENJ. SIMON: After mother's death
lend all the above lands to BENJAMIN SIMON during his
life. After his death I give above lands to poor of
Beaufort Co. on following conditions: that they never
be sold, but held as a stock belonging to said poor,
subject to be rented, cultivated or leased as the war-
dens or managers of the poor may deem most desirable,
but never to be left for longer term than seven years
and no more timber to be used than is necessary for
use of farms. I give to BEN SIMON, 200 A tract which
will more fully appear by a deed from I. J. BLOUNT to
FORBES GERRAD, also 100 A tract adjoining the two
above as will more fully appear by Grant from State to
FORBES GARRAD. GEORGE GERRAD, 200 A tract S side Pam-
lico River near Flat Swamp and road from Bath to Newbern as will appear by grant from State to FORBES
GERRAD, University of N. C.: Give 13,000 A in Tenn-
eysee, on condition the trustees or persons having
charge of property of University shall not suffer any
part to be forfeited and sold for taxes, or sell any
part in less than 7 yrs. after my death, on pain of
forfeiting whole property, further no part of tract
of land for my own service in Army shall never be
sold but remain a stock belonging to the University,
subject to be cultivated, rented or leased but for no
longer than 7 yrs. and no more timber used than is
necessary for operation of farms. The tract for my
service in Army contains 2560 A, S. side Cumberland
River, including mouth of Yellow Creek. Friend & Exr:

THOMAS BLOUNT, sword and $25 for a ring of remembrance.
Friend: GEN. WILLIAM BRICKELL, my pistols and all money he may owe me on my private affairs, either Bond
or otherways. Sell following: All land in New Hanover
and lot in Raleigh and all naggs not mentioned above;
all residue of moneys to be paid wife, ELIZABETH
GERRAD, Wit: H. HAYWOOD, GEORGE W. OGG.

GEWIN (GWIN?), CHRISTOPHER
     Apr. 2, 1748. Feb. Ct., 1749. Son & Exr:
CHRISTOPHER. Dau & Extx: MARY HARRELL; Gr. sons: LOT,
plantation whereon I live on Tar River, Conetoe Swamp
and on Burton's lines; ABELL and CHRISTOPHER, remainder
of land. Wit: JAMES BRASWELL, BENJAMIN BRASWELL,
ABRAHAM DEW.

GIBBS, FREDERICK
     Dec. 19, 1780. Aug. Ct., 1781. Son-in-law:
THEOPHILUS THOMAS, 1 S sterling of Great Britain; bro-
in-law & Exr: JOHN THOMAS, 5 negroes, and my wearing
apparel, all residue of estate; Cousin: FREDERICK
GIBBLE THOMAS, 1 negro; sister-in-law: PATIENCE
THOMAS: 4 negroes, mare and colt; also bolster and
pillows, and 2 sheets left in care of TIMOTHY DURGIN;
Cousins: ROBERT THOMAS and JOHN THOMAS, all I left in
care of ROBT NETTLES and FRANCIS SPIVEY. Wit: JESSE
PITMAN, WILLIAM MORRIS, JOSEPH BARNES.

GILCHRIST, THOMAS
     Aug. 6, 1789. Nov. Ct., 1789. Wife & Extx: MARTHA,
devise to wife and WILLIE JONES and ELLEN JONES land
purchased of my late son-in-law THOMAS HOGG situate
on Little Alligator in TIRREL (Tyrel) County; also
land purchased of RICHARD HENDERSON, belonging to
RICHARD HENDERSON CO. either in this state or Va. Lots
and tenements in Tarborough to wife her lifetime, reversion to son ALLEN. Bro-in-law (?) & Exr: WILLIE
JONES; Sister-in-law & Extx: ELLEN JONES. Son: ALLEN
GILCHRIST; Dau: ELIZABETH HOGG, 1 negro; Dau: GRIZIE
GILCHRIST, 2 negroes, money for wedding clothes at
Mother's descretion. After Mother's death 2/3 of resi-
due to ALLEN, 1/3 divided between daus. Wit: W. R.
DAVIE, J. W. CLENABAR (?).

GILL, TAYLOR
Oct. 22, 1792. Feb. Ct., 1793. Wife & Extx: MOLLEY
GILL, lend her 1/3 estate for her lifetime. Other 2/3
to be divided between chil. Sons: WILLIAM TAYLOR GILL
and THOMAS GILL; Dau: NANCY GILL. Wit: AUGUSTIN
COPPEDGE, HARTWELL WILLEFORD, HARDY TODD.

GILL, WILLIAM (of Northumberland Co., Va.)
Sept. 19, 1794. Nov. Ct., 1794. Sis: MARY GILL, 2
negroes, all furn. I have possest to her and all money
I have by keeping school. Bro & Exr: RICHARD GILL, 1
negro, my saling boat named Vecommecoe. Bro & Exr:
WINDER GILL, 1 negro. Wit: JOHN WILLEFORD, MARTIN
PITMAN, EDWARD PITMAN.

GLOVER, GEORGE
Jan. 29, 1768. No probate date. Wife & Extx:
FAITHFULL, use of plantation during widowhood; at her
death divided between sons, give 1 negro. Give residue
Estate to wife for widowhood, reversion to 3 chil.
Sons: JOHN, PERSONS (PARSONS); Dau: MARY. Exr: HENRY
HART. Wit: JAS. HASSELL, JOS. HART, MOSES MOORE.

GODWIN, WILLIAM
Dec. 4, 1779. Aug. Ct., 1783. Wife: TABITHA. Gr.
son: JOHN GODWIN, pot, frying pan, 4 cows and calves,
horse, bridle, and saddle, 8 sheep. Remainder estate
to chil. (Unnamed). Exr: DAVID GODWIN, THOMAS GODWIN
(Sons?). Wit: CORNELIUS JORDAN, SR., WILLIAM BOND
WHITHEAD, PENELOPY BARNES.

GOODSON, THOMAS
Nov. 13, 1761. June Ct., 1762. Wife & Extx:
ELIZABETH, ½ of lot and remainder of estate during her
life. At her death all to be divided equally between
other 4 daus. Dau: WINNIE GOODSON, ½ profit of my lot
in Tarborough Town number 57; after Mother's death,
Daus: MARY MERRIT, SARAH GUNTER, ELIZABETH MERIT,
OLOEF WHITEHEAD. Exr: JOHN GUNTER, WILLIAM MERIT. Wit:
BENJ. BUNN, JR., JOHN IRWIN, WILLIAM STANDARD.

GOODWIN, WILLIAM
May 25, 1780. Aug. Ct., 1781. Wife & Extx: TABITHA.
Lend houses & lott in town of Tarborough, also personal

estate during her widowhood. Each child to receive
theirs when of age if necessary; no names given. Exr:
THOMAS H. HALL. Wit: H. IRWIN TOOL, EDWARD HALL.

GORDON, ROSS (of Baltimore)
Sept. 21, 1799. Feb. Ct., 1800 Mother: ANN GORDON,
$80. Sisters: ANN GORDON, HANNAH GORDON, MARY GORDON,
each $80. Bro: WILLIAM GORDON, $150, he assisted me
when I began business. Father: WILLIAM GORDON, $80.
Bros: ALEXANDER and AARON, $80. Friend and Exr: JOSEPH
ROSS of Petersburg. Wit: HENRY DUKE HART, SAMUEL McCRAE,
Authentic copy signed by WILLIAM BUCHANAN, Regs'r.
Baltimore Co., 23, Jan. 1800.

GOSNEY, JOHN (planter)
Apr. 5, 1779. No probate date. Wife: MARTHA, all
estate during natural life; Dau: ONEY GRIFFES, after
Mother's death 1 negro; rest of estate to be equally
divided between 2 daus. Dau: HENRIETTA MARIA SASNET.
Exr: WILLIAM GRIFFES, RICHARD SASNET. Wit: AQUILA SUGG,
WM. HAYWOOD, LOT MOORE.

GOX, RICHARD
Apr. 12, 1779. May Ct., 1779. Children, but does
not name them. Exr: H. IRWIN TOOLE, BARTHOLOMEW KELLY.
Wit: DON SOUTHERLAND, DENNIS OBRYAN, MARTHA JONES.

GRAY, BENJAMIN
Oct. 31, 1817. Nov. Ct., 1817. Bk. E, p 168. Wife:
POLLY, lend 1/3 lands including buildings; give her all
property she possessed at our marriage. Son: PETER,
$100; Daus: ELIZABETH, large trunk, 1 cow and calf;
GODITHA, 1 walnut desk, 1 cow and calf; REBECKAH PEAL,
1 cow and calf. Gr. daus: POLLY GRAY; CHARLOTTE PEAL,
PEGGY PEAL, $10 each. Exr: Friend, REDMUN CURL. Wit:
JOSHUA TAYLOR, WILLIAM TAYLOR, WILLIE BUNN.

GRAY, CHARLES
June 18, 1811. Aug. Ct., 1811. Bk. E, p 21. Wife
& Extx: NANCY. Exrs to sell all lands in Ga. purchased
of JACOB BATTLE, and after debts paid, residue to be
given to wife and sons ETHELRED & WILLIAM HENRY GRAY.
Lend wife 2 slaves her natural life; give her my best

horse and riding chair, harness, also all stock of
cattle, and hoggs, ½ all crop, also my chest of drawers, ½ remaining furniture. Sons: ETHELRED GRAY, and
WM. HENRY GRAY, 1 negro each, also another at wife's
death. Residue to sons. Exr: JAMES W. CLARK, SHERWOOD
HAYWOOD. Wit: ELISHA BATTLE, SR., JACOB BATTLE.

GRAY, ETHELRED
    July 15, 1788. Feb. Ct., 1790. Bk. 3, p 124. Son
& Exr: WILLIAM ROBERT GRAY, 714 A plantation whereon
he now lives on S side Tar River, also 580 A tract
called Norsworthy's, and 12 negroes. Son & Exr:
CHARLES GRAY, plantation whereon I live, it with tract
called Walnut Creek containing 875 A, 400 A tract lying N side Tar River, 200 A tract lying S side Tar R.
purchased of NEWIT PITMAN, and 11 negroes. Dau:
ELIZABETH GRAY, money from sale of 250 A tract of land
in Pitt Co., 6 negroes, ₤ 250 current money of Va. Wit:
MICAJAH HOLT, WILLIAM EMSON, DEMSEY VANN.

GRAY, ETHELDRED
    Mar. 5, 1846. May Ct., 1846. Bk. F, pp 341-2. Wife:
MARY, profits from residue of my estate shall be applied
first to support and education of my youngest daughters,
VIRGINIA GRAY and HELEN B. GRAY until they attain the
age of sixteen years; profits and residue divided between all my chil: MARTHA ANN, MARY E., WILLIAM,
FRANCES, CAROLINE, VIRGINIA and HELEN B. GRAY. Family
to have use of home as long as Children and Wife remain single, and have use and possession of my house
in Rocky Mount, with lots adjoining. Exr: WILLIAM
NORFLEET. Wit: W. WESTON, D. FERGUSON.

GRAY, JAMES
    May 4, 1797. Aug. Ct., 1797. Neph: JAMES GRAY of
Southhampton Co., Va., 2 negroes; Kinsman: CHARLES
GRAY of Edgecombe, 2 negroes and all remainder of es-
tate. Exr: LAMON RUFFIN, Kinsman. Wit: JOHN J.
DAVIDSON, WILLIAM DAVIDSON.

GRAY, JOHN
    June 11, 1776. Apr. Ct., 1777. Bros & Exrs:
JOSEPH GRAY, JAMES GRAY, estate divided equally bet-

ween Bros. Wit: JETHRO PITMAN, BENJAMIN BUNN.

GRAY, ROBERT
    Feb. 18, 1781. Aug. Ct., 1781. Wife: MARY, 1 negro, silver watch, silver shoe, knee and band buckles; also lend during her life labour of 6 negroes. Son & Exr: ETHELRED, (alias NICHOLSON), my plantation lying on N side Tar River, purchased of WILLIAM LASSITER, also 2 tracts which my son SIMON GRAY gave me by his last will, one lying in Edgecombe, one in Pitt; 17 negroes, all stock of cattle, hogs, sheep and all stock and utensils and tools belonging to plantation whereon my son SIMON GRAY died, 1 negro at Mother's death. Daus: HANNAH HAYWOOD, reversion in 3 negroes, I bequeath 10 negroes; MARY JEFFREYS, reversion in 2 negroes. I now bequeath 11 negroes. Gr. son: ETHELRED GRAY, all my lands and Plantation lying in Va. and N. side of Blackwater Swamp in County of Surry. Residue divided between wife and chil. Exr: Son-in-law, WILLIAM JEFFREYS. Wit: AQUILLA COHOON, JOHN SIKES, JOEL BRIGGS.

GRIFFIN, BENJAMIN
    Apr. 11, 1808. May Ct., 1808. Wife: PURRITY, ½ tract land adjoining ZAKARIAH GRIFFIN and FRANCIS DANCY, including houses, 1 horse, saddle and bridle, all Bacon fatt, corn, 1 cow and yearling, 1 cow and calf, her choice, 1 sow, 8 pigs, 1 chest, 1 table, her choice. Bros: ZAKARIAH GRIFFIN, JOHN GRIFFIN, LEWIS GRIFFIN, these three to have residue of land whereon I live; also tract purchased of FREDERICK PHILIPS equally divided between them. Nephs: JOHN, RICHARD and WILLIAM POND, sons of STEPHENSON POND and MOURNING POND, $200 divided equally. Residue sold & divided between wife and 3 bros. Exr: Bro., ZAKARIAH GRIFFIN, WILLIAM BALFOUR. Wit: LAMON RUFFIN, MICHAEL WILLIAMS.

GRIFFIN, HENRY (SEN.)
    Feb. 27, 1819. Aug. Ct., 1819. Bk. E, p, 220. Wife & Extx: ELIZABETH, lend all lands during life or widowhood, reversion to chil. Dau: ELIZABETH, 1 chest; Son: WILLIS, 1 horse, 12 months schooling. Exr: Son, ICHTY GRIFFIN, JAMES BRASWELL. Wit: EDWIN BULLOCK, DANIEL LAND.

GRIFFIN, JOHN
Mar. 23, 1761. Sept. Ct., 1761. Sons: LEWIS, 250
A plantation whereon I live also 100 A adjoining; if
he should die without lawful heirs, it shall be divided equally between my chil., 5 cows and calves, 1
horse; JOHN, £ 5 Va. money; JOSEPH, 3 cows and calves;
HARDY (Exr), 3 cows and calves, DEMCEY, 1 horse, 5
cows and calves; Daus: MILENDER (MILDRED, according
to Olds Abstracts); ANNE (ANNA, according to Olds
Abstracts); MARY (MAY, according to Olds Abstracts);
all three , 5 cows and calves, £ 5 Va. currency;
DELILAH, 5 cows and calves, £ 10 Va. currency. In
naming 8 chil. HARDY'S name is first, so perhaps he
is oldest child, others as follows: HARDY, JOSEPH,
DEMCEY, LEWIS, MILENDER, ANNE, MARY, DELILAH. Exr:
THOMAS MANN, MATTHEW DRAKE. Wit: WILLIAM DRAKE, JUN.,
JONAS WILLIAMS, JUN., JOHN WILLIAMS, JUN.

GRIFFIN, SUSAN
Oct. 1, 1839. Nov. Ct., 1855. Bk. G, p 116. Dau:
MARY ANN SUSAN GRIFFIN, negroes Jo and Fillis. All of
my property of every description. Adm. JAMES EDGE.
Wit: G. W. KILLEBREW, C. B. KILLEBREW.

GRIFFIN, WILLIAM
Mar. 12, 1813. May Ct., 1813. Bk. E, p 57. Wife:
ONEY, all things on plantation her lifetime, except 1
mare, bridle and saddle, reversion to chil. Sons &
Exrs: ZAKARIAH, JOHN. Son: LEWIS. My chil. and Gr.
chil: SEALAH LONG, ANN ELIZA HARDY, MIKE WILLIAMS,
JOSEPH WILLIAMS, JOHN PEAL. Wit: MARMADUKE BELL,
WILLIAM WALKER.

GRIFFIN, ZACHERIAH
Apr. 26, 1837. No probate date. Wife & Extx:
MARGARETT, lend tract whereon I live on lines of JOHN
ANDERSON, now LOT STALLINGS line on E side of Grassy
Branch; 1 negro, pot, and hooks, Dutch oven, pr. flat
irons, griddle, skillet, mare, side saddle, bridle,
china press and contents, riding chair and harness,
stone jar, 4 good sitting chairs, trunk, chest, table,
sow and 14 pigs, shoats, cow and calf or yearling,
loom and gear, 6 geese, pork, corn, wheat, 20 lbs.

sugar, 10 lbs. coffee, 3 bu. salt, 5 gal. molasses.
Daus: MARIA RUFFIN, wife of JOHN RUFFIN, land whereon
they live; MARTHA HAWKINS, wife of FREDERICK HAWKINS,
land whereon they live; the two tracts being lands
bought of DAVID BARNES and JAMES GRIFFIN. Residue to
be divided between: — Dau: ELIZABETH SPICER, Heirs of
JAMES GRIFFIN, Heirs of ONY HILL, REBECCA MOORE,
WINNEFRED SAWYER, MARIAH RUFFIN, MARTHA HAWKINS. Exr:
JESSE C. KNIGHT. Wit: WILLIAM HINTON, DAVID MATTHEWS.

GRIFFIS, JOHN
      Oct. 21, 1796. Nov. Ct., 1799. Dau: SARAH
BLOODWORTH, wife of THOMAS BLOODWORTH, 1 bed and furn.
etc. in her possession. Sons: JOHN; DEMSEY; FRANCIS,
1 cow and calf in his possession; FREDERICH, horse etc.
in his possession; dau: POLLY MACE, 1 parcel of feathers,
1 nice Redpainted chest etc. in her possession; Son &
Exr: WILLIAM, 3 horses, 6 cattle, 2 pine chests, all
residue of my estate. Wit: LAMON RUFFIN, JOHN SASNETT,

GRIMES, THOMAS
      Sept. 12, 1795. May Ct., 1797. Dau: FRANCES HATTON,
wife of FRANCIS HATTON, I lend 1 negro girl, her & her
increase to be divided between her chil. Son & Exr:
LEWELLING, 1 negro, 20 geese. Son: WILLIAM, land where-
on he lives, 1 cow and calf. JOHN C. GRIMES (does not
say son), land whereon he lives, also £ 5. Son & Exr:
THOMAS, 1 negro. Son: JAMES, 1 negro and mare; Daus:
CHLOE, SARAH, ELIZABETH and MARY, 1 negro each. Son:
GEORGE, 2 negroes. Exr: JNO. LEWELLING. Wit: LEMUEL
DAVIDSON, THOMAS BEST.

GRIMES, WILLIAM
      May 21, 1850. Nov. Ct., 1850. Bk. F, p 450. Wife:
TABITHA, 1/3 all lands including house etc., 6 negroes
her choice, 1/3 furniture, 1/3 tools, gig and harness,
2 horses, 3 cows and calves, 6 sheep, 2 sows, bees,
1000 lbs. pork, 50 bbls. corn, 10 bu. peas, 200 lbs.
cotton, 10 lbs. wool, 50 lbs. coffee, 100 lbs. sugar,
10 gal. molasses, 5 gal. honey, 5 bu. salt, 1 bbl.
flour, all soap, poultry and $200. Daus: JULIA CHERRY,
MARY MOORE, TABITHA LANIER, all $500. Reversion to
TABITHA'S chil. LYDIA (dec'd ? dau), to chil. which
                            147

ASA JONES had by her, $500 between them. Son: THOMAS,
Residue sold and equally divided in 5 shares, one for
each of my chil. and chil. of LYDIA by ASA JONES to have
one share. Wit: H. WARD, JOHN KNIGHT, SR., HAMON (?)
WARD being dec'd, will proven by oaths of JOHN KNIGHT,
SR. and JOHN NORFLEET. No Exr named Adm. granted
THOMAS GRIMES and WILLIAM R. CHERRY. Bond of $50,000
with R. MAYO, HENRY R. CHERRY, LEWIS PERRY, and JOHN
KNIGHT, SR., Securities.

GUION, SARAH

Sept. 17, 1827. No probate. Bk. F, p 83. Dau-in-
law: SUSAN GUION, wife of my son ISAAC D. GUION, lend
all personal property; reversion to her chil. if she
has any. Should she leave no child, all aforesaid property shall go to friend BARTHOLOMEW BOWEN. Son & Exr:
ISAAC D. GUION. Wit: THOMAS GRIFFIN, RICHARD THOMAS.
Exr. refused to qualify. Adm. granted BARTHOLOMEW
BOWEN. Bond $3000. MARMADUKE BELL & SOLOMON PENDER,
Securities.

GUION, THOMAS

No. date. Nov. Ct., 1822. Bk. E, p 315. Wife:
SALLY (SARAH), lend lands whereon I live, adjoining
JAMES SOUTHERLAND and HENRY SHIRLEY, during her life;
also give her 3 negroes, all furniture, best riding
chair, 2 horses, all cattle, hogs, 2 carts, etc. Son:
ISAAC D. GUION. 4 negroes; reversion in all lands,"on
condition he pay my daughter JANIS C. GUION, $1500."
Dau: JANIS C. GUION, 2 negroes, $1500 at death of her
mother. Exr: Friends, SPENCER D. COTTON, DAVID BARNES.
Wit: NO Wit. No Signature. Will caveated but duly
proved by the following jury: ASA JONES, BLAKE H.
WIGGINS, RICHARD PARKER, CHARLES WILKINSON, JACOB
DUNN, ASAEL FARMER, WILLIAM GOFF, JOHN L. MAYO, JOHN
R. SCARBOROUGH, JESSE LITTLE, GEO. W. KILLIBREW,
ROBT. FOXHALL. Nov. County Ct., 1822. N. MATHEWSON,
CLK.

GUNTER, JOAB

Jan. 4, 1818. Feb. Ct., 1826. Bk. F, p 53. Wife:
PRISCILLA, 2 negroes, and all furniture. Negroes lent
her for lifetime; reversion to chil: HENRY, PEGGY,
and DRURY, all other divided between wife & chil.

148

Exr: Friend, GRISHAM PITMAN. Wit: J. BENTON. Since
JAMES BENTON was dead his handwriting proven by oath
of SPIER WHITAKER.

GUNTER, PRISCILLA
     Dec. 26, 1844. May Ct., 1846. Bk. F, p 339. Son:
HENRY, $1. Dau: MARGARET MERITT, $1. Son & Exr:
DREW, whole state including my interest in land
whereon I reside, on Fishing Creek, adjoining G. C.
PITTMAN. Wit:(REDDIN) PITTMAN, GRESHAM C. PITTMAN.

GWIN, DANIEL
     Sept. 6, 1795. Aug. Ct., 1796. Wife & Extx:
ELIZABETH, lend all property her lifetime. Daus: POLLY;
SUSANNA PROCTOR, 1 cow and calf at mother's death. Son
& Exr: WILLIAM GWIN, reversion in 75 A of "land lying
in Nancimond Co., Va., it being given me by deed of
Gift which I left in my brother's possession. Also I
give him 100 A land in state of Cumberland on Stones
River, purchased from LOTT MOUND. All remaining estate
to be equally divided between son & dau. Wit: DRURY
STOKES, OLIVE BOAZMAN, PATTY BROARDSTREET, ELISHA EDGE.

HALL, CHARLES
     July 5, 1791. Probate date, 1791. Land in Wake Co.
lately given me by my father, I leave to my two youngest brothers, THOMAS and RALPH, to be applied toward
schooling and better maintenance and hire of negro.
Exrs. to be their Gdns. Sisters: HARRIETT, horse now
in possession of my father; DOLLY, riding horse, or
negro whichever Exr. and my Mother shall think best.
All remaining personal property to be sold and divided between my sisters. Exr: Friend and Kinsman (Uncle),
EDWARD HALL, If he should be called away during minority
of legatees, I request MR. ALLEN ATKINSON to continue
as Exr. Wit: THOMAS BLOUNT, WILLIAM POPE.

HALL, EDWARD
     Jan. 3, 1821. Nov. Ct., 1823. Wife: LUCY, lend plan-
tation whereon I live, also all negroes and all personal property except Bank stock and note due me by
HUGH TELFAIR for $1000. The interest of these I give
her for her better maintenance. Son-in-law & Exr:
149

MICHAEL HEARN and Dau: MARTHA HEARN, bequeath all lands
on N side Tar River; all lotts in Tarborough, already
in their possession. Gr. son: LAWRENCE HENRY HEARN, at
death of wife, I give him all land & plantation whereon I live, also 1 A of land on Hatcher's Swamp intended for site of a Mill, 5 negroes purchased of MARTHA
HARDAWAY'S estate, 10 negroes out of my own family,
all remainder personal estate, including Bank stock
which may assist in educating him. At the death of wife
I will all remaining negroes to my Gr. chil., the chil.
of MICHAEL & MARTHA HEARN. Exr: Son-in-law, MICHAEL
HEARN. Wit: BEN B. HUNTER, DAVID DANCY. Codicil, 25
of Jan. 1821. Wit: BEN B. HUNTER, G. COLLINS.

HALL, JAMES
     Oct. 8, 1772. Nov. Ct., 1772. Wife & 2 chil.
(unnamed). Debts to ROB'T BIGNALL & WALLACE McCLELLAN,
ordered paid. Exr: Bros. THOMAS HALL, EDWARD HALL. Wit:
JOHN MARSHALL, JOHN HALL.

HALL, JOHN
     Aug. 23, 1782. Feb. Ct., 1783. Sons: ROBERT,
BOLLING, WILLIAM, 1 negro each. Residue of estate
divided between son, WILLIAM and dau. MASON. Daus:
MARTHA, 1 bed of furn.; ANN HARDAWAY 1 case of knives
and forks, 1 doz. silver spoons; MASON HALL. Exr:
Neph., EDWARD HALL. Wit: MARTHA HALL, WILLIAM KENT.

HALL, THOMAS
     Oct. 22, 1816. Feb. Ct., 1819. Bk. E, p 212. Wife:
POLLY, plantation whereon I live for her lifetime provided she live on it. If not, I leave it to Gr. son:
THOMAS GAY. Bequeath to her 1 negro and all furniture.
Wife & Gr. dau. to use brandy still until Gr. son Thos,
GAY, comes of age, then to be his. Stock and cattle
and tools to wife POLLY. Gr. dau: LAVINIA GAY, 1 little
chist, all swamplands. Exr: ELI AMASON. Wit: ELLENDER
AMASON, SALLY AMASON. Exr: refused to qualify; Adm.
granted to EPHRAIM DANIEL who entered bond for $1500
with ELI AMASON and WILLIAM WHITE, guarantors.

HALL, THOMAS H.
     May 4. 1850. Aug. Ct., 1853. Estate to be sold

and proceeds divided between bro. RALPH HALL, and
sister MRS. DOLLY WOOD, living in Vicksburg, Mississippi. If these be dead, to the daus. of FRANCIS
HALL, dec'd and of EDMUND HALL, dec'd. Found among
the papers of THOS. H. HALL and handwriting proved
by HENRY T. CLARK, JOHN T. BRIDGERS and WILLIAM STATON.

HAMMONS, SHADRACH
     Aug. 26, 1824. Aug. Ct., 1828. Bk. F, p 92. Dau:
URIDICE. Sons: WILLIS, 1 horse in his possession;
ELIJAH, 1 horse in his possession; JAMES, 1 cow and
calf in his possession. DELILA REVEL, 1 bedstead in
her possession. Daus: SUSANNA, ROSANNA and ELIZABETH,
all lands, stock, furn. etc. if any married, reversion
to the other; if all marry divided equally. Exr: WM.
H. DICKEN, EPENETUS DICKEN. Wit: WILLIAM DICKEN,
WILLIAM H. DICKEN.

HANSON, JOHN
     Jan. 6, 1849. Feb. Ct., 1849. Bk. F, p 417. Wife:
MARY, lend land whereon I live, also tract bought of
SAWNY IRVIN, where ELIZABETH COBB now lives; hogs, cows,
cattle, etc. corn, wheat, peas, etc., furn. and tools.
Son: WILLIAM, reversion home plantation provided dau,
ELIZABETH, is to live with him all her life or until
marriage. Son: JESSE, reversion in land bought of SAWNY
IRVIN where ELIZABETH COBB lives provided dau SALLY
may live with him for her life or until marriage. Son:
JAMES, $1. Exr: JAMES LAWRENCE. Wit: JOHN H. DANIEL,
JESSE HARRELL.

HARDAWAY, JANE
     Oct. 19, 1820. Feb. Ct., 1821. Bk. E, p 261.
LAWRENCE HENRY HEARN, son of MICHAEL HEARN, 1 negro,
reserving her services for my sister LUCY HALL for her
lifetime. Niece: LUCY ANN STITH, wife of JOHN STITH,
$600. nieces: ANN H. HARDAWAY and KATHERINE J.
HARDAWAY, daughters of my bro. JOSEPH HARDAWAY, $100
each and residue from sale of land, household furn.,
beds, bed clothing, wearing apparel and all other
personal property. Exr. & Gdn of Nieces: EDWARD HALL,
Wit: BENJA. B. HUNTER, EDWARD C. BELLAMY.

HARDY, ROBERT

May 2, 1820. Aug. Ct., 1820. Bk. E, p 239. Daus:
POLLY CHERRY, ½ lands, all property in her possession
and also ½ of residue; JUDITH HARDY, ½ lands for life,
reversion to 3 Gr. chil.: PEGGY HARDY, LYDDA HARDY and
RUFFIN HARDY. Also to JUDITH HARDY all property now in
her possession and ½ residue. Exr: EATON COBB and Son-
in-law, WILLIE CHERRY. Wit: HOWELL THIGPEN, MICHAEL
HARDY.

HARE, JESSE

May 28, 1770. Apr. Ct., 1774. Wife: BETTY, reserve
for her use 4 negroes, plantation whereon I live and
land joining thereto, to the line formerly dividing
WILLIAM LASATER and WILLIAM MOORE, for her life or
widowhood, provided she live on plantation and never
move negroes out of this province. Nor should she offer
to claim and sue for her right of dower in any land I
have sold since we were married. Bequeath to her ₤ 40
Va. money. If she marry, should she or her husband
offer to claim or sue for dower or move negroes out of
province, all negroes, land and money shall be forfeited
and it shall become property of my 2 daus. Daus:
ELIZABETH MARY ANN KING HARE, reversion in plantation
and land left her mother; ANNE, plantation and land
bought of WM. HAYWOOD and which he bought of WM .MOORE.
Exr: WILLIAM HAYWOOD, JOHN HAYWOOD. Wit: WILLIAM HALL,
JAMES HILL, (CHRISTOPHER) LAKEY.

HARRELL, CHRISTOPHER

Oct 18, 1843. Feb. Ct., 1844. Bk. F, p 307. Wife:
MARGARET, lend 3 negroes, 2 horses, 3 cows and calves
and all furniture. Dau(?): ELIZABETH CHERRY, $300 held
by Exr. for her benefit. Sons: LEWIS HARRELL and wife
TAMSEY have use of 100 A land whereon they live on
lines of JESSE HARRELL to Hardy's corner, reversion
to their chil; DAVID HARRELL, 100 A tract on lines of
Hardy's Swamp. WILLIAM HARRELL and JESSE HARRELL. Dau:
SALLY BROWN, $300 held by Exr. for her support, also
all money owed me by THEOPHILUS BROWN. Daus: MARTHA
MOORE, LUCY LEIGH, POLLY LEIGH, NANCY HARRELL, and
REBECCA 'MOORE, $400 each. Gr. chil: MARTHA HARRELL,
LEWELLING HARRELL, MARGARET HARRELL, LEWIZA HARRELL,

$10 each. Son & Exr: JESSE HARRELL. Son: WILLIAM HARRELL, Son: LEVI HARRELL, $600. Wit: EATON COBB, JOSEPH COBB.

HARRELL, SAMUEL
Jan. 23, 1825. Feb. Ct., 1825. Bk. F, p 32. Wife: (no name), plantation and 3 negroes for lifetime. Son & Exr: DAVID HARRELL, reversion in plantation and 1 negro. Gr. dau: MILLEY HARRELL, 1 negro. Gr. dau: MAYMY (or MARY?) CORBITT, 1 negro. Sons: EANAS HARRELL, LEWIS HARRELL. Son & Exr: ELISHA HARRELL. Dau: POLLY BRINKLEY. Wit: R. OWENS, WILLIAM CORBITT.

HARRELL, THOMAS
Apr. 24, 1763. July Ct., 1763. Note:- Some error caused probate to be made at Oct. Ct., 1763. Wife: REBECCA, use of 1 negro and residue of estate. Plantation on N side Ronoak R in Bartee County to be sold for education of 4 youngest chil. (not named). Sons: SIMON, 200 A land purchased of ROBERT DUNBAR and 1 negro; EDMOND, 160 A manner plantation with 100 A N side Tar River purchased of THOS. SPELL, and 1 negro. Daus: SEALE POWELL (HARRELL?), ELVEY, BARBERY CAIN, ELIZABETH BRYANT, and SABRA BOND, 1 negro and L 40 pro. money each. Exr: WILLIAM BRYANT, JONATHAN CANE (CAINE). Wit: CHARLES EVANS, THOMAS BELLCHER, SOLOMON NETTLES.

HARRIS, ARTHUR
Mar. 20, 1784. Aug. Ct., 1784. Wife: LIDIA, lend plantation whereon I live, all equipment and stock provided she maintain chil. properly; otherwise, Exrs to make equal division between wife and chil. Son: JESSE, 2 negroes. Dau: BETSEY, 1 negro. Son: THOMAS, 1 negro and reversion in plantation. Residue divided equally between 3 chil. Exr: WILLIAM RENN, LEWIS BAILEY. Wit: HENRY IRWIN, ABRAM FOWLER, WILLIAM RENN.

HARRIS, JAMES
Jan. 10, 1749-50. Feb. Ct., 1749-50. Wife & Extx: CHEARY, plantation in Southhampton Co. Sons: JAMES, ½ of 100 A plantation whereon I live on E side Deep Creek; ELI, remainder of plantation. Exr: MATHEW JOYNER. Wit: WILLIAM SKINNER, JOHN BLOUNT, JOHN CRUMPTON.

HARRIS, NATHAN
Nov. 30, 1809. May Ct., 1810. Bk. D, p 360. Wife:
MOLLY, lend during widowhood: 5 negroes, 1 horse, 1
mare, 1/3 of stock of every kind, horses excepted, 1/3
furniture and plantation utensils, sider still, also
houses and land on Whiteoak Swamp. Friend: WILLIAM
EXUM, 1 negro. Dau: POLLY DICKEN, 100 A on Watery
Branch where RICHARD DICKEN lives. Gr. dau: FRANKEY
DICKEN, 2 negroes. At wife's death all to be divided
between POLLY DICKEN and her chil. said son-in-law
RICHARD DICKEN to never have any part of it in his
possession. Exr: ELIAS BRYANT, DAVID COFFIELD. Wit:
DAVID BRADLEY, LEVI DENTON, HARRISON PITMAN. EXUM
LEWIS became Exr. in Nov. Ct., 1821.

HARRIS, THOMAS
May 12, 1786. Feb. Ct., 1787. Wife: SARAH, all estate her natural life; at her death personal estate
divided equally among chil. Son: WILLIAM, plantation
whereon I live. Gr. chil: JOHN and ELIZABETH HARRIS,
chil. of my son JAMES HARRIS, to have one share. Remaining chil: THOMAS, JOSEPH, OLIF SANDIFOR, ELIZABETH
BRYAN, SARAH FORT, ANN HARRIS, MARY HARRIS and PHEBY
HARRIS. Exr: BRITTAIN BRYAN and his wife, ELIZABETH
BRYAN. Wit: JOHN DOLVIN, REBECKAH DOLVIN, SARAH EDWARDS.

HARRISON, MARY ANN
Nov. 19, 1790. Nov. Ct., 1792. Sons & Exrs: HENERY
(eldest) 3 negroes; RICHARD, 3 negroes; DAVID COFFIELD,
1 negro. Daus: MARGARET, MARY and NANCEY, remainder of
negroes; residue divided between 3 daus. Wit: JOHN
GOODMAN, MALACIAH SORY, MARGARET W. MICHAL.

HARRISON, SALLY
Dec. 21, 1834. May Ct., 1835. Bk. F, p 170. Dau:
NARCISSA, 7 sheep, 2 cows and calves, sows, 6 geese;
2 pots, 4 pot hooks, oven, skillet, frying pan, 2
chists, 7 sitting chairs, 1 bofat and it's contents,
and all residue. Exr: SPENCER L. HART. Wit: JESSE C.
KNIGHT.

HART, HENRY
Oct. 4, 1780. Feb. Ct., 1785. Wife & Extx:

PRISCILLA, bequeath 1 mare, saddle, 1 iron pot, all
pewter, 4 sows and pigs, 10 cattle, 6 sheep, 1 guilt
trunk, 1 large chest, box iron and heater, linnen
wheel and wollen wheel; lend use of 4 negroes for
widowhood, negroes to revert to CLARY and MARY. Daus:
CLARY, 1 negro, also half those lent wife, iron pot,
2 cows and calves and 4 sheep; MARY, 1 negro also half
of those lent wife, iron pot, 4 cows and calves and
4 sheep. Son & Exr: JOSEPH, manner plantation, with
exception of orchard where MARY BRADDY lives which I
lent to RICHARD for 4 yrs., reversion to JOSEPH; 2
negroes, mare, 2 cows and calves, iron pot, sow and
pigs, all tools, ½ still, and ½ cyder hogsheads. Son:
RICHARD, plantation I bought of PILRIM POPE and his
son; 2 negroes, 1 colt, 4 cattle, copper kettle, whipsaw, shoemakers tools, ½ cyder hogsheads, and ½ still.
Daus: SARAH, 2 negroes, 2 cows and calves, 4 sheep
and iron pot; ZADA, 2 negroes, iron pot, 2 cows and
calves and 4 sheep. Exr. to sell my brandy and proceeds
of orchard and some colts in order to discharge a bond
to ELIJAH POPE for land given to RICHARD. Exr: ISAAC
SESSUMS. Wit: EDWARD HALL, WILLIAM FORT.

HART, PRISCILLA
      Aug. 13, 1798. Nov. Ct., 1798. Son: RICHARD, 1 large
iron pot, 1 chest, ½ of cattle, except 1 cow and calf,
½ sheep, 1 pr. fire irons, my large Church Bible, 1 iron
pot rack, Brass kittle and copper kittle. Daus: SARAH
ELIZABETH, she and MARY to have all hogs, crop of corn
and plantation tools; MARY, ½ cattle, ½ sheep, all
kitchen furniture, 1 feather bed, new feathers for another bed, 1 pr. new cotton sheets, chest, 2 wool blankets, 1 Rose blanket, 2 hackles, 1 pr. flat irons and
1 horse; ELIZABETH BIGGS, 1 heffer, the bed I brought
from my mothers' and small pine chest; and NANCY FORT,
cow and calf, 1 hackle and my mare. Money in house to
satisfy debt due TELFAIR from HENRY HART, Dec'd. Exr:
EXUM PHILIPS. Wit: KIZZIAH DAVIS, STARLING DIGGS.

HART, SPENCER L.
      _____? 1847. Aug. Ct., 1853. Bk. F, p 513. Wife:
LOUISANNA, 280 A tract whereon I live together with
mill thereon, adjoining RICHARD HARRISON and JAMES

BATTLE, another tract of 500 A adjoining, known as
HARDIWAY tract, 8 slaves and their chil., hogs, cattle,
cows and calves, etc. Reversion of her land to son
SPENCER L. Dau: MARGARET, 500 A tract where I formerly
lived adjoining my HARDIWAY, NEUSOM and DICKERSON
tracts. Dau: MARTHA ANN, my 300 A NEWSOM tract adjoining land of WILLIAM PENDER and that given dau. MARGARET.
Dau: ELLEN L., 136 A DICKERSON tract, also an adjoining 100 A tract bought of JAMES BATTLE "my old home
tract", NEUSOM tract and lands of JAMES S. BATTLE. Son:
BENJAMIN, if I die before education completed, he is
to have $500 for that purpose. Son & Exr: WILLIAM. Sons
FRANKLIN and ALMON. Land on N side Tar River and all
residue of negroes to be sold at direction of Exr.
and divided equally between chil. Gdn. for minors and
Exr: ROBERT R. BRIDGERS. Wit: ROBERT H. PENDER, JOSHUA
D. HORN.

HARVEY, ANNA (widow)
     Aug. 2, 1802. Aug. Ct., 1805. Bro: JOHN GRAY BLOUNT,
25 negroes, now estimated at value of $3500. Nieces:
POLLY ANN BLOUNT, dau; of JOHN GRAY BLOUNT, $700, my
silver tankard within 12 mo. after her marriage or at
21 yrs; LOUISA ANN BLOUNT, dau. of my bro. READING
BLOUNT, my silver soup spoon and $400, to be same as
above niece; POLLY HARVEY BLOUNT, dau. of my bro.
READING BLOUNT, 1 pianoforte of value of $150 to be
purchased when she arrives at 12 yrs of age; CAROLINE
JONES BLOUNT, dau. of READING BLOUNT, 1 pianoforte
value $150, delivered when she arrives at 12 yrs;
NANCY BLOUNT, dau of my dec'd bro. JACOB BLOUNT, $50
to purchase a mourning locket and ring; BETSEY BLOUNT,
dau. of dec'd bro. JACOB BLOUNT, $50 to purchase a
mourning locket and ring; ANNE BLOUNT TOOLE, dau. of
dec'd bro. WM. BLOUNT, 4 negroes, all household furniture except that which remains at Blount Hall, horse
and chair, cow and calf and 1/3 of debt of $600 due
me from JAMES ARMSTRONG of Pitt Co.; MARY LOUISA
BLOUNT MILLER, dau of my dec'd bro. WM. BLOUNT, my
gold watch and $50 to purchase a mounring locket and
ring. Neph: WILLIAM GRAINGER BLOUNT, son of dec'd
bro. WM. BLOUNT a collection of law books, the value
of $250 selected and purchased under discretion of

my bro. THOS. BLOUNT, who has authority to sell 1
negro to pay for same, also 2/3 part of debt due from
JAMES ARMSTRONG of Pitt Co. Nieces: BARBARA BLOUNT,
dau. of dec'd bro. WM. BLOUNT, money for education
at direction of my bro. WILLIE BLOUNT; ELIZA BLOUNT,
dau. of dec'd bro. WM. BLOUNT, money for education
at direction of my bro. WILLIE BLOUNT. Nephs:
RICHARD BLACKLEDGE BLOUNT, and JACOB BLOUNT, & nieces:
BARBARA BLOUNT and ELIZA BLOUNT, the four youngest chil.
of my dec'd bro. WM. BLOUNT I devise all my lands in
state of Tenn. purchased of JAMES ARMSTRONG and
CASWELL ARMSTRONG, 2 of the heirs of the late Gen.
JAMES ARMSTRONG, this to be managed by my bro. WILLIE
BLOUNT. All of the legacies unless otherwise noted to
be paid for by Bro: JOHN GRAY BLOUNT and charged against the 25 negroes left to him. At his death residue to,
be divided among his children. One faithful old negro
left in care of Bro: READING BLOUNT, 2 faithful old
negroes in care of Bro: THOMAS BLOUNT. Exrs: Bros.
JOHN GRAY BLOUNT, READING BLOUNT, THOMAS BLOUNT.
Wit: JOHN HUDSON, WM. STANTACK.

HARWOOD, JOSEPH
     May 30, 1769. Feb. Ct., 1770. Wife & Extx: SARAH,
benefits and profits of all estate, real and personal,
during natural life or widowhood. Sons & Exrs: JOSEPH,
130 A plantation he lives on bought of STEPHEN WILLS,
after mother's death, 3 negroes, cow and calf, ½ sheep
and 1 horse; ABSOLOM, plantation whereon I live after
Mother's death, tract bought of JOHN BAKER, 2 cows and
calves, 1 negro, ½ sheep, horse and mare. Dau: REBECCA,
1 bed of furn. after Mother's death. Gr. sons: HAMLET
UNDERWOOD, cow and calf, my gun after wife's death;
HOWELL HARWOOD, 1 negro after his father's death;
TURNER HARWOOD, 1 negro after his father's death;
JESSE and WM. HARWOOD. Wit: DUNCAN LAMON, ARCHIBALD
LAMON, MARGARET LAMON.

HATCHER, JOHN
     Oct. 1, 1765. Jan. Ct., 1766. Wife: DOROTY, remain-
der of land for lifetime; reversion to dau. SARAH. Son:
JEREMIAH, 100 A land. Daus: SARAH, 1 bed furn. and
cow and calf; MARY, 1 bed of furn. and cow and calf.

Son & Exr: HANCOCK. Son: JOHN, 10 S. ARTHUR PITMAN,
10 S. Residue to 5 chil. Wit: JOHN MIAL, JETHRO PITMAN.

HATTON, FRANCIS
    Dec. 6, 1827. May Ct., 1828. Bk. F, p 86. Wife:
FRANCES, lend use of all negroes during lifetime. Exr:
to sell all land and property not bequeathed in will
and use money to move family to Ala. Residue of money
to be equally divided between SALLY, POLLY, JULEY,
NANCEY, and JAMES HATTON. At wife's death all negroes
to be sold and return equally divided as above. Sons
& Exrs: JAMES, and SAMUEL, 1 negro each. Dau: BETSEY,
1 negro. Wit: JAMES DOWNING, SR., JOHN EDMONDSON. Exr
herein named refusing to qualify, RODERICK STATON made
Adm., entering bond of $2000 with ALLEN JONES and
LAWRENCE STATON, Securities.

HAWKINS, ELZA
    June 16, 1828. Feb. Ct., 1837. Wife: GRACY, all
estate. It is my will that my boys have 2 yrs schooling each out of my estate, and that between the age
of 12 and 18 not be bound out, but to be supported
out of my estate. It is my will that my oldest dau.
MIZY HARRISS shall never have any part of my estate
as 1 have given her $100 which I think is an equal
share. Mother-in-law: TABBITHA TAYLOR, lend feather bed
and furniture. Children unnamed. Wit: EDWARD G. HAMMOND,
LEVIN LEGGITT. There being no Exr. named, Adm. granted
to DEMPSEY BRYAN who entered into bond in sum of $2000
with RODERICK PURVIS and LEVIN LEGGITT, Securities.

HAYWOOD, JOHN
    July 23, 1756. Dec. Ct., 1758. Sons: WILLIAM, JOHN,
EGBERT and HARWOOD. Daus: DEBORAH and MARY HAYWOOD,
213 A land to daus. All 6 chil. appointed Exrs. Wit:
EDWARD CROWELL, WILLIAM CAMPBELL, THOMAS MERRITT.

HAYWOOD, JOHN
    Feb. 18, 1758. June Ct., 1758. Bros: EGBERT,
WILLIAM and SHERWOOD HAYWOOD. Sisters: DEBORAH and
MARY HAYWOOD. Father, not named. Exr: EGBERT HAYWOOD.
Wit: ROBERT WARREN, JOSEPH POPE, SAMUEL PITMAN.

HAYWOOD, SHERWOOD

Mar. 10, 1780. May Ct., 1780. Wife & Extx: HANNAH, bequeath 10 negroes, ½ all household goods, ½ of all stock, also Ł 100 paper currency, lend plantation during widowhood, and use of 5 negroes. Son: ADAM JOHN HAYWOOD, Ł 220 in gold and silver, plantation whereon I live, all adjoining lands, also tract called Doe Head, also tract lying in Fork of Falling Run called the Quarter, also all land S side of Tar River on Walnut Creek and ELVINGTON'S Branch and 21 negroes. If unborn child is boy, shall have 350 A land on Falling Run called the Quarter, also that on Walnut Creek and Elvington's Branch. If child is girl, she shall have only 6 negroes. If chil. die before maturity property shall be divided between JOHN & SHERWOOD HAYWOOD, sons of WILLIAM HAYWOOD and JOHN & THOMAS HAYWOOD, sons of EGBERT HAYWOOD. Exr: ROBERT DIGGES, EGBERT HAYWOOD, JOHN HAYWOOD, SEN., ETHELRED RUFFIN, JOHN HAYWOOD, JR. Wit: WILLIAM DANCY, RICHARD STROTHER, JOHN SUMNER, ABRAHAM EVINS.

HAYWOOD, WILLIAM

Nov. 25, 1779. Feb. Ct., 1780. Wife: CHARITY, rid-ing chair and harness, lend 270 A plantation bought of JESSE NARE whereon I live, provided she lives on it, all household goods and stock of horses, cattle, hogs, sheep, also use of 13 negroes. Son & Exr: JOHN HAYWOOD, tract taking up deed out of Earl of Granville for 450 A lying on DELOACH'S or Folk's Branch, also tract sur-veyed by CARTRIGHT adjoining WILLIAM DELOACH and WILLIAM SHERROD and 2 negroes. Daus: MARY RUFFIN, 2 ne-groes; ELIZABETH TOOLE, 3 negroes. Son & Exr: SHERWOOD H., other part of tract given son JOHN lying on E of DELOACH'S Branch, also 1 negro. Daus: ANNE, JEMIMA, CHARITY, 1 negro each. Son: WILLIAM HENRY, 400 A lying both sides of middle prong of Walnut Creek also 128 A on Walnut Creek granted to MOSES NARE of Hertford Co., also 1 negro. Son: STEPHEN, 270 A plantation whereon I live that I had of JESSE NARE and 1 negro. Exr: Bros, SHERWOOD HAYWOOD, EGBERT HAYWOOD. Wit: WILLIAM WILSON, JAMES WILSON, GEORGE WEATHERS. Codicil signed, 1779. Same witnesses.

HEARN, MICHAEL
Nov. 15, 1787. Jan. Ct., 1788. Bk. B, p 59. Wife
& Extx: MARY, lend 4 negroes, reversion to chil. houses
and improvements in Tarborough, reversion to sons
MICHAEL & LAWRENCE HENRY HEARN. Mentions children but
gives neither number nor names. Wit: AMOS JOHNSTON,
NOAH SUGG.

HEDGEPETH, JOHN
Sept. 4, 1816. Aug. Ct., 1823. Bk. E, p 337. Wife:
ELIZABETH, lend 82 1/2 A tract N side of road adjoining tract in Nash Co. and tract on S side of road. Bequeath $120 to buy 2 horses, sell my horses, 5 cows
and calves, all hogs, furniture and saddle. Son: ARTHUR,
Mother's land after death. 250 A tract in Nash Co. where
sister MARY SANDERS lives and 2 negroes to be sold and
returns divided between daus: TABITHA, AGATHA and
PENNINAH. Exr: WM. HORN, BARTLEY DEANS. Wit: ELI MERCER,
LITHA HEDGEPETH.

HENDRICK, WM.
Jan. 1, 1766. Jan. Ct., 1767. All property sold,
money divided between 4 chil. Son: JOSHUA. Son & Exr:
WILLIAM. Daus: SARAH BECKINGHAM, MARY HOOD. Gr. chil:
JEREMIAH HEDRICK, WILLIAM BUSBY, MILDRED COKER, 5 S
each. Wit: WILLIAM BLACKBURN, JOHN NICHOLSON,
WILLIAM PRITCHET.

HERN, JAMES (HEARN)
Aug. 27, 1783. No probate date. Bk. B, p 129. Wife:
ELIZABETH HERN, all my estate for the purpose of main-
taining her and raising the children. Wit: TEAGLE
TAYLOR, DANIEL WALKER.

HICKMAN, NATHANIEL
Mar. 10, 1790. Nov. Ct., 1795. Wife: SARAH, lend
350 A plantation whereon I live, also land on branch
of Town Creek and all remainder estate for life. Sons:
NATHANIEL, reversion 150 A, upper part plantation
whereon I live; WILLIAM, reversion 150 A lower part
plantation whereon I live. Gr. son & Exr: SNODON
HICKMAN, 200 A tract on Town Creek, 1 negro, 1/3
cattle, horses, hogs, sheep and tools. Gr. dau: NANCY

CLARK, 1/3 cattle, horses, hogs and sheep, woolen
wheel and linen wheel. Dau: MORENING PITMAN, 1/3
cattle, horses, hogs, sheep, tools and 1 negro. Daus:
ELIZABETH VIVRETT, SARAH DIXON and MARY STRICKLEN, 5
S each. Exr: DEMSEY DAWSON. Wit: DEMSEY DAWSON, ROLAND
ROBBINS.

HICKS, JAMES
    Aug. 11, 1840. May Ct., 1841. Bk. F, p 254. Wife:
MARY HICKS, cow and calf, etc. for life. Property sold
for division among heirs: LAMON, STARLING, REDEN,
CHARLOTTE BILLUPS, SPENCER HICKS, and BRITTANIA HARRIS.
Son & Exr: SPENCER HICKS. Wit: WM. THIGPEN, WILLIAM
MAYO.

HILL, PENELOPE
    Feb. 8, 1826. Aug. Ct., 1826. Bk. F, p 59. PEOPLES
HILL, 2 negroes, note he owes me for $53.56 and cow
and calf. CATHERINE LONG, all wearing apparel except
1 habbit. WHITMILL WILLIAMS, $20 and cow and calf.
BENNETT LONG, $10. Remaining estate sold and residue
divided between legatees. Exr: ROBERT BARNES. Wit:
ELIZABETH LONG, ORREN D. COHOON.

HILLIARD, JACOB
    Dec. 14, 1763. Jan. Ct., 1764. Wife: ELIZABETH, be-
queath 2 negroes, ½ household goods, 3 horses, 1 colt,
all cider casks, 8 cows and calves, 2 steers, 12 sows,
30 barrous and sows, sheep, 15 bu. wheat, 35 bbl. corn,
5 sows and 23 pigs now on market. Lend use of 1 negro
til dau. ELIZABETH comes of age or marries, use of plantation whereon I dwell, only ½ of orchard after son
JEREMIAH comes of age and use of still; all this during
widowhood. Son: JEREMIAH, reversion in all lands and
3 negroes. Dau: ELIZABETH, 3 negroes; residue sold,
money divided between children JEREMIAH and ELIZABETH.
Exr: ELISHA BATTLE, WILLIAM HORN, son of HENRY. Wit:
HENRY HORN, GEORGE WIMBERLY, MARY HORN.

HILLIARD, ROBERT
    Apr. 13, 1743. May Ct., 1751. Devisees and legatees:
Wife, CHARITY; Cousins, JACOB and ROBERT HILLIARD, sons
of JEREMIAH HILLIARD, dec'd, my plantation. Cousin,

JEREMIAH, son of JEREMIAH HILLIARD, my 622 A plantation on the falls of Teare River where my bro. JEREMIAH HILLIARD (dec'd) did live. Cousins: SAMSONE and MARY, chil of JEREMIAH HILLIARD, dec'd; WILLIAM H. son of WILLIAM and ANN HILLIARD, £ 50; JEAMES H. son of WILLIAM and ANN HILLIARD, £ 20. Exr: WILLIAM HILLIARD and OSBORNE JEFFREYS. Wit: SAMUEL HOLLIMAN, WILLIAM SERGINER, BENJA. BOYKIN.

HINES, KINCHEN
    Dec. 28, 1829. May Ct., 1830. Bk. F, p 116. Wife & Extx: CHARITY ANN, all estate including 11 negroes. Lend 8 negroes, reversion to my brothers and sisters, the negroes having privilege of choosing their masters. Bro: JOHN HINES, $250. Wit: JAMES J. PHILIPS, ELIZABETH GEORGE.

HINES, PETER (SR.)
    Nov. 15, 1783. Nov. Ct., 1783. Sons & Exrs: HENRY, all lands in Edgecombe on lines of JOHN ELLIS, OARIUS COWEN, Tar River and road that leads up Town Creek from River road to Gouger Branch, and ½ my part of grist mill across Town Creek, 5 negroes beside all that already in his possession; PETER, all remainder of lands adjoining above, other ½ my part of mill across Town Creek, 8 negroes, mare, case of bottles and all that already in his possession. Daus: ELIZABETH ELLIS, 10 negroes, reversion to her chil. and all that already in her possession; ANN EVANS, 3 negroes and all their chil. and all that already in her possession; MARY CONON (CONARE ? or CONNOR ?): 8 negroes, large church Bible, 6 ewes and lambs and all that already in her possession. Gr. son: PETER HINES, son of HENRY HINES, 1 negro. To sons all money, housed tobacco, clothes and cloth. Residue divided between 3 daus. Wit: WILLIAM QUINN, JESSE PROCTOR, STERLING DUPREE, PETER CARTRIGHT, JAMES JOHNSTON.

HINES, PETER (SR.)
    Feb. 27, 1804. Feb. Ct., 1805. Bk. D, p 215. Son & Exr: PETER, plantation whereon I live, all lands S side Town Creek, land bought of BOLING MARLEY, also 30 A bought of NATHAN MARLEY; 9 negroes, mare, yoke

of oxen I purchased of JETHRO HARRISON, shotgun, and
all furniture belonging to my Hall Room. Son: RICHARD,
land already given him, 10·negroes, filly, 2 steers
and $100. Should he die before maturity son PETER to
have all land. Dau: SALLEY, 13 negroes, riding chair
and harness, mare and colt. Gr. daus: AGNES H. SPRUILL
and ROSANNA E. H. SPRUILL, chil. of BENJ. SPRUILL and
wife ELIZABETH, 7 negroes, 1 of which I bought of
JESSE DRAKE, also $400. AMOS JOHNSTON, Esq., MAJOR
PETER HINES. Wit: WILLIAM WILKINS, PETER EVANS, JAMES
WILKINS.

HINES, PRUDENCE
    May 12, 1850. No probate date. Son & Exr: PETER E.
HINES, all land on SE side of Beaver Dam Swamp on lines
of JOHN A. VINES, PETER EVANS and heirs of ISAAC EASON.
All negroes and residue divided between 2 chil. Dau:
CATHERINE W. BYNUM, wife of BENJAMIN BYNUM. Wit: JOHN
HARRELL, JONATHAN ROBERSON. Exr: refused to serve. Adm.
granted BENJAMIN BYNUM. Bond $15,000. JOHN A. VINES
and REDMOND DUPREE, Securities.

HINES, RICHARD
    Feb. 1, 1781. Aug. Ct., 1781. Wife & Extx: MARY,
bequeath walnut chest, saddle, ·bridle, 8 chairs, 2
tables, 1 bell mettal, skillet, lend land and plantation whereon I live, residue to son JESSE, lend all
negroes, 1/3 of all cattle, hogs, sheep, pewter, tools,
etc. to go to each son at maturity, other 1/3 to wife,
reversion to sons. Sons: JESSE HINES, 2 negroes, 2
horses; RICHARD, 2 negroes, mare and colt, "shottgun",
razor and hone. If either son die before maturity his
negroes go to surviving son; if both die under age,
they go to daus. Daus: ANN THOMPKINS; MARY BELCHER,
MARTHA STOCDALE, SARAH STURDIVANT, 1 negro and cow
and calf each; HANNAH HINES, cow and calf, looking
glass, 1 pr. cotton cards, linen wheel, trunk and 2
chairs. Exr: BEVERLY BELCHER, WILLIAM VANN (?). Wit:
GABRIEL ALLEN, OWEN CRAVEY, JOHN MIAL (?).

HINES, W. H.
    Mar. 29, 1853. Feb. Ct., 1854. Wife: MALVINA. Be-
queath to friend JESSE MERCER, trustee.... negro,

MARIAH, 2 horses, buggy, crockery, including 1 set of
table and 1 set of teaspoons and child's part of all
negroes. $100 to hold in trust for wife MALVINA, re-
version to 4 sons. Sons: JESSE, old fashioned London
watch and ivory headed walking cane left me by my
father: WILLIAM R., double cased watch and silver-
headed walking cane marked W. H. H.; JOSIAH H.; PETER
E.: 4 sons to have all remainder of property, including
all my books. Negroes Adeline and Harriett to be sold,
proceeds to wife and son. If negro woman, Grace lives
till she become disabled she shall be comfortably provided for by all my heirs. Gdn.: JOHN B. MERCER, request him to give them a liberal education. Exr: JAMES
F. JENKINS, JESSE MERCER. Codicil, May 9, 1853. ADELINE
& HARRIETT (negroes) not to be sold, but equally divided between heirs. No Witnesses. Proven by oaths of
JOHN R. MERCER, J. L. HORNE, JAMES A. ARMSTRONG.

HINES, WILLIAM W.
        Dec. 14, 1820. Aug. Ct., 1822. Bk. E, p 305. Wife:
LUCY, all property during widowhood or until son
WILLIAM HENRY HINES reaches maturity. In either case,
property, real and personal shall be equally divided
between mother and WILLIAM HENRY HINES. Son: WILLIAM
HENRY, sleeve buttons, Ivory head walking cane, half
stocked shot gun, shot bag and powder horn, Morses'
Geography, Morses' Gazetteers, Walker's Dictionary,
my Cyphering book, Dilworth's Arithmetick, Marray's
Grammar, Medical Companion. Afflicted Man's Companion,
silver watch, State and Cary's Atlas. Exr: TURNER
BYNUM, SAM'L H. JENKINS. Wit: STEPHEN WOOTEN, EPHRAIM
WOOTEN.

HINES, WILLIAM
        Aug. 14, 1816. Nov. Ct., 1818. Bk. E, p 205.
Mother: CATHERINE JOHNSTON, widow of AMOS JOHNSTON,
dec'd, all lands and 8 negroes for her lifetime, reversion of land and negroes to neph. WILLIAM HINES,
son of Col. PETER HINES. If he should die before maturity, to be equally divided between my bros: PETER
HINES and ROBT. W. HINES, Executors; to have £ 50
each for their service. Wit: SAMUEL RUFFIN, WILLIAM
J. RUFFIN.

HINTON, WILLIAM
　　May 17, 1841. May Ct., 1841. Bk. F, p 254. Mother
& Extx: RACHEL HINTON, lend land bought of the late
ELISHA LEWIS, the TART land where my mother now lives,
notes, horses, reversion to bro. & Exr: JAMES HINTON,
also carpenter's tools. Residue to JAMES and sisters:
CIDDY, ELIZABETH, LUCY and SALLY. Wit: MOSES BAKER,
HENRY WHITEHEAD, HILLIARY PEELE.

HOBBS, MARY
　　May 23, 1819. Aug. Ct., 1819. Bk. E, p 222. Dau:
SUSANNA DUNFORD, brindle cow, all money (about $35),
owed me by my son ISAAC HOBBS. Gr. dau: NANCY DUNFORD,
dau of SUSANNA DUNFORD, cow and yearling; gr. dau:
JULAN WHITTY, dau. of JESSE WHITTY, dau: NANCY WHITTY,
wife of JESSE WHITTY. Residue divided between 2 daus.
No Exr. No Adm. Wit: BENJA. SHARPE, JOHN WILKINSON.

HOBBY, JACOB
　　Jan. 22, 1758. Sept. Ct., 1758. Wife & Extx:
JEMIME. Son: MATTHEW, all my land. Daus: RHODA, SARAH,
FRANCES. Exr: JOHN BAKER. Wit: ANDREW IRWING,
BRACEWELL BRIDGERS, JOSEPH KELLY.

HODGES, ANTHONY
　　Feb. 28, 1811. May Ct., 1811. Bk. E, p 17. Neph:
KINNY HODGES, 1 negro. Niece: NANCY DIGGES, ½ land and
½ my interest in land at my mother's death. Sister:
PENNY HODGES, ½ land and ½ my interest in land at my
mother's death. Sisters: NANCY SMITH, SARAH CLAUD, and
ELIZABETH DIGGES, 5 S each. Exr: ELIAS BRYANT, WILLIAM
BELLAMY. Wit: ALLEN SESSUMS, JACOB SESSUMS.

HODGES, SARAH
　　Dec. 18, 1822. May Ct., 1828. Bk. F, p 88. All property sold. Residue divided between 4 daus. as well as
clothing. Daus: POLLY LATHAN, ₤ 40; PENNY ABBINGTON
₤ 30; NANCY SMITH: SARA CLOUD. Gr. son: WILLIAM HENRY
HODGES, ₤ 30. Exr: EPHRAIM DICKEN. Wit: JACOB SESSUM,
EPHRAIM DICKEN.

HODGES, THOMAS
　　Feb. 19, 1800. May Ct., 1806. Wife: SALLY, lend

plantation whereon I live, 5 negroes, old riding chair,
harness, horse, the buffat and all furniture that belongs to it. One doz. mulberry chairs, 1 walnut table,
2 pine tables, 1 chest, 1 set bed curtains, 2 cows and
calves. Dau: NANCY SMITH, tract bought of LEMUEL JELKS
and by him of HENRY PHILIPS, 4 negroes, property already in her possession. Dau: ELIZABETH DIGGES, tract
bought of LEMUEL **JELKS** and JELKS of JOHN DOLVIN,
DOLVIN of GEO. COTTEN, adjoining MOSES SMITH; 2 negroes,
side saddle, bed clothing she got by her own industry
and horse; lend tract over Crooked Swamp, I purchased
of LEMUEL JELKS, JELKS of JOHN DOLVIN and DOLVIN of
JOSHUA PROCTOR to use until gr. son HENRY WILLIAM
HODGES arrives at 10 yrs of age, she to have sole, entire and separate use and enjoyment of said property
without same being liable or subject to molestation of
her husband, ,STARLING DIGGES, nor shall same be to pay
any debts made by STARLING DIGGES. Reversion to her
children. Dau: SALLY HODGES, 5 negroes, some were purchased of DOCTOR HAYWOOD, bed and window curtains,
quilts she acquired by her own industry, new riding
chair and 1 horse purchased of JOHN BOLT, 1 trunk and
side saddle. Son: THOMAS, plantation whereon I live,
1 negro, colt, and saddle, tract purchased of RICHARD
SESSUMS during life of his mother. Son: ANTHONY, reversion in plantation purchased of RICHARD SESSUMS except 20 A purchased of WILLIAM BRYAN, 1 negro, 1 horse
and saddle. Dau: PENNY, 4 negroes, 1 filly, and trunk.
Gr. dau: NANCY DIGGES, 2 negroes and parcel of feathers.
Gr. son: HENRY WM. HODGES, tract lying over Crooked
Swamp, this being land lent dau., ELIZABETH DIGGES,
also 1 negro. Exr: JEREMIAH HILLIARD, JACOB BATTLE,
DEMSEY BATTLE. Wit: RICHARD HARRISON, RICHARD HART
Executors refused to qualify and RANDOLPH COTTEN Adm.

HOGG, THOMAS
    May 11, 1789. Nov. Ct., 1789. Bk. 3, p 117. Wife
& Extx: ELIZA, whole estate for life or until eldest
son comes of age, at which time all shall be divided
equally between wife and 2 sons: SAMUEL and JOHN
BAPTIST; Exrs: Bro. SAMUEL HOGG, THOMAS GILCHRIST. Wit:
SAMUEL OWENS, ELIZA THOMPSON, BENJAMIN CHERRY.

HOLLAND, JACOB

May 15, 1798. Feb. Ct., 1799. Wife & Extx: PEGGA, lend all land during widowhood; bequeath horse, side saddle and bridle, hogs, sheep, 3 cows and calves, iron pott, pr pott hooks, 1 pewter dish, pewter bason, 2 pewter plates, 3 sitting chairs, 1 chest; lend 2 pewter basons, 4 pewter plates, 1 pewter dish, 1 flesh fork, bred gridale, iron spoon, looking glass, 1 tub, pail, piggen meal sifter, bread board, pr tin candle "mouldas", cyder casks, barrels, guns, tray, cart and wheels, 2 plow frames, 2 plow hoes, grubbing hoes, rakes, weeding hoes, juggs, bottles, sweet gumwood table, flax hackle, pr wool cards, all flax, cotten, meate and corn. At wife's death, land to be divided between my 7 sons. All other lent wife to be divided between all children. Sons & Exrs: JAMES and RICHARD, cow and calf; sons: JACOB and LAMON, cow and calf. Daus: BARSHEBA BRAKE, wife of NATHAN BRAKE; ABRA HOLLAND; SARAH HOLLAND. Sons: DAVID, HARDY, DIOLACAN (?). Wit: LAMON RUFFIN, AARON PROCTOR, UNITY HARGROVES.

HOLLON (HOLLIN, HOLLAND?), DAVID

Jan. 14, 1847. May Ct., 1848. Bk. F, p 394. Wife: life estate in house and land for her own support, furniture, cow and calf, $25.00, loom, gear, 400 lbs pork, 10 bbls corn, 50 lbs. lard, 50 lbs. flour, 15 lbs coffee, 30 lbs sugar, 1000 lbs fodder. Son: EPENETUS HOLLON, $100.00 cash and bind him to take care of his mother; my brandy still, worm, benefit of my orchard, apple mill, still shelter and acre of land whereon it stands. Sons: JOHN and EPENETUS, all my lands, they to pay my dau. MARTHA ANN STALLINGS $75 each. Exr: LEMUEL C. PENDER. Wit: WILLIAM PENDER, L. C. PENDER.

HOLMES, JOHN

Feb. 28, 1735 - 1736. May Ct., 1736. Son: JOHN; son & Exr: HARDY, parcel of land between BEAVERDAM Swamp and the Marsh; Son: EDWARD, land whereon I dwell; Son: GABRIEL, land purchased of JAMES SAUNDERS. Daus: ANN SANDERS, CHARITY BROWN, DOROTHY SPIER, BEATRIX SPEIR, ROSE HOLMES and MARY HOLMES (youngest child). Wit: EDWARD BUXTON, WILLIAM DAVIES, ELIZABETH WELCH.

HOPKINS, DANIEL
Apr. 10, 1845. Aug. Ct., 1846. Wife: MARY, 5 negroes,
gig and harness; dau-in-law: JULIA HOPKINS, widow of
WILLIAM D. HOPKINS; gr. dau: JENNET, dau of WILLIAM
D. HOPKINS, 4 negroes, 300 A tract called Shivers
Tracts adjoining FREDERICK HOPKINS; son & Exr: JARRET,
tract called Billy Place adjoining FREDERICK HOPKINS,
and 8 negroes; dau: HARRIET STANSELL, 650 A tract pur-
chased of AARON ATKINSON, adjoining WILLIAM C. LEIGH,
DAVID MAYO, WILLIAM HARRELL and 8 negroes; son: HENRY
A, 300 A tract bought of WILLIAM CHERRY and ASA BROWN
and 9 negroes; son: THOMAS C., land whereon I live,
tract bought of BRITAIN SPELLINGS, also tract bought
of ELIJAH PRICE, in all 900 A and 9 negroes; gr. daus:
JENNET LOUESER (LOUISA) JENKINS and MARY ELIZABETH
JENKINS, 2 lots in Tarborough known as the Lackey Lot
and the Guyon lot and 5 negroes. Exr: JESSEY STANSELL
(STANCIL). Wit: JOHN PORTER, HENRY STANSELL. Codicil,
May 15, 1846. Slight change in legacy and giving
ARSENA MAYO $50. Wit: WILLIAM C. LEIGH, JESSE W. LEIGH.

HOPKINS, SAVORY
Mar. 23, 1853. May Ct., 1853. Bk. F, p 524. All
estate, including 6 slaves to be divided between Gr.
sons: FREDERICK JENKINS, JOHN McGILBRA (McGILVERY)
JENKINS and JOSEPH VANBUREN JENKINS. Niece: NANCY
STATON. Exr: Gr. son: FREDERICK JENKINS; Neph. CARSOL
STATON. Wit: JOHN WARREN, JESSE STANCIL.

HORN, ELIJAH
Mar. 27, 1804. Feb. Ct., 1815. Bk. E, p 83. Wife:
SUSANNA, lend 20 A land called School house ridge,
with a good comfortable log house built thereon by
direction of executors, 18'x14' planked flour and door
and dirt chimney, shingled roof, at expense of my son
BYTHAL HORN from his legacy and with help of my negro
man Buggin; bequeath 10 hogs, 20 bbl. good sound corn,
fodder, bacon, fatt, soap and corn sufficient to support her and son HENRY until Dec. next. Son & Exr:
SIMEON, all land W side of branch formerly called
Griffin's Branch now called Rice Pond Branch adjoin-

ing THOS. DEAVER'S line including 200 A plantation whereon he now lives; cow and calf, 5 sheep, beside what he already has. Son: JAMES, 200 A where he now lives and adjoining MOSES PRICE, CHARLES GRAY, JESSE CLARK, the land called ADAM HAYWOOD'S and land hereinafter bequeathed to my son BYTHAL; 5 sheep besides what he already has. Son: WILLIE, 200 A tract on Rice Pond Branch, mouth of Maple Pond Branch bounded by THOMAS DEAVER, SIMEON HORN and Cool Spring Branch; 1 negro, matt and card, 2 Rose Blankets, beside what he already has. Son: BYTHAL, all residue of lands, 300 A plantation whereon I live bounded by lines of HENRY WILLIAMS, dec'd, and the land called ADAM . HAYWOOD'Son Great Pocosin, 1 negro, horse, colt, 4 sheets, 4 Rose Blankets, 2 matts and cards, bridle and saddle, all geese, 2 cows and calves, 1 pr. Oxen and geer, cart and wheels, 3 sows and pigs, 15 hogs, walnut desk, pine chest, pine table, large iron kettle, large iron pott, potthooks, tools, 6 sheep, pewter dish, 6 pewter plates, 6 pewter spoons, 3 cups and saucers, large butter pott, 6 knives and forks, pr. warping bars and axes, meal tub, flour tub, 5 cyder hogsheads, 2 cyder barrels, 4 casks, 2 tubs, 1 pail, piggin meal sifter, bread tray, wooden bowl, glass tumbler, Bible, hymn book, table cloth, wiping towel, glass decanter, claw hammer, wedges, saw, drawing knife, 4 bbl. corn and forage. Dau: RHODA WARD, wife of MERCER WARD, 2 cows and calves. Dau: SELAH DEW, wife of SAM'L DEW, cow and calf. Son: (?): HORN, $500 silver (no given name). Residue equally divided between sons: SIMEON, LEVY, MICHAEL and WILLIE. Wit: LAMON RUFFIN, ETHELRED RUFFIN;_____ . SIMEON HORN was resident of State of Georgia at time of probate. Adm. granted to WILLIE HORN and MOSES SPICER. They entered bond of L 3000, with SPENCER S. HART and THOMAS B. HORN, Securities.

HORN, ELISHA
    Mar. 16, 1765. April Ct., 1765. Wife: RACHEL, bequeath mare and colt, saddle and bridle, 2 spinning wheels, all puter, 1 pot, 1 "friing" pan, skillet, "acks", saw, 4 sows and pigs, all corn and fodder, 2 cows and calves, chist and trunk. Son: EDWARD, all rest

of estate. Exr: DANIEL ROSS, MICHAEL HORN. Wit: MICHAEL
HORN, JOSIAH TAYLOR, ELIJAH HORN.

HORN, HENRY
     Mar. 29, 1761. June Ct., 1761. Wife & Extx:
ELIZABETH, all estate during lifetime. At her death
land to be sold and money equally divided between daus,
RUTH, MIRRIUM and ZERAIAH. Personal estate sold and di-
vided between all chil. viz: Sons, SION and JOSIAH;
dau, PENSTOPE (PENELOPE?) NUNRY. Exr: Bro., MOSES
HORN, JOHN SCOTT. Wit: GRIFEN NUNRY, JAMES PERRY,
REUBEN WHITFIELD.

HORN, JACOB
     Sept. 18, 1826. Feb. Ct., 1827. Bk. F, p 68. Dau:
MILICENT FARMER, 1 negro. Gr. dau: POLLY TUCKER, tract
land on Little Swamp; dau: MOURNING COBB, horse; Gr.
chil: THOMAS HORN and SALLY HORN, all property bought
at sale of their father's property, sold by DEMSEY
DEANS, to satisfy judgements I held against THOS. HORN,
SEN.; dau: EDIE SIMMS; son: WILLIAM HORN. Sons & Exrs:
HENRY HORN and JEREMIAH HORN. Son: J. R. HORN. Residue
divided between all chil. Wit: SETH WARD, JAMES
PERMENTER.

HORN, JAMES
     Aug. 27, 1783. 9th year American Independence.
Nov. Ct., 1783. Wife & Adm: ELIZABETH, to have all
estate for her life in order to maintain chil. which
"is" now with her. Reversion to children. Wit: TEAGLE
TAYLOR, DANIEL WALKER.

HORN, JOEL
     Feb. 15, 1785. May Ct., 1785. Wife: ANN, lend all
estate, except 2 negroes and 1 barrel Brandy to be
sold. Money put at interest and divided between chil.
when they come of age. Son & Exr: ELIJAH, reversion
in all land and 1 negro; he and uncle, WILLIAM HORN
to own still. Son: THOMAS, 1 negro. Residue divided
between all children. Bro: WILLIAM HORN. Daus: MARY,
MARGRIT, ECLOWE (?) and PENELEPA. Exr: Bro, ELISHA
HORN. Wit: JETHRO PITMAN, JOEL HORN, JOSEPH PRICE.

HORN, MARY
Oct. 5, 1783. Feb. Ct., 1785. Son & Exr: ABISHA, 1
negro. Son & Exr: MOSES, 1 negro for money I owe him,
and all my part of crop. Son: WILLIAM, 1 negro, also
1 other negro if he pay Ł 40 into estate. Sons: JOAB
and JOEL. Residue divided between all children. Daus:
MARY, KIZIA, DRUSILLA, ELISABETH, JEAN and SARAH. Wit:
HOWARD HARRIS, JESSE GREEN.

HORN, MICHAEL
? torn 6, 1785. No probate date. Wife & Extx:
SURANY, all household and kitchen furniture and stock,
reversion to 3 youngest sons: ABSALOM, CASWELL and
MICHAEL; daus: DELILAH ANDERSON, DICEY WATKINS and
CHARITY COHOON, feather bed and furniture each; dau:
ELIZABETH, 10 S; youngest daus: BEERSHABA and POLLY;
gr. son: MATTHEW HORN, 10 S. Sons & Exrs: ELISHA,
grindstone; ELIAS, colt. Wit: DANIEL ROSS, ELISHA HORN,
ELIAS HORN.

HORN, MICHAEL
Sept. 24, 1814. Nov. Ct., 1814. Bk. E, p 74. Nephs:
JOHN ROBBINS HORN, 1 negro; ISAAC HORN, my horse;
CAZWELL HORN, by bridle, saddle and shot gun. Bro &
Exr: ABSALOM HORN. Sisters: BARSHABA HORN and POLLY
BARNES, all stocks of cattle. Residue to Mother and
Bro, ABSALOM HORN. Exr: THOMAS B. HORN. Wit: MOSES
SPEAR, JOSIAH HORN.

HORN, PRISCILLA
Feb. 26, 1837. Aug. Ct., 1850. Nov. Ct., 1851.
JESSE A. COTTON, son of ELIZABETH COTTON, widow, of
Mississippi, $300 at discretion of Gdn. Remainder of
the money and notes, whether in gold, silver, Bank
notes, or notes against individuals, together with my
breast pin, be given unconditionally to JAMES M. BATTLE,
of Edgecombe County. All my wearing apparel... trunks,
chests, boxes of all sorts, side saddle, and all my
property not otherwise disposed of, to FRANCIS FORT,
dau. of PRISCILLA FORT. Exr: neighbor, JOSEPH S. BATTLE.
In case of his death, or refusal to act, my esteemed
neighbor, Doctor JAMES PHILLIPS. Wit: BENNETT H. BUNN,
JOHN H. DANIEL.

HORN, RUTH

May 20, 1803. Aug. Ct., 1803. Mother: RUTH HORN.
Estate equally divided between the following PATIENCE
(?) WOOD (illegible), CHARITY HORN, RACHEL JONES, ANN
HORN. Exr: JEREMIAH HILLIARD, JETHRO BATTLE. Wit: JOHN
BRAKE, JONATHAN PRICE.

HORN, RUTH

Aug. 16, 1803. Nov. Ct., 1803. Daus: JEMIMAH
GLANDEN, side saddle and 5 S; PATIENCE WOOD, cow;
CHARITY HORN, 6 pewter plates, jug, butter pott, 2
chairs, ½ my part of whole crop after JOHN BRAKE has
his part, ½ hogs, "weading" hoe, "shovle" and tongs,
1/3 my sheep and 1/3 my leather; RACHEL JONES, 1 pott,
1 dish, ½ crop, half my hogs, 1/3 my sheep and 1/3
leather; ANN HORN, "Linning" wheel, pewter bason,
earthen bason, 1/4 part said crop, 1/3 sheep and 1/3
leather. Gr. daus: ELIZABETH GLANDEN, my cloak; POLLY
HORN, "beahive and beas". Exr: JOEL PRICE. Wit:
JEREMIAH HILLIARD, JOHN BRAKE.

HORN, SARAH

No date. Feb. Ct., 1799. Son & Exr: JEREMIAH
HILLIARD, my horse and colt and large "Bell-meattle"
skillet. Dau: CHARITY BUNN, colt, new saddle $10 and
1/4 "wearing clothes"; son: HENRY, all spun thread
and colt; daus: ELIZABETH FORT, PIETY FORT, and SEELY
SUGG, all my wearing clothes. Residue to 6 children.
Wit: ELISHA BATTLE, JR., JACOB BATTLE.

HORN, WILLIAM

Mar. 15, 1795. May Ct., 1795. Wife & Extx: RUTH,
lend remainder of estate, reversion to JEMIMA GLANDEN,
CHARITY HORN, RACHEL HORN and RUTH HORN. Perishable
estate divided between PATIENCE and ANN HORN. Daus:
PATIENCE, 1 cow; CHARITY, 1 pewter dish and bason she
bought, 1 cow, saddle and 3 chairs she bought; RACHEL,
1 cow, 1 saddle and bridle, and 3 chairs she bought;
ANN, 1 puter dish and earthenware she bought, 1 cow;
RUTH, 1 cow; gr. son: WM. GLANDEN, gun. Exr: MAZAH
GLANDEN. Wit: JONATHAN PRICE, W. COTTEN.

HOUSE, JOHN

Mar. 11, 1791. May Ct., 1791. Bk. C, p 167. Wife.
MARY, lend use of 275 A plantation where I now live,
with reversion to youngest sons: ISRAEL, ISAAC and
JOSEPH, he to have that part where house stands; dau:
UNATY ADAMS, 40 S; son: JESSE, 30 S; daus: SARAH, 1
sheat, 1 counterpin and bed cover; FAITH, 30 S; MOURNING
and CHARLOTTE, L 5 current money; son: JOHN, 200 A plan-
tation where I formerly lived, filly and musket; dau:
RACHEL, L 10 current money. Exr: JACOB HOUSE, SEN.,
JESSE JOHNSON, ETHELRED PHILLIPS. Wit: EXUM PHILLIPS,
BENJAMIN PHILLIPS, WILLIAM ROSE.

HOWARD, ELIAS
    Jan. 2, 1798. Probate date, 1799. Mother: SARAH, all
estate during lifetime, reversion to all brothers and
sisters. Bro: JOHN, $10. Exr: HARDY HOWARD, WILSON
HOWARD. Wit: SAMUEL GATER, WM. EDMUNDSON.

HOWARD, EVAN
    Oct. 21, 1847. Nov. Ct., 1847. Bk. F, p 381. Wife:
SARAH, 2 milk cows, heifer, yearlings, mare and gig,
hogs, 2 sows and pigs, 6 chairs, chest, bofat, all bee
hives, cart, 1 negro, 1/3 all land, it being tract N
side Little Contentney Creek, all this for life or
widowhood. A line shall be run between corner my land,
ABNER EASON and FANNA (FENNER?) SIKES' corner thence
to a hickory in RICHARD HOCOTT'S line on the road. Oldest son: EDMOND, land on S side above line. Youngest
son: BENJAMIN, land on N side of line. Daus: ABSILLA
DILDA, wife of BENJAMIN DILDA, to her children, I leave
$50; ELIZABETH, cow and calf, sow and pigs, chest and
$100; DELPHA EDWARDS, wife of WILLIAM EDWARDS, cow and
calf, sow and pigs, chest and $75. Whereas EDMOND will
not arrive at age of 21 yrs until April 13, 1852, and
BENJAMIN A. will not arrive at age of 21 yrs. until
April 6, 1864, therefore I wish WILLIAM ELLIS, son of
COFFIELD ELLIS, to be appt'd gdn. for my minor sons.
Exr: ICHABOD MOORE of Pitt Co. Wit: JOHN H. JENKINS,
DANIEL HOCOTT.

HOWARD, STEPHEN
    Aug. 13, 1782. May Ct., 1788. Bk. C, P 71. Wife:
SARAH, lend plantation I live on with reversion to son,

JAMES HOWARD. Son: WILLIAM, tract he lives on. Son &
Exr: WILSON, bed. Sons: HARDY, horse; ELIAS and JOHN,
bed each. Son & Exr: WILLIS, 5 S. Daus: ANNE HODGES,
CLOVIA HOWARD, HULDAY and ORPHEY, 5 S each. Wit: JOHN
HUDNALL, PETER KNIGHT, ENOCH FLOOD.

HOWARD STEPHEN
    Aug. 2, 1834. Nov. Ct., 1838. Daus: ELIZABETH
EVINGS (EVANS?), 60 A on Ortere's (Otter's) Creek, by
deed of gift of earlier date, and furniture; MARY
HOWARD, 60 A at head of Orter's (Otter's) Creek, furniture by deed of gift of earlier date. Three youngest
daus: KIDDEY (KITTY), WINEY (WINNY) and SEALLEY (SEALY);
youngest son, WILEY, my home plantation on N side of
String (stream or spring?), called the Bet Bagit String;
land on S side of Bet Bagit String divided between
sons: STEPHEN and IVEY. Exr: RICHARD HOCOTT. Wit:
MARTHEY BRUCE, BRAY HARRELL.

HOWELL, JAMES D.
    Aug. 27, 1849. May Ct., 1850. Bk. F, p 444. Estate
divided between heirs, unnamed. Exr: CHARLES C. BONNER.
Wit: JAMES A. BOYD, OSCAR F. ADAMS. Exr refused to
serve. Adm. granted MATHEW WEDDELL. Bond $10,000, with
BAKER STATON and JAMES WINSTEAD, securities (all illegible).

HOWELL, JOHN
    Nov. 3, 1845. No probate date. Bk. F, p 364. Wife:
POLLY, lend 145 A land whereon I live, 2 horses, 2
cows and calves, 4 ewes and lambs, cart and wheels,
whatever furniture she needs and 2 negroes; daus:
POLLY HOWARD, lend 5 A land where she now lives;
BETSEY, reversion of land loaned wife, chest, and
saddle; NANCY, tract bought of DREW PENDER, also tract
bought of WILLIAM BIGGS adjoining sd PENDER tract containing altogether 157 A; JACK ELIZER PRICE. Sons:
CLINCH and CANADY (CANADA), 20 S each and no more. Son:
ELIJAH, also have tract called BRASEL Tract; 2 others
which I bought of CLINCH HOWELL and he bought of
CHARLES and NATHAN FREEMAN joining the BRASEL tract to
be sold and residue divided between heirs excepting
POLLY HOWARD, ELIZABETH HOWELL, JACK ELIZER PRICE.

Will names NANCY STRICKLING and BETSEY WHITEHEAD, but
does not give relationship. Exr: BYTHAL HOWELL. Wit:
MILES LANDING (Clerk shows MILLS), JOSEPH KNIGHT.

HOWELL, JOSEPH
Jan. 10, 1749. May Ct., 1750. Wife & Extx: MARGETT.
Son & Exr: JOSEPH. Son: THOMAS, land on Herrick's Creek.
Daus: MARY, MURPHREY and MARTHA. Exr: Col. J. DAWSON,
SAMUEL RUFFIN, THOMAS HOWELL, JOSEPH HENDERSON. Wit:
JOSEPH WILLIAMSON, JAMES BARRON, THOMAS BARRON.

HOWENTON (HOWERTON?), WILLIAM
Nov. 22, 1843. Feb. Ct., 1844. Bk. F, p 300. All
my property to be divided between my children: Sons:
THOMAS, WILLIAM. Dau: NANCY. Sons: HENRY, BAKER,
ALEXANDER. Exr. and Gdn: MAT. C. WHITAKER. Wit: JAMES
C. KNIGHT, WILLIAM H. KNIGHT.

HOWERTON, EZEKIEL
Apr. 5, 1828. May Ct., 1828. Bk. F, p 84. Wife &
Extx: MARY ANN; all estate, including land on both
sides Griffin Swamp purchased of JAMES KNIGHT and
DANIEL BARKSDALE. Exr: GRISHAM C. PITMAN. Wit: R.
PITTMAN, JAMES ETHEREDGE.

HOWERTON, THOMAS
Apr. 10, 1816. May Ct., 1818. Bk. E, p 189. Wife:
SOPHIA, 1/3 land during life; 1/5 all personal and
perishable property. Son & Exr: EZEKIEL, son: WILLIAM.
Dau: ELIZABETH. Sons to have remaining land. Exr to
sell residue and divide between chil., each to have
1/4; 1/4 to remain in estate. He mentions some BOYKIN
grandchil. but doesn't say that they are ELIZABETH'S.
Exr: JAMES BENTON. Wit: ROBERT MASON, DAVID MORRIS.

HUDNALL, ROBERT
Jan. 30, 1762. Jan. Ct., 1763. Wife & Extx:
ELIZABETH, plantation on Deep Creek bought of WILLIAM
NEWMAN, negroes and still with reversion to son, WILLIS.
Residue, with reversion to all children. Chil: WILLIAM,
Ł 20 current money; ROBERT, Ł 15 current money; MARY
DOWNING, 1/2 cattle bought of WILLIAM COLSON and a
mare; JOHN, Ł 20 current money; AMOS, Ł 25 current

money at age 21; LYDIA, ₤ 20 current money of N. C.
and MARTHA, ₤ 20 current money at age of 18 or marriage.
Son & Exr: WILLIS, 183 A land S side Fishing Creek,
100 ₤ current money, my watch and gun. Wit: BOOZ (BOAZ)
KITCHING, ELIAS GEORGE, ANDREW IRVING.

HUMPHREY, ROBERT
     Sept. 9, 1785. Feb. Ct., 1785. Wife: MURPHREY, 3
negroes, all estate, mare, all cattle and household
furniture, except that my mother has in her possession.
Exr: JOSEPH HOWELL. Wit: STARLING WALLER, ANN HOWELL.

HURSEY, JESSE M.
     Oct. 22, 1849. Nov. Ct., 1849. Wife: JENNET, whole
estate. Exr: HENRY P. BRYAN. Wit: GEORGE THOMAS, FRANCIS
L. BOND.

HUSSEY, EMELIZA
     July 13, 1854. Aug. Ct., 1854. Bk. G, p 78. Estate
to all children as provided by deed executed previous
to my marriage to THOMAS HUSSEY (July 7, 1849) to
WILLIAM NORFLEET, trustee for my heirs. (EMMA ELIZA
As signed). Wit: JOHN H. MATHEWSON, JOHN LAWRENCE.

HYETT, THOMAS
     Jan. 18, 1781. Feb. Ct., 1783. Son & Exr: WILLIS,
upper part plantation whereon I live on Fishing Creek
and Cow Lick Run; son and exr: DAVID, whipsaw, file
and cow and calf; son: JOHN THOMAS HYETT, lower part
plantation and 1 negro; dau: ELIZABETH, small trunk,
woman's saddle, flax wheel, etc. Negroes divided between 3 sons, WILLIS SPEAR and NANCY SPEAR, (chil. of
dau. FATHY SPEAR), and daus: ELIZABETH WILLS, ANNEY
BRADLEY and PENELOPE ALSOBROOK. RICHARD WILLS shall
have liberty of living on son, JOHN THOMAS' land until
JOHN reaches 18 yrs. old. Wit: ISAAC SESSUMS, DAVID
SMITH.

HYMAN, KENNETH
     Apr. 12, 1834. Nov. Ct., 1834. Bk. F, p 165. Wife
& Extx: PEGGY, lend all land whereon I live, also 6
negroes, furniture, 3 (choice) horses, 3 cows and
calves, 4 sows and pigs, 20 sheep, farming utensils,

3000 lb. pork, 100 Bbl corn, fodder, 1 breach and harness and all poultry. As each child comes of age or marries, they are to have 1 f. bed of furn., also $1000. Also give wife $100. . . I wish that the school house built on my land by myself, JOSHUA PENDER and THEOPHILUS PENDER should remain on the lot whereon it now stands for the use of a school house and nothing else. Exr: WILLIAM HYMAN, THEOPHILUS CHERRY, JOSHUA PENDER. Wit: DANIEL PARRISH, SAMUEL HYMAN.

HYMAN, THEOPHILUS
     Sept. 10, 1839. May Ct., 1841. Bk. F, p 255. Bro. & Exr: HENRY HYMAN, my interest in the store of H. and T. HYMAN, all other property, money, lands, servants, should I not marry. Wit: C. L. DICKEN, EPHRAIM DICKEN.

HYMAN, THOMAS
     Jan. 28, 1796. May Ct., 1796. Bro and Exr: WILLIAM HYMAN, 1 negro and all land. Bro: JOHN. Sis: CLOANNA DUGGAN. Daus: of CLOANNA: MARY DUGGAN and ELIZABETH CONE. Residue divided between these nieces. Wit: NATHAN MAYO, FREDERICK MAYO.

ING, JOSEPH
     Dec. 10, 1773. Oct. Ct., 1774. Wife & Exr: ANNE, all residue. Son: JOSEPH, reversion in mother's estate provided he pay each Bro £ 10. Va. currency when of age. Daus: SARAH; LYDDA, cow and calf and 2 breeding sows each. Sons: CHRISTOPHER and MATTHEW. Exr: JOHN HOUSE. Wit: ETHELRED EXUM, JAMES COKER, SR., JAMES COKER, JR..

IRWIN, ANDREW
     Undated. May Ct., 1772. Wife & Extx: MARY, part of manner (manor) plantation her lifetime. Eldest son: JOHN, 200 A land in Halifax Co., on Spring Pocasin adjoining lines of MICHAEL DARMON, WILLIAM HUDNALL, DIXON and BRIDGERS. Sons: JEREMIAH, part of 460 A in Edgecombe Co. adjoining DIXON and BRIDGER'S corner and cow and calf; JAMES, 175 A and cow and calf. Eldest daus: MARTHA DIXON, 20 S; ELIZABETH, 20 S. Son & Exr: ANDREW, manner (manor) plantation and remaining estate. Wit: THOMAS HARRIS, JESSE POPE, ARTHUR HARRIS, ARTHUR BRYAN.

IRWIN, HENRY
    Mar. 3, 1773. Aug. Ct., 1773. Bk. B, p 228. Desire
to be buried in the garden beside my dear wife, BETY.
Son: HENRY, 6 negroes, saw mill and 108 A land bought
of JAMES DUNLAP, being part of RICHARD GORE'S land,
land called "the Old Mill", new survey, silver watch
and new gun. Son: LEWIS, 4 negroes, 300 A land called
"the Old Plantation", land called COWELL'S Survey, also
50 A of town land. Son: JOHN ALEXANDER, 4 negroes,
land bought of BENJ. BARNES, houses and lot I bought
of PARTICK MCDOWELL and now live on. Dau: ELIZABETH,
4 negroes, the lot and houses I bought of COTTON that
MR. STOCKDALE now lives on; also my single riding
chair, mare, and all her mother's clothes. Dau: POLLY,
5 negroes, and their increase. Executors empowered to
keep some furniture for children not of legal age; considerable sum of money to be put out at interest. Sons
to be bound to good masters in Virginia for training,
education and to receive £ 100 Virginia money Daus.
entitled to receive their shares at age of 18, or 16
if they may be married. None of my clothes shall be
sold. My children be kept together as long as it may
be found prudent. Exr: RICHARD LAKEY (LAKER?), HENRY
IRWIN TOOLE, ELIAS FORT, HENRY IRWIN (son), JOHN WEBB,
Esq. Wit: CHRISTOPHER LACKEY, JENNY TOOLE, MARY TOOLE.
Codicil: My good cousin POLLY TOOLE, £ 10 Virginia
money a year as long as she remains single and will
keep house for my children.

IRWIN, HENRY
    Feb. 29, 1792. Feb. 29, 1792. Nunc. Will. Younger
and only Bro: SAMEY (?) IRWIN possess his estate.
GEORGE WASHINGTON, of Tarboro, £ 100. Wit: THOMAS
LYON, ANNIS ROBERTSON. Proved before AMOS JOHNSTON.

IVEY, ADAM
    June 10, 1762. Sept. Ct., 1762. Wife: (Unnamed),
side saddle, linning wheel, wooling wheel, 600 lbs.
pork, 400 lbs. beef, 10 bbls. Indian corn 'til son
GEORGE comes of age, dwelling and cleared land for
5 yrs , £ 50 Proc. money, Sons: FRANCIS and ADAM, 5
S each; they having received their inheritance. Daus:
ELIZABETH, side saddle, linen wheel and £ 20 Proc.

money; SARAH, ↳ 25 Proc. money; MARY, ↳ 25 Proc. money
at 20 yrs. of age. Sons: LEWIS, old 200 A plantation
bought of WILLIAM REGISTER, horse, saddle, all cattle
with half moon in ear, ↳ 50 Proc. money and 1 riffle
gun; GEORGE reversion in his mother's property. Son
& Exr: BENJAMIN, 285 A plantation. Wit: ROBERT SIMMS,
NATHAN BARNES, JOSEPH SIMMS.

JACKSON, JOHN J.
Jan. 19, 1779. Feb. Ct., 1799. Masonic rites re-
quested. Debts to be settled by notes due and sale of
land lying on Cokey Swamp, purchased of SAMUEL DELOACH.
Wife & Extx: CHARLOTTE, all property and child NANCY
boarded and clothed in as genteel manner as case may
admit. Neither property in Cumberland Co., Tenn. nor
any of negroes to be sold or disposed of by gift. In
case wife and dau. die without heirs, estate to be
divided between FIGURES, SALLY and NANCY PHILLIPS, bro.
and sis. of my wife. Exr: JEREMIAH HILLIARD. Wit: WM.
HAYWOOD RUFFIN, JANE PHILLIPS.

JELKS, WILLIAM
Dec. 4, 1781. Feb. Ct., 1782. Mother: ANN JELKS,
lands and plantation, 3 negroes, horses, cattle and
sheep, reversion to: Bro & Exr: LEMUEL, ½ residue. Sis:
TABY BELL, 1 negro and ½ of residue. Sis: MARY MORGAN,
1 negro. Exr: BENJAMIN BELL. Wit: THOMAS PORTER,
BENJAMIN ATKINSON, MARY BARLOW.

JINKINGS, DEMPSEY
Apr. 12, 1822. May Ct., 1822. Bk. E, .p 295. Wife:
MARY, her lifetime, 1/3 real estate, and 4 negroes.
Dau: SARAH, all stock in State Bank of N. C., Tarboro
and 1 negro. Sons: JOSIAH, JAMES F., each to have ½
all real estate in Edgecombe. Dau: ELIZABETH; dau:
SARAH and sons to have residue. HENRY HORN, 3 negroes
bought of him. JOHN GARRETT, 2 negroes now in his po-
ssession. Exr: BENJAMIN SHARP, JOHN WILKINSON. Wit:
BENJAMIN BOYKIN, WILLIS WILKINS, JESSE CROWELL.

JENKINS, NOAH
May 2, 1812. May Ct., 1812. Bk. E, p 30. Movable
property to be sold. Exr: Mother of Noah Jenkins,

BENJAMIN SHARP. Wit: BENJAMIN SHARP, ELIZABETH JENKINS.

JINKINS, JOHN
    Nov. 18, 1807. Aug. Ct., 1808. Bk. D, p 321. Wife
& Extx: (not named), land on W side Peacock's Road.
Sons: NOAH JINKINS, land E side road, blacksmith's
tools to be sold. All other property to be used to
raise my little children; MARTIN, land lent my wife.
Daus: ELIZABETH, MILLEY and REBECCA, residue divided
between these three. Exr: DEMSY SKINNER, SR., Wit:
PHILLIP CAUSEY.

JOHNSON, BENJAMIN
    Sept. 27, 1763. Oct. Ct., 1763. Wife & Extx: JEAN,
mainor (manor) plantation, reversion to son & Exr:
CORNEALUS, at age 18 he may have cow and calf, basin,
plate, 3 spoons and £ 5 money, this Province, to school
him. Son: SAMSON, horse, bridle and saddle, cow and
calf, 2 sows and pigs, 1 dish, bason, 3 spoons and £
5 money of this Province. To the following chil:
BENJAMIN, ANNE and MARY, 20 S sterling money of Great
Britton each. Wit: JOHN HINNANT, JOHN FOLK.

JOHNSON, NATHAN
    Mar. 5, 1829. May Ct., 1829. Bk. F, p 100. Wife:
RANY, house and land, half the orchard, corn, bacon,
horse, 12 cows, 1 pot and rack, pig and 4 sheep. Son:
THOMAS, reversion in land where I live. Dau: NANCY
WHITLEY, 60 A land bought of JESSE BARNES, filly, 4
cows and yearling, calf, 4 ewes, sow and pigs, 8 shoats,
painted chest, painted table, pot and hooks, old pot
rack, dish, ½ doz spoons, plates, wooling wheel, pr.
cards, 2 setting chairs, 4 geese and Dutch oven. Gr.
dau: PENINA JOHNSON, 4½ A land bought of JESSE BARNES,
45 A bought of ROBERT COLEMAN and 2 cows etc Son &
Exr: THOMAS JOHNSON. Son-in-law: DAVID WHITLEY. Wit:
JAMES W. BARNES, JOHN COLEMAN.

JOHNSON, SIMON
    Feb. 1, 1789. May Ct., 1789 Bk 3, p 101 Wife:
MARTHA, land and plantation, 3 negroes, mare and horse,
woman's saddle, man's saddle, 2 bridles, cattle, hogs,
sheep and kitchen furniture. Gr. chil: JESSE HINTON

and MARTHA HINTON, 1 negro each. Son-in-law & Exr:
WILLIAM HINTON, 10 S current money. Son & Exr: JESSE,
land and 3 negroes. Wit: JOSIAH POPE, CHRISTOPHER ING.

JOHNSTON, AMOS
     Dec. 20, 1814. May Ct., 1816. Bk. E, p 133. Wife:
CATHERINE, plantation, 6 negroes, household, kitchen
furniture utensils, horses, creatures, yoke of oxen,
silver, chiney, mare, 12 cattle, 12 sheep, riding chair
and harness. Daus: ESTHER WILKINS, wife of JAMES WILKINS,
land S side Town Creek bought of SARAH and DREWERY DRAKE
on'lines of JOS. PITT, Horsepen Branch, the Meeting
House Road, JONAS WALSTON, DEMPSEY SKINNER, Mill Swamp
to Town Creek; large Bible that was my father's, my
pocket Hymn Book and oavl walnut table; dau: MARY BATTLE,
wife of JOEL BATTLE, land on Town Creek, on lines of
DREWERY WILLIAMS and HARDY FLOWERS and also 400 A formerly owned by MARTIN GARDNER, which I purchased of
JAMES WILKINS, my small church Bible and 2 vols of
Erskine's works; dau: NANCY EVANS, wife of PETER EVANS,
400 A land on Tar River, bought of JOHN ANDREWS, WILLIAM
COPELAND and heirs of DEMPSEY COPELAND, also land on S
side Town Creek bought of RICHARD JOHNSTON (dec'd),
including tract I gave my son RICHARD W. JOHNSTON called the CARTWRIGHT Place, 360 A, several other tracts;
200 A bought of PETER CARTWRIGHT, 440 A bought of
CHRISTOPHER EDWARDS, tract bought of ALEXANDER BALKUM,
243 A bought of AMOS HEARN and JOHN DOWDEN where JOHN
EVERETT lives, 530 A tract bought of EDWARD SUMMERLIN
in all 2600 A, also my new church Bible and Concordance.
Gr. son: AMOS JOHNSTON WILKINS, son of JAMES WILKINS,
900 A plantation where I live adjoining land bought of
HEZEKIAH CARTWRIGHT. Gr. son: AMOS JOHNSTON BATTLE,
land on S side Town Creek where WILLIAM CLARK lives,
on lines of DEMPSEY and JONATHAN GARNER, BENJAMIN SHARP,
and LAZARUS GARNER, 900 A in all including plantation
where REDDICK BARNETT lives. Gr. son: WILLIAM HORN
BATTLE, $1000 in good notes. Gr. daus: SUSAN D. WILKINS
and MARY ANN EVANS, $1000 each in good notes. Dau-in-law:
NANCY JOHNSTON Exrs: Friend, Dr. ROBERT WILLIAMS, of
Pitt. Co.; Neph, PETER HINES; Sons-in-law: JAMES WILKINS
and PETER EVANS. Wit: SAMUEL RUFFIN, JOHN R. SCARBOROUGH.

181

JOHNSTON, CATHERINE

Jan. 31, 1842. Aug Ct , 1842. Bk. F, p 268. Son:
PETER HINES, negro, sideboard and the glass on it,
feather bed and maple bedstead and furn attached to
same, half doz. silver tablespoons with A. I. on them.
Gr. dau: CATHERINE WILLIAMS BYNUM, wife of BENJAMIN
BYNUM, 3 negroes, also 1 mohogany bedstead, bed, curtains and other furniture attached to same, set of Tea
China and all table furniture, 6 silver desert spoons,
6 silver teaspoons with initials C. J. on both kinds,
trunk covered with skin and its contents. Gr. son:
WILLIAM H HINES, son of Col. PETER HINES, 1 negro,
mule, f. bed and common bedstead and curtains and furniture attached; also lend the "OWEN Place" (about 240
A) which I purchased of JOHN SKINNER, JR. Reversion to
his sons: JOHN HENRY HINES, ROBERT WILLIAM HINES, and
AMOS JOHNSTON HINES. Residue equally divided between
son Col. PETER HINES and Gr. son: WILLIAM H. HINES.
Exr: PETER E. HINES of Green Co., N. C. TURNER BYNUM.
Wit: JOHN F. HUGHES, ROBERT BELCHER. JOHN F. HUGHES
out of the state, PHEASANTON S. SUGG, proved signature of HUGHES.

JOHNSTON EDWARD

Sept. 2, 1778. Nov. Ct., 1778. Wife: MARY, 1 rug,
1 blanket, 2 sheets, 4 cows and calves, 1 gilt trunk,
5 sheep and Ł 50. BETTY BATHANY, 1 rug, 1 blanket,
2 sheets, Ł 50. Gr. dau: PATIENCE DAVIS, Ł 100. WILSON
NELSON, 1 rug, 1 blanket, 1 sheet and all my wearing
clothes. Son: SIMON, all that is left after death of
my wife. Exr: ETHELRED EXUM Wit: ETHELRED EXUM, WEST
POPE, JR.

JOHNSTON, ELISHA

June 4, 1800. Aug. Ct., 1800. Wife: FANNY, household furniture, estate to be sold and money divided
between: Son & Exr: PURVIS, and child expected. Exr:
GRAY LITTLE, JAMES ADAMS. Wit: JESSE LITTLE, EPHRAIM
THIGPEN.

JOHNSTON, EMILY

Aug. 4, 1841. Nov. Ct., 1841. Bk. F, p 264. Dau:
ELIZABETH $500. Residue to son: WILLIAM H.; Daus:

MARGARET E. , MARY C. ,Exr: Bro, ROBERT NORFLEET   Wit:
JOSIAH LAWRENCE, ARABELLA E. CLARK.

JOHNSTON, ESTHER
     July 4, 1840 Feb Ct , 1841. Bk. F, p 249. Daus:
PRUDENCE HINES, MARY RUFFIN, 2 negroes and wearing
apparel, each. Gr. chil: RICHARD HINES, JONAS J CARR;
ESTHER J. BLOUNT, WINNEFRED W. EASON and chil of
LUCILLA PRINCE, proceeds from sale of two negroes, chil.
of LUCILLA PRINCE to have one fourth part. Residue to
be divided into 4 equal parts, 1 part to PRUDENCE
HINES; 1 part to MARY RUFFIN; 1 part to RICHARD HINES;
1 part to be divided between 2 gr. sons: JONAS J. BELL,
WILLIAM J. ANDREWS; gr. daus: MARGARET TURNER, 1 negro;
MARY M. PHILLIPS, bed and furniture; Niece: ELIZABETH
PHILLIPS, $50. Exr: Son-in-law, PETER HINES; Gr. son:
JONAS J. CARR. Wit: AMOS WALSTON, PETER P. PHILLIPS.

JOHNSTON, JACOB
     Feb. 27, 1780 Feb Ct., 1782. Wife: MARY, use of
remainder of estate, reversion to sons JACOB and AMOS
and Gr. son JORDAN JOHNSTON, son of NATHAN Son & Exr:
NATHAN. Son & Exr: JACOB; son: AMOS, 5 S each. Gr. son:
HUGH CRAVEY, son of OWEN CRAVEY, and my dau. SELEY ,
his former wife, 2000 ₺ of current money of the State
to be left in care of my son, AMOS. Gr. chil: daus.
and son of JONAS JOHNSTON and of OWEN CRAVEY and
SELEY, his former wife. Exr: HUGH CRAVEY. Wit: RICHARD
TOMLINSON, PHILIP BELCHER (?) DEMCY SKINNER.

JOHNSTON, JACOB
     Mar 27, 1807 Nov Ct., 1808 Bk. D, p 330. Neph:
AMOS WIKINS, son of ESTHER WILKINS, 1 negro; niece:
SUSANNA D. WILKINS, dau of ESTHER WILKINS, 1 negro,
Sisters: MARY BATTLE, NANCY EVANS, 1 negro each. Bro
& Exr: RICHARD W JOHNSTON, 6 negroes, goods, chattels.
Wit: WILLIAM OWENS, JOHN ELLIS, E. CRUMPLER.

JOHNSTON, JONAS
     Mar. 22, 1779 Aug. Ct., 1779. Wife & Extx: EASTER,
3 negroes, mare, 2 horses, 6 cows and calves, 6 ewes
and lambs, furniture, real estate etc. for life. Daus:
SELAH JOHNSTON, ELIZABETH MAUND JOHNSTON, PRUDENCE

JOHNSTON, MARY JOHNSTON, 2 negroes each. Son: WILLIAM
JOHNSTON, plantation lands and lots. Exr: Bro, AMOS
JOHNSTON; ELIAS FORT; MALICHI MAUND. Wit: WILLIAM
MAUND, WILLIAM CORBITT, CHARLES EDWARDS.

JOHNSTON, RICHARD W.
    Apr. 14, 1814. Date of probate not recorded. Wife:
NANCY, life state in plantation where I now live; also
the TAYLOR place, willed to me by my bro. JACOB
JOHNSTON, also the FLEMING'S Places, and the DRAKE
place; interest in grist and saw mills, agreeable to
my father, AMOS JOHNSTON; 10 negroes, 4 choice bedsteads, household furniture, plantation tools, riding
chair, gear, 4 choice nags, 4 choice cows and calves,
10 cattle, 2 yoke oxen, sheep, carriages, carts, shoats,
hogs. Residue to be sold Sis: ESTHER WILKINS, POLLY
(MARY) BATTLE, NANCY EVANS, Niece: by marriage: PATSY
BOONE, 1 negro. ROBT. W. HINES, for service rendered,
Aunt CATHERINE JOHNSTON, plantation called CARTWRIGHT
Place. Wit: JOHN HEARN, LUCY JENKINS, MARY RUFFIN.

JOINER (JOYNER), DREWRY
    June 3, 1820. Aug. Ct., 1821 Bk E, p 274. Wife:
CEALY life estate or widowhood. Daus: ELIZABETH, furn-
iture, cow and calf, stock of bees; SUSANNAH HOWARD;
MARTHA OWENS, 7 S and sixpence, each. Son & Exr:
ELVENSON. Exr: Friend, BENJAMIN MOORE. Wit: JOHN R.
SCARBOROUGH, PROVIDENCE VICK. Filed as DRURY JOYNER.

JONES, FRANCIS
    Jan. 14, 1750. Aug. Ct., 1755. Wife & Extx: JEMIMA.
Son & Exr: NATHANIEL; son: TIGNALL, both land on Crab-
tree Creek in Johnston Co.; JOHN, land on Crabtree
Creek; MATTHEW, land on Swift Creek in Johnston Co.;
FRANCIS, land on Jackit Swamp, Edgecombe Co.;
ALBRIDGTON (ALBRITTON?); RIDLEY. Son-in-law: JOHN
CULLERS, land on Crabtree Creek. Daus: JUDITH WILSON,
MARY CULLERS, LUCY JONES, BETTE DAY JONES, LYDIA JONES,
JEMIMA JONES. Wit: THOS. WIGGINS, FRANCIS DRAKE.

JONES, FREDERICK
    Oct. 4, 1807. Nov. Ct., 1808. Bk. D, p 334. Wife
& Extx: ELIZABETH JONES, 2 negroes, riding chair and

harness, 4 cows and calves, furniture, 20 bbls. corn,
etc., 6 setting chairs, 1 chest; plantation, and land
adj. LAWRENCE O'BRIANS line, half of my still, Puter,
Wench, Bofat, furniture. Sons: ALLEN, land joining
EZEKIAL STATON'S, furniture; ASA, land whereon Father
lived, LAWRENCE O'BRIANS line, furniture; RICKEY, land
between ASA JONES and WALKER KNIGHT and furniture;
FREDERICK, land, 1/2 orchard, furniture. Daus: ELIZABETH
and TEMPY JONES, 2 negroes, furniture, each. Exr: JOHN
LEWELLING, JOHN W. MAYO. Wit: LEWELLEN STATON, JAMES
KNIGHT.

JONES, HARDY
     Aug. 2, 1796. Aug. Ct., 1796. Wife & Extx: HANNER,
life interest or widowhood, home plantation, furniture,
cattle, stock. Sons & Exrs: ABRAHAM, land, cattle,
stock; JESSE, cattle. Sons: RUBIN, JOHN, 5 S each. Daus:
CRYSTAL ALEXANDER (?) and ELSBETH BAGGET, 5 S each.
Wit: JOSEPH WIMBERLEY, WILLIAM BROADRIBB.

JONES, ISAM
     Apr. 24, 1753. Nov. Ct., 1753. Wife: MARY. Dau:
CREACY. Men he left to make division of land: JOHN
HATLY, THOMAS THROWE, RICHARD BURD. Exr: WALLIS JONES.
Wit: RICHARD BURD, MATTHEW JONES.

(See Errata page 376 for John and Nancy Jones)
JONES SAMUEL
     Dec. 7, 1776. Nov. Ct , 1779, Wife: PATIENCE, life
or widowhood, then to my children, (unnamed) Exr:
BENJAMIN SHERROD, BENJAMIN FORT. Wit: ABSOLAM BARNES,
ASIEL BARNES, JESSE AMASON.

JONES, WILLIAM
     Nov. 27, 1749 Aug. Ct   1750. Wife & Extx: SARA
(SARAH), sons: DRUERY; PETER, plantation whereon I
live, ISAM, grist watter mill and all land formerly
belonging to WILLIAM HICKMAN, also land purchased of
ROBERT STANFIALD. Arbitrators to divide land; THOMAS
HILL, GEORGE NICHOLSON, JOHN CLARK, WALLIS JONES. Ex:
WALLIS JONES Wit: THOMAS THROWER, WILLIAM ATKINSON,
WINNEFRED ATKISON.

JORDAN, CORNELIUS (SR.)
     Apr. 8, 1792. Feb. Ct , 1794. Gr son: JOSHUA,

land, 308 A on Hominy Swamp. Gr. son: CORNELIUS JORDAN,
JR., land 150 A on N side Great Swamp, 200 A granted
land. HENRY, my manor Plantation with 150 A land and
250 A of my granted land. Gr. son: LEVI JORDAN, 200 A
of my granted land joining his father's (CORNELIUS
JORDAN) land. Sons-in-law: THOMAS SANDERS, ISHAM EVINS.
Wit: JOSEPH BARNES, ROBERT COLEMAN, WILLIAM WHITE.

JORDAN, CORNELIUS
     July 4, 1854. Aug. Ct., 1854. Bk. G, p 83. Son
& Exr: JAMES, tract whereon he lives provided he pay
his proportionate part of my debts. Son: JOSIAH, tract
adjoining son, JAMES, same proviso. Son & Exr: THOMAS,
tract whereon I live, same proviso. Son: CORNELIUS,
tract where son THOMAS formerly lived, adjoining
PATSY VASER, same proviso. All negroes to be sold,
proceeds divided between 4 sons. Dau: not named, $4.
Wit: WESLEY SWIFT, JESSE MORRIS.

JORDAN, EDITH
     Sept. 11, 1833. Nov. Ct., 1835. Gr. sons: JOSIAH,
4 negroes; DAVID, 3 negroes; JESSE, 2 negroes. Gt. gr.
dau: SARAH DEANS dau. of BARTLEY DEANS, Jr. and wife
ELIZABETH, 2 negroes, bed & furn., 4 chairs. Residue
divided between grandchildren. Exr: BARTLEY DEANS. Wit:
WILLIAM HAYNES, JOHN GRICE.

JORDAN, GRAY
     July 26, 1814. Nov. Ct., 1841. Bk. F, p 263. Son:
GRAY, all my land, Black mare, stock, household furn-
iture, farming tools. Wit: JAMES RICKS, ROBERT RICKS,
JONATHAN BAILEY.

JORDAN, HENRY
     Oct. 7, 1836. Nov. Ct., 1837. Wife: POLLY, 100 A
of land, and dwelling house adjoining the Great Swamp,
and lands of CORNELIUS, for life or widowhood, 5 negroes, horse, bridle, saddle, 2 cows and sow and pigs,
8 hogs, 4 ewes, 8 setting chairs, 2 tables, painted
chest, 3 tables, 3 pots, 3 puter basons, 6 puter plates;
case of knives and forks; linnen wheel; 2 woollen
wheels; provisions for herself and family one year.
Daus: RHODA TAYLOR, 3 negroes, painted chest without

drawers; ELIZABETH STRICKLIN, 2 negroes, chest with drawers; SALLY COLEMAN, 3 negroes and walnut table. Son & Exr: JOSIAH JORDAN, 3 negroes, 1 Bofat, all land, one Church Bible. Exr: ISAAC STRICKLIN, JOSIAH JORDAN, JOHN COLEMAN. Wit: CORNELIUS JORDAN, WILLIAM HAYNES.

JORDAN, JOSHAWAY
Mar. 30, 1791. Nov. Ct., 1791. Bk. 3, p 175. Wife: EDEY, my manner (manor) plantation, life or widowhood; stock, cattle, furniture. Sons: JESSE; STEPHEN. land in Nash County, 1 negro boy; negro girl, furniture, stock, cattle, sheep, etc.; HENRY, horse and saddle, sheep, furniture, gun; JOSHAWAY, furniture, money to buy horse saddle and 4 cows, sheep, hogs. Daus: EDEY, furniture, cattle; ELIZABETH JORDAN, cattle, silver money to buy furniture. Exr: THOMAS SANDERS, SEN., CHARLES COLEMAN. Wit: JOHN HEDGEPETH, ARTHUR HEDGEPETH, JETHRO HARRISON.

JORDAN, JOSHUA
Dec. 29, 1840. Aug. Ct., 1842. Bk. F, pp 275, 76, 77. Wife: JULAN, land lying on E side of branch this side LEWIS ELLIS, on lines of JACOB TAYLOR, feather bed and furn., chest, trunk, side board, kitchen furniture, pork corn, 2 cows and calves, 6 ewes and lambs, hogs and hat came from MARY BARNES, horse, gig, harness, utensils, cart and wheels, bbl brandy; executor and EDWIN BARNES to buy 2 negroes for wife. Reversion of all property to daughter MARYAN. Exr: LARRY DEW. Wit: EDWIN BARNES, JACOB TAYLOR. Aug. Ct., 1842. LARRY DEW, Adm., Bond $10,000 with BENJAMIN SIMMS, JOSHUA BARNES, Securities. Nov. Ct., 1843. Jury: JEREMIAH BATTS, WILLIAM HEARN, ELIJAH WILLIAMS, JOSEPH KNIGHT, KENNETH THIGPEN, DAVID P. SHALLINGTON, THOMAS EVANS, JAMES C. KNIGHT, JOHN HARRELL, JACOB D. ROBBINS, DIXON RANDALL, WILLIAM SKINNER. Jury found it to be last will and Test. of JOSHUA JORDAN.

JORDAN, JOSIAH (JORDIN)
Sept. 30, 1846. Feb. Ct., 1848. Bk. F, p 388. Son: WILLIAM H. JORDAN, all property. Should he die before reaching age 21 years, without heir, it shall go to my cousin, DAVID JORDIN. Exr: DAVID JORDIN. Wit: JOHN W. FARMER, JAMES D. BARNES.

JUDKINS, JOHN E.
     No date. May Ct., 1802. Son: JOSEPH BRYANT JUDKINS,
house and lot in town of Greenville, Nos. 67, 55, 45
and 31. Land and negroes to be sold for schooling, etc.
SALLY RITTY WHITE, dau. of SARAH WHITE, $300. Dau:
REBECCA JUDKINS, land, etc. money for education from
land bought of WILLIAM and HOPEWELL ADAMS, 150 A including storehouse and ferry, land and negroes be sold
for maintenance and schooling. Exr: GEORGE EVANS, of
Pitt Co. Note:- Refused to serve. Wit: RICHARD WILLIAMS,
RICHARD RIVES.

KEA, FAITHY
     Oct. 29, 1814. Feb. Ct., 1815. Bk. E, p 88. Estate
equally divided between my chil: WILLIAM KEA, PATSY
FOUNTAIN; SALLY KEA and NANCY FORT, wife of JOSEPH
FORT. Exr: FREDERICK PHILIPS. Wit: MATHEW PHILIPS,
LOCKY SAVAGE.

KEA, HENRY
     No Date. Nov. Ct., 1842. Bk. F, pp 242, 43. Dau:
ELIZABETH OWEN. Son: WILLIAM, and dau: MARY KEA, 40
S each. Son & Exr: JOHN, 2 negroes. Son: WILLIE, 1
negro. Dau: NANCY BELL, 4 negroes, reversion to her
children. Exr: WILLIAM BELL. Wit: JAMES BIGGS.

KEA, SARAH
     Jan. 24, 1850. Feb. Ct., 1850. Bk. F, p 438.
MARTHA E. LACKEY, 1/3 of my bed clothing and wearing
apparel. Sis: MARTHA ALSBROOK, 1/3 of same, and my old
negro woman, Pink, and residue of my estate; SARA E.
HOWELL, 1/3 bed clothing. Exr: Friend, PATRICK McDOWELL.
Wit: JOHN W. WILKINSON, LEWIS M. ALSBROOK.

KEA, WILLIAM
     Dec. 22, 1803. Feb. Ct., 1804. Wife & Extx: FAITH
KEA, whole of my estate her lifetime provided she keep
my children together, educate and maintain them, until
of lawful age. As each one comes of age, a horse, bridle
and saddle. Exr: Friend, FREDERICK PHILIPS.

KEEFE, PATRICK (of Tarborough, N. C.)
     Feb. 21, 1809. Feb. Ct., 1809. Wife & Extx: MARY,

land, tenaments, goods and chattles. Child: PATRICK,
of MARY PERRY, $100 and schooling. Exr: Friend, SOLOMON
SESSOMS. Wit: DANIEL REDMOND, GEORGE W. WATSON.

KEELAND, JOHN
Jan. 21, 1752. Mar. 24, 1752. Exr & Sole Legatee:
JAMES CARTER. Nunc. Will, proven before "His Excellency,
GABRIEL JOHNSTON, Esq., His Majesty's Captain General,
Governor and Commander-in-chief over the Province of
N. C." by the oaths of: WILLIAM HORNSBY, WILLIAM TAYLOR,
CATTREN CARTER.

KELLEY, ALEXANDER (Parish of St. Mary's, Colony of
North Carolina.)
Sept. 4, 1764. Apr. Ct., 1765. Wife: MARGARET,
estate, real and personal. Wit: HENRY HART, THOS. HARRIS,
MICAJAH PETTAWAY.

KELLEY, JOHN
May 24, 1783. Nov. Ct., 1783. Wife: ELIZABETH, land
and plantation, personal effects, life or widowhood.
Support and educate son: JOSEPH KELLEY and my 3 daus
(unnamed). Exr: JOHN MILBURN, JAMES ADAMS. Wit: JOHN
HINES, SIMON NUSOM, CHARLES MARLOW.

KILLEBREW, JOSHUA
Jan. 4, 1793. Feb. Ct., 1793. Wife: SUSANNAH, all
my estate one year, lawful dower during widowhood, 1/3
of my grist mill, 2 negroes, stock, cattle and furniture. Chil: CHARLOTTE, LOVEL, GERALDOS and DOLLY, 1
negro and furniture each. Son: GEORGE WASHINGTON
KILLEBREW, $50 silver. Friend: RICHARD WELLS, grey
filley. Exr: LAMON RUFFIN, JESSE DELOACH, DAVID
BULLOCK, AMOS JOHNSTON. Wit: JOHN WILSON, AGNES
BULLOCK, JOHN STRINGER.

KILLEBREW, REBECHA
Apr. 16, 1839. No Probate Date. Son & Exr: JOSHUA,
lend all land and property except that given gr. chil.
unless my son CALDWELL KILLEBREW return to his county.
in which case, he shall share equally with his bro:
JOSHUA. Gr. sons: JOSHUA ROBERSON and DAVID ROBERSON,
$6 each; JOHN ROBERSON, 1 pr. shoes. Gr. daus: SUSAN

ROBERSON, 1 table; REBECCA ROBERSON, all the furn.
also red chest and all wearing apparel; EMILY KILLEBREW,
dau of JOSHUA, 2 sheets, 2 quilts, 1 bolster, 1 pillow.
Wit: W. F. EAGLES, JOHN HASSELL.

KILLINGSWORTH, RICHARD
    Dec. 3, 1733. No Probate Date. Wife & Extx: MARY.
Legatee: Counsin, RICHARD KILLINGSWORTH, son of
WILLIAM KILLINGSWORTH. Wit: BENJAMIN WOOD, FRANCIS
WOOD, JOHN SPIER.

KINCHEN, WILLIAM (JR)
    Nov. 6, 1758. Dec. Ct., 1758. Son & Exr: JOHN,
land on the river adjoining Craghill, also 1/2 my land
in NORTHHAMPTON Co., that is to say: Upper part of
my land on both sides of Roanoke River has been sold
to PAUL PATRICK, the deed not yet delivered. Son:
WILLIAM, remainder of my land. Daus: MARTHA, ELIZABETH,
MARY, TEMPERANCE. Exr: Bros: BLAKE BAKER, HENRY DAWSON.
Wit: HENRY CAMPBELL, PETER JONES, WILLIAM MOORE.

KINCHEN, WILLIAM
    July 4, 1779. Nov. Ct., 1779. Wife: SARAH, plan-
tation and lands during life, negroes, horses, furniture, cattle, hogs, etc. Son: MATTHEW, 14 negroes,
Brandy still, Blacksmith tools, silver tankard, 3
silver spoons, furniture. Dau: MOURNING BALL, side
saddle, furniture and utensils. Exr: ETHELRED PHILIPS.
Wit: ETHELRED PHILIPS, JOSEPH PHILIPS, URIAH SMITH.

KING, WILLIAM (Planter)
    May 17, 1751. No Probate Date. Wife & Extx:
ELIZABETH, everything during her widowhood. Son & Exr:
JOHN, reversion in plantation and land. The balance
divided among the rest of my children, my son JOHN,
excepted. Wit: JOHN FOUNTAINE, PHILIP PETTYPOOL,
HUMPHREY JOANS (JONES).

KING, WILLIAM C.
    June 20 (?), 1813. Nov. Ct., 1818. Bk. E, p 208.
Wife: HARDY, lend part of plantation (to ARTHUR PHILIPS
line), 1 negro, horse, bridle, saddle, riding chair,
stock, a Burch table, dressing table, furniture and

$300. Dau: FANNY, negro man, furniture, bridle, saddle,
dressing table, etc. Son: THOMAS, 2 negroes, horse,
bridle, saddle, gun, small house with brick chimney,
pair wheels, cart, furniture, cow, etc., large red chest.
Dau: SALLY, 1 negro, bed and furniture. Sons: COFFIELD,
AUGUST, JOHN R. and HENRY, 1 negro each. Balance, after
debts paid, to be equally divided. Exr: BENJAMIN
COFFIELD, SEN'R, EXUM LEWIS, SAMUEL BRANTLEY, DAVID
BRADLEY. Wit: ELIAS BRYAN, MOODY PORTER, DAVID BRADLEY,

KITCHEN, ELIZABETH
     July 1, 1825. Aug. Ct., 1825. Bk. F, p 44. MICAJAH
E. BRADLEY, a tract of land I bought of JOHN KNIGHT;
another tract I bought of JOHN PARKER. Gr. son: MICAJAH
EDWARDS, 1 negro when he reaches 21 yrs. ELIZABETH
BRADLEY, negro woman. Remainder of estate, after debts
be paid, divided between: MARTHA MANNIN (MANNING?),
ELIZABETH BRADLEY, SUSANNAH HARPER, MARY EDWARDS, DICIE
HOWELL. Wit: JOB BRADLEY, JAMES WEEKS, FRANCIS WEEKS.
Probated by WILLIS BRADLEY, Exr. Caveated by BRITAIN
HOWELL, STEPHEN HARPER, JOHN MANNING and MARY EDWARDS.

KITCHING, BOAZ
     June 8, 1767. Nov. Ct., 1776. Wife: (unnamed), 6
pieces of Puter, horse, bridle, saddle, 4 cows, 1 negro,
during her widowhood. Daus: LUCRESIA HUDNALL, cattle;
LURANEY, 1 negro, furniture. Son: WILLIAM, 100 A land,
part of CAIN'S patent on Deep Creek to Cabin Branch.
Son & Exr: BOAZ, 160 A plantation, still and 1 negro.
Dau: CHRISTIAN, 1 negro. Son: LARRENCE (LAWRENCE), 1
negro and 10 cattle. Gr. dau: MOURNING HUDNALL, £ 13-8.
Estate to be equally divided after wife's widowhood.
Wit: THOMAS JOYNER, BENJAMIN BATTS, MARY JOYNER. Aug.,
1772. Registered, BOAZ KITCHEN in presence of AMOS
HUDNALL delivered to his son JETHRO a little negro boy,
Buck as a gift. About same time LURENA KITCHEN was
called upon by me and BOAZ and saw him deliver said
slave to his said son as an absolute gift. Signed by
AMOS HUDNALL. AMOS HUDNALL and LUCRENA KITCHING made
oath to above Test.

KITCHING, MARY
     Jan. 13, 1782. Feb. Ct., 1785. Son: JETHRO, plan—

tation, mare, colt, furniture. Gr. dau: LUCRESSY
HUDNALL, dish, plate, and box iron. Son: LAWRENCE, jug,
bason, plate and chair. Rest of my estate to be divided
between my sons and daus. Exr: BOAZ KITCHEN, ROBERT
HUDNALL. Wit: WM. HACKNEY, THOMAS WELLS.

KNIGHT, ANN
    Aug. 24, 1816. Nov. Ct., 1820. Bk. E, p 247. Gr.
son: JOHN LAWRENCE, son of JOSHUA LAWRENCE, featherbed
and furniture. It is my desire my negro woman Judah
shall have her freedom, etc. after my death. Exr:
JOSHUA LAWRENCE, refused to serve; unable. Wit: WM.
HAYNES, SR., BYTHAL HAYNES.

KNIGHT, ARTHUR
    Apr. 25, 1829. Aug. Ct., 1824. Wife: SALLY, be-
queath 340 A land whereon I live, reversion to "friend
and relative by affinity", ARTHUR BARLOW. If ARTHUR
BARLOW die before reaching age 21 yrs, reversion shall
be to JOSEPH KNIGHT, son of my bro. JOHN KNIGHT, also
11 negroes, etc. to my wife. ARTHUR BARLOW and DAVID
BARLOW to share my right in land called BISHOP Land
which I purchased at ARTHUR BISHOP'S sale. Exr:
BENJAMIN BATTS; JOHN LAWRENCE, son of JOSHUA LAWRENCE.
Wit: J. R. LLOYD, BENJAMIN BOYKIN. Exr. refused to
serve, SALLY KNIGHT appointed as Adm., entered into
bond of $20,000 with ARTHUR K. BARLOW and DAVID BARLOW,
Securities.

KNIGHT, B. F.
    Feb. 1, 1854. May Ct., 1854. Bk. G, p 56. It is my
will that my negroes be taken to Richmond and sold, by
the MESSRS. DICKINSON, thereby placing them as near as
possible upon the same footing as when I purchased
them. I give to my father, JESSE C. KNIGHT, the proceeds of the sale of said negroes, together with the
balance of my entire estate. Father and Exr: JESSE C.
KNIGHT. Holograph Will. WILLIAM H. JONES, W. T. DORTCH
and JOHN NORFLEET, sworn, said they could identify the
writing of B. F. KNIGHT.

KNIGHT, FRANCIS
    June 23, 1808. Aug. Ct., 1808. Bk. D, p 324. The

whole estate be kept together during widowhood of my
wife, or until son HENRY arrive at 21. Son: JESSE C.,
1 negro, all my lands, tenements, and $500. Son & Exr:
HENRY, to have equivalent. Should sons die, without
heirs, my negro man Dick, shall fall to BETSY COOPER,
dau. of SUCKEY COOPER of Southampton, Virginia. Negro
Tom to my bro. LEWIS KNIGHT'S son, DANIEL; negro girl
Silvy go to SARAH HOWARD; negro man Pat to the chil.
of REBECCA MAYO, wife of LIVENTON (LIVINGSTON?) MAYO.
Everything else to my 2 bros. CHARLES J. and JOHN. Exr:
Bro., CHARLES KNIGHT. Wit: NATHAN MAYO, SARAH HOWARD.

KNIGHT, JAMES
     Nov. 2, 1786. Feb. Ct., 1794. Wife: PRISCILLA, my
estate and 2 negroes her widowhood. Sons: JAMES, plan-
tation and land where I now live on N side of GRIFFIN'S
Swamp; WILLIAM, all land lying on S side of GRIFFIN'S
Swamp and W side of Bair Branch, 1 negro and horse;
MOOR(MOORE), negro gal, and negro woman; JACOB, ₤ 10
and crosscut saw. Daus: ELIZABETH COFFIELD, DILLY
MORRIS, and SARAH KNIGHT, 6 negroes between them. Gr.
chil. heirs of JACOB: 2 negroes and all WINFIELD
WRIGHT estate, I bought of said KNIGHT. Exr: BENJ.
COFFIELD, JAMES JONES. Wit: MALA (MALACHI?) NICHOLSON,
FRANCES PARKER, JOHN BOYKIN. Widow of JAMES KNIGHT
dissented. Exrs. refused to qualify. Adm. granted
KINDRED KNIGHT.

KNIGHT, JAMES
     July 20, 1844. Nov. Ct., 1847. Bk. F, p 384. Wife:
(unnamed), lend all lands, negroes, dwelling house,
furniture, mules, cattle, horses, sheep, hogs, bacon,
pork, cotton, wool, etc. during her life. Son: JAMES
W., lend all land at death of her mother. If he dies
without heir, lend it to VIRGINIA STATON, WILLIAM ANN
STATON and SIMMONS B. D. STATON. If all of them die
without an heir, I give said land to 2 eldest sons of
LUNSFORD R. CHERRY. Also lend son JAMES, 1/2 valuation
of negroes, to be left in same way as above. VIRGINIA
STATON, WILLIAM ANN STATON, SIMMONS B. D. STATON, other
half of negroes. No Exr: Wit: H. WARD, ALSTON SAVIDGE.
Adm. granted H (?) WARD. Bond $20,000 with JOSEPH
JOHN PIPPEN, JOHN KNIGHT and WILLIAM R. CHERRY, Secur-

ities.

KNIGHT, JESSE

Dec. 16, 1815. Feb. Ct., 1816. Bk. E, p 122. Wife: MARY, during her widowhood, plantation and land, 2 negroes, stock, cattle, furniture, cotton wheel, cotton cards, flax wheel, case of knives and forks, iron pot and hooks, Duch Oven, chairs, table, riding chair, Brandy still, 12 months provisions, etc. Son & Exr: ALLEN, land and plantation I purchased of AMOS JOHNSTON, also furniture, etc. Daus: ELIZABETH BATTS, mare, bridle, saddle, furniture, etc.; TEMPERENCE KNIGHT, bed furniture, $350; MARTHA MILLER, furniture and $350. Son: PETER, land purchased of HENRY ANDERSON and JAMES COOK, also piece purchased of SAMUEL WREN. Dau: NANCY, 1 negro. My two sons: JESSE B. and EDWIN KNIGHT, 6 negroes. Dau: LYDIA, 1 negro. Sons: LEWIS, land purchased of NOAH PIPPIN and BENJAMIN PIPPIN, another piece purchased of JOHN KNOX; Son: ARTHUR, land and plantation my father gave me and two other tracts I took up adjoining same. Dau: SYLVIAH, 1 negro.. Property lent wife during widowhood be sold and equally divided. Exr: EATON COBB. Wit: JOHN W. CHERRY, THEOPHILUS CHERRY.

KNIGHT, JOHN

Oct. 10, 1769. Nov. Ct., 1770. Wife: ISABELL, riding horse, whole estate, both land and money during her widowhood. Then to be divided. Son: JAMES, both plantations where I now live, square table, Pewter dish, Pewter Bason. Sons & Exrs: JOHN, case of bottles, chest, hand mill, 2 iron pots, wearing clothes; MOSES, Desk, Brandy still, and 1 negro. Gr. son: KINDRED KNIGHT, son of MOSES KNIGHT, 1 negro. Daus: JUDAH FOREMAN, SARAH BOYKIN, RACHEL HACKNEY, and MARY FOREMAN, 5 S each. Gr. son: SPIER KNIGHT, 5 S and gun. Remainder of estate to be divided after widowhood of my wife. Wit: ETHELRED EXUM, ABRAHAM SAULS, REBECCAH POPE.

KNIGHT, MOSES

June 14, 1781. No Probate Date. Wife & Extx: CHARITY, use of my estate during her life or widowhood. Sons: KINDRED, 3 negroes at legal age; ALAN, 100 A land lying on Wolfpit Branch, purchased of ROBERT

PARKER, 1/2 of new entry lying on N side of Whiteoak
Swamp, furniture, 3 negroes, at legal age; JOHN CARTER
KNIGHT, plantation where I live with remainder of my
land, 5 negroes, furniture, gun, sword, and case of
bottles. Daus: SARAH PACE, MARY KNIGHT and PHEREBY
KNIGHT, 1 negro girl each. Shall receive their negroes
at age of eighteen years or marriage. Exr: JOHN
NICHOLSON, JAMES PACE. Wit: JONATHAN POPE, EXUM LEWIS,
SPIER KNIGHT.

KNIGHT, PETER
    May 9, 1809. Nov. Ct., 1811. Bk. E, p 25. Wife &
Extx: ANN, I lend plantation I now live on reversion
to son: PETER EPPS KNIGHT, 1 negro wench, cattle, sheep,
stock, furniture, loom and weaving gear, ploughs, cart,
puter dishes, basons, 12 spoons, etc. Son & Exr: JESSE
tract of land bought of JOHN HODGE, also 73 A I took
up adjoining same. Son: ARTHUR, tract bought of JAMES
JONES, another tract bought of BENJAMIN PIPPEN, tract
adjoining JAMES ADAMS and my own land. Son & Exr: JOHN,
tract of land lying on Fishing Creek, bought of JOSEPH
HART. Son: WILLIS, I lend plantation bought of ALLEN
HARDY during his life, reversion to his son, JORDON
KNIGHT. Dau: LUCY BATTS, 2 negroes. Son: CHARLES,
plantation bought of ELIAS FORT, also tract I took up
adjoining BENJAMIN BATTS and 1 negro. Dau: MARY
LAWRENCE, 1 negro. Son: PETER EPPS KNIGHT, 110 A tract
of land bought of JAMES HOWARD, and 1 negro boy. Dau:
ELIZABETH KNIGHT, negro. WALKER KNIGHT'S 5 youngest
chil: JAMES, MARTHA, SISLEY, JOHN and CHARLES KNIGHT,
Ł 25 each. Wit: DAVID LAWRENCE, JAMES WEEKS.

KNIGHT, ROBERT
    Jan. 30, 1761. June Ct., 1761. Wife: TERECE (?)
1/3 my plantation and estate, negroes, household goods
for widowhood. Son: SPIER, 150 A plantation I now live
on. Chil: SPIER, PENELOPE and FRANCES KNIGHT and child
unborn, to share equally. Exr: Bro., JAMES KNIGHT;
JAMES SPIER. Wit: ROBERT ROBISON, CHARLES PORTER, JOHN
JONES.

KNIGHT, SALLY
    June 3, 1843. Aug. Ct., 1847. Bk. F, p 368. Neph:

DAVID BARLOW, 2 negroes, all stock, sheep, mare, mule, 3 cows and calves, 4 sows and pigs, 2 chests, 1/2 bees, 6 newest sitting chairs and 1/2 kitchen furniture. Neph. & Exr: ARTHUR K. BARLOW, residue. Wit: WILLIAM R. LONG, HENRY L. STATON, WILLIAM S. LONG.

KNIGHT, WALKER
Apr. 15, 1830. No Probate Date. Bk. F, p 143. Wife: ELIZABETH, lend to wife and son CHARLES E. KNIGHT all furniture, 4 sows and pigs, 3 cows and calves, 2 horses, 8 sheep, also lend plantation on which I live containing 3 tracts, wiz: the JOHN EVANS tract, the LEMUEL EDMERSON tract, and the ASA JONES tract, also 12 negroes; reversion of all moveable property to all chil; reversion of land to son CHARLES. sons: CHARLES, 1 negro and plantation at descease of mother; JAMES, plantation bought of JAMES and GEO DOWNING, 1 negro; daus: MARTHA BRYAN, 2 negroes; CECELIA STATON, 2 negroes; son: JOHN, plantation bought of WILLIAM SAVAGE, 1 negro, $600; dau: LUCY L. HAMMOND, 2 negroes. Exr: BENJAMIN BOYKIN, JOSHUA PENDER. Wit: BENJAMIN BOYKIN, JOSHUA PENDER. Exrs: refused to qualify, Adm, granted to JAMES KNIGHT and EDWARD G. HAMMOND; bond $15000, JOHN MOORING and JOSHUA PENDER, securities.

KNIGHT, WILLIS
July 22, 1845. May Ct., 1846. Bk. F, p 343. Wife: POLLY, land, 2 horses, 12 sitting chairs, 3 tables, best bofat, all crockery, chest, tools, furniture, gig and harness, 20 pigs of her choice, 2 cows and calves, 4 ewes and lambs, bacon, corn, coffee, beehives, etc.; lend her dower which fell to her from her former husband JESSE KNIGHT, land bought of SILAS WILKERSON and LEWIS KNIGHT, also land bought of PETER KNIGHT, called the ANDERSON and WREN land, also lend her $400, 2 negroes, brandy still, apple mill, 40 cider barrels, and presses. LITTLEBERRY BROWN'S daus: REBECCA, PATSEY, POLLY AND LIDDIA ANN BROWN, reversion of $400 left wife. Son: JORDAN, land whereon he lives. Son & Exr: WILLIAM, plantation whereon he lives adjoining land bought of CULLEN ADAMS, and tract bought of MICHAEL HEARN, and RANDOLPH COTTON, adjoining same; 1/4 Light Tract, deeded to myself and JOSEPH R. LLOYD by

MICHAEL HEARN, also 1 bought of ASA BROWN and wife, and JOHN BUNTIN and wife; 1 negro. Son & Exr: JOHN, land bought of PETER KNIGHT, after wife's death, tract bought of SILAS WILKERSON, except wife's dower; and 1/4 of Light Tract; Dau: NANCY MAYO, now living in Mississippi, 2 negroes, and those she has already; $600 also lend her 4 negroes, reversion to her heirs, also $50. Dau: HARRIETT LITTLE, 3 negroes. Wit: WILLIAM C. LEIGH, JESSE W. LEIGH.

LAKEY, RICHARD
No. Date. July Ct., 1777. Wife & Extx: MARY, lend 2 negroes, riding chair, plantation, cattle and stock, until my first dau. marries; then a division. Son & Exr: CHRISTOPHER, plantation bought of HENRY IRWIN, a bond of GEORGE RYAN'S of Ł 75 Proc. money, 1 negro boy, desk and bookcase. Dau: ELIZABETH, 1 negro, reserving child she will have, which I give to my dau. ANN along with another negro. Dau: MARY, 2 negroes. Exrs. sell my tools, if wife thinks proper, to pay debts. Exr: HENRY IRWIN. Wit: ARTHUR HARRIS, HENRY KEA, HENRY IRWIN. Codicil (not dated). Wife appointed Gdn. to ELIZABETH, MARY and ANN. Wife to have use of legacy until they marry. Wit: HENRY KEA, ARTHUR HARRIS, HENRY IRWIN.

LANCASTER, BENJAMIN
Sept. 24, 1793. Nov. Ct., 1793. Wife: (unnamed), 280 A , where I live, horse, bridle, saddle, stock, cattle, etc. for life, or widowhood. Son: BENJAMIN LANCASTER, 100 A land, furniture, pewter and loom. THOMAS BOYET, furniture, 50 A of land whereon I live, and to his son: BENJAMIN BOYET, gun and my wearing apparel. Son: ROBERT LANCASTER, furniture, pewter dish and plates, basin, 2 hoes and drawing Knife. Son & Exr: ELIJAH LANCASTER, furniture, horse, bridle, saddle, etc. pewter plates, basin, gun, 280 A land after death of his mother. Son: LEVI BOYET, bed and gun. Remainder estate to be divided betwixt my 2 sons: ROBERT and ELIJAH LANCASTER. BENJAMIN LANCASTER, JACOB BOYET and THOMAS BOYET have received full legacies. Wit: THOMAS MERRIT, SAMUEL MERRITT.

LAND, CHARLES

May 23, 1838. Aug. Ct., 1838. Wife: MARY, use of
plantation, residue. Son: HENRY LAND, horse, furniture,
etc. Daus: FANNY WHITEHEAD and POLLY WEAVER, $1.00 each;
they have had their portion. Sons & Exrs: CHARLES LAND,
land on S side of Calvin Branch, etc; JOHN LAND, my
still, and contents, half of my household furniture.
Son: JESSE LAND, $1.00, Gr. dau: SOPHY BRASWELL, 1
pine chest. Wit: JOHN BEELAND.

LAND, LITTLEBERRY
    Dec. 20, 1827. Aug. Ct., 1829. Bk. F, p 102. Wife:
MARY, plantation where I live, 4 negroes, cattle, stock,
Brandy still, furniture, utensils for widowhood or life.
Son & Exr: DANIEL, negro woman and increase. Son:
BURREL, 100 A land and 2 negroes. Daus: POLLY LANCASTER,
2 negroes and their increase; AMY JOYNER, 2 negroes
and $50. Son & Exr: BIRD LAND, 150 A of land, 1 negro
girl and Brandy still after death of wife. Dau: SALLY
HARGROVE, 2 negroes. Wit: D. WILLIAMS, MATTHEW
WHITEHEAD.

LANDING, MARTHA ANN
    No date. Aug. Ct., 1855. Bk. G, p 109. Neph. & Exr:
JAMES THOMAS HYDE, 80 A land whereon I live on lines
of WILLIAM BELL and AARON DAVIS. REBECCA SAVAGE, cow,
calf, and trunk. STEPHEN HYDE, son of JOHN HYDE, cow
and calf, sow and pigs. Remainder to 2 sisters (not
named). Wit: AARON DAVIS, WILLIAM F. COOPER.

LANE, CHRISTIAN
    Oct..5, 1747. May Ct., 1748. Son: ABRAHAM. Daus:
SARAH, S side land on Spring Branch; MARY, N side land
on Spring Branch. CHRISTIAN HILL. Exr: ABRAHAM HILL.
Wit: STEPHEN JACKSON, SARAH HILL.

LANE, JAMES
    No date. Aug. Ct., 1789. Bk. 3, p 103. Wife: SARAH,
currency to purchase 1 negro boy; plantation during
widowhood or life with reversion to son & exr: JAMES,
he also to have cattle. Son: ETHELRED, 1 negro woman.
Daus: ELIZABETH FAIRCLOTH, L 1 currency; ANN HALL, L
10 currency; MIRIAM and ZILPAH, bed and furniture
each. Remainder divided between my 5 youngest chil:

JAMES LAND, MARY BELCHER, SARAH BRAKE, MIRIAM LANE,
ZILPAH LANE. Wit: EDWARD ARNOLD, ELISABETH ARNOLD.

LANE, JOSEPH
    Dec. 6, 1757. Nov. Ct., 1758. Bros: WILLIAM LANE,
plantation whereon I live, also land where WILLIAM
GRISSUM now lives, cattle, hogs, etc. and 5 negroes;
NEWIT LANE. Sisters: FAITH BYNUM and DREWSILLER BRYANT.
Legatee: WINIFRED POPE. Father: "I lend use of two
negroes." Kinswoman: MARY McKINNE. Exr: JOHN BRADFORD,
HENRY POPE. Wit: BENJAMIN MERRYMAN, BARNABAS LANE,
DAVID DICKSON.

LANGLEY, JOHN
    Aug. 4, 1827. Feb. Ct., 1830. Bk. F, p 113. Wife:
FEBBEY, residue, lifetime, then divided among: ISAIH
LANGLEY, ROBERT ELLIS, WILLIAM PAGE. SHADRACH LANGLEY,
$10 worth wearing apparel, his full share of my estate.
Friend, JOHN CHESTER, 100 A land in Pitt Co. adjoining
STEPHENSON PAGE and SETH BOWLTON, horse and cow. Exr:
Friend, LITTLETON WALSTON. Wit: R. OWENS, SETH BOWLTON.

LANGLEY, WILLIAM
    Feb. 12, 1790. May Ct., 1790. Wife: MARTHA, lend
mare, £ 10 money, bed, furniture, reversion to my dau.
FERRIBE. Daus: MARY LANGLEY, £ 10; FEREBEE LANGLEY,
chest and £ 10; ELIZABETH LANGLEY, £ 10 money. Son:
WILLIAM LANGLEY, plantation and negro. Exr: BENJAMIN
MATTHIS, JOSIAH POPE. Wit: JEREMIAH HILLIARD,
CHRISTOPHER ING.

LANGSTON, ANN
    Aug. 2, 1788. Feb. Ct., 1789. Bk. 3, p 84. Gr. son
& Exr: ISAAC LANGSTON, all my estate. Wit: THEOPHILUS
THOMAS, MARTHA (?) WOODARD, JOHN WOODARD.

LANGSTON, LEONARD
    Aug. 8, 1780. Nov. Ct., 1780. Wife: (unnamed), lend
plantation and 1 negro with reversion to my gr. son
LUKE BOLTON. LEWIS BANDY, pinewoods plantation, cattle,
sheep, mare with crooked leg, chist that I had of
JAMES BROWN, and negro wench. WILLIAM DANIELL is not
to be interrupted till LEWIS BANDY is of age. Gr. son:

ISAAC LANGSTON, bed, furniture and chest I call mine.
Gr. son: LUKE BOLTON, 250 A plantation and negro wench.
Gr. dau: ELIZABETH BOLTON, my desk and negro girl. Exr:
ELISHA WOODARD, JOSEPH COX. Wit: EPHRAIM BARNES, JOSEPH
COCKS, ELIZABETH AMASON.

LASETER, HARDY
    Oct. 9, 1851. May Ct., 1853. Bk. F, p 502. Sons:
SILAS, tract known as the TOMLINSON Tract, 81 A, ad-
joining land of BENJAMIN SIMMS and a mare; MATTHEW,
GREEN and HARDY, all the tract whereon I live, equally
divided, HARDY to have the part whereon the house stands,
as the dowery part, and mare, Bunch; MATTHEW to have
my sorrel horse, Doctor; GREEN to have sorrell horse,
John. Daus: TREACY; PENNY, or her heirs, and SALLY
ARTICE, $50 each; RACHEL, bed and furniture, known as
my bed I occupy, cow and $30. Little Gr. dau: ELVY
LASETER, $10. Residue divided. Exr: JOHN W. FARMER.
Wit: WILLIAM TOMLINSON, JOSIAH FARMER.

LAURENCE, JOHN
    Mar. 7, 1795. Aug. Ct., 1797. Wife: ABSEL, land
and plantation, except mill; negro woman, negro man,
horse, 4 cows, bed, furniture, chest, pewter, during
her life. Sons: JOHN, plantation bought of WILLIAM
KITCHEN on Cabin Branch, also mill, 350 A land after
wife's decease; negro woman and 80 gal. still; DAVID,
plantation bought of JOHN SWALES on Tar River, plantation bought of WILLEBE WELLS, 2 negroes; after wife's
widowhood or decease; 40 gal. still, furniture;
RODERICK, plantation purchased of MORGAN. Also plantation purchased of WILLIAM KITCHEN, and 2 negroes,
1/2 interest in 40 gal. still; and furniture. Daus:
MARY, plantation bought of THOMAS JOYNER, negro girl,
and furniture; FEREBEE, land I got of JETHRO KITCHEN
and land of JAMES DOWNING. I lend to MARY BRADY, sister of JOSEPH BRADY plantation whereon Widow SAVAGE
now lives, during her life. Also produce. Exr:
BENJAMIN BATTS, JOHN LAWRENCE, JOSHUA LAWRENCE. Wit:
JACOB MURRILL, FREDERIC SAVAGE, MARY KITCHEN.

LAURENCE (LAWRENCE), JOHN
    Nov. 22, 1799. Feb. Ct., 1805. Bk. D, p 218. Mother:

ABSAL STATON, 10 S. Bros: JOSHUA LAWRENCE, all my ne-
groes; DAVID LAWRENCE, plantation, on road where
WILLIAM KITCHEN lived; PHELORICK LAWRENCE, the rest of
my land, he to pay $800 to his sisters, POLLY and
FEREBEE LAWRENCE. Exr: ISAAC BATTS. Wit: ORREN
KITCHEN, JAMES WEEKS, BENJAMIN WEEKS.

LAURENCE, SOLOMON
    Oct. 30, 1801. May Ct., 1804. Sons: JOHN, HENRY,
MILES and SOLOMON, 10 S each; property already poss-
essed. WILLIS, plantation where I now live, cattle,
and furniture; LEMUEL, property already possessed. Daus:
SARAH TAYLOR, property already possessed; MILDRED
LAWRENCE, furniture, cattle, horse, woollen wheel;
MARTHA TAYLOR, furniture. Exr: JOHN LAWRENCE, WILLIS
LAWRENCE. Wit: JESSE LITTLE, JOHN BILLUPS.

LAURENCE (LAWRENCE), THOMAS
    Apr. 18, 1791. Aug. Ct., 1794. Wife: COMFORT, 4
daus: LYDDA, LUCY, SARAH and MARY LAWRENCE, 50 A land
whereon my son, JESSE, lived as long as he was single,
then to my son THOMAS, JR. Dau: ELIZABETH LAWRENCE, £
10 current money. Exr: THOMAS CROMWELL, JOHN BELL. Wit:
MILES HODGE, PAUL LAWRENCE, MARTHA LAURENCE.

LAURENCE, EPHRAIM
    Aug. 14, 1777. Oct. Ct., 1777. Wife & Extx: BETTY,
lend use of Estate during widowhood for raising my
chil.; 1/2 personal estate if she remarries, use of
half Plantation for life. Son: JESSE LAWRENCE, plantation after death of wife. Remainder divided among
children. Wit: REBECCA LAWRENCE, JO'N THOMAS.

LAWRENCE, JAMES
    Oct. 28, 1784. No Probate Date. Wife: ELIZABETH,
bed and covers. Estate to be sold and divided between
5 sons: When JOEL (?) and JAMES come of age, and not
before. Remainder divided among all my children. Wit:
TEAGLE TAYLOR, JAMES LAWRENCE.

LAWRENCE, JOHN
    Nov. 25, 1841. Aug. Ct., 1844. Bk. F, p 310. Wife:
SARAH, lend Conetoe tract adjoining lands of JOHN

DANIEL, WM. KNIGHT, MICHAEL HEARN, also all negroes.
Friend: WILLIAM KNIGHT, son of WILLIS KNIGHT, 306 A
tract bought of BENNETT BARROW, that he shall hold it
in trust for my 3 chil: GAY LAWRENCE, BOYKIN LAWRENCE
and POLLY HARDY. Upper river tract, bought of Dr. BENJ.
BOYKIN adjoining land of EPENETUS CROMWELL, FREDERICK
O. LITTLE and JOHN MAY; 650 A to go to JAMES, JESSE
and JOSEPH, and 1 negro each. At wife's death, remain-
ing negroes to be divided between 4 youngest daus:
MARIA, NANCY, EVELINA, CATHERINE, ELENY HENLY, PEGGY
SINGLETON and BETSY LAWRENCE. Sons and Exrs: JAMES
LAWRENCE, JOSEPH LAWRENCE. Wit: WM. NORFLEET, JESSE
C. KNIGHT.

LAWRENCE, JOSHUA
    Oct. 16, 1841. Feb. Ct., 1843. Bk. F, pp 282-88.
Wife: MARY, land on Fishing Creek, Mill Branch and
lines of HUDNALL and FOXHALL; reversion to son THOMAS;
also lend my wife, 6 negroes, 2 cows and calves, 3
sows and pigs, 10 sheep, all poltry, corn, fodder, peas,
2000 lb. pork, farm tools, carts and wheels, furniture,
2 birch tables, 1 beaufat, sideboard, all earthen ware
and glass, loom & gear, 2 woolen wheels, 1 flax wheel,
doz. sitting chairs, doz. knives and forks, 3 chests,
gig and harness, also $50. Son: JOHN, land purchased
of JOHN KNIGHT with all property given him before and
1 negro. Gr. dau: LUCY, dau. of JOHN LAWRENCE, 1 negro.
Gr. dau: ANNALIZA, $400. Son: JAMES MCDONALD LAWRENCE,
$25, he nor his mother or their descendants to the
fourth generation to have any further part of my estate.
Son: JOSIAH, house I built in Tarboro for a doctor's
shop and 1 negro with all other property I've given
him. Gr. dau: MARGARETT, dau of JOSIAH LAWRENCE, 1
negro. Gr. son: WILLIAM JOSHUA LAWRENCE, tract I
purchased, in Franklin Co., of Mrs. TOOL, widow of
GERALDUS TOOL, This property reserved for use of
ELIZABETH LAWRENCE, widow of my bro. DAVID LAWRENCE,
during her lifetime. After that, WILLIAM JOSHUA
LAWRENCE shall have it. Dau: LOUISA BURK, $500. It is
understood that she nor any of her future increase to
the fourth generation shall have any further part of
my estate. Be it also understood that the land on which
she lives and negroes in her possession are mine neither

lent nor given to her. Gr. sons: GEORGE WASHINGTON
KNIGHT, and JOHN KNIGHT, $25 each, Son: JOSHUA
LAWRENCE, land on Fishing Creek and Tar River, Wolf
Pit, between the GEORGE BRYAN tract and HUDSON tract
to near the gate of ROBERT FOXHALL. Also 2 negroes
after mother's death. Son: BENNETT B. LAWRENCE and his
wife, FRANCES, lend lands bought of ROBERT SORY and
GEORGE FORT lying in Nash and Edgecombe Counties, 3
negroes, $500 and all perishable property already
given him. Dau: PHEREBE LAWRENCE, lend 4 negroes, furniture, also 215 A plantation bought of WILLIAM KEY;
should she die without issue, said land shall be equally
divided between my daus: MARTHA and DELLAH. Son: THOMAS
DAVID LAWRENCE, bequeath his mother's land at her death,
also adjoining land on lines of DREWERY BRYAN, JOSIAH
SESSUMS, ROBERT FOXHALL and JOSHUA L. LAWRENCE and
HUDNALL, being the land purchased of WILLIAM FOXHALL.
His mother's land was given me by my father and purchased of WILLIS HUDNALL; 4 negroes, boufat, 1 doz.
chairs, still, 8 cider hogsheads, 2 presses, furniture,
$800, for the purpose of finishing his education. Also
given him my long gun, which I call Liverpool, my watch,
all books in which his name is wrote by his own hand.
If he die before reaching 21, and leave no lawful
issue, I leave land to my daus. SARA LOUISA and EDER
DELLAH, daus of BENNETT B. LAWRENCE. Gr. Sons, sons
of JOSHUA L. LAWRENCE; JOHN JOSHUA LAWRENCE, THADDEUS
MAYO LAWRENCE to have following lands, HUDSON BRYAN
Tract bought at sale of IRVIN BRYAN, dec'd, also land
adjoining bought of BURWELL DUN, also piece I took up
adjoining said HUDSON tract, for which there is a
grant from N. C. Also sein place bought of WM. DUPREY
and wife, the whole containing 300 1/4 A. Exr: Sons,
JOHN LAWRENCE, JOSIAH LAWRENCE, JOSHUA L. LAWRENCE,
BENNETT B. LAWRENCE, THOMAS D. LAWRENCE. Wit: DANIEL
PARRISH, ROBERT FOXHALL, GEORGE A. MEEKS. Codicil,
Nov. 18, 1842. Feb. Ct., 1843. Lend to son BENNETT
B. LAWRENCE, 64 A tract called the WEAVER Place, also
1 negro. Wit: JOHN BEDFORD, THOMAS D. LAWRENCE.

LAWRENCE, LEMUEL
     Jan. 16, 1831. Aug. Ct., 1838. Wife: GRACY
LAWRENCE, all of my property remaining after payment

of debts, 5 negroes and their increase, stock, horses,
cattle, sheep, hogs, household and kitchen furniture,
gig and harness, saddle, etc. Exr: Friend, CHARLES
MABREY. Wit: JESSE HAYES, CHARLES MABREY.

LAWRENCE, PETER, P. (Tarboro)
    Apr. 21, 1852. Feb. Ct., 1855. Bk. G, p 101. Wife
& Extx: ABBY P., 60 shares stock of Bank of Cape Fear,
reversion to NATHAN, lend house and lot in Tarboro, re-
version to oldest chil: DAVID, JOHN W., RICHARD C. and
MARY E. A. HORNE. Furniture, reversion to youngest daus:
E. A. HOSKINS, M. O. JONES, H. J. LAWRENCE. "Books and
pamphlets I wish to be divided between all my chil. and
hope they may make a wise improvement of them." No
Witnesses. Proven by oaths of NATHAN MATHEWSON, JOHN
NORFLEET and RUSSEL CHAPMAN.

LEE, HENRY
    Sept. 23, 1812. Nov. Ct., 1812. Wife & Extx:
ELIZABETH, plantation which lyeth on the E side of
Tyancoque Road, and land on E side of Georgia Road to
JESSE FRYAR'S (?) line, her widowhood, plantation in
forks of SASSNETT'S Mill Swamp, until son WILLIAM is
21; pay for use of sd. negroes, $40 a year benefit of
my estate. Furniture, pewter, plates, woollen wheel, pr.
cotton cards, utensils for farming, etc. Son: JOHN,
tract he is now living on, provided he pay SARAH PORCH
$50, I owe her. Dau: NANCY, furniture and $20. Son:
HENRY, tract of land, negro boy, furniture, gun, year-
old filly, when he reaches 21. Son: WILLIAM, plantation,
etc. when of legal age. Son: JEREMIAH, plantation on
E side of Tyancoque Road and Georgia Road. Property to
be sold and residue divided among my daus: SARAH RUFFIN,
wife of JESSE RUFFIN; ELIZABETH BULLUCK, wife of EDWIN
BULLUCK and NANCY LEE. Exr: STARLING WALLER. Wit: ENOS
GREEN, ELIJAH STANLEY.

LEE, JAMES
    Jan. 4, 1771. Oct. Ct., 1777. Wife: AGNES LEE,
slaves, land, etc., life interest. Sons & Exrs: JAMES,
3 negroes, horse, suit of clothes, hat, stockings,
trunk, half of my mill; ROBERT, land, negroes, suit
clothes, cattle, sheep, geese. Son: WILLIAM, land on

SMITH'S Creek, negroes, stock, cattle, at JOHN PINNER'S
furniture and gun. Daus: WINNEY WILDER, land on Smith's
Creek, in Johnston's County, etc.; TABITHA, negroes,
stock, cattle, geese, Pewter dishes, etc.; MARY
CARPENTER (?), sheep, geese, etc. Sons: JAMES BUDD LEE,
plantation, stock, cattle, 1/2 interest in mill, negroes,
etc.; PHILIP LEE, negroes, stock, cattle, sheep, and
furniture; JOHN LEE, negroes, cattle, stock, sheep,
geese and horse. Daus: BEDANCE (OBEDIENCE) LEE, cattle,
sheep, mare, negroes; MILBREY LEE, negro boy, cattle,
sheep, geese, 1 great white pacing mare; SARAH LEE,
negroes, cattle, sheep, gray mare, 2 fillies. Wit:
JOHN O'NEAL, WINNY WILDER.

LEE, JOSHUA
       Mar. 29, 1767. Apr. Ct., 1774. Wife: ELEANOR, I
lend personal and real estate. At her decease to my
dau & Extx: MARY, wife of THOMAS POPE. Sons: JOHN LEE,
JOSHUA LEE, 5 S' each. Daus: SARAH, ELIZABETH, ANN and
NAOMY, 5 S each. Have had equal parts already. Gr. dau:
ANN WATSON, cow and calf, yearling heifer, all hogs
marked with a swallow fork in ye right ear and half
moon under same. Bed I now lie in and furniture. Wit:
BENJAMIN BRAND (?), CHARLES LEE, DAVID LEE.

LEE, RICHARD
       Apr. 4, 1756. May Ct., 1756. Sons: TIMOTHY,
100 A on Contenteny Creek in JAMES ROBERT'S Patent;
ARTHUR, RICHARD, 50 A whereon he lives; SOLOMON, "manured plantation which I now live on . . it is my will
and desire that he maintain and provide for his mother."
Daus: ELIZABETH LEE, RACHEL BRADLEY, SARAH HORN and
MARTHA LEE. No Exr. Wit: ABSALOM HOLLIMON, WILLIAM
FOKES, JAMES PERMENTER. Stock mark of the Testator is
described as being "swallow fork in the right ear and
a crop and half crop in ye Left Ear."

LEE, SOLOMON, Planter
       Mar. 8, 1762. Mar. Ct., 1762. Wife: (unnamed)
(illegible). Mother: Feather bed, etc. Sons: BRIAN, L
90 and 10 S Virginia Money, shot gun, 10 head of cattle,
half of my hogs, 4 sheep, etc., plantation whereon I
live; RICHARD, land lying above my home plantation,

and ₤ 10 and 10 S Virginia money, and everything I have
besides except what I give to (my) son: CHARLES. Exr:
JEREMIAH LEE, ARTHUR LEE, JAMES PERMENTER. Wit: JOHN
WARD, JR., WILLIAM BARRON.

LEGGET, NOAH
    May 22, 1823. Feb. Ct., 1825. Bk. F, p 33. Wife:
SINA LEGGET, all property now in her possession by
Contract with PITTMAN WORSLEY and .50¢ in cash. Son:
RANDOLPH'S chil: all property he received. Daus:
TEMPERENCE WHITE, furniture, two heifers and property
received from me and furniture, side saddle and negro
woman, Alice; TERRESSA LEGGET, negro boy, Frank, furniture, her choice, Woman's saddle, small table, bandbox,
tin trunk, chest. Son: NOAH LEGGET, land on lines of
LEAVIN LEGGET, ELIZA HAWKINS, RODERICK STATON'S line.,
Little Contentnea Creek... and Mayo Mill pond... furniture, filly called Fly, bridle and saddle. If he dies
without heirs, then to son: SAMUEL LEGGET, land, adjoining land I gave son RANDOLPH on lines of BYTHAL
STATON'S... REDDICK STATON... LEAVIN STATON, horse,
Darby, $20, cash; furniture. If he dies without heirs
to heirs of son NOAH LEGGET. Dau: SARAH LEGGET, furniture, chest, side saddle, negro girl. Gr. son: WILLIAM
R. LEGGET, $100. Gr. son: EZEKIEL S. WHITE, furniture
in possession of JOHN WHITE and property I lent my dau
NICEY WHITE. Residue divide among all my heirs. Exr:
WM. R. LONG, LEAVIN LEGGET. No Witnesses.

LEGGETT, LEVIN
    Feb. 10, 1854. Feb. Ct., 1855. Bk. G, p 102. Son:
JAMES ROBERT ALEXANDER LEGGETT, all lands except that
lying on E side of road which passes near my residence
and leads from the crossroads meeting house to Green-
ville; bridle and saddle, gun, also $150; slaves to be
divided between all my chil. Daus: ELIZABETH and
MELISSA ANN, $150; MAHALA WARD, SUSAN PERKINS, TABITHA
WARD, ISABELLA WHITE, PAMELIA WHITE. No Exr. Wit:
WILLIAM NORFLEET, WILLIAM H. JOHNSTON. JAMES A. WHITE,
Adm. Bond $22,000. JOHN WHITE, LEMUEL A. SAVAGE,
Securities.

LEIGH, FRANCIS. Tarboro, N. C.

Mar. 17, 1798. Aug. Ct., 1798. Bro: WILLIAM LEIGH,
2 negro men and the family watch. Neph: JOHN L.
WILLOUGHBY, negro boy and all my books. Niece:
ELIZABETH WILLOUGHBY, negro girl, with her increase, a
locket and ring. Perishable property sold, divided
between Bro: WILLIAM LEIGH and RANDOLPH COTTON. Exr:
RANDOLPH COTTON. Wit: W. T. COTTON, SPENCER D. COTTON.

LEIGH, WILLIAM C.
Nov. 6, 1854. Feb. Ct., 1855. Wife: LUCY, lend
furniture, plantation called BROWN field, wagon, gear,
barouche and harness, house field and ginhouse, 2 cows
and calves, 2 sows and pigs, horse or mule, cart and
wheels, all slaves, reversion of land to FRANCIS and
WILLIAM. JESSE W., $800 and mare; Dau: TEMPERENCE
HARRELL, wife of WM. HARRELL, $200; son & exr: JOHN H.,
$700; Dau: MARTHA A; Sons: FRANCIS and WM. to have
SCOTT land, CHERRY tract, the TEMPERANCE PIPPIN tract
and tract purchased of CHRISTOPHER HARRELL; WILLIAM
also to have gun. Exr: WM. HARRELL. Wit: JESSE HARRELL,
DAVID COBB.

LENOIR, THOMAS. Parish of St. Mary's Province of No.
Car.
May 14, 1765. July Ct., 1765. Wife & Extx:
MOURNING, life estate in real and personal property.
Son: ROBERT, 1 S. Daus: ANN WESTMORLAND and BETTY
LATTIMORE, 1 prayer book each. Lands, lot in Tarborough
Town to be sold, money divided between my five sons:
THOMAS, ISAAC (Exr); LEWIS, and when he comes of age,
JOHN and WILLIAM LENOIR. Daus: LEAH WHITAKER, and MARY
PERRY, personal estate. Wit: JAMES ATKINSON, JOSHUA
POLLARD.

LESTER, MOSES
Apr. 26, 1825. May Ct., 1826. Bk. F, p 38. Gr. dau:
CEALY OWENS, land I now live on; Gr. son: JOHN EASON,
tract I purchased of EASON up Iron Branch known as
SHADERICK LANGLEY land; daus: FRANCES EASON, furniture,
her life, then to Fr. son, OBED EASON; ANN WEBB, negro
man, Deed of Trust on land of JEREMIAH LESTER. Fr. dau:
FRANCES OWENS, furniture. Dau: NANCY OWENS, negro man,
land, cattle, sheep, stock, money. I desire my negro

Woman, Anniky, choose her own master. Exr: STEPHEN
WOOTTEN, EPHRAIM WOOTTEN. Wit: RICHARD JOHNSON, HEZAKIAH
LANGLEY, ELIJAH OWENS.

LEWELLENG, ALEXANDER
    June 20, 1791. Feb. Ct., 1792. Wife & Extx:
ELIZABETH, my estate, furniture, stock, cattle, tools,
etc. Son: EDMUND, 5 S; son-in-law: BENJAMIN AMASON.
Sons: JAMES, JOHN and Dau: FANNY, 5 S each. Wit:
EDMUND STUCKEY, JAMES LEWELLING.

LEWELLING, JOHN (of Martin County, N. C.)
    Oct. 2, 1793. Aug. Ct., 1794. Wife's dau: MARY
BOWERS, 6 pewter plates, pewter dish, 3 negroes after
decease of my wife; then to chil. of MARY BOWERS. Wife's
dau: CHLOE BOWERS, 6 pewter plates, plate and 3 negroes,
her husband WILLIAM BOWERS, after decease of my wife,
then to chil. of sd CHLOE. Wife's dau: CLARY
SOUTHERLAND, 6 pewter plates and 1 dish; 3 negroes
after death of wife, during lifetime of CLARY and husband JOHN SOUTHERLAND, then to their chil. Wife's
dau: CHARLOTTE STATON, 5 pewter plates, dish, a negro
girl be purchased for CHARLOTTE and husband ARTHUR
STATON; also negro girl child Chane; after death of
my wife, negro man, Isaac, then to their chil. (Relation not given), GRACEY MOORING, 6 pewter plates,
1 dish, 1 negro girl, Trebaney, negro boy, Charles;
after death of my wife; negro man, Lewis, to GRACEY
and her husband, JOHN MOORING. Wife's dau: ANNEYS
MOORE, negro girl, Nance, negro woman, Chane; after
death of my wife, negro man, Toney; after death of
ANNEYS and WILLIAM MOORE, to their chil. Wife's
dau: SUSANNAH MOORING, 6 pewter plates, pewter dish,
negro girl, Hasty, negro Boy, Sampson, after death of
my wife, 1 negro man Luke; after death of SUSANNAH and
husband, JAMES MOORING, then to their chil. Wife's
son: JOHN LEWELLING, my negro man, Philip, negro man,
America, negro boy, Harry, Mulatto girl, Charlotte,
negro man, Bob; my will and desire Bob shall make my
wife's shoes during her life. Negro girl, Bett; 1/2
household and kitchen furniture, utensils, tools,
horses, cattle, sheep; also half water Grist mill, and
still; wife to have liberty of stilling her liquor.

Toney, Isaac, Neptune, Sam, Lewis and Luke to be hired
out to give my wife a genteel maintenance; others to
be kept on Plantation. My son & Exr: JOHN LEWELLING,
all my lands, except what his mother can tend with 2
hands and 1/4 of the orchard, for life estate. Exr:
Col. NATHAN MAYO, WILLIAM WALLACE. Wit: MATTHEW BURNETT,
MATTHEW CROSS, FRANCIS BURNETT.

LEWIS, ANN
    Dec. 9, 1843. Feb. Ct., 1844. Son & Exr: KENELM H.
Son: WILLIAM F.; Gr. son: JOEL B. LEWIS, the 1/8 part
which his dec'd father JOHN W. LEWIS, would have in-
herited. Dau: ELIZABETH F. WHITAKER. Son: RICHARD H.
LEWIS. Daus: MARY ANN HUNTER and EMMA SPEIGHT. Son:
EXUM LEWIS. Each to have 1/8 of estate. Wit: JESSE H.
POWELL, JOSEPH J. W. POWELL.

LEWIS, EXUM
    June 26, 1790. Aug. Ct., 1790. Wife: ELIZABETH,
life estate. Son: THOMAS, plantation where he now lives,
on the Reedy or Great Branch to low grounds of Swift
Creek..W to GEORGE FOREMAN'S line..S by P. FOREMAN'S
line, 200 A; 2 negroes. Son: GREEN, 420 A plantation
I now live on, near run of Swift Creek N by GEORGE
FOREMAN'S to mouth of Reedy or Great Branch, up Mirey
Branch, E to FIGURES LEWIS, to GEORGE LINCHE'S 2 negroes, cattle, furniture, pewter dishes, $50 when 20
yrs. of age. Son: BARTHOLOMEW, 793 A of land adjoining
lands given, Sons: THOMAS & GREEN LEWIS, negro girl,
cows and calves, furniture, pewter, dishes, Basins,
6 plates, $180 cash. Sons: EXUM & EDWIN, moeny goods
in the store, Pork, Bacon, Brandy, lands, when EDWIN
arrives at age 20. Son: EXUM, negro boy, Cato, horse,
Marcus, bridle and saddle, cows and calves, Bed and
furniture, 2 pewter basins, pewter dishes, 6 pewter
plates, etc. Dau: ELIZABETH, 2 negro women, bay mare,
Silver Heels, bridle and saddle, 2 cows and calves,
furniture, 2 Pewter dishes, 2 Pewter basins, 1 flax
wheel. Dau: SALLY MOORE, negro girl. Sons: THOMAS,
BARTHOLOMEW and GREEN LEWIS, the use of my brandy
still. Residue of property lent to wife, ELIZABETH.
Exr: sons: FIGURES LEWIS and EXUM LEWIS; son-in-law:
JESSE JOHNSON. Wit: NATHAN HARRIS, ELI B. WHITAKER,

JAMES WHITAKER. Probate date, 1795.

LEWIS, EXUM
   Mar. 30, 1831. Feb. Ct., 1839. Wife: ANN, 8 negroes,
4 horses, 6 cows and calves, 6 young cattle, furniture
and utensils. Lend plantation whereon I live, including
lands purch'ed of JOHN WILLIAMS on E side road I live
on, also 200 A that I purchased of NORSWORTHY MIAL on
W side sd road, containing altogether 316 3/4 A. Remainder equally divided among 4 children. Sons & Exrs:
JOHN W., RICHARD H. Daus: BETSY and MARY ANN LEWIS.
Sons-in-law & Exrs: SPIER WHITAKER, THOMAS HUNTER. No
Witnesses. Proved by oaths of L. D. WILSON, H. BRYAN
and JESSE H. POWELL.

LEWIS, GREEN
   Feb. 6, 1814. Feb. Ct., 1814. Bk. E, p 64. Wife
& Extx: PATSEY, plantation, negroes, and stock. Dau:
SALLY ADDELINE, when she arrives at age 18 shall draw
a propertionable part of my negroes. HENRY EXUM, at
the age of 20, agreeable to a law provided in such
cases. Likewise for the rest of my chil. should wife
have another birth. Exr: EXUM LEWIS. No Witnesses;...
found among other valuable papers and proved by oaths
of ORREN LINCH, EATON LINCH, and MATTHEW PHILIPS as
being hand-writing of GREEN LEWIS.

LEWIS, JAMES
   Aug. 10, 1844. Nov. Ct., 1846. Bk. F, p 350. Wife:
(unnamed), bed and chair, lend 182 A land, nag, cow
and calf, 2 sows and pigs, 2 ewes etc., largest bofat
and clock. Gr. dau: PENNY FORBES, $__; Dau: FANNY
ELLIS (dec'd), her chil. to have her share of property.
Equal Division between chil: CHARLOTTY HARPER, SALLY
WEBB, ELIZABETH PAGE, JAMES E. LEWIS, REDDIN S. LEWIS,
KINCHEN LEWIS, MARY EDWARD and REBECCA MERCER. Exr:
son, REDDIN S. LEWIS, RICHARD T. EAGLES. Wit: ABNER
C. WILKINSON, HENRY GAY.

LINCH, GEORGE
   Dec. 30, 1808. Feb. Ct., 1810. Bk. D, p 354. Wife:
OLIVE, remainder estate, personal and otherwise, life
est.; she to provide schooling for READING and HANCE,

210

unmarried chil. to live on plantation and enjoy man-
shion (mansion) lent to my wife, until her death. Daus:
PATTY KNIGHT, TAZZY (?) PITMAN, and MARY PITMAN, 4 negroes each. Son & Exr: ORREN, all my lands on S side
of Whiteoak Swamp, lines of EATON LINCH and JAMES
BOYKIN; Whiteoak bridge towards Enfield road, to former
plantation of JACOB COKER, where the old road inter-
cepted same...Indian Cabin Branch... the road to Tarborough to Enfield...Little Branch...MOODY PORTER'S
and my own line, E toward DANIELS Meeting House...
GREEN LEWIS' line... agreeable to Deeds from GREEN
LEWIS and EZEKIAL COKER...Tracts I purchased of WM.
MORGAN, SEN'R; also negro man. Daus: OLIVE LINCH, 3
negroes, after death of my wife, MILLY LINCH, 3 negroes. Son & Exr: EATON, all my lands lying below road
each side of Whiteoak Swamp, purchased of WILLIAM
MORGAN, JR., JANE EDWARDS, NATHANIEL COKER and EZEKIAL
COKER; 1 negro. Son & Exr: GREEN LINCH, negro boy, 3
year old Filly, saddle and bridle of $16 value. Dau:
BEEDY, 3 negroes, saddle and bridle, value of $16. Sons;
READING, 1 negro, horse, saddle, bridle, value about
$100; HANCE, 2 negroes, horse, saddle bridle, value
about $100. Wit: JEREMIAH MARSHALL, GREEN LEWIS, B.
LEWIS.

LINCH, OLIVE (SR.)
    July 30, 1824. Feb. Ct., and May Ct., 1825. Bk. F,
p 36. Son & Exr: REDDIN, whole crop of corn, cotton,
fodder, etc. and stock. Dau: MILLY, sow, shotes, all
money in hand, and due me, except $40 due from dau,
OLIVE, which I give OLIVE'S son MARK, to apply on his
education; Dau: MARY PITTMAN, small low bed I now
occupy. Residue of estate divided among my son HANCEL,
and my 4 gr. chil., chil. of EATON LINCH. Gr. son & Exr:
REDDIN PITTMAN. Wit: EXUM LEWIS.

LINCH, ORREN
    Sept. 9, 1822. Nov. Ct., 1822. Bk. E, p 312. Es-
tate to be sold, just debts paid. Interest to be
appropriated to the maintenance of PENELOPE DIXON and
her 4 chil: CLARENDA, VINEY, ORREN D. L., and ALLY
DIXON, as long as she remains single. Estate divide
equally at lawful age. Exr & Gdn: SPIER W. COFFIELD.

Wit: REDDIN LINCH, EXUM LEWIS.

LITTLE, ABRAHAM
Mar. 15, 1785. Feb. Ct., 1789. Bk. C, p 85. Wife:
AMY, entire estate except land, reversion of 1 negro
to each child; son & exr: WILLIAM, 150 A whereon he
live, reversion in 1/2 still and all tools; son:
FREDERICK; son & exr: JESSE, 300 A in Dobbs Co., pur-
chased of JAMES ADAIR, horse, bridle and saddle; son:
JOHN, plantation whereon I live, reversion in 1/2 still.
Daus: SELAH TAYLOR, SARAH BELCHER, ANN GARDNER and
ELIZABETH GARDNER. Wit: WILLIAM LITTLE, AXUM LITTLE.

LITTLE, BENJAMIN G.
Jan. 7, 1847. Aug. Ct., 1847. Bk. F, p 367. I have
left all estate in hands of friend W. D. PETWAY, native
of Edgecombe County, N. C. WILLIAM E., JESSE C., SARAH
E., LAWRENCE D., MARY A., and MARGARET A. LITTLE, to
have all my estate in N. C. provided I never return
from the army. Exr: Uncle, EATON COBB. Wit: JNO. G.
WILLIAMS, L. WILLIAMS.

LITTLE, JACOB
May 19, 1787. Feb. Ct., 1791. Bk. C, p 157. Wife:
MARY, residue during widowhood, reversion of plantation to ASA. Son & Exr: NAM (NAHUM), 2 negroes, deske,
chist. Dau: JANNE, 1 negro, cow and calf, lume and
geare, tea table, saddle and iron skillet. Son: ASA,
1 negro, chist, cow and calf, horse, saddle, L 25
specie. Exr: JAMES LITTLE, JACOB GREMMER. Wit: ROB'T
GREMMER, JOSHUA SHARP, JOHN SHARP.

LITTLE, JANE
Jan. 1, 1833. No Probate date. Neph: JACOB VINES
LITTLE, lend 2 negroes, reversion to his heirs. If no
heir, reversion to nieces: SARAH WALKER, FRANCIS
CUTLER, JANE ALLEGOOD and LOUISA NARON. Bro: NAHUM
LITTLE, 1 negro, reversion to his heirs. No Exr. Wit:
JORDAN KNIGHT, F. D. LITTLE. No Clerk.

LITTLE, JESSE
Oct. 11, 1824. Aug. Ct., 1825. Bk. F, p 42. Wife:
FRANCES, lend plantation whereon I live, also tract

212

lying on Cheek's Creek bought of SAMUEL WILLIAMS, Extr.
of Col. JOHN DONASON, dec'd, 1/2 my "sein" place on
Tarr River opposite mouth of Town Creek, 11 negroes,
negroes to revert to chil., and all residue. Son:
JOHN A., all property I have possessed him of except
plantation whereon he lives, which I give to his chil.
at death of my wife FRANCES; all money he owes me and
I desire the bonds to be given up to him by my Exrs.
Son & Exr: FREDERICK D., 125 A tract bought of JOHN
COBB, reversion in plantation whereon I live, 1/2 "sein"
place, 1 negro, filly, saddle and smal trunk. Daus:
ELIZABETH SKINNER, land now in her possession, lend her
7 negroes with reversion to her chil; SARAH FLEMING,
3 negroes, all property now in her possession; FRANCES
A. and ANN, 2 negroes, large trunk and saddle, each.
Exr: DAVID BARNES, DANIEL HOPKINS. No Wit. Proven by
oaths of: CULLEN LITTLE, SOLOMON PENDER, JOSIAH PENDER,
BENJAMIN MILLER.

LITTLE, MICHAEL
    Jan. 30, 1826. Feb. Ct., 1826. Bk. F, p 51. Wearing
apparel to 6 bros. and father. Sister: ELIZABETH LITTLE,
all remainder. Exr: JAMES BARRON. Wit: JOSEPH ANSLEY,
JORDAN AMBROSE.

LITTLE, SYLVIA
    July 25, 1827. Feb. Ct., 1831. Bk. F, p 124. Dau:
PENINNAH CROMWELL, negro girl, small blue chest. Sons:
GRAY, WILLIAM and SETH, 6 negroes and their increase,
stock of every description, household and kitchen furniture, brandy still, and 2 kettles. Son & Exr: GRAY, 2
doz. silver spoons, and a ladle. Wit: EATON COBB,
JAMES THIGPEN.

LITTLE, WILLIAM
    May 4, 1790. Nov. Ct., 1794. Bk. C, p 293. Wife:
ELIZABETH, lend plantation whereon I live, and 1 negro,
reversion to chil. Sons & Exrs: EXUM, 150 A; GRAY, Ł
25, reversion in 1 negro. Dau: TEMPY. Son: MAC, horse,
bridle, saddle and gun; reversion in plantation whereon I live. Daus: ELSEY, FANNY, POLLY and ELIZABETH
LITTLE. Wit: JESSE LITTLE, JOHN LITTLE, MARY
SCARBOROUGH.

LLOYD, JOSEPH R.
Dec. 20, 1839. Feb. Ct., 1841. Bk. F, p 250. I
appoint GEORGE W. MORDICAI, Gdn. of my children. Chil:
HENRY S., MARY LOUISE, JOSEPH, GEORGE MORDICAI, and
WHITMELL PUGH LLOYDE, to be reared and educated in the
State of N. C. If he refuses, then B. F. MOORE. Wife:
MARIA AUGUSTUS LLOYD, carriage and horses, household
and kitchen furniture, use of lands and negroes 1 year
for support of my family. Real and personal estate and
residence to be sold and residue divided and invested
to best interest. Exr: BARTHOLOMEW F. MOORE, of Halifax
County.

LLOYD, NICHOLAS
Feb. 24, 1781. Nov. Ct., 1781. Wife & Extx: SARAH,
lend 2 negroes, plantation bought of JOSEPH MOORE'S
estate, and residue. Son: RODERICK, bequeath 2 negroes,
lend plantation whereon I live bought of NEEDHAM BRYAN,
plantation whereon SAMUEL GATER now lives, also plantation on the road, bought of JOSEPH MOORE estate,
with reversion to his son. It is my will that my son
be bound to Mr. NOAH HINTON to learn his trade and to
be kept at school while (until) he has sufficient
learning. If Mr. HINTON will not take him, I leave
him in the care of ISAAC SESSOMS and JOHN LLEWELLING.
Daus: SALIE GOLDSMITH BELL, ELIZABETH SESSOMS and
MARTHA ADDAMS, 5 S each; MARY, 2 negroes. I desire
she be put to Mr. and Mrs. SOLOMON SESSUMS until 18
or marries; FRANCES, 2 negroes, lend her plantation
whereon Widow RAINER lives, reversion to heirs law-
fully begotten of her body. I desire she be put out
to Mr. NOAH THOMPSON and his wife, until 18 or marries.
If they will not take her, it is left to the discretion of ISAAC SESSOMS and JOHN LLEWELLING. Exr:
NOAH HINTON, NOAH THOMPSON, WILLIS HUDNALL, ISAAC
SESSOMS, JOHN LLEWELLING. Wit: WILLIAM HAYNES, JOHN
HUDNALL, THEANEY ALSOBROOK.

LODGE, JOHN
Sept. 7, 1804. Nov. 1804. Bk. D, p 214. I lend
plantation whereon I live to Mother, MARY LODGE and
sister, VICEY LODGE, with reversion to bro., ROBERT,
he also to have all residue. Exr: WILLIAM BALFOUR.

Wit: WINNEFRED LODGE, MARGARET GRIFFIN.

LODGE, LUIS
     Jan. 24, 1794. Feb. Ct., 1794. Wife: MARY, lend
whole estate during lifetime with reversion to sons
JOHN, ROBERT and REDDICK. Son-in-law: OGBURN
NORSWORTHY, breeding sow. Son: JOSIAH, breeding sow.
Son: LUIS, 6 bbls corn, also part of a note of hand
against my son-in-law, ISAAC LANGLEY. Son-in-law: ISAAC
LANGLEY, remainder of note. Exr & Son: JOHN LODGE. Wit:
SAMUEL RUFFIN, JOHN WILSON, WILLIAM SAUNDERS.

LODGE, NANCY
     Jan. 15, 1848. No Probate date. I direct that all
my property of whatsoever kind, after paying my just
debts, be handed over to ROENA COBB. Exr: My esteemed
neighbor: J. W. JENKINS. Wit: JOSEPH G. GARRETT.

LOHON, ELIZABETH
     Nov. 27, 1788. Feb. Ct., 1791. Bk. 3, p 160. Friend
& Exr: JAMES COKER, JR.; all estate. Wit: NATHANIEL
COKER, JAMES NELSON, JAMES COKER, SR., SAMUEL JONES
NUNARY.

LONG, WILLIAM R.
     Dec. 21, 1848. Aug. Ct., 1849. Bk. F, p 432. Wife:
ANNIS, lend 234 A tract land whereon I reside, 8 negroes, horses, cows, pigs, etc., corn, fodder, pork,
3 chests, walnut table, 3 pine tables, 6 stools, 6
rush bottom chairs, side saddle and bridle, also
"secretary", china press, all pewter, tin, earthern
and glassware, case of knives and forks, tools and
kitchen utensils, loom and gear, linning wheel, 2
wolling wheels, 2 pr. cotton cards, 1 pr. wool cards,
all soap on hand. Daus: MANIZE DANIEL, $100; HENRYETTA
NOWELL, what I have already given her. Son & Exr:
JAMES S. LONG, all I have given him and my brandy still;
daus: TABITHA SAVAGE, $100; MARY ANN REAVES, all I have
given her. Son: WILLIAM S., chest of tools and all I
have given him. Exr: LEMUEL L. SAVAGE. Wit: BENJAMIN
STATON, LEVIN LEGGITT, JAMES B. STATON, MACK JONES.

LOWRY, ROBERT

215

July 4, 1768. Apr. Ct., 1774. Wife & Extx: ANN,
lend whole estate for widowhood or life; reversion to
son & Exr: JOHN, all land, houses, orchards, etc. Sons:
LEWIS, PETER and RICHARD, ₤ 15 sterling equally divided.
Daus: FRANKEY LANGFORD and JEMIMIAH WATTS, ₤ 20 current
money. Residue divided among: Sons: WILLIAM, ROBERT,
LEWIS, (Exr:) PETER, RICHARD, JAMES, and Daus: MARY
COLLINS, ANN DICKENS, BETTY STANFIELD, SARAH MAY,
FRANKEY LANGFORD and JAMIMA WATTS. Wit: WM. COOK,
ISAAC BEACHAM, ALEXANDER CLARK. Codicil: June 12, 1773.
If JOHN LOWRY dies without lawful heirs, land to be
sold and money divided between my other children. Like-
wise, youngest child of WM. LOWRY to have no part in
my estate. Exr: BENJ. DICKEN; Wife: ANN LOWRY; Son,
JOHN LOWRY. Same Witnesses.

LUPO, JAMES
Mar. 26, 1811. Aug. Ct., 1811. Bk. E, p 20. Nunc.
Will. Wife: ANNE, all estate with reversion to chil-
dren: ZACHARIAH, ANNE LANCASTER, MOLAN, PHEBE and
PHILIP LUPO. Proven by oaths of: WILLIAM DIXON, FANES
DIXON.

LUPO, ZACHARIAH
Oct. 27, 1821. Nov. Ct., 1821. Bk. E, p 281. Wife
& Extx: PATSY, land and estate for life or widowhood;
mentions reversion to children, but no names. Wit:
JO(AB) P. PITT, MOSES BAKER.

LYNCH, EATON
Mar. 11, 1851. Nov. Ct., 1851. Sister: MILLY LYNCH,
I lend to sister her life, the whole of my estate, including 2 negroes, all money due me and all money on
hand. Sons & Exrs: ADOLPHUS B. LYNCH and GEORGE G.
LYNCH, the whole of my estate, however reserving to
my sister MILLY her life estate, excepting 2 beds and
furniture, 1 painted chest, 1 trunk and $10.00. My
sons are to support, board and clothe my dau:
ELIZABETH A. E. A. LYNCH during her life, also pay 1
year's tuition for HESTER M. F. CUTCHINS children;
all the said property I give to my said sons and their
heirs. Dau: HESTER M. F. CUTCHIN, bed and furniture,
1 green painted chest (she has received) and $5 in

216

money. Wit: HENRY HYMAN, HENRY A. DOUB, WILLIE BRADLEY.

LYNCH, WILLIAM, Tarborough, N C.
Dec. 30, 1787. Jan. Ct., 1788. Bk. 3, p 361.
(Lengthy, complicated Will dealing with business firms
in Richmond and Balitmore.) Legatees: MICHAEL HENDRUN,
of Tarborough, DOMINICK JORDAN, of Baltimore, L 40
silver to be laid out for such mourning wanted for wife
in Baltimore, is only reference to family. Exr: DOMINICK
JORDAN, HENRY J. O'TOOLE, MAJ. JOHN INGLES, Merchants
of Baltimore. Wit: D. SUTHERLAND, TIMOTHY CAHILLE.

LYON, THOMAS
June 1, 1834. Feb. Ct., 1836. Bk. F, p 186. Wife:
DELPHIA, land at the mouth of Fishing Creek, then along
the lane to the negroe's graveyard; 6 negroes, 2 cows
and calves, 2 sows and pigs, sheep (her choice), still,
new gig, and harness, cart and wheels, tools, household
and kitchen furniture, 1500 lbs. pork, 25 bbls corn,
50 lbs sugar, 30 lbs coffee, fodder to feed her horse
one year. Dau: PATSY D. GRAY, wife of ETHELRED GRAY,
1 negro; after her death all negroes before given her
go to her chil. Son & Exr: HENRY J., 2 negroes, mare,
cow and calf, sow and pigs, trunk, and $700, being for
land sold to JAMES C. WHITAKER. Son & Exr: BENNET T.,
1/2 COFFIELD land, and 1/2 FLANNINGAN land, cow and
calf, sow and pigs, trunk and 2 negroes. Daus: NANCY
and SUSAN, 8 negroes and their increase, 2 trunks, 2
cows and calves and 2 horses. Dau: DELPHIA WHITAKER,
1 negro woman and all her increase; except Judy and
Simon, trunk, cow and calf, sow and pigs. Son & Exr:
JOSHUA, 1/2 land whereon I live, reversion in the
other half, also tract called the HINE'S tract, 2
negroes, mare, got by SIMON'S horse, cow and calf, sow
and pigs and trunk. Other property not given to be
sold and divided among all my children. Wit: EDWIN L.
MOORE, WILLIAM B. WHITAKER.

MABRY, WILKINSON
Dec. 17, 1833. No Probate Date. Bk____, p 231.
Daus: REBECAH BASS and her husband TURNER BASS, I lend
5 negroes, reversion to their chil. Bequeath 1 mare and
all remaining property of mine in their possession;

217

MELISHA BASS and her husband JOHN BASS, I lend 4 negroes, reversion to their chil. Bequeath all property
of mine in their possession. Gr. dau: ELIZABETH
DICKENS, 1 negro. Sister: TEMPERANCE MABRY, $200, 4 f.
beds, 4 blankets, 2 counterpins, 2 sheets, bedstead,
2 cows and calves, etc., reversion to CHARLES. Son &
Exr: CHARLES, all land. Exr: Sons-in-law, TURNER BASS,
JOHN BASS. Wit: JOSEPH EDMONDSON, WILLIAM BATTS.

MACDADE, WILLIS
    Apr. 20, 1820. Nov. Ct., 1823. Bk. F, p 8. Sons:
JOHN and WILLIE, 100 A both sides Great Branch, joining PHILANDA TISDALE, FREDERICK PHILIPS and AARON
PROCTOR. Dau: RHODY MACDADE, $25.00. CATHERINE YORK,
wife of JOHN YORK, 30 A where son JOHN formerly lived,
between JOSEPH GRIFFIN, the large Branch and lands of
sons: JOHN and WILLIE. Daus & Extx: MARY, ELIZABETH
and DELILIAH MACDADE, remainder of lands and all residue.
Wit: WEEKS PARKER, JONATHAN JOINER.

MACNAIR, EDMUND D.
    Sept. 6, 1842. Feb. Ct., 1843. Bk. F, p 274. Wife:
ELIZA B., estate divided between wife and her children.
Son: RALPH, having sold plantation (called Shabane)
which I designed to give my son RALPH, I desire that
he may receive from my estate $3500 which, with that
he already has received, will probably make a full
share when my late losses are considered. Dau: SUSAN
M. TANNABILE, wife of WILLIAM TANNABILE. Gr. daus:
MARY KIRTLAMD and SUSAN KIRTLAND, $1000 each. Sons
& Exrs: RALPH E. MACNAIR, THOMAS A. MCNAIR. Other
chil. not named. No Wit. This paper proven by oaths
of JOHN NORFLEET and CHRISTOPHER L. DICKEN to have
been found locked among valuable papers of EDMUND D.
MACNAIR. Handwriting proved by oaths of THEOPHILUS
PARKER, LOUIS D. WILSON and BENJAMIN M. JACKSON. Note:-
Splendid Will written by EDMUND MACNAIR.

MANER, AARON
    Feb. 7, 1825. May Ct., 1826. Bk. F, p 58. Son &
Exr: ZACHARIAH, plantation. Gr. son: MARMADUKE, horse.
Negroes, brandy stills, stock, equally divided be-
tween all my chil. LEVI & PATSY, chil. of AARON MANER,

dec'd. Old Esther may choose her master at her pleasure
and they are to support her during her life. Exr: HENRY
BRYAN. Wit: FREDERICK PHILIPS, JAMES PHILIPS.

MANNING, THOMAS
June 6, 1823. Nov. Ct., 1823. Bk. F, p 1. Wife:
MOURNING, lend land adjoining POPE, PHILIPS and NATHAN
MANNING. Also Black Walnut chest, 8 chair frames, table,
6 earthen plates, 2 pewter dishes, 6 knives and forks,
2 pots, 1 pan, Dutch oven, spider, breadbaker, earthen
dish bowl, bason, 6 cups and saucers, teapot, sugar
dish, butter pot, jug, fire tongs and shovel, pr. flat
irons, tools, woolen wheel, flax wheel and hackle, side
saddle, Testament, hymn book, 2 washing tubs, 1 can,
1 water piggin, bee hive, cart and wheels and geer,
mare, stock, 1 negro. Sons & Exrs: RICHARD, he and
EXUM to share land on E side Mirey Branch, except 1
1/2 A around about the Meeting House, 1 Bbl Brandy,
horse, stock, $46.63; EXUM, desk, horse, stock and
$46.63. Sons: NATHAN and THOMAS, to share land W of
Mirey Branch, horse, stock, Bbl Brandy, $3 to pay for
schooling and $46.63; THOMAS, horse, stock, 1 bbl.
Brandy, gun, $30, 1 slate, $6 to pay for schooling and
$46.63. Books, tools, beehives, stock, cattle, to be
divided equally between 4 sons. Wit: WILLIAM POPE,
MOURNING MANNING.

MARLAN, CHARLES
Oct. 19, 1782. May Ct., 1784. Wife: SARAH, all
estate for life; reversion to unnamed children. Wit:
THOMAS CROMWELL, SELAH CROMWELL.

MARLEY, ANN
Apr. 5, 1799. May Ct., 1799. Son: BOLING, 2 S 6
pence. Daus: SARAH, 2 S 6 pence; NANCY, residue. Exr:
WILLIAM DRAKE, HINES DRAKE. Wit: DELILIAH SHURLEY,
ELIZABETH BARFIELD.

MARLEY, NATHAN
Jan. 15, 1824. Feb. Ct., 1831. Bk. I, p 124. Wife:
RACHEL all estate during her lifetime or widowhood,
then to be divided between my 12 chil: CATHERINE,
MARY ANN, BENJAMIN, JANE, WILLIAM, NATHAN, ELIZABETH,

HENRY, JAMES, JOHN & ABRAHAM MARLEY. Exr: WILLIS
WILKINS, Esq. Wit: BEN I. SPRUILL, PETER EVANS.

MARSHALL, JOHN
    Oct. 24, 1757. Feb. Ct., 1758. Wife & Extx: AMY
Son & Exr: JOHN, plantation. Sons: HUMPHREY, planta-
tion over Tar River at head of Middle Creek; ABSALEM &
WILLIAM, plantation whereon I live on Elbe Creek. Daus:
ELiZABETH and PRISCILLA MARSHALL; GOODWIN TUCKER and
PENELOPE MARSHALL, To all daus are given negroes. Wit:
BENJA. HAILE, BENJA. NEVILLE, THOMAS MARSHALL.

MATTHEWSON, NATHAN
    Started July 30, 1826; finished Aug. 3, 1826. Aug.
Ct., 1832. Bk. F, p 133. Son: JOHN H., my watch, the
reason for no other legacy is that his grandfather has
left him out of his estate, more than I can give my
other children. Sister-in-law: SABRA PARKER, it is my
will that Family Bible and "portrate" of my picture
be left with my sister-in-law for later use of my
family. Daus: ABBY PECK, the "escrutor" and work table
purchased in Providence, R. I.; ELIZA (?) CAROLINE,
chest of drawers with glass knobs purchased in Providence, R. I., all silver spoons, silver sugar tongs,
casters and the 4 large salt "sellers"; SALLY MARGARET,
my executors shall purchase a chest the same kind that
ELIZA CAROLINE has. Sons; PASCAL POOLY, income from
4 negroes, 1 lot of land in Providence, R. I., which
was made over to my bro. to pay a legacy from my father
in his lifetime to my mother-in-law (step-mother?)
HANNAH MATTHEWSON. All my other property in Providence
to be sold by exr. and returns added to my estate;
NATHAN, (youngest son), house and lot in Tarboro where
I live. Bro-in-law (Step-bro?): MICHAEL HEARN, large
silver ladle, an old family piece, with his father's
and mother's name on it. My family to live in present
home for 1 yr. and have use of all negroes excepting
1 who will be hired out to help in their support. All
residue to be divided between 3 minor chil. Exr:
MICHAEL HEARN, BENJAMIN MANN JACKSON. No Wit. Proved
in court by oaths of GRAY LITTLE, BENJAMIN R. HINES.

MAUND, MARY

Sept. 27, 1795. Nov. Ct., 1795. Sons: LOTT, HARDY
and dau: REBEKAH KILLEBREW, 2 S 6 pence, each. Daus:
NANCY DRAKE, 2 S 6 pence, Ŀ 4 used as Exr. see fit for
her use; POLLY, large chest "cauled mine", also all
cotton and flax as she can spin while family remains
together. Chil of REBEKAH; LOTT and BARBARY KILLEBREW,
1 negro. Sons: MALLACHIA MAUND and DANIEL CHAMPIN TRAVIS
CARTER BOLING NICHOLS MAUND, these 2 sons share all remaining estate for their schooling. Exr: WILLIAM DRAKE,
NATHAN EDWARDS, JR. Wit: AMOS JOHNSTON, JOSIAH BOAZMAN,
SHADRACK HADDOCK.

MAUND, NOAH
Feb. 1, 1752. Feb. Ct., 1752. This is a Nuncupative
Will proven before SAMUEL WILLIAMS by ELIZA WEBB and
JOSEPH ISENMANGER, in which all estate of testator is
left to AQUILA SUGG, who is appointed Exr.

MAUND, WILLIAM. Parish of St. Mary's
Feb. 7, 1761. No Probate Date. Wife: MARY, stock,
furniture, household goods, lend 2 negroes. Son: HARDIE,
remaining estate. Exr: ROBERT WRIGHT; uncle: AQUILA
SUGG. Wit: JAS. BOAZMAN, DAVID ? MATE, MURFOR (?)
(MURFREE?) HOWELL.

MAYO, DAVID
Feb. 25, 1832. Feb. Ct., 1834. Bk. F, p 154. Wife:
SARAH, lend 7 negroes; after her death to be sold and
proceeds divided between: LEVI MAYO, PEGGA HARRELL,
MARTHA LEWIS, LUCY LAWRENCE, MARTHA BROWN, ELIZABETH
WILKERSON, LIZER WILKERSON and LYDIA WILKERSON. Also
lend her all horses, stock, cattle, and furniture,
reversion to my grandchil. named above. LEWIS MAYO, 1
negro; MARTHA BROWN, lend 1 negro. Dau: LUCY LAWRENCE,
$600. Exr: WILLIAM D. HOPKINS, WILLIAM THIGPEN. Wit:
SILAS EVERITT, L. B. BROWN.

MAYO, JOHN W.
July 12, 1824. Feb. Ct., 1825. Bk. F, p 28. Wife:
NANCY S. S. D. MAYO, 4 negroes, stock, cattle, etc.,
tools, provisions, $100. Lend land known as Staghead,
to branch dividing land owned by heirs of ARTHUR
STATON, dec'd and myself, still and cider utensils,

household and kitchen furniture, 2 negroes, At wife's death all to be divided equally. Son: LAWRENCE, all notes I hold against him, also money for upkeep. Son & Exr: JAMES, $5 in addition to that already given him. Daus: MERINA BEMBREY, $25 in addition to that already given her; NANCY SOUTHERLAND, $100 in addition to that already given her. Son: FREDERICK, tract known as BEMBRY Place, 1 negro, stock, cattle, etc. No Wit. Proven by oaths of JOHN L. SOUTHERLAND, KENNETH C. STATON, SPENCER L. HART, WILLIAM R. LONG, SOLOMON T. BRADDY.

MAYO, NATHAN
    Dec. 2, 1808. May Ct., 1811. Bk. E, p 11. Wife: ELIZABETH, lend 1/3 houses, lands, whereon I live and child's part in rest of property. Land purchased of Col. ARTHUR STATON and ZADOK STATON to be kept for use of mill. Son: FREDERICK (dec'd), leaving widow and her 2 chil. also natural son AGA JOHNSTON; it is my will that his name be changed to AGA MAYO and that he be entitled to share alike in my property with the heirs of sd son FREDERICK, dec'd., viz: JOHN LEWELLING MAYO, SUSANNAH MAYO and AGA MAYO. Tract in Islands of Cone-toe, equally divided among chil. of my first wife, viz: MICAJAH MAYO, TABITHA GRIMES, JOHN W. MAYO and heirs of my son FREDERICK, dec'd. Dau: TABITHA GRIMES, tract on lines of BARFIELD, Muddy Branch, Woolfpit and WILLIAM GRIMES' below BARNES' field and RAINES' field. Sons & Exrs: JOHN W., tract leased to ISAAC CUSHING dec'd, also 1/2 all land I hold W side of Swamp including that purchased of HEARN, joining HYMAN, BATTLE, BARFIELD, etc.; NATHAN, plantation whereon I live together with other half of that bought of HEARN. Sister: DELILAH MAYO, a home in house wherein I live during lifetime. WILLIAM HYMAN, son of my wife, $300. Son & Exr: MICAJAH MAYO. Wit: JOHN LEWELLING, SOLOMON STALLINGS.

MAYO, REBECCA
    Feb. 3, 1846. Aug. Ct., 1847. Bk. F, p 369. Gr. dau: DRUCILLA REDDICK, loom and gear. Gr. son: GRAY BUNTIN, chest. Son: WILLIAM MAYO, bofat. No Exr: Wit: JESSE HARRELL, LLEWELING HARRELL.

MAYO, WILLIAM
    Dec. 31, 1853. Feb. Ct., 1854. Bk. G, p 54. Wife &
Extx: ABBA (ABBY) MAYO, Residue of my property during
widowhood for benefit of raising my 3 youngest chil:
WILLIAM H., AGNES and MARGARET F. MAYO. Daus: MARY
SHELTON, SALLY ANN HARRELL, ELIZABETH, MARTHA ANN and
LOUISE MAYO and son: WILLIAM HENRY MAYO, cow and calf
and feather bed each. Oldest son: ANDREW JACKSON MAYO,
dark bay horse. Wit: PATRICK LANE, JAMES H. HICKS.

McDADE, MARY
    Aug. 16, 1832. No Probate Date. Sisters: RHODY and
ELIZABETH McDADE, all land to be divided equally be-
tween these 2; reversion to sister SARAH PRICE and
THOMAS McDEVER YORK. Sister: DELILAH MITCHEL, 2 A on
S side of road adjoining her dwelling. Bros: WILLIS,
JOHN and THOMAS McDADE, remainder of land. Residue
divided between RHODY WILLIS, ELIZABETH, SARAH PRICE,
DELILIAH MITCHEL, heirs of JOHN McDADE, and 1 part to
heirs of CATHERINE YORK. Exr: MOSES PRICE. Wit: WILLIAM
D. PETWAY, JOHN RICKS.

McDANIEL, CAMEIL (CAMPBELL)
    Dec. 15, 1807. Feb. Ct., 1808. Bk. D, p 302. Daus:
MARIAM McDANIEL, HARIAT McDANIEL, side saddle each and
1 negro between them. Residue divided between 4 daus.
Daus: AGNES DENTON, OLIVE COURKER (COKER). Exr: DAVID
COFFIELD. Wit: CARY WHITAKER, THOMAS LYON, FANNY COTTEN.

McDANIEL, DANIEL (Torn)
    June 5, 1768. Feb. Ct., 1769. Eldest son & Exr:
DANIEL McDANIEL, plantation on which he lives, all
stock, etc. in his possession. Dau: ANN ANDERSON, 20
S. Sons: ARCHIBLE (ARCHIBALD ?), stock, 1000 lbs. pork;
DAVID, 100 A lying on Wood Pocoson, 1/2 corn crop, and
horse; CAMEL (CAMPBELL), plantation whereon I live.
Son: JOHN, mare. Dau: ELIZABETH, _____?(torn),Sons
& Exrs: DANIEL McDANIEL, also Gdns to youngest chil:
ELIZABETH and CAMEL. Wit: _____? (torn), WM.
THRAILKILL, WM. CLARK, SPIER COFFIELD.

McDANIEL, DANIEL
    Nov. 20, 1792. Nov. Ct., 1792. Wife: MARY ANN,

lend plantation whereon I live, for life. Son & Exr:
JOHN, 300 A (the Mill Tract). Son: CHARLES plantation
of mother after her death. Daus: MARY ANN McDANIEL,
100 A Piney Woods land whereon J. HORN lives; SALLY
ANN McDANIEL. Bro. & Exr: CAMEL McDANIEL. Wit: D.
COFFIELD, RICHARD HARRISON, THOMAS BANKS.

McDANIEL, MARIAN
Nov. 15, 1793. Nov. Ct., 1793. Daus: SARAH (SALLY?)
ANN and MARY ANN, residue. Sons: JOHN and CHARLES
McDANIEL, 5 S each. Exr: CAMEL McDANIEL. Wit: _____?
HORN, MARY SESSOMS, D. COFFIELD.

McDOWELL, ELIZABETH
Sept. 2, 1831. Aug. Ct., 1835. Bk. F, p 177. Dau:
NANCY CAUSWAY and son: PATRICK McDOWELL, $1 each. Dau:
MARTHA CROMWELL, all property, real and personal. Exr:
NEWSOM CROMWELL. Wit: WILLIAM DANCY, MARTHA SAVAGE.

McDOWELL, JOHN
Feb. 10, 1825. May Ct., 1829. Bk. F, p 99. Wife:
ELIZABETH, lend all land N of Maple Swamp, 1 negro,
1/2 stock, riding chair, harness, saddle, bridle,
Brandy Still, cider casks, apple Mill and press for
life. Reversion to dau MARTHA. Daus: MARTHA, 1 negro;
NANCY CASWAY, wife of LEVEN (SEVEN?) CASWAY, 10 S. Son
& Exr: PATRICK, all land S of Maple Swamp, 1 negro, all
tools, 1/2 stock, all money. Wit: BEN DICKEN, WILLIAM
DANCY, SENR.

McKINNE, BARNABEE, JR.
Oct. 13, 1736. Nov. Ct., 1736. Wife and Extx: MARY,
5 negroes. Daus: PATIENCE and MARY, land, Legatees:
BARNABY, son of JOSEPH LANE: BARNABY, son of WILLIAM
McKINNE; JOSEPH LANE; JOHN POPE; JAMES NOWELL. Bros:
WILLIAM McKINNE, ROBERT McKINNE and JOHN McKINNE. Le-
gatees: NATHANIEL COOPER and JOHN LANE. Livestock and
land to legatees. Wit: NATHANIEL COOPER, JOHN CROWELL,
JOHN WATFORD. Note:- Original of this Will missing.
Abstract made from recorded copy No. 58 in Grant Book,
No. 4.

McKINNE, JOHN

Feb. 28, 1753. May Ct., 1753. Wife & Extx: MARY,
"I give and bequeath to my loving wife Mary the use of
my grist mill on Great Quonkee two years next ensuing
for pay for the giving each of my children before mentioned two years schooling." Son: BARNABY, horse I had
of WILLIAM WYNSTON. Daus: MARY, MARTHA, PATIENCE,
ANGELINA PARISH. Friend: CANNON CUMBO. Exr: MONTFORT
ELBECK. Wit: MONTFORT ELBECK, WILLIAM GADDY, MARY ELBECK.

McKINNE, MARY
        Oct. 13, 1754. Nov. Ct., 1754. "Imprimis, I most
humbly bequeath my Soul to God my Maker beseeching His
most Gracious reception of it through all the sufficient
merits and Meditations of my Most Compassionate Redeemer
Jesus Christ, who gave himself to be an atonement for
my sins, and is able to save to the uttermost all that
come unto God by him, Seeing He ever liveth to make
intercession for them, and who, I trust will not reject
me a returning penitent sinner, when I come to him for
mercy; in this Hope & confidence I render up my soul
with comfort humbly beseeching the most Blessed and
Glorious Trinity, one God most holy, most merciful and
gracious to prepare me for the time of my dissolution,
and then to take me to himself unto that Place of Rest
and incomparable Felicity which he has prepared for
all that Love and fear his holy name Amen Blessed be
God."According to Grime's Abstracts, the above preamble
is typical of the wills of that period. Sons: JOHN,
BARNABY. Daus: ANGELEANY POPE, MARY, MARTHA, PATIENCE,
McKINNE. Exr: BARNABY POPE. Wit: DAVID CRAWLEY, WM.
GADDY, ROBERT BELCHER.

McKINNE, RICHARD
        Aug. 10, 1751. Aug. Ct., 1755. Wife & Extx: MARY.
Bro: ROBERT McKINNE. Neph: BARNABY McKINNE. Exr:
WILLIAM KINCHEN, WILLIAM KINCHEN, JR. Wit: W. KINCHEN,
WM. BAKER, LEMUEL KINCHEN.

McMILLAN, WILLIAM
        Oct. 26, 1730. Nov. Ct., 1784. Wife & Extx:
(Unnamed), all residue. Sons: NEALLY McMILLAN and
ROBERT McMILLAN, all land. Exr: N. COTTEN. Wit: ARTHUR
HARGROVE, MOSES HARGROVE.

McWILLIAMS, MARY

Apr. 7, 1847. May Ct., 1848. Bk. F, p 396. Son:
WILLIAM HENRY McWILLIAMS, 2 negroes, 2/7 of estate;
dau: ELLEN FRANCES McWILLIAMS, 2 negroes, 5/7 of
estate. In case either child die without heir, the
other shall have whole estate, in case both die without
heir, estate shall be divided equally between my bros
JOSEPH and JACOB HIGGS and the chil of dec'd bros
WILLIE and REUBEN and chil of dec'd sister SALLY
WHITEHEAD. Exr: Bro, JACOB HIGGS. Wit: W. F. DANCY,
GEORGE HOWARD.

MERCER, MARGARET (Wife of JESSE MERCER)

Apr. 2, 1852. Nov. Ct., 1852. Bk. F, p 491. Being
authorized by a certain deed from the said JESSE MERCER
to JOHN NORFLEET as trustee dated June 4, 1847 to con-
vey property therein mentioned in writing by will or
otherwise I do make and publish and declare this my
Last Will and Testament. Bro: BENJAMIN NORFLEET, all
my interest in lands which descended to me from my
father, the late ISAM NORFLEET, and lands which descended to me from my sister the late SARAH NORFLEET,
the former being one ninth part and the latter being
one eighth part. Bro & Exr: THOMAS NORFLEET, $300.
Neph: WILLIAM H. JOHNSTON, $500. Bro: JOSEPH NORFLEET,
residue divided between brothers BENJAMIN, THOMAS and
JOSEPH. Exr: JOHN NORFLEET. Wit: A. J. M. WHITEHEAD,
JOHN S. DUGGAN.

MERRETT, THOMAS

Aug. 29, 1757. No Probate Date. Wife & Extx: MARY,
100 A whereon I live including mill, for her lifetime,
HH goods, stock, cattle and hogs. Sons: WILLIAM, 200 A
I had of MITCHEL, tools, etc.; BENJAMIN, 100 A I had
of TAYLOR; 100 adjoining, and plantation and mill after
wife's death. Daus: MARY INGRAM and MARTHA MERRETT, 100
A; MARGAIT (Olds, MARAGARET) and BARBARY (Olds,
BARBARA), 100 A S side of mill; JANNEY (Olds, FANNY)
and CHARLOTTY (Olds, SHALATY), 50 A each in Granville
Co. Son: JAMES, 300 A in Granville Co. and mill thereon. Wit: SHER'D HAYWOOD, ELIZABETH GOODSON, JOHN STONE.

MERRITT, JOHN

Jan. 13, 1757. Nov. Ct., 1757. Wife & Extx: MARY.
Sons: THOMAS and JOHN. Daus: PEGEE, wife of JOHN STONE;
AMEE, wife of WILLIAM HANBY and BETTY MERRITT. Wit: JNO.
HAYWOOD, THOS. MERRITT.

MERRITT, MARY
June 9, 1778. Aug. Ct., 1778. Nunc. Will. ANNE ?
BURN, wife of MICH'L BOURN, made oath before me that
MRS. MARY MERRITT when in good senses said she wished
her property should be inherited by her grandson,
EMANUEL MERRITT. Signed: ROBERT BIGNALL. Wit: ANNE
BOURN.

MERRITT, NATHANIEL. (of BARTIE PRESCINT IN ROANOKE)
Apr. 10, 1735. Feb. Ct., 1735. Wife & Extx: MARY.
Sons: NATHANIEL, plantation whereon I live; EFRUM,
5000 lbs. of "drest" pork; BENJAMIN, 1 negro. Daus:
SARAH and MARY. Wit: FRANCES WELDON, HENRY JONES.

MEWBORN, THOMAS
Apr. 22, 1782. Aug. Ct., 1782. Wife: GRACE, 1 negro, reversion to dau. SOOKEY and residue. Son: GEORGE,
plantation including all my land between Little Swamp
and Great Branch. Daus: SOOKEY, NANCY and PATTY, 1 negro each. JOHN CANNADY, cow and calf. Son: THOMAS
MEWBORN. Exr: CHARLES LEE, Bro. JOHN MEWBORN. Wit:
JACOB GRICE, SARAH STOKES.

MIAL, JOHN
Feb. 9, 1775. Feb. Ct., 1778. Sons: THOMAS, JOHN,
JETHRO, and dau: CHARITY LANGLEY, 5 S each. Son & Exr:
NORSWORTHY, remainder of estate, land, etc. Wit:
ETHELRED EXUM, JOHN EXUM.

MIDDLETON, JOHN
July 20, 1750. Nov. Ct., 1750. Wife & Extx: MARY.
Sons: JAMES, EDWARD. Daus: ELIZABETH PERREY, wife of
BENJAMIN PERREY; JANE; SARAH and MILDRED. Wit: AMBROSE
JOSHUA SMITH, JUDITH SMITH.

MILLER, JOHN
Sept. 26, 1816. Nov. Ct., 1823. Bk. F, p 10. Wife:
DOLLY, lend 2 fields, (mill field and house field),

furniture, corner cubard, burow, chist, chairs, loom,
2 wheels and cards, kitchen utensils, remainder (mill,
cotton gin, orchard, etc.) to be rented, money put to
interest for provision of "a generous country education" for son. Son: FREDERICK, residue. Exr: STEPHAN
ROBBINS, JOHN BEELAND. Wit: REDDICK BARNES, MICAJAH
PETTAWAY, JOHN MORGAN. Exr. refused to qualify. Adm.
by wife, DOLLY MILLER. Surety: MICAJAH PETTAWAY,
STEPHEN ROBBINS.

MILLER, JOSHUA
   May 27, 1806. Aug. Ct., 1806. Bk. D, p 249. Wife
& Extx: POLLEY, land on Causey Branch, Cheek's Creek
and MANNING'S line and horses and cattle, to be sold,
remainder divided equally between wife and 5 children.
JULIA, BENJAMIN, SARAH, HENRY & NOAH MILLER. Exr: JESSE
LITTLE, GRAY LITTLE. Wit: DRURY MAY, JAMES HICKS.

MILLER, MARY
   May 18, 1802. Aug. Ct., 1802. Son: WILLIS ETHERIDGE,
50 A land, tools, furniture, etc. Remainder sold and
divided between 2 daus: MARY and BETSY. Bro and Exr:
NATHAN ETHEREDGE. Wit: MICAJAH PETTAWAY, EDWARD PITTMAN.

MILLER, STEPHEN
   Dec. 9, 1802. Feb. Ct., 1803. Wife & Extx: LUCRESY,
whole estate for life, reversion to 2 daus: ELIZABETH
and ANN. Wit: SALLY GOLDSMITH BELL, JAMES ADAMS.

MITCHELL, PETER
   Apr. 14, 1770. No Probate Date. Wife: Unnamed. All
perishable estate for widowhood. Reversion to SUSANNA.
Daus: HANNAH RICHARDSON, MARTHA HARDY (?), ELIZABETH
EVINS, and sons: STEVEN and ISAAC (Exr), 5 S each. Son:
JOHN, plantation whereon I live and 1 negro. Dau:
SUSANNA. Exr: BEVERLY BELCHER. Wit: JOHN SKINNER,
ELIZABETH SPARON, MARY MITCHELL.

MITCHELL, RANDALL
   Sept. 24, 1756. June Ct., 1758. Wife & Extx: MARY.
Bro: WILLIAM MITCHELL. Dau-in-law: ELIZABETH LEAVET.
Exr: AQUILLA SUGG. Wit: BAURLEAY (BEVERLY) BELCHER,
JOSEPH HOWELL, BENJAMIN MITCHELL.

MOBLEY, JOHN (of Lunenburg Co. Va.?)
Aug. 5, 1752. May Ct., 1753. Wife & Extx: RACHEL,
2 negroes. Sons: JOHN, MORDECA, EDWARD (Exr), and HAMON
(HARMON), 1 negro each. Bro: EDWARD MOBLEY. Wit: JOHN
WILLIAMS, JOHN WARD, LEWIS ATKINS.

MOOR, AMOS
Feb. 18, 1788. May Ct., 1789. Bk. Q, p 99. Wife:
ELIZABETH, lend all land and personal property for life
or widowhood. Son: NUETON, all land at mother's death.
Daus: CHARRITY and DAUGHRITY, personal property divided
between 3 chil. Exr: BYTHAL BELL, JOHN FOXHALL. Wit:
CHARLES CAPELL, ELIZABETH CAPELL.

MOORE, ELIJAH
Feb. 10, 1820. Feb. Ct., 1833. Bk. F, p 140. Wife:
MARY, lend tract laid off and alloted to my son ELIJAH
MOORE whereon I live, it lying on lines of LAMON RUFFIN,
JOHN RUFFIN, DAVEE BULLUCK, the lines having been surveyed by WILLIAM WILKINS, which divided the lands of
my sons ELIJAH and ETHELRED, also all furniture, 1 cow
and calf, mare, 1 sow and pigs, 5 sheep. Sons:
ETHELRED, balance said tract whereon he lives, 1 small
pot and hooks, 3 gal. jug, 1/2 gal. jug, gin jug, 1
gal. pewter bason, 1/2 still, etc.; ELIJAH, tract lent
to wife, at her death, 4 gal. jug, large decanter, 2
black bottles, still jug, 1 gal. pewter bason, cow and
calf, 5 sheep, 1 chest, 1 table, 1/2 cider barrels and
stands, 1/2 still, tools, etc. Dau: ZADA WILLIAMS, wife
of JOSIAH WILLIAMS, 1 flax wheel. Sons & Exrs:
THEOPHILUS, SAMUEL. Son: EXUM. Dau: MARTHA ROBBINS,
wife of ELIJAH MOORE, residue divided between all chil.
Wit: MOSES SPICER, JOHN LONG, SR.

MOORE, ELIZABETH
Sept. 6, 1851. Feb. Ct., 1852. Exr to dispose of
all property. Proceeds to go to Dau: SALLY ANN TEALE,
reversion to her daus: MARGARET C. and FLORENCE C.
TEALE, $1 each. Exr: LITTLEBERRY MANNING. Wit: WILLIAM
S. BAKER, J. J. N. MARK.

MOORE, ETHELRED
Mar. 27, 1838. No probate Date. Bk. F, p 245. Wife

& Extx: SALLEY, lend all property, also lend to 6 daus.
all household and k. furniture and 2 negroes so long as
they remain at present residence. Mentions 6 daus and
3 sons but does not name them. Wit: BENNETT BRADLEY,
ORREN BULLUCK. Codicil: June 1, 1840. I give to son
MOSES MOORE, 1 note for $105 with int. from Dec. 28.,
1839. I give unto my dau, PENNY, $10; I give unto my 6
daus: 3 notes totalling $165.20 to be equally divided
between them. Sworn to before D. J. BAKER, J. P., June
9, 1840. Wit: EXUM MOORE, JAMES RUFFIN.

MOORE, JOSEPH
     Feb. 15, 1753. Feb. Ct., 1757. Wife & Extx: ANN,
Sons & Exrs: JOSEPH, plantation in Edgecombe Co. on
Little Swamp, also plantation in Bertie Co. on Rock-
quies Swamp where WILLIAM BRYANT formerly lived; JAMES,
100 A land bought of WM. McGEE on S side Conetoe pocosin;
HODGES, 100 A land on N side Conohoe Swamp; JESSE, plantation on Mill Branch and MONTGOMERY'S line whereon I
live; EZEKIEL and JESSE to have my water mill. Son-in-
law: (unnamed), tract of land on Conetoe Swamp. Daus:
ANN MAGEE, MARTHA HINTON, CELIA MOORE. All chil. get
negroes. MELIA MOORE. Wit: ELIZABETH WILLIAMS, MARY
WHITMILL, WM. WILLIAMS.

MOORE, JOSEPH
     Oct. 6, 1775. Jan. Ct., 1776. Wife: ANN, lend plan-
tation whereon I live and that which joins it purchased
of JAMES DUNLOP and 3 negroes; remaining negroes to be
hired out for benefit of wife etc. Bequeath £ 500 for
her pocket money. Each trustee or Exr to be paid £ 100
Proc. money. £ 200 to the poor. ZEKEL MOORE, tract
whereon he lives, 1 negro and £ 100. JOSEPH MOORE, son
of JAMES MOORE, £ 100. HENRY IRWIN, son of HENRY IRWIN
of Tarboro, £ 100. POLLY TOOLE, £ 50. JOSEPH MOORE
IRWIN, son of HENRY IRWIN. JEAN TOOLE, £ 50. HENRY
IRWIN TOOLE. Exr. to use remainder of income to relieve
and support any poor of the Church of England, not being
dissenters for 10 yrs. Exr: WILLIAM WILLIAMS of Martin
Co., HENRY IRWIN, HENRY IRWIN TOOLE, JAMES MOORE. Wit:
GERALDUS TOOLE, MARY TOOLE, JINEY TOOLE.

MOORE, JOSEPH
Oct. 7, 1775 (?). Jan. Ct., 1778. Nunc. Will.
Leaving wife (unnamed), household goods, crop, etc.
Statement sworn to before ROBERT BIGNALL. Proved by
oath of HENRY IRWIN.

MOORE, MARTHA
Apr. 9, 1853. Aug. Ct., 1853. Bk. F, p 518. Estate
divided between 4 chil. and gr. dau. Daus: MARTHA E.,
POLLY P. and ANNAMARIA B. (?), and Son: WILLIAM B. Gr.
dau: MILICENT MOORE. No Exr. Wit: ABNER EASON, BENNET
BURRUS.

MOORE, MOSES
Apr. 2, 1802. May Ct., 1802. Wife: SUSANNA, lend
120 A S side Tyancokey Swamp, also 1 negro, for widow-
hood; stock, cattle, tools, furniture and $5. Son:
GEORGE, $1 silver beside that already given him.
WILLIAM, son of GEORGE, and wife ELIZABETH, $100 sil-
ver. Sons: HARTWELL, JOSEPH, MOSES, MARK, JOHN, $100
silver each. All land divided between latter 4 sons.
Daus: NANCY, ELIZABETH, REBECCA, ESTHER, $24 each. Exr:
LAMON RUFFIN, SIMEON HORN, DEMPSEY JENKINS, MARK
DILLARD. Wit: H. HAYWOOD, ETHELRED RUFFIN, SAMUEL
HANDBY.

MOORE, RUTHA
Sept. 14, 1850. Nov. Ct., 1850. Bk. F, p 449.
MARTHA ANN COBB, dau of JOSEPH COBB, 1 wheel and trunk
after the death of my dau SARAH COBB. Gr. dau: MARGRETT
COBB, loom and gear after death of my dau SARAH COBB,
1 safe, butter pot, 2 unfinished quilts. Gr. dau:
SARAH COBB, bed and clothing, 1 blue grounded wooling
blanket; all this loaned to dau SARAH COBB then to
daus. Sons: JAMES CARNEY (Exr), walnut chest, large
decanter, large flowered tumbler; WRIGHT CARNEY. Dau:
ELIZABETH CARNEY, red chest. Wit: JESSE HARRELL, DAVID
M. COBB.

MOORE, SAMUEL
Jan. 17, 1793. Nov. Ct., 1794. Wife & Extx:
ELENDER, lend plantation, all land, 3 negroes for
widowhood. Daus: ELIZABETH DAVIS, DELILAH WOODARD,

SARAH PARISH, 5 ₺ each; MOLLY HARRELL, 5 S, also lend
1 negro, reversion to her chil. at her death. Daus:
JERUSHA AMERSON, ELLENDER and SINTHA MOORE, 1 negro
each at mother's death. Dau: JEMIMA, all land and plantation, also 1 negro at mother's death; 1 negro shall
choose his mistress among MOLLY HARRELL, JERUSHA
AMERSON, ELENDER, SINTHA and JEMIMA. Exr: WILLIAM
AMERSON. Wit: ETHELRED RUFFIN, ELI AMERSON, JAMES
JOHNSTON.

MORGAN, JAMES S.
    Dec. 18, 1848. Feb. Ct., 1849. Bk. F, p 419.
Father and Mother: HENRY MORGAN and MILBRY MORGAN,
$200 and 2 negroes. Reversion to bros. Bro and Exr:
HENRY W. MORGAN, horse. Bros: LEMUEL and FRANCIS
MORGAN. Sisters: FELECIA and CATHERINE MORGAN, 1 negro;
MAHALA MORGAN, $75; DELPHIA HOCOTT of Tenn., $25. Wit:
WILLIAM NORFLEET, JOHN S. DANCY.

MORGAN, JOSEPH
    May 5, 1791. Nov. Ct., 1792. Wife: MARY, formerly
called MARY ATKINSON. Sons: DAVID, JOSEPH, JOHN. Dau:
ANNE CAUSEY. Exr: SOLOMON SESSUMS, Esqr., Capt. JOHN
WHITE. Wit: D. SUTHERLAND, EZEKIEL CAUSEY, BENJAMIN
SMALL. Exrs. refused to qualify, JOSEPH MORGAN, Admt'r.
Will very illegible. (See duplicate will of Joseph
Morgan made 5 July, 1790.)

MORGAN, WILLIAM
    Nov. 10, 1794. Feb. Ct., 1795. Son: WILLIAM, all
land. Gr. son: DAVID MORGAN, mare and stock. Daus:
MARTHA PRICE and KEDDY JENKINS. Residue divided between 3 chil. and gr. son. Exr: HORATIO DURLEY. Wit:
JACOB COKER, JOHN MORGAN.

MORGAN, WILLIAM
    Oct. 1, 1837. Probated in 1837. Gr. son:
THEOPHILUS MORGAN, 214½ A plantation and land whereon
I now live; Son: WILLIS, $75.00. Exr and Worthy Friend:
WILLIAM D. BRYAN. Wit: THOMAS MAYO, JAS. C. MARKE.

MORGIN, JOSEPH
    July 5, 1790. No Probate Date. Not Recorded? Wife:

MARY MORGIN, or MARY ATKINSON, all land and personal
property during widowhood. Personal to be divided between 4 sons. DAVID and ROBERT to live with mother until maturity, to have 3 yrs. schooling. Sons: DAVID,
tract running from old river landing to great public
road, Sein place to DAVID and ROBERT; ROBERT, tract adjoining DAVID'S having houses etc. on it (whereon I
live); JOSEPH, all money and interest due me, including
Bond for $316 2/3 by JOHN LAWRENCE; JOHN. ANN CAUSAY,
10 S. At death wife, 1 negro to be freed. Exr: Capt.
IRWIN TOOLE, SOLOMON SESSUMS. Wit: NOAH SUGG, NOAH
SUGG, JR., WILLIAM KEY.

MORRIS, JESSE
       Aug. 19, 1778. Nov. Ct., 1778. Sons: CHESTON,
(CHESTER?) Exr: HENRY; SAM DAVIS; JAMES MORRIS; JABAS
(JABEZ, Olds), equal division. Dau: SUSANNAH MORRIS.
Wit: JOSEPH SUMNER, JR., ELISHA SUMNER, JOSEPH SUMNER.

MORRIS, JOHN, SENR.
       Feb. 24, 1800. May Ct., 1800. Wife: CHRISTIAN (?),
lend plantation and all land in Edgecombe Co. during
widowhood, farm tools, etc. and orchard to be divided between wife and son BENJAMIN when he reaches
maturity. Son: BENJAMIN, 297 1/2 A tract in Nash Co.
Exr: DEMPSEY BARNES. Wit: WM. DEW, NATHAN JOHNSON,
MARY JOHNSON.

MORRIS, JOHN
       Feb. 15, 1838. Feb. Ct., 1838. Wife: MARTHA, furn-
iture, pot, dish, bole (bowl), griddle, pan, set of
knives and forks, set table spoons; also lend unto
her the hole of my lands during her natural life or
widowhood. Reversion to 3 youngest sons: BENJAMIN,
THOMAS and JESSE MORRIS, my horses, stock, cattle,
Daus: SUSAN, ANNEY and SARAH, bed, bedstead, furniture each. Residue to be divided between my 6 chil.
now living with me: SUSAN, ANNY, SARAH, THOMAS,
BENJAMIN and JESSE. Son & Exr: JOHN MORRIS, JR. Wit:
WM. BARNES.

MORRIS, NATHAN
       Dec. 30, 1820. Nov. Ct., 1829. Bk. F, p 106. Wife

& Extx: FEBY, lend all property to wife for widowhood
Mother-in-law: ELIZABETH HUNT, cow and calf. Wit: JAMES
W. BARNES, DEMSEY D. BARNES, HENRY HORN.

MOYE, IRWIN
June 1, 1832. Nov. Ct., 1832. Bk. F, p 137. Wife:
SUSANNAH, 2 negroes, my clothing, hats and shoes, large
Bible, Hymn Book, all cloth. Sons: WILLIAM H., LEMUEL
H. and dau: MARY JANE, $750.00 and 1 negro each. All
other negroes and Green Co. land to be sold and residue
divided equally between wife and chil. Bro & Exr: WYATT
MOYE. No Wit: broken open in prescence of LEM HARDY,
MACON MOYE. Proven by oaths of MACON MOYE, WILLIAM MOYE,
ASA AMASON.

MOYE, WILLIAM H.
Jan. 2, 1847. Feb. Ct., 1848. Bk. F, p 389. Exr.
to pay note for $230 due JOHN WILKINSON dated Jan. 2,
1847, also note for $90 due LEWIS J. DORTCH dated Dec.
1846. Estate to legal heirs. Exr: WYATT MOYE. Wit:
HENRY M. THOMPSON, A. E. GILL.

MULKEY, PHILIP
Dec. 17, 1736. May Ct., 1737. Wife & Extx: SARAH .
Sons: DAVID (eldest), land on Beaver Pond; PHILIP "2nd
son, my plantation". Daus: JANE (eldest), mare in the
hands of ROBERT LEE; EVE, ELIZABETH, SCARBOROUGH,
JUDITH. Son-in-law: GEORGE LAWS. Friends: RACKLEY
KIMBROUGH, 100 A; JOHN HARDY, 100 A at Plum Tree;
NATHANIEL BYZALL (illegible), 80 A he bought. Exr:
JAMES SMITH. Wit: RICHARD HERRING, JOHN CALIHAN,
JONATHAN MULKEY.

MURPHY, WILLIAM
Jan. 23, 1736. May Ct., 1737. Wife & Extx: ANN.
Daus: MARY, 100 A S side Cooch Swamp called Busby's
Cabbin, also negroes; MARTHA, 240 A S side Cooch Swamp,
also negroes; ESTHER, negroes. Kinsman: WILLIAM HURST,
100 A adjoining CUTLER POLLOCK, former patent of
WILLIAM OPICE (?) JOSEPH BRADSHAW, 200 A S side
Cooch Swamp. Exr: JOHN EDWARDS, ISAAC RICKS. Wit: JOHN
POPE, WM. GOODWIN, JOHN STRICKLAND.

NELSON, JAMES
        Oct. 30, 1766. Apr. Ct., 1767. Son: WILLIAM, 5 S
sterling. Daus: SARAH, 5 S sterling; ELVEY, cow, calves,
mare, etc.; Plantation to be sold and revenue divided
between daus: CHARITY, VIOLETTA and BETTY, and son:
WILLIAM. Exr: JACOB BETHANY, horse; LAZARUS WHITEHEAD.
Wit: WILLIAM BLACKBURN, MOLLY DORTCH, LEWIS DORTCH,
LAZARUS WHITEHEAD, JR.

NELSON, JAMES
        Oct. 10, 1795. Feb. Ct., 1797. Wife: JUDAH NELSON,
all estate. Exr: JACOB HOUSE. Wit: JAMES COKER, JR.,
HOSEA DURLEY, JR.

NETTLE, JOHN
        Jan. 6, 1830. Feb. Ct., 1830. Bk. F, p 115. Daus:
MOURNING, to share land whereon I live, also 45 A re-
cently taken up adjoining it, with ELIZABETH, also 2
negroes; ELIZABETH, negroes, chest, negress Hannah to
choose her master and to be supported by my family;
POLLY DRAKE; Gr. son: JOHN NETTLE, brandy still, tub
and worm; Gr. dau: ANN NETTLE, $50; son: ALLEN, $50.
OLLIFF FOREHAND. Residue divided between POLLY DRAKE,
OLIFF FOREHAND, ELIZABETH NETTLE, MOURNING NETTLE. Exr:
WILLIS WILKINS. Wit: JOHN GARRETT, ELISHA PEEL.

NETTLES, JACOB
        Nov. 12, 1837. May Ct., 1838. I wish my Executors
hereinafter named to sell my lands, crops, stock, provisions, and furniture in such way as they deem most
proper and prudent...no part of furniture and clothing
and furniture, which my negro woman Sarah, or any other
of my slaves may have, is to be taken from them whatsoever. The money arising from sale...it is my will
that so much as may be necessary therefrom that my
Executors devote to the purpose of transporting safely
and comfortably to the State of Indiana, or some other
State in the Union provided there is no prohibitory
law in regard to people of colour going, or emigrating
thereto, where they may forever enjoy their freedom...
namely, Sarah, a negro woman about 45 or 50 years;
Blount, who was born the 15th day of February, 1821;
Washington, born July 20, 1827; Sarah Ann born March

235

31, 1829, as their ages are set down in my Bible, and
Wedley, aged about 4 years, of whose precise age I have
no record. All the last named being the children of the
first named, Sarah.

If it so happens that from any cause my Executors
cannot legally comply with my will and desire to send
my negroes above named to some State in this Union
where they may enjoy their freedom, as I wish them to
do, then, and in that case, I wish my Executors shall
permit and allow my said servants to live and enjoy
themselves as free persons of colour in this State,
and that they purchase or provide out of the funds
which may be in their hands, a small tract of land,
such as they may think sufficient for their comfortable support and maintenance, and that from time to
time they see and attend to them in such a way as they
may deem best to carry into effect my will as set forth,
devoting to that purpose all necessary funds as aforesaid, and further, I hereby Enjoin it upon my servants
Blount, Washington, Laura Ann and Wedley, and wish my
Executors to see that they comply with this request
that in the event that their mother wherever she may
be, shall be kindly treated and comfortably maintained
by them, should necessity require their attendance and
assistance.

Item 3rd. In the event that there now be or hereafter may be any law or other impediment which may
prevent compliance with my will...and it should be
necessary that any or all of my servants should be
sold...then, in that case they be allowed the privilege
of selecting and choosing their own masters.

It is my earnest wish and desire that none of my
servants herebefore named may ever under any circumstances be slaves or bondsmen to any person whatsoever,
and more especially do I enjoin it upon my Executors
never to permit any of my relations, whether connected
to me by either consanguinity or affinity to have any
right management, supervision or control over any of
my said servants...and I do further request and enjoin
it upon my Executors to comply with my will in every
particular by no means failing or neglecting to provide if possible, for the freedom and comfortable support of my said slaves, provided they are unable to

secure their full freedom and entire emancipation... that they do all in their power to prevent their falling into the hands of improper persons, and be treated as nearly as possible as free persons.

Item 6th. It is my will and desire that if it should so happen that my said servants, or any of them, shall be sold or hired out, or there is a surplus of funds in anywise belonging to my estate after my Executors have done all in their power to carry into effect my will, then in that case I give all such surplus, whether it be money, notes or any other species of property to ELI PORTER, of the town of Tarborough, etc. Exr: BENJAMIN THORPE, JOSEPH JOHN PORTER. Wit: BENJAMIN DUNN, MARTIN GARDNER, B. R. HINES.

NEWSOM, THOMAS
Nov. 16, 1778. Feb. Ct., 1779. Wife & Extx: HANNAH, 1/2 remaining personal estate, use of 1/3 of land, reversion to son JOSEPH. Son & Exr: JOSEPH, remainder of land and 1/2 remaining personal estate. Chil: PATTEY BOOTHE, 20 S; THOMAS, L 40; KISIAH, L____ (? torn), FANNEY, MARY, PRISCILLA, DELANE and HANNAH, 40 S each. Wit: ROB'T BOOTH, JOHN BONNER, J. W. WHITE.

NICHOLSON, JOHN
Jan. 18, 1799. Feb. Ct., 1799. Wife: PENELOPE, lend plantation whereon I live, 5 negroes, horses, cows, cattle, etc., 6 flagbottom chairs, 2 tables and desk. Dau: MATILDA, L 10 Va. money. Son & Exr: TIMOTHY M., 250 A plantation on Fishing Creek (fell to me from my bro. ABSALOM.) Also Mother's land at her death; 2 negroes and L 300. Land adjoining Fishing Creek and MALICHI NICHOLSON to be sold and money divided between daus. Also land purchased of JOHN ROBERTSON to be sold after death of wife and money along with 1 negro each to daus: SARAH M., PENELOPE, MARTHA, MARY, FEREBY, ELIZABETH, ANN and LATITIA CROWELL. Remaining negroes to be divided equally among chil. Exr: Son-in-law, SAMUEL CROWELL. Wit: JOHN NICHOLSON, JR., DUNCAN CAIN.

NICHOLSON, PENELOPE
Jan. 24, 1820. Aug. Ct., 1820. Bk. E, p 238. PENELOPE WHITFIELD, 1 negro purchased of HARDY

WHITFIELD, reversion to her chil. All remaining pro-
perty to be sold and revenue divided between PENELOPE
WHITFIELD and: MARTHA JENKINS, PHERIBA SHELTON, POLLY
JELKS, ELIZABETH PHILIPS, NANCY BELLAMY, HEIRS OF
LETITIA CROWELL, SALLEY M. PHILIPS, TIMOTHY M.
NICHOLSON. Exr: Son-in-law MATTHEW PHILIPS. Wit:
CORNELIUS FORMAN.

NOBLELAND, JOHN
    Aug. 12, 1755. Nov. Ct., 1755. Wife & Extx: MARY.
Daus: MATHEW, REBECCA and MARY COTTON. Wit: WILLIAM
OGILVIE, NATHANIEL MERRITT, WILLIAM RAINWATER.

NORFLEET, CHRISTIANA
    Apr. 27, 1852. Aug. Ct., 1853. Bk. F, p 509. Dau:
MARGARET NORFLEET. Son & Exr: THOMAS, and sons:
BENJAMIN and JOSEPH, all residue; Gr. chil: WILLIAM H.
$100 and MARY C. JOHNSTON. Son & Exr: JOHN. Wit: A. J.
M. WHITEHEAD, JOHN S. DUGGAN. Codicil Feb. 17, 1853,
revoke bequest of $100 to WILLIAM H. JOHNSTON and
bequeath same to son JOSEPH, also give to friend REPSA
PEEL dau of WILLIAM PEEL bureau which did belong to
my late dau MARGARET MERCER signed CHRISTIANA NORFLEET
same Wit.

NORFLEET, THOMAS
    Jan. 23, 1745. Aug. Ct., 1746. Wife: RUTH. Sons:
THOMAS 300 A where I live (part of tract purchased of
JOHN SPEARS) also land at Conetoe, 3 negroes, silver
punch bowl, cows and calves, furniture, case of pistols, and holsters, large new Bible and large brass
kettle; MARMADUKE 300 A land, 3 negroes silver tankard,
cows and calves, furniture, still and worms, large
walnut table and large Bible. Daus: SARAH, FARBEY,
SUSANNAH, MARY, ELIZABETH, each dau to have furniture,
1 negro, cow and calf and silver spoons. Exr. and Bro:
MARMADUKE NORFLEET. Wit: ROBERT HILLIARD, JOHN BLUNT.

NORRIS, CHARITY
    Dec. 6, 1807. Feb. Ct., 1808. Bk. D, p 310. Heirs
of my dau ELIZABETH LAWRENCE 3 negroes one of them 1
"pound" to JOSEPH BELL, he to be paid in full for her.
Exr: GERALDUS TOOLE, JOHN WEEKS, Wit: WILLIAM HAYNES,
JOHN WEEKS.

NORRISS JOHN
    July 23, 1801. Aug. Ct., 1801. Wife & Extx: CHARITY,
lend plantation whereon I live, all negroes, riding
chair, all cattle, hogs, horses, tools, etc. I wish
her to keep my gr. chil. WEALTHY NOWELS & BETTAY NOWELS
and I bequeath $100 to each of them; sons & Exr: LUKE,
lend 133 1/2 A plantation whereon he lives, and 1 negro, reversion to his sons LUKE & JAMES; daus: SILVAH
SAVAGE, lend 100 A on Avaries Swamp, and 1 negro, reversion to her chil, POLLY C ?; DELILIAH, 200 A on
SAVIDGE and BURNETT lines, and 1 negro; son: URIAH, 1
negro, horse and saddle; daus: CHARLOTTE, 133 1/3 A
and 2 negroes; ELIZABETH, 133 1/3 A and 1 negro. Exr:
ISAAC BATTS, SAM GATER. Wit: SARAH KNIGHT, SAM GATER,
ALLIN SAVIDGE.

NORSWORTHY, WILLIAM
    Nov. 13, 1778. Aug. Ct., 1781. Wife & Extx:
ELIZABETH, lend all estate, to be divided among chil
after they are of lawful age; son, JOHN, to have the
land; Chil: TRISTROM, SAMUEL, SARAH, OGBURN, LEAH,
NICKLES and PATEY APPLEWHIGHT 5 S each. Wit: WILLIAM
BLOODWORTH, SAMUEL RUFFIN.

NORTHEN, WILLIAM
    July 18, 1790. Feb. Ct., 1793. Sons: EDMUND,
WILLIAM, MYNTA, JOHN and GEO. 10 S each; daus: SARAH,
$100, MARGARET, ANN, MARY, LAUNNER and son; REUBEN, 10
S each; son: PETER all lands lying in Richmond Co.,Va.
all stock on that plantation except 2 negroes; sons:
MEREMAN and KILBEY 10 S each; daus: all lands & negroes
in Edgecombe Co., my negroes in Va.; all stock of every
kind, household goods, money in the house, debts due
me to be divided between Daus: CATEY, NELLIE and LUCY
when CATEY becomes 21; ELIZABETH 10 S. Exr: JACOB
SESSUMS, THOMAS HODGES. Wit: ALEXANDER SESSUM. Proven
by oaths of ALEXANDER SESSUMS, ALICE SESSUMS, REBEKAH
SESSUMS and POLLEY SESSUMS.

NORVEL, CHAPMAN
    Apr. 28, 1850. May Ct., 1850. Bk. F, p 441. Wife:

LUCINDA, lend 1/2 lands whereon I live 2 negroes, furniture, horse, cow and calf etc; son: HYMAN 150 A land adjoining that lent to mother, also on Otter's Creek and lines of BURTON, BRYANT EDWARDS, SR., HARMON EDWARDS, and filly provided he pay to AMOS WOOTEN and my son HARDY NORVEL $50 each; son: LITTLEBERRY, land lent to his mother, horse, 10 bbls corn and 500 lbs pork; dau: ARRENA PHILIPS, her share to be divided with her chil & any negroes she may draw, to be held in common stock between her and her chil until oldest arrive at 21 yrs. Son & Exr: HARDY, 50 A bought of SIMON EDWARDS. Exr: son-in-law, AMOS WOOTEN. Wit: P. S. SUGG, RICHARD T. EAGLES.

NORVILLE, RUEL
July 11, 1848. Aug. Ct., 1848. Bk. F, p 401. Cousin: HARDY NORVILLE, for the benefit and support of my mother as he may think proper for her comfort, $100.00; Balance to my bros. and sisters, except ALLEN NORVILLE, who lives in Tennessee, I leave nothing. Wit: THOMAS SMITH, F. G. PITT.

O'BRYAN, ELIZABETH
Jan. 3, 1811. May Ct., 1811. Gr. son: DENNIS GERALDUS O'BRYAN. Gr. daus: NANCY O'BRYAN and SUSANNA O'BRYAN, 1 negro each. Gr. son: LAWRENCE DENNIS, GERALDUS O'BRYAN, my house, lot and 2 negroes; son: LAWRENCE O'BRYAN 1 negro, also all remaining personal property. Exr. Son: LAWRENCE O'BRYAN. Wit: NATHAN MATHEWSON, MICHAEL HEARN. The Executor having died, DENNIS O'BRYAN served as Adm.

ODUM, ABRAHAM
Dec. 24, 1826. Feb. Ct., 1827. Bk. F, p 66. CATHERINE ODUM, mare. SEALY STALINS, POLLEY ODUM, BECKA ODUM, PRISCILLA ODUM, ARON ODUM, brother in S. C. bro: DEMSEY ODUM. Exr: JAMES STALINS. Wit: JAMES MINOR, HENRY ADAMS.

OGG, GEORGE
Mar. 10, 1800. May Ct., 1800. WILLIAM BALFOUR, 1000 A in Franklin Co., State of Ga., in possession of GEORGE HANNAH, also 1000 A in Franklin Co., Ga.,

now in possession of JOHN BRANCH of Halifax Co., N. C.,
which he holds as guarantee for payment of £ 112, the
monies arising on the lawsuit in Superior Court of
Halifax against JOHN GRAY BLOUNT, of Beaufort Co.,
N. C., also all monies from a covenant I hold against
DAVID ELLISON & heirs, late of Phil. on acc't of
500.000 A, entered in State of N. C. No exr. WILLIAM
BALFOUR. Adm. Wit: RANDOLPH COTTON.

O'NEAL, EDMUND (EDMON)
     Dec. 19, 1843. May Ct., 1844. Bk. F, p 309. Wife:
FANNY, to be provided for by Exr: dau: MOLLY EXUM; dau:
NANCY O'NEAL, plantation whereon I live, all hogs also
2/3 residue; sons: ARTHUR O'NEAL and WHITMILL O'NEAL
to have 1/3 residue. Exr: JOHN COKER. Wit: JAMES COKER,
STEPHEN COKER, widow dessented.

O'NEAL, ELISHA
     Jan. 19, 1850. Feb. Ct., 1855. Bk. G, p 95. Wife:
SUSAN, knives, forks and $10; sons: BENNETT and WYATT
10 S each. Gr. son: JOHN O'NEAL, all land and residue.
Exr: LITTLEBERRY BRADLEY. Wit: JOHN W. JOHNSON, DAVID
B. BELL.

O'NEAL, FRANCES
     Aug. 23, 1854. Aug. Ct., 1854. Bk. G, p 74. Dau-
in-law: POLLY O'NEAL, all my crop, crockery, knives,
forks and 50 lbs. bacon. Friend & Exr: LUNSFORD R.
CHERRY, the residue of my estate. Wit: J. B. LEWIS,
EVERIT MILLS.

ONEEL, ISHAM
     Feb. 13, 1811. Feb. Ct., 1811. Bk. E, p 7. Wife:
ELIZABETH, I lend part of plantation whereon I live,
lying on MOORE Swamp, and LAZARUS ONEEL lines, mare,
during widowhood and 1/3 all hogs, 1/2 all bacon and
lard, household goods, etc. Sons: LAZARUS, EDMUND and
ELISHA all perishable estate and all land lent mother;
residue sold and divided between 3 sons and daus:
POLLEY PRICE, PATIENCE ANDERSON, wife of JAMES ANDERSON,
10 S. Exr: JONATHAN PRICE. Wit: BENJAMIN BRADLEY, LEVI
DENTON.

ONEIL, ELIZABETH
    Sept. 13, 1827. Nov. Ct., 1827. Bk. F, p 71. EDWIN
EXUM, furniture, 2 punch bowls, 3 saucers, 3 cups, 3
spoons. JOHN P. MANNING, residue of Estate. Exr:
LUNSFORD R. CHERRY. Wit: GREEN EXUM, WINNEFRED KING.
Exr. refusing to qualify, JOHN BELLAMY adm. Bond $500
with JAMES COKER, JR. & DAVID BRADLEY, securities.

OWENS, ELISHA
    June 7, 1817. Aug. Ct., 1817. Bk. E, p 156. Wife:
AMEY, I lend 100 A plantation lying on lines of ROBERT
OWENS, THOMAS JENKINS, and ARTHUR FORBES on Harricane
Branch, reversion to son ELIJAH, also my tools, stock,
chest, furniture. ELIJAH to receive mother's land at
her death; dau: NANCY, a chest. Remainder to be divided
between sons: JOHN, ETHELRED, ROBERT and ALPHA, and
dau NANCY. Exr: JOHN and ROBERT OWENS. Wit: JAMES LEWIS,
CHARLOTTE LEWIS.

OWNEEL (ONEIL- ?) JOHN
    Dec. 19, 1783. Nov. Ct., 1784. Wife: SARAH all
estate during widowhood daus: SARAH, 107 A tract whereon I live. GRACE, L 30. Exr: bro ISHAM OWNEEL, ELISHA
STALLINGS. Wit: JACOB DICKINSON, ELIAS FORTE, DANIEL
HOLLAND.

PARKER, FRANCIS
    Apr. 26, 1746. Aug. Ct., 1747. Wife & Extx:
ELIZABETH, sons: FRANCIS, JOSEPH, Exr: SIMON, 200 A
whereon I live, 80 A whereon he lives also another
200 A tract. Daus: ELIZABETH FOREMAN, CHARITY BRETT,
CATHERINE HODGES. Wit: GERRARD WALL, JOHN KNIGHT,
WALTER MCFARLAN.

PARKER, FRANCIS
    Undated. Apr. Ct., 1774. Wife: lend house wherein
I dwell, furniture, pine chest, horse, pewter, stock,
tools. linen & wooling wheels, reversion to son
FRANCIS; Son & Exr: FRANCIS all lands at Mother's
death, 4 negroes, horses, cattle, etc. Daus: SARAH
RAKLEY, ANN, ELIZABETH and PENELOPE 1 negro, each,
pewter, linen wheel, chist, bottles, tubs, etc. Exr:
MATTHEW DRAKE. Wit: WIL? MEARN, WILLIAM DRAKE.

PARKER, HARDY

June 16, 1852. Aug. Ct., 1854. Bk. G, p 78. Wife
& Extx: HARRIETT PARKER, I lend lands and tenaments
where I now live, S side of Deep Creek, life estate,
then divided between dau MARY R. PARKER and son JOSEPH
H. PARKER, perishable property to be sold after wife's
death, residue divided between daus: ELIZA BIGGS, NANCY
B. EDMUNDSON, MARY R. PARKER, and son JOSEPH H. PARKER,
and DAVID PARKER'S 2 sons; Eldest Dau: ELIZA BIGGS and
her chil perishble property and 10 S; Dau: NANCY B.
EDMONDSON and her chil. furniture. Son: PAUL A. PARKER
and chil 10 S and property in his possession; Dau:
MARY B. PARKER 1/2 my land at mother's decease, line
of BLOUNT COOPER, Gum Swamp, to the Canal WEEKS PARKERS
and COOPER'S Canal, life estate then to my 2 gr. sons
SIMMONS B. PARKER and CHARLES D. PARKER. Son & Exr:
JOSEPH H. PARKER, other half of my land between JOSEPH
and dau. Mary at wife's decease, etc. Wit: BLOUNT
COOPER, BYTHEL HOWELL.

PARKER, JOHN

May 11, 1761. Sept. Ct., 1761. Wife & Extx: MARY,
I lend land and plantation her lifetime; bequeath all
remaining estate to chil: GABRIEL, plantation after
mother's decease, horse, cow, and 2 sows; JOHN, 1 cow,
son ARON, 1 sow, cow, furniture; WILLIAM AMMONS, "hefer",
SARAH 2 "hefers", 1 sow; MARGRIT, cow, sow; ELIZABETH,
cow 2 hogs that "yous to be called hers." Exr: THOMAS
HORN, SR., THOMAS HART. Wit: JOHN DEW, MARY DEW,
CORNELIUS JORDAN.

PARKER, JOHN

Aug. 24, 1836. Nov. Ct., 1836. Bk. F, p 196. Wife
& Extx: CHARITY, all estate; reversion to unnamed
chil. Exr: WILLIS BRADLEY. Wit: CLINCH HOWELL, JOSEPH
EDMONDSON.

PARKER, JONAS

Feb. 18, 1807. May Ct., 1808. Wife and Extx:
ZILPHEA, lend plantation bought of WM. PATON, reversion to BETSEY, PATSEY & CHARLOTTE; lend all land
to wife until 3 sons reach maturity, to school and

243

raze my children; 8 negroes, all household and farm
equipment, still and cash; Daus: BETSEY, PATSEY,
CHARLOTTE, SUSANNAH and OLIVE BELL 1 negro and furni-
ture each; Sons: JAMES, plantation bought of JAMES
IRWIN, 1 negro, horse, saddle, bridle; SAMUEL, land
bought of ZACK HACKNEY, 1 negro, horse, bridle, saddle,
JOHN, plantation whereon I live, 1 negro, horse, bridle,
saddle; WILLIS 1 negro and £ 50. Exr: SAMUEL PARKER of
NorthHampton Co. WILLIS PARKER. Wit: JAMES CHAMPION,
THOMAS HACKNEY.

PARKER, MARY
    Aug. 11, 1753. Aug. Ct., 1754. Gr. son, and sole
legatee: EDMOND GODWIN. No. Exr: Wit: BENJAMIN BRAND,
MOSES COLEMAN, CORNELIUS JORDAN.

PARKER, MARY, widow of WILLIAM PARKER, dec'd.
    Feb. 28, 1817. May Ct., 1817. Bk. E, p 151. Sons:
WILLIAM, JOHN and LEMUEL; daus: TEMPY BARNES and
DOLLY, 5 S each. Sons: FREDERICK and RICHARD, £ 30
each; Son & Exr: WILAH (?) BISHOP lend 2 negroes, reversion to his chil. If he dies without lawful heir,
to be divided between my 3 youngest sons: LEMUEL,
FREDERICK and RICHARD. Wit: JAMES BIGGS, NANCY WORREL.

PARKER, SIMMONS B.
    Apr. 21, 1846. May Ct., 1846. Wife: EMILY ANN
PARKER 1/2 my real, personal, and mixed estate. Son:
WEEKS PARKER, the other half. In event of his death
before reaching 21 yrs, reversion to EMILY ANN PARKER.
Exr: NATHAN MATTHEWSON. Wit: WM. H. HINES, JESSE
PRICE.

PARKER, SIMON
    Dec. 31, 1758. Mar. Ct., 1759. Wife: JUDAH. Sons:
FRANCIS, plantation whereon I live also 150 A adjoin-
ing; SIMON, 200 A tract called the Black Ridge;
WILLIAM 85 A; ROBERT 100 A on Wolf Pit Branch; JAMES.
Daus: JUDAH, SARAH, WINNE, CHARITY and RUTH. Exr:
bro., FRANCIS PARKER, bro-in-law, JAMES KNIGHT. Wit:
CHARLES DANIEL, GIRRARD WALL, MARY CULLENDER.

PARKER, SIMON
    May 20, 1781. Aug. Ct., 1781. Wife & Extx: JERUSEY,

mare, saddle, briddle and furniture; reversion to chil.
Son: JETHRO, 400 A, 1 negro, 1 "coult" daus: JUDITH,
PATTY and PENELOPE, 1 filly and furniture each. Exr:
JONATHAN GODWIN. Wit: JEREMIAH KIRKLEY, FRANCIS PARKER.

PARKER, THEOPHILUS, Tarboro
Aug. 31, 1848. Feb. Ct., 1849. Bk. F, p 414. Wife:
MARY, house in Tarboro and lots 20, 21, 31 & 32 on
which it is situated, all furniture, carriage, harness
and horses used with it; such negroes as she chooses
to equal a chil's part. Son: JOHN HAYWOOD PARKER, already provided for. Property in St. Francisville, La.,
4 lots in Tarboro, 800 A in Obion Co., Tenn. to be
sold and equally divided between wife and chil excepting JOHN HAYWOOD; all negroes, after wife's portion
taken out, divided among chil, excepting JOHN HAYWOOD.
Daus: MARY W. HARGROVE, CAROLINE C. HARGROVE and ARABELL
C. PARKER and son: FRANCIS M. PARKER. Gdn. for ARABELL:
BENJ. M. JACKSON. Exr: JAMES WEDDELL, ROBERT R. BRIDGERS
Wit: RUSSELL CHAPMAN, MATHEW WEDDELL.

PARKER, WEEKS SEN'R
July 31, 1843. Feb. Ct., 1844. Bk. F, pp 303-4-5-6
Wife: SABRA I. PARKER, entire residue of estate for
life, or widowhood; lands, houses, slaves, stock,
cattle, carriage all property, real and personal, "except my watch and seal (ring) which I now wear". Son
& Exr: SIMMONS B. PARKER, at decease of wife, all
property, real and personal, (except slaves otherwise
devised), and 20 slaves, Daus: MARGARET H. BATTLE, wife
of REV. AMOS J. BATTLE, slaves to be hired out and for
her own income, not to be controlled by her present
or any future husband; HENRIETTA S. H. BATTLE, wife of
COL. BENJAMIN BATTLE, lands, slaves. Dr. JOHN H. PARKER,
dec'd in Florida, lands and slaves to be sold and
monies due me from COL. ROBERT JOYNER, executor of est.
of JOHN H. PARKER, I bequeath 1/3 to SIMON B. PARKER,
1/3 to HENRIETTA, S. H. BATTLE and chil of MARGARET
H. BATTLE now born and hereafter to be born unto her.
Exr: COL. WILLIAM H. HINES, NATHAN MATHEWSON. Wit:
WHITMELL WILLIAMS, GABRIEL E. ARMSTRONG. Codicil 20
Dec. 1843. Amending bequest to dau MARGARET, allowing
Exr: SIMMONS B. PARKER to make payments of income to

MARGARET H. BATTLE at proper occasions for her and her chil. Wit: JNO H. MATTHEWSON, WILLIAM NORFLEET, Feb. Court 1844.

PARRISHE, WILLIAM
    Jan. 20, 1735 – 1736. Aug. Ct., 1736. Wife & Extx: MARY, Dau: SARAH PARRISH. Wit: BUCKLEY KIMBROUGH, ISAAC WINSTON.

PASSMORE, JOHN
    May 10, 1754. Nov. Ct., 1754. Wife: SARAH, Sons & Exrs: GEORGE, JOHN, ROBERT, JOSEPH, 100 A plantation whereon I live. Daus: ELIZABETH SAMMON (SALMON?) 100 A part of my plantation; SARAH PASSMORE, 100 A, part of my plantation. Wit: JOHN JACKSON, MOSES PENDRY, JAMES SAMON (SALMON?)

PEACOCK, ZADOCK
    June 16, 1852. Aug. Ct., 1852. Bk. F, p 479. Wife: SALLY, lend 275 A land bought of ARTHUR SPEIGHT, crop that is on Toisnot Swamp, all negroes, tools, furniture, blacksmith tools, remaining stock, all carts, buggy and harness, meat, lard, soap, all old corn, reversion of land to SALLY M. and JAMES B. PEACOCK. Son & Exr: WILLIAM, 180 A land bought of JAMES SPEIGHT; and filly, Dau: SALLY M., my "poianna", (piano?) colt, 6 sitting chairs; Sons: JAMES B., colt; 'CALVIN' GASTIN, $450 per yr for 4 yrs; JOSEPH M. and LAWRENCE, residue divided between all chil. Wit: J. W. (?) THOMPSON, NATHAN P. DANIEL.

PEELE, ABNER
    July 18, 1798. Nov. Ct., 1798. Bro: JOHN PEELE all land. Residue divided between bros and sisters (unnamed) Exr: JOSEPH HALL, Wit: ROBERT PEELE, CHAS. COLEMAN, JOHN HAILS.

PEELE, CATHERINE
    June 17, 1812. Nov. Ct., 1814. Bk. E, p 71. Gr. son: ENOS TART, 1 negro; he to be allowed to take up the 4 negroes at their valuation, if he chooses; 4 negroes to be allowed to choose with whom they wish to live, in which case their masters are to pay into

estate value placed on them by appraisal of 3 men appointed by the court; or else they to be hired out; revenue to be divided between gr. dau: CATHERINE SPATES
and gr. son: ELNATH (ELNATHAN) EASON. Gr. dau:
CATHERINE SPATES (SPEIGHT?) "chainia" (china) press
and its furn., 1 led "coulard" chist, ironbound trunk,
bed with calico curtains, also $100, 1/2 kitchen furn;
gr. son: ELNATH (ELNATHAN?) EASON "my housedesk"; gr.
daus: CATHERINE TART, dau of ENOS TART, bed, furniture
also its curtains; MARGARET PHILLIPS, dau of FREDERICK
PHILIPS, bed, furniture also silk rug. Dau: ELIZABETH
FARMER, 10 S; gr. dau: SALLEY PHILIPS, 1/3 my pewter,
my riding chair & geare to be sold, money to her; dau:
MARTHA EASON, 1/2 kitchen furn. Pen, old negro woman
to be free to choose with whom she will live, supported
by my estate, bequeath my lume and geare also wheele
and cards she has generally used in my service. MARY
PRICE (PIERCE?) $5.00 paid yearly as long as she lives.
Neph: JOHN GORRELL, 1 negro. Residue of estate sold
and money therefrom divided thus: $1000 to heirs of
gr. dau SALLEY PHILIPS, remainder to heirs of dau
MARTHA EASON; gr. son: JAMES JONES PHILIPS, son of
FREDERICK PHILIPS, case of white bottles; gr. dau:
PHEREBY, dau of FREDERICK PHILIPS, 1 blew chest. Exr:
Nephew, ENOS TART, CHARLES COLEMAN, EPHRAIM DANIEL.
WIT: LEMUEL DANIEL, JOHN COLEMAN.

PEEL, HILLARY
     July 4, 1849. May Ct., 1853. Bk. F, p 500. Son:
WILLIAM. My 5 daus: EASTER MOORE, wife of MOSES MOORE,
negro and $100; NANCY LANGLEY, wife of WILLIS LANGLEY,
MARY STALLINGS, wife of JAMES STALLINGS, LYDIA WARD,
wife of JOHN WARD, ELIZABETH DAVIS, wife of JOHN DAVIS,
all lands, and other property sold and divided between
my daus; gr. dau: DELLAR ROGERS $50. Exr: JAMES F.
JENKINS to have $35 for his services. Commissioners
for div. of notes: MOSES BAKER, J. J. GARRETT, JOSIAH
D. JENKINS. Wit: CHARLES H. JENKINS, S. P. JENKINS.
In a will written Sept. 27, 1850 but not proven in
court, there is a legatee, gr. son: STEPHEN RODGERS.
Wit: MAGY MORE, W. G. BULLUCK.

PEELE, JOHN, SEN.

May 24, 1817. Aug. Ct., 1818. Bk. E, p 198. Wife: LUCY, lend for life furniture, 2 iron pots, mare, bridle and saddle, 1 negro, Dutch oven, skillet, "chist", table 6 sitting chairs, farm and household tools, 500 lb. pork, 20 bbls corn, cow and calf, sow and pigs, all dishes, basons, plates, knives and forks, beaufat, forage, also all land and plantation. Son & Exr: JOHN, furniture; daus: PHERABY and PEGGY, furniture. Residue sold and divided among 3 chil. Exr: HILLARY PEELE. Wit: DEMPSEY JENKINS, JOHN HYMAN.

PEEL, JOHN, SENIOR
Apr. 14, 1843. Feb. Ct., 1847. Bk. F, p 355. Wife: PATSY for widowhood or life, land where I now live, stock of every discription, household and kitchen furniture. At her remarriage, or death, reversion to my dau SUSAN PEEL. No Exr. named. Wit: J. C. KNIGHT, BUSHROD WASHINGTON VICK.

PEELE, ROBERT
Feb. 24, 1803. Feb. Ct., 1803. Wife: ESTHER, during widowhood land and plantation whereon I live. If she marries, what part thereof the law provides. Also lend 3 beds, large blew chest, all house chairs, 2 spinning wheels, 1 wool 1 linen, loom & geer, beaufat and furn., all pewter, iron pots, & hooks, skillet, all knives & forks, small trunk, looking glass, hand bellows, flaxhackle, pine table, all cotten cards. Also mare, 3 cows and calves, all sheep, 29 hogs (being peanut fed in the piny woods) all geese, 35 bbls corn, all fodder all flax and cotton, all farming tools, tea- kettle, firetongs, and shovel, washing tub, 2 piggins, lard, 2 saddles, all sweetening belonging to the house, 1 sugar tub. In case wife marries, to have no more than law provides. Bequeath 1 pr. cart wheels and cart. Son: JOSIAH, all lands and plantation, excepting his mother's third as above; bridle and saddle; daus: TEMPY and MARY, all personal property at mother's death. Exr: JACOB HORN, JESSE FARMER. Wit: ROBERT PEELE, SR., JOHN PEELE, ELIZABETH PEELE.

PEELE, ROBERT
Sept. 15, 1807. Nov. Ct., 1808. Bk. D, p 332. Wife:

CATHERINE, 7 negroes, all horses, stock, household furn-
iture, farming tools, utensils of every kind, and crop
on plantation, at my decease; dau: MARY DAVIS, wife of
RICHARD DAVIS, Ł 100 placed in hands of JOSEE (?)
HOLEWELL for her use, reversion to her chil. Sons:
JESSE, WILLIS and JOHN 10 S each. Gr. son: FLETCHER
PEELE, son of DAVID PEELE, dec'd. $100 silver; gr.
dau: MARY HALL, daus: FERIBY HORN and MARGARET OUTLAND,
these share residue of estate with dau MARY DAVIS, also
Ł 20, and chest of waring apparel to 3 sons. Exr: ENOS
TART, CHAS. COLEMAN. Wit: JESSE FARMER, RICHARD SANDERS.

PERRY, JOHN
        Jan. 27, 1752. Sept. Ct., 1758. Vol. 1 p 1 (filed
in Halifax Crt. House). Loving wife (unnamed), household goods. Son: WILLIAM PERRY, 400 A of land. No Exr.
Wit: THOS. GOOD, JOHN MILLS, ELIZA MILLS.

PENDER, CELIA
        Sept. 6, 1820. May Ct., 1821. Bk. E, p 267. Son:
JOSIAH, horse, bed; daus: DELPHIA, boufat; LOUISIANNA,
bed, furniture; JULIA, bed, furniture, and colt. Residue divided among chil. Exr: SPENCER L. HART, AARON
ATKINSON. Wit: WILLIAM O. CARTER, ELISHA ELLIS.

PENDER, JOHN
        Mar. 8, 1818. May Ct., 1818. Bk. E, p 186. Wife:
NANCY, lend dwelling and as much land as she thinks
proper. Bequeath furniture, cow and calf, sow and pigs,
lend 1 writing desk, loom, wheels, and cards, kitchen
furn., provisions for support of self and family and
brandy still. Daus: ELIZABETH HOPKINS; at mother's
death all personal property to be sold and revenue
divided. MARTHA and POLLY, furniture, cow and calf,
each. Sons: SOLOMON (Exr); JOSHUA; WILLIAM, mare;
JAMES, bed and furniture. These 4 sons to have $100
in hand for support of JOHN. Exr: CHARLES W. KNIGHT.
Wit: S. L. HART.

PENDER, JOSEPH
        Feb. 26, 1799 (?) No record of Probation. Wife &
Extx: SELAH, 2 negroes, bed and furniture, mare, 2
cows and calves, 2 sows and pigs, ewes and lambs; lend

houses on plantation where I formerly lived, with plantation belonging thereto. Son & Exr: EDWIN, all my
land E side FORT Branch adjacent to Town Creek; Son:
JAMES, all my land lying W side FORT Branch adjacent
to Town Creek, also 1 negro. Daus: NANCY, POLLY, MARTHA,
PATIENCE, RHODA, ZILPHA, DELPHIA, 1 negro each. Land
on pocoson, near Whiteoak Swamp, to be sold and revenue
divided between 7 daus. Remaining negroes divided between all chil; stock and household K furn. to be sold
and divided between wife & chil. Exr: JAMES WILLIAMS,
JOHN WILLIAMS of Town Creek Edgecombe Co. Wit: CHAS.
LEE, DAVID STOKES.

PENDER, JOSIAH
    Feb. 28, 1823. May Ct., 1823. Bk. E, p 329. Wife:
SARAH, furniture, 2 cows and calves, $100; lend
dwelling house, and outhouses, a home for her during
her widowhood, 8 negroes, stock, horses, cattle, etc.
The plantation to continue during widowhood of wife.
Reversion of negroes to nephews SOLOMON, JOSHUA and
WILLIAM PENDER. Nephs: SOLOMON PENDER, note against him
for $460.15 with int. from 26 March 1821; JOSHUA PENDER;
WILLIAM PENDER, land purchased of him; RUFFIN PENDER
and JOSIAH PENDER, sons of SOLOMON PENDER, tract of
400 A whereon I live provided wife stays there during
widowhood; JAMES PENDER, remainder of land purchased
of JOSHUA PENDER, MARTHA, dau of JOHN PENDER, dec'd.,
10 A whereon she hath built her house (part of tract
purchased of JOSHUA PENDER) also $50. LUCINDA PENDER,
dau of SOLOMON PENDER, $400; neph: JOSEPH JOHN PENDER,
son of SOLOMON PENDER, $400; Sisters: SELAH WEEKS, $100.
reversion to her son JAMES WEEKS; SARAH TREVATHAN, wife
of LEWIS TREVATHAN, $100 reversion to JAMES PENDER, son
of JOHN PENDER, dec'd. Nephs: JAMES WEEKS, son of sister SELAH WEEKS, $100; JOSHUA PENDER, $400; NAPOLIAN
PENDER, son of JOSHUA PENDER, $400. Desire Exr. have
negroes mak a "parcell" of brick next fall and com-
pletely and decently wall in a graveyard wherein I
may be buried. Exr: SOLOMON PENDER, JOSHUA PENDER.
Wit: STARLING WALLER, WARREN WALLER.

PENDER, MARTHA
    Mar. 18, 1854. Aug. Ct., 1854. Bro: JAMES PENDER

to be paid interest from my investment , so long as he
may live; then to his living chil following his death.
Exr and Neph: JOSEPH J. B. PENDER. Wit: DEMPSEY D. BRYAN,
BATTLE BRYAN.

PENDER, SARAH
     Feb. Ct., 1836. Bk. F, p 187. Sons: JAMES TURNER,
$200; chil of my son JOHN G. TURNER: JOHN G. TURNER,
CHARLES TURNER, and MAY TURNER, ELIZABETH TURNER, as
was, HENRY TURNER $225 each; dau: ELIZABETH BEEMAN, all
wearing apparel, new cloth, all spun? of every description, together with all I have heretofore given
her; gr. chil: ELIZABETH BEEMAN, that was, ANN BEEMAN
and LEMUEL BEEMAN, 1 featherbed each; PARKS BEEMAN, 1
large trunk and $10; JULIUS BEEMAN, $300, in trust for
benefit of his mother ELIZABETH BEEMAN, hoping and
believing that he will faithfully and honestly apply
same to the comfort and support of his mother as a good,
affectionate and dutiful son ought to do. Exr: SPENCER
D. COTTEN, WILLIS WILKINS. Wit: C. P. ALLEN, JOHN W.
COTTEN. Codicil Oct. 8 1835. Ordering change in will:
$100 taken from legacy left to chil of son JOHN G.
TURNER, and same to be added to my son, JAMES TURNER.
Wit: J. W. COTTEN.

PENDER, SOLOMON
     No date. Feb. Ct., 1783. Daus: SELAH WEEKS, $2 sil-
ver, armchair; SARAH DEVATHAN ? (TREVATHAN) $1 silver.
Sons: JOSIAH, furniture, razar, hone, gun, 6 soop plates,
6 mettle spoons, pottle bason, 1 gal. ditto, other 3
of my cattle; residue divided between 2 sons. Son:
JOHN, gun, small deep dish, gallon bason, 4 plates,
remainder pewter and 3 cows; Exr: friends JOHN PENDER,
JOSIAH PENDER. Wit: JOHN WHITE, MATTHEW HUMPHREY.

PENDER, WILLIAM
     Nov. 6, 1850. Aug. Ct., 1852. Bk. F, p 480. Wife
& Extx: ELLEN, horse, cow and calf, 2 sows and pigs,
50 bbl corn, 1000 lbs. pork, bbl. flour, fodder 25 lbs
coffee, 50 lbs sugar, molasses, cart and wheels, buggy
and harness, tools, 3 negroes, 2 tracts land purchased
of REDDING SUGG and WEEKS PARKER, except 50 A of SUGG
tract which I hereinafter bequeath to my dau: JANIS ?

PENDER. Daus: WILLIAM ANN PENDER, ELLEN, JANIS ? PENDER, wife of ROBERT H. PENDER, 50 A land on line of RICHARD HARRISON, CHARLOTTE DANCY. WILLIAM NORFLEET, my saw and grist mill to hold in trust and for benefit of MARY M. PENDER, wife of my son LEWIS C. PENDER; reversion to their chil. JOSHUA & LEWIS PENDER. Son & Exr: LEWIS Exr: ROBERT PENDER. Wit: L. L. DANCY, RICHARD BRACEWELL.

PENNEY, THOMAS
    May 12, 1780. Aug. Ct., 1780. Wife & Extx: MARY, lend movable estate; sons: MALEKIAH, plantation where- on I live and 1/2 land belonging to it; JOHN (Exr.) re- maining land with an entry joining the other. Plantation in Norfolk Co., Va. to be sold and revenue divided among all my chil. Wit: LAMENTATION ONEIL, CHRISTIAN SPEIR, JOHN SPEIR.

PERMENTER, JAMES
    July 9, 1789. Nov. Ct., 1789. Bk. No. 3, p 106. Wife & Extx: MARGARET, lend remaining estate except 3 negroes, also use of plantation whereon I live during her life; son: JOHN, 5 S; JAMES, son of JOHN, 1 negro; Son & Exr: JAMES, 2 negroes; son: NATHANIEL, all land E of Miry Branch, being part of tract whereon I live, tools, 4 cattle, bed and furniture; MALACHI, son of NATHANIEL, 1 negro; daus: MARY BRASWELL, 1 negro, 4 cattle; MARTHA SWEARINGAN, 10 S; MARY SWEARINGAN, dau. of MARTHA SWEARINGAN, L 50; LIDIA SWEARINGAN, L 50. JOHN QUINN, all land W side Mirey Branch, being plan- tation whereon I live, along with tract adjoining on S side; also all other estate lent wife. Exr: JOSEPH PENDER, Esq. Wit: URIAH ASKEW, JOSIAH ASKEW, RUTH MAY.

PERRITT, ANN
    Aug. 15, 1788. No record probation. All estate to 3 gr. chil; ISAAC PERRY, FEREBY PRICE, LEWIS PRICE. Exr: JOHN GOODMAN. Wit: WM. COTTEN, SEN., MARY GOODMAN.

PERRITT, LEWIS
    Dec. 6, 1785. May Ct., 1786. Wife: ANN, lend house- hold furniture, reversion to son; son-in-law: JOHN PRICE, bed, L 1 current money; son & Exr: SOLOMON, all estate provided he care for mother. Wit: DAVID HYATT, DAVID COKER.

PERRITT, PRISCILLA
Mar. 9, 1761. June Ct., 1761. Bro: WILLIAM PERRITT,
bed and furniture; AGNES PERRITT, wife of JOHN PERRITT,
my bro. lining wheel; aunt: LUCY PERRITT, wife of
NICHOLAS PERRITT, all my wearing close, pewter, saddle;
any money after debts paid goes to uncle NICHOLAS
PERRITT. Exr & uncles, LEWIS PERRITT, JOHN PERRITT. Wit:
BENJ. HART, JESSE HART, JOHN DILLARD.

PETTAWAY, WILLIAM
Mar. 19, 1786. Feb. Ct., 1787. Wife: ELIZABETH,
lend all estate; at her death to be divided as follows:
friend, DAVID BARLOW, 150 A plantation whereon I live;
3 negroes and all brandy. LUCY BRYANT, wife of SMITH
BRYANT, 1 negro. Remainder divided equally between
DAVID BARLOW and LUCY BRYANT. Exr: DAVID BARLOW. Wit:
ETHELRED PHILIPS, BRITTAIN BRYAN, JACOB PROCTOR.

PHILLIPS, ARTHOR
Feb. 4, 1789. Nov. Ct., 1790. Wife: ELIZABETH, lend
all land and plantation whereon I live, 3 negroes, 3
beds and furniture, farming utensils, brandy still, all
stock; at her death to be divided thus: perishable
estate divided between: MARTHA PHILLIPS, MARY HARRIS,
SARAH PHILLIPS, PATIENCE MANNING and PLEASANT PHILLIPS.
Dau: SARAH, all land W side Whiteoak, 4 negroes; JOHN
ADKINS, plantation whereon he lives; dau: LEWSEY (LUCY)
ADKINS, 20 S; daus: MARY HARRIS, 1 negro; MARTHA
PHILLIPS, 2 negroes; PATIENCE MANNING, 1 negro;
PLEASANT PHILLIPS, 3 negroes, 1 likely horse or mair
(her choice). Remaining land sold, money divided bet-
ween MARTHA, MARY HARRIS, PATIENCE MANNING, SARAH &
PLEASANT. Exrs: WILLIAM COTTEN, RANDOLPH HAND (?),
JOHN NICHOLSON, JOHN GOODMAN. Wit: BARNABY EXUM,
MOODY PORTER, MARY GOODMAN.

PHILIPS, ETHELRED
May Ct., 1795. Bk. C, p 329. Son: EXUM PHILIPS,
474 A plantation and lands purchased of WM. ANDERSON
SR. AND WM. ANDERSON, JR. and ELIJAH PRICE, also 1/2
of water grist mill, with about 18 A of land on Swift

253

Creek, known as the Creek Mill, reserving etc... Son:
EATON PHILIPS, the plantation and land whereon I live,
also land adjoining etc; interest in grist mill, saw
mill, and Brandy still. Negroes and other estate to be
kept together for support of my wife and chil until
son EXUM arrives at lawful age; chil to be educated
and brought up in a good manner. Exr: Bro, BENJAMIN
PHILIPS; Bros-in-law, FIGURES LEWIS, EXUM LEWIS. Proved
by EXUM PHILIPS, JOHN INGLES, BYTHAL BELL.

PHILIPS, JOSEPH
Nov. 6, 1779. Nov. Ct., 1784. Bk. B, p 147. Wife:
SARAH, lend use of 582 A land in 3 tracts, adjoining
plantation where I now live; 162 A whereon JOSHUA
SIKES formerly lived, being the remainder of the
School Survey; 320 A to be possessed and enjoyed by
her until son JOSEPH PHILIPS shall arrive at 21; 8
negroes, household goods, plantation utensils, stock
of all kinds. Sons: ETHELRED, 270 A tract-of land
whereon he lives, which I purchased of HANCOCK HATCHER,
also tract adjoining aforesaid, being the lower part
of a survey called the School House Tract, to WILLIAM
ANDERSON'S Corner; negro girl; BENJAMIN, 700 A tract
of land, granted me by a Deed bearing date 15th day
Oct. 1761, lease plantation, mill and appurtenances
which I purchased of JAMES GRAY on the S side of Tar
River where my son BENJAMIN now lives, all stock and
cattle on said plantation; and negro girl; EXUM, 660
A tract of land purchased of ELIAS HILLIARD, lying on
the S side of Swift Creek, also late entry adjoining
said tract and JACOB HOUSE; negro boy, mare he now
has in his possession, 2 cows and calves, etc; MATTHEW,
300 A tract of land on S side of Swift Creek which I
purchased of WILLIAM KINCHEN, whereon JOHN SYKES
formerly lived, also 700 A tract adjoining, negro boy,
bay horse, bed and furniture, 2 cows and calves, 3
ewes and lambs, 2 likely sows and pigs, 20 bbls of corn,
350 weight of pork, half bu of salt, plow, weeding hoe,
and axe. Daus: SARAH PHILIPS, negro girl, my exr to
purchase healthy negro, male or female between 6 and
10 yrs of age out of my estate for my dau SARAH, purchase for her a good horse, saddle, and briddle, and
if she should choose to take a bay filly which I have

in my possession instead of horse to be purchased, she can have 2 cows, 2 calves, 3 ewes and lambs, 2 sows and pigs, 10 bbl of corn, and furniture, at day of marriage or age 21 yrs; MARTHA PHILIPS, negro girl and other property as described for my dau SARAH, also horse, saddle, bridle, furniture, 2 cows, calves, 3 ewes and lambs, 2 sows and pigs, 10 bbl of corn at marriage or age 21. Son: JOSEPH PHILIPS, 582 A in 3 tracts adjoining plantation whereon I now live, and other 2 tracts when he shall become 21, negro boy, bay mare (9 yrs old) 2 cows and calves, 3 ewes and lambs, 2 sows and pigs, furniture, my saddler's tools, 20 bbl of corn, 350 weight of pork, half bu salt, plain hoe, 1 weeding hoe, etc. Exrs to purchase for each of my chil: BENJAMIN, EXUM, MATTHEW, JOSEPH, SARAH and MARTHA, 2 sizable iron pots, 1 frying pan, 2 pewter dishes, 2 basons, 6 plates, when they receive their legacies. Mill on Swift Creek and all appurtenences to my 4 sons, ETHELRED, EXUM, MATTHEW and JOSEPH, with 6 A of land on Swift Creek, lending use to JOSEPH until he is 21 yrs old. Also Brandy still to be jointly possessed by my sons, JOSEPH'S part to be lent to my wife until JOSEPH is of age. It is my desire that my exrs cause to be built a good frame house 20 ft long and 12 ft wide on land given my son MATTHEW, also saddle and briddle for sons, EXUM, MATTHEW and JOSEPH. Exrs: Sons, ETHELRED PHILIPS, BENJAMIN PHILIPS, EXUM PHILIPS, MATTHEW PHILIPS. Wit: ROBERT DIGGES, JOHN CURL.

PHILIPS, JOSEPH
Dec. 23, 1819. Feb. Ct., 1822. Wife: NANCY, lend whole of my lands, 650 A lying S side Swift Creek, boundaries ascertained reference division land of my father EXUM PHILIPS and deed of sale from HORATIO E. HALL, reversion to chil, 10 negroes, all h. hold and kitchen furn, also sufficient pork and corn to serve her and her family for 1 yr. Dau: MARY, 10 negroes. Unborn child to share equally with MARY. JOHN TAYLOR, of Martin Co., father-in-law. Dr. John F. Ward, Gdn for MARY. Exrs: father-in-law, JOHN TAYLOR; bro, MATTHEW PHILIPS; ELIAS BRYAN, EXUM LEWIS. Wit: JAMES J. PHILIPS, ETHELRED PHILIPS, JOHN F. WARD.

PIPPEN, JOSEPH

Apr. 3, 1791. May Ct., 1791. Bk. 3, p 190. Wife:
BARBERY, lend plantation whereon I live, all stock,
consisting of 3 horses, 6 cattle, 7 sheep, 43 hogs,
loom, 3 pots, Dutch oven, pewter, plantation tools,
house and furniture during widowhood and no longer;
gr. dau: POLLY GARROT (GARRETT), cow and calf, ewe and
lamb; gr. son: CALEB DAVIS, cow and calf, ewe and lamb;
residue at wife's death to be divided between all lawful begotten chil; sons: WILLIAM, JOHN and ARTHUR. Exr:
JOHN LARRENCE (LAWRENCE), WILLIAM PIPPEN. Wit. not mentioned.

PIPPEN, JOSEPH

Sept. 14, 1827. May Ct., 1833. Bk. F, p 146. Wife:
TEMPERANCE, I lend 1 negro, reversion to 4 daus: tract
adjoining WILLIS KNIGHT and NANCY WARD, give furniture,
cow and calf, 2 sows and pigs, 2 ewes and lambs, 1 horse,
$55, port, corn, etc; reversion of land to son JOSEPH
JOHN; daus: NANCY WARD, lend 1 negro, reversion to her
dau: HARRIETT MAY; LYDIA AUSTIN, 3 negroes; MARTHA
PORTER, 2 negroes; LUVINA SPELLING, 300 A tract whereon she lives; lend 4 negroes, reversion to her heirs,
give her 2 notes, value $100, one given by her, the
other by BRITAIN SPELLING, also $50 each; Son: JOSEPH
JOHN PIPPEN, plantation whereon I live with exception
of that lent wife; gr. son: WILLIAM S. BRYAN, lend 7
negroes; reversion to his heairs. Exr: HENRY AUSTIN,
ELY PORTER. Wit: W. M. HOPKINS, DANIEL HOPKINS.

PIPPEN, JOSEPH L.

July 18, 1851. Nov. Ct., 1853. Bk. F, p 519. Wife:
TABITHA, 460 A land touching Ballahac, conveyed to me
by my father the late JOSEPH PIPPEN, by his will, live
stock of all kinds, tools, furniture, also $100; re-
version of land to son, NATHAN. Son & Exr: JOHN W.,
550 A land bought of ARTHUR K. BARLOW adjoining BRITTON
HOWELL, ALLEN JONES and Dr. C. L. DICKENS; sons:
JOSEPH H, 2 tracts lands, one, part of BARLOW tract
other bought of WINFIELD D. STATON and NANCY WARD;
JAMES S 300 A land bought of THEOPHILUS CHERRY, also
tract of land on Ballahac Swamp and $500; FLAVIUS A,
300 A land bought of MICHAEL HEARN and wife, adjoining

DR. C. L. DICKENS, JOHN W. DANIEL and RANDOLPH COTTEN;
CULLEN A., 400 A tract conveyed me by my father during
his lifetime; WILLIAM M, .already provided him with
$2500; bequeath him 25¢; daus: CATHERINE E. WARD, has
already had $1300, bequeath her slaves to value of
$1200; BETHINAE M. BROWN, has already had $1100, bequeath slaves to value of $1400; ELIZABETH A. COBB,
has already had $290, bequeath slaves to value $2210;
NANCY J. PIPPEN, slaves to value $2500; TABITHA L. M.
PIPPEN, slaves to value $2700. As far as I have been
able to, I have given each child either lands, money
or slaves to the value of $2500. Exr: Neph, ROBERT H.
AUSTIN. Wit: WILLIAM NORFLEET, WILLIAM S. LONG, JAMES
F. JENKINS. Codicil Apr. 15, 1852. Whereas since making
my will I have advanced to my dau: ELIZABETH A. COBB
and her husband $840. I hereby revoke the legacy given
her, and in lieu thereof, hereby bequeath unto her
slaves to the value of $1300. Wit: MAYO WORSLEY,
WILLIAM NORFLEET. Codicil Apr. 8, 1853. Give unto JOHN
W. PIPPEN the whole of tract known as BARLOW land, purchased of ARTHUR K. BARLOW, revoking that item of my
will which bequeathed a part of it to son JOSEPH H.
PIPPEN; JOHN W. shall have no part of division of residue. Wit: WILLIAM THIGPEN, LEVIN LEGGITT, WM. NORFLEET.

PIPPEN, MARY
     May 3, 1805. Aug. Ct., 1805. Bk. D, p 235, land
bought of THOMAS NEWSOME to be rented until son JOHN
reaches maturity, then sold and equally divided between
3 chil: POLLEY BROWN, JOHN and LUCINDY PIPPEN. Exr:
ASA BROWN, THOMAS NEWSOME. Wit: JESSE KNIGHT, MARY KNOX,
REBECKER PIPPEN.

PIPPEN, SPICY
     Nov. 2, 1849. No Probate date. Bk. F, p 518. Gr.
daus: MARTHA PIPPEN, chest and checked sheet; MARY
S. PIPPEN, bed. No Exr. Wit: JESSE HARRELL, JAMES
THIGPEN.

PIPPEN, TEMPERENCE
     Dec. 16, 1852. Aug. Ct., 1854. Bk. G, p 84. MARY
F. ABRAMS, wife of ELIJAH ABRAMS, dau of WILLIAM R.
DUPREE, $300; TEMPERENCE DeSHIELDS, of the State of

Arkansas, infant dau of MARTHA DeSHIELDS, wife of NOAH
DeSHIELDS, and dau of WILLIAM R. DUPREE of Edgecombe
Co., $100; gr. son & Exr: JESSE W. LEIGH, desk made of
walnut, and 1 negro; gr. son & Exr: JOHN H. LEIGH, beau-
fat and 1 negro man; gr. dau: MARTHA A. LEIGH, chest
and 1 negro; gr. dau: TEMPERENCE HARRELL, wife of
WILLIAM HARRELL, 1 negro; my 4 gr. chil; JESSE W., JOHN
H., MARTHA A. and TEMPERENCE HARRELL, the residue of
slaves, etc; son: WILLIAM C. LEIGH, slaves etc; Wit:
KENNETH THIGPEN, HENRY STANCIL. Codicil appointing
JOHN H. LEIGH Co-exr with JESSE W. LEIGH. Wit: IRVIN
THIGPEN, WM. NORFLEET.

PIPPEN, WILLIAM
     Nov. 14, 1849. May Ct., 1852. Bk. F, p 473. Wife:
WINNEFRED, lend all cleared land with houses, etc, it
being on PETER E. KNIGHT'S line, furniture, utensils,
cows and hogs, sheep and my mare; all except land to
be sold at her death, reversion to MARY, MARTHA and
JOSEPH JOHN PIPPEN; daus: MARY DREW PIPPEN, land;
MARTHA, negro; son: JOSEPH JOHN PIPPEN, all remainder
of land. Exr: WILLIAM S. LONG. Wit: PETER E. KNIGHT,
ANDREW J. KNIGHT.

PIRENT, JAMES
     Mar. 7, 1757. May Ct., 1757. Son: JAMES, plantation
whereon I live; Daus: TATION, (?) MARY and SARAH, each
child received negroes. Exr: ARTHUR BELL, JOSHUA BELL.
Wit: JAMES HOGAN, JOSHUA BELL, WILLIAM HOLLOWAY.

PITMAN, BENJAMIN
     Aug. 3, 1755. May Ct., 1756. Wife & Extx: ANN;
sons: MOSES, MICAH, SAMSON and JACOB, he to have
plantation whereon I live; daus: PATIENCE FAULK, MARY
BOTTOM, ABIGAL, LUCY, CELA and JEMIMA PITMAN. Wit:
JOHN STREATER, JOHN JAMESON, JOHN MURPHREE.

PITMAN, HARROD
     Nov. 30, 1836. Nov. Ct., 1836. Bk. F, p 197. Wife:
ELIZABETH, I wish all my negroes and property of all
kinds sold, the money to be divided equally between
my wife and chil (unnamed), unless my wife prefer to
keep her portion of negroes. In which case, after my

wife takes her share, proceeds of sale together with my
Bank stock and money be placed at interest for benefit
support and education of my chil. Boys to receive their
portion of estate at the age of 21, girls at like age
or marriage. Exr: REDMOND BUNN, HENRY BRYAN. No Wit.
Proven by oaths of JOSIAH ELLINOR, WILLIAM BILLUPS.

PITMAN, JESSE
    Aug. 6, 1793. Nov. Ct., 1793. Wife: MOURNING, lend
household chattels, all cattle and hogs, 1 horse, bridle
and saddle, reversion to son: HICKMAN who, also shall
have my manured plantation of 250 A; other chil: FELIX,
JESSE, ROBERT, PATIENCE and CHRISTIAN (?) PITMAN, 5 S
each; Exr: HICKMAN DIXON. Wit: NATHAN HICKMAN, JR.,
HARDY ALLEN, W. HICKMAN.

PITMAN, JOSEPH
    Dec. 18, 1786. Feb. Ct., 1787. Wife: HANAH, bequeath
5 negroes, bed of furn. it being the estate I had with
her by "maregd" (marriage); when ISAAC reaches maturity
residue divided between chil: ABNER, ISAAC, ELIZABETH,
HANAH and CHARITY PITMAN. Exr: ROBERT BOOTHE, REUBEN
JONES, SION TREVATHAN. Wit: WILLIAM EMSON (AMASON),
ROBERT TREVATHAN, FREDERICK TREVATHAN.

PITMAN, NANCY
    June 20, 1842. Nov. Ct., 1842. Bk. F, p 271. Bro:
STEPHEN PITMAN, all my land; residue divided between:
SUSANNA, JOHN and STEPHEN PITMAN and MARY TEAT. No
Exr; no Wit.

PITMAN, MOSES
    Mar. 24, 1759. Dec. Ct., 1760. Wife & Extx:
ELIZABETH, 1/3 estate; remaining estate equally divided
between 3 chil: JAMES, MOSES and MARY. Exr: ANDREW ROSS,
JR. Wit: JOSEPH PITMAN (Quaker), JOHN GAY, JESSE GREEN.

PITMAN, SALLY
    Oct. 2, 1833. May Ct., 1834. Bk. F, p 156. Chil:
AMY O'BERRY, chest, wearing apparel, large pewter bason
and 6 pewter plates; and WILLIAM PITMAN, spotted chest
and all cloth contained therein. Exr: MOSES SPICER.
Wit: LEVI WILKINSON, THOMAS DICKINSON.

PITMAN, THOMAS
 Apr. 4, 1754. Feb. Ct., 1755. Wife: ANNE; sons: LOT,
320 A and THOMAS (EXR); 7 other sons mentioned but not
named; daus: 2 mentioned but not named. Exr: bros,
ROBERT PITMAN, AMBROSE PITMAN. Wit: JNO. HOPKINS,
AMBROSE PITMAN, JOHN FORT.

PITT, ANN
 Oct. 10, 1809. Feb. Ct., 1821. Bk. E, p 264. Daus:
WEST BANKS, cotton loom; MOLEY (MOLLIE) STEWART, bed;
SARY PITMAN, fore Dolers ($4); son & Exr: RICHARD PITT,
1 negro, all stock hoses (horses), cattle, hoggs and
sheep and furniture etc. Exr: WILLIAM STEWART. Wit:
E. HUMPHRESS, ELIZABETH HUMPHRESS.

PITT, CATHRAIN
 Nov. 25, 1837. May Ct., 1838. Sons: JOHN, Brandy
still; JAMES, my roan horse, buofat, walnut table and
negro man; gr. daus: EMILY CATHERINE PITT, chest;
CATHERINE WARD, chest; POLLY DUNN, bed; SALLY CARTER,
$30. Property to be sold, residue to be divided be-
tween WILLIE PITT, JAMES PITT and ARTHUR PITT. No exr.
Wit: MOSES BAKER. Caveated by: JACOB DUNN, DEMPSEY
OWENS, JOHN R. PITT, ZACKARIAH CARTER, WILLIE WILLIAMS,
JOHN MERCER, JUN.

PITT, ETHELRED
 Dec. 28, 1798. Feb. Ct., 1799. Bro & Exr: RICHARD
PITT, land whereon I live; sister: MARY STEWART, after
death of my mother, ANN PITT, my part of 2 negroes,
which were left me by my father, JAMES PITT; mother,
ANN PITT, lend all residue of estate, reversion to
bro. and sisters. Exr: THOMAS BANKS. Wit: EXUM PHILIPS,
SEN., LEWIS DIRKEN, ABNER PITMAN.

PITT, JAMES
 Jan. 5, 1797. Feb. Ct., 1797. Wife: ANN, lend 2
negroes, and plantation whereon I live, bequeath horse,
colt, corn, meat, hogs, flaxwheel, cotton wheel, weaving loom and gear. Lend her brandy still, reversion to
son ETHELRED. Bequeath 2 cows and calves, 2 yokes of
stears, yokes, all sheep, hogs and all brandy; residue

divided between RICHARD & ETHELRED. Sons & Exrs:
RICHARD, plantation purchased of BENJAMIN ONEAL
I negro and reversion in 1 negro; Son & Exr: ETHELRED,
reversion in plantation whereon I live, and reversion
in 1 negro; daus: WEST, 2 negroes, mare, cow and calf
and flaxwheel; MOLLEY STEWART, 2 negroes, mare, cow
and calf and flaxwheel; SARAH PITMAN, 1 negro and mare.
Exr: JACOB BATTLE. Wit: WILLIAM JONES, GEORGE GRIFFIS.

PITT, JAMES, SEN.
     June 21, 1830. Feb. Ct., 1831. Bk. F, p 121. Young-
est son: BENNETT, 170 A land purchased of HENRY PITT
and JOSEPH PITT, tract on lines of SILAS WARD, E of
Great Meadows Branch and Little Branch, $200 and 2
negroes and horse. Remaining land divided between 4
oldest sons: JO (JOAB) P. PITT (Exr); JOHN (Exr), 2
negroes and horse each; DAWSIN, 1 negro and horse;
RALPH, 2 negroes, horse and $50; daus: REBECCA JINKENS,
2 negroes; PERNITEE (?) BRIDGERS, 2 negroes and $80;
and JEDIDAH, 2 negroes and $200. Wit: W. D. PETWAY,
MOSES BAKER.

PITT, JAMES
     Mar. 30, 1849. May Ct., 1850. Bk. F, p 443. Wife:
REBECCA, lend 1/3 my land, 2 negroes, sideboard, buffet,
2 horses, 2 cows and calves, 2 ewes and lambs, 2 sows
and pigs, 25 bbl corn, 1500 lbs. pork, fodder, 50 lbs
picked cotton, $20 in cash, brandy still, tools, etc.
Residue sold and proceeds divided between all chil.
Sons & Exrs: PERRY & WARREN. Wit: J. C. KNIGHT, WRIGHT
BARNES.

PITT, JOAB P.
     Aug. 7, 1754. Aug. Ct., 1854. Bk., G, p 80. Wife:
(unnamed), during widowhood, 1/2 of the tract of land
whereon I live, the house to be allowed to her; also
lend her 6 negroes, cow and calf, horse, stock, 2000
lbs. pork, yoke of oxen, 4 bu. salt, 10 bu. wheat, 2
cast plows, utensils, sugar, coffee, doz. chairs,
tables, blue chest and $25; dau: JOHN ELLA (JOHN ELLIS
?), reversion in 6 negroes and land; sons: ROBERT S.,
FRANKLIN G. (Exr.), and JOSEPH I. T. PITT, all my
"White House" lands, called the ELLIS tract, the RAYNER

Tract, the BATTLE Tract, the Big Hole Tract, some 1200 A; daus: REBECCA, 160 A tract lying near the Pitt Co. line, known as the Dr. WILLIAMS land, 1 negro, lot lying near River Bridge at Sparta, about 2 A; GATSY, lot in Tarborough No. 113; son MARK BENNETT, 1/2 my house plantation on which I now live; my 4 chil: REBECCA, GATSY, MARK and JOHN ELLIS (?), the dividend of my 16 shares of Wilmington Railroad stock; residue divided. Wit: THOS SMITH, KINCHEN HARRELL.

PITT, THOMAS
    Sept. 4, 1820. Nov. Ct., 1820. Bk. E, p 243. Land to be divided into 2 parts; beginning at mouth of Redland Branch, on HOLLOMAN'S line, S side Town Creek to mouth Littleton Branch thence to Littleton Pond, so as to strike center of land at WILEY PITT'S line; wife: CATHERINE, lend all land on W side of line containing buildings and orchard, reversion to son JOHN, and 2 negroes; dau: SUSANNAH, all land E of line. Residue of estate to be sold and returns divided between wife and chil, provided "them that is marryed render a true account of what they have received and that to be counted as part of their legacy." Son & Exr: JAMES PITT. Exr: JONATHAN BULLUCK, MOSES BAKER. Wit: JO P. PITT, JAMES PITT.

PITTMAN, AMEY (AMY)
    Nov. 3, 1790. Feb. Ct., 1791. Bk. 3, p 165. Dau: ELIZABETH, mare, bridle, saddle and 4 cattle. Residue sold, money put at interest until maturity. Exr: ABISHAI HORN. Wit: EDWARD VANN, WILLIAMSON BARNES.

PITMAN, ELIJAH
    Mar. 10, 1790. May Ct., 1799. Sons: HARRISON, 250 A tract lying on White Oak Swamp and 3 negroes; GRESHAM (?) COFFIELD PITTMAN, 1/2 plantation with adjoining land lying in Halifax Co. and on Fishing Creek, 3 negroes, 1 mare and $50 silver; BENJAMIN PITTMAN, remaining half of above land, 3 negroes and mare; dau: ELIZABETH, 4 negroes. All tools, stears, carts and wheels, cattle etc. left on plantation in care of son GRESHAM; remainder of personal estate and land lying on Beach Swamp in Halifax Co. to be sold, residue,

after debts paid, divided between 4 chil. Exr: DAVID
COFFIELD. Wit: RICHARD COKER, NATHANIEL COKER, WILLIAM
MANNING.

PITTMAN, GRESHAM C.
    July 12, 1845. Feb. Ct., 1853. Bk. F, p 496. Gr.
dau: MARY A. S. PITTMAN, 1 negro; son & exr: REDDIN,
the whole of my estate, land lying on the S side of
Fishing Creek, adjoining the land of WELLS DRAUGHAN and
other; tract in Halifax Co. on the N side of said Creek
adjoining the lands of J. DAVIS and W. W. TAYLOR; all
my negroes in Halifax and Edgecombe Cos., all my money,
bonds, notes, Bank and Railroad stock, horses, cattle,
hogs, sheep, household and kitchen furniture, etc. Wit:
W. D. BRYAN, JOS. JNO. B. PENDER.

PITTMAN, JOSEPH
    Oct. 9, 1762. July Ct., 1763. Wife & Extx: ANN, all
estate except land divided equally between wife and
chil; son, JETHRO, all land; daus: ANN and CLOE. Exr:
DANIEL ROSS. Wit: JAMES HORN, JACOB PITMAN, MARY GREEN.
Trustys (Trustees) DANIEL ROSS, JESSE GREEN, JACOB
PITTMAN.

PITTMAN, REDDIN
    Dec. 11, 1853. May Ct., 1854. Wife: MARTHA PITTMAN,
during widowhood 2 parcels of land on the new road
leading from Coffield Bridge to the head of the South
Prong of Miry Branch, on the lines of Cockelshell
Branch, Shell Bank Marlbed, Old Quarter Spring, Gallberry Pocossin, Coker Old Field, Hebron Meeting House,
Bridge, Maple Swamp, Grimes' island field, Hillside
and Coker field branch; 14 negroes and their increase,
carriage, harness, pair of horses bought of D. W.
BULLUCK, buggy and harness, gold watch, locket and
chain, bureau with glass knobs and mirror, tin safe,
clothing, blankets, mohair rocker, etc., $3000, 40
shares Bank stock, State of N. C., Bank of Washington
etc; sons: OLIVER P. PITTMAN 770 A tract in Halifax
Co. N side of Fishing Creek, devised to me by my
father GRISHAM C. PITTMAN, same conveyed to him by the
Hon. JOHN BRANCH 4th day of Feb., 1835, Halifax Book
#29 p, 217; BEVERLY T. PITTMAN, land in Edgecombe Co.

on S side Fishing Creek on lines of NORFLEET CUTCHIN,
Cockelshell Branch, WILLIAM S. PITT, JAMES MOORE,
COFFIELD Bridge, Mirey Branch, Marl path. Old Quarter
Spring and Grimes Island; also 200 A parcel of land
in Halifax on N side of Fishing Creek, HILLIARD FORT
conveyed to my father by Deed 1, Jan. 1847; Son: REDDIN
GRISHAM PITTMAN, land in Edgecombe on Fishing Creek,
Maple Swamp, Hebron Meeting House and Coker Old Field,
etc; dau: MARTHA B. PITMAN, 1013 A land conveyed to me
by WILLIAM D. BRYAN 10 Jan., 1848 & 13 Nov. 1850; son:
WILLIAM D. PITTMAN, lands in Edgecombe already possessed.
Exr: LOUIS H. B. WHITAKER of Halifax, HENRY HYMAN, Dr.
NEWSOM J. PITTMAN, JESSE POWELL, WILLIAM NORFLEET. Wit:
LUNSFORD R. CHERRY, L. B. MANNING, NORFLEET CUTCHIN.
A long, interesting will of many pages.

POND, RICHARD
    Feb. 13, 1848. Aug. Ct., 1852. Bk., F, p 478. Wife
& Extx: MILBRY, whole estate. Wit: SAMUEL D. PROCTOR,
JESSE C. KNIGHT.

POND, STEPHENSON
    May 30, 1806. Aug. Ct., 1806. Bk. D, p 251. Wife:
MOURNING, lend use of plantation and all land; be-
queath her choice of my horse creatures, also saddle,
bridle, and residue. Reversion of everything to chil:
JOHN, RICHARD, WILLIAM, CELAH and ZACHARIAH POND. Exr:
Father-in-law and friend, WILLIAM GRIFFIS, LAMON RUFFIN.
Wit: JOHN GRIFFIS, JUN., WILLIAM MACE.

POPE, JACOB
    Mar. 1, 1770. May Ct., 1772. Wife: JANE, largest
iron pot, 1 puter bason, 1 of my best dishes, 3 puter
plates, breeding sow, lend 1 cow, 1/3 land, 1/3 orchard
with reversion to gr. son: ELIJAH POPE, also lend her
1 negro, reverson to son, PILGRIM; Son: SAMPSON, 5 S;
daus: MOURNING WIMBERLEY, REBECCAH SYKES and MARY
SURGINER, 5 S each; son & Exr: PILGRIM, residue consisting of cattle, hogs and sheep, furniture of every
kind etc. Wit: ROB (ER)T DIGGS, JOHN SURGINER, SARAH
SURGINER (SURGEONER) by The Clerk.

POPE, MARY

July 8, 1837. Nov. Ct , 1844. Bk. F, p 315. Chil:
MARTHA TREVATHAN, JESSE J. POPE and CHARLOTTE POPE,
$1 each; residue divided between son & exr: WILLIAM E.
POPE and dau: RHODA POPE. Wit: BRYANT G. POPE, MARTIN
T. POPE.

POPE, WILLIAM

Jan. 15, 1749. Feb. Ct., 1749. Sons: JACOB, 3 negroes; WEST, 1 negro; STEPHEN, 1 negro and plantation
whereon I formerly lived in Isle of Wight; daus:
REBECCA POPE and JULIAN NEWSOME; gr. sons: WILLIAM
TAYLOR, 2 negroes, and WILLIAM POPE, son of JACOB, my
plantation whereon I live; should he die without issue,
reversion to his bro. RICHARD POPE. Son & Exr: JACOB
POPE; son-in-law & exr: JOSEPH NEWSOME. Wit: HENRY WEST,
JOSEPH PEARCE, ARTHUR WALL, JOHN JORDAN. In probate
notes by BENJAMIN WYNNS, C. C. Testator came to this
state from Isle of Wight County, in Virginia, and devised to son STEPHEN plantation in said County.

PORTER, CHARLES

Sept. 28, 1794. Nov. Ct., 1794. Chil: SILVEA,
CHARLES, 1 negro each; THOMAS (Exr), 1 negro, 1/2
brandy still; ELIZABETH COKER, 2 negroes; KISSIAH
COKER, 1 negro; MARTHA, 1 negro; MOODY (Exr), 1 negro,
horse, 1/2 brandy still. Wit: GEO. SINET, JESSE
JOHNSON.

PORTER, ELY, Tarboro, N. C.

June 2, 1842. Feb. Ct., 1843. Bk. F, pp 279-82.
Wife: MARTHA, lend 11 negroes and their increase, that
came from her father's estate, reversion to MARTHA E.
and JOSEPH JOHN PORTER, dwelling house and where we
now live (No 36 and lot No 47) and use of 95 A land
adjoining NORFLEET, her life, bureau, desk, sideboard,
china press, horse, gig, harness, etc., and money lent
to BENNETT BUNN, REDMOND BUNN, Security. Daus: NANCY
PORTER, piano, 2 negroes, $400 shee can use to buy man
servant, bureau, looking glass, 1 Doz. silver tea spoons,
lots No 36 & 47 in which her mother has life estate;
MARTHA E. HYMAN, negro girl and her increase, for which
I paid $485, deed of gift to MARTHA and her husband
HENRY HYMAN, $200 cash, 1 negro man, 2 doz. silver tea

spoons; bureau, looking glass, Lots #34 and 35 with improvements, reserving small plot where I may be buried; son & exr: JOSEPH J. PORTER, $385, watch, ($100), negro man, $50 more in cash; 1/2 of lot #15 which I purchased of WILLIAM H. WILLS; my storehouse and lot No 50; 184 1/2 A land adjoining LEVI DENTON'S (deceased) be sold and divided among my children; my 10 shares in Bank of State of N. C. and 10 shares in Bank of Cape Fear, divided between wife and chil, etc. Exr: Son-in-law, HENRY HYMAN. Wit: GEO. HOWARD, WILLIAM L. DOZIER.

PORTER, MARTHA
    Apr. 6, 1845. Nov. Ct., 1845. Bk. F, p 330. Son & Exr: JOSEPH JOHN PORTER, $1000, desk, bookcase, my interest in negroes left me by my sisters LYDIA AUSTIN and NANCY WARD, by my father JOSEPH PIPPEN, after the death of his wife TEMPERANCE PIPPIN, blue silk umbrella, also give him $1000 to be held in trust for my dau. ELIZABETH HYMAN, for her support to be kept free from control of her husband HENRY HYMAN, reversion to be held in trust for her child or chil; daus: ELIZABETH HYMAN, lend 6 silver tablespoons, reversion to her chil; NANCY PORTER, 12 chairs, carpet, sideboard, mohogany dining table, pr. brass andirons, shovel, tongs and fender, sofa, rocking chair, clock, double washstand, side saddle, curtain, bedstead, red chest, window curtains, candlestand, unmade curtains, calico, buggy, harness, Brittania Teapot, 8 silver tablespoons, 14 silver teaspoons, pr. sugar tongs, my interest in 10 shares stock in Bank of the State of N. C. and 5 shares stock in Bank of Cape Fear; gr. daus: ANN E. HYMAN, my bureau and glass, and MARTHA S. HYMAN. All bedclothes, glass, china, knives, forks divided into 3 parts for my 3 chil. In case son may not serve as Exr. I nominate nephew, ROBERT H. AUSTIN, of Tarboro, as Exr. and Trustee for dau MARTHA HYMAN and her chil. No Wit.

PORTIS, GEORGE
    Oct. 5, 1775. Jan. Ct., 1776. Dau & Extx: ANN, choice of beds and furniture; son: WILLIAM, 5 S sterling of Great Britain; son & Exr: JOHN FLOYD alias PORTIS, he and dau ANN to have remainder of estate. Wit:

ABSOLOM LANCASTER, WILLIAM CONNELL, BENJN. FLOYD, HENRY
GAINER.

POWEL(L), BENJAMIN
    Feb. 4, 1819. Feb. Ct., 1824. Bk. F, p 17. Wife:
ANN, residue for her widowhood, should she marry 1/2
of her property goes to son NAUM; son: NAUM, 4 "cheers",
1/2 puter, 1 pot, saddle, gun, 1/2 cattle, sow and pigs,
pork, crib of corn, ax, weeding noe, plow hoe, chains,
tools, etc. Wit: BENJAMIN WHITFIELD, FREDERICK MAYO.
There being no exr NAUM POWELL, was Adm. and entered
$1000 bond, securities were BENJAMIN WHITFIELD and
RODERICK CHERRY.

POWELL, NANCY
    May 29, 1809. Aug. Ct., 1809. Bk. D, p 348. Rela-
tions' chil: NANCY FOORT and ELIZABETH FOORT, 21 A
land lying N side Griffin's Swamp adjoining THOMAS
WIGGINS, THOMAS DOZIER and JOHN WIGGINS and 1 negro
to be sold and all remaining property to be sold and
money to be divided between and for use of these chil.
If they should die before maturity, property to go to
relation REBECCAH LEE, dau of JOHN LEE and wife BETSEY.
Exr: THOMAS WIGGINS. Wit: JAMES HUNTER, NANCY YOUNG.

POWELL, NATHANIEL
    Dec. 19, 1770. Apr. Ct., 1777. Wife & Extx: SARAH,
all estate of negroes and chattels for her widowhood,
reversion to chil. Son: WILLOUGHBY, 500 A lying in
fork of Beaver Dam Swamp; younger sons: NATHANIEL and
NATHAN, my manor plantation. Exr: JAMES WYATT, JUN.
Wit: JOHN PACE, LYDIE POWELL.

POWELL, WILLIAM
    June 12, 1792. Nov. Ct., 1793. Wife: NANCY, 1 negro,
choice of horses, 3 cows and calves, 1/4 of all corn
and meat, 1/2 all wheat, money sufficient to put a
good outside chimney to my dwelling house, 2 tables,
her choice of 1 chest, 1 trunk, 6 "chears", 2 dishes,
2 basons, 6 pewter plates, all earthenware, woolen
wheel, linen wheel, pr cotton cards, tub, pail, piggen,
pot, pan, iron, spice mortor, all poultry, lawn seve,
hair seve, all knives and forks, spoons, looking glass,

2 trays, saddle, 1/4 all hogs, lend her 2 negroes her
lifetime, residue to be divided between wife and chil:
ZACARIAH, JOHN (Exr), MARY JONES, ELIZABETH ROBERTSON,
SARAH COLEMAN and CHRISTIAN ROANE, all these now living.
Dec'd chil: WILLIAM, GEORGE, JESSE and CANDACE POWELL.
Their part to be divided between their chil. Exr:
MALACHI NICHOLSON. Wit: CALEB ETHERIDGE, ADLEY MORRISS,
JESSE WYATT.

PRICE, CHARITY
    Aug. 7, 1824. May Ct., 1826. Bk. F, p 55. Heirs
of JESSE BRAKE and wife, PATIENCE: RACHEL, WILLIE,
JOSEPH, WILLIAM and PENINA BRAKE, large blue painted
chest, 2 iron pots and hooks, 1 iron skillet, griddle,
frying pan, all this with remaining perishable property
to be sold and money to be divided between these 5.
Exr: JACOB BATTLE, MOSES SPICER. Wit: MOSES SPICER,
JOSIAH SPICER.

PRICE, ELIJAH
    Apr. 10, 1792. Aug. Ct., 1792. Wife: JEAN, lend
whole estate during widowhood for comfort and a support of herself and my chil, at her remarriage or
death to be divided among all my chil (unnamed). Exr:
EXUM PHILIPS, JESSE JOHNSON. Wit: ETHELRED PHILIPS,
JOEL PRICE.

PRICE, JESSE
    Nov. Ct., 1812. Bk. E, p 47. Wife: PATIENCE, lend
plantation whereon I live, orchards, crop of corn that
is on it, house, except 1 dau., CHARITY lives in,
horse of her choice, cow, 2 yearlings, 1 sow and pigs,
2 ewes and lambs, 2 spinning wheels (flax and wollen)
for her widowhood; reversion to chil and heirs of
PATIENCE BRAKE; sons & exrs: JOEL, all land S side
of Beach Run adjoining JETHRO MARNER; JONATHAN, remainder of land S of that I give son JOEL; dau: CHARITY,
$200; dec'd dau: PATIENCE BRAKE, $200 to her chil;
residue sold and divided between wife, 2 sons, CHARITY
and chil of dec'd dau, PATIENCE BRAKE. Exr: CHARLES
COLEMAN, Wit: MITCHEL WATKINS, JOHN COLEMAN.

PRICE, JOSEPH

July 16, 1811. Feb. Ct., 1815. Bk. E, p 78. Wife: MARY, all lands and one negro for widowhood, reversion to gr. son, JOSEPH JAMES PRICE, son of MOSES PRICE; remainder estate to be equally divided between wife, son and exr: MOSES and dau BETSEY, wife of JAMES HORN. Wit: JAMES W. CLARK, ELISHA VANN.

PRICE, THOMAS
Aug. 24, 1750. May Ct., 1751. Wife not named. Sons: WILLIAM, THOMAS and JOHN; daus: ELIZABETH and RACHEL. No Exr. Wit: JOHN HOOKS, WILLIAM RADDOM (?), JOHN HOOKS, JR.

PRICE, THOMAS
Mar. 13, 1779. Aug. Ct., 1781. Wife: ELIZABETH, lend 1/2 plantation, orchards thereon, use of houses where I live, tools and chattels; reversion to ELIZABETH and MARY. Chil: JESSE, WILLIAM, CADER (?), JOSEPH, MONEN (MOURNING) ANDREWS (?), KIZIAH COLEMAN, ANN GWIN and RACHEL ALLEN, 5 S each; son and exr: ELIGE (ELIJAH), plantation where I live with 100 A belonging thereto; daus: ELIZABETH and MARY, cow and calf each. Exr: bro, JOSEPH PRICE. Wit: AARON ODOM, AARON MARVEN (?), RICHARD ODOM.

PRICE, WILLIAM
Jan. 11, 1793. May Ct._____ Wife & Extx: SARAH, lend "manner" plantation whereon I live, stock, and household goods; chil: MACKINGAIN, plantation at mother's death or marriage; BARBARY, 3 A; SARAH DAVIS, PRISCILLA FOSSET (?), ELIZABETH FAITHFUL, SAMUEL and Child of dau NANNEY FOSSET, 5 S each; JAMES, 150 A the upper part of land whereon he lives, reversion to his son WILLIAM; JOHN, remainder of land whereon son JAMES now lives; WINNEY, at mother's death, cow and calf, sow and pigs. Wit: CHARLES COTTEN, FREDERICK COTTEN, HENRY HARRISON

PRIDGEN, WILLIAM, Saint Mary's Parish
May 11, 1762. No Probate date. Wife: MOURNING, all that part of my estate that belonged to her before her marriage, provided she makes up money "dew" to her chil, left them by their father, out of her part; sons

269

& exrs: THOMAS, 100 A S side Tar River, purchased of
WILLIAM GAINEY, 1 negro, black cattle, in JONATHAN
WEAVER'S care, 2 pewter dishes, 2 basons and 4 plates;
Son & Exr: DAVID, negro, horse, cattle in WILLIAM
DAFFNEL'S (illegible) care; likewise 2 dishes, 2 basons,
and 4 plates; sons: JESSE, 250 A purchased of JOHN
LAWHORN (?), 1 negro, 1 dish, bason and 4 plates;
WILLIAM, 180 A plantation whereon I live with all
apurtenances belonging thereto, also 2 basons, 1 dish
and 4 plates; Son, DREWERY, still, £ 30 Proc. money;
daus: MARY, feathers sufficient to make 1 bed; SELAH,
1 negro, 2 dishes, basons and 4 plates; LEVI, £ 33
6 S 8 pence Proc. money, 2 small basons, 2 dishes and
4 plates; ELIZABETH, £ 33 6 S 8 p Proc. money, 2 small
basons, 2 dishes and 4 plates; gr. daus; daus of MARY
WHIBLEY (WHITLEY), to wit: MARGARET, MARY and RODICE (?)
£ 11 Proc. money when 18, or at their marriage. Wit:
DUNCAN LAMON, DANIEL WILLS, JOHN LESLIE (?).

PROCTOR, AARON
     Apr. 13, 1821. Aug. Ct., 1821. Bk, E p 272. Wife:
CHARITY, 2 horse creatures, 2 "wooling" wheels, 2
cotton cards, 2 flax wheels, 2 puter plates, 2 dishes,
3 puter basons, 2 iron pots and hooks, frying pan,
spider, 6 cattle, 6 ewes, all hoggs, tools, table,
pine chist, 14 cider barrels, all pig bacon, hog lard,
all corn now in barn, 10 geese, all chicken fouls,
land and plantation whereon I live for life or widowhood; all land together, with that of Mother at her
death to be equally divided between sons YOUNG and
WRIGHT; daus: PATEY (PATTY), RHODA, CHARLOTTE and
BETTY PROCTOR. MARY WILLIAMS, provision for support
for which I am bound; 2 negroes, to be hired out and
income go to all 6 chil. and support of MARY WILLIAMS,
1 negro and horse to be sold to pay debts. Exr:
AUGUSTIN WHITEHEAD. Wit: MOSES SPICER, WILLIAM SPICER,
JR.

PROCTOR, JOHN
     Dec. 21, 1761. (?) Feb. Ct., 1772. Wife & Extx:.
ANN, manor plantation during her life or widowhood,
reversion of said land along with additional 200 A
land, to son MOSES; sons: JOHN, my survey of land

adjoining JESSE FLOWERS, to ARTHUR WILLIAMS' survay;
SHADRACK, 175 A adjoining my son JOHN PROCTOR; AARON,
100 A where JACOB BRAKE lived, it being the upper part
of a 200 A survey; SAMSON, 100 A the other half of
above survey; dau: PATIENCE JONES, 5 S sterling. Exr:
JOHN MORRIS. Wit: MARY MORRIS, DEBERIAH MATE.

PROCTOR, JOHN
    Jan. 23, 1790. Probated 1794. Wife: EDEA, saddle,
dovetail chest; lend use of land and plantation whereon I live during her natural life, give her all spinning
wheels and cards and all provisions. Remainder of property to be equally divided between wife and chil;
son: JOHN, 80 A plantation whereon I live. Exr: WILLIAM
ROBERT GAY. Wit: WILLIAM ROBERT GRAY, JAMES WILLIFORD.

PROCTOR, JOSHUA
    Jan. 23, 1785. May Ct., 1785. Chil: RICHARD, 1 ne-
gro; son & exr: JACOB, plantation and land adjoining
whereon I live and 2 negroes; NANNEY BARLOW, and
CHERRY PROCTOR, 1 negro each; residue divided between
JACOB, NANNEY BARLOW and CHERRY PROCTOR. Exr: son-in-
law, DAVID BARLOW. Wit: ETHELRED PHILIPS, MATTHEW
WILLIAMS, JOS. FORT.

PROCTOR, WILLIAM
    Oct. 5, 1779. May Ct., 1780. Wife & Extx: JENE
(JEAN) lend 500 A land, mare, colt, 10 cattle, 21
sheep, all furniture, during life or widowhood; reversion of land to STEPHEN, JESSEY and MORRIS; MORRIS
to have the plantation for his part; daus: MARY HARREL,
BETTEY TOMMAS (THOMAS) and son JOHN, 20 S each; dau:
LUCY, 3 cattle and all their increase that THOMAS
MESSER is to have upon stocks, likewise 3 ewes and
their increase that JACOB HOLLON has upon stock; residue divided between son & exr: STEPHEN, JESSEY and
MORRIS. Wit: GEORGE SMITH, WILLIAM BLOODWORTH.

PURVIS, LEWIS
    Mar. 11, 1851. May Ct., 1851. Bk. F, p 454. Wife:
DINAH, for life or widowhood, all land on side of the
road on which house stands, except the long field, til
son LEWIS KINDRED PURVIS comes of age, one years pro-

visions, choice of my horses, mules, cows, stock, 5
negroes, chest, sideboard, press, and contents, half
doz. knives, forks, 6 setting chairs; dau: JULIA
COUNSELL, cow, calf, chest, dressing table, 2 negroes,
and their increase; son: JOHN A., filly, cow and calf,
cattle, 2 negroes, and their increase; dau: ELIZABETH,
chest, dressing table, 3 negroes, cow and calf; son:
REUBEN T., horse, cow and calf, 2 sows and pigs, chest,
2 negroes and increase; daus: HANNAH E. DANIEL, 4 sheep,
chest, dressing table, 3 negroes and increase; ISEA B.,
1 chest, dressing table, cow and calf, 2 negroes and
increase; ELIZAR, chest, dressing table, cow and calf,
3 negroes and their increase; sons: ANDREW, cow and
calf, sow and pigs, horse, mule, desk, all my MANNING
land on the E side of Coneta Creek; 3 negroes and their
increase; LEWIS K., all my home and TAYLOR lands, but
this is not to interfere with land I left my wife her
life or widowhood, 2 negroes, cow and calf, horse or
mule, sideboard and press after death of my wife. If
any of my heirs be not free at my death, they shall
receive their property at the age of 20 years. No Exr
or Wit.

PURYER, ROBERT
    Dec. 25, 1758. June Ct., 1759. Wife & Extx: FRANCES;
sons: ROBERT, my plantation; WILLIAM; daus: MARY,
MARGARET, ELIZABETH and ANN. Exr: MOSES HORNE. Wit:
WILLIAM HOBGOOD, RACHEL TANER.

QUINN, WILLIAM
    Aug. 7, 1790. Nov. Ct., 1790. Wife: MILLY, all
residue, reversion to JAMES, THOMAS, WILLIAM, SALLY,
JOHN and PAULLY; chil: PATTY JONES, NANCY SANDISER, (?)
JAMES, THOMAS, WILLIAM, SALLY, JOHN and PAULLY (son
or dau?); Exr: HENRY HINES, AMOS JOHNSTON, PETER HINES.
Wit: HUGH CRAVEY, BENJ. BLACKBURN, EZEKIEL CAUSEY,
RICHARD SHIRLEY.

RANDOLPH, DAVID
    Feb. 10, 1822. Aug. Ct., 1829. HENRY, negro slave
to be given his freedom and bequeath all blacksmith
tools to him. Orphans of PAUL RANDOLPH: PEGGY, WILLIAM
and MARY RANDOLPH, all remaining estate. Exr: ROBERT

JOYNER. Wit: ROBERT FOXHALL, JAMES ELLINOR, JR.

RAWLINGS, BENJAMIN
Dec. 10, 1738. Feb. Ct., 1738. Parcel land N side
Fishing Crk purchased of EDWARD PARKER to be sold;
legatees: ROBERT LOCKLEAR, DAVID COLTRAINE, DR. JAMES
FLOOD, EDMOND KEARNY, son of THOS. and SARAH, 300 A
N side Swift Creek and plantation whereon I live;
BENJAMIN HILL, JR son of BENJ and SARAH, silver shoe
and knee buckels; HENRY HILL, son of BENJ. and SARAH,
my silver spoons; SARAH KEARNY, wife of THOMAS, horse;
ELIZABETH ALSTON, wife of my good friend, JOSEPH JOHN
ALSTON, all earthenware and looking glass; THOMAS
KEARNEY, all pewter, iron and brass; WILLIAM ALSTON;
ELIZABETH WILLIAMS, wife of SAMUEL. Exr: THOS KEARNY,
DAVID COLTRAINE. Wit: SAM'L WILLIAMS, R. WHITTINGTON,
WILLIAM LEE.

REASONS, RAULEY
Apr. 3, 1841. Nov. Ct., 1841. Wife: MARY, cow, pot,
frying pan, coffee pot, woolen wheel and cards, horse,
etc; son: RICHARD W. REASONS, all land I possess, except 1/3 reserved for wife her lifetime with reversion
to RICHARD; daus: SALLEY, NANCY, and PENNY, feather bed
and furniture each; residue sold and money divided.
Exr: STEPHEN WOOTEN. Wit: WILLIAM M. CRISP, WILLIE
WHITLEY.

RENFROW, JOHN
May 30, 1748. Aug. Ct., 1748. Wife & Extx: TOMESON;
sons: ENOCH, JACOB, GEORGE, WILLIAM and JAMES Exr:
MATTHEW McKINNE. Wit: JOHN HAYWOOD, NATHANIEL HOLLY,
JOHN EVANS.

RENN, JAMES
Dec. 9, 1794. Feb. Ct., 1795. DAVID, all land, 4
negroes, entire estate. Exr: EDWARD HALL. Wit: WM.
LEIGH, SIMON HARRELL.

RENN, WILLIAM
Jan. 12, 1792. Feb. Ct., 1792. Chil: JAMES, 3 ne-
groes, all stock and furniture; ANN, 3 negroes and mare;
ELIZABETH, 3 negroes; and PATSEY, 4 negroes; land

whereon I live to be sold and money divided between
2 sons: DAVID and ARCHIBALD and 3 negroes each. Residue divided between ANN, ELIZABETH, PATSEY, DAVID and
ARCHIBALD. Exr: ETHELRED PHILIPS, LEWIS IRWIN. Wit:
J. H. HALL, WM. WILLIAMS.

RHOADES (RHOADS), ABRAHAM
    Oct. 28, 1819. Aug. Ct., 1821. Bk. E, p 269. Son
& Exr: JOHN, land and plantation whereon I live, lying
on both sides of Town Creek and Tyancoque Swamp, small
tract I purchased of JOHN HUBBARD and 2 negroes; dau:
POLLY WHITE, wife of HENRY WHITE, 2 negroes, reversion
to her chil; $750 put to interest for support of POLLY
WHITE and chil. Residue divided between son JOHN and
chil of POLLY WHITE; children's portion left in hands
of Exr. for their support. Exr: STARLING WALLER. Wit:
JAMES GARRETT, JOSIAH FREEMAN.

RHOADS, ANN (Clerk's spelling RHODES)
    Aug. 3, 1822. May Ct., 1826. Bk. F, p 54. Gr. dau:
ELIZABETH PITMAN, all estate. No Exr. ISAAC NORFLEET
became Adm. gave $1000 Bond, HENRY AUSTIN security.
Wit: ISAAC NORFLEET, CHRISTIANA NORFLEET.

RHODES, ANTHONY
    Nov. 26, 1797. Feb. Ct., 1798 Wife & Extx: MARY,
whole estate. Wit: WM. HAYNES, THOS. CUTCHIN

RICHARDS, RICHARD
    Oct. 23, 1758. Dec. Ct., 1758. Wife & Extx:
REBECCA; sons: JOHN, JESSE and RICHARD, tract of land
to each son. Exr: DAVID CRAWLEY. Wit: WM. KINCHEN,
WM. HAYES, JOHN GREEN.

RICHMOND, SKIPWITH
    July 26, 1774. Oct. Ct., 1774. Sis: SARAH RICHMOND,
tract of land in Bute Co., adjoining WILLIAM HILL and
old Mr. BIRD and 1 negro; aunt; DOROTHY MEARNS, lend
2 negroes, reversion to my cousin WILLIAM SKIPWITH;
cousin: WILLIAM SKIPWITH MEARNS, 540 A tract on Roanoke
River in Halifax Co., it being a tract my father
WILLIAM RICHMOND purchased of WILLIAM HURSTT bearing
date May 1, 1751, a tract known as the Fork land

adjoining COL. JOSEPH MONTFORT on Conaquanary Swamp
in Halifax Co; 522 A tract lying in Granville (or Bute)
Co. on both sides of Jolley's Creek which was granted
to my father WILLIAM RICHMOND by deed from Earl of
Granville 20 Sept. 1758, 3 negroes, 2 horses and mare.
All remainder of estate. Exr: WILLIAM SKIPWITH MEARNS.
Wit: EDMUND DRAKE, MARY DRAKE, ROBERT CLARK.

RICKS, BENJAMIN
    May 5, 1774. Apr. Ct., 1775. Wife: PATIENCE, 80 A
tract S side ____ Branch, which I settle on her as a
dowery; chil: LEWIS, BENJAMIN, JACOB, JOHN (exr), MARY,
JOEL, WILLIAM, SARAH, MEREDITH, THOMAS, PATIENCE and
JOSIAH, 5 S each; son: ABRAHAM, residue, real and
personal. Exr: Cousin, JOHN RICKS. Wit: DUNCAN LAMON,
JACOB FLOWERS, ARCHIBALD LAMON.

RICKS, ISAAC
    Mar. 11, 1748. Oct. 28, 1748. Wife & Extx: SARAH;
sons: ABRAHAM, plantation where I live, 3 negroes,
pewter, tools household furniture, horse and saddle;
ROBERT, 400 A S side of Connowan Swamp, which did
belong to ROBERT SIMMS; pewter, cattle, stock etc.
and 2 negroes; JOHN, £ 80, stock, cattle, furniture
etc. and 2 negroes; daus: MARY POP (POPE), 2 negroes;
MARTHA RICKS, 3 negroes. Wit: JOHN CROWELL, RICHARD
RICHARDS.

RICKS, ISAAC
    Apr. 15, 1760. Dec. Ct., 1760. Son & Exr: JAMES,
250 A whereon I live, 200 A purchased of GEORGE
GOODSON, with 1/2 grist mill, he allowing JOSEPH
HENDERSON his part; use of negro for 1 yr, reversion
of negro to chil: JAMES, JOHN and SARAH ROSS; Dau:
SARAH ROSS; son & Exr: JOHN, 128 A plantation whereon
he lives, and 73 A adjoining and 1/2 grist mill; gr.
son: ISAAC RICKS, son of JOHN, £ 4 for schooling;
residue to JAMES. Wit: EDWARD MOORE, JAMES ROSS,
WILLIAM HORN.

RICKS, ISAAC
    May 29, 1825. Aug. Ct., 1828. Bk. F, p 90. Wife:
ANNE, lend 140 A on N end with houses and outhouses

whereon I live, 1 flaxwheel, cotton wheel, 2 pr. cards,
loom and geer, 8 setting chairs, stables, 3 chests,
watter pails, pigin, can, 3 tubs, 2 trays, 1 meal sifter,
1/2 bu. measure, 2 puter dishes, 6 ditto plates, 3 ditto
basons, 6 ditto spoons, 3 earthen dishes, 1 dz. ditto
plates, 2 ditto bowls, 2 ditto pitchers, 2 ditto chamber
pots, 2 sets cups and saucers, all glassware, 2 iron
pots and hooks, griddle, dutch oven, frying pan, skillet,
2 sad irons, 2 sets knives and forks, mare, briddle and
saddle, cart and wheels, gear, all tools and cyder
casks; son & Exr: WILLIE, all lands not lent wife, also
horse, saddle, shotgun; reversion in 140 A cart and
wheels, tools, cyder casks and 1/2 bu measure; residue
divided between chil: DELILAH, NANCY, RICHARD, $15;
SALLY, JOHN. Exr: JOEL BATTLE. Wit: JOHN J. BUNN, EATON
GAY, JAMES G. BARNES.

RICKS, JAMES
    Mar. 13, 1792. May Ct., 1792. Wife: PHEBE, lend
1/2 plantation whereon I live, 1/2 grees Mill, negro,
2 horses, 3 cows and calves, 6 sheep, 20 hogs, 50 bbl
corn, 2 sows and pigs, copper skillet, 2 irons, 3 iron
pots, 1/2 geese, 1/2 wear in my cubbert, 2 large dishes,
2 small dishes, 6 pewter plates, 2 basons, 6 spoons,
cart and wheels, tools, kitchen utensils, knives and
forks, looking glass, blew chest, 6 cheers, trunk,
pine table, 20 sider casks, large stone gugg, 2 butter
pots, loom and gear, 2 flaxwheels and hackels, all
flax, cotton and wool, all my salt, during her widowhood; bequeath 1 negro, saddle and bridle; son-in-law
and exr: ABISHA HORN, 1 negro; chil: ANN HORN, ₤ 10
current money; JUDITH MOORE, 1 negro; MOURNING
ARRINGTON, 1 negro; RHODA BATTLE, 2 negroes; ROBERT,
100 A on the river adjoining REDMUN BUNN called the
Goodson Place, plantation bought of RICHARD RICKS,
10 A in Folly Island of the river, 1 negro, mill, 1/2
grist, colt, saddle and bridle, 3 cows and calves,
2 sows and pigs, 1/2 geese, Bible, sifering book, slate,
ink stand, crosscut saw, all carpenter's tools, 6
cheers, folding table, chest, 8 sheep, shot gun, 2
pr. stilliard, 2 large dishes, large stone gug, frying
pan, pot, Dutch oven, potrack, 20 cider casks; 560
A in piney woods to be divided between ROBERT, ELI .

HENRY and JOSIAH; dau: CHARITY, 1 negro, mare, saddle
and bridle, Testament, spelling book, 2 cows and calves,
6 sheep; son: ELIE, reversion in 240 A plantation whereon I live, 100 A above the falls mill, it being part of
the Goodson Place, 2 negroes; HENRY 2 negroes and reversion in 1 other; JOSIAH, 1 negro, reversion in mill
and 1 other negro, 1/2 grist, he and HENRY to share
240 A plantation bought of JOHN FLOWERS; residue at
wife's death or marriage to be equally divided between
ROBERT, ELI, HENRY and JOSIAH and CHARITY. Exr: REDMUN
BUNN, JOHN BATTLE. Wit: REDMUN BUNN, JOEL HORN, DANIEL
ROSS.

RICKS, PHEBE
    Oct. 22, 1806. May Ct., 1812. Bk. E, p 36. Sons:
ELI, 3 sheep, all corn and fodder divided between ELI
and HENRY; HENRY, mare, 2 cows and calves, 3 sheep,
sow, 7 shoats and 5 pigs; son-in-law and exr: NATHAN
GILBERT, residue divided between sons ELI, HENRY, son-
in-law NATHAN GILBERT, and heirs of ROBERT RICKS, dec'd,
(the heirs to divide 1/4 part between them). The exr.
having died, HENRY RICKS was made Adm. Wit: REDMUN
BUNN, BENJAMIN BUNN.

RICKS, WILLIAM
    Jan. 10, 1771. No Probate date. Son: BENJAMIN,
cooper's tools; gr. sons: JOHN RICKS, 5 A land, chest
with lock and key, and 3 sheep; gr. son: JACOB RICKS,
my horse, bridle and saddle, 6 horned cattle, 3 sheep,
pork I killed for years provision, ax, carpenter's
tools, and all wearing apparel; gr. dau: MARY RICKS,
2 year old heffer; gr. son: exr: LEWIS RICKS, 200 A
plantation whereon I live, on lines of BENJAMIN RICKS,
MICAJAH THOMAS and JOHN RICKS. Wit: DUNCAN LAMON,
RICHARD VICK, MERIDA RICKS.

ROBBINS, ISAAC
    June 26, 1847. Aug. Ct., 1847. Bk. F, p 370. Wife:
CATHERINE, plantations, lands, household and kitchen
furniture, all goods and chattles for life, or widowhood; no Exr. named; Wit: EATON GAY, I. W. WOODRUFF.

ROBBINS, JOHN

Feb. 17, 1819. May Ct., 1819. Bk. E, p 217. Daus:
ELIZABETH PENDER, NANCY EMASON, L 25 each; BEADY
ROBBINS, whole of my land, plantation whereon I live,
also still, blacksmith tools and 8 negroes; son-in-law:
THOMAS EMASON (AMASON), 1 negro and note I hold against
him for $350; gr. dau: CATHERINE WILLIAMS, 3 negroes,
2 cows and calves, remaining negroes to be hired out
until gr. chil come of age, then to be divided equally
among them; residue estate to be sold and money divid-
ed between all gr. chil. Exr: JOHN MERCER, JOHN BRIDGERS,
THOMAS EMASON. Wit: E. BULLUCK, HENRY DIXON, BURRELL
BARNES, Will contested by THOMAS AMASON and wife NANCY,
ELIZABETH PENDER and CATHERINE WILLIAMS (an infant by
EGBERT H. WILLIAMS). Court ordered will submitted to
jury to decide whether it was will of sd JOHN ROBBINS
or not. Jury: MUNDY (MOODY)WILLIFORD, JOHN ELLIS, MOSES
PRICE, HILLARY PEEL, JACOB BARNES, ELIJAH HORN, JOSEPH
BARNES, SR., JOHN LAWRENCE, JR., KINCHEN GAY, ELIJAH
PRICE, JOSHUA PENDER, JAMES THIGPEN. Jury find it to be
the will of JOHN ROBBINS and order probation.

ROBBINS, ROLAND
Sept. 6, 1822. No Probate date. Bk. F, p 139. Wife:
ALECEY; sons and exrs: ARTHUR and SIMON to share all
land and property. Wit: JAMES W. BARNES, DEMPSEY BARNES.

ROBBINS, SARAH
Apr. 29, 1809. Aug. Ct., 1809. Bk. D, p 346. Chil:
ROLAND, LEDY ROGERS and MILLEY ROGERS, 5 S each; dau:
ZILLEY ROBBINS, colt; gr. son: SIMON PARKER, cow, 3
yearlings, tub, piggin, 2 yews and lams, 1/2 hogs,
saddle and shotgun; dau: ELIZABETH ROBBINS, remainder
of estate. Exr: JOSEPH BARNES. Wit: THOMAS DIXON, JAMES
BARNES. Codicil Aug. 7, 1809. Give to gr. son SIMON
PARKER 1/3 my brandy. Wit: JAS. BARNES.

ROBBINS, SIMON
_____ 1848. Feb. Ct., 1850. Bk. F, p 339. Wife:
ELIZABETH, Iend 2 negroes and $50 current money; dau:
JANE BARNES, 3 negroes; son & exr: WILLIE or WILLIS,
3 negroes, $800 current money and all land; EDWIN,
$700 current money; residue sold and divided equally
among 3 chil. Wit: JOHN FARMER, WILLIAM L. FARMER.

ROBBINS, WILLIAM
Apr. 7, 1779. Nov. Ct., 1781. Sons: ARTHUR, WILLIAM,
JETHRO and THOMAS, ₤ 5 each; gr. son: JESSEY GREEN, ₤
20; daus: LURANEY HORN, lend melato garl, reversion to
my gr. son ELIAS HORN, and bequeath 5 sheep; ELIZABETH
WILLIAMS, wife of THOMAS WILLIAMS, 1 negro; CHARITY,
wife of DAVID SEARS, ₤ 15; MILLEY ROBBINS, 1 negro;
son: JOHN, all land, 7 negroes, residue both real and
personal. Exr: JOHN WILLIAMS, JOHN ROBBINS. Wit:
BENJAMIN WE(A)VER, JACOB ROBBINS, MARY ROBBINS.

ROBBINS, WILLIAM
Oct. 2, 1826. Feb. Ct., 1831. Wife: PHEBE, lend
plantation and land, household and kitchen furniture,
utensils and tools, mare, briddle and saddle, 12 hogs,
her choice, cow and calf; son: WILLIAM ROBBINS, 1 S;
gr. sons: MOSES ROBBINS, son of ELIJAH ROBBINS, and
WILEY, son of ELI ROBBINS, all my land to be equally
divided at decease of my wife; residue to sons:
STEPHEN (Exr), ELIJAH, ELEY, and dau CHARITY BRASWELL,
wife of ISAAC BRASWELL, SR. Wit: BRITAIN WILLIFORD,
CALEB DAVIS, MORGAN JACKSON.

ROBERSON, ARCHELAUS
Jan. 11, 1803. May Ct., 1804. Wife & Extx: MARY,
336 A tract adjoining Beaverdam Swamp, SAMUEL RUFFIN,
JONATHAN ROBERSON, RHODA ROBERSON, Stokes old field,
and Bryry Branch during life or widowhood, reversion
to son JAMES; wife also to have perishable estate,
cattle, etc., furn. tools for widowhood or life,
reversion to chil; dau: MARY JOHNSON, 100 A tract on
lines of SAMUEL RUFFIN, SAMUEL TAYLOR, ? DUNFORD ?
EVERITT; sons: ELIJAH, 100 A tract on lines of MARY
JOHNSON, ? TAYLOR, ? EVAN'S Road; JONATHAN, 100 A
tract on lines of SAMUEL RUFFIN, RHODA ROBERSON, and
MARY JOHNSON; dau: RHODA ROBERSON, 75 A tract on lines
of ELIJAH ROBERSON, MARCUS STOKES, EVANS' Road, 2 cows
and calves. Exr: SAMUEL RUFFIN. Wit: KETON EVERITT,
PHILIP DUNFORD, JOHN EVERITT.

ROBERTSON, HARDY
Jan. 9, 1795. Feb. Ct., 1795. ANN GRIMES and RHODA
GRIMES, daus of PHEREBY GRIMES; PATSEY PARISH, dau of

ELLENDER PARISH. Estate divided between chil when they
come of lawful age. Exr: CHARLES COLEMAN, MOSES
ROUNTREE. Wit: BENJAMIN SIMS, FRANCES ROUNTREE.

ROBERTSON, HENRY
     June 23, 1749. Feb. Ct., 1752. Sons: HIGDON, HENRY,
PETER, LEWIS, 100 A tract on both sides of Choeyot
Creek purchased of MARMADUKE KIMBROUGH for £ 100 tho
deed not yet delivered. If sale consumated, I leave
85 A to PETER and 75 A to son & exr: LEWIS; daus:
DEBROAH ROBERTSON, TEMPERANCE WEST. Wit: A. J. SMITH,
WILLIAM OGILVIE, CHRISTOPHER OGILVIE.

ROBERTSON, PETER
     Dec. 12, 1823. Nov. Ct., 1824. Bk. F, p 27. Wife
(not named) to have estate for her life. After wife's
death, lend to dau NANCY and her dau POLLY WILLIAMS,
plantation and house during their single life. After
their decease or marriage, reverts to chil of my son
ALLEN ROBERTSON; dau: NANCY ROBERTSON, 2 tables,
earthenware; gr. dau: POLLY WILLIAMS, dau of NANCY,
furniture, chest, $10; gr. chil: REBECCAH, JAMES A.,
RHODA, ALLEN, chil of my son, ALLEN ROBERTSON; dau-
in-law: POLLY ROBERTSON, be allowed to live where she
now is during life or widowhood and have privilege of
path beginning at road near W. ADAMS, (M or W)
STALLINGS path; son: JOHN $1; residue divided between
3 daus NANCY ROBERTSON, BETSEY WATKINS, RHODA POPE.
Exr: RICHMOND DOZIER, JOHN POPE. Wit: HENRY ADAMS, E.
EXUM.

ROBINS, THOMAS (Planter)
     Dec. 4, 1770. Jan. Ct., 1776. Wife: (unnamed),
lend plantation whereon I live, 1 negro, 2 mares,
cattle, sheep, hogs and geese, 2 cows and calves,
sheep and sows, reversion of all to WILLIAM, all furn.,
reversion to daus; son & exr: ROWLAND, plantation
whereon he lives bought of BOYETT, 1 negro, colt and
horse; sons: SIMON, plantation bought of MILLS
BAREFIELD, 1 negro, mare, horse, cattle, sheep, hogs
and geese bought of MILLS BAREFIELD; remainder cattle
hogs and sheep to be divided equally between daus;
Son: WILLIAM, remainder household goods, tools and

conveniences at mother's death. Exr: WILLIAM BLACKBURN.
Wit: WILLIAM ROBINS, ROBERT ROGERS, WILLIAM ROGERS.
Will drawn by WILLIAM BLACKBURN.

ROBINSON, JONATHAN
     Oct. 14, 1784. Nov. Ct., 1784. Wife: PATIENCE, all
land, household furn., horse, mare, all cattle, sheep,
hogs: At her death land divided between 7 chil; sons:
WILLIS, WILEY, JOHN and REDDIN, all land sold and
divided equally between 4 sons; daus: WINEA, MILBERRY
and ELVY, stallion to be sold money divided between
3 daus; 2 mares to be sold, money divided between all
chil. Exr: ROBERT PEAL, WILLIAM DICKINSON. Wit: EDMUND
STUCKEY, WILLIAM ATKINSON.

RODGERS, TRISTRAM
     Jan. 16, 1799. Aug. Ct., 1799. Wife (unnamed),
lend plantation with all utensils, furniture, stock
of horses, cattle, hogs and sheep, provisions for her
life or widowhood. Residue of personal property to be
divided equally among all chil; son ?: DANIEL, land
on E side of Spring Branch adjoining WILLIAM ELLIS;
sons: WILLIS' land E side Spring Branch adjoining
JOSHUA BENTLEY; LEVI, Manor Plantation lying between
Spring Branch and Long Branch, furniture, colt; STEPHEN,
furniture; daus: WINNAFORD WHITLEY, ELIZABETH and
DOICY RODGERS furniture each. Exr: WILLIAM ELLIS, LEVI
RODGERS. Wit: SOLOMON BARFIELD, JOSEPH WINSLOW, MATTHEW
SPEIGHT.

ROGERS, JOHN, SEN'R
     No Date. Nov. Ct., 1770. Wife & Extx: RACHEL, all
estate for her life, reversion to chil of deceased son,
JOHN ROGERS. Exr: JOHN ROGERS, JR. Wit: WILLIAM MIZELL,
BENJAMIN PIPPEN, WILLIAM ROGERS.

ROGERS, JOSIAH
     Mar. 22, 1844. Nov. Ct., 1844. Bk. F, p 316. Wife:
ELIZABETH residue of all my property, widowhood or life
estate; Chil: BENJAMIN; DANIEL, bay horse; dau: NANCY
ROGERS; JOHN ROGERS, 50¢; daus: SALLEY HINSON and hus-
band and RICHARD HINSON, 50¢; ADALINE (?) AMANDA ROGERS.
Exr: BENJAMIN C. D. EASON (of Green Co), MARIANNA ALLEN.

No Wit mentioned.

ROSE, CHRISTAN (CHRISTIAN)
    Dec. 14, 1829. May Ct., 1830. Bk. F, p 116. (Relation of legatees not stated) KINCHEN ROSE, furniture, cow and calf; WILLIS WELLS of Edgecombe Co., 2 hogs; MICAJAH ROSE, of Edgecombe Co., 2 hogs; residue to be equally divided amongst the hears; Note:- No Executor, no witnesses. MICAJAH ROSE, ADM. Entered into $200 bond, JOHN PARKER, GRAY LITTLE, Securities.

ROSE, ROBERT
    May 29, 1816. Nov. Ct., 1820. Bk. E, p 245. Son: REUBEN, 5 S; daus: ELIZABETH TREVATHAN, wife of HENRY TREVATHAN, Ⳑ 12 - 10 S; SARAH CANADY, Ⳑ 21 - 10 S, furniture; residue divided equally between 5 chil; WILLIAM (Exr), AARON, MATTHEW ROSE, and SARAH CANADY and ELIZABETH TREVATHAN. Exr: JACOB ING. Wit: ISRAEL HOUSE, MOSES JOHNSON (JOHNSTON in Clerk's notation).

ROSS, ANDREW
    Apr. 14, 1761. June Ct., 1761. Wife & Extx: SARAH, all moveable estate during life or widowhood, reversion to chil; daus: SARAH, plantation at Sappony Meadows; JUDITH, tract on Sappony Creek, also 1 on Stony Creek; ANN, to her and her heirs, plantation on Stony Creek whereon my son JAMES lived; MARY, plantation on which I live; dau-in-law: ESTHER ROSS, plantation where my late son ANDREW ROSS lived, during widowhood, reversion to my dau ELIZABETH; ELIZABETH, 1 negro at death of mother; sons-in-law: WILLABY TUCKER, WILLIAM PITTMAN, JAMES STALLINGS, my wearing apparel. Exrs: WILLABY TUCKER, WILLIAM PITTMAN, JAMES STALLINGS. Wit: JOHN MOORE, WM. ANDERSON, THOMAS PRICE.

ROSS, DANIEL
    Apr. 6, 1761. June Ct., 1761. Father & exr: ANDREW ROSS, all real and personal property. Exr: WILLIBEA (WILLOUBY ?) TUCKER, WILLIAM PITTMAN, JAMES STALLIENS (STALLINGS). Wit: SHERROD HAYWOOD, MARY ROSS (a Quaker), SARAY TUCKER.

ROSS, DANIEL

July 3, 1781. Aug. Ct., 1781. Wife: SARAH, lend
during life or widowhood all land, 1 negro, 10 cows
and calves, 5 young cattle, 20 sheep, furn., tools, 2
mares, 3 negroes, all pewter, 1 distill, blacksmith
tools, 36 hogs, also desire my mother and father-in-
law to be supported out of my estate for 12 mo.; lend
unto my mother 1 cow and calf until my son DANIEL come
of age, 5 beds of furn., to deliver 1 to each child at
maturity, also lend my wife, horse, side saddle, saddle
cloth, loom and gear, 6 cattle, 8 sheep, 10 hogs until
dau ANN comes of age, also lend wife, horse, flaxwheel,
5 cattle, 8 sheep, 10 hogs until dau JUDITH come of
age, also lend all residue; reversion to daus ANN &
JUDITH; son: DANIEL, all lands, 1 negro, distill,
blacksmith tools lent his mother, 1 cow and calf and
saddle; daus: MARY and SARAH, 1 negro each; ANN, JUDITH.
Exr: JOHN BATTLE, REDMUN BUNN. Wit: ELISHA BATTLE, JR.,
MICHAL HORN, LURANA HORN.

ROSS, JOHN S. (Planter)
June 9, 1826. May Ct., 1828. Bk. F, p 87. Sister:
MARGARET SIMPSON ROSS, to share with sister ELEANOR
the plantation whereon I live, cattle, horses, etc.,
also my right to property in Washington, inherited
from our Mother, give to her negro and chil; sister
ELEANOR POLLOCK ROSS, 1 negro and chil; it is my desire that they have all negroes, and that they should
remain on plantation until ELEANOR reaches maturity,
then property divided, and by no means to have negroes
ill used or separated one from another. Negro Ned to
have a small place on farm to live and he not to be
made to work, but be well taken care of. Exr: father,
WILLIAM ROSS, EDMUND D. MACNAIR. Codicil mentions
Little friend THOMAS A. MACNAIR. Will written in own
handwriting, no witnesses, proven by oaths of RALPH
E. MCNAIR, EPHRAIM DICKEN, DANFORD RICHARDS.

ROSS, KALLUM
Dec. 8, 1760. Dec. Ct., 1760. Wife & Extx:
ELIZABETH, furn, 1 mare, 2 pewter dishes, 6 pewter
plates, 2 basons, Iron Pott, large chest, lend 1 ne-
gro for widowhood, reversion to son DANIEL; son & exr:
DANIEL, negro, all rest estate; daus: JUDE RICKS and

ANN RICKS, 1 negro each. Wit: JACOB HILLIARD, THOMAS
WILLIAMS, WILLIAM ROBINSON.

ROSS, WILLIAM
    Dec. 8, 1760. Dec. Ct., 17__ (torn) Bk. A, p 7.
Wife & Extx: ELIZABETH, furniture, 2 pewter dishes,
6 pewter plates, 2 basons, 1 iron pot, 1 large chest;
negro wench, Sarah; daus: JUDA RICKS, negro boy, Pompey;
ANN RICKS, negro, Dinah; son & exr: DANIEL ROSS, negro
boy, Jacob. Wit: JACOB HILLIARD, JUN'R, THOMAS WILLIAMS,
JUN'R, WILLIAM ROBESON, JUN'R.

ROUNDTREE, LEWIS
    Sept. 20, 1849. May Ct., 1850. Bk. F, p 445. Wife:
ELIZABETH, lend 230 A of tract on which I live, including mansion house, outhouses, etc, in lieu of her
dower; 2 negroes, George and Fanney, all horses not
herein disposed of, all cattle, sheep and hogs, household and kitchen furniture, family carriage, all carts,
crop and provisions, tools, cider barrels, brandy still,
poultry, reversion of negroes and perishable property
to daus; sons: NATHAN and LEWIS, each to have 1/2
residue of land whereon I live, also horse; SARAH
JORDAN, wife of THOMAS JORDAN, negro Sam and $1000;
daus: ELIZA DANIEL, (wife of WILLIE DANIEL); HARRIET
ELLIS (wife of J. G. ELLIS); PENELOPE; ELIZABETH;
TREASEA, $500 for education; and, MARGARET ROUNDTREE,
$500 for education. These 6 daus to have 32 negroes.
Sons & Exrs: MOSES, $300, to equalize his portion;
WILLIE, $600 to equalize his portion. Wit: JACOB S.
BURNES, BARRON (?) WATSON, ELISHA BARNES.

ROUNTREE, NATHAN H.
    Sept. 4, 1837. Nov. Ct., 1837. Wife: EMELIZA,
estate in fee simple... provision for maintaining and
education of chil: THADEUS and MARGARET ROUNTREE. Exr
and friends: JOSEPH R. LLOYD, CLEMENS DARDEN. Wit:
BEN M. JACKSON, NATHANIEL M. TERRELL.

ROUNDTREE, WILLIE
    May 12, 1847. May Ct., 1847. Bk. F, pp 362-3. Sons:
WILLIE ROUNTREE, land on Contentnea Creek, known as
the BARNES Place, on the Creek...to JAMES SIMMES; land

on N side of Hominy Swamp, beginning at Hominy Swamp
Bridge...EDWIN BARNES (deceased) line...CADER ROUNTREE'S
line to ELIZABETH AMASON'S line; son: JONATHAN ROUNTREE,
tract on the S side of Hominy Swamp, adjoining land of
SETH WARD, BRIANT BARNES and his bro. WILLIE ROUNTREE,
land on S side of Hominy Swamp known as the Old Place,
or "Rich Neck". Gr. dau: MARY ANN ROUNTREE, 1/2 share;
my girl chil. (unnamed), share equally in residue, negroes and land. Exr: JOHN W. FARMER, JAMES J. TAYLOR.
Wit: WESTRY SWIFT, WILLIAM MUMFORD.

ROUTH, WILLIAM
    Mar. 9, 1803. May Ct., 1803. Son: ROBERT, 210 A
manner (manor) plantation also 6 1/2 A adjoining bought
of JOHN MERCER, also 55 A pine woods land by name of
Occoneches, adjoining JOHN MERCER and BAKER, 1 negro;
daus: NANCY, ELIZABETH, SALLY, CATHERINE, $600; 2 ne-
groes each. All other land, stock, chattels etc to be
sold, residue divided between NANCY, ELIZABETH and
SALLY. Exr: JAMES WILKINS, JOHN MERCER. Wit: THOMAS
WELLS, DOWNIN HENDREN. (?).

ROW, WILLIAM
    Mar. 31, 1761. June Ct., 1761. Wife & Extx:
CHRISTIAN ROW, all lands and living for her widowhood,
reversion to chil (unnamed). Wit: CORNELIUS JORDAN,
QUINN BEST, MOSES COLEMAN.

RUFFIN, BENJAMIN
    Mar. 27, 1795. May Ct., 1795. Wife: SARAH, lend
my land and "Little Improvement" whereon I live, residue; daus: WINEFRED DILLIARD, wife of LUKE DILLIARD,
furniture; LUCY, colt, 1 whitefaced heiffer and 3
piggs; son: GRAY, horse and bridle, red cow bought at
sale of estate of JESSE DELOACH, dec'd; dau: PURITY,
furniture, 4 pigs; son: WILLIAM, filly, 1 heiffer,
sow and 4 pigs; daus: POLLY, speckled cow, spotted
sow; FAITHEY and PENNY, furniture; sons: JOHN and LAMON
(Exr), reversion in land. Wit: ELIJAH HORN, JOHN RUFFIN,
SIMEON HORN.

RUFFIN, ELIZABETH
    June 3, 1850. Aug. Ct., 1851. Bk. F, pp 458-9

ELIZABETH FRANCIS RUFFIN, bed and stead and its necessary furnishings, black chest; SALLY RUFFIN, 1/2 doz blue edge plates, 1 large pot, and 1/2 doz. cups and saucers; POLLY TAYLOR, a spider with a lid on it, a desk and 1/2 doz. plates; ELIZABETH ANN THOMAS, 1 black safe, pr. flat irons, half doz. table spoons, coffee pot, glass sugar dish; SAMUEL H. RUFFIN, 1 bottle, a pitcher, a hard jug, and a hammer. Residue to be given SALLY RUFFIN. Wit: C(HURCHILL) B. KILLEBREW, C. H. JENKINS.

RUFFIN, LUCY
    Undated. Prob. May Ct., 1838. Son: JACOB RUFFIN, saddle, bridle and shotgun; residue to be sold and divided amongst my 4 sons: JACOB, THOMAS, DAVID and DICKINSON RUFFIN as they arrive at the age of 21 yrs. Exr and Friend: JESSE KNIGHT. Wit: BRYAN B. GATLIN, RICHARD POND.

RUFFIN, LAMON
    Nov. 3, 1809. Aug. Ct., 1828. Bk. F, p 93. HENRY JOHN GRAY RUFFIN son of my bro. ETHELRED RUFFIN, and his wife MARY, residue and remainder of my estate. Exr: Bro. ETHELRED RUFFIN; neph, HENRY J. G. RUFFIN. No Wit., proven by oaths of SPENCER L. HART, MOSES SPICER, RANDOLPH COTTEN. Caveat: JOSEPH R. LLOYD, Esq. (Tarboro, N. C.) in order to try the validity of the paper writing purporting to be the last will and testament of LAMON RUFFIN, dec'd, now in Edgecombe Court of Pleas Sessions you are at liberty to enter a caveat thereto in my name if you think proper. Respectfully yr. obs. (signed) SALLY KILPATRICK; Franklin County, Aug. 20, 1828.

RUFFIN, MARY
    Feb. 12, 1817. Aug. Ct., 1818. Bk. E, p 203. Daus: SALLY HAYWOOD, 2 negroes; CHARITY ANN WOOD, 1 negro, furniture and looking glass; sons: WILLIAM H., furniture; JAMES L., shall be relieved of obligation for notes for money which I may hold against him; residue divided amongst 3 sons; Exr & son: HENRY J. G. RUFFIN. Wit: JOHN R. THOMAS.

RUFFIN, SAMUEL

Nov. 8, 1798. Nov. Ct., 1798. Bro: HENRY JOHN GRAY
RUFFIN, negro, also $400, this money to be raised and
gotten from the debts due on Medical Books of Dr.
HAYWOOD and myself, this money I want laid out by executor for purpose of giving said HENRY a liberal education, my will and desire is that sd HENRY be first
sent to W. COLWELL, of Guilford Co., 1 yr. at least.
Any residue after the debts due on the books to be divided between my father ETHELRED RUFFIN and DR. HAYWOOD.
Bro: WILLIAM H. RUFFIN, all wearing apparel, saddle and
bridle; father and exr: ETHELRED RUFFIN, all residue.
Exr: DR. HENRY HAYWOOD, LAMON RUFFIN. Wit: R. COTTEN,
SPENCER D. COTTEN.

RUFFIN, SAMUEL

Jan. 4, 1826. Aug. Ct., 1826. Bk. F, p 60. It is
my will and desire that my debts be paid by crop of
turpentine, together with moneys due me. Should that
be insufficient, ex's may sell negro, also lot in town
of Smithfield; Wife & Extx: MARY, residue from sale of
3 negroes, all pork and corn on hand; also large new
Bible, Benedict's "History of the Baptists", (2 vols.)
Booth's, "Reign of Grace", "Profession of Faith",
"Pilgram's Progress", Clay & Daniel's Hymn Books and all
residue; lend wife 70 A tract adjoining lines of THOMAS
DUNFORD, JONATHAN ROBERSON, Evan's old road and WILLIAM
J. RUFFIN. Son: WILLIAM J., furniture, horses, hogs and
1 negro; daus: ELIZABETH M. RUFFIN, 2 negroes, furniture,
1 chest or trunk; ESTHER J. TYSON, 2 negroes, furniture;
CECELIA O. RUFFIN, 2 negroes, furniture, 1 family trunk;
remaining negroes to be hired out and money equally
divided between daus: MARGARET H., JACQUE, MARY A. and
PRUDENCE S. RUFFIN. Exr: son-in-law: WILLIAM TYSON;
READING SUGG. Wit: ASA GRISWOLD, ELIJAH ROBERSON.

RUFFIN, SARAH

Dec. 4, 1779. Feb. Ct., 1780. Dau: OLIVE RUFFIN,
10 cattle, 2 ewes, lambs and 1 negro; gr. daus:
BETTY PRIDGEN, 1 negro; NANCY SHEPPARD, 2 cows and
calves; residue divided between sons and exrs: GRAY
and LAMON. Son & Exr: ETHELRED RUFFIN. Wit: JESSE

DELOACH, PETER STEPHENSON.

RUFFIN, WILLIAM
    July 28, 1830. Aug. Ct., 1831. Bk. F, p 126. All
my property of every kind to be divided between my
bro and exr: JAMES RUFFIN, and 2 sis: RACHEL RUFFIN
and ELIZABETH RUFFIN. Wit: MOSES BAKER, ORREN BULLUCK.

SANDERS, THOMAS
    May 22, 1801. May Ct., 1802. Land in Johnston Co.
where JESSE SANDERS lives, also tract on Mash (Marsh?)
Swamp, Nash Co, to be sold in order to settle just
debts; wife: SARAH, lend plantation and remaining land,
furniture, stock, etc. during her life. Reversion to
sons: CORNELIUS, ISAAC and LUKE SANDERS, and gr. sons
THOMAS SANDERS, son of THOMAS SANDERS, and WILLIAM.
SANDERS, son of ELISHA; daus: ELENDER and MARY, bed
and furniture, each; residue divided between my chil.
and heirs of THOMAS SANDERS, ELISHA SANDERS and SARAH
BARFOOT; each family to have 1/8. Exr: CHARLES COLEMAN,
ISAAC SANDERS. Wit: BAS SIMMS, JETHRO HARRISON, WILLIAM
WHITE, THOMAS HORN.

SANDERS, WILLIAM
    June 5, 1756. Feb. Ct., 1757. Sons: HENRY, 200 A
S side Panther Branch; WILLIAM, 230 A "Mannor planta-
tion"; wife and daus not named Exr: JOSEPH SHAW, JR.
(SHANE?), JOHN BRADFORD, TRISTRIM LOWTHER, SOLOMON
WILLIAMS. Wit: WM. IRBY, JOHN GRICE, WM. HORNSBY.

SARSNETT, HENRIETTA
    May 9, 1820. Nov. Ct., 1820. Bk. E, p 251. Son &
Exr: JOSHUA, negro, furniture, 3 pewter plates, 1
pewter dish, cow and calf; dau: MARTHA LODGE, wife of
LEWIS LODGE, lend 1 negro, reversion to her chil, also
lend furniture, cow and calf, 4 pewter plates, and
dish. Bequeath saddle and all wearing clothes; son &
exr: ZACHARIAH SARSNETT, 1 negro, furniture, 1/2 grist
mill, 1 pewter dish, 3 pewter plates, walnut table,
cow and yearling; son: JOHN SARSNETT, negro, furniture;
gr. son: JAMES, son of RICHARD SARSNETT dec'd, 1 negro,
2 yearlings, 1 pewter bason, 4 pewter plates, iron pot,
$200 divided between chil and gr. son, JAMES SARSNETT,

it being part of note I hold against JOSHUA SARSNETT
and STARLING WALLER, dated Nov. 6, 1818. Exr: STARLING
WALLER. Wit: JOHN RHOADS, MARTHA HAIL.

SARSNETT, RICHARD
 Aug. 6, 1794. Nov. Ct., 1795. Wife & Extx:
HENRIETTA, lend plantation whereon I live, use of all
land, all stock of hogs, cattle, etc. not given away,
remainder of household goods, tools etc during widowhood, use of 2 negroes, reversion of residue to all
chil; son: JOHN, 200 A tract; son & exr: JOSHUA, 200
A plantation whereon I live, with 1/2 grist mill, mare,
cow and calf, heifer, ewe and lambs; Son: ZACHARIAH,
200 A, mare, cow and calf, heifer, ewe and lambs and
furniture; RICHARD, 1/2 grist mill; MARTHA LODGE, negro at mother's death. Wit: STARLING WALLER, JAMES
WILSON.

SASNETT, JOSHUA
 Oct. 12, 1833. Aug. Ct., 1834. Wife & Extx:
ELIZABETH, 2 negroes, furniture, all cattle, hogs,
sheep, mare, riding chair and gear, 2 tables, 6
sitting chairs, sideboard and press; Lend 2 negroes,
and all lands N side Beaver Dam Swamp; reversion to
BERRY and HENRY; sons: READING, 3 negroes, 100 A land
S side of Beaver Dam Swamp; BERRY, negroes; ESTHER
WIGGINS, wife of LAURENCE WIGGINS, chest, table, 1
negro; daus: FANNY, table, 1 negro, 70 A land on
Beaver Dam Swamp near ZACKARIAH SASNETT; MARY DUGGIN,
75 A whereon my house and orchard is situated. Exr:
READING SUGG. Wit: EDWIN BULLUCK, HARMON STALLINGS.

SASNETT, LUCY
 Jan. 11, 1846. Aug. Ct., 1854. Bk. G, p 75. Dau:
ELIZABETH, trunk, bandbox, set of silver teaspoons,
also all remaining estate, 2 negroes, land etc. No
exr; JESSE A. B. THORN, Adm. Wit: JESSE C. KNIGHT,
R. B. SASNETT.

SAUL, ABRAHAM
 Feb. 17, 1769. May Ct., 1771. Wife & Extx: ANN,
lend 2 negroes during widowhood or life; reversion
to gr. sons ABRAHAM and ABSALOM; residue of estate

reversion to 4 gr. chil; Gr. son: ABRAHAM SAUL, 217 A
S side Beaver Dam Swamp or Plat Stone Swamp and lower
side of Lower Grist Branch, 1 negro and, 1 at death of
my wife, furniture, 2 pewter dishes and saw; ABSALOM
SAUL remaining 117 A portion of above tract, 2 iron
wedges, 1 negro now, 1 at death of my wife, furniture,
tools, 2 pewter dishes, 6 deep pewter plates; gr. daus:
MARY SAUL and DORCAS SAUL, 1 negro each; son-in-law:
HENRY SCRUES, still; dau: MARY SCRUES, L 15 – 6 S –
8 d. Exr: JOHN JONES, SR., DAVIS CONNELL. Wit: JAMES
CHURCHWILL, SUCKEY CONNELL, CATY CONNELL.

SAVAGE, CHARLES
    July 4, 1789. Nov. Ct., 1794. Wife: ANN, lend all
estate; reversion to my 8 chil; MILLEY, ZILPHAH, MARY,
RHODAH and PENELOPY; THOMAS, SAMUEL and JOSHUA SAVAGE.
Exr: son-in-law, JAMES IRVIN, ROBERT SAVAGE. Wit:
JAMES BARROW, SION TREVATHAN.

SAVAGE, FRANCES
    Sept. 19, 1843. Nov. Ct., 1845. Bk. F pp 328-30.
Sons: ALSTON, 3 slaves, lent him, to be sold after
his death, and divided among his chil; WARREN, I lend
negro Quay, at his death, to his wife during widowhood. Also negroes Isaac, Jacob and Hannah, and notes
I hold against him, to be cancelled. Saddle, mare and
mule; land E side of road, bought of BAKER STATON; son
& exr: LEMUEL, I lend 5 negroes to be divided among
his chil. I give notes held at my death. Also, my
horse Robnay and land not lent; dau: ELIZABETH SHERROD,
9 negroes during her life, then to her chil, should
any be living. If not, reversion to my chil; also $300,
bed and furniture; gr. dau: FRANCES SAVAGE, 1 negro.
If dies without heirs, to JOSEPH LLOYD SAVAGE and
EMMA ELIZA SAVAGE; MARGARETTA JANE SAVAGE, negro,
Ransom; ALSTON SAVAGE, all land on W side of the road
bought of BAKER STATON. Wit: WM. R. CHERRY, JAMES
KNIGHT, HENRY L. STATON.

SAVAGE, JAMES
    Jan___1834. Nov. Ct., 1834. Bk. F, p 164. Son-
in-law & exr: WILLIAM G. RAWLING, 1/3 all my land and
son-in-law JOHN BARFIELD, 1/3 all my land; EMMY, my

youngest dau, 1/3 all my land, also $100. Wit: JAMES
H. SAVEDGE, CORNELIUS FORMAN.

SAVAGE, LOVELISS (LOVELACE ?)
    May 24, 1802. May Ct., 1807. Dau: KEZZIAH, formerly
wife of JOHN COTTEN, now said to be married to one
JOHN EVANS, 5 S; gr. daus: CHARITY FOUNTAIN, REBECKAH
BRADDY, and dau: MARY ALLEN, 5 S each; gr. sons: LOCK
SAVAGE and ROBERT SAVAGE, 5 S each; WILLIAM SAVAGE,
all land, 1 negro, all cattle, etc. Exr: DEMSEY BRYAN,
RICHARD HART. Wit: JAMES BRYAN, WYATT E. HINES.

SAVAGE, STERLING
    Aug. 13, 1794. Nov. Ct., 1794. Wife & Extx:
SUSANNAH, lend home plantation, 1/2 apple orchard,
negro; Bequeath mare 1/6 stock of cattle, all sheep,
3 sows and pigs, utensils, spinning wheels, chest all
"cheers", all copperware for house, tools, case and
bottles, stone jugs, pare of cotton cards, cart and
wheels, pare iron wedges, 2 pare sheres, all cotton,
flax, wheat, bees, 25 bbl corn, 1200 lb. good pork,
1/3 pewter, 1 raw cowhide and £ 5; sons: STERLING
KING SAVAGE, all my land on the Road, adjoining that
bought of ISAAC HILL, also tract my father gave me,
joining the Road Plantation, 2 negroes, furniture,
colt, 3 bbl corn, 1/6 stock and cattle; JESSE, my part
of land formerly belonging to LOVELISS SAVIDGE, dec'd
negro, £ 25, 1/6 stock and cattle; LOVELISS (LOVELACE),
at mother's death, the manor plantation whereon I live,
land I bought of SLAUGHTER HILL for my son, negro, 1/2
my Savanah land, 1/6 stock and cattle; daus: ELIZABETH,
negro, bed and bedstead, chest, 1/6 cattle, 1/3 pewter;
BRITANNA, negro, bed and furn., trunk, 1/6 cattle,
1/3 pewter. Exr: WARREN SAVIDGE. Wit: W. HYMAN, ROBERT
SAVIDGE.

SAVIDGE, ABSALOM
    Nov. 27, 1815. Feb. Ct., 1816. Bk. E, p 119. Wife:
MARTHA, lend plantation whereon she lives, crop of
corn, fodder, furn., plantation utensils, cider
barrels, and hogshead, mare, saddle and bridle, all
cattle and hogs; dau and extx: ELIZABETH McDOWELL,
10 S; deceased son's chil (unnamed), 10 S each; daus:

SALLY KITCHEN, horse; MARTHA, 10 S; gr. son: PATRICK
McDOWELL, all blacksmith's tools, tar barrels, timber
in cooper's shop, still kettle and worm; gr. dau: NANCY
McDOWELL, residue. Exr: JOHN McDOWELL. Wit: JACOB
SESSUMS, RCHD HARRISON.

SAVIDGE, ALLEIN (ALLEN)
     Apr. 19, 1813. May Ct., 1816. Wife: SARAH, lend
160 A tract whereon I live adjoining lines of WILLIAM
STATON, WILLIAM HOWELL, on S side mill Swamp. Bequeath
all cattle, sheep, hogs, tools, furniture, horse; lend
her negro until dau BRITTANA reaches 18 yrs., at which
time to be divided equally between wife, BRITTANA and
child my wife now goes with; son: SHERROD, 100 A plantation in Conetoe, adjoining CHRISTOPHER HARRELL, 1
negro and chest; sons: KITCHEN and HENRY, negro, bed
and furniture each; dau: BRITTANNA, negro, black walnut table and chest. Exr: FRANCIS HATTON, JAMES DOWNING.
Wit: JOHN C. GRIMES, SARAH HAYNES.

SAVIDGE (SAVAGE), ROBERT
     Mar 12, 1796. May Ct., 1796. Wife: RHODA, lend all
land during life or widowhood. Bequeath bed and furniture, stock, of all kinds. If she should marry, she
to have 1/3 land; daus: MARY and RHODA, bed and furniture each; son: WILLIAM, furniture, and plantation
whereon I live. Residue divided between 3 chil. Exr:
NATHAN MAYO, WILLIAM HYMAN. Wit: DAVID DAVIDSON,
KITCHEN SAVIDGE.

SCARBOROUGH, DAVID
     Nov. 20, 1773. July Ct., 1774. Wife: SARAH, lend
houses and chattels during widowhood; reversion to
2 younger sons: JOEL and LABE (?); residue divided
between other 7 chil: JAMES, TABITHY, SAMUEL, ADORSON,
(ADDISON), SHADRACK, RHODA, SALLEY, JOEL, LABE. No
Exr: Wit: WILLIAM DRAKE, JAMES SCARBOROUGH.

SCARBOROUGH, DAVID
     Apr. 4, 1775. Apr. Ct., 1775. Wife: NANNY, lend
negro, plantation on which we now live, reversion of
land to son HARDY. Bequeath best bed and furn., 1/3
all household goods, 1/3 cattle, sheep and hogs, mare;

sóns: HARDY, and ENOCH, share plantation, GEORGE SMITH,
₤ 5 and 2 yrs later ₤ 5 more; JOHN DUNN, SENIOR, and
wife, EASTER, to be taken care of. Exr: MILES
SCARBOROUGH, WILLIAM SCARBOROUGH.

SCARBOROUGH, JAMES
    May 12, 1835. May Ct., 1836. Bk. F, p 189. Wife:
MARTHA; dau: ZILLY, plantation on the N side of the
Swamp, with all my crop, household and kitchen furni-
ture, brandy still, and cider emplements; 9 negroes
with increase; these negroes by no means to be hired
out, but to remain on the plantation to labor for them
during their natural lives; stock, etc; gr. daus:
MILLISCENT, ELIZABETH and MARTHA EASON and gr. son:
JAMES S. EASON, daus and son of JOSHUA B. EASON; son:
JOHN R. SCARBOROUGH; dau: POLLY P. EASON, wife of
JOSHUA B. EASON; gr. dau: PENELOPY EASON (now EAGLES).
I have given my son JOHN R. SCARBOROUGH the land
whereon he lived, 196 A, also 3 likely negroes when
he went away, and now I give him 4 more, Luke, Gifford,
Orange and Willis, not to be carried away without Law-
ful authority. Exr: STEPHEN WOOTTEN, RICHARD T. EAGLES.
Wit: STEPHEN EDWARDS, RIAL EDWARDS.

SCHENCK, JOHN G. S., Tarborough
    June 8, 1804. Feb. Ct., 1807. JOHN HUDSON, Tarbo-
rough, friend, all lands in Edgecombe Co., town of
Tarborough, Franklin Co., lot in Raleigh to be sold
for benefit of estate; Betty, slave to be set free and
provided with $25 per annum in consideration of her
faithful service. Remaining negroes to be sold, wish
them sold in families only, and to such persons as
will be likely to treat them well and by no means to
speculators who may carry them for a distance; Mrs.
MARY JONES (widow of WILLIE JONES, Esq.), $1000 as
small mark of my respect and esteem; PATSEY JONES,
dau of MRS. MARY JONES, $1000 to be at her disposal
whether she is of age or not, also my set of Curtiss'
Botanical Magazine, also set of silver service for a
Tea Table, consisting of coffee pot, Teapot, 2 sugar
dishes, pair sugar tongs, 2 cream Potts, 4 doz. silver spoons, to be made by best workmen to the north-
ward; SALLY JONES, dau of Mrs. JONES, $1000 at her

disposal after she arrives at age of 15; MRS. ANN
MARIA LITTLEJOHN, silver service same as above; WILLIE
WILLIAM JONES, gold watch value of guinea, procured
from best watchmaker in London. Friends: ROBERT A. JONES,
my little friend, watch like one above; Friends:
BENJAMIN WILLIAMSON, of Northhampton Co, $1000; SAMUEL
McCULLOCH, $1000; BENJAMIN McCULLOCH, $1000; WILLIAM
ROSS of Washington, $1000; JOHN HUDSON of Tarborough,
$1000; JAMES COFFIELD, $1000 to be paid him when he
pays up that sum that may be due on account of the
profits made by the concern, SCHENK & COFFIELD; THOMAS
BLOUNT of Tarborough, $1000; residue of estate after
paying debts and legacies to be divided thus: ANDRENAS
GEORGE SCHENCK, bro of Riga, Russia, 1/4 residue;
GUSTAVE THEODORE SCHENCK, bro of Riga; CARL HEINRICH
SCHENCK, bro of Riga, these 2 bros. to share remaining
3/4 residue, upon express condition that they pay my
dear mother, if living, $200 per year. Reversion to
chil of bros. However, if bros. die childless I wish
my exr to provide my mother $200 per annum in manner
as they may judge best as long as she lives. And in
case Brothers die childless, their part to be divided
between the following: MRS. MARY JONES, 1/10; PATSEY
JONES, 1/10; ROBERT ALLEN JONES, 1/10; SALLY JONES,
1/10; MRS. ANN MARIA LITTLEJOHN, 1/20; BENJ. WILLIAMSON
(Northampton), 1/10; SAMUEL McCULLOCH, 1/10; BENJ.
McCULLOCH, 1/10; WM ROSS (Washington), 1/10; THOMAS
BLOUNT, 1/20.
    It is my wish that my Exr. make earliest inquiry
about my brothers and their situation and should they
be in needy circumstances, that they be so good as to
make them such remittances from time to time as they
with propriety can do. I do not wish them on hearing
of legacies left them to be tempted to leave home and
occupation, which might tend to injure them more than
the value of legacy they are to receive. Exr: WILLIAM
ROSS, of Washington, N. C.; JOHN HUDSON, Tarborough.
Note:- Interesting Will.
    Codicil Oct. 3, 1806. JOHN SCHENCK ROSS, son of
WILLIAM ROSS of Washington, N. C. To him I bequeath
plantation near Tarborough, now under lease to JOHN
FELEADER, who shall be discharged of one years rent;
WILLIAM BOYLAN, Raleigh, N. C. my house and lot in

Raleigh; DANIEL REDMOND, $500, also pay him any debt
that I may owe him; WILLIAM ROSS, Washington, N. C.,
$2000; Miss MARIA BAKER, dau of JACOB BAKER, merchant
of Phila., $500, also my gold watch with suitable chain;
MRS. CATHERINE COMEGYS, wife of CORNELIUS COMEGYS of
Baltimore, $500; JOHN COMEGYS, merchant of Baltimore,
my pheton, and pair small bay horses; BENJAMIN COMEGYS,
merchant of Baltimore, my pr. large bay horses.

In case none of my Brother nor their children may
be found their legacies to be divided between BENJAMIN
COMEGYS, JOHN COMEGYS and CORNELIUS COMEGYS, jointly
with legatees of residue estate mentioned in will. I
request friends COMEGYS to assist ex's in search for
brotners or their children. LEWIS, slave, if he wishes
to become free, JOHN COMEGYS shall see that he is man-
umitted in legal and proper manner. Wit: ROB'T DONALDSON,
WILLIAM H. TOD, JOHN W. BAKER.

SCRUSE, WILLIAM
    Dec.24, 1760. Mar Ct., 1761. Bk. 8, p 23. Wife &
Extx: ANNE life estate; son: JOHN, 100 A land joining
land purchased of JOHN PARISH; 150 A land lying on
Griffin's Swamp; son: HENRY SCRUSE, 100 A land where
I now live, and 150 A land on Griffin's Swamp; dau:
MARY SCREWS, 1 long chest. Exr: FRANCIS SPIVEY (?).
Wit: ISAAC FARGUSON, BENNET CREED (?) CREECH (?),
THOMAS DANIEL, JOHN J. BYNUM.

SELLERS, BENJAMIN
    Jan. 3, 1761. Mar. Ct., 1761. Wife & Extx: SARAH,
life estate; reversion to youngest son: SIMON SELLERS;
sons: ELISHA SELLERS, and BENJAMIN SELLERS, 5 S each;
residue to be divided between wife and chil now living
with her. Exr: WILLIAM DORTCH. Wit: ROBERT THOMPSON,
CATTREN SELLERS, MATTHEW SELLERS.

SESSOMS, ELIZABETH
    May 6, 1797. Nov. Ct., 1798. Son & Exr: JOSEPH,
2 mares, colt, still, pot and 2 chairs; daus: AMEY,
MILDRED and CLAREY SESSUMS, a chest and furniture,
each; gr. dau: ROSANA SESSUMS, furniture; ELIJAH
MOORE and RICHARD BELL (does not state relationship),
10 S each; son: ELMORE SESSUMS, 10 S; residue to be

sold and divided between JOHN, JOSEPH, MILDRED and
CLARY SESSUMS. Wit: JOHN BATTS, WILKINSON MABRY.

SESSUMS, RICHARD
     Apr. 22, 1769. May Ct., 1769. Bk. E, p 173. Wife
& Extx: SARAH use of 5 negroes her lifetime and horse;
dau (illegible) HART, 5 S; son: JACOB SESSUMS, land
lying on Coneto Swamp, I purchased of THOMAS WILLS,
known as BRYANT Islands; 3 negroes, cattle, stock, 1/2
my great still containing about 75 gals; son & exr:
ISAAC SESSUMS, all remaining land and tenaments on N
side of Maple Swamp; Grist mill and all my land on S
side of said Swamp, negroes, Benborough, Simon and
George, negro girl, Nell, after wife's decease. She
to have remainder of my great still, Blacksmith's tools,
bed and furniture, 15 head cattle; dau: PATIENCE COFEL
(COFFIELD ?), 2 negro girls, furniture, 4 head cattle;
son: SOLOMON SESSUMS, 360 A land on N side of Tar
River bought of ROBERT CLARY; 2 negro boys, 1 girl and
her increase after decease of my wife SARAH; L 50 Va.
money; horse Dolphin, bed, fruniture, stock. Wit:
MICAJAH LITTLE, SARAH BRYAN.

SESSUMS, ELIZABETH, Town of Tarborough
     Oct. 5, 1834. May Ct., 1835. Bk. F, p 173. Son
& Exr: ISAAC, all lands devised to me by my husband
SOLOMON SESSUMS and which lie N side Tar River, 4
negroes, the bedstead that stands in my bedroom, sideboard and all glass and crockery that stand on it, my
still, 1 mule, gig, all stoneware and kitchen furn.,
my silver tablespoons, farming utensils, 2 brass
candlesticks, brass kettle, 1/2 my sitting chairs,
1 pr. andirons which are in my bedroom, blacksmith's
tools, the trunk which belonged to his bro: NOAH, and
a paper trunk in which I keep my papers. Dau:
CHARLOTTE DANCY, 2 negroes, china press, all crockery—
ware not given away; large work basket, parasol, hackle,
1/2 sitting chairs, linen wheel, large wash tub, all
wearing apparel, bed clothes, looking glass, table
cloths, towels and carpets, also andirons which stand
upstairs, loom gear, my trunk that stands in a fram;
gr. dau: DELBI (?) DANCY, 1 negro, bed and furniture
with a pair of net valances, silk quilt, dressing

box, small trunk; gr. sons: WILLIAM DANCY, filly, $150; JOHN, 1 negro; and gr. dau: ELIZABETH DANCY, small bed, paint box and $100; gr. son: DAVID SESSUMS, 1 negro; (?) PENELOPE ABBINGTON, bureau; gr. sons: HENRY L. IRWIN, THOMAS B. IRWIN, these 2 to have 1 negro, 1 bed and furniture, knives and forks, silver spoons, wire siene, shovel and tongs, and cow and calf; (?) ALAVANA BELL bed and bedstead, 1 sheet and counterpane, pillows & bolster; (?) EMILIZA ROUNTREE, bed, sheet, counterpane, pillows and bolster; (?) MARY WILSON, same as above; Sis: MARY GREGORY, large china bowl; (?) MARY KILLABREW, banbox, bonnet, safe, cloak, also $50; (?) POLLY LANGSTON, $20. Wit: JOSEPH R. FLOYD, EPHRAIN DICKEN.

SESSUMS, ISAAC
Nov. 14, 1784. Feb. Ct., 1785. Son: RICHARD SESSUMS, all my estate, lands, negroes; sell perishables, discharge just debts. Exr: THOMAS HODGES. Wit: ROBT. DIGGES, JOHN DOLVIN.

SESSUMS, JACOB
Apr. 6, 1792. May Ct., 1792. Wife: FRANCES, lend use of 2 negroes, a horse named Fly, furniture, 3 cows, calves, stock, 10 head sheep; dwelling, land where I now live, bought of JOHN NORWOOD; son & Exr: ALEX SESSUMS' land bought of WILLIAMS NELMS; daus: ALICE and REBECCA SESSUMS, 2 negroes, furniture, and £ 20 each; POLLY and ELIZABETH SESSUMS, 2 negroes and furniture, each; sons: ROBERT SESSUMS, land I bought of ELISHA RHODES in fork of Moore's Swamp and Maple Swamp, joining tract I bought of DAVID WYAT; 1 negro, bed and furniture; JACOB SESSUMS' tract of land I bought of WILLIAM BYRD; tract I bought of RICHARD SHIP, dwelling house, manor plantation where I now live. Exr: bro, SOLOMON SESSUMS.Wit: ARCHD DANCY, EDWIN DANCY, THOMAS TERRY.

SESSUMS, NICHOLAS
May 28, 1764. Oct. Ct., 1764. Wife: ELIZABETH SESSUMS, use of my whole estate her lifetime; son: THOMAS SESSUMS, furniture, my wearing clothes, 1/2 my still, 1/2 my orchard, horse, and mare for use on plantation; daus: ELIZABETH DUFFIELD, RACHEL PARKER, LURANA DUNN, ANN DUNN, SARAH MARLEY, 5 S each; sons: WILLIAM SESSUMS, 100 A of land joining SIZEMORE'S

line in Contenea in Edgecombe Co; NICHOLAS SESSUMS,
whole of my estate after my wife's decease to take
care of his younger bro. THOMAS SESSUMS during his life;
1/2 my still and orchard; shall help maintain my wife.
Exr: NICHOLAS SESSUMS. Wit: JOHN SKINNER, BENJAMIN
FAIRCLOTH.

SESSUMS, SOLOMON, Town of Tarborough
     Nov. 22, 1817. Feb. Ct., 1818. Wife: ELIZABETH, lot
where I now live; land purchased of SIMON NEWSOME; negroes Sterling, old Charles, Celia, Old Gen. Nell and
Rose; horse bought of LEMUEL THIGPEN, riding chair,
2 beds, bedsteads, sideboard, chairs, china, glass
and crockeryware, tables, kitchen furniture; 4 cows
and calves; 1 yoke young steers; china press and things
kept in it, to have the use of her life; then disposed
of as herein directed, the right to cut timber use of
lot I devised to her and $900; dau: SALLY IRWIN, wife
of JOHN ALEXANDER IRWIN, negroes Moses, Pat, Chane,
at her decease divided among her chil, interest on
$400 annually; son & exr: ISAAC, in fee simple lands
on N side of Tar River, subject to provision made for
my wife etc; 140 A of land in Tennessee, storehouse
and lot in town of Tarborough fronting Court House
Square; negroes, John, Adam, Lucy and Little Jin. Dau:
ELIZABETH SESSUMS, negroes, Simon, Silvia, Mary and
chil: Daniel, Julia, Sophia and John; lot in town of
Tarborough on which my blacksmith shop stands; dau:
CHARLOTTE DANCY, negroes Charles, Ben, Lucy and her
2 chil Old Sylvia, a new negro; $400 in money, also
negro Nell and her increase etc; daus: ELIZABETH
SESSUMS and CHARLOTTE DANCY, my Tavern lot and Stable
lot in town of Tarborough, etc; residue to be sold,
debts paid, divided etc. Exr: JOSHUA LAWRENCE. Wit:
JOSEPH BELL, HENRY AUSTIN.

SESSUMS, WILSON
     Mar. 24, 1848. Feb. Ct., 1849. Bk. F, p 423. Wife:
MARY ANN, lend 4 negroes, reversion to chil; bequeath
2 mares, furniture, hogs, cows etc; exr to sell all
land and buy tract for $2500 for home for family, which
I lend to wife MARY, reversion to chil; children to be
educated. Exr: JESSE H POWELL, HENRY FOXHALL. Wit:
JOHN G. RIVES, DUKE W. MANN.

SHARP, JOHN
Dec. 12, 1784. Nov. Ct., 1798. Cousin (nephew) &
Exr: JOSHUA (?) SHARP, son of ANN SHARP, all my lands,
plantation I now live on, all my estate, real and per-
sonal, after paying Ŀ 12 to THOMAS LAWRENCE, son of
THOMAS LAWRENCE in schooling; sis: ANN SHARP, in quiet
and peaceful possession during her life, then her son
JOSHUA shall have it all. Wit: JOHN TAYLOR, TEAGLE
TAYLOR, WILLIAM LITTLE.

SHARPE, JOHN P.
Dec. 8, 1845. No Probate Date. Bk. F, p 336. Wife:
NANCY, 1/3 of whole estate; sis: MAHALY BARNES and her
chil, 2/3 whole estate. Exr: ELIAS BARNES, to manage
sister's portion. Wit: JOSIAH LAWRENCE, HENRY B. S.
PITT.

SHEARLEY, HENRY
Nov. 1, 1849. Probated 1849. Wife: ELIZABETH, my
Southerland plantation lifetime,10 negroes in fee simple,
(her choice), half household and kitchen furniture, 5
cows and calves; 4 horses, 4 mules, $1000 cash from
sale of negroes; WILLIAM S. BAKER, negro, Frank; JOSEPH
H. BAKER, $7000 cash; LAURA BAKER, $7000; MARGARET
BAKER, $7000; REDMUND R. DUPREE, $2000, negroes (2)
in trust for benefit of MARTHA BELCHER, wife of HENRY
BELCHER and pay her interest arising, at mother's death
to be divided among her chil; REDMOND DUPREE, $2000
to hold for benefit of ELIZA DUPREE, wife of LEWIS
B. DUPREE, paying annual interest, then to her chil;
DAVID BARLOW $1800 in trust for benefit of HENRY
SHEARLY, JR., interest annually; gr. child, child of
JESSE HYATT:_____HYATT, $200; my dau: PENINA
$10,000 her life; then to her heirs; farm known as the
Hines Place be sold etc. DAVID BARLOW, 5 negroes; Exr:
JOHN L. BRIDGERS. Names of Witnesses blotted out.

SHEARLEY, RICHARD
Mar. 20, 1816. Nov. Ct., 1823. Wife: DELILAH, life
estate; chil NANCY EDWARDS, BYRD, NATHAN; dau: MURPHY
SHEARLEY, $100 each; ELSEY MARLEY, $12; at death of
wife land to be sold, money divided among my chil:
JOHN, HENRY, JAMES, STARLING, RICHARD, DAVIS, and URIAH

SHEARLEY and NANCY EDWARDS, MURPHY SHEARLEY, BYRD
SHEARLEY and NATHAN SHEARLEY. Exr: EDMUND EDWARDS. Wit:
JACOB NETTLES, ELISHA PEELE.

SHEARLY, DELILAH
    Mar. 1, 1827. Aug. Ct., 1827. Bk. F, p 70. Sons:
NATHAN, land, he to pay my son BYRD SHEARLY $12; dau:
MURPHEY WEAVER, $12; dau: NANCY EDWARDS' chil, $12;
BYRD SHEARLY, featherbed and furniture; NATHAN SHEARLY,
featherbed and furniture. Balance to be sold on credit
of 6 mos and divided between sons BYRD SHEARLY and
NATHAN SHEARLY and daus MURPHY WEAVER, NANCY EDWARDS'
Chil etc. Exr: BENJAMIN WEAVER. Wit: ELISHA PEEL, ALLEN
NETTLES, THOMAS TAYLOR.

SHELLEY, JOHN PHILIP
    June 28, 1749. Aug. Ct., 1749. Sons: PHILIP, land
on Swift Creek, 10 cows and calves, 2 mares, 1 brass
Kettle, 1 iron Kettle and 4 negroes; DANIEL, 100 A on
Swift Creek at the mouth of Tumbling Run, all steers
and hogs and 2 negroes; dau: JUDETH SHELLEY, 2 negroes,
1 large brass Kettle, 1 large iron pot, and Linen
wheel. Remainder of household goods to be sold, and
£ 8 money put to the use of schooling my 3 chil. Exr:
THOMAS MANN. Wit: WILLIAM SMITHES, JEREMIAH MALPASS,
MARGARET TERRY. Impression of head on seal.

SHELTON, WILLIAM
    Apr. 30, 1827. Nov. Ct., 1829. Bk. E, p 107. Wife:
LYDIA SHELTON, life estate; dau: HARRIET HOWARD, 30 A
land, adjoining JAMES; son & exr: JOHN, land, property
sold at wife's decease and divided. Exr: Friend,
FREDERICK LITTLE. Wit: JOHN COBB, AMOS COBB.

SHERROD, J. WILLIAMS
    May 1, 1778. May Ct., 1778. Wife: UNITY, life
estate in plantation I now live on at mouth of Sue (?)
Branch, on the lines of Hatcher's Swamp to Rooty
Branch, up Ruty Branch, Tyancoco Swamp; use of 2 negroes Jack and Cad; use of household goods, stock of
all kinds; chil. not married come of age or marry,
wife to give each 3 cows and calves, bed, 2 sheets,
bolster, horse, sheep; dau: CATRON SUMNER, 1 bed,

2 sheets, bolster; I desire my negroes Jack and Cad
to be kept together for use in raising my chil til
youngest is of age; moveable property sold for ready
money, divided between my 8 chil: RHODA, SOLOMON,
CATHERAIN SUMNER, RACHEL SHERROD, ROBERT JOLLY WILLIAMS,
UNITY and JOHN SHERROD; I lend the use of my still to
my wife while my son JOHN comes of age then to JOHN
SHERROD; Plantation to son: WILLIAMS SHERROD; sons:
JOHN SHERROD, land S side of Ruty Branch where land
lent my wife leaves Unity Branch, strikes Tyancoco
path etc; JOLLY SHERROD, land on Ruty Branch, Jack's
Branch, mouth of Unity Branch, and Hatcher's Swamp;
ROBERT SHERROD, land Jack's Branch and JOHN DIKINSON'S
line, down Hatcher's Swamp to WILLIAM FORT'S line;
cousin (?): JOHN SHERROD, land at mouth of Sue Branch,
Hatcher's Swamp; horse, Gilbert, money in my care be-
longing to him. Exr: ROBERT COLEMAN, JOHN SUMNER,
JAMES WILSON. Wit: W. HAYWOOD, GEORGE LINCH, OLIVE
LINCH.

SHERROD, JAMES
    Jan. 15, 1849. No Probate or Registry. Wife &
Extx: NANCY, all estate during life or widowhood;
should she marry she to have child's part; chil. not
named. Exr: BENNETT BRADLEY. Wit: L. M. WALKER, SAMUEL
D. PROCTOR, S. C. PENDER.

SHIP, RICHARD
    Aug. 23, 1778. Nov. Ct., 1778. Wife & Extx:
ELIZABETH, estate, real and personal, life, when she
doth die my lands in Wake Co. near Nuce river, (Neuse)
to be divided between my 2 sons: EPHRAIM SHIP and TILLER
SHIP; at wife's decease property sold and divided; son
& exr: BENJAMIN SHIP; daus: MARY HOLLOWAY, SUKEY WALL;
sons: RICHARD SHIP, L 5 Proc. money each; Son: WILLIAM
SHIP colt which he has had in his possession and L 150;
Wit: SAMUEL PRICE, SARAH THOMAS, RICHARD SHIP.

SHURLEY, (SHEARLEY-SHIRLEY), SUSAN
    Oct. 3, 1848. Feb. Ct., 1849. Bk. F, p 413. Neph:
HUGH WILKINSON, whole estate for education and support.
JOHN WILKINSON, act as Gdn. Exr: EDWIN B. BRIDGERS.

Wit: ZADOC PEACOCK, WASHINGTON BARNES.

SIMES, CHRISTER (CHRISTOPHER)
Mar. 15, 1833. Nov. Ct., 1833. Not registered. Son:
GARRY, all land, if he should die without heir, rever-
sion to sons: BENJAMIN SIMES and JAMES SIMES; and 2
negroes. Exr: BENJAMIN C. D. EASON. Wit: EDWIN STOKES,
JOHN T. EASON.

SIMMONS (SIMMS ?), EDWARD
Oct. 5, 1735. Oct. Ct., 1746. Wife & Extx: MARY,
dwelling, plantation; daus: ELIZABETH HOLLEY, 40 S;
JANE HOLLEY, 150 A on lower side of Watery Branch;
MARTHA, 3 cows and calves; 2 pewter basons, 3 large
new pewter dishes; 4 pewter plates, 1 5 gal. pott;
TOMAZIN, 3 cows and calves, 2 large pewter basons, 3
large pewter dishes, 4 pewter plates and 3 gal. iron
pott; HANNAH, 3 cows and calves, 2 large pewter basons,
3 large pewter dishes, 4 pewter plates, 1 4 gal. iron
pott; gr. chil: JOHN JACKSON and MARY JACKSON, 2 year
old heifer each. Wit: ANDREW JOHNSON, FRANCES JOHNSON,
BENJ. RAWLINGS.

SIMMS, BENJAMIN
Sept. 17, 1814. Feb. Ct., 1815. Bk. E, p 79. Wife:
CRITTA, for life, house and half of the WILLS and;
the negroes, Jack, Jim and Doll; 4 cows and calves,
10 head sheep, 4 hogs, furniture, and riding chair;
daus: POLLY MINSHEW, negro woman Luce; PATSEY BARNES,
3 negroes Sesar, Jenna and Danson and property given
her at marriage; son & exr: JOHN SIMMS the CHESTER
tract of land; also the RUFFIN land, 2 negroes, Prince
and Dinah, stock etc; 2 sons: BENJAMIN and JAMES SIMMS,
tract of land whereon they now live; 4 negroes Bob,
Jack and Sarah and Venus, equally divided; daus:
SALLEY BARGAM (?), 3 negroes Dick, Peg and Rachel,
horse and 6 head sheep, and property given her at her
marriage; NANCY SIMMS, 4 negroes, Snipe, Hannah,
Champion, Jude; furniture and $200; son: JARREY (?)
SIMMS, half of the WILLS land and after mother's decease the whole WILLS tract, negro Roger; Jack, Jim
and Doll after mother's decease, horse, bridle and
saddle, 6 head sheep, hogs, furniture and Blacksmith

tools; dau: PENINAH SIMMS, 3 negroes Bryant, Anna and
Peter, 174 A of land in Johnston Co. on prong of Black
Creek, furniture, and $100; balance to be equally di-
vided among my heirs. Exr: ELI AMASON. Wit: DAVID JONES,
THEOPHILUS EASON.

SIMMS, JAMES
Sept. 29, 1846. Aug. Ct., 1847. Bk. F, p 377. Wife:
(unnamed), 250 A on Harmony Swamp, the EDWIN field,
ARMSTEAD field, reversion to son BENJAMIN, 6 negroes,
4 horses, 2 mules, 4 cows and calves, 5 sows and pigs,
10 sheep, buggy and harness; sons: (eldest) WILLIE,
929 A tract whereon he lives and 8 negroes; (youngest)
BENJAMIN, tract called THOMAS GRIMES' tract, also home
tract, containing 1093 3/4 A; also 8 negroes, 4 horses,
2 mules, bridle and saddle, 4 cows and calves, 5 sows
and pigs and 6 sheep; daus: ELIZABETH (eldest), wife
of EDWIN BARNES, 432 A tract N side Contentnea Creek,
6 negroes, filley, also $1000; (next oldest) MARTHA,
wife of JOHN DEW, 373 A tract known as Bridge Tract
and ROBBINS tract, 7 negroes, mule, also $1000; PATIENCE,
7 negroes and $5000; MARIAH (MARIA ?), 6 negroes, $5000.
Exr: EDWIN BARNES. Wit: WILLIE DANIEL, ELIAS D. POPE.

SIMMS, JOSEPH
Sept. 12, 1795. Nov. Ct., 1795. Sons: SHADRICK, 1
negro man Aberdeen, negro boy Jim, $500 silver dollars;
SIMON, land he now lives on, appurtenances thereto and
negro Cadge; BENJAMIN, land he lives on etc., negro
Jack; WILLIAM, land he lives on and negro Peter; GARRY
SIMMS, land he lives on etc., negro Aram and Hannah
and $100 silver, sorrel horse; cattle, hogs, sheep,
furniture; daus: PATTY GRICE, negro woman Lil, negro
girl, Jenny, negro Tab, negro boy Aram; SENAH DOWDNA
(?), negro woman Ester, negro girl Rose, negro boy
Cesar, negro boy Linas and $60 silver. Balance divided
among all my chil; brandy still and Blacksmith Tools,
etc. Exr: Sons, SIMON SIMMS, BENJAMIN SIMMS, WILLIAM
SIMMS, GARRY SIMMS (only GARRY SIMMS qualified). Wit:
JESSE FARMER (Quaker.)

SIMMS, WILLIAM
Sept. 2, 1827. Nov. Ct., 1827. Wife: EDE SIMMS,

303

life estate, negroes: Bosun, George, Jude and Chane; 3
horses; furniture, 3 cows and calves (her choice), 2
tables walnut and pine, desk, 3 pots and pot hooks,
Dutch oven, frying pan, griddle, all earthen and crockery
ware, Glassware in cupboard, all my silver spoons, chest,
Weaving loom and gear, 10 head choice sheep, 4 sows
and shoats, 6 choice plows, weeding hoes, 2 axes, 2
iron wedges, all my knives and forks, spade, cycle, 2
barrels brandy, all my cider casks, until my son LEROY
becomes 21, or she marry. Then casks to be divided between children, land adj. HENRY HORNE'S, JAMES SIMMS'
line, Branch in WHITLEY'S line to Great Branch,
DICKERSON'S corner, house, 170 barrels of corn, 4000
lbs of good pork; cart and wheels, riding chair, 35
bu, wheat, 600 lbs. seed cotton, present crop, etc;
sons: JACOB, 3 negroes: Peter, Sary and Wright, rest
of Sary's chil. (names not known); 300 A land in
Johnston Co., sorrel, filly; JESSE, 3 negroes, Tanner,
Peter and John; daus: CHARITY, 2 negroes Ned and
Dililah, mare Lib, 4 head cattle, 6 head sheep, trunk,
called hers, negro boy Charles, also old Bosun at her
mother's death; SALLY SIMMS, 2 negroes, Arthur and
Dinah; Black mare, 4 head cattle, 6 head sheep, and
trunk called hers, also negro boy Mathew; son: THOMAS,
land lying on Great Branch, to HENRY HORN'S Corner to
JUDY DANIEL'S line, negro, Young Bosun; sorrel mare,
with blaze face, sows, pigs that fed at new ground,
3 doz. plain ones, saddle, called his and gun; dau:
POLLY GOIN (?), negroes Stephen and Viney, bay mare
colt, Dymont; 4 head cattle, 6 head sheep, furniture,
trunk negroes Jude and Mann, at her mother's death;
son: LEROY, land, negro boy Joiner, furniture, when
of age, Bay filly, saddle, etc.; dau: PATIENCE SIMMS,
2 negroes, Abby and Washington, when she marries or
is of age; Bunn, a child and George (negroes); sons:
JACOB & JESSE, the residue of my property. Exr: Friend,
JOHN HORN, BENJ. SIMMS. No witnesses mentioned.

SIMMS, ZILLAH
    Mar. 22, 1851. Nov. Ct., 1851. Bk. F, pp 459-60.
Daus: PATIENCE, tract of land known as the PATTY SIMMS
tract adjoining lands of STEVEN WOODARD, negro boy,
furniture; MARIAH SIMMS' land adjoining BENJAMIN SIMMS,

and furniture; MARTHA DEW, negroes; her lifetime, then
to her chil; PATIENCE and MARIAH SIMMS, my gray horse,
buggy and gear; balance to be divided between my sons
BENJAMIN SIMMS and my daus ELIZABETH BARNES and MARTHA
DEW. Son & Exr: WILLIE SIMMS. Wit: JOHN W. FARMER,
JOHN SMITH.

SIMPSON, WILLIAM
Dec. 28, 1822. Feb. Ct., 1823. Bk. E, p 318. Wife:
MOURNING, 1 roan mare, choice of cows and calves, hogs,
etc, $15 in money, etc; at death of wife stock, tena-
manents, etc. to Dau: TEMPEY SIMPSON, also 2 tracts
adj. ROBERT HODGE, COFFIELD'S, ARCHABLE PITTS'___.
Killebrew's Mill Branch, bought of MATTHEW WHITEHEAD,
WILLIS PEELE, JOHN HODGE. Exr: BENJAMIN WILKINSON,
NATHANIEL BILBERY. Wit: WILLIAM W. ARMSTRONG, JOHN
GRIFFIN.

SINGLETON, JOHN
May 16, 1762. Jan. Ct., 1763. Wife & Extx: MARY,
plantation where I now live S of Bear Branch, life
interest and household goods, except 1 chest; son &
exr: JOHN, lands on N side of Bear Branch with new
survey; chest with drawers and all that is in it, new
board whipsaw, furniture etc; son: JAMES, my cupper's
(Cooper's) tools and old whip saw, (out of order);
residue of estate to wife MARY for her own disposing.
Wit: JONATHAN (?) THOMAS, THOMAS AMASON.

SKINNER, DEMPSEY
Apr. 11, 1827. Nov. Ct., 1827. Bk. F, p 74. Wife:
LYDIA, plantation where I now live; 2 negroes, 2 cows
and calves, hogs, 2 mares, riding chair, furniture,
my setting chairs, knives and forks, tables, corn and
fodder, bacon, farming utensils, 4 head sheep, also
Brandy still; Son: WILLIAM, furniture, all property I
am possessed with I have not loaned unto my wife I
wish sold to pay debts, present crop stands for de-
ficiency, if any, residue divided; gr. dau: LYDIA
EASON to have $5 ; Exr: JAMES BARRON. Wit: WM. D.
JENKINS, ENOS HARRELL.

SKINNER, HENRY

Undated. Nov. Ct., 1825. Bk. F, p 49. Wife & Extx:
ELIZABETH (VINES ?) SKINNER, residue of my estate, life
or widowhood, to enable her to raise my chil. in a de-
cent manner. After her death, or marriage, property to
be divided among my chil: LYDIA SKINNER, SALLIE SKINNER,
WILLIAM HASLETON SKINNER, JESSE LITTLE SKINNER, ROBERT
AUGUSTUS SKINNER, GENERAL JACKSON SKINNER, JAMES SKINNER,
AMEY ANN SKINNER, FELITIA LAVINIA SKINNER. Wit: J. S.
SCARBOROUGH, A. ATKINSON, ENOS HARRELL.

SMITH, JOSEPH
Undated. Apr. Ct., 1764. Wife: ELIZABETH, furniture,
horse, stock, etc.; lume (loom), use of plantation
during widowhood, rest of my household goods and movable
effects, etc.; dau: (BARBARA ?), furniture, etc.; sons:
ARCHIBALD, iron pot, 2 iron wedges; NEHIMAH, my biggest
iron pot; ABRAM, a large Puter dish and 3 puter plates;
to my 3 sons all my lands, equally, and never to sell
any one except it be to each other above named, then
to heirs. Exr: WILLIAM HORN, HENRY HORN, SR. Wit:
JOHN MOORE, JOHN THOMAS.

SMITH, RICHARD
Dec. 17, 1756. May Ct., 1757. Wife & Extx: SARAH;
sons: RICHARD, STEPHEN, WILLIAM, 73 A of land each;
BENJAMIN, my plantation; all residue after decease of
wife SARAH to be equally divided between my 6 chil.
Wit: JOHN DOYLE, CHARLES DODSON.

SMITH, THOMAS
Mar. 10, 1757. May Ct., 1757. Wife & Extx: (not
named), Exr: BENJAMIN HALL (HALE). Wit: JOHN JONES,
SUSANNA JONES.

SOARY, ANDREW
Mar. 22, 1818. May Ct., 1818. Bk. E, p 185. Wife:
LUCY, residue of my estate during widowhood, then
divided between all the chil. of SALLY THOMAS and
POLLY BRASWELL; gr. son: HENRY, son of SOLOMON SOARY
(son), furniture, and all the rest of my property lent
to my son SOLOMON SOARY; gr. daus: NANCY and POLLY,
his (SOLOMON'S) daus: SOLOMON SOARY, $25 to pay a debt
to ELI PORTER (?); son: WILLIAM, furniture, shot gun,

Pewter basin, iron pot, etc.; also note I hold against
my son; JOSIAH SOARY, sum of $25. I give son JOSIAH
SOARY all my cider casks, cooper's tools, broad axe,
Pewter basin, small iron pot, and man's saddle; gr. dau:
ELIZABETH SOARY, and dau of LILY THOMAS, furniture;
dau: POLLY BRASWELL, $1, furniture. Exr: ZADOC BRASWELL,
SOLOMON SOARY. Wit: DANIEL LAND, EDWIN BULLUCK.

SOARY, SOLOMON
     Feb. 6, 1850. Aug. Ct., 1855. Bk. G, p 113. Wife
& Extx: CHARLOTTE, all residue of my estate of every
description; dau: LUCY MORGAN, furniture, etc.; gr.
son: RICHARD LODGE and my gr. dau: LYDIA MARGARET
LODGE, chil. of JOSHUA LODGE, dec'd, 25¢ each. Wit:
J(ESSE) C. KNIGHT, P. S. SUGG, JOSHUA KILLEBREW, Esq.
was appointed Adm. and gave bond with W. A. JONES and
JAMES JENKINS.

SOREY, LUCY
     Mar. 24, 1836. Feb. Ct., 1842. Bk. F, p 265. Gr.
dau: MARY SOREY, bed stead and furniture, formerly
belonging to my son WILLIAM, dec'd, 1 table and washing tub; gr. dau: ELIZA SOREY, dau. of my son JOSIAH,
furniture; property divided between my chil: SOLOMON
SOREY (Exr), SARAH THOMAS, POLLY BRACEWELL, JOSIAH
SOREY. No Wit.

SOUTHERLAND, JOHN (SENIOR)
     Jan. 16, 1796. Feb. Ct., 1798. Sons & Exrs: JOHN
JUN'R, negro slave; JAMES, plantation whereon I live;
negro slave, Bofat standing in the house; dutiful dau:
MARTHA SOUTHERLAND, 1 negro girl; dutiful dau: ABBY
SOUTHERLAND, negro girl; dutiful dau: SALLEY SOUTHERLAND,
negro man slave, slaves: Eneh, Vilet, Will and Dick
to be divided amongst my 5 chil. Wit: JOHN INGLES, W.
CLEMENTS, NATHAN MATHEWSON.

SPARKMAN, THOMAS
     Feb. 25, 1808. May Ct., 1808. Bk. D, p 317. Wife
& Extx: WINIFRED, land, plantation, houses, orchards
for life, for support of family til chil. come of age;
filly, briddle, saddle, furniture, 2 pots, Dutch oven,
1 pan, 1 kettle, chest, 2 tables, chairs; 1 negro

$350 to buy a negro boy to serve her; 5 head cattle, 5 sheep, 9 hogs, 4 wheels; sons: REDDICK SPARKMAN, horse, bridle, saddle and gun; WILLIE and THOMAS SPARKMAN to have horse, bridle and saddle each at age of 20; Daus: ELIZABETH, NANCY and SINTHEE, when arrive at age 18 each shall have bed, furniture, etc.; gr. dau: MARTHA SPARKMAN, dau of ELIZABETH at age of 18, bed and furniture; estate divided among 6 heirs, after death of my wife. Exr: WILLIE STANTON. Wit: JAMES SPARKMAN.

SPELL, DREWRY
    Dec. 16, 1781. Feb. Ct., 1782. Son: (not named, evidently infant and motherless). Exrs shall have the keeping and disposal of property as they think best for my son. Father and mother to have use of plantation till son comes of age. If son dies, Brother LEWIS SPELL shall have it. If son dies before he is of age, Father shall have all my personal estate. Exr: Father; Bro., LEWIS SPELL. Wit: M. C. BELCHER, JOHN SPELL.

SPELL, JOHN
    Oct. 7, 1784. Nov. Ct., 1784. Wife: ELIZABETH, lend use of negro girl, Rachel, and her increase, widowhood, reversion to my sons and daus, stock, (illegible) negro Chloe and increase, 150 A of land on the River joining BROWNRIGG, MRS. EVANS and SOUTHERLAND'S lines, sons & exrs: LEWIS, land and negroes; JOHN, land adjoining TEMPLEY'S Survey, SOUTHERLAND and Mrs. EVANS, about 300 A, it being the land he lives on and 1 negro; dau: MARTHA, 1 negro and increase, after death of my wife. Exr: Father (unnamed). Wit: NOAH SUGG, RICHARD SHEARLY.

SPICER, WILLIAM
    June 6, 1820. Nov. Ct., 1822. Bk. E, p 308. Wife: NANCY, bed, 2 sheets, homespun blanket, small poplar bedstead, woman's side saddle, sow and pigs, 300 weight good pork, 3 barrels good sound corn, all the cotton that is now growing, small iron pot, and hooks, 2 Pewter plates, 1 griddle, cow and calf; daus: KESIAH BAILEY (?) furniture; SALLY PITTMAN furniture; son: JAMES SPICER'S deceased heirs, 20 S; daus: MARY JONES and MARGARET JONES, furniture; sons: WILLIAM SPICER,

$50; MOSES SPICER, gray horse, bay mare and colt, 1 ash, banister bedstead, 1 poplar bedstead, all my cooper's tools. Balance estate sold, debts paid, residue divided. Exr: MOSES SPICER. Wit: ORREN D. COHOON (CALHOUN ?), ETHELRED COHOON.

SPIER, JAMES
      Jan. 12, 1761. Mar. Ct., 1761. Wife & Extx: ELIZABETH, have use of plantation, etc. life, or widowhood; son & exr: JOHN, 1 S; sons: JAMES, 1 S; NATHANEIL, Ł 25 Va. money; DEMPSEY, Ł 25 Va. money; son & exr: WILLIAM, 250 A of land on S side of Fishing Creek, plantation he now lives on, and 1 A on N side of Fishing Creek at his landing, in Halifax Co.; son-in-law: ROBERT KNIGHT, 40 S Va. money; son-in-law: FREDERICK SAULS (?) and my dau FRANCES SAULS, negro girl Rose, said negro girl to my gr. son: MOSES (NORRIS ?) SPIER, son of JOHN, sons: WRIGHT, negro girl and 200 A of land, adjoining his bro WILLIAM, land; DAVID, negro boy, Robin, plantation I now live on; KINDRED, negro boy Ned and land. Negro Wench, Cate, be sold to pay debts. Wit: ROBERT ROBESON, DANIEL DOUGHTIE, DEMPSEY DOUGHTIE, JOHN HENNEGAN.

SPIER, JOHN (School Master)
      June 18, 1783. Feb. Ct., 1790. Wife & Extx: CHRISTIAN, estate for life unless she waste it, then sold and divided amongst my chil; son: JOHN, plantation; daus: ROSY, furniture; ABSALA PITMAN' if dies without heirs, her part to be divided between PHILIP SPIER and BENTON SPEIR. Son and Exr: HARRIS SPIER. Wit: WILLIAM SPEIR, ANN SPEIR, MOOR SPIER, MATHEW ING.

SPIER, WRIGHT
      Jan. 31, 1777. No probate date. Wife & Extx: ELIZABETH and son & exr: WILLIE (?) SPIER, all my Estate, after debts are paid. Land to be sold and other land bought more satisfactory to my wife and son. Wit: BENJ. COFFIELD, THOS. DURLEY, BRUMBLE COKER.

STALLINGS, ELISHA
      Feb. 23, 1790. Feb. Ct., 1792. Wife & Extx: MARY, Chil: HARDY, ORPHA, REDICK, LOTT, JOSEPH, ELIJAH and

NATHAN STALLINGS, land, utensils, etc; Exr: WILLIAM
BROADRIBB, WILLIAM FORT. Wit: JOHN MURPHREE, ELIJAH
STALLINGS, MOSES WOODARD.

STALLINGS, JAMES
    May 20, 1830. May Ct., 1834. Bk. F, p 157. Gr. son:
WILLIAM POPE, son of WILLIAM POPE of Tenn, 1 negro; gr.
chil: JOSEPH, MARY ANN, SALLEY, ADELINE, and THOMAS
WEST POPE, chil. of WILLIAM POPE of Tennessee, 1 negro
each; gr. dau: TABITHA ROBERTSON, dau of WILLIAM
ROBERTSON, dec'd, $150; chil of my dau MARTHA by her
late husband JOHN DRAUGHON; $900; gr. dau: REBECAH
TAYLOR, wife of ALLEN TAYLOR, 200 A tract on S side
Swift Creek, known as JOSIAH POPE tract for her life,
reversion to her chil. that shall be living; grt. gr.
chil, born of my gr. dau: REBECCAH TAYLOR, 700 A tract
lying S side Swift Creek known as WM. POPE Tract, to
be equally divided; sister: SELAH STALLINGS and to my
old negro woman Esther, lend 50 A tract lying on S
side Brown's Branch, known as the Thorn Tract, and at
their deaths I give and bequeath said land to son-in-
law WILLIAM POPE of Tenn; "My will and desire is that
my old negro woman Esther be liberated from slavery
for her meritorious services, that a sufficiency of
my estate be reserved for to support her comfortably
during her natural life, that she be not removed from
these parts to no other, contrary to her wish, and request, and appoint my friend JACOB ING, who is one of
my executors to look specially to the care of said negro Esther."
    Son-in-law: WILLIAM POPE of Tenn., all residue of
my lands not previously bequeathed in this will. Remaining residue to be divided thus: 1/2 to WM. POPE,
other half to chil of my dau MARTHA, dec'd, by her
first husband WM. ROBERTSON and last husband, JOHN
DRAUGHON. Exr: JACOB ING; son-in-law, WILLIAM POPE.
Wit: HENRY ADAMS, TABITHA VARDEN.

STALLINGS, JOHN
    Dec. 31, 1779. Aug. Ct., 1780. Residue to wife:
JUDA STALLINGS, plantation and land, reversion to son:
SIMON; sons: JAMES, WILLIS (Exr), and JOHN, 5 S each.
Exr: ELISHA STALLINGS. Wit: JAMES EDWARDS, ELISHA
STALLINGS.

STALLIONS, GRIGGRE

Aug. 15. 1788. May Ct., 1790. Wife & Extx:
ELIZABETH, residue of estate; sons: ELISHA, shop, tools,
grindston, stilliards, etc.; SYMOND (?); WILIE JONES
(at age 21) should he die, to his bro ALLEN JONES; daus:
SARAH O'NEAL, MARY O'NEAL, HANNAH EMESON, ABSLE (ABSALA?)
BRAKE, RACHEL JONES, 5 S each; stepdau: LUCY CASTRIGN
(?) cow, calf, furniture, pewter plates, etc. Exr: JACOB
BRAKE, ISHAM O'NEAL. Wit: WHITFIELD WILSON, ROBERT
ROGERS, ELISHA STALLIONS.

STALLIONS (STALLINGS), JAMES

Feb. 26, 1764. Apr. Ct., 1764. Wife: ANN, if she
shall be with child, she to have the second living
child of my wench Bridget, estate her widowhood, after-
ward I give said wench to son JACOB STALLIONS; also
all my land and 1 negro boy; daus: ESTHER STALLIONS,
negro boy; ELIZABETH STALLIONS, first born living
child of my negro wench, Bridget; remainder of estate
to be divided between my wife and chil. Exr: HENRY
HORN. Wit: ETHELRED EXUM, ELISHA STALLIONS, JOHN
STALLIONS.

STANTON, LEMON P.

Oct. 12, 1845. Feb. Ct., 1846. Bk. F, p 334. Neph:
GEORGE W. STANTON, son of WM. STANTON, negro Harry;
Niece and neph: LOUEAZER, S. E. DEBERRY and LEMUEL J.
DEBERRY, heirs of LEMUEL and ELIZABETH DEBERRY, negro
slaves, etc.; nieces SALLIE, JULIA and REBECCA STANTON,
$100 each; LEMUEL DEBERRY, SENIOR, chest and contents
that sets by the fireplace up the stairs; W. M. STANTON
$300; Exr: Bro. WASHINGTON M. STANTON. Feb. Term 186_
No Wit. Will found among papers of deceased, proved by
NATHAN P. DANIEL and oaths of JOSHUA BARNES & ELIAS
BARNES to be in handwriting of LEMON P. STANTON, de-
ceased.

STATON, ARTHUR

Nov. 24, 1821. May Ct., 1822. Bk. E, p 300. Wife:
CHARLOTTE, land bought of NATHAN MAYO and WILLIAM
BARFIELD; liberty to distill her liquor in still I
give to KENNETH C. STATON, my hand mill, negro boy,
horse, bay mare, 4 sows and pigs, 12 shoats, 10 head

sheep, furniture, riding chair, and harness, cart and
wheels, plow stocks, hoes and gear, 2 weeding hoes, 2
grubbing hoes, 2 Pewter dishes, 3 earthen dishes, 1
doz. earthen plates, 1 doz. cups and saucers, half
doz. knives and forks, half doz. tablespoons, 2 pots
and hangers, half doz. setting chairs, 1 walnut table,
2 chests, Beaufot, that has no glass, 1 looking glass,
pr. of firedogs, tongs and shovel, 2 Pewter Basins, 2
earthen basins, 2 butter pots, 2 chump bottles, 2 jugs,
half doz. milk cups, 2 bowls, 1 decanter, 2 tumblers,
1 small trunk, 1 loom and gear, 2 tubs, 2 pails, 2
woollen wheels, 1 flax wheel, 1 skillet, 1 Dutch Oven,
1 frying pan, 1 gridiron, 1 griddle, 1 noggin, half
my cider casks, having her choice of everything, except
otherwise described during her natural life and 3 negroes; son & exr: WINFIELD D. STATON, the Savanah land
bought of WARREN SAVIDGE, 100 A, 50 A I bought of JAMES
BRYAN and 150 A I bought of JOHN GRIFFIN, WILLIAM HANSEL,
LEWIS BRYAN and JAMES BRYAN and $100; dau: NICEY HOUSE,
$350 to pay for negro woman Lewcy, mare, bridle, saddle,
furniture, 2 cows and calves, 1/2 the land I bought of
NATHAN MAYO, 1/2 land I bought of WILLIAM BARFIELD, at
death of my wife; dau. & Extx: SUSANNAH MOORING, negro
woman Faun, $50, mare, briddle, saddle, 3 cows and
calves, lands; son & exr: KENNETH C. STATON, plantation
and lands I bought of ISAAC HILL, DAVID DAVIDSON and
JOHN H. JONES, and 100 A bought of WILLIAM JONES, 100
A of JOHN BURNETT, 50 A of THOMAS BRYAN, and 32 A of
new entered land, my still and 1/2 my cider casks,
horse, briddle and saddle, furniture, 3 cows and calves,
etc.; gr. son: ARTHUR S. COTTON, $300 to buy him a
negro boy, horse, briddle, saddle, etc.; sons: WINFIELD
D. STATON and KENNETH C. STATON and dau: SUSANNAH, grist
mill known as Mayo Mill. Exr: JOHN MOORING, JUN'R.
Wit: THOS. EDMONDSON.

STATON, EZEKIAL
    Feb. 25, 1815. Nov. Ct., 1815. Bk. E, p 113. Wife:
MARY STATON, life or widowhood, plantation where I
now live, formerly belonging to BENJAMIN PIPPEN, half
the house of said plantation, the partition in the hall
room to be the dividing line, she to have the small
rooms she generally stays in both upstairs and below,

also 3 negroes, 1 horse, riding chair, harness, 3 cows
and calves, 3 ewes and lambs, furniture, 3 green and
3 yellow Windsor chairs, 6 rush bottom chairs, large
iron pot, frying pan, 6 Pewter Plates, 1 Pewter dish,
pewter spoons, 2 Pewter basins, case of knives and
forks, 2 plow hoes, 2 weeding hoes, 1 disc, all her
choice, chest, 1 black walnut table, black walnut desk,
small Beaufat, all earthenware, corn and bacon, sufficient quantity to support self and family; gr. chil:
POLLY and JOHN HOWELL, chil. of GRACIE HOWELL, my dau,
negro woman Esther and her chil. When Gr. son arrives
at 21, negro man Davey to be sold, and money divided;
son: WILLIAM STATON, 545 A I purchased of JAMES IVES,
$100 in part to pay for a negro girl, I am to pay $125
further for said negro girl and two negroes; son:
JAMES, 2 negroes and increase, inlaid black walnut
desk, plainest black walnut table, etc.; dau: NANCY
WHITLEY, 5 negroes and their increase, negro man WILLIS,
2 negro boys Bob and Frank; dau: ANNIS LONG, negro
woman Nan, 4 negroes and their increase; dau: SABRY
HOPKINS, 5 negroes and their increase; dau: BYTHA
JONES, 6 negroes and their increase; son: REDDING
STATON, 3 plantations purchased of ISAAC HILL, JAMES
STATON and JOHN BARFIELD, 5 negroes and their increase,
horse SeaGull and mare purchased from JOHN SMITH, etc.;
son: RICKEY, lands, plantations, old place where I
formerly lived the CARRAWAY Place and the new purchased
place, near JESSE HAWKIN'S place, head of Branch running into Poplar Branch, 8 negroes and increase, horse,
Bull, mare, briddle, saddle, etc. Exr: EDWARD POWER,
NOAH LEGGETT. No witnesses mentioned.

STATON, JESSE
    Oct. 8, 1812. May Ct., 1813. Bk. E, p 58. Wife:
REBECCA, land, house, 2 negroes her choice or horses,
furniture, table and Bofat, pr. of firedogs, cart and
wheels, 2 sitting chairs, choice of stock, sheep, sows,
shoats, 2 weeding hoes, 2 plow hoes, loom and gear,
trunk, looking glass, 10 choice casks, riding chair,
household and kitchen furniture, that she brought with
her, beehives, provisions, fowls; son: FREDERICK STATON,
1 negro man, furniture, the whole of my wearing apparel;
son and exr: THOMAS, negroes; daus: SARAH MANNING, $10;
LOVEY ANDREWS, after wife's death, negroes; son and

exr: BYTHAL, land, plantation, bofat, walnut table, after death of my wife, stock and cattle. Exr: MICAJAH MAYO. Wit: WILLIAM BARFIELD, JAMES STATON.

STATON, MARY
Apr. 15, 1836. May Ct., 1836. Bk. F, p 192. Son & exr: EZEKIEL, all my money and notes I possess, all property of every description. Wit: SILAS WILKINSON, MAYO WORSLEY.

STATON, NEHEMIAH
Aug. 26, 1820. May Ct., 1822. Bk. E, p 297. Wife: ELIZABETH, 4 negroes, life estate, land to the run of CONETA Creek, still, etc.; dau: ELIZABETH BARFIELD, negroes after death of wife, her lifetime; reversion to her chil: LITTLE B., CHARLOTTE and ALFRED BARFIELD, ₤ 3 in money; son: WILLIAM STATON, ₤ 3; dau: TALITHA DREW, negro girl, after death of my wife, her natural life, then to gr. dau: CHARLOTTE DREW with increase, if any, divided between heirs of TALITHA DREW, and ₤ 3; gr. dau: SARAH DREW, after death of my wife, negro girl; gr. chil: ELIZABETH STATON, ALLEN WILLIAMS, TEMPY WILLIAMS, RODERICK WILLIAMS and MARY WILLIAMS. Exrs: WILLIAM HYMAN, WINFIELD D. STATON. Wit: ARTHUR STATON, THOMAS EDMONDSON.

STATON, REBECCA
Oct. 8, 1824. Feb. Ct., 1830. Bk. F, p 110. THOMAS EVERETT, son of KINCHEN EVERETT, my negro man Pompey; if he dies without heirs, then to POLLY WATSON, dau of THOMAS WATSON, horse, colt, furniture, 2 heifers, etc. Exr: JOURDON WATSON. Wit: W. D. STATON.

STEPHENS, SHADRACK
Undated. Feb. Ct., 1790. Wife: LUCY, my 2 yr old roan, filly, choice of stock, cattle, sheep, geese, hogs; all my household and kitchen furniture, plantation, tools, land, etc; ₤ 15 after debts are paid, to be equally divided among my chil: GEORGE, TABITHA, BETSEY and JAMES STEPHENS. Sons: GEORGE and JAMES STEPHENS, all my lands lent my wife after her marriage or death. Exr: JOSHUA KILLEBREW, JESSE DELOACH. Wit: S. RUFFIN, WM. DELOACH, STEPHENSON POND (?).

STEPHENSON, GEORGE
    June 25, 1753. Aug. Ct., 1754. Nephs: JOSEPH
STEPHENSON, son of bro. WILLIAM; 1 negro, 1 bed and
furniture, 25 lbs. feathers, and 1 bolster; JESSE
STEPHENSON, son of bro. CHARLES, 2 negroes, 6 cows and
calves; WILLIAM STEPHENSON, son of bro. CHARLES, 3 negroes, my plantation, cattle, hogs, household and kitchen furniture, goods and implements. Exr: WILLIAM
STEPHENSON. Wit: HENRY HORNE, ELIZABETH HORNE, SION
HORNE.

STEVENS, EDMUND H.
    Mar. 24, 1853. Aug. Ct., 1853. Bk. F, p 507. Wife:
SARAH A. E. STEVENS, during her widowhood, all property
I may own at death, on condition she pay all my just
debts and raise my chil (unnamed). No Exr. named. JAMES
J. TAYLOR appointed by Court. Wit: L(ARRY) D. FARMER,
J(AMES) J. TAYLOR.

STILMAN, SAMUEL Town of Tarborough
    No Date. Nov. Ct., 1827. Bk. F, p 81. Wife: RACHEL
my estate being small, it is my desire after just debts
are paid, balance be left in her hands for maintainance
of herself and chil (names not given). Exr: BENJAMIN
M. JACKSON. No Wit mentioned.

STOCKDALE, JAMES
    Dec. 7, 1789. May Ct., 1790. Bk. 3, p 139. Wife:
PATSY, life estate, remainder to chil: MARY ANN and
JOHN STOCKDALE. Exr: BEVERLY BELSHER. Wit: DENNIS
STOCKDALE, MATTHEW STOCKDALE.

STOCKDALE, JOHN
    July 25, 1773. Apr. Ct., 1774. Wife & Extx, and
Gdn. to my Chil: ANN. all my estate after debts are
paid. Wit: HENRY IRWIN, MARY SKINNER, JOHN STOCKDALE.

STOKES, J. J. F. (JACOB J. F.)
    Jan. 2, 1847. May Ct., 1847. Bro-in-law: THOMAS
JOHNSON, my right in 225 A tract of land we purchased
of HARDY COBB, S side Town Creek, E side Page Branch,
all farming utensils, 2 hare trunks, small tin trunk,
looking glass, table, all this being left in his care
until I return from Mexico war. Exr: BENNETT P. PITT.

Wit: BENNET P. PITT, KETURAH PITT. Exr. renounced executorship. Adm. granted THOMAS JOHNSON, Bond $200,
JAMES F. and AMOS W. COBB, Securities. Note:- "Testator
was soldier in war waged by U. S. against Mexico, and
died from sickness on board a steamboat out of San
Francisco, as I have been informed." Sgn: JOHN NORFLEET,
C. C.

STOKES, JOHN
    May 8, 1783. Feb. Ct., 1784. Wife: ELIZABETH, manor
plantation, other lands and residue of my estate, her
life, no longer; reversion of my residue to my chil:
WILLIAM, son & Exr: SHARACK, 200 A, DAVID and DEMSEY
STOKES; son: WILLIAM 200 A land, son & exr: MARCUS
STOKES, my manner (mana) plantation, and other lands
after decease of his loving mother, my distill and
Blacksmith tools, etc.; son: DEMSEY 640 A of land lying
on both sides of Briary Branch, etc.; dau: BETTY TOLER
(?), negro girl; gr. son: WILLIAM JOHNSON, 5 S, no more.
Exr: JOHN WILLIAMS. Wit: PETER CARTWRIGHT, THOS. N.
CARTWRIGHT, HEZEKIAH CARTWRIGHT.

STOKES, MARCUS
    June 1784. Nov. Ct., 1784. My wife: BETHINIA STOKES,
life estate, then reversion to my chil: EPHRIAM, MILLEY,
MARTIN and MARCUS STOKES; son: MARCUS STOKES, plantation
where I now live, being a part of my father's estate
after the death of my beloved mother, ELIZABETH STOKES,
and my distill. Exr: Brother-in-law: SOLOMON WARD; bro.
SHADRACK STOKES. Wit: DAVID STOKES, JOHN STOKES, DEMSEY
STOKES. (Will very fadded and difficult to read.)

STOKES, SHADRACK
    Nunc. Will Proved in Open Ct., 1784. JOHN CANNADY
and DAVID STOKES being sworn deposed that they heard
SHADRACK STOKES declare his last Will and Testament:
that his bro. should have his mare, and the rest of his
estate be divided among his bros and sisters (?); that
CHARLES LEE write it down, that said SHADRACK STOKES
has not altered said Will as it was the night before
he was deceased this morning about 7 o'clock. This 4th
day of October (about 10 o'clock) 1784. Wit: AMOS
JOHNSTON, J. P.

SUGG, LEMUEL

No Date. Nov. Ct., 1780. Wife (unnamed) plantation during widowhood or life (very faded will difficult to decipher) land, 2 negroes, my water grist mill with 2 1/2 A lots; son: NOAH, all that tract and plantation on S side of old road (illegible) son: LEMUEL SUGG (illegible); son: DAVID (DAVIS ?), ___?; son: READING, tract I purchased of WILLIAM SUGG; daus: MARY, negro girl; FRANCES, negro girl, land (illegible). Exr: (Illegible). Wit: AQUILLA SUGG, WILLIAM LONG, ESTHER HOWELL.

SUGG, NOAH

Mar. 31, 1804. May Ct., 1804. Bk. D, p 207. Neph: WILLIAM PETTAWAY, son of MICAJAH PETTAWAY, 20 S; Niece: POLLY PETTAWAY, dau of MICAJAH PETTAWAY, 20 S; MICAJAH PETTAWAY, 5 S; bros: LEMUEL SUGG, 20 S; READING SUGG, all remainder of estate which is not given away, reserving use of my negro woman Rose, unto my loving mother so long as she does not give or bestow on MICAJAH PETTAWAY. Exr: READING SUGG, JAMES SOUTHERLAND. Wit: JERMIAH BATTLE, WM. A. WHITE.

SUGG, REDDING

Nov. 18, 1840. Aug. Ct., 1841. Bk. F, p 257. Wife & Extx: MARGARETT, lend plantation whereon I live on N side Jerries Creek, and lines of STATON and WALTER, reversion to gr. son, READING WILLIAMS, 25 negroes, cattle, stock, etc., still, wine and vinegar all provisions; dau: FRANCES WILLIAMS, 16 slaves; son & exr: PHEASANTON, 7 negroes also my half of EVANS tract land; son: JOEL S., all lands on Swift Creek and Tar River, purchased of SAMUEL FARMER and EXUM LEWIS, including mill, etc., also 16 negroes, utensils, tools, etc., bees and honey; gr. dau: MARY M. ROUTH, 6 negroes, residue to 3 chil. Wit: TAYLOR MEEKS, WILLIAM D. PETWAY.

SUGG, WILLIAM

Dec. 24, 1787. Jan. Ct., 1788. Bk. 3, p 57. Son: JOSIAH, plantation whereon I live, all lands to the new road, excepting 100 A I give to MATTHEW STOCKDALE; 5 negroes, horse, I purchased of NOAH SUGG, JUN'R. cows and calves, wearing apparel, bed and furniture;

317

daus: EAUPHANIA (EUPHEMIA ?) STOCKDALE, 5 negroes, 2
cows and calves, bay mare purchased of GABRIEL ALLEN,
furniture, MARY SUGG, 4 negroes, bay horse, 2 cows and
calves, furniture, all my lands on other side of new
road, joining JOHN MITCHELL'S line to READING SUGG'S,
3 negroes, with crop of corn, sold, to discharge debts.
Any residue divided among chil, all debts, bonds, and
notes of hand, due me, I give my son: JOSIAH SUGG.
Balance divided equally. Exr: MATTHEW STOCKDALE, AMOS
JOHNSTON, BEVERLY BELCHER. Wit: JOHN BARNHILL, D.
SUTHERLAND, ESTHER HOWELL.

SUMMERLIN, BARNES
    Sept. 7, 1815. Nov. Ct., 1817. Bk. E, p 162. Wife:
ANNA, during life or widowhood, 150 A plantation I now
live on; 20 A on S side of High Hill Branch, land where
my dau POLLY PITTMAN lived when she dyed; 2 negroes,
sorrel mare, riding chair, and as much of my other
stock, household and kitchen furniture as may be proper;
son: WILIE, 300 A plantation where he now lives, 2
negroes, all the property I had before put in his
possession; son: ASA, 150 A plantation he now lives
on, lying on W side of Georgia Road, joining the land
of JESSE RUFFIN, also plantation of 150 A lent to my
wife where I now live, after her death, 1 negro boy,
horse, furniture, all property I put in his possession,
2 cows and calves, 6 head sheep...negro woman, Mourning
and her increase, after death of my wife, be divided
between my sons WILIE and ASA SUMMERLIN...negro girl
Dice lent to my wife and her increase and after decease of wife to be divided between my gr. chil: PATSEY
and TEMPY PITMAN, Chil of my dau: POLLY PITTMAN, deceased, and my gr. dau: TEMPY, dau of SILAS WATSON,
etc.; gr. dau: ELIZABETH PITTMAN, dau of POLLY PITTMAN,
21 A of land, together with plantation on S side of
High Hill Branch, on the Georgia Road, between land
of ASA SUMMERLIN, the GARRETTS and JESSE RUFFIN, land
lent my wife. Exr: WILLIE SUMMERLIN, STARLING WALLER.
Wit: NATHAN SESSOMS, TIMOTHY (illegible), JOSIAH
FREEMAN.

SUMMERVILE (SUMMERAL), JACOB
    July 4, 1761. Mar Ct., 1762. 265 A plantation and

land I now live on be sold to discharge my just debts, remainder to my daus: SARAH and MARY SUMMERVILE; wife & extx: ROSANA, 1/3 of est. for life. Exr: JOHN PURVIS. Wit: DEMPSEY SPIER, ELIZABETH SPIER, MARY SPIER.

SUMNER, JOHN
Apr. 4, 1797. May Ct., 1797. Wife: MARY, 2 negroes, riding chair, harnes, briddle, bay mare, which she generally rides, 6 turned chairs, stool chair, I lend 2 negroes, my still, my desk, plantation where I now live, all my land on E side of Beach Run Swamp during widowhood, or until my son JOSEPH arrives at 21 years; son: EDWIN, plantation and land on Tar River which my father purchased of JESSE GREEN; and shot gun, I purchased for him; son: DANIEL SUMNER, remainder of my land on W side of Beach Swamp, joining land of JACOB BATTLE and JOSEPH SUMNER, dec'd, and shot gun; to my 4 daus: NANCY, ELIZABETH, CATHERIN, and FEREBY SUMNER, Ł 50 current money of this State, a hunting saddle and bridle, each. All negroes (not given my wife) to my 7 chil: EDWIN, NANCY, ELIZABETH, CATHERINE, DANIEL, FEREBE and JOSEPH SUMNER. My still provided my wife keep York and Cudge, and the still and they are lent to her. Also bed, furniture, 3 sows, Piggs, 2 cows and calves, etc. Exr: JACOB BATTLE, DEMSEY BATTLE. Wit: MALACHI MURPHREE, MARTHA SUMNER, JACOB BATTLE.

SUMNER, JOSEPH
Jan. 11, 1783. May Ct., 1785. Wife: ANNA, 2 negroes, furniture, 4 cows and calves, 2 sows and pigs, 1 stear, Black mare, side saddle and bridle, 3 turned chears, chest, 1/2 my Pewter and iron pots, plantation, land, I purchased of ABRAHAM ODOM, also land on the River I purchased of JESSE GREEN, as she may think property to sow flax on for her own use; son: JOHN, all the negroes and their increase and other things I have given into his keeping, land and plantation on Tar River, except the privilege of wife's sowing flax during her widowhood; son: JOSEPH, all their increase which I have given into his possession, land lying in Edgecombe Co.; dau: CHARLOTTE, all lands I hold in Nash Co.; also 2 negroes, young mare, side saddle and bridle, furniture, chest, 1/2 my Pewter and

319

iron pots, 4 cows, and calves, and other stock; gr.
son: DUKE WILLIAM SUMNER, negro, still. Residue of
estate to wife, ANNA, and chil: JOHN, JOSEPH and
CHARLOTTE SUMNER, not to be sold by them. Exr: son,
JOSEPH SUMNER, JACOB BATTLE. Wit: ELISHA BATTLE, JETHRO
BATTLE, DEMSEY BATTLE.

SUMNER, JOSEPH
    Dec. 7, 1793. May Ct., 1795. Wife: MARTHA, 300 A
of land on Beach Run Swamp and the Purchase Patent,
including plantation where I now live, which I had
lent to her during widowhood; 4 negroes, mare, saddle,
bridle, horse, my riding chair, 3 cows and calves, 6
ewes and lambs, 3 sows and pigs; 1 grass stear, furniture, 2 chests, 1/2 doz. knives and forks, 1/2 doz.
Pewter plates, 2 basins, 2 dishes, large iron pot,
hooks and rack, 1 flax and 1 woollen wheel, etc.; sons:
DUKE WILLIAM SUMNER; now under age; if not living then,
the next oldest of my five sons: DUKE WILLIAM SUMNER,
TOBIAS, JOSEPH, EXUM and JACOB SUMNER. Estate to be
sold, except land and negroes, which should maintain
and educate them; dau: SARAH. Exr: ETHELRED PHILLIPS,
JACOB BATTLE, DEMSEY BATTLE. Wit: JACOB BATTLE,
WILLIAMSON BARNES, NATHAN BARNES. (Interesting will).

SURGINER, ROBERT
    Aug. 7, 1773. Aug. Ct., 1778. Wife: CATHERINE, all
my lands, and plantation, stock, cattle, furniture,
utensils during widowhood, reversion to chil; son &
exr: JOHN, shall have, hold and enjoy all my land,
furniture, stock, etc.; sons: WILLIAM and BENJAMIN,
1 S each; dau: SARAH SURGINER, OLIVE POPE and HANNAH
SIKES, 1 S each. Wit: ROBERT DIGGES, WM. WILLIAMS,
URIAH WILLIAMS.

SUTHERLAND, DANIEL
    Sept. 9, 1792. Nov. Ct., 1792. Son: PATRICK, $500
2 negroes and my shaving utensils; daus: ISABELL, 3
negroes; ELIZABETH, 1 negro woman; MARGARET, 1 negro
woman. Estate to be sold, debts paid, remainder divided
between all my.chil. It is my will and desire that if
any of my daus should marry an Irishman without the
consent of Gdn. or bro., she shall forfeit her legacy

to the other 3 chil. Exr: Maj. CHARLES GERROD (GERARD),
JOHN WHITE. Wit: WILLIAM WILKINS, JOHN BILLUPS.

SWALES, MARY
　　Mar. 11, 1796. May Ct., 1800. Aged and Infirm, I
make my Will. It is my will and desire that my negro
woman Nell, for her long and faithful services may
have her freedom; dau: ANN SMITH' wife of REUBEN SMITH;
dau: SUSANNAH HILL, wife of HENRY HILL, share equally
in all my personal property, except the negro boy Jerry;
son: ENOCH SWAILS, Negro boy Jerry. Exr & sons-in-law:
REUBEN SMITH, HENRY HILL. Wit: ISAAC HILL, JACOB MURRELL,
MILLY MURRELL.

SWINNY, NANCY
　　Sept. 10, 1816. Feb. Ct., 1817. Bk. E, p 150. Gr.
dau: NANCY KNIGHT, $100; son & exr: ROBERT FOXHALL,
furniture, and choice of my bed quilts; all the rest
of my estate after debts are paid. Wit:____?,
BILBERRAY, JOSHUA LAURENCE.

SYMS, WILLIAM
　　Oct. 24, 1755. No Probate Date. Dau: SARAH WHOOPER
(HOOPER), plantation lying on Kehukey; son: WILLIAM.
Exr: JOHN WHITAKER. Wit: THOS. TAYLOR, MARY TREE, EXTR
(CHRISTOPHER ?) HAYNES.

TART, ELNATHAN
　　Sept. 24, 1795. Feb. Ct., 1796. Wife: OBEDIENCE,
life estate in land on Whiteoak Swamp, Wolf Pit Branch.
Godwin's Branch, dwelling, all pertaining thereto,
lend 4 negroes, stock, cattle and 1 Barrel of Brandy,
annually, until my son: JAMES, comes of age. I desire
my negroes remain at their respective plantations for
the purpose of keeping up their farms, raising stock
of every kind. Estate, bonds, notes and 1 negro each
to be divided between my 4 chil as they come of age:
PENNINAH, POLLY, JAMES and THOMAS TART. Whereas my
father JONATHAN TART in his last will and testament
left 4 negroes: to be divided between myself JAMES,
ENOS and SALLY TART, after a term of 10 years, it is
my will and desire said negroes continue at the
Plantation where they now live. If negroes are sold
my Executors may purchase them at their discretion

and if Tom, Jack or Venus should fall to my part, they
may have choice to live with which of my sons they
please after THOMAS comes of age. I also bequeath my
chil above named 4 negroes Banus, Fillis, Tamer and
Sal when of age, or marry. All my lands, Tools equally
to my sons JAMES and THOMAS. To all 4 chil equally my
part of $1,200.54 in Funded Certificates.

It is my will and earnest desire that my Exrs be
careful to have my chil educated in the best manner
the situation of this part of the country will admit
of. Exr: CHARLES COLEMAN, J. S. BARNES, JACOB HORN,
ICHABOD THOMAS. Wit: THEOPHILUS THOMAS, WILLIAM AMASON,
JOSEPH MAYO.

TART, JONATHAN
Undated. May Ct., 1789. Bk. 3, p 87. Wife:
CATHERINE, 2 negro boys and Lin for 10 yrs., when he
shall be free man, and shall have the corn field,
orchard and house now known as his property; sons:
ELNATHAN, 2 negroes, girl Tamer; JAMES, 2 negro boys;
daus: ELIZABETH WALTON (WALSTON ?), negro woman and
her increase; MARTHA EASON, 350 A of land, MILLS
(MILES ?) BARFIELD now lives on E side of Toisnot and
Whiteoak Swamps, 2 negroes; cousins: JOHN WEST, ⅃ 70
current money of N. C.; FEREBY FAIL, ⅃ 70 current
money of N. C.; son: ELNATHAN TART, I lend the plantation JOHN BRADSHAR lives on, and 2 negro men for
term of 6 yrs.; gr. son: ENOS TART, 4470 A plantation
JOHN BRADSHAR now lives on, negro man; gr. dau: SARAH
TART, 1 negro; and as for my negroes Jack, Venus,
John and Sal I lend to my son ELNATHAN 10 yrs.; after-
wards (they and their increase) to be divided between
my sons ELNATHAN and JAMES TART and 2 gr. chil: ENOS
and SARAH TART, my brandy still to my sons ELNATHAN
and JAMES and gr. son, ENOS TART; son: JAMES TART,
⅃ 60; other money equally divided between wife, sons
ELNATHAN, JAMES and dau MARTHA EASON, and my Loan
office ticket money and 2 negroes, Buster and Sharp,
in like manner and Plantation on Toisnot Swamp to son
JAMES, my wife to have her share her lifetime. Exr;
JOHN BRADSHAR, JAMES GANES, MARTHA BENTLEY. No Wit
named.

TATUM, NATHANIEL

Nov. 9, 1750. Feb. Ct., 1750. Wife & Extx:
ELIZABETH; sons: EDWARD, NATHANIEL, PETER, JOSE
(JESSE ?) and dau: REBECKA, lands divided among gr. chil.
Wit: JAMES CANE, ELENER WEAVER, REBECCA CANE.

TAYLOR, ARTHUR
Aug. 9, 1765. Oct. Ct., 1765. Dau: MARTHA DEW,
negro boy Sam; son & exr: BENJAMIN, 1 negro his lifetime, reversion to his son BENJAMIN; son: JAMES, riffle
and iron kettle; gr. sons: JOHN, 160 A land on S side
of Tar River, in Edgecombe Co., purchased of CHRISTOPHER
CLINCH; SAMUEL, negro boy; sons: WILSON, 400 A land on
S side of Tar River in Edgecombe Co., mouth of Wolf
Trap Branch, negro man, 4 cows and calves, etc.; DREWRY,
80 A plantation whereon I now live, and another 370 A
Tract adjoining, lying below the mouth of Wolf Trap
Branch, S side of Tar River, negro boy, 4 cows and
calves, furniture which I desire not be sold but kep
for the boy to lay on while he is small. I desire
LAZARUS (?) POPE have the care of the child till my
son WILSON be of age to care for him; daus: PRISCILLA,
furniture and negro girl; ANN, negro boy; son: KITT,
400 A tract of land on S side Tar River by name of
BRITT'S (BURT'S ?) Plantation, Long Branch, 1 negro,
12 cows and calves; daus: SALLY (SEELY ?), 1 negro,
bed, furniture; MOLLY, negro girl Lucy; son: JOHN,
1 negro, cow and calf, yearling, etc. It is my desire
that JACOB STRICKLAND have the care of my 2 chil KITT
and SEELY (SALLY ?) and their estates. Remainder of
my estate divided among my chil. Exr: JOHN TAYLOR.
Wit: LAZARUS POPE, GALE BRYANT.

TAYLOR, JAMES
Aug. 10, 1782. May Ct., 1783. Son & Exr: SAMUEL,
land and plantation where I now live (except what is
reserved), stock, cattle, etc., mare, colt, filly,
wearing apparel, tools and household furniture; gr.
son: JAMES, son of JOHN TAYLOR, land lying over Deep
Branch, etc.; gr. son: HODGE, son of JAMES TAYLOR 5
S; daus: SUSANNA ALLEN and ELIZABETH JORDAN, 5 S each.
Wit: ELIZABETH STOKES, PETER CARTWRIGHT, ANN CARTWRIGHT.

TAYLOR, JOHN

Mar. 21, 1823. Aug. Ct., 1825. Wife: ELON (ELLEN ?),
land and plantation, houses, etc._____ Branch on the
lines of CRISP and ROBERT BEST'S line, furniture, chest,
mare, saddle, etc., 2 cows and calves, 2 ewes and lambs;
2 plough hoes, gear, 2 axes, hand saw, drawing knife,
hatchet, 2 weeding hoes, loom and gear, pot and hooks,
Dutch oven, Pewter plates, basin, Cart and wheels,
Woollen wheel and cotton cards, flaxwheel, apple (cider)
mill and Press, 8 cedar barrels, 1 hogshead, Tub, pail,
gallon Piggen (noggin ?). Her first choice of everything.
All provisions on hand to remain for family use. Sons:
MARCUM, furniture, etc.; FREDERICK, and dau ELON BENNETT,
$5 each. Dau: CINDERILLA, furniture and cow; gr. dau:
MATILDA WHITFIELD, land and property lent to wife. Exr:
MARCUM TAYLOR, JOHN MOORING. Wit: WILLIAM BEST, JOHN
BEST.

TAYLOR, MARTHA
    Feb. 27, 1828. May Ct., 1828. Bk. F, p 85. Sister:
LUVENIAH TAYLOR, furniture, chest, table, 6 chairs,
loom and harness and all my clothes, etc. Exr: GEORGE
PURVIS, WILLIAM W. K. PHILPOTT. Wit: CHARLOTY PURVIS,
RODERICK PURVIS.

TAYLOR, MARY E.
    Aug. 21, 1843. Nov. 1843. Bk. F, p 294. Niece:
MARIAN SUSAN BATTLE, my gig, horse also 1/3 remainder
estate; nephs: JAMES L. BATTLE, 1/3 estate; JETHRO D.
BATTLE, 1/3 estate, to be held in trust by JAMES L.
BATTLE. No Exr. Wit: JAMES J. PHILIPS, CHARLES
HARRISON. Adm. granted JAMES L. LITTLE, Bond $10,000;
Securities, JAMES S. BATTLE, JOSEPH BATTLE.

TAYLOR, ROBERT
    Undated. Sept. Ct., 1758. Wife & Extx: ANN; sons:
ROBERT, EDWARD, JOSEPH; son & exr: WILLIAM, HENRY,
RICHARD, THOMAS, BILLINGTON, NIMROD and HUDSON and
Daus: JUDITH and RACHEL TAYLOR and ANNE HUISE, 1 S
each. Wit: WILLIAM HUDSON, JAMES VAULX (?), WILLIAM
HUDSON, JR.

TAYLOR, STEPHEN
    Mar. 20, 1848. May Ct., 1848. Bk. F, p 391. Wife:

NANCY, lend 5 negroes reversion to chil; daus: SARAH
TISE (TICE?), ELIZABETH SHARPE, NANCY VIVRET, MILBERY
WIGGINS, and PATSY VIVRET; sons: EGBERT TAYLOR, horse;
WILLIE GRAY TAYLOR, $30; gr. chil: JOHN SHARP'S child:
GRAY, DAVID and MARGARET SHARP, $300; son: JESSE, $200.
Exr. & sons-in-law: WASHINGTON TICE, JAMES WIGGINS.
Wit: JOHN G. WILLIAMS, WILLIAM W. BATTS.

TAYLOR, TEAGLE
    Mar. 10, 1823. Nov. Ct., 1826. Bk. F, p 64. Dau:
REBECCA TAYLOR, furniture. Residue of my estate after
death of myself and wife, CELIA, shall be equally
divided among our chil living at that time. Exr:
STEPHEN TAYLOR. Wit: E. BULLOCK, BENJAMIN LANCASTER,
BRITAIN WILLIFORD.

TAYLOR, THOMAS
    Feb. 27, 1773. Apr. Ct., 1774. Wife & Extx:
ELIZABETH, all rest of my estate of whatever nature,
life or widowhood, residue equally divided between my
chil; son: WILLIAM, 150 A land on Town Creek and line
of WILLIAM HINES'...JOHNSTON'S Mill Creek. Chil:
CASSANDRA TAYLOR, MARY BERGGIN, ELIZABETH and JOHN
BERGIN. Exr. & Bro: JOHN TAYLOR. Wit: DEMSEY SKINNER,
MARCUM BELSHER, LAZARUS DRAKE.

TAYLOR, THOMAS
    Nunc. Will. On the 15th of this month, I was with
THOMAS TAYLOR; he then complaining of the headache,
and appearing very unwell, in consequence of which I
asked what he intended to do with his property if he
should die before he came of age. He said he would
give it to WILLIAM ANDERSON. It was quite clear to me
that it was his determination to do so from the manner
in which he spoke of it to me and others. 27th March,
1802. Sgd/ ANN HOWELL. Wit: JOHN WOMBLE.

TAYLOR, WILLIAM
    Dec. 10, 1783. Aug. Ct., 1786. Wife: MARY, plan-
tation and land on S side of Beach run, 1 negro,
riding horse, all household and kitchen furniture of
her choice, stock, cattle, hogs and sheep, land on
N side of Beach Run; dau: RACHEL WHITLEY, 200 A land

on Brown's Branch, Deed of Grant dated 10th day of
July 1762; son: DAVID, after his mother's death or
marriage, my land on S side of Beach Run; daus:
SUSANNAH, MARY and RACHEL, household and kitchen furn-
iture after wife's decease; my 8 chil: JOSIAH, REUBEN,
WILLIAM, MILLS, DAVID, SUSANNA, MARY and RACHEL, all
my estate lent to my wife after her death or marriage.
Exr: son: REUBEN TAYLOR; JACOB BATTLE. Wit: ELISHA
BATTLE, JETHRO BATTLE, DEMSEY BATTLE.

TAYLOR, WILLIAM
    Apr. 19, 1831. Feb. Ct., 1833. Bk. F, p 142. Wife
(?) 1/3 personal estate, lend all lands, reversion to
Bro: ALLEN TAYLOR, 2/3 personal estate. Exr: JAMES J.
PHILIPS, JAMES S. BATTLE. Wit: BENNETT HARPER, JOSEPH
J. SPELLINGS.

THIGPEN, GILLIAD
    Nov. 24, 1831. May Ct., 1838. Wife: ELIZABETH,
land, stock of all descriptions, life estate; son:
REDDING THIGPEN'S heirs $1; dau: VICEY (VINEY) EASON'S
heirs, $1; gr. son: GEORGE WASHINGTON THIGPEN, $25
for his schooling; son: JOHN THIGPEN, all land and
appurtenances; dau: SALLY GAY; residue to be divided
between son: JOHN and dau SALLY GAY and heirs. Son &
Exr: JOHN THIGPEN, friend: BURREL GAY. Wit: JAMES
PAGE, BENJ. MOORE.

THIGPEN, JAMES
    Apr. 30, 1840. Feb. Ct., 1849. Bk. F, pp 420-422.
Wife: PATSY, 2 negroes, $1000 cash, table, necessary
furniture, chest, trunk, dining table, chairs, china,
spining wheel, pair of cotton cards, horse, years'
provisions, lend wife land whereon I live and 1 negro;
dau: FANNIE LITTLE, 7 negroes; sons: WILLIAM, land
whereon he now lives, furniture, and $330 cash;
LITTLEBERRY, tract whereon he lives, furniture, horse,
bridle, saddle and $330; L. B. THIGPEN, $500 cash;
dau: LYDIA COBB, 5 negroes; sons: JOB THIGPEN, 2 negroes; property already received; BEN ASHLEY THIGPEN,
4 negroes, $150 cash, horse, bridle, saddle; B. A.
THIGPEN, 2 negroes, furniture, for his life then to his
heirs; SPENCER, land on which he lives, horse, bridle

and saddle, furniture, 3 negroes; KENNETH, land where-
on he lives, joining OLLIN COBB, ALLEN WARREN, WILLIAM
THIGPEN, & SPENCER THIGPEN. Also land known as the
KELLY land, etc. Exr: Eldest son: WILLIAM THIGPEN;
Second son: JOB THIGPEN. Wit: ALLEN WARREN, ALLEN MAYO.

THIGPEN, LEMUEL
    Dec. 2, 1839. May Ct., 1841. Bk. F, p 258. Wife:
ANN, land whereon I live..to EATON COBB'S line, 3 negroes, household and kitchen furniture, choice of my
horses, cows, etc.; daus: ELIZABETH WARREN, PENNETTA
SMITH and LYDIA THIGPEN, negro woman each; sons: IRVIN,
1/2 my land, negro boy and furniture; JAMES, 1/2 my
land, negro boy and furniture; residue to my 5 chil.
Exr & Sons-in-law: RICHARD WARREN, WILLIAM SMITH. Wit:
JORDAN KNIGHT, SALLY ALFORD.

THOMAS, JACOB
    July 19, 1833. May Ct., 1840. Bk. F, p 243. Dau:
MARY ELIZABETH AMANDA THOMAS, lands and negroes, if
dies without heirs to ELIZABETH BUNN, MARTHA ANN, MARY
VINSON VAUGHAN, and ROENA W. VAUGHAN. Exr. & Bro-in-
law: DAVID BUNN. Wit: WILLIAM GAY, JOHN W. LEWIS.

THOMAS, JAMES
    Jan. 12, 1777. Oct. Ct., 1777. Bk. A, pp 261-2.
Wife & Extx: ELIZABETH, all my estate during life;
reversion to my chil (unnamed). Exr: SAMUEL SKINNER,
THOMAS WILLIS. Wit: MOSES WILSON, EMANUEL SKINNER,
BARBARY SMITH.

THOMAS, JOHN R.
    Feb. 1, 1826. Feb. Ct., 1826. Five negroes, to be
sold to pay my debts; wife: MARY, 3 negroes for life;
1/2 my household and kitchen furniture with china,
crockeryware, silver and plate; I lend her all my land
on Toisnot Swamp, and Fort Branch, between me and
ELISHA FELTON, Little Prong of Fort Branch to line of
ICHABOD THOMAS to AMASON'S and appurtanances, her life;
4 cows and calves, choice of my flock, yoke of steers,
all my sheep, hogs, etc.; son: ELNATHAN HOOKER THOMAS,
after his mother's decease said property between me
and NATHAN AMASON and heirs of ELI AMASON, land on

Toisnot Swamp; negroes to be divided between my 3 daus:
ELIZA ANN HOOKER THOMAS, PENNINA ROGERS THOMAS, and
MARY ELIZABETH THOMAS when they marry, or arrive at
21 years; residue of my estate to be sold and divided;
sons: HYMERIC H. and WILLIAM J. R. H. THOMAS, my plantation with all appurtenances when oldest son reaches
age 21, and 2 negro boys each. Exr: REDIC BARNES. Wit:
WILLIE BROWNRIGG, THEO. S. SIMMS, MICAJAH AMASON.

THOMAS, JOHN
     Apr. 21, 1788. Feb. Ct., 1789. Bk. 3, p 80. Wife:
CHRISTINALOR (CHRISTIANA), lend all my Estate for her
maintenance in care of my son: THEOPHILUS THOMAS, and
JACOB THOMAS, as overlooker to see she is properly
cared for, then to my son: JOHN THOMAS, £ 5 besides
what I have already given him; gr. son: JONATHAN, son
of JONATHAN THOMAS, £ 5 besides what I have already
given him; daus: TREASEY HILL, £ 5 besides what I have
given her and her husband; MILLISON (MILLICENT ?) HORN
(?), negro woman; son: THEOPHILUS THOMAS, 8 negroes,
my still, cap and worm and all the rest of my estate.
Exr: THEOPHILUS THOMAS, JACOB HORN (?). Wit: ELI AMASON,
WILLIAM AMASON, MANOAH AMASON.

THOMAS, JOHN Parish of St. Elizabeth, N. C.
     Nov. 24, 1774. Apr. Ct., 1777. Wife: (Unnamed), re-
mainder of my estate, during widowhood, then to my chil:
JOHN, ABISHAG and CHLOE; RICHARD, chest, stilliards;
JESSE (?), 1/2 the Barfield timber; SARAH MELTON, other
half barfield timber; MARY SMITH, 5 S; JOHN chest and
furniture; ABISHAG, lining wheel and hackle; CHLOE, box
iron and heater. Exr: son, JESSY THOMAS. Wit: THOS.
WHITFIELD, SEN'R, THOMAS WHITFIELD, JUN'R, JOHN THOMAS.

THOMAS, JONATHAN
     Jan. 17, 1775. Apr. Ct., 1775. Wife & Extx: MARY,
horse, desk, walnut table, all Pewter, Potts and hooks,
side table, stock, cattle, sheep, etc.; negro to be
at her own disposing. I lend her the use and benefit
of my plantation, and all land belonging during widowhood, or til my son JONATHAN comes of age, then the
upper part, lying on Buck Branch, at Meeting House
Branch, give to my son JONATHAN THOMAS at marriage or

death and plantation whereon I now live. I lend my wife
the rest of my estate for use in raising and schooling
my chil, till my youngest dau MOURNING, is of age; daus:
ELIZABETH, CHRISTIANA, TREACEY, SARAH, CHARITY and
MOURNING THOMAS, furniture and L 5 Proc. money each.
Exr: Bro, JOHN THOMAS. Wit: JONATHAN THOMAS, LISHA
SPIVEY, THEOPHILUS THOMAS.

THOMAS, JOSEPH
Oct. 24, 1757. June Ct., 1758. Wife & Extx:
MOURNING, L 15 for schooling chil; daus: MARY, lower
tract on Pig Basket Creek, 1 negro, Black Walnut Chest;
furniture; PRISCILLA, tract bought of JOHN WOTTSON
(WATSON), on Pig Basket Creek, also tract on N side
of Pig Basket Creek, Black Walnut Chest, furniture,
1 negro; CHARITY, tract on Pig Basket Creek, deed not
taken out of office, Black Walnut Chest, L 45 and 1
negro; MOURNING, my plantation and all my lands on
Peachtree Creek, adjoining my plantation, Black Walnut
Chest and L 20 and 1 negro. Bro. and Exr: JOHN THOMAS.
Wit: MICAJAH THOMAS, WILLIAM DEFNALL (DEVANAL?),
MOURNING THOMAS.

THOMAS, LUKE
June 20, 1751. Aug. Ct., 1751. Bro. & Exr: JACOB
THOMAS, my plantation, 1 negro, 1 stallion; sister:
MARY THOMAS, 1 negro, stallion, mare, 2 cows and
calves, 2 pewter dishes and basons; EZEKIAL KEEL, L
10. Wit: EDWARD BROWN, JOHN TANNER, ELIZABETH KEEL.

THOMAS, MARY
Jan. 18, 1810. May Ct., 1810. Bk. D, p 363. 2
negro wenches, my riding chair, my stock and cattle,
except 2 work stears and sheep to be sold to pay just
debts; son: MICAJAH THOMAS, walnut table and 1 candle-
stand, etc.; son & exr: JOHN THOMAS, hogs, etc.; son:
THEOPHILUS THOMAS, sorrel mare, yoke of oxen, etc.;
daus: ELIZABETH COBB, sorrel mare, 1/2 doz. sitting
chairs; NANCY THOMAS, bridle, saddle, $350 to school,
clothe and board her; OBEDIENCE BROWNRIGG, MILICENT
SIMMS, TREACEY TART and TABITHA SIMMS, 5 S each; sons:
ICHABOD and BENJAMIN THOMAS, 5 S each; Residue of my
Estate between my 3 sons MICAJAH, JOHN and THEOPHILUS

THOMAS. Wit: JAMES BARNES, H. HAYWOOD, JNO. B. COBB.

THOMAS, MARY
    May 29, 1802. Aug. Ct., 1802. daus: ELIZABETH
BARNES, saddle, horse; CHRISTIAN SIMMS, sorrel mare;
SALLY DEW, sorrel mare, and furniture, etc; POLLY
BRANTLEY, 1 negro and furniture etc.; gr. dau: MOLLY
BRANTLEY, furniture; dau: CHARITY WATKINS, 1 negro,
etc.; gr. dau: MOLLY WATKINS, bed and furniture; gr.
son: HILLIARD THOMAS, Brandy still, reversion use until
my ensuing crop of liquor is distilled; gr. son:
JONATHAN THOMAS, my whipsaw, cross saw, etc.; gr. son:
EASON THOMAS, 6 sitting chairs, walnut table, desk,
reserving use to his mother until he comes of age; gr.
dau: NANCY THOMAS, bed and furniture; gr. dau: POLLY
THOMAS, my sugar Cannister and Tea Kettle, etc.; dau:
MOURNING WILKINSON, furniture, large Pott and hooks,
spice mortar, flax Hackle, glass Cannister, large
Pewter dish; gr. dau: ELIZABETH ROUNTREE, Pewter Basin,
Dish and Plate, etc.; gr. dau: TREASIA ROUNTREE, flax
wheel, pewter Basin, etc.; gr. dau: SALLY ROUNTREE,
woollen wheel, pair of cotton cards; gr. son: LEWIS
ROUNTREE, sorrell, colt; gr. chil: POLLY, WILIE,
ELIZABETH, LEWIS (OR LOUISE), TREASEA and SALLY
ROUNTREE, $150 cash to be divided among them. Stock
of cattle, hogs, etc. be fattened, sold, divided
between my daus: ELIZABETH BARNES, CHRISTIAN SIMMS and
SALLY DEW. Negro man Samuel to be sold, debts of de-
ceased son JONATHAN THOMAS be paid; gr. dau: POLLY
DEW, pine chest. Exr & Sons-in-law: JOHN DEW, WILLIAM
WILKINSON. Wit: JOHN HORN, JACOB HORN, EDWARD PITTMAN.

THOMAS, MICAJAH Parish of St. Mary
    Dec. 4, 1769. Feb. Ct., 1770. Wife: MOURNING, mare,
saddle, bridle, furniture, use of 18 negroes during
life, or widowhood; also use of plantation and another
on Tar River bought from THOMAS HERSEY, another plantation bought from THOMAS POLLARD, 20 cows, 20 calves
and yearlings, 10 barren cows, 7000 wt. Bacon for use
of family and to support carpenters, joiner and other
workmen, 20 sows, 40 other hogs under 18 mos. old, 50
bu. salt, 2 bbls brown sugar, etc., still, 6 horses,
Smith tools, etc.; dau: BATHSHEBA, 10 negroes, 2 tracts

land I bought from THOMAS HARDIMAN etc., tracts bought
of WILLIAM HARRIS on Peachtree Creek, 1340 A tract
bought of WILLOUGHBY TUCKER on Back Swamp, 100 A tract
bought of PETER HEDGEPETH, 700 A land on Pig Basket
Creek, tract bought of JOSHUA WOMBLE; son: MICAJAH,
lands, negroes, cattle, stock, etc.; Exr: ELISHA BATTLE,
SEN'R, NATHAN BODDIE. Wit: DUNCAN LAMON, NATHAN BODDIE.

THOMAS, PHILIP
     Oct. 13, 1786. No Probate Date. Sons: JORDAN, 2
negroes, whipsaw, etc.; JACOB, 590 A plantation and
land whereon I live, crosscut saw, sheep, 2 negroes,
20 bbls of corn; daus: FAITHY, flaxwheel and 40 S;
ANN, 1 negro, 320 A land on prong of Horne's Creek,
2 beds and furniture, flaxwheel, horse, geese, sheep;
MARY, land, 200 A and plantation whereon WILLIAM
BARNES formerly lived, sheep, flaxwheel, geese, chest,
desk, bay mare; 172 A of land on Tyancoke Swamp sold
and debts paid. Exr: JOHN BATTLE, SAMUEL SKINNER, JUN'R.
Wit: REDMUND BUNN, SAMUEL SKINNER, WILLIAMSON BARNES.

THOMAS, THEOPHILUS
     June 25, 1803. Nov. Ct., 1803. Bk. D, p 172. Wife:
MARY, negro girl Clarey, for her own use; furniture
and set of curtains, 4 cows and calves, 10 head of
sheep, my flock of geese, my sorrel mare, 4 sows and
pigs, 10 head of 2 yr. old hogs, and 2 of my best
Beef Cattle, except my yoke of oxen; also lend unto
my wife 2 negroes, with the Plantation, I now live on,
all land on W side of road from White Oak Swamp, up
to my son MICAJAH'S line, near the Gallberry Pocosin
and cornfield on E side of road, joining the Swamp;
also my still, cap and worm, (but she shall not be
moved off the plantation where she now stands by no
person whatever till my youngest son comes of age to
take it in his possession), large pine chest, Beauphat,
2 pine tables, large spice mortar, brass skillet, 5
of the best chairs in the house, my hunting gun,
Blacksmith tools, 2 large iron potracks and iron
bearers, and after death of my wife I give the above
mentioned articles to my son THEOPHILUS and my yoke
of oxen, etc. Plantation tools, axes, hoes, barrels,
hogsheads, and all my lumber etc. Books to be divided

between 3 youngest sons and 2 youngest daus (names not
mentioned) and it is my desire nothing that I have
given to any of my chil shall be sold, but kept for
them until they shall be able to possess them. My 4
daus: OBEDIENCE BROWNRIGG, MILLISCENT EASON, TREASY
TART, TABITHA SIMMS, 5 S each; son & exr: ICHABOD,
2 negroes, besides what I have already given him; son:
BENJAMIN, 1 negro beside what I have already given him;
son & exr: MICAJAH, my 640 A plantation lying on the
road from Tarborough to Stanton's Bridge on Contentnea
Creek, with all my land from White Oak Swamp to my
back line on a branch of Little Contennea Creek, except
on new entry joining THOMAS WILLS' lines; 4 negroes,
Sorrell mare, bridle, saddle, cow and calf and heifer,
3 ewes and lambs, 4 sows and pigs, called his own,
furniture, chest and gun, called his own, large pewter
dish, large pewter basin, 6 new pewter plates, 1 large
brass candlestick, bbl of Brandy, my Law book, called
Iredell's Revisal with all the acts of the Assembly,
my whipsaw, jointer, stock, jack, and smoothing plain,
my plain (plane), irons and large hand vise, I give
him 3 sitting chairs, 1 small stew pot of mixed mettle,
1 small jointer's saw, and a pair of iron traces. My
will is that my son MICAJAH shall be of age to act
for himself at the age of 18 in the same manner as if
he was 21 years old. Son: JOHN, plantation bought of
JAMES BARNES, lying on S side of Oak Swamp, with land
beginning at the run of Whiteoak, through my cornfield.
..to old Wolf Pit, on side of the road along plantation.
.. JOHN AMASON'S corner...small branch...Big Branch...
South Branch to Whiteoak Swamp...with new entry of land
joining THOMAS WELLS and DAVID WOODARD'S line; 4 negroes, filly, black walnut table, small pine chest,
bbl of Brandy, cow and calf, heifer, 3 ewes and lambs,
large brass candlestick, 3 sitting chairs, saddle,
bridle, 2 sows and pigs, saddle bags, lock and key,
small set of fire dogs, my crosscut saw, small iron
skillet. It is my will and desire my son JOHN shall
be free to act and do for himself at the age of 18.
Son: THEOPHILUS, all my land on E side of road as far
as the Wolf Pit except cornfield joining swamp and
road, 3 negroes, sorrel filley, 2 sows and pigs, cow
and calf, heifer, 3 ewes and lambs, bridle and saddle,

furniture, and my shot molds and ladle to melt lead, a
book called The Young Man's Companion.
    My will is if either of my sons die before marrying,
or come to lawful age, the other shall have the deceased's property, except in case of my son JOHN or
THEOPHILUS, should either die before marriage or legal
age, the other shall have deceased's land; rest be
divided among 2 youngest sons, 800 A on both sides of
road from Tarborough to Godwin's Bridge on head of
Beaverdam Branch joining ENOS TART'S line, with negro
woman Loose (Lucy) be sold to pay debts. If not sufficient, stock, cattle, hogs, sheep, at public or
private sale. Dau: ELIZABETH, 2 negro girls, furniture,
set of curtains, chest of drawers, saddle and bridle.
Dau: NANCY, 2 negroes, and furniture, set of curtains,
bridle and saddle, black walnut desk.
    Young negro James to be hired out for my 2 youngest
daus: ELIZABETH and NANCY, till marriage or come to
age of 18, or either die, then shall be divided to all
the deceased's property, etc. Wit: C. H. PICKERING,
WILLIE BARNES, ELI AMASON.

THOMAS, WILLIAM
    Feb. 22, 1776. Apr. Ct., 1777. Cousins: ELIZABETH,
JAMES and NANCY HILLIARD, chil of ISAAC HILLIARD and
LEAH, his wife, all my land and tenements in S. C.
equally divided between them; cousins: WILLIAM CRAWFORD
HILLIARD, son of ISAAC HILLIARD and wife, LEAH, 1
negro and her increase; ISAAC HILLIARD, son of ISAAC
HILLIARD and wife, LEAH, 1 negro and her increase;
STARLING THOMAS, son of MARY BARNES, 1 mare; HENRY
HILLIARD, son of ELIAS. Exr: ISAAC HILLIARD, WILLIAM
SKIPWITH MEARNS. Wit: FRANCES HAMILTON, ELIZABETH
CRAWFORD, CATY CORNWELL.

THOMPSON, ELIZABETH
    Apr. 12, 1790. Nov. Ct., 1792. If my husband JOHN
THOMPSON ever returns to this County it is my will
that he may enjoy the profits and use of my house and
lots in Halifax that were formerly his, during his
life; neph: JOHN H. HALL, 1 negro and horse; niece:
MARY ANN HALL, negro girl and horse; neph: JAMES HALL,
2 negroes; I bequeath to WILLIAM THOMPSON, 1 negro

to HARRIETT HALL, 1 negro; I give and bequeath to
DOLLY HALL, 1 negro...to MARTHA HALL, 1 negro. It is
my will that my negro Mary shall have her freedom
forever. I give to EDWARD HALL, my riding chair. Residue of estate be divided between the chil of my deceased sister DOLLY McNAIR, and the chil of my sister
PAULINE TELFAIR after my debts are paid, etc...to remain in the hands of EDWARD HALL and by him managed
until they come of age. If my husband should return
to this country, as above said, he is to have the use
of 4 negroes. Exr: Bro, EDWARD HALL; neph: JOHN H. HALL.
Wit: CHARLES HALL, MASON HALL, THOMAS HALL.

THOMPSON, JOHN
    Oct. 21, 1791. Nov. Ct., 1791. Bk. 3, p 174.
Sister: ANN THOMPSON, all my estate; Father & Exr:
ROBERT THOMPSON. Wit: JOHN NICHOLSON, PETER ROBERSON,
LETITIA NICHOLSON.

THOMPSON, MARY
    Sept. 28, 1849. Feb. Ct., 1853. Bk. F, p 495. Dau:
JACQUE ANDERSON, house and lot during widowhood; gr.
dau: SUSAN CARTER, house and lot after death or widowhood of JACQUE ANDERSON. Estate to be equally shared.
Exr: GREEN CARTER. Wit: JO LAURENCE, N(ATHAN) MATHEWSON.

THORN (HORN ?) NICHOLAS
    Sept. 13, 1788. May Ct., 1789. Bk. 3, p 95. Wife
& Extx: RACHEL, all land; sons: THOMAS and MARTIN,
furniture and cow and calf to each; dau: ELIZABETH,
furniture and chest; some of this will illegible. Wit:
GEORGE EZELL, FRANCES EZELL.

THORNEL, BENJAMIN
    June 20, 1810. Aug. Ct., 1810. Bk. D, p 365. Wife:
CONSTANT, lend use of land and plantation during
widowhood or life, reversion to sons BENJAMIN and
HENRY; daus: SALLY JORDAN and DOLLY BROWN, 10 S each;
residue divided between wife, BENJ. JR., HENRY and
POLLY. Exr: JOHN BELAND, RANDOLPH JORDAN. Wit: JOHN
ROBBINS, THOMAS DIXON.

THORP, SOLOMON

Sept. 29, 1788. Nov. Ct., 1793. JOB BRADDY, son of
PATRICK BRADDY, 283 A plantation I now live on; MARY
BRADDY and SARAH PITMAN, $10 each; rest to be divided
between JOHN ANDREWS and DAVID ANDREWS, JOSEPH BRADDY
and JOB BRADDY. Exr: ROBERT HUDNALL, JOSEPH BRADDY.
Wit: ANDREW IRWIN (?), JOHN LASKEY, SAMUEL CUTCHINS.

TISDAL, RENISON
        Sept. 26, 1808. Feb. Ct., 1811. Bk. E, p 2. Wife:
(not named) furniture, horse, mare, saddle, bridle,
30 hogs, 3 cows and calves. Lend 850 A land whereon
I live during widowhood, 4 negroes furniture, 1/4
still; reversion of land to PHILANDER; sons: HENRY and
WILLIAM, 1 negro each; EDWARD, 1 negro and set of
blacksmith's tools; and PHILANDER (Exrs), 3 negroes
and saddler's shop and tools, still to be shared with
EDWARD and mother; dau: ELIZABETH PEARCE, Ł 2; gr. sons:
JOEL and JOSIAH PRIDGEN, 1 negro to be shared; son-in-
law: HARDY PRIDGEN, Ł 2; son-in-law: ELISHA HORN, Ł 2;
gr. daus: HANSEL and TABITHA HORN, to share 1 negro
at death of gr. mother; gr. son: MARTIN HORN, 1 negro
at death of gr. mother; gr. son: SARKY PRIDGEN, 1
negro; dau: ONEY BARNES, 1 negro; gr. dau: LEVISA
TISDALE, furniture (all new), cow and calf and $50;
gr. dau: ELIZABETH TISDALE, 1 negro, residue divided
between wife and 6 chil and 6 gr. chil. Wit: PETER
GRAY, BENJAMIN GRAY, REBEKAH GRAY, ELIZABETH GRAY,
JAS. WILLIAMS.

TISDALE, MARY
        No Date. May Ct., 1820. Bk. E, p 234. Gr. dau:
TABITH JOYNER wife of WRIGHTSON JOYNER, 1/2 wearing
app'l, 1/2 4 stone jugs, 1/2 4 black bottles, cow,
all this to TABITHA; ELIZABETH TISDALE, dau of
EDWARD TISDALE, cow and yearling, also furniture,
1/2 earing app'l, 1/2 of 4 stone jugs, 1/2 of 4 stone
bottles, and trunk. Residue divided between gr. daus:
TABITHA JOYNER and ELIZABETH TISDALE. Exr: WRIGHTSON
W. JOYNER. Wit: PHILIP STALLINGS, BENJAMIN THORNELL.

TOLSON, WINDER
        Jan. 19, 1837. Probated in 1837. Wife: FANNY, a
good featherbed and furniture; chil: TELLITHA PIPPEN,

MARY PRICE, ELIZABETH, ANN; EXUM and WILLIAM RUFFIN,
each child to have bed and furniture; WILLIAM RUFFIN
to have 121½ A I now live on; residue to be equally
divided between wife and chil. Wit: F. D. LITTLE,
WILLIS FLEMING.

TOMPKINS, JOHN S.
Aug. 21, 1823. Aug. Ct., 1824. Bk. F, p 21. Wife:
ROSANNAH, whole estate. Exr: PETER EVANS, RICHARD HINES.
Wit: WILL J. ANDREWS, WM. W. GARRETT.

TOOLE, ELIZABETH
Mar. 27, 1832. Nov. Ct., 1832. Bk. F, p 136. Gr.
son: JOHN HAYWOOD PARKER, claim of $1000 due me from
THEOPHILUS PARKER; gr. sons: HENRY TOOLE and HENRY T.
CLARK, 20 shares of Bank stock in the State Book of
North Carolina; gr. daus: MARY E. TOOLE and LAURA P.
CLARK, 10 shares of stock in Bank of Cape Fear; gr.
dau: MARIA T. CLARK, my bureau, 3 negroes; gr. dau:
CAROLINA C. S. PARKER, 1 negro woman; gr. dau:
ELIZABETH T. PARKER, 2 negroes; gr. daus: MARY SUMNER
CLARK, MARY WEEKS PARKER, bed and bureau each;
THEOPHILUS PARKER and JAMES W. CLARK, residue of
estate. Exr: THEOPHILUS PARKER, JAMES W. CLARK. Wit:
BENJAMIN BOYKIN, JOHN PARKER.

TOOLE, GERALDUS
July 8, 1834. Probated...1834. Wife: ELIZABETH,
25 negroes, carriage and horses, all household and
kitchen furniture in Franklin Co.; all horses, cattle,
sheep, hogs and farming utensils. Lend Plantation
whereon I live in Franklin Co., reversion to dau:
MARY L. TOOLE; dau: ANN ELIZA ROBARDS, lend 100 A adjoining River Tract on lines of MOORE, KNIGHT and
LAWRENCE, bequeath 25 negroes, lend 1/2 my MOORE
Plantation in Franklin Co., River Tract in Edgecombe
on lines of ROBARDS and FERGUSON, also 140 A of HEARN
Tract adjoining WM. LONG, all these lands to her for
her life, reversion to her chil. I have given deeds
to Mr. ROBARDS for BURNET and EDMONDSON Tracts; dau:
AMELIA RIDLEY, following tracts of land, 1/4 of MOORE
tract, in Franklin Co., land in Edgecombe purchased
of Mrs. HEARN, the JOHN EDMONDSON tract, bought of

SLATER & EDMONDSON, also reversion to her chil., and
the DAVID LAWRENCE tract with 26 negroes; dau: MARY
LAVINIA TOOLE, following lands, tract in Edgecombe on
which I reside, purchased from HALL, 120 A of MORRIS
Tract, several tracts of vacant land taken up by me,
1 50 A, the other 180 A, also my Shiloh plantation
purchased of HENRY TOOLE which, being highly prized
for family recollection. I desire to perpetuate it as
long as possible to my own descendants, therefore I
give it to my dau MARY for her life, then to her chil
and theirs (Torn), and 28 negroes; to MARY LAVINIA,
my clock, piano and bookcase, balance of furniture to
be divided between SUSAN IRWIN and MARY; dau: SUSAN
IRWIN TOOLE, 1/4 MOORE lands in Franklin Co., tract
purchased of CHARLES KNIGHT, a part of FERGUSON Tract,
also 27 negroes; gr. son: SAMUEL GERALDUS WILLIAMS,
6 negroes, also Green Tract in Franklin Co.; SUSAN
and MARY are minors. Mrs. NANCY O'BRIEN to have use
of my house and lot in Tarboro or to be rented for
her, also $25 per year. Exr: JAMES W. CLARK of
Edgecombe, JOEL KING of Franklin. Wit: HENRY T. CLARK,
JOHN WILLIAMS,

TOOLE, HENRY I.
   Oct. 2, 1813. Nov. Ct., 1816. Bk. E, p 147. Mother
and Extx: (not named), 2 negroes with request that they
be liberated and given a home on my farm in Nash Co.;
3 other negroes continued on same farm and profits
given to my mother during her lifetime. Reversion to
son, MATHUSELAH TOOLE, desire that he be raised, and
educated in N. C.; wife: (not named), land in Edgecombe
equal to that set aside for her in Nash. Her proportion
of my negroes shall be allotted out of such as I acquired from her relations by marriage or gift. Desire
that none of wife's relations shall have anything to do
with management of my estate. Exr: Uncle, GERALDUS
TOOLE. Wit: JAMES ADAMS, G. TOOLE. Exr refusing to
qualify, Adm. granted THEOPHILUS PARKER, who entered
Bond of $15,000 with GERALDUS TOOLE and BENNETT
BARROW, Securities.

TOOLE, LAURENCE
   No. Date. Dec. Ct., 1761. Wife & Extx: SABRA, lend

plantation furniture, tools, use of 3 negroes, cattle, hogs, horses, etc.; son & exr: LAURENCE, plantation whereon I live, at death of his mother, also her negroes; sons: HENRY IRWIN TOOLE plantation bought of RICHARDSON and 2 negroes; GERALDUS, plantation bought of PETTYPOOL and 2 negroes; dau: ELIZABETH O'BRYAN, money from sale of 1 negro, also money MacMANAS owes me; daus: ANN, MARY, SABRA, JENNY, 1 negro each; at wife's death cattle etc. divided between 3 sons. Exr: GERALDUS O'BRYAN. Wit: HENRY HART, WILLIAM BRACEWELL, PRISCILLA HART.

TREVATHAN, ROBERT
     Apr. 22, 1790. May Ct., 1791. Bk. 3, p 171. Wife: PRUDENCE, lend bed, bedstead, 2 sheets, reversion to son WILLIS; son: WILLIAM, 5 S; dau: ELIZABETH, mare, saddle and bridle, furniture, rug, 1 sheet, cow, heifer, box iron and heater and looking glass; son: WILLIS; son & exr: ROBERT, tract land in Gates Co. on Bennett's Creek adjoining REUBEN LASSITER, 7 hogs, furniture; sons: FREDERICK and LEWIS, 1 S each; son & exr: HENRY, furniture, 2 sheets; son: SION, 20 S; residue divided between WILLIS, ROBERT, HENRY and ELIZABETH. Wit: JESSE JOHNSON, SETH GARRET, AMOUS ROSE.

TREVATHAN, ROBERT
     Mar. 2, 1824. Aug. Ct., 1824. Bk. F, p 24. Wife: GRACE, lend use of all property, land reverting to JONAS and DEMPSEY; chil: JONAS, DEMPSEY, ROBERT, furniture each; ELIZABETH, $45, furniture; son: JOHN, furniture, mare, cow and calf, 3 sheep (value $43), exclusive of bed; daus: SALLY ROSE, furniture, cow and yearling (value $10); CATHERINE, furniture, cow and calf; residue divided between ROBERT, JOHN, ELIZABETH, SALLY, CATHERINE, after wife's death. Exr: HENRY BRYAN, RICHMOND DOZIER. Wit: HENRY TREVATHAN, ELI TREVATHAN.

TURNER, HENRY
     Jan. 20, 1748. Feb. Ct., 1748. Wife & Extx: MARY, yuse of 3 negroes, slave Jude to be sold, money put in hands of my friend MATTHEW JOYNER to be let out upon interest until my dau MARY TURNER comes of age or marries; should wife decease or marry my son

SOLOMON shall have my negro boy Burrell, and my dau
OLLIF (OLIVE ?) shall have the child my wench Rachel
now goeth with. Each son a horse, called his. Residue
divided. Sons: JOSEPH, 150 A of land bought of DANIEL
McDOWELL, SW of Cat tale Marsh; stock, cattle to be
sold, money laid up for youse of my son JOSEPH when
he comes of age of 21; THOMAS, plantation bought of
ROBERT COUNCIL likewise 150 A plantation whereon I now
live, on E side of Cat tale Marsh, reversing youse of
my land to my beloved wife MARY during her widowhood;
SOLOMON, 200 A land lying on W side of Deep Creek. Exr:
Friend, MATTHEW JOYNER. Wit: MATTHEW JOYNER, JAMES
HARRIS, MARMADUKE NORFLEET.

TURNER, HENRY
    Aug. 25, 1819. Nov. Ct., 1819. Wife: POLLY, all
residue; chil: JACOB, ETHELRED, WINNY HEDGEPETH,
PATIENCE, MOURNING, 1 sheep and ewe each. Exr: JOSEPH
LEE. Wit: W. BUNN, ETHELRED EXUM, RACHEL BUNN.

TYSON, WILLIAM
    Oct. 10, 1826. Feb. Ct., 1828. Bk. F, p 82. Wife:
ESTHER J. TYSON, whole estate; if she should have a
child and remarry she shall have half personal property,
the other half and all land shall go to our child. If
child should not live to maturity it's share to go to
MARY RUFFIN, grandmother of said child. Written in
own hand. No Wit. Proven in Ct. by oaths of RICHARD
HINES, Esq., ELNATHAN TART, and WM. GARRETT.

UMPHREY, ROBERT
    Mar. 20, 1761. No record of Recording. Wife & Extx:
MATHEW (MARTHA ?), 2 negroes, lend all cattle, hogs,
mare, household goods, tools, cider casks during widowhood; son: THOMAS, 100 A tract on Mill Creek, horse,
bridle, saddle, cattle, hogs, etc. called "THOMASES"
and ewe and lamb; sons: ISUM and ROBERT ₺ 10 in gold
and silver coins each; money to be used to take up
land for them; son: MATTHEW, plantation whereon I live,
except 100 A given THOMAS. Daus: ELESE, MARY and PATIENCE
and sons ISUM and ROBERT to share residue at mother's
death. Exr: JOSEPH HOWELL. Wit: BENJA. HART, BENJA.
BUNN, THOS. UNDERWOOD.

VASSER, TEMPERANCE
    Sept. 7, 1839. Aug. Ct., 1840. Bk. F, p 245. All
property to mother (unnamed); reversion to sister and
Extx: MARTHA VASSER. Wit: JAMES JORDAN, BENJAMIN WHITE.

VICKERS, JOHN "of greate age and low condition"
    Feb. 21, 1784. Nov. Ct., 1784. Wife & Extx: MARY,
plantation whereon I live, also all moveable estate
for her life or widowhood; reversion to 3 sons JOSHUA,
RALF and JOSEPH. Sons: ABRAM and JACOB, to them and
their heirs, 1 S; JOHN, 360 A plantation whereon he
lives and all land in that survey; My deceased son's
(GEORGE) heirs; DAVID and GEORGE, 200 A plantation E
side Williamson's Branch whereon my son lived; SABRINA
and SARA, daus of deceased son GEORGE, 1 S each, and
1/2 of all moveable property except still & tools; son:
BENJAMIN, 1 S; son & exr: RALF, 200 A plantation whereon I live on lines of Town Creek, Williamson's Branch
& JOHN MORRIS; JOSHUA, 40 S Va. money; JOSEPH, 40 S
money, blacksmith's tools and still at mother's death;
STEPHEN, 1 S; daus: MARTHA HATCHER, MARY MORRIS,
PATIENCE STOKES, 1 S each; gr. dau: BETSY STOKES, dau
of PATIENCE, ELIZABETH WHITE, 1 S each; gr. dau BETSEY,
L 10 after death of wife; Exr: son-in-law: JOHN MORRIS,
to be paid 5 S each for serving; Wit: BRITON BRIDGERS,
SAMUEL VICKERS.

VICKERS. RALPH, Parish of St. Mary's
    Aug. 11, 1761. Sept. Ct., 1762. Wife & Extx:
SARAH, lend plantation whereon I live, reversion to
youngest son ABRAHAM, 1 negro to be sold at her death,
money divided between 4 youngest chil., horse, saddle,
bridle, 2 pewter dishes, pewter tankard, 6 pewter
plates, best iron pot and frying pan; Eldest son &
Exr: RALPH, plantation bought of WILLIAM WILLIAMSON,
horse, large gun, sword; sons: JOHN, plantation bought
of JOHN MOORE, also horse and gun; ABRAHAM, mare
bought of EDWARD BURTON to be shared with SARA; SARA,
furniture, residue to be divided between wife SARAH
and her four chil, MARY BAKER, RACHEL SCARBOROUGH,
eldest daus, L 2 - 15 S each. Wit: MOSES BAKER,
BENJAMIN BRAND, AARON BAKER.

VICKERS, SARAH
Feb. 7, 1781. Aug. Ct., 1783. Sons & Exrs: ABRAHAM,
plantation whereon I live, as provided in his father's
will, all estate; JOHN, use of still. Wit: JOHN
PERMENTER, MARY HEAD, JOHN VICKERS.

VINES, CHARLES
June 10, 1823. Aug. Ct., 1823. Bk. E, p 334.
THIGPEN land lying S side Autry (Otter's) Creek also
1 negro to be sold to pay just debts; SOFFIA (wife ?),
lend 1/3 land, child's part of residue; lend 1 negro,
reversion to ALLEN & LEMUEL. Mother: LUCY O'NEAL lend
2 A, all my rite in 3 negroes. Exr: SAMUEL VINES, JONAH
WOOTEN. Wit: BENJAMIN MOORE, HEZEKIAH LANGLEY, ENOS
ELLIS.

WALL, DORCET (DOCET)
Dec. 30, 1760. June Ct., 1761. Wife: MARTHA, residue to be divided between her and daus: MASSEY, plantation whereon I live; FANNEY, tract lying on Pine-
logg Swamp; dec'd bro: MOSES WALL, tract that falls
to me from him as well as all my cattle and stock to
be divided between my daus. Exr: JOHN JONES, JAMES
DUGLESS. Wit: DAVIS CONNELL, FREDERICK SAULS, ABSALOM
SAULS.

WALL, ELIJAH
Dec. 28, 1760. Mar. Ct., 1761. Wife (unnamed),
bequeath 1/3 movable estate and all movable for her
life or widowhood; eldest son: ELISHA, 90 A plantation
I live on adjoining JAMES WALL; son: HARDY, 90 A plantation whereon SARAH WALL did live where ELIJAH WALL
now lives; Exr: JAMES WIET, ABRAHAM SAULS. Wit: THOMAS
DANIELL (?), JOHN WIET, CHARITY WALL.

WALL, GERRAD (GERRARD ?)
Dec. 14, 1760. Mar. Ct., 1761. Wife: RACHEL, lend
200 A plantation whereon I live, reversion to my 4th
son: JAMES, bequeath 1/3 residue; eldest son: DORSET,
64 A tract along Pinelog Creek, ABRAHAM SAULS' with
the hard money I have reserved to save it with, also
150 A tract where he lives; 2nd son: ELIJAH, 180 A
plantation where he now lives and heifer; gr. son:

ELISHA, son of ELIJAH, 100 A on Griffin's Swamp; 3rd
son: MOSES, 500 A on Griffin's Swamp, also 1 heifer;
daus: CHARITY, linen wheel; MARTHA, linen wheel, residue to be divided between 6 chil. Exr: Bro-in-law:
WILLIAM SCREWS, CHARLES DANIELL. Wit: FRANCIS SPIVEY,
CHARLES DANIELL, ELIJAH WALL, SUSANNAH WIET.

WALL, JOHN (of Halifax Co. N. C.)
    Sept. 15, 1778. May Ct., 1779. Son & Exr: JESSE,
plantation whereon I live; daus: ELIZABETH WEEKS, cow
and calf, side saddle, 2 pewter dishes, 6 plates and
iron pot; THENAH (PHEBY) ALSOBROOK, 5 S; daus: SELAH
KELLEY, FAITHEY GRIFFITH and HANNAH; gr. chil:
PRISCILLA, HANNAH and RODAH ALSOBROOK, chil of DAVID
ALSOBROOK. Exr: Son-in-law: GILES KELLEY. Wit: R.
COTTEN, ARCHELUS WEEKS.

WALL, SARAH
    Nov. 2, 1754. June Ct., 1756. Sons: HENRY, ARTHUR
and JOHN, bed each at her death, a large chest with
lock and key and 20 S; gr. son: WILLIAM FRENCH, 3 deep
new pewter dishes, 1/2 pewter plates, 2 3-qt pewter
basons, 1 3-gal iron pot and all residue; dau: FAITHE,
5 S; Exr: JOHN WALL. Wit: HENRY HORN, ELIZABETH HORN,
SIHON HORN.

WALLER, JAMES
    Apr. 23, 1808. May Ct., 1808. Bk. D, p 315. Wife:
REBECCA, life estate in house and lands, 1 negro, $100,
2 cows and calves, 2 sows and pigs, beaufat, household
furniture, and provisions for ensuing year; gr. son:
URIAH SHIRLEY, 50 A land adjoining land bequeathed my
wife, reversion in land I bequeathed my wife REBECCA,
gr. son URIAH SHIRLEY, 1 negro, bridle and saddle,
sow and pigs, 2 cows, 2 yearlings and heifer. If dies
without reaching legal age, estate to be divided between surviving gr. chil; daus: JENNY MORGAN (?) and
her chil for support, Ł 20 per year; dau: NANCY HOWELL,
Ł 5 per year during her life; dau: MARY TAYLOR and her
chil, 1 negro wench; gr. son: JOHN SHIRLEY, 20 S in
full for his share. Sell remaining land not bequeathed
and put money to interest, 3 negroes be hired out for
20 years and money divided between my gr. chil, except

SHIRLEY; if advantageous, negroes can be sold. Exr: son, STARLING WALLER, JAMES SOUTHERLAND, THOMAS D. GUION. Wit: THOMAS GUION, JOSIAH PENDER.

WALLER, MARGARET
　　July 13, 1829. Feb. Ct., 1830. Bk. F, p 109. Bro: JAMES WALLER, all my land and 1 negro; MARGARET GRIFFIN, dau of THOMAS GRIFFIN, $50; LUCY WALLER, dau of EDWARD WALLER, $40; Mother (unnamed) and single sisters, use of negroes and stock of all kind, provided they remain on plantation; reversion to bro and exr: JAMES WALLER. Wit: READING SUGG, ROBT. H. WATKINS.

WALSTON, JONAS
　　May 7, 1806. Feb. Ct., 1813 (?) 1815 (?). Bk. E, p 125. Wife & Extx: CHARLOTTE, 100 A plantation, being same land I bought from REUBEN ELLIS. Wit: AMOS JOHNSTON, WILLIAM JOHNSTON.

WALSTON, SILAS
　　Nov. 16, 1815. Nov. Ct., 1815. Bk. E, p 109. Wife: RACHEL, all personal property; use of plantation during life. Exr: LEVI MERCER, JACOB MERCER. Wit: GILLIAD THIGPEN, JOSHUA B. EASON.

WARD, CHARLOTTE
　　May 26, 1855. Aug. Ct., 1855. Bk. G, p 111. Nephew & Exr: ETHELRED PHILIPS, of Florida, all my lands, ne-groes and property of every description during his life, then to his chil, in consideration of which he will continue the farm, keep my negroes together, and pay to JOSEPH I. PORTER a legacy of $500, pay all my debts, that he shall keep graveyard where my late hus-band JOHN WARD and my son JOSEPH are buried, and where I wish to be buried, and well enclose said graveyard, place tombstone to each grave, or suitable monument for the whole, etc. If nephew does not choose to ac-cept terms, property to be sold and will carried out. Wit: JAMES I. PHILIPS, W. F. LEWIS. Codicil: To the daus of ETHELRED GRAY, deceased, MARTHA ANN HOWELL, MARY, WILLIAM F. & VIRGINIA and HELEN B. GRAY and the child of CAROLINE GRAY BONNER, 7 slaves. Wit: JAMES I. PHILIPS, JOHN G. RIVES.

WARD, JOHN D.

Sept. 4, 1823. Nov. Ct., 1823. Bk. F, p 4. Wife &
Extx: CHARLOTTE, have use of all my property in this
State until my son JOSEPH J. E. WARD reaches lawful
age; support and education be provided wife and son,
and all my property in this State at death of my wife;
sons: DAVID E. WARD, all my property in Tennessee;
JOSEPH J. E. WARD, all my property in this State after
death of my wife. Exr and testamentary Gdn. to my son
JOSEPH J (?) E. WARD, LOUIS D. WILSON, S. WHITAKER,
Bro: DICKEN WARD, my Exr in the State of Tenn. and Gdn.
to my son DAVID C. WARD. Wit: NANCY PHILIPS, JOHN N.
PHILIPS, TIMOTHY M. PHILIPS.

WARD, LUKE (SENR)

Oct. 16, 1838 Probated 1838. Wife: NANCY, all
farming utensils, cart, gig, and harness, 2 horses,
3 cows and calves, (her choice), 20 hogs, 3 sows and
pigs, 1500 lbs pork or bacon; half the crop of corn,
fodder on hand; bbl of brandy, bbl of wine, 15 gal of
honey, 11 negroes, land in Edgecombe County her lifetime; son & exr: RIPPON, tract of land in Pitt Co. and
negroes; son & exr: DANIEL, land in Pitt Co. and 3
negroes; son & exr: HARMON, 1 negro. Wit: JOS. JOHN
PIPPEN, WILSON HOWARD, JUN.

WARD, NANCY

Nov. 26, 1853. May Ct., 1854. Bk. G, 57. Dau:
HARRIET P. LAURENCE, wife of JOSHUA L. LAURENCE, lands
in Edgecombe and Martin Cos. adjoining lands of GABRIEL
PURVIS, JOHN A. PURVIS, LUNSFORD BROWN, Miss NANCY MAYO,
about 800 A; gr. chil; chil of HARRIET P. LAURENCE,
all my monies, bonds, notes and accounts, my 5 slaves
to be hired out and fund to be kept at interest and
paid to him or her at age of 21 yrs; No Exr. Wit:
WILLIAM NORFLEET, R. H. AUSTIN.

WARD, SILAS

Apr. 3, 1832. Aug. Ct., 1832. Bk. F, p 135. Wife
& Extx: SALLY, raise and keep together chil, using
whatever necessary to support family; should there .
be any residue, I desire it paid to my dear wife, then
divided among chil, at her marriage or death. Exr:

344

JOAB P. PITT. Wit: JAMES PITT.

WARD, SOLOMON
     Dec. 9, 1826. Feb. Ct., 1827. Bk. F, p 67. Wife:
MICHAEL, negro girl, life estate; daus: ANNIS, 1 negro;
RHODA, 1 negro; sons: SOLOMON and JOHN WARD; all my land
and Brandy still, balance of my negroes and their in-
crease. Exr: MOSES BAKER. Wit: W. G. BULLUCK, HILLIARY
PEALE.

WARD, SOLOMON
     Oct. 21, 1837. Nov. Ct., 1843. Bk. F, p 293. Wife:
ZILPHA, whole estate. Exr: EDWIN BARNES. Exr. dec'd,
Adm. granted JAMES D. BARNES.

WARREN, PRISCILLA, of Pitt County, N. C.
     Jan. 11, 1811. Nov. Ct., 1820. Bk. E, p 256. My
six oldest chil: ELIZABETH LANG (?), STEPHEN ROGERS,
SARAH WOOTTEN, PRISCILLA TURLINGTON, WILLIAM ROGERS,
JOHN ROGERS, Estate equally divided after debts are
paid. Exr. and Worthy friends: JOHN LANG, JOSIAH
WOOTTEN. Wit: ANNA BROWN, (illegible), BENJAMIN WALSTON.

WARREN, ROBERT
     Undated. June Ct., 1759. Wife & Extx: MARGRET, 3
negroes, also all remainder of real and personal estate;
daus: MARY, 1 negro, 3 cows and calves, dwelling plantation on Great Branch and 1 mare; SARAH, 1 negro, 3
cows and calves; JANE, 1 negro, 3 cows and calves, land
on E side of Great Branch, known as Co. (Col ?) RUSSEL'S
Old Field; MILYSON (MILLISCENT ?), 3 cows and calves.
Exr: GEORGE DAWKINS. Wit: BENJAMIN MERRYMAN, WILLIAM
LANE.

WEAVER, BENJAMIN
     Apr. 5, 1812. Aug. Ct., (4th) 1815. Bk. E, p 107.
Wife: OLIVE, shall hold possession, and continue on
that part of my land given my son ZACARIAH with him
during widowhood, cow, calf; my 4 sons: JONATHAN,
BENJAMIN, JETHRO and ZACKARIAH, all my lands equally
divided. It is my desire my son ZACKARIAH, have the
portion that contains houses and orchards, sorrel mare,
cow and calf; daus: CHARITY and ELIZABETH WEAVER,

furniture each. Balance divided between my wife OLIVE,
and chil: JONATHAN, BENJAMIN, JEREMIAH, PIETY LAND,
JETHRO, MOURNING TAYLOR, CHARITY, ELIZABETH and
ZACHARIAH WEAVER. Exr: JONATHAN WEAVER, BENJAMIN WEAVER.
Wit: JOHN WEAVER, WILLIAM LANGLEY, CHARLES LAND.

WEAVER, JONATHAN W.
Jan. 1, 1847. Feb. Ct., 1848. Bk. F, p 389. Sisters:
ELIZA BRITT and OBEDIENCE SKINNER. Estate to children
of sisters. Exr: JOHN PITT. Wit: WILLIAM NORFLEET, JOHN
NORFLEET.

WEBB, JOHN
Jan. 23, 1785. May Ct., 1785. Wife: PATIENCE,
furniture, loom, geese, 2 Lining wheels, and wooling
wheel, 2 pots, 2 hooks, 2 pewter basons, 2 dishes, 6
plates, 6 spoons, flacks (flax), Hackle, box iron and
heaters, also 1 chest, 4 head horses, 2 cows and calves,
6 head sheep; dau: MARY JONES, ₺ 15; sons: JOHN, tract
of land in Scotland Neck, 1 negro, horse, furniture,
2 cheers, 2 cows and calves; if he died without heirs
the negro fellow Tobe returns to my son JAMES; THOMAS,
plantation I now live on... run of Little Swamp, up
Marsh Branch, furniture, desk, 2 cows and calves, and
1 negro; WILLIAM, tract on S side of the Little Branch
by the run of said Swamp... on lines of JAMES DOWNING,
MICAJAH LITTLE, EPHRIAM ADDAMS and JOHN OWENS, negro
Wench, still, worm and cap, furniture, 2 cows and calves,
4 head sheep; dau: PENELOPE, ₺ 125 to buy her a negro
girl; JAMES, negro fellow Jacob and ₺ 60 to buy him
another negro. Exr: THOMAS BOYKIN, SAMUEL GAINER. Wit:
JOHN HUDNALL, JOSEPH SWALES.

WEBB, JOHN (SENIOR) "Feeble and advanced in age."
Mar. 2, 1841. Nov. Ct., 1842. Bk. F, p 271. Sons:
DAVID, tract known as ANDREW OWEN tracts whereon I now
liveth, about 200 A; Tract known as STEPHEN HARRELL
tract, (2) the Rakestraw tract about 95 A; (3) EDWARD
GWIN, about 95 A adjoining the DEMPSEY WEBB tract and
my home tract, known as the BRAZIER (BRASWELL ?) land
on the S side of the mill pond, adjoining the HADDOCK
land, about 100 A; WILLIAM have tract known as EASON
land, adjoining land of WILLIAM PATE, about 182 A;

DEMPSEY 95 A tract known as the GAY land; JOHN, 95 A
tract known as the ELISHA FELTON land, joining the Mill
Pond, also $35; residue to be divided between POLLY
WALSTON, WILLIE WEBB'S chil, to wit: WEALTHY, DELPHA,
REDDIC and ELI WEBB and CYPY SMITH and CHARLOTTE
HARRELL, lands and negroes. Exr: JOAB P. PITT. Wit:
ELISHA HARRELL, HENRY BRINKLEY.

WEBB, JOHN
     Oct. 19, 1845. Aug. Ct., 1853. Sons: JOHN, 5 ne-
groes and a colt; DANIEL, 3 negroes; NATHAN, 5 negroes and land on Reedy Branch adjoining JOHN ELLIS,
another tract adjoining CHARLES ELLIS, bought of
JOSEPH KELLY, tract adjoining JOHN CARTER and JAMES
BARRON (BARROW ?); ORMEN, 2 negroes; WILLIS, 2 negroes; daus: ANNA, 2 negroes; TEMPERENCE, tract
whereon I now live, 100 A, S side of a large Pocosin
Branch from Tarborough Road to Whiteoak Swamp adjoining land of JOB FELTON; gr. dau: MARANDA WEBB,
$200; daus: NANCY, 50 A part of the old tract given
me by my father whereon HENRY WEBB did live; CELIA
HARREL, $150; sons: DAVID and JOHN, all my lands not
disposed of; DAVID to have my saddle horse; gr. son:
GARRET WEBB $300; gr. chil: chil of DELPHIA ELLIS,
ELIZABETH HARRELL, MARTHA ANN OWEN, SYNTHIA JONES,
CELIA HARREL, NANCY WEBB and TEMPERENCE WEBB, share
equally in the residue of my estate. Exr & Worthy
Friend: DAVID WILLIAMS. Wit: JNO. G. WILLIAMS, J. L.
HORN.

WEBB, WILLIAM
     Feb. 28, 1848. May Ct., 1848. Bk. F, p 399. Wife:
SALLY, lend all land (2 tracts) and all residue, 3
chil to have schooling; daus: MALVINA, CELIANN (?);
son: WILLIAM FRANKLIN WEBB. Exr: RICHARD T. EAGLES.
Wit: JOHN R. MERCER, JOHN FELTON.

WEEKS, (WEAKS), CELY
     July 26, 1827. Nov. Ct., 1827. Bk. F, p 77. Son:
ARCHER WEAKS surviving Heirs and dau: ELIZABETH KITCHEN'S
Heirs 10 S; son: JAMES WEAKS; gr. daus: TEMPY BATTS
and SARAH HARPER; daus: MARY PIPPEN and MARTHA BRYAN;
son: SOLOMON WEAKES; son & Exr: PENDER WEAKES, 10 S

each; residue to 2 gr. sons JACK D. WEAKS and SOLOMON P. WEAKS. Wit: JAMES BIGGS.

WEEKS, JAMES
    Nov. 11, 1809. May Ct., 1815. Bk. E, p 93. Wife: SELAH, during life, the manor Plantation whereon I live, 1 negro, furniture, mare, named Blaze, 2 cows and calves, ewe and lamb, 2 iron pots, bason, dish, half doz. plates (which is to be Pewter), 1 case of knives and forks, black walnut table, Trunk, woman's saddle, bridle, cupboard, sow and pigs, and woodenware belonging to the house; son: JAMES, 1 negro after my wife's decease, furniture; son & exr: PENDER, land and plantation where I now live after my dear wife SELAH'S decease, 1 negro and still; deceased son ARCHIBALD'S heirs: the sum of 10 S; daus: MARY PIPPEN (life), 1 negro; SARAH HARPER (life), 1 negro Violet and to her heirs, furniture now in her possession; ELIZABETH KITCHEN and heirs L 25; SELAH PIPPEN and heirs, L 25; MARTHA BRYAN and heirs, L 25. Exr: Friends, JOB BRADDY, HARDY PARKER. Wit: HARDY HOWARD, EDWARD POWER, JACK M. HACKNEY.

WEEKS, JAMES
    Oct. 25, 1837. 1837. Wife & Extx: TINCY, during her widowhood or life, 120 A land reversion to son GEORGE WASHINGTON WEEKS, horse, bridle, and saddle; daus: unnamed except SUSANNAH, whom he had provided for. Wit: CYRUS M. BRYAN, LITTLEBERRY BRYAN.

WEEKS, JOHN (WEAKS)
    May 28, 1810. Aug. Ct., 1810. Bk. D, p 367. Wife: CHARLOTTE land I bought of DAVID LAWRENCE, my negro Ned, for widowhood; son: BYTHAL, and the child that my wife is now with, all my property at wife's death or marriage. Exr and Friends: THOMAS CUTCHIN, WILLIAM HAYNES. Wit: SELAH PIPPEN, SARAH HAYNES.

WEEKS, SARAH
    Oct. 12, 1792. Nov. Ct., 1792. Gr. son: BENJAMIN WEEKS, horse, bridle and saddle; daus: MARTHA, wife of WILLIAM HACKNEY, L 10 lawful money of this State; ANN, wife of KADAH PARKER, 5 S; property to be sold

and divided among my 4 other chil, after paying said
MARTHY HACKNEY and ANN PARKER; my sons: JAMES, (Exr),
JOHN and ARTHUR WEEKS and MARY PARKER. Wit: JOSEPH
BRADLEY, PHILIP POPE, WILLIAM PIPPEN.

WELLS, MATTHEW
June 23, 1834. Aug. Ct., 1836. Bk. F, p 194. Wife:
HONOR, plantation where I now live, and remainder of
estate for life or widowhood, then to my dau: HONOR
MORE (MOORE) and BENJAMIN MORE, then to their chil;
wife's gr. son: ELKANA BAILEY, cattle in his possession
and my gun; residue to be divided between HONOR MORE
AND ELKANA BAILEY. Exr: REDDICK BARNES. Wit: COFFIELD
ELLIS, EDWIN STOKES, ELBERT AMASON.

WELLS, STEPHEN, Parish of St. Mary's Province of North
Carolina
Mar. 10, 1773. Apr. Ct., 1775. Wife & Extx:
PRISCILLA, 200 A plantation for life only, use of
personal estate, L 10 current money of Va., which she
is to make use of in bringing up my gr. son. ELIJAH
WELLS; sons: STEPHEN, land N side Tar River beginning
in Co. of Edgecombe at the River, EDMOND SHERROD'S
Corner, down the River, 150 A etc; 1 heifer, after
his mother's decease; REDMON, FREDERICK and JOSHUA,
land on N side of Tar River in Edgecombe Co., mouth
of Wild Cat Branch, original Deed called for 300 A;
SOLOMON, 200 A plantation I now live on, after his
mother's death; DANIEL, cow and calf; daus: MARY
ROBBINS, sow and pigs; BETTY STERLING, ewe and lambs;
WINY POOVY, ewe and lamb after wife's death; PRISCILLA
POPE, sow and pigs, etc. Wit: DUNCAN LAMON, JOSEPH
CROWELL, ROSAMOND JACKSON.

WELLS, THOMAS
May 26, 1800. Aug. Ct., 1801. Son: LEONARD, 300 A
of land on S side of Goff Swamp, mouth of Gum Branch,
and furniture; daus: MARY, 100 A plantation whereon
WILLIAM DANIEL formerly lived between Goff Swamp and
Gum Branch, 2 cows and calves; TEMPY WATSON, 100 A
plantation whereon she now lives, on Buzzardnest
Branch, and Little Branch, various courses, to Branch
called Tar Kiln, during life; reversion to her 3 daus

SARAH, ELIZABETH and ANN WATSON, furniture, etc; son
& exr: MATTHEW, 417 A land on N side of Goff Swamp,
furniture; daus: ANN WELLS and RACHEL JOHNSTON (?),
furniture each; SARAH DANIEL, 10 S; gr. son: FRANCIS
DANIEL, furniture; residue divided among all my chil:
LEONARD, MATHEW, MARY, TEMPERENCE WATSON and ANN and
RACHEL WELLS. Exr: ELI AMASON. Wit: EDWARD MAYO, NATHAN
SESSUMS (QUAKERS).

WEST, WILLIAM
     Nov. 26, 1748. Feb. Ct., 1749. Son: WILLIAM, JR.,
200 A S side of Rocky Swamp together with water mill;
bro: HENRY WEST; neph: WILLIAM, son of HENRY WEST,
breeding mare, 2 cows and calves, 2 sows and pigs;
dau: MARY WILLIAMS, 5 S in confirmation of what I
have given her before and after marriage; Exr: WILLIAM
WEST. Wit: WALLIS JONES, JOHN LONG, JOEL JONES.

WESTON, AMOS
     Nov. 1, 1811. Nov. Ct., 1811. Bk. E, p 28. Wife
& Extx: WINNIE, stock of all kinds, household and
kitchen furniture, farming utensils for life; reversion to my 5 chil: SALLEY, AMOS, WINNEY, REUBIN
and HARDY WESTON; son: EZEKIEL WESTON, 10 S; dau:
NANCY, wife of WILLIS WALLER, 10 S. Wit: WILKINSON
MABREY, CARL ALSOBROOK.

WHEATLY (WHITLEY ?), GEORGE (SENR) St. Mary's Parish
Province of North Carolina
     Oct. 2, 1765. Oct. Ct., 1766. Son: GEORGE, cow and
calf; dau: ELIZABETH, cow and calf, furniture, her
choice; son: NATHAN, 170 A plantation and appurtenances;
residue divided among my chil. I appoint MOSES ADKINSON,
Trustee for my sons: BRITAIN and NATHAN, and desire
he may instruct NATHAN in the mystery of his trade;
to have management of estate until they arrive at 21.
Exr: MOSES ADKINSON. Wit: DUNCAN LAMON, WM. EASON,
EDWARD SHERRARD.

WHEELESS, BENJAMIN
     Nov. 22, 1772. Nov. Ct., 1772. Wife: MILDRED,
large chest, use of plantation (widowhood), 5 cows,
her choice, horse and L 25 Proc. money; son: AMOS,

Rifle gun, now called his, my Blacksmith tools; residue divided among chil: if child wife now goes with,
male or female, shall have share alike, with all other
chil: AMOS, WILLIAM, JESSE, and SARAH WHEELESS. Exr:
ISAM WHEELESS, Mr. JAMES DRAKE, SENR. Wit: THOS. MANN,
JOSEPH HOBDY, WILLIAM WHEELESS.

WHITE, ANN
     Feb. 3, 1805. Aug. Ct., 1810. Son: DANIEL, shall
have my horse and nothing more; dau: HANNAH, furniture
and nothing more; residue to be divided between my sons:
LUKE and JOSHUA WHITE; dau: SARY GINER (JOYNER?). Son
& Exr: WILLIAM WHITE. Wit: DAWSON VASSER, JOSHUA WHITE.

WHITE, ARCHIBALD
     Dec. 28, 1782. Feb. Ct., 1783. Wife: MURPREY, houses,
lots, furniture, use of lands, young trotting mare,
saddle, bridle, 1 negro, furniture, use of my estate
during widowhood for support and schooling my chil;
after her marriage or death, estate sold and divided
among my 3 sons: WILLIAM, ALEXANDER, HENRY and
ARCHIBALD, when my son WILLIAM ALEXANDER arrives at 21.
Exr. & Friends: WILLIAM FORT, JOHN HAYWOOD, JAMES WILSON.
Wit: ELIAS FORT, STARLING WALLER, ESTHER HOWELL.

WHITE, BENJAMIN
     Oct. 22, 1807. May Ct., 1808. Wife & Extx: unnamed,
lend plantation, remainder of stock, household and
kitchen furniture, my negro woman Chaney and child be.
sold, money used for raising my chil; daus: POLLY,
ELIZABETH and TREASEY, furniture, 2 cows and calves
each. Exr & Bro: WILLIAM WHITE, SENR. Wit: HARDY FLOWERS,
MARY FLOWERS.

WHITE, GEORGE
     Nov. 27, 1777. Feb. Ct., 1782. Wife: Unnamed, during
widowhood, plantation I now live on; reversion to my son:
WILLIAM, at my wife's decease or marriage, also land I
bought of my son JACOB, horse and bason; son: GEORGE,
tract of land I took up, joining JACOB ROBINS, featherbed, horse, Bason; dau: NANCY, furniture; son: BENJAMIN,
lower part of my land, run off by a new line, horse,
Plate mold and small ladle; dau: MARY, furniture and

pot. Son & Exr: JACOB WHITE. Wit: JOHN WILLIAMS, AARON PROCTOR, RALPH VICKERS.

WHITE, JOHN
Undated. May Ct., 1800. Daus: SARAH HAMMOND, NANCY, POLLY and PENELOPE WHITE, furniture, 2 cows and calves each; son & Exr: JOHN WHITE, all my land, furniture, 2 cows and calves, 2 negroes, for maintenance and supporting his sister, my dau NANCY WHITE. Exr: JOHN BILLUP, JOHN BONNER. No Witnesses.

WHITE, JOHN
Aug. 25, 1803. May Ct., 1804. Wife: ANN, child's part of my personal estate; daus: COMFORT, ANN and SARAH, what they have already had; sons: DANIEL, LUKE and JOSHAWAY, what they have already had; WILLIAM, 1 negro Woman, my still and cider casks; residue to be divided between wife ANN and son WILLIAM; gr. son: JOSHAWAY WHITE, negro boy; dau: HANNAH, negro boy; negro boy Ishmael be set free at age of 21. Exr & Friend: WILLIAM WHITE, JR. Wit: WILLIAM ROSS, ELI MERCER, WILLIAM ROBINS, SENR.

WHITE, MARTHA
Jan. 26, 1838. May Ct., 1840. Daus: EDITH DAWSON and MARTHA WHITE, and son: BENJAMIN, 1 negro each; I wish my negro Tab to choose which of my chil she pleases to live with and old negro Nan to be maintained during her life; sons: JOSHUA, and WILLIAM, $5 each. Exr: EDWIN BARNES. Wit: JOSHUA BARNES, JAMES D. BARNES.

WHITE, REUBEN
Sept. 11, 1803. May Ct., 1804. Wife: ELLENDER, 1 negro life estate, then to child my wife goes with; residue of estate, wife to use; Exr: WILLIAM WHITE, SENIOR, WILLIAM WHITE, JUNIOR. Wit: ELI MERCER, WILLIAM WHITE, (son of WILLIAM WHITE, SENIOR).

WHITEHEAD, AUGUSTINE
Jan. 6, 1846. Feb. Ct., 1847. Bk. F, pp 357-361. Wife: MARY, life or widowhood, land where I now live, all improvements, utensils, stock, crop, provisions, household and kitchen and furniture, 6 negroes, to

reside on, and keep up plantation, support all the negroes in my possession; son, HENRY; Exrs: HENRY
WHITEHEAD and gr. son, JAMES W. LANCASTER, to have
management of 313 A property given my dau PRUDENCE,
wife of JESSE LANCASTER, whereon she and JESSE now reside, at her decease to be divided between my 4 gr.
sons: WILLIE, DOSSEY, DAVID and ROBERT LANCASTER, negroes, lands, etc; son: HENRY WHITEHEAD; 50 A W of
his house S of the Branch, land E side of his line,
due S from end of the land leading to his house, to my
old place, then to the Mill Branch to WILLIAM MERCER'S
line, etc., lands, negroes; son: ROBERT, provided for.
Wit: JAMES D. THOMAS, JACOB PROCTOR, WILLIAM PROCTOR.
Nov. Ct., 1846 Will caveated by HENRY WHITEHEAD and
JESSE LANCASTER to prove writing of AUGUSTINE WHITEHEAD.
Feb. Ct., 1847. Jury: JAMES LITTLE, WILLIAM TAYLOR,
DAVID STANCIL, JOSEPH HOWARD, LAWRENCE WALKER, JOHN
FULLER (?), JOHN DAWES, JOSHUA L. LAWRENCE, DAVID
SHALLINGTON, WRIGHT WIGGINS, COFFIELD KING, and WILLIAM
H. HINES who find the writing to be that of AUGUSTINE
WHITEHEAD and ordered it recorded.

WHITEHEAD, HENRY
     July 29, 1847. Aug. Ct., 1848. Bk. F, p 400. Wife:
PIETY, the whole of my property that came by my father,
AUGUSTINE WHITEHEAD, 133 A, 3 negroes, for life. Balance of my estate in fee simple, viz: house, furniture,
utensils, stock of every description, provisions, all
monies and evidence of money, 75 A of land and 4 negroes. Exr: WM. H. HINES. Wit: BYTHAL G. BROWN, BAKER
S. BROWN.

WHITEHEAD, MATTHEW (SENIOR)
     Feb. 21, 1846. Feb. Ct., 1848. Son: MATTHEW, plan-
tation and land where I now live; dau: MARGARET, wife
of JAMES GRIFFIN, cow and calf, my desk, walnut table,
chest, etc.; son: JOHN, land adjoining JEREMIAH BATTS
and 92 A land where I now live; JAMES, WILLIAM, FRANCIS,
and CAROLINA WHITEHEAD, land adjoining JEREMIAH BATTS,
each 92 A; dau: THANEY, wife of THEOPHILUS THOMAS,
cow and my clock. Exr: JOHN WHITEHEAD. Wit: BRITAIN
WILLIFORD.

WHITEHEAD, SARAH

Jan. 31, 1808. Feb. Ct., 1810. Dau: SUSANNAH
ROUNTREE, all my corn, wheat, bacon, clothes, Barrel
Brandy and $100; son: JAMES, 2 cows; daus: ELIZABETH
COLEMAN and SARAH BARNES, $100 each; residue of
estate to daus. Exr: WILLIAM WHITE, JUNIOR, JOSEPH
BARNES. Wit: Z. W. BAKER, EDWARD YORK.

WHITEHEAD, WILLIAM BOND

Oct. 4, 1805. Aug. Ct., 1807. Bk. D, p 286. Wife:
SARAH, plantation and lands, line to be run from my
line and DEMPSEY BARNES' lines where join in Toisnot
Swamp, thence, up said Swamp to mouth of Little Swamp,
where Brook Cobb Bridge stood. Run so as to leave 250
A to old plantation, 4 negroes (widowhood); all stock,
except horse, 3 cows and calves, household and kitchen
furniture, plantation tools, brandy still, cidar Press,
and $300; son: JAMES, remainder of land, 1 negro and
$150; daus: ELIZABETH COLEMAN, 2 negroes; NANCY WHITE
$150; SARAH BARNES, $200 and 1 negro; SUSANNAH ROUNTREE,
$200, land lent to wife, 3 negroes, Brandy still and
cider press; gr. son: WILLIAM, 1 negro; gr. daus: MARY
ROUNTREE, 2 cows and calves; PENELOPE ROUNTREE, horse,
furniture; SARAH ROUNTREE, 1 negro. Exr: son-in-law,
JOSEPH BARNES; WILLIAM WHITE, son of JOHN WHITE. Wit:
CHARLES COLEMAN, JOHN DEW.

WHITTENTON, RICHARD

Dec. 9, 1760. Mar. Ct., 1761. Nunc. Will. Then
came before me PATIENCE COX and made oath that RICHARD
WHITTENTON, late of this County, departed this life
on the eighth of this instant, heard the said RICHARD
WHITTENTON make a verbal will in manner following:
That his personal Estate be kept together to raise
his children upon; that the money in RICHARD THOMAS'
hands might be kept for taking a Deed out of the
Earl of Granville's office for a tract of land
lying on Swift Creek, which he gave to his youngest
son RICHARD WHITTENTON. MICAJAH THOMAS.

WIGGINS, BLAKE H.

Sept. 2, 1823. Feb. Ct., 1828. Bk. F, p 83. Wife:
NANCY, all my property of every species, real, personal,

perishable, her life, then to her heir, if there be any,
by me; bro: ROWLAND WIGGINS, if no child born, inherits
at decease of my wife. Wit: DAVID DANCY.

WIGGINS, JAMES
Jan. 25, 1789. Nov. Ct., 1794. Wife: WINNAFORD (life)
all my estate; at her decease, sold to highest bidder,
money divided among my chil (not named); Exr: MOSES
POWELL, CALEB ETHERIDGE. Wit: FIGURES LEWIS, ALANSON
POWELL, MARY MINTON.

WIGGINS, JAMES
Mar. 13, 1823. Aug. Ct., 1823. Bk. E, p 339. Wife:
SARAH, the residue of my land (life), furniture, 4
head cattle, stock, white horse; my 2 sons: ELISHA
& LAWRENCE, all the land on E side of Dunn's Branch
equally; son: RICHARD, land at decease of my wife. Exr:
ELISHA WIGGINS, JOHN GARRETT. Wit: ALLEN NETTLES, JACOB
NETTLES.

WIGGINS, LAWRENCE
June 25, 1847. Aug. Ct., 1847. Bk. F, p 373. Crop
to be housed and considered part of my Estate; son:
WILLIAM LAWRENCE WIGGINS, all my lands, S side of road
from Wiggins' Cross Roads towards Sparta; dau: ELIZABETH
SARAH WIGGINS, balance of my lands; all my estate, ex-
cept slaves, be sold, and divided. Exr: JESSE C. KNIGHT.
Wit: ALLEN NETTLES, JAMES STALLINGS.

WIGGINS, RICHARD
Sept. 9 (year not given). Apr. Ct., 1775. Wife:
SARAH, all lands, livings, and possessions, during
widowhood, then sold and divided among my chil, (un-
named except LEWIS, eldest son and Exr. Exr: JOHN HOUSE.)
Wit: WILLIAM DIXON, JOHN MIALS (MILES ?).

WIGGINS, ROBERT
Apr. 30, 1803. Aug. Ct., 1803. Bros: JOHN, 20 S,
it is my will he shall keep the land he intended to
give me, and my estate pay him $300 for negro Will
that I bought of him; THOMAS, 3 negroes, the said
THOMAS paying to my estate $250; sister: CATHERINE
WHITAKER, 1 negro; bro: JESSE B. WIGGINS, 2 negroes;

355

sister: POLLY KING, $250; THOMAS CROWELL, son of my
sister NANCY CROWELL, deceased, wife of EDWARD CROWELL,
residue, if any, left after debts and other legacies
are paid. Exr & Bros: THOMAS WIGGINS, JOHN WIGGINS,
JESSE WIGGINS. Wit: D. BARKSDALE, THOMAS CROWELL.

WILKINS, THOMAS M.
    Dec. 15, 1849. Aug. Ct., 1854. Bk. G, p 69. The
residue of my estate I give to my sisters (unnamed);
Mother, (unnamed), I give and bequeath my slaves to my
mother, her life, then to my sisters and their heirs,
but not to their husbands. Two slaves recently purchased
of R. D. BATTLE, Jason and Eliza, I give in trust to
R. D. BATTLE to be disposed of as he may see fit, binding
myself to make good to my sisters and their children
$300 and interest from the first of September 1849 etc.
Also life policy of $5000. Exr: ROBERT R. BRIDGERS. Wit:
THOS. NEWBY, W. J. BATTLE.

WILKINS, WILLIAM
    Aug. 22, 1810. Aug. Ct., 1816. Bk. E, p 144. Wife
& Extx: NANCY, have as much of my estate of every kind
whatsoever, sufficient for her support during her life;
at her decease divided between my chil: WILLIS, HENRY,
NANCY ELLIS and PATSY WILKINS; sons & exrs: JAMES, plantation whereon he lives, 1 negro, mare, which he already
hath; WILLIAM, plantation he is living on, 1 negro and
mare; sons: WILLIS all land I possess lying E of North
Creek, of my mill joining land of JOHN SPELL (SPIER ?).
PETER EVANS, READING SUGG, and NATHANIEL BILBARY; half
of my water Grist mill owned by me and PETER EVANS, 1
negro, mare, called Molly, bridle, and saddle, 2 cows
and calves, furniture, chest, 2 sows and pigs; HENRY,
the residue of my land not given away, including plantation I live on, joining land given son: WILLIS, PHILIP
CAREY (?), PETER EVANS and JOHN SPELL; reserving the
whole unto my wife NANCY, her life, or widowhood; 1 negro, horse, bridle, saddle, 2 cows and calves, 2 sows
and pigs, furniture; daus: NANCY wife of GRAY ELLIS, 2
negroes, sorrel mare, bridle, saddle, 2 cows and calves,
furniture, and 1 chest in her possession; PATSY WILKINS,
2 negroes, horse, bridle, saddle, 2 cows and calves,
furniture and 1 chest; gr. daus: SARAH ROUTH, dau of

WILLIAM ROUTH, deceased, 1 negro given her by will of
her father; CATHERINE ROUTH, dau of WILLIAM ROUTH,
furniture. Wit: JOHN SPELL, ?_____.

WILKINSON, BENJAMIN
      Feb. 6, 1837. No Probate date. Wife: OBEDIENCE,
estate widowhood, or life, or until my youngest child
is 12 yrs. of age. If she wishes to move South, she
may carry all my movable personal Estate. Lawsuits
pending in Edgecomb Court. Exr: JESSE C. KNIGHT. Wit:
BENNETT BRADLEY, JOHN GARRETT.

WILKINSON, JAMES
      Mar. 25, 1855. May Ct., 1855. Bk. G, p 107. Wife
& Extx: JULIA, $2000; WILLIAM ESLER, $1000 to be held
in trust for LAURA ESLER; dau: MARY, $50; son:
WASHINGTON, $2000 when arrives at 21 yrs; all remainder
to JULIA and her heirs. Buried Blandwood Cemetery,
Petersburg, Va. Wit: GEORGE HOWARD, L. D. PENDER.

WILKINSON, JOSHUA
      Oct. 29, 1817. Aug. Ct., 1819. Bk. E, p 194. Wife:
MILDRED, during widowhood, land on E side of Branch adjoining lands of ROBERT CHERRY and WILLIAM WORSLEY. It
is my will my Exr cause a frame house 12 x 16, with
brick chimney to be built on said land; I further lend
my wife MILDRED, 2 negroes, mare, riding chair and
harness, furniture, cow and calf (her choice); son &
exr: JOHN, 2 negroes, part of the water grist, saw and
boelting mill on Town Creek and all property I have
heretofore given him; daus: SARAH MORRIS, 2 negroes
with all property I have heretofore given her; MARY
DUNN and EDITH KNIGHT, 2 negroes each with all property
I have given them; son & exr: CHARLES, the plantation
and land whereon he now lives (being land I bought of
JOHN BONNER), on southside of Kokey (Cokey) Swamp, 2
negroes together with all property I have heretofore
delivered to him; sons: BENJAMIN, land and plantation
I bought of GUARRALELIUS (GERALDOS ?) J. KILLEBREW,
on the N side of Kokey Swamp, adjoining land I gave my
son CHARLES, 2 negroe boys, horse called Jack, bridle,
saddle, furniture, cow and calf, yoke of work steers,
and my still; JOSHUA, land and Plantation I bought of

357

WALKER KNIGHT, except the highland lying on the S side
of the Cypress Pocosin and Dam Branch down to Ballihack
Swamp. 2 negroes, mare colt, bridle and saddle now
called his; SILAS, land and plantation whereon I now
live, with all the rest of my lands not disposed of,
2 negroes, bedstead and furniture, cow and calf (or
yearling), $75; gr. sons: JOEL WHITFIELD and BENJAMIN
WHITFIELD, $250 each; gr. dau: ALBENATH WHITFIELD, 1
negro. Exr: BENJAMIN WHITFIELD. Wit: FREDERICK MAYO,
WILLIAM WORSLEY.

WILKINSON, MILLY
    June 28, 1840. Nov. Ct., 1845. Bk. F, p 325. Gr.
dau: SARY ANN WORSELEY, all my 3 negroes and increase,
residue of my estate of every kind including monies
due me. Exrs & Friends: JESSE C. KNIGHT, JOHN GARRETT.
Wit: BENJ. F. KNIGHT, JOSEPH J. GARRETT. Exrs renounced
executorship. ELIZA TAYLOR appointed; bonded $400 with
NEWTON TAYLOR and ISAAC ROBBINS for securities.

WILLIAMS, ABSALOM
    Oct. 4, 1802. Feb. Ct., 1814. Bk. E, p 63. Sister:
ANNA PROCTOR and her heirs, all my lands and all other
property whatsoever. Wit: AUGUSTINE WHITEHEAD, AARON
PROCTOR, BURREL WILLIAMS.

WILLIAMS, ANN D.
    Mar. 10, 1852. Aug. Ct., 1853. Bk. F, pp 515-518.
My estate to be equally divided between my 3 chil;
daus: Mrs. MARY C. JANNETT, Mrs. MARIA LOUISA PENDER,
INDIANA E. WILLIAMS. Exr: MARY C. JANNETT, THOMAS S.
GHOLSON. Wit: F. H. ROBERTSON, JOHN WALSH, DAVID G.
POTTS. This Will was filed in Petersburg, Va., 19th
March 1852 and in Edgecombe County, Tarborough, N. C.,
August Term 1853.

WILLIAMS, ARTHUR
    July 29, 1779. Nov. Ct., 1779. Wife: UNITY, residue
of estate and use of plantation, all privileges during
life. To be divided at her decease among my 6 chil:
JOSEPH, HENRY, SARAH, ABSALOM, NANCY and NOAH; eldest
son: HEROD, 20 S; son: THOMAS, 20 S; dau: MARY, now
wife of JACOB WHITE, 20 S; son: ABSALOM 260 A land I

purchased of JOHN PROCTOR, adjoining WILLIAM PROCTOR;
NOAH, 320 A plantation whereon I now live, entry of
100 A adjoining land where I now live. Exr: JOHN WILLIAMS.
Wit: BENJAMIN WILLIAMS, JOSEPH WILLIAMS, HENRY WILLIAMS.

WILLIAMS, BENJAMIN
    July 28, 1793. Nov. Ct., 1793. Wife: MARY, life
estate; oldest son: JOHN, 40 S; dau: PENNELOPHE, cow,
yearling, 5 sheep, furniture, 2 dishes, 6 plates, etc.;
sons: MICAJAH, furniture, 2 cows and calves, etc., 2
sows and pigs, 2 ewes and lambs; WILLIAM, furniture,
cow and calf, 2 ewes and lambs; dau: ELIZABETH, furniture, cow and yearling, 5 sheep, 2 dishes and 6 plates,
etc.; sons: BENJAMIN, furniture, mare etc.; SIMEON,
entry of 150 A of land adjoining JACOB WHITE; colt
foaled last Spring etc.; ELISHA, plantation whereon I
now live, etc., with reservation to wife MARY, lifetime;
entry of land purchased of PETER CARTWRIGHT beginning
at SAMUEL RUFFIN'S Corner; bro: JOHN WILLIAMS. Wit:
ABSALOM WILLIAMS, JACOB WHITE, PENELOPHE WILLIAMS.

WILLIAMS, BURREL
    July 29, 1811. Aug. Ct., 1811. Wife: WINNIFRED,
all my estate during widowhood, reversion to my only
son: WILIE WILLIAMS; my daus: SALLY, CATY, LOOLY (?)
and PATSEY WILLIAMS shall have $50 each out of my per-
sonal estate and furniture; residue to be divided.
Exr. & Worthy friend: AUGUSTINE WHITEHEAD. Wit: E.
BULLOCK, NATHAN TART.

WILLIAMS, DREWRY
    Nov. 29, 1830. Probated 1831. Bk. F, p 125. Wife:
ELIZABETH, 3 negroes, her life, then divided between
my sons WILLIAM, JOSIAH and DAVID; also lend her negro George for life, then to my son DAVID, 2 horses,
4 cows and calves, 3 sows and pigs, 10 shoats, and
furniture. My Estate of every description be sold,
residue divided; sons: WILLIAM and JOSIAH WILLIAMS,
1 negro each; gr. daus: SALLY CURL and POLLY CURL negro girl each, and furniture; son & exr: DAVID WILLIAMS,
3 negroes and land whereon I live, with still and all
my cider casks. Exr: Friend, EGBERT H. WILLIAMS. Wit:
JOHN MERCER, DAVID CHERRY.

WILLIAMS, ELISHA

Aug. 13, 1751. Feb. Ct., 1755. Bros: SOLOMON, 2
negroes, 6 cows and calves; GEORGE, Ŀ 20; DANIEL, Ŀ
15; JOSHUA, plantation, all lands, 2 negroes; JOHN;
nephew: RICHARD WILLIAMS, son of JOHN, sisters: MARY
CARR, 1 negro and Ŀ 10; ELIZABETH DAUGHTRY, Ŀ 15 and
young horse; MARY DICKENS, 4 cows and calves. Exr:
JOSHUA WILLIAMS. Wit: JAMES SMITH, DREW SMITH, GEORGE
BELL.

WILLIAMS, GEORGE, of Northampton Co.

Jan. 6, 1749-50. No Probate date. Wife: SARAH, plantation and land adjoining after her decease to my son
ROBERT; I also lend her 4 negroes, after decease, give
Harry to SARAH, her dau, and Peter to my son GEORGE,
and Tona to her dau MILDRED, and if said Phillis do
bring a negro child to live, I give same to her dau
ANN, and said Phillis unto her son ROBERT; my son:
ROBERT, after my decease, my negro Simon; land lying
at head of Howell Spring Branch; my son: GEORGE, the
old patent land I purchased of MATTHEW KINCHEN of Isle
of Wight Co., and 1 negro; my son: SAMUEL, survey of
land on S side Creek near THOMAS WILLIAMS, 1 negro
(illegible), bed called his Uncle Samuel's daus: ANN,
SARAH and MILDRED, 1 negro each; sons: JACOB and
WILLIAM, 2 negroes each. Exr: JOHN (illegible), ROBERT
WILLIAMS (son). Codicil ETHELRED TAYLOR, JAMES TURNER,
JUNIOR and JOHN De BERRY to divide remainder of my
Estate between my wife & chil. Wit: ETHELRED TAYLOR,
NICHOLAS MONGER, WILLIAM MONGER. Northhampton Co., N. C.
Will exhibited in Court by JOHN PITTMAN and ROBERT
WILLIAMS, and proved by oaths of ETHELRED TAYLOR and
WILLIAM MONGER, Wit.

WILLIAMS, GEORGE

July 19, 1758. June Ct., 1759. Wife & Extx:
PRISCILLA; sons: GEORGE, my 100 A plantation; SAMUEL,
land on Deer Creek bought of WILLIAM WHITEHEAD; dau:
CLOE; deceased sister: LUCRETIA WILLIAMS. Wit:_____?,
MOSES BAKER, JOHN NORWOOD.

WILLIAMS, JAMES

July 8, 1800. Court held at Dinnwiddie Co., Va.

Monday 15th September 1800. It is my will and desire
that my negro woman Nan, with all her chil: LONDON,
BECK, SAL, PENN (?) and the one she was pregnant with
when I left the State last Spring, be absolute free
without interruption, etc. under the care and guardian-
ship of my executor until they arrive at age 21; residue of my estate my attorney GEORGE LOYD, will trans-
mit to my bro JOHN WILLIAMS. Exr & Friend: FREDERICK
PHILIPS. Wit: SAMUEL T. KIRBY, FREDERICK BONNER,
WILLIAM PERKINS. C. C.: JOHN NICHOLAS, Dinwiddie Co.,
Va.

Dinwiddie, Va. I do hereby certify that JOHN
NICHOLAS is clerk of Dinwiddie County Court and that
all due credence ought to be given to his certificate.
Given under my hand and seal as first acting Justice
in the said County this 18th day of September 1800.
Sgn/ JOSEPH JONES, J. P.

WILLIAMS, JAMES
    Feb. 16, 1789. May Ct., 1789. Bk. 3, p 91. Wife:
ELIZABETH, shall have use of lands I have given my
sons JAMES and ETHELRED; also the negroes I have given
them, mill, etc.; her life, stock, etc. until they
come of lawful age etc. My 4 sons: JOHN, MATHEW, JAMES
and ETHELRED WILLIAMS, my water, grist and saw mill,
all that part of land purchased from MARY BELLAMY,
blacksmith's tools; sons: JAMES, 160 A plantation, on
land known as "the old place", another late survey
adjoining, 71 A remainder of tract bought of MARY
BELLAMY, which I have not already given away, with the
mill, and negro girl; ETHELRED, 221 A plantation whereon I now live, and negro boy; JOHN, a negro girl;
MATTHEW, a negro boy, dau. CHARITY HARRISON, 15 S; gr.
dau. ELIZABETH HARRISON, 1 negro; gr. son: JAMES
HARRISON, negro boy; son: ETHELRED, my brandy still,
but lend use of same to my beloved wife, and all my sons
have the liberty of stilling their own liquor in her.
Exr: JOHN WILLIAMS, MATTHEW WILLIAMS. Wit: ETHELRED
PHILLIPS, EXUM COBB, SARAH WIGGINS.

WILLIAMS, JOHN
    No date. Prob. Aug. Ct., 1737. Wife and Extx: ANN,
best bed and furniture, 6 cattle, 1 horse, 2 mares,

1 iron pot, 1 chest, pine chest with lock and key, 1
pot, 1 skillet; sons: JOHN, 1 S; JOSHUA, 200 A plantation adjoining land and mill, 6 breeding cattle; dau:
MARY, 6 breeding cattle, 1 pewter bason, 1 pot, 1 skillet. Wit: HENRY TANTON, THOMAS CARTA (CARTER).

WILLIAMS, JOHN
    Mar. 14, 1792. Aug. Ct., 1793. Wife & Extx:
MOURNING, life interest in Estate, liberty of plantation,
5 cows and calves, 2 two-year old stears, 10 two-year
old hogs; 10 1-year old hogs, 3 sows and pigs, horse,
mare, 2 negroes, 2 dishes, 4 basons, 6 plates and case
of knives and forks, chest, 2 weeding hoes, 2 plows,
woollen wheel, lining wheel, all stock sheep, 6 chairs,
etc.; reversion to Betsey; son: BENJAMIN, 1 horse, colt;
dau: MARY, wife of ROBERT LANCASTOR, 1 horse, also all
now in their possession; son: JESSE; daus: MILBERRY
(MILBRE) and NANCY, plantation whereon JESSE formerly
lived to be divided by the schoolhouse Branch, MILBERRY
to have the plantation and lower end of the land; NANCY,
the upper end etc.; son & exr: JOHN, 294 A tract joining himself and HARDY TODD; dau: LUCY, wife of JOHN
BELL, 1 negro woman and her increase; son: DRURY, plantation whereon I live, also land on N side of Town
Creek, dau: BETSEY, 1 negro, 178 A tract purchased of
SHADRACK PROCTOR, 2 cows and calves; etc; No Witnesses mentioned.

WILLIAMS, JOHN
    Oct. 15, 1817. Nov. Ct., 1817. Wife (unnamed),
lend all land on N side of new road, except the land
belonging to son EGBERT H., for her lifetime; son &
Exr: EGBERT H., tract on lines of Great Swamp and lines
sons, HENRY and JOHN GRAY WILLIAMS and the new road;
sons: JOHN GRAY, tract N side new road; HENRY, tract
S side new road; daus: PATSEY, POLLY, CATY, BETSY & LUCY.
Each child to have mare or horse, bridle and saddle,
cow and calf, 2 ewes and lambs. Exr: Friend, DREWRY
WILLIAMS. Wit: DEMPSEY JENKINS, STEPHEN TAYLOR,
BENJAMIN WILLIAMS.

WILLIAMS, JOHN
    Oct. 3, 1819. Nov. Ct., 1819. Bk. E p 228. Wife:

MARTHA, residue of estate her lifetime, provided she
have my gr. son: JOHN READ educated so far as to under-
stand the rule of threes, and my gr. dau: MARTHA READ,
to read and write, and will board my said gr. chil,
and my dau, SALLY WILLIAMS and RHODA READ during life
or until they should marry, etc. At death of wife, estate to be divided between daus SALLY WILLIAMS and
RHODA READ; gr. son: JOHN READ, 1 negro; gr. dau:
MARTHA READ, 1 negro. Exr: RHODA READ, EXUM LEWIS. Wit:
BENJAMIN BRADLEY, RICHARD S. HART.

WILLIAMS, JOHN
Nov. 25, 1844. Feb. Ct., 1849. Wife & Extx: CAROLINE,
house and lot whereon I now live, household and kitchen
furniture during her widowhood; all monies due me
collected and laid out in bank stock; my 2 farms kept
up, all my property kept together until my chil become of age and shares delivered when each child reaches
legal age. Wit: JOHN H. MATHESON, S. BAKER PARKER. Oath
of NATHAN MATHESON proved signature of S. BAKER PARKER.

WILLIAMS, JOSEPH
Sept. 1, 1808. Nov. Ct., 1808. Bk. D, p 338. Son
& Exr: WILLIAM, land and plantation whereon I live,
with all improvements, home to be kept intact as long
as all agree. Residue to be divided. Wit: THOMAS WELLS,
SAMUEL RUFFIN.

WILLIAMS, JOSHUA
Mar. 31, 1798. May Ct., 1798. Wife & Extx: EASTER,
plantation whereon I live, with all tenaments etc.
during life or widowhood, after her marriage or decease; reversion to Bro: COLDING WILLIAMS. Exr: WILLIAM
BELL. Wit: WHITMELL BELL, DEMPSEY BRYAN, JAMES
BRACEWELL.

WILLIAMS, PHILLIS
June 4, 1760. Dec. Ct., 1760. Chil: JOHN WILLIAMS,
ROBERT, and JOSEPH SIMONS (or SIMMS?), SARAH WILKINSON,
KEZIA (CASIAH) PAUL (BALL?), and LUCY ALSTON, 1 S each;
MARTHA GRIFFIN, my side saddle; residue of estate to
be equally divided between my 2 gr. chil, SIMON SIMMS
(?) and PATTY SIMES, son and dau of my son JOSEPH

363

SIMMONS (SIMMS?), illegible. Exr: Son, JOSEPH SIMONS
(SIMMES?). Wit: JESSE LEE, ELIZABETH LEE, JOHN SUTTON.

WILLIAMS, PILGRIM
    Apr. 1, 1764. July Ct., 1764. Wife: SARAH, mare,
5 cows and calves, 2 basins, 2 dishes, 6 plates, 6
spoons, 1 iron pot, 10 sheep, 20 two-yr old hogs,
woolling wheel, and cards, during her life. It is my
desire that my executors divide my pewter as equally
as possible between my children hereafter named, remainder to be sold to best advantage without the sheriff,
and money equally divided among my children: JONAS,
JOELL, BILLY, NATHAN, DREWRY, ANN and MOURNING WILLIAMS;
son & exr: ROWLAND, 100 A land on N side of Toisnot
Swamp purchased of MARGRIT TAYLOR, 1 negro, 12 cattle,
1 horse, saddle and bridle, iron pot and Ł 2, 13 S 4
p Proc. money to him and his heirs; sons: JONAS, reversion in plantation whereon I live, horse, bridle
and saddle, and my wearing clothes; JOEL, 1 negro;
BILLY, 1 negro; NATHAN, 144 A of land on S side of
Toisnot Swamp, joining land of THOMAS HORNE, also 5 lbs
feathers for bed, Ł 10 gold or silver, etc.; DREWRY,
Ł 10 gold or silver. Exr & Bro: SAMUEL WILLIAMS. Wit:
EDWARD MOORE, JOHN DEES (DEW?), HENRY FLOWERS.

WILLIAMS, THOMAS
    June 26, 1825. Nov. Ct., 1827. Bk. F, p 72. Wife:
SALLY, sufficient for herself and family for 1 yr. 1
work creature (horse, mule ?), 2 sows and pigs, 4 ewes,
all residue of household and kitchen furniture, not
hereinafter given away, her lifetime, or widowhood, 2
negroes to work for her as they ever have done but
nevertheless, shall be under the command of my son
JOHN WILLIAMS to see that they work for their mistress,
1/3 my lands with dwelling house thereto belonging,
life or widowhood; believe it will be advantageous to
both parties that my son JOHN WILLIAMS crop it yearly,
and attend to her business as they may agree, dividing
the profits; etc; son & exr: JOHN, all my lands of
every description except 1/3 already lent to wife; 3
negroes, 2 work horses and 2 work stears; son: THOMAS,
1 negro; dau: CHARITY PROCTOR, my cider casks of every
kind, stocks of Bees shall continue on my plantation

for the use of my wife SALLY and son JOHN WILLIAMS.
Residue to be disposed of and divided equally amongst
all my chil living at that time and their heirs, etc;
Exr and Friend: DAVID WILLIAMS; Wit: E(DWIN) BULLOCK,
ZADOC BRASWELL.

WILLIAMS, SAMUEL
    Nov. 18, 1748. Feb. Ct., 1748. Wife & Extx: JANE.
Sons: SAMPSON and WILLIAM, "land adjoining to the
TAYLOR'S in the island as I leased of Mrs. JOHNSTON";
JACOB and GEORGE, the manner plantation and land on
Beaverdam Swamp; SAMUEL, dau: CREESE, to sons and dau
are bequeathed 5 negroes. Wit: JOHN POPE, JOHN CRUDUP,
MOURNING CRUDUP.

WILLIAMS, SAMUEL
    Oct. 21, 1753. Feb. Ct., 1754. Wife: ELIZABETH;
sons: WILLIAM, SOLOMON and SAMUEL, land on Mush Island,
bought of ROBERT LANG; JOSEPH JOHN, about 800 A bought
of JOHN BURT and JOHN EGERTON and adjoining YANCEY'S
line and the Reedy Branch. To JOSEPH JOHN and SAMUEL,
11 negroes; gr. son: SAMUEL WILLIAMS. Exr: PHILIP
ALSTON, BENJ. WYNNS. Wit: THOMAS KEARNEY, EDMUND
KEARNEY, JAMES ALSTON.

WILLIAMS, WILLIAM
    Aug. 15, 1843. Nov. Ct., 1843. Bk. F, p 294. Wife:
CATHERINE, property, land and negroes for widowhood or
life, horse and cattle of her choice, etc. furniture,
Bofat, sitting chairs, tables and geese; sons: DREWRY,
lands on S side of Straight Branch, etc; BARTLEY, land
on N side of Straight Branch; daus: MOURNING, trunk
and NANCY. Exr: DREWRY WILLIAMS, DAVID WILLIAMS. Wit:
WILLIE BRIDGERS, KINCHEN CORBETT.

WILLIAMS, WINIFRED
    Mar. 6, 1848. Feb. Ct., 1849. Bk. F, pp 416-17.
Gr. son: JOHN R. WILLIAMS, 1 negro, all lands and im-
provements, lying on W side of the big ditch, running
along the Branch; gr. dau: PHARABE WILLIAMS; dau of
SARAH WILLIAMS, $75; dau: POLLY DUNN, wife of LARRY
DUNN, 1 negro; dau: MARTHA WILLIAMS, wife of HENRY
WILLIAMS, in trust of my friend WM. H. HINES, free

from control of her present or any future husband, negro to be sold and funds, and money divided among
MARTHA'S chil; gr. son: THOMAS P. PITT and JESSE C. K.
WILLIAMS, the balance of my lands. Perishable estate
to be sold and divided: wearing apparel, bed clothing
divided between daus MARTHA WILLIAMS and POLLY DUNN,
gr. dau: PHARABY, dau of SARAH WILLIAMS, and WILLIE
WILLIAMS, deceased. Exr & Friend: ROBERT R. BRASWELL.
Wit: L. S. COBB, THOMAS CURL.

WILLIAMSON, HARDY
      Feb. 25, 1761. Mar. Ct., 1761. Wife & Extx:
LUCRESY, lend the labor of my negroes for term of 8
yrs; son: BELLAJAH WILLIAMSON, 1 negro. If he should
die before reaching age of 21, then said negro to my
beloved wife, 1 cow and calf, land on Deerman's (Durman?)
Branch, Edgecombe Co., etc. Exr: JOSEPH COTTON, the
Elder JOSEPH WILLIAMSON. Wit: WILLIAM SHERROD, JAMES
GRAY.

WILLIFORD, WILLIS
      Feb. 20, 1824. Nov. Ct., 1825. Bk. F, p 50. MARY
ODOM, $4; REDDIN DAUGHTRY, the rest of my estate. Exr:
JOSEPH GRIFFIN. Wit: WILLIS WILLIFORD, ROBERT W. BARNES,
REDMUN CURL. Bond of $1000 with MOSES PRICE and
BENJAMIN WILKINSON, Securities.

WILLIS, WILLIAM
      Jan. 5, 1776. Probated in year 1776. son: THOMAS,
150 A of land whereon I live; daus: MARTHA, 2 negroes;
ANN ARRINGTON, 2 negroes; RHODA BECKWITH (?), 1 negro;
SARAH DANIEL, 5 S sterling. Remainder of estate to be
divided between my son (THOMAS) and 3 daus: MARTHA,
ANN and RHODA. Exr & Sons-in-law: THOMAS JAMES
ARRINGTON, AMOS BECKWITH. Wit: RICHARD VICK, BENJAMIN
VICK, BENJAMIN EVANS.

WILLS, THOMAS
      Apr. 8, 1761. July Ct., 1766. Wife: MARY, 1 negro.
She shall be quietly possessed with all my other
household goods, stock, cattle, hogs, sheep her lifetime, reversion to chil; sons: WILLIS, 400 A plantation
I bought of my bro RICHARD WILLS; WILLIBEE, 200 A
366

plantation I bought of JOSEPH MOOR; THOMAS BARNES WILLS,
plantation I live on after wife's decease; eldest son:
WILLIAM WILLS plantation lying on Little Conetoe; daus:
MARY, OLIVE and CATTREN WILLS, 1 negro each. Exr & Bro:
JAMES BARNES, RICHARD WILLS. Wit: JOHN SCOTT (?), JAMES
FRENCH, LOVE SAVAGE.

WILSON, ISAAC
     July 29, 1779. Aug. Ct., 1779. Wife: SUSANNAH, the
use of 3 negroes her lifetime, horse, and filly, saddle
and bridle; son: WILLIAM, plantation whereon he lives,
at the mouth of Running Branch, 1 negro, 1 filly and
other articles he now has in his possession; son & exr:
JAMES, upper part of my plantation, whereon I live, on
river bank, near Gosney's Old Ford etc.; 1 negro, mare,
and her 2 colts; son: WILLIS, (illegible), below part
I gave my son JAMES WILSON, should he not live to the
age of 21, or die without issue, then to son: WILLIE
(WYLIE ?), 5 negroes; son: JOHN, plantation I bought
of RICHARD SASNETT, lying on Killebrew's Mill Swamp,
mare, and her colt, horse, saddle and bridle; dau:
ANNY COTTON, 2 negroes, after wife's decease, my riding mare, and her colt that now sucks, looking glass
and 6 sheep. Still and worm to my son JAMES; wife
SUSANNA to have care and brining up of my son WILLIE,
to give him sufficient schooling, and take into her
possession all his legacy and have the use of it until
he reaches the age of 14 yrs. In case my wife SUSANNA
should marry, or die, before my son WILLIE comes to
aforesaid age, it is my will my son JAMES, should have
the care, etc. Exr: ELIAS FORT. Wit: WILLIAM FORT,
JOHN SIKES, JOHN SHERROD.

WILSON, LOUIS D.
     May 26, 1833. Nov. Ct., 1847. Bk. F, p 380. Sister:
MARY, $500; sister: NANCY, lend land and plantation
inherited from my father, bequeathed to my brother and
myself; and my negroes; I give the Chairman of the
County Court of Edgecombe and his successors in office
the residue of my estate real and personal, for the
use and benefit of the Poor (Paupers) of said County;
I give my Town lots Nos. 27 and 28 to ELIZA COTTON,
now ELIZA THOMPSON. The foregoing paper purporting to

be the last Will and Testament of the late LOUIS D.
WILSON, Esq., is offered for probate; JAMES A. BATTLE
and MARY A. BATTLE, nearest of kin, waiving all ob-
jection to probate, said paper is duly proved as last
Will and Testament and ordered recorded. Note:- LOUIS
D. WILSON, Esq. of Edgecombe Co. died the 6th day of
August, 1847, at Vera Cruz, in Mexico, aged 58 years,
3 mos. He was a Colonel in the 12th Reg. of the 12th
Infantry. Wilson County was named in his honor.

WILSON, MARY
     May 31, 1855. Aug. Ct., 1855. Bk. G, p 110. Nephew:
JOHN WILSON, all estate; If he should not survive me,
shall go to CHARLOTTE DANCY and DELHA M. FREEMAN;
ELIZABETH M. BATTLE, wife of WM. S. BATTLE; Mrs.
CHARLOTTE DANCY, all wearing apparel, 2 trunks; Wit:
WILLIAM F. DANCY, N. MATHEWSON. No Exr, WILLIAM F.
DANCY Adm. $2000 Bond KENNETH THIGPEN, WM. NORFLEET,
Securities.

WILSON, WILLIAM
     June 16, 1804. Aug. Ct., 1807. Bk. D, p 280. Wife:
ELIZABETH, use of plantation during life or widowhood
and 3 negroes; after her decease, etc. these 3 negroes,
furniture and residue be divided between my 3 daus:
NANCY, SUSANNAH and POLLY WILSON. Sons: JAMES, lower
part of plantation whereon I live, on the river bank,
near Gosney's Old Ford, running Branch... to the river's
various courses, etc. In case my son JAMES WILSON should
not live to the age of 21 or die without issue, reversion to my son LEWIS D. WILSON, and 1 negro; son: LOUIS
D. WILSON, remaining part of my land and plantation.
In case my son LOUIS D. WILSON should not live to age
21, or die without issue, the property go to my son
JAMES WILSON, and 1 negro boy. Exr. & Friend: BENJAMIN
DICKEN. Wit: JNO. WILSON, JAMES WILLIFORD.

WIMBERLEY, GEORGE (SEN'R) - PLANTER
     May 26, 1764. May Ct., 1768. Wife: MOURNING, all
of the estate I had with her at the day of marriage
and the increase of the same at the day of my death;
son & exr: GEORGE, where I formerly lived, and all land
N side of Tar River, 2 grants, containing 1010 A, 3

negroes and horse; daus: ZILPHA COTTON, 3 negroes;
SARAH, 2 negroes, mare, 2 cows and calves; black wal-
nut chest and lining wheel. If SARAH die without heirs,
then all the Estate and every article I have given her,
shall return to be the property of my son GEORGE
WIMBERLEY, etc; dau: PHARIBY. Exr and Trusty Friend:
ELIAS FORT. Wit: SHERROD HAYWOOD, JACOB DICKINSON,
CHARITY THOMAS.

WIMBERLEY, GEORGE
    Mar. 13, 1790. May Ct., 1790. Bk. 3, p 132. Sons:
JOSEPH, 324 A he now lives upon, which I purchased of
JAMES ROBARDS, and that tract of land I leased to.
JOSIAH MURPHREE, 3 negroes and mare; GEORGE, 344 1/2
A, part of plantation I live on, on the river bank,
thence to South Branch...to the corner my grant calls
for and thence along the river bank, 1 negro Old Dick,
for this reason, that he may have sufficient support
without any abuse; JONATHAN, remaining 344 1/2 A not
given my son GEORGE in this will etc. when he shall
arrive to 21 years of age; dau: MOURNING where my negro man Tony now lives in the County of Nash on the
N side of Pig Basket Creek, est. 80 A, 1 large Black
walnut chest, and all her mother's wearing apparel. It
is my will my man Tony be let live his own life, free
from service, or servitude from me and my heirs. It is
my desire that Tony have the labor of a negro woman
named Moll, he claims for his wife, or while they continue to cohabit together, as man and wife, but Tony
is at liberty to deliver the said woman, Moll, to my
heirs when he shall think proper; Tony shall have use
of the land and house whereon he lives his lifetime,
without molestation, stock of hogs, 2 cows and calves,
breeding mare, all crop of corn now on his place,
all the sheep; at his decease same goes to my dau
MOURNING WIMBERLEY. Residue to be equally divided between my 3 chil. Exrs and Friends: ELIAS FORT, JACOB
DICKINSON, GEORGE WIMBERLEY. Wit: JOHN MURPHREE, NOAH
WOODARD.

WINSTEAD, JEREMIAH
    Sept. 5, 1850. Nov. Ct., 1851. Bk. F, p 463. Wife:
NANCY, for life or widowhood, lands, 4 setting chairs,

cow and calf (her choice) sow, 6 pigs, or shoats, horse, household and kitchen furniture, loom and gear, and 1 chist. After death, property to be sold, and proceeds divided equally between chil: MARTHA, MARY, JINCY, and SALLY; if GILBERT PARKER stays until he is free, he is to have $10 and 1 bed; residue to be divided. Exr & Friend: JOHN G. WILLIAMS. Wit: JAS. W. BARNES, J. H. BARNES.

WINSTEAD, JOSEPH (SENIOR)
Aug. 7, 1823. Aug. Ct., 1823. Bk. E, p 336. Wife: SARAH, lend 300 A of land whereon I live, at her decease same to my son and exr: JOSEPH WINSTEAD, negro Jim, 6 cattle, cart and wheels, mare; son & exr: ELIJAH, the residue sold and divided among all my chil. Wit: E(DWIN) BULLOCK, WILLIAM DAUGHTRY.

WINSTEAD, RICHARD
Dec. 6, 1791. Aug. Ct., 1792. Wife & Extx: SUSANNAH, mare, bridle and saddle, 3 cows, all hogs, sheep, cattle, corn and meat; son: SAMUEL, small shot gun; It is my desire my stock of cattle be let out until my chil come of age then divided equally between my 2 chil; lands, household furniture, etc., I lend my wife, lifetime or widowhood, then divided between my chil. Exr: Bro, PETER WINSTEAD, BENJAMIN BISHOP. Wit: EDWARD JACKSON, WILLIAM BOYETT, JORDEN BOYETT.

WINSTEAD, SALLY, "Old and infirm"
Feb. 5, 1837. Aug. Ct., 1838. Daus: ZILPHA DAVENPORT, PENNY WINSTEAD, NANCY WINSTEAD, CHANEY WILLIFORD, CHARITY WILLIFORD and Gr. dau: PENNY DEANS $1.00. Sons & exrs: JOSEPH and ELIJAH WINSTEAD $100.00 Wit: JOSIAH VICK.

WOOD, JOSEPH
Apr. 24, 1783. Nov. Ct., 1785. Wife & Extx: ANN, lend remainder of my estate during her widowhood. It is my desire my chil be brought up by my beloved wife ANN WOOD. Estate after decease of wife divided between son FRANCIS MARBREW WOOD, and dau ELIZABETH FRAZER WOOD. It is my will and desire the mare by name of Genediver, and sorrel colt, named Bunch be sold when

fit and money put to interest for son: FRANCIS MARBREW
WOOD; dau: ELIZABETH FRAZOR WOOD, maple desk, at the
date of marriage or age of 18; son: JOHN HORN WOOD, 1
set of raisors, stock buckle, and knee buckles, 1 gun
and land I live on. Exr: JOHN MILBRON. Wit: JAMES
BOOTH, JOSEPH NEWSOME.

WOOD, JOSIAH
    Dec. 12, 1817. Feb. Ct., 1818. Wife & Extx: TABITHY,
tract of land I live on her lifetime or widowhood, 2
negroes, mare, bowfat, 10 sitting chairs, apple mill
and 12 bbls, cow and calf, 2 sows and pigs and 9 shoats;
dau: NANCY H., 1 negro when she arrives at age of 21
yrs; son: JOSEPH JOHN WOOD; reversion in tract of land
I live on; also if my wife is now pregnant, and if the
child be a son, I give him tract of land I bought of
NOAH PIPPEN and JAMES NEWSOM, and if it should be a
girl, 1 negro etc. Exr: FRANCES M. WOOD. Wit: LOT
PENDER,_____ PENDER, E. CROMWELL. Note:- Wife did not
survive to serve as Co-Extx with FRANCIS M. WOOD.

WOODARD, DAVID
    July 30, 1798. No date of recording. Loving wife
(unnamed), plantation whereon I now live, mare, 3 cows,
2 calves, yearling, beaufat, all my pewter and earthenware, 2 spinning wheels and (cotton) cards, all my
chairs, and chest, cart and wheels, plows, hoes, wheat
and wheat box, meat, feed, vessels, hogs, sows, pigs,
my knives, forks, 2 pots and hooks, skillet, 2 stands,
2 axes, grubbing hoe, griddle, corn growing and in the
crib, and all that is made in the JOHNSTON field, the
bread tray and meal sifter, during life or widowhood,
then to my 3 chil: JAMES, WILLIAM, SARAH WOODARD. Sons
to have 347 1/2 A land on N side of Bear Branch, being
in 3 separate deeds, also part of another tract lying
on the S side of Little Quotankney Creek which LEWIS
BANDY sold me; dau: SARAH land lying on the N side of
Little Quotankney Creek, LEWIS BANDY conveyed to me
my deed. Exr: ELISHA WOODARD, EDWARD MAYO. Wit: WM.
ELLIS, WILLIAM ELLIS (SENIOR), WILLIAM JOSEY.

WOODARD, ELISHA
    Mar. 26, 1798. Nov. Ct., 1798. I give and bequeath

to the five chil of my son JOSHUA WOODARD, namely:
JAMES, JESSE, ELIZABETH, MARGARET and ANNA WOODARD, 5
S Merlen Money each; to my gr. son: JESSE WOODARD, 1
brindled heiffer and her increase; my son & Exr: ELISHA,
the 490 A plantation whereon he lives, tract patented
by my father, JOHN WOODARD, deceased, bounded by
WILLIAM BARNES' Corner.. banks of Contentnea Creek,
and various courses of said Creek; an 83 A tract adjoining ROBERT PEELE, and others, land JACOB ALMOND
settled and sold to me, crosscut saw, carpenters' addz,
etc; son & exr: JOHN, 300 A plantation whereon he now
lives, S side Great Contentnea Creek, in the County of
Wayne, land purchased at public sale of JOHN WEAVER,
re-entered, and secured under present Government;
another 309 A parcel of land in said County of Wayne
on N side of Black Creek whereon JAMES HASTY now lives,
purchased of ARMAGER HALL and DAVID BOND, taken up by
ROBT SIMMES, Esq. all in one survey, also my old horse
and mare, cow and calf; son: DAVID, 175 A land in
County of Edgecombe, on Bear Branch, whereon he lives,
conveyed to me by SPENCER BOLD (BALL?); Also 100 A
land adjoining same, being land on which JOHN BULLOCK
formerly settled, and by JOHN CHARLES conveyed to me;
3 cows and yearlen, and 2 calves, etc; son: LEMUEL,
20 S current money of N. C.; daus: MARY DANIEL, wife of
ELIAS DANIEL, 1 pine chest, 2 pewter basons, and 10
silver dollars; MARTHA AMERSON, wife of BENJAMIN
AMERSON, 1 cow and yearling, middle size pot; DELANAH
AMERSON, my natural dau, wife to ISAAC AMERSON, 1 cow
and calf; my 3 gr. sons: ASA, THOMAS and LEVI JORDEN,
sons to CORNELIUS JORDEN, JUN'R, deceased, 5 S sterling
money each. Wit: ARCHELUAS BARNES, WILLIE STANTON,
ROBERT PEELE.

WOODARD, JOHN Parish of St. Mary's
Feb. 11, 1765. July Ct., 1765. Wife: MARGARET,
plantation I live on, 2 negroes, during widowhood,
reversion of plantation and negro Sam to son: ELIJAH;
son: JOHN, 1 still and 1 negro, after wife's decease;
dau: MARY LEE, 1 negro and lend use of negro her
lifetime, then to gr. dau: MARGARET BROWN, dau of
MARY LEE to have said negro Hannah; son-in-law and
dau: LEONARD LANGSTON and wife, ANN, lend use of 2

negroes, lifetime, reversion to gr. daus: SARAH and
ELIZABETH LANGSTON; son-in-law and dau ? : JAMES HOLLAND
and SARAH his wife, for life, the use of negro Rose
then to gr. son: JOHN HOLLAND, forever; son & exr:
THOMAS, horse and Ł 5 Proclamation money. Wit: STEPHEN
COBB, JAMES BARNES, JOHN DREW.

WOODMAN, GEORGE W.
Aug. 11, 1832. Nov. Ct., 1833. Estate to be held
by Exr until death of 2 sisters, annual income from
same to be paid 1/3 to each sister, remaining third
paid to 2 neices; sisters: NANCY WOODMAN of Newport
R. I.; MARY HEATH, of New Bedford, Mass.; nieces:-
ELIZA WOODMAN, dau of my deceased bro RICHARD WOODMAN;
and NANCY WOODMAN dau of my deceased bro RICHARD WOODMAN;
Uncles: EDWARD WOODMAN, ROBERT WOODMAN, JOB COOK. Exr:
LOUIS D. WILSON. Wit: LEWIS BOND, HENRY JOHNSTON.

WOOTEN, ABSALOM
Undated. Aug. Ct., 1836. Bk. F, p 193. Wife:
FANNIE, all my property, land, house, household and
kitchen furniture, cattle, hogs, and farming utensils,
during her life; child: WILLIAM, HARDY, ELI, JESSE,
STEPHEN, EPHRAIM and AMOS WOOTEN, SILEY EDWARDS and
NANNEY EDWARDS, JOHN and WINNIE COBB, BRIANT and
ELIZABETH EDWARDS, DEMPSEY and MILLY CORBETT, $1 each;
ABSALOM WOOTEN, son of JESSE WOOTEN, 100 A of land on
Cow Branch Creek; WESTON CORBET, son of REDDING CORBET,
102 1/2 A on the Creek. Exr and Bro: AMOS WOOTEN. Wit:
R. T. EAGLES, RIAL EDWARDS.

WOOTEN, AMOS
Apr. 11, 1811. May Ct., 1812. Bk. E, p 31. Wife:
PRISCILLA, for life or widowhood, land at mouth of
Long Point Creek at the head of the Marsh, on HARDY
NORVELL'S line, including Dwelling House, and improvements, 2 negroes, 6 chairs, chest, flax wheel,
woolen wheel, man's saddle, woman's saddle, 2 horses,
3 cows and calves, 2 sows and pigs, cart, gun; her
choice of Pewter dishes, 6 plates, 4 basons, 12 spoons,
2 pots, frying pan and skillet, Dutch oven, 6 knives
and forks, 2 Bee Hives, 30 bbls corn, 1500 lbs. pork,
2 stacks of Blade Fodder, 200 lbs. seed cotton, box

iron and heater, 2 tubs, 2 water pails, all cider
barrels, 2 ewes and lambs, 3 weeding hoes, grubbing
hoe, 2 axes, 2 plow teams with gear. At wife's decease
or marriage, to my chil (unnamed). Exr: STEPHEN and
AMOS WOOTTEN. Wit: HENRY B. DAVIS, WILLIAM WOOTTEN,
BRYANT EDWARDS.

WOOTTEN, JAMES
    Apr. 21, 1821. May Ct., 1821. Bk. E, p 265. Wife:
MARTHA, all household goods, such as she may care for,
residue to be sold, money applied to her own use, horse,
stock of cattle, sheep, hogs, etc. dau: SALLY TAYLOR
and JOSEPH TAYLOR'S chil all the land lying on the E
side of the Branch, called the Eagle land; also 50 A
land where JOSEPH TAYLOR lives, their natural life,
by paying to my 2 gr. sons: JOHN and JAMES TAYLOR, $1
yearly; gr. chil: that is HENRY WOOTTEN'S chil, all
my land not already given, except 100 A adjoining land
of JORDAN JOHNSTON, and CHARLIE VINES, known as the
Spain land, to be sold to pay the loan except my son
and exr: HENRY, pays loan for me, in that case he is
to have the land. Wit: EDWIN NORVILL, JOHN S. EDWARDS.
Will was caveated by JOSEPH TAYLOR and wife, SARAH.

WOOTTEN, JESSE
    Jan. 25, 1826. Nov. Ct., 1827. Bk. F, p 62. Wife:
TABITHA, for widowhood or life, lands, etc. Desire she
shall keep my chil together until they are of age,
furniture as her own property forever; residue to be
divided among my chil: LUANSA, REDMON, SPENCER D.,
EPHRAIM, ABSALAM, and ASIA WOOTTEN. Exr & Bro: AMOS
WOOTTEN. Wit: STEPHEN WOOTTEN, EPHRAIM WOOTTEN.

WOOTTEN, PRISCILLA
    Mar. 2, 1815. May Ct., 1815. Bk. E, p 101. Nunc
Will. She did give and bequeath to her son EPHRAIM
1 featherbed, 5 bbls corn, sow and pigs, etc.; to her
son: DAVID, 15 bbls corn, sow and pigs; son: AMOS, sow
and pigs, etc. No Exr named, SAMUEL RUFFIN appointed;
GRAY LITTLE & BENJAMIN SHARP, Securities. Wit: PHANUEL
WOOTTEN, NANCY WOOTTEN.

374

WOOTEN, WILLIAM
Apr. 27, 1792. May Ct , 1792. Wife: ANN, all my
property, except a piece of land lying between Hog Pen
Branch and Causway Branch, which is for JAMES WOOTEN.
Wit: JOEL WOOTEN, JOSHUA WOOTEN.

WORSLEY, DICY
Apr. 7, 1831. Aug. Ct., 1833. Daus & Extx: POLLY
and ELIZABETH, all furniture divided between 2 daus,
also 1 cow and calf each; son: LITTLE, colt, cow and
calf; residue divided between 3 chil. Wit: WILLIS KNIGHT.

WRIGHT, WILLIAM
Jan. 18, 1763. Apr. Ct., 1763. Bk. A, p 116. Wife
& Extx: (name illegible), plantation and lands on the
N side of Nuce (Neuse) River in Dobbs Co. during widow-
hood, then to my dau (name illegible) son: GEORGE WRIGHT
L 20 Proc. money at legal age, 300 A of land, S side
of Tar River in Edgecombe Co. Wit: SOLOMON WRIGHT,
SARAH WRIGHT, JOHN AVERITT.

WINN, JOHN M.
Oct. 18, 1847. Feb. Ct., 1848. Bk. F, p 387. It is
my will that my wife and family take $300 or $400 and
buy land to settle upon which land I lend my wife for
a home for herself and children. Reversion to all children. Wife: LUCY; sons: JOHN, 2 years schooling; ROBERT,
3 years schooling Wit: WILLIAM J. ARMSTRONG, JOHN
WHITEHEAD. No Exr. Adm. given MATHEW WHITEHEAD. Bond
$3000 with JOHN _____? and JOHN WHITEHEAD, Securities.

HADDOCK, SHADRACH
Jan. 8, 1807. Prob. 1817. Lend wife, ELIZABETH,
198 A land whereon I live adjoining WILLIAM CORBITT,
NICHOLAS CORBITT, SAMUEL HARRI (HARRIS?) and JOHN WEBB,
SR., as well as all personal estate. Reversion to sons:
JOHN and SHADRACH. Exr: JOHN OWENS. Wit: PENNY HADDOCK
and POLLY RETTOR.

HUNTER, HENRY
Oct. 3, 1805. Nov. Ct., 1823. Wife & Extx:
ELIZABETH, all property I became possessed of in con-
sequence of my intermarriage with her. Remainder of
property to be equally divided between my children:
HENRY B. HUNTER, BENJ. B. HUNTER, MARY B. HUNTER,
McGILLIRY B. HUNTER. Exr: BENNETT BARROW and sons:
HENRY B. HUNTER and BENJ. B. HUNTER. No Wit. Proven
by oath of SPENCER L. HART.

JONES, JOHN
Oct. 24, 1757. June Ct., 1758. Son & Exr: WALLIS.
Sons: ETHELRED, JOHN and FREDERICK. Sons-in-law: THOMAS
SPELL, CHARLES JERKINS, PETER MITCHELL, LAW THOMAS. Gr.
son: JOHN, son of WALLIS JONES. Dau: SARAH JERKINS. Gr.
daus: ANN RICHARDSON, wife of BENJ. RICHARDSON and dau
of THOMAS SPELL; MARY, dau of CHAS. and SARAH JERKINS
(JENKINS?). Wit: HENRY HORN, SION HORN, JOSIAH HORN.
Codicil, Dec. 17, 1757. Makes bequests to sons. Same
witnesses.

JONES, NANCY
Sept. 24, 1794. Nov. Ct., 1794. Mother: RACHEL JONES,
2 negroes, stock, cattle, furniture, $10. Bro & Exr:
JOHN HIGGINS JONES, L 50 currency of this State, stock,
Linnen wheel. Bro: WILLIAM JONES, stock, cattle, furni-
ture. MARY ANN GRIMES, negro girl. FREDERICK JONES,
negro woman, furniture, after his mother's decease.
JOHN DAVIDSON, horse, Crockery, pewter. Wit: ISAAC HILL,
MARY BEST.

PLACES and NAMES INDEX

93-101; Turner, 57; Wm. 33-58-59-60-80-93-153-230
Buchanan, Wm. 143
Bulluck (Bullock), Agnes 61-190; Bennett, 22; Betty, 61; David, 61-94-190; D. W. 263; E. 278-325-359; Edward, 61; Edwin, 51-145-204-289-307-365-370; Eliz. 204; Gray, 61; Jesse, 15-18; Jonathan, 61-262; John, 61-109-372; Josiah, 32; Lucy, 31; Martha, 22; Nathaniel, 61; Orrin, 61-230-288; Patty, 61; Polly, 31; Robt. 61; Susannah, 61; Wm. G. 31-247-345; Whitmel K. 31-61-
Bumpass, John, 61-121; John W. 62; Martha, 62-121; Mary, 62; Phereby, 62
Bunn, Ann, 62; Benj. 129, 131, 142, 145, 277, 339; Bennett, 44-265; Bennett H. 171-277; Charity, 25-172; David, 62-327; Eliz. 327; John, 62-267; Mary, 129; Mary H. 57; Redmond, 93-259-265-276-277-283-331-339; W. 339; Willie, 93-143
Buntin (Bunting), Creesy, 62; Eliz. 87; Gray 222; John, 62-197; Mary, 62; Rich. 62; Wm. 62
Buntyn (Bunting?), Amy, 8; Benj. 8; Elsey, 8; Everitt, 8; Jas. 8; Sally, 8
Burd (Byrd), Rich. 185
Burden, Maria, 54
Burgess, Joel, 83; Burk, Louisa, 202
Burn, Aaron, 62; Ann, 62; Michael, 62
Burnett, Francis, 209; John, 312; Matthew, 209
Burrus (Burrous), Bennett, 231; Jane, 83
Burt, John, 365
Burton, Edward, 340; Col. Hutchins G. 42-43; Sally, 42-43
Busby, Wm. 160
Buxton, Edward, 167
Bynum, Absala, 63; Allen, 62; Benj. 22-163-182; Catherine, 163-182; Eliz. V. 63; Faith, 199; John, 295; Jos. 62; Julia, 63; Mary, 107; Reuben, 62-63-119; Sally, 62; Sam. 63; Turner, 164-182
Byrd, Wm. 297
Byrn, Mary, 54
Byrum, Jacob, 63; John, 63; Moses, 63; Thos. 63; Minneford, 63

–C–

Cahille, Timothy, 217
Cain (Caine), Ann, 64; Abijah, 64; Barbara, 153; Delilah, 64; Duncan, 237; Eliz. 64; Hardy, 24-63-64; Isobel, 63; Jacob, 64; James, 24-63-64-122; Jerusha, 64; Jordan, 63; Jonathan, 63; Mary, 64; Penelope, 64; Peurity, 63; Rachel, 63; Rebecah, 35; Sarah, 50-63; Wm. 35; Zaporrah, 64
Caland, Eliz. 103
Calihan, John, 234
Cameron, Duncan, 42
Calhoon, Andrew A. 14-64-65; Eliz. 128; Hardy G. 65; J. W. 21-52-65; John, 128; Nancy, 64; Orren D. 14-21-54; Pherebe, 65; Polly, 50; Pricilla, 128
Camp, Richard, 59
Campbell, Henry, 190; Wm. 158
Cannady, John, 227-316 Sarah, 282
Cane, Archy, 65; Elisha, 65; Eliz. 177; Jas. 323; Sarah J. 65; Jonathan, 153; Rebecca, 323; Wm. 65
Capell, Chas. 229; Eliz. 229
Carlile (Carlisle), Cary, 66; Clark, 65; Coleman, 65; Edwin, 65; Jno. 65; Jos. 65; Liddy, 65; Martha, 66; Mary Ann, 65; Millie, 66; Nancy, 65-66; Rhoda, 65; Robt. 36-65-66-74; Sarah, 65-66; Simon, 65; Susannah, 65; Wm. 66
Carney, Eliz. 231; Jas. 231; Rich. 132; Stephen W. 132; Wright, 231
Carpenter, Mary, 205
Curr, Celia, 66; Elias, 6-66-67; Jonas, 68; Jonas J. 66-67-183; Lucretia, 67-68; Mary, 360; Mary B. 67; Milly, 112; Wm. 67-68; Wm. B. 67
Carrel, James, 63
Carson, Sarah, 68
Cartu, Thomas, 362

Cartwright, Ann, 323; Chas. Evans, 69; Hezikiah, 69-181-316; John, 68-69; Mat. 69; Peter, 69-162-181-316-323-359; Rich. 181; Sarah, 69; Susannah, 69; Thos. 69
Carver, Cath. 35
Castrign, Lucy. 311
Caswell, Saray, 53; John Rodney, 53
Casway (Cassway), Absalom, 44; Leven, 224; Nancy, 224
Caulwell, Mary, 69
Causey, Ann, 232-233; Cullen, 69; Ezek. 232-272; Greenberry, 69; Leavin, 69; Nancy, 69; Philip, 69-99-180; Rachel, 69
Causway, Nancy, 224; Philip, 134; Rachel, 98
Cavena, Aquilla, 70; Arthur, 70; Chas. 70; David, 70; Henry, 70; Mary, 70; Memorial, 70; Needham, 70; Nicholas, 70; Wm. 70
Champion, James, 244
Channel, Rufe, 32
Chapman, R. 32; Russel, 32-95-204-245
Charles, John, 372
Chevrollie (Chevrolet), Mary Littlejohn, 42; Mr. 42
Cherry, Aaron, 70; Chas. 71; Charlotte, 87; Clary, 71-87; Dav. 70-359; Eliz. 70-152; Emily, 32; Henry R. 148; Julia, 147; John, 71; John W. 194; Kiuchen, 111; Lewis K. 70; Lunsford R. 10-47-55-70-79-193-241-242-264; Mary, 71; Obed, 92; Peggy, 71; Polly, 152; Robt. 71-296-357; Rod. 71-90-267; Sam. 71; Sary, 70; Sarah, 71; Solomon, 71; Sukey, 193; Susannah, 71; Tabitha, 71; Theophilus, 71-177-194-256; Thos. B. 32-71; Willie, 152; Wm. 71-87-168; Wm. R. 31-148-193-290
Cheshire, Jas. 290; Mary (Polly), 71
Chester, John, 199
Churchwell, Jas. 290; Mary (Polly), 71
Clark, Aaron, 73; Alex. 216; Arabella E. 72-183; Chas. 72; Charlotte, 58; Clary, 72; Frances, 72; Franky, 72; Henry, 72; Henry J. 87; Henry T. 8-72-87-94-151-336-337; Jas. M. 42-72-144-269-336-337; Jean, 73; Jesse, 58-169; John, 185; Laura R. 336; Levi, 73; Maria T. 72-336; Mary S. 42-43-72; Mary Sumner, 336; Moses, 73; Nancy, 161; Nathan, 72; Penny, 72; Pennina, 49; Polly, 58; Rich. 72-99-112-136; Robt. 73-275; Sealey, 72; Thos. 136; Wm. 45-73-181-223
Claud, Sara, 165
Clements, W. 38-307
Clenabar, J. W. 141
Clinch, Christopher, 323; Duncan L. 42; Joseph J. 36
Clyburn, Jean, 73
Cobb, Allen, 122; Amos W. 73-128-300 316; Eaton, 73-152-153-194-212-213-327; David, 207; David M. 73-231; Edward, 14-73-115; Eliz. 151-257-329; E. E. 73-128; Elsey, 44; Exum, 361; Fannie Eliza, 73; Gray, 73; Hardy, 315; Jas. F. 316; James M. 119; John 73-213-300-373; Jonas, 73-115, Jos. 40-153-231; Josiah, 44; Lucinda, 73; Lydia, 326; Lydia Luella, 73; L. S. 366; Mary, 14; Margarett, 231; Martha Ann, 231; Mourning, 170; Ollin, 327; Roena, 215; Sarah, 231; Stephen, 73-373; Thomas N. 73; Winnefred, 73; Winnie, 373
Cockburn, Eliz. 74; Frances, 74; Geo. 74; Marie, 74; Mary, 74; Theo. 74; Winifred, 74
Cohoon, Anderson, 95; Andrew A. 77; Avy, 77; Aquilla, 53-145; Charity, 77-78-171; Etheldred, 309; Hardy, 77; Hardy G. 77; Jemimah, 107; Joel, 77; John, 77; John W. 77; Mary, 77-78; Orren D. 77-95-161-309; Penelope, 78; Pharaba, 77; Prisilla, 77; Prusilla, 78; Sarah, 70; Simon, 77; Sollomon, 78; Tresy (Teresa), 78; Wm. S. 78
Coffield, Benj. 74-79-110-132-191-193-309; D. 224; David, 47-75-76-77-106-132-154-223-263; Eliz. 58-75-77-193; Eliz. Ann, 76; Eliz. W. 75; John W. 75; Mary, 74; Martha C. 76; Nancy, 77; Patience, 296; Penelope, 74; Polly, 58; Roseanah, 74; Sally, 76; Sarah, 75; Sarah Spier William, 76; Spier C. 38; Spier William 75; Spier W. 74-75-76-84-211-233; Thos. 58-76; Prisc. West, 76; West, 77

Coker, Abi, 79; Agnes, 78; Brumblea, 78; Brumbly, 79; Brumble, 309; Caleb, 78-79-124; David, 79-252; Eliz. 78-265; Ezek. 78-211; Geor. 139; Jacob, 78-211-232; Jas. 78-79-80-177-215-235-241; John, 79-241; Jos. 120; Kessiah, 265; Lovey, 139; Mary, 78; Marg. 78; Martha, 79; Mildred, 160; Nancy, 139; Nath. 78-211-215-263; Olive, 79-223; Patsey, 79; Rebecca, 139; Rich. 78-79-80-263; Sarah, 78; Stephen, 75-79-117-241; Tirzah, 79; Thomas, 78; Wm. 78-79-80-139
Coleman, Aaron, 24-53-80-81-82-105; Abagal, 80; Alex. 75; Allen, 82; Amos, 81; Benj. 99; Cadar, 81; Chas. 11-80-82-126-187-246-247-249-268-280-288-322-354; Christian, 81; Eliz. 354; Esther, 82; Grace, 81; Harde, 80; Hardy, 81; Jaconias, 81; Jane, 82; John, 19-81-82-180-187-247-268; Jonathan, 80-138; Josiah, 81; Kizah, 269; Mary, 81-82; Moses, 81-82-244-285; Patience, 80; Rachel, 2-80; Robt. 15-81-82-180-186-301; Samuel, 82; Sampson, 82; Sarah (Sally), 2-81-82-187-268; Sely, 81; Sela, 82; Silpha, 81; Stephen, 36-53-81-82-94; Susanor, 81-82; Willie, 82; Wm. 82
Collins, Alley, 83; Blount, 83; Dav. 97; Eliz. 82-83; Grizzy, 82; G. 150; John, 82-83-135; Josiah, 83; Mary, 216; Shadarack, 49-82;
Colson, William, 175
Coltraine, David, 273
Colwell, Eliz. 45-83; Mary, 83; Sarah, 83; W. 287; Wm. 83
Conner, Mrs. of Craven. 41
Coniga, Wm. 71
Connell, Cath. 83-290; Davis, 290-341; Simon, 83; Suckey, 290; Thos. 83; Wm. 83-267;
Comegys, Benj. 295; Mrs. Cath. 295; Cornelius, 295; John, 295
Contech, Kennedoy. 55
Cook, Courtney, 109; Jas. 194; Job, 373; Judea, 224; Wm. 216; Woodard, 18-22;
Cooper, Betsey, 193; Blount, 83-243; Drusilla, 135; Nath. 224; Sophia, 84; Wm. F. 198
Copeland, Demsey, 181; Wm. 181
Coppedge, Augustin, 84-142; Charlot, 84; Griffin, 84; Mary, 84; Willmuth, 84; Corbin, Polly, 37
Corbit, Ann, 84; Dempsey, 373; John, 84; Johnston, 84; Kinchen, 365; Mary, 84; Maymy, 153; Milly, 373; Nich. 82-84-376; Redding, 373; Richard, 84; Sarah, 84; Tempy, 84; Weston, 373; Winifred, 84; Wm. 82-84-153-184-376
Corey, Mary, 17
Cornwell, Katie, 333
Cotten, Alex, 84-85-86; Amos. 84-117-131; Annie, 367; Arabella Clark, 86; Arthur, 84-85-312; Benj. 85; Betsey, 87; Chas. 269; Dan. 132; Edward L. 112; Eliz. 85-87-171; Fanny, 85-87; Florida Coll. 86; Fred, 80-84-85-86-126-127-269; Fred R. 85-86; Geo. 84-166; Godwin, 85; Henry, 129; Jas. 84; Jamison Godwin, 85; Jesse A. 171; John, 86-87-251; Joseph, 84-365; Kezziah, 291; Laura P. 72-86; Mrs. M. G. 43; Mary, 84-85-86-238; Marg. 42-43-86; Mary Godwin, 85; N. 222; Pheribe, 85; Polly, 87; R. 87-90-134-287-342; Randolph, 80-84-85-86-99-166-196-207-241-257-286; Sally, 85; Spencer D. 42-43-76-84-85-86-148-207-251-287; W. 172; Wm. 127-262-253; Willie, 87; Wimberley, 84; W. T. 207; Zilpah, 84; Zilpha, 369
Council, Bennett, 87; Chas. 87; Christian, 88; Clary, 88; Dice, 87; Hardy, 87; John, 87; Joshua, 87-88; Julia, 272; Mary, 88; Reddick, 87; Silvia, 87; Tempy, 87; Temperance, 88; Wiley 87; Willie, 87; William, 71
Cowell, Berward, 88; Drusilla, 88
Cowen (Cowon), Mary, 162; Darius, 162
Cox, Eliz. 86; Jemimia, 88; John, 88; Jos. 88-120-200; Nathan, 88; Patience, 354; Patsey, 88; Robert, 88; Seth, 88; Wm. 88
Cravey, Hugh, 89-183-272; Jas. 88; Owen, 163-183; Seley, 183
Crawley, David, 225-274
Crenshaw, Cath. Eliz. 8
Crisp, Benj. Frank, 89; Ellender, 89; Eliza, 89; Francis, 90; George, 90;

387

www.ingramcontent.com/pod-product-compliance
Lightning Source LLC
Chambersburg PA
CBHW021844020426
42334CB00013B/185